A Contemporary Cuba Reader

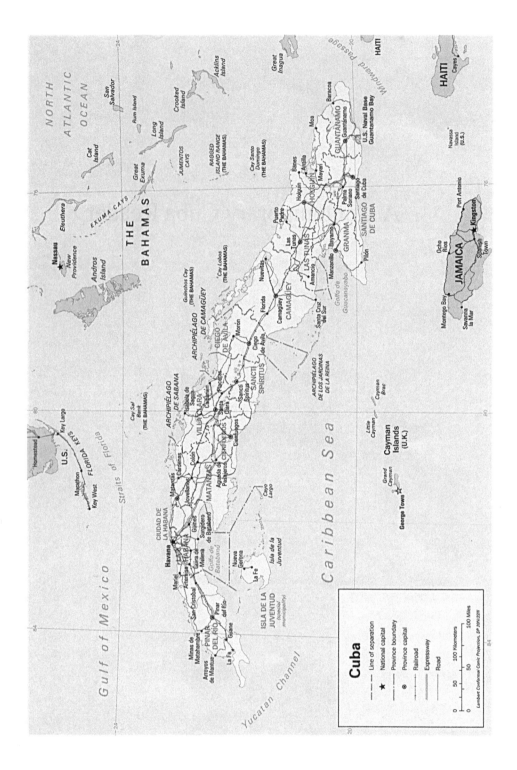

A Contemporary Cuba Reader

The Revolution under Raúl Castro

Second Edition

Edited by Philip Brenner, Marguerite Rose Jiménez,
John M. Kirk, and William M. LeoGrande

ROWMAN & LITTLEFIELD
Lanham • Boulder • New York • London

Published by Rowman & Littlefield
A wholly owned subsidiary of The Rowman & Littlefield Publishing Group, Inc.
4501 Forbes Boulevard, Suite 200, Lanham, Maryland 20706
www.rowman.com

16 Carlisle Street, London W1D 3BT, United Kingdom

British Library Cataloguing in Publication Information Available

Library of Congress Cataloging-in-Publication Data
A contemporary Cuba reader : the revolution under Raúl Castro / edited by Philip Brenner, Marguerite Rose Jiménez, John M. Kirk, and William M. LeoGrande.—Second edition.
pages cm
Includes bibliographical references and index.
ISBN 978-1-4422-3098-9 (cloth : alk. paper)—ISBN 978-1-4422-3099-6 (pbk. : alk. paper)—ISBN 978-1-4422-3100-9 (electronic)
1. Cuba—History—1990- I. Brenner, Philip, editor of compilation, author. II. Jiménez, Marguerite Rose, 1982- editor of compilation, author. III. Kirk, John M., 1951- editor of compilation, author. IV. LeoGrande, William M., editor of compilation, author.
F1788.C67 2014
972.9107—dc23
2014008031

Printed in the United States of America

Contents

List of Tables

Preface

On July 31, 2006, the Cuban government announced that President Fidel Castro Ruz had relinquished temporarily all of his government and party responsibilities. Nearly dead from complications due to abdominal surgery, the iconic Cuban leader had designated his younger brother, Raúl Castro Ruz, to serve as provisional president, head of the Cuban Communist Party, and commander in chief of the armed forces. Over the next eighteen months as the elder Castro recuperated but lacked the physical ability to resume any of his previous official roles, it became clear that a peaceful succession of power had occurred in Cuba.

This book examines the consequences of the succession by focusing both on the changes that have occurred since mid-2006 in Cuba's economics, politics, social relations, culture, and relations with other countries and on the continuities, especially how the country has attempted to maintain its social safety net, guarantee of good health care and education to everyone, and prestige among Third World nations as well as a tradition of collective responsibility and shared burden in the face of increasing individualism.

In assembling chapters for this edition of *A Contemporary Cuba Reader*, we faced the challenge that Cuba is a rapidly moving subject. To prevent this collection from becoming obsolete within months of publication, we commissioned a larger percentage of original chapters for this edition than we did for the first, asking authors to identify the dynamics of their subjects in order to provide readers with a sense of what drivers lie behind the process of change. Moreover, we have created for readers a continually updated website that includes data on Cuba's demography and economy, information about current political events and political leaders in Cuba and Cuba's international relations, and links to films, music, photos, and topical articles.

The first edition of *A Contemporary Cuba Reader* examined what President Fidel Castro declared in 1990 to be a "Special Period in a Time of Peace"—a period of extreme hardship that led to a dramatic reversal in the quality of life for most people on the island. The collapse of the socialist trading bloc in 1989 and the subsequent breakup of the Soviet Union caused the Cuban economy to decline by nearly 30 percent in four years. The first edition described and analyzed both the myriad ways that Cubans had reinvented their Revolution during the "Special Period" and the way that some changes, such as the dual currency, contributed to undermining fundamental goals of the Revolution by increasing inequality and diminishing the value of education. The government still has not officially announced an end of the Special Period, but we would argue that by 2006 it was over, as the Cuban economy was again expanding and the worst years seemed past. In 2006, Cuba hosted the summit of the 116-

nation Non-Aligned Movement, elevating Cuba once again to a position of Third World leadership. Cuban music and the arts were flourishing, and there was a new openness on the island in discussions about Cuba's future.

Still, as Raúl Castro took the baton from his brother, there was considerable uncertainty about the path he would take in leading the country. There was even the question of his own ability to replace Fidel, a giant whose charismatic relationship with Cubans had conferred legitimacy on his authority even in the worst times.[1] In Washington, fears of turmoil and a possible onslaught of Cubans trying to enter the United States led President George W. Bush to warn Cubans not to leave the island. Yet no hint of turmoil followed the announcement of Raúl's assumption of leadership. As Julia Sweig wrote in the first edition of *A Contemporary Cuba Reader*, "Despite Fidel's overwhelming personal authority and Raúl's critical institution-building abilities, the government rests on far more than just the charisma, authority, and legend of these two figures."[2] Indeed, while there is little doubt that Fidel Castro played the central role in determining the character, the successes, and the failures of the Cuban Revolution, it had not been "Castro's Revolution." The calm that ensued after he stepped down suggested both that he was replaceable and that the Revolution he led had been forged by the Cuban people who continued to support its fundamental goals of national independence and social justice. As we highlight in the introduction to this book, contemporary Cubans carry with them the legacy of many prior generations who were determined to build a Cuba independent of foreign domination—whether by Spain, the United States, or the Soviet Union—and at least since 1959 to foster an ethos of egalitarianism.

Raúl Castro has thus sought to retain the wide-ranging social programs that have provided substantial benefits to the Cuban population while introducing a series of measures intended to modernize the economic structure and provide incentives to the growing self-employed sector. This has resulted in a radically new stage of the Cuban revolutionary process, significantly different from anything seen to date—yet with the same underpinnings of revolutionary society as found before. Although Raúl Castro's era is not over yet—he has announced that he will serve as president until the end of his current term in 2018—he has determined Cuba's path clearly enough that we can ascribe the period since 2006 as the Revolution under his leadership.

Several people have assisted us as we worked on *A Contemporary Cuba Reader*. We thank Amy Ruddle, Kia Hall, Uri Lerner, and Alex D'Agostino for their research assistance, and Will Pittinos for his work on the index. We have benefited from the advice and contributions given to us by numerous colleagues at American University, Dalhousie University, the University of Havana, and Cuba's *Instituto Superior de Relaciones Internacionales* and from anonymous reviewers and students and faculty who have used the book. Officials at the U.S. Interests Section in Havana and the Cuban Interests Section in Washington, D.C., have facilitated our travel and research. Our families have been generous with their support and patience. All of the editors' royalties from the sale of this book will be donated to MEDICC (Medical Education Cooperation with Cuba), a U.S. nonprofit organization working to enhance cooperation among U.S., Cuban, and global health communities. The second edition of *A Contemporary Cuba Reader*—like the first—would not have been possible without our editor at Rowman & Littlefield, Susan McEachern, who engaged in this project with the spirit of a team captain, combining her collegiality and gentle pressure with experienced judgment and a shared appreciation for the editors' objectives.

We dedicate this edition of *A Contemporary Cuba Reader* to Saul Landau, who died in September 2013. As he was to countless students of Cuba, Saul was to us a dear friend, a mentor, and a colleague who encouraged us to know Cuba from the perspective of Cubans, to write about Cuba honestly, and to work tirelessly to improve U.S.-Cuba relations for the benefit of people in both countries.

Philip Brenner
Marguerite Rose Jiménez
John M. Kirk
William M. LeoGrande
May 2014

NOTES

1. Nelson P. Valdes, "The Revolutionary and Political Content of Fidel Castro's Charismatic Authority," in *A Contemporary Cuba Reader: Reinventing the Revolution*, edited by Philip Brenner, Marguerite Rose Jiménez, John M. Kirk, and William M. LeoGrande (Lanham, MD: Rowman & Littlefield, 2008).
2. Julia E. Sweig, "Fidel's Final Victory," in Brenner et al., *A Contemporary Cuba Reader*, 237.

Introduction

History as Prologue: Cuba before 2006

Philip Brenner, Marguerite Rose Jiménez, John M. Kirk, and William M. LeoGrande

On July 31, 2006, a gravely ill Fidel Castro handed his conductor's baton to Raúl Castro. The younger brother of Cuba's larger-than-life revolutionary leader accepted the provisional reins of power as head of state, first secretary of Cuba's Communist Party, and commander in chief of the Revolutionary Armed Forces. A new era had begun.

It was the moment about which U.S. policymakers and many Cuban exiles had been dreaming, when chaos would ensue and the revolutionary regime would collapse. Fearing its wishes might come true, the Bush administration warned Cubans "against leaving the island"[1] as it anticipated a massive exodus. But there was no turmoil, no rush for the exit. The transition occurred almost seamlessly. Historian Julia Sweig aptly characterized the handover as the Cuban leader's "final victory."[2]

Fidel Castro was the indispensable person without whom the Cuban Revolution would have taken a different course. But he was not a traditional Latin American caudillo. From 1959 to 2006, the country's economy, politics, foreign policy, culture, and social organization were not merely a reflection of Castro's personality and personal predilections because the Cuban Revolution had an organic quality. It grew from below and was shaped by the relationship between leader and followers. As sociologist Nelson Valdés explains, Castro was a *charismatic* leader. "His charismatic authority would not have been possible without the revolutionary practices which the Cuban populace embraced."[3]

For a government to remain legitimate after the passing of its charismatic leader, it needs to substitute one of two other forms of legitimacy, which sociologist Max Weber termed traditional and legal-institutional.[4] Consider that the U.S. federal government at first relied on George Washington's charismatic leadership for its legitimacy and then turned to tradition. Succeeding presidents through John Quincy Adams endowed the new government with legitimacy by their ties to the American Revolution. But fifty-three years after the start of the Independence War, the revolutionary heroes or their sons were no longer available. President Andrew Jackson of Tennessee, who took office in 1829, had been born outside one of the original thirteen states and was only nine years old when the Revolution began. He ushered in a new era during which the right to vote was expanded significantly to non–property owners, which contributed to the government's legal-institutional legitimacy.[5]

Establishing governmental legitimacy was a primary task that confronted Raúl Castro in 2006. Of course, as one of the Cuban Revolution's leaders, he could rely on traditional

1

authority. And at first he did surround himself with leaders whose right to rule derived from their personal participation in the Revolution. But Raúl was seventy-six years old, and his colleagues—the "historical" generation that overthrew Fulgencio Batista in 1959—were of the same vintage. High on his agenda was reinforcing the legal-institutional authority that would be necessary to sustain the Cuban Revolution in the future.[6] At the same time, he had to bring about change, to lead the country toward a model appropriate for the twenty-first century that would enable it to develop independently, maintain its commitment to providing basic needs equally for all Cubans, and sustain Cuba's high standing in Latin America and the Third World. This book examines how Cuba has attempted to fulfill this agenda since 2006.

Such an examination necessarily includes a review of the way in which the country's prior experiences prepared Cubans for the changes they experienced and instilled in them a tradition of independence. A central dynamic during Cuba's last five centuries has been the Cubans' struggle against domination by an external power (Spain, the United States, or the Soviet Union) that prevented the island from developing full political and economic independence.

FIRST FOUR CENTURIES OF COLONIALISM

Christopher Columbus "discovered" Cuba on his first voyage across the Atlantic in 1492, claiming it on behalf of the Spanish Crown. Prior to Columbus's discovery, native tribes of Cuba—largely *Arawak* and *Ciboney*—had lived in peace for centuries in basic harmony with their neighbors and nature. The Spaniards outlawed the tribes' religious practices, stole their collective property, and made them slaves for the benefit of the Crown. In contrast to the indigenous population of mainland Spanish America, the native peoples of Cuba virtually disappeared within a generation of Spain's arrival, wiped out by overwork, disease, and mass suicides.[7] A notable exception were the *Taino Arawaks*, who waged a fierce struggle against the Spanish. Their example of resistance is still celebrated in Cuba, and *Taino* tribal leader Hatuey is a national hero.

For much of its time as a colony, Cuba languished as a backwater in the Spanish Empire. It possessed few minerals of real worth; its value lay in its strategic location. The Spanish Crown maintained a monopoly on all of Cuba's trade, stifled attempts to develop indigenous industry, and imposed high taxes on all imports and exports. As in other colonies, political control in Cuba remained with governors and administrators from the mother country, and Spanish soldiers enforced colonial rule. The Crown rewarded Spanish settlers who came to live in the "most lovely land that eyes have ever seen," as Columbus described Cuba, with immense tracts of land. In the mid-eighteenth century, they began to transform their agricultural production from basic food staples to sugar, in response to European popular demand. Sugar was cultivated most efficiently on large plantations, and its harvesting was a labor-intensive process. With profits waiting to be earned and a shortage of workers on the island, Spain legalized slavery, and an active trade in African slaves began in 1763. Slave traders brought approximately 750,000 Africans to Cuba in the next 100 years. In 1862, Afro-Cubans accounted for more than half of the 1.4 million people on the island, and Cuba produced one-third of the world's sugar supply. Slavery did not end in Cuba until 1886.

The Spanish colonial government encouraged the racial divide that slavery produced, doling out almost all prestigious positions in the military and government to whites born in Spain, known as the *peninsulares*—those born on the peninsula of Spain. Children born in the "colonies" to Spanish parents—the *criollos*, or "creoles"—were branded with an original sin of inferiority despite being "white." The end result was a racist society in which one's status, privileges, and rights were based on the color of one's skin and the location of one's birth.

Spanish Catholic bishops accommodated and reinforced this standard by allowing only white Spanish priests—many of whom were "parachuted" in for limited-term appointments—to officiate in Cuban churches.

Between 1810 and 1821, people throughout South America successfully struggled to end colonialism, developing national boundaries more or less along the lines of the current configuration of Latin America—but not in Cuba, where the prosperity brought by sugar and fears of a slave uprising like Haiti's dampened immediate demands for independence. Cuba became the refuge for the Spanish soldiers defeated in the wars of independence, and they tended to reinforce the authoritarianism, rigidity, and racism already prevalent in Cuba. The consequent tension was heightened by Cuba's uneven development, which produced great disparities in wealth between Cubans and between regions within Cuba. This volatile mixture came to a head in 1868, when Cubans began a ten-year war for independence that would unfold over the following ninety years.

The Ten-Year War

Agitation for independence had been building for nearly two decades, particularly in the eastern part of the island, when plantation owner Carlos Manuel de Céspedes proclaimed Cuba's freedom from Spain on October 10, 1868. Joined by other planters, he freed his slaves and declared the *Grito de Yara* (Cry of Yara)—a call for revolution. Starting with fewer than 200 volunteers, the rebel army (called the *mambises*) grew within a few months to 12,000, gathering small farmers, laborers, and freed slaves. This was a conservative revolution in most aspects other than ending slavery, as the planters resented the increases in Spanish taxes and sought political power for themselves. Although Western sugar plantation owners, who depended on slavery, opposed the revolutionary effort, it was able to accumulate many successes. The rebels defeated superior Spanish forces in several battles, captured cities such as Bayamo, and established a new government and democratic constitution. But both the rebels and the Spaniards were exhausted after ten years of fighting, which left 50,000 soldiers and civilians dead. In February 1878, they signed a treaty that freed some slaves, promised future reforms, and left Cuba as a Spanish colony. Unwilling to accept continued foreign rule, rebel officers led by Antonio Maceo penned "The Protest of Baraguá," a pledge to continue the independence war. Cuban leaders today still refer to Baraguá as a symbol of defiance against external dominance.[8]

Maceo had to abandon the fight within a few months, after the Spanish military captured and exiled him. He did not return to Cuba until March 1895, one month after the renewed independence war began. Yet he had been working with others, such as Máximo Gómez, to plan for the war. In 1892, José Martí gathered the opposition under the banner of the Cuban Revolutionary Party as he coordinated preparations for the coming struggle. The son of poor Spanish immigrants, Martí began his first attacks on Spanish colonial rule in *La Patria Libre* (Free Fatherland), a newspaper he started in 1869 at the age of sixteen. Jailed for his political activities, he was then exiled to Spain in 1871. In 1881, he moved to New York, where he worked as a journalist, covering U.S. politics for several Latin American newspapers, and wrote poetry and novels.

Cuba was experiencing a severe depression in 1895, in part caused by a U.S. tariff on sugar imposed the year before. This contributed to the widespread support the rebels received. They started their campaign in the east (Oriente Province), and by the end of the year the struggle for independence had engulfed the entire island. Martí was killed in combat on May 19, 1895, only six weeks after returning to Cuba with General Gómez. Yet his concept of *Cuba Libre* continued to inspire the new *mambises*. It also set the stage for an inevitable clash with the

United States. As historian Louis Pérez explains, *"Cuba Libre* had come to signify more than separation from Spain. . . . The *independentista* formula was simple: Cuba for Cubans—the one eventuality which nearly one hundred years of North American policy had been dedicated to preventing."[9]

Meanwhile, Spain fought back against the revolutionaries with enormous brutality, razing villages and driving Cubans out of their homes. The 200,000-soldier Spanish garrison at first seemed sufficient to counter the *independentistas*. But by 1898, the army's morale was low, and Spanish repression had stimulated support for the revolutionaries. Both Madrid and Washington assessed that the rebels would likely win the war by year's end.

"A Splendid Little War"

The U.S. declaration of war against Spain in April 1898 did not result merely from a sudden burst of popular passion—fueled by the "yellow" journalism of William Randolph Hearst and Joseph Pulitzer's competing newspapers—after a U.S. battleship exploded in Havana harbor killing 260 U.S. seamen. Many factors contributed to the U.S. intervention. U.S. business barons, for example, feared that a rebel victory would mean a Cuba run by Cubans, which might undermine their holdings and privileged trade deals. Even before the war, the United States had supplanted Spain as Cuba's main trading partner.[10] It was in response to concerns about property owned by Americans—and perhaps about the lives of U.S. citizens—that President William McKinley dispatched the USS *Maine* to Cuba in January. Yet there also were U.S. political leaders who convinced themselves that intervention would be a humane and selfless action because an independent Cuba could not govern itself.[11] The "splendid little war"– as Secretary of State John Hay described the 1898 conflict—resulted in the transfer of the Philippines, Guam, and Puerto Rico from Spain's colonial control to that of the United States. Cuba also was a U.S. prize from the war, but annexation was blocked by the Teller Amendment that the U.S. Congress had added to the declaration of war against Spain.

The *Maine*'s explosion on February 15, 1898, occurred as the rebels were preparing their final offensives. U.S. intervention effectively stole from Cubans the fruits of their thirty years of fighting. Four months after the United States declared war, it signed a bilateral peace treaty with Spain without any Cuban participation. The name commonly applied to the conflict in the United States—"Spanish American War"—betrays an ignorance about the limited importance of the U.S. contribution in securing victory. It also obscures the U.S. suppression of Cuban hopes for full independence. In Cuba, the conflict is known as the Cuban War of Independence.[12]

DE FACTO COLONIALISM:
CUBA'S SPECIAL RELATIONSHIP WITH THE UNITED STATES

Although Cuba was nominally independent from 1903 to 1959, it was a de facto colony of the United States. The United States withdrew its occupation forces from Cuba in 1902 on the condition that the new constitution would include the Platt Amendment, a provision that permitted U.S. unilateral intervention on the island. During the period when the Platt Amendment was in force, from 1903 to 1934, the United States occupied Cuba with troops on three different occasions. At the same time, U.S. corporations and investment banks gained control of Cuba's basic infrastructure. Formal independence did not bring about meaningful sovereignty; Cuba was once again controlled by a foreign country.

The U.S. occupation began on January 1, 1899. Leonard Wood, the second U.S. governor-general, revealed in a letter to President McKinley the patronizing attitude the new rulers had toward their subjects. He wrote that "we are dealing with a race that has steadily been going down for a hundred years and into which we have to infuse new life, new principles and new methods of doing things."[13] Indeed, while the Platt Amendment was couched in the language of protecting liberty, life, property, and stability on the island, historian Lars Schoultz explains that its purpose was to "maintain control over people whom they [U.S. officials] considered unfit for self-government," without continuing military occupation of the island.[14] In developing the Platt Amendment as a mechanism for intervention, Senator Orville Platt and Secretary of War Elihu Root manifested President McKinley's vision that Cuba and the United States should have a "special relationship" with "ties of singular intimacy."

In practice, the special relationship stifled Cuban development. Spurred by special concessions that the occupation government granted to U.S. investors, the North American hold over Cuban sugar plantations quickly led to U.S. domination of Cuba's nonsugar industries. Sugar operations were quite large, and the *centrales* became thoroughly integrated small cities that linked key sectors of the Cuban economy, most of which were controlled by U.S. firms. Consider that in the mid-1920s, as a result of ties between sugar mills and railroads, U.S. companies owned 22 percent of Cuba's land area.[15] Moreover, U.S.-Cuban trade agreements opened Cuba to inexpensive manufactured goods, suppressing the creation of an indigenous manufacturing sector. The U.S. sugar quota, which specified how much sugar Cuba could sell at a subsidized price, became the most important determinant of year-to-year survival for Cuba's sugar workers and for Cuba's economic planning. A "wrong" decision that might upset one U.S. senator could lead to a filibuster against Cuba's quota. And so, for example, although Cuba had the potential to produce tomatoes and even tomato catsup commercially, both were imported from the United States because of U.S. tomato growers.

By the mid-1950s, 90 percent of Cuba's telephone and electrical services, 50 percent of public service railways, 40 percent of raw sugar production, and 23 percent of nonsugar industries were U.S. owned. The United States was Cuba's largest export market and the main source for its imports: 59 percent of the value of Cuban exports—including 80 percent of its exported sugar—went to the United States. Notably, 76 percent of Cuba's imports originated in the United States. This reflected, in part, U.S.-owned firms buying from their own subsidiaries. As important, Cuba needed to import basic foods because its dependence on sugar for hard currency reduced its ability to produce rice, wheat, and flour. One-third of U.S. rice exports were sold to Cuba in the 1950s.[16]

As U.S. businesses rapidly took root in Cuba, demand for the services of English-speaking Cubans increased. This led members of the Cuban elite to send their children to U.S. universities and even high schools so that they subsequently could take up management positions with U.S. companies on the island. Not surprisingly, the Cuban upper class came to identify with U.S. cultural values. During the first half of the twentieth century, the Americanization of the creole middle class followed the accelerating conversion of the elites, and Cuban society as a whole became imbued with a North American perspective. Baseball became the national pastime. The use of U.S. products conveyed a sense of higher status, and soon anything American was deemed better than anything Cuban—from the arts to the design of buildings to business strategies. Louis Pérez well describes the profound influence this process of acculturation had on Cubans' worldview:

> The well-being of many people, specifically as it related to economic development and prosperity, which also implies social peace and political order, was increasingly linked to the United States: entry to its markets, access to its products, use of its capital, application of its technology. . . .

These were complex social processes, for they involved the incorporation of a new hierarchy of values into Cuban life. Tens of thousands of Cubans of all classes—children and adults, men and women, black and white—were integrated directly into North American structures at virtually every turn; as customers, clients, coworkers, as employees and business partners, in professional organizations and voluntary associations, at school and in social clubs, in church and on teams. [17]

During the period of the special relationship, a limited form of democracy did emerge on the island, but it was one that Cubans associated with corruption and foreign domination. The U.S. Marines occupied Cuba from 1906 to 1909, for a short time in 1912, and from 1917 to 1922. In 1933, President Franklin Delano Roosevelt (FDR) feared that the unpopularity of Cuba's president—the dictatorial Gerardo Machado—might lead to instability and a radical government. He dispatched a personal emissary, Ambassador Sumner Welles, who persuaded Machado to resign, and arranged for his replacement by a reformer who would comply with U.S. requests.

Within weeks, a popular uprising—sparked by a sergeants' revolt with Fulgencio Batista in the lead—ousted the U.S.-approved president and established a provisional government. The new government proclaimed that it would bring about national "economic reconstruction" as it began "the march toward the creation of a new Cuba founded . . . upon the most modern concept of democracy."[18] Welles made clear his disapproval of the revolutionaries' chosen leader, Ramón Grau San Martín, and FDR refused to recognize Grau's government. Welles then worked behind the scenes to entice key backers, particularly Batista and the military, to defect from the revolutionary coalition, which lasted only four months before being over-thrown by the army. Batista continued to be a dependable U.S. surrogate for the next quarter of a century. Cubans learned that FDR's "Good Neighbor Policy" meant only that the United States would not intervene *militarily*. The U.S. success in suppressing Cuban nationalism, though, led nationalist populism to become the dominant theme of Cuban politics in the following twenty-five years.

When Batista overthrew the constitutional government in 1952, ending Cuba's experience with "democracy," there was little public outcry. Nelson Valdés observes that many in the Cuban elite had abandoned the concept of a distinctive Cuban national identity. In addition, the mass of Cubans associated democratic elections with the theft of Cuban nationalism, either by the *mafia* or the U.S. government. The revolutionary movement that triumphed in 1959 in part derived its legitimacy from its devotion to Cuban nationalism. This placed the new regime on an inevitable collision course with the United States.

THE 1959 REVOLUTION

Active opposition to the Batista dictatorship was organized by several groups and was spread across the island, especially in the cities. Each group of revolutionaries had distinctive goals, but together they shared a desire to rid Cuba of corruption, to modernize the country, and to raise living standards for the vast majority of the population. It was not until mid-1958 that the combined revolutionary organizations came together as a unified force, though they did not acknowledge anyone as their single leader. The 26th of July Movement had become the largest and most dynamic group, gaining increased support as it won military victories in the summer of 1958. The movement took its name from the date in 1953 on which Fidel Castro and some 160 others stormed the Moncada garrison in Santiago in a failed attempt to spark a general uprising to overthrow the Batista dictatorship. As founder of the rebel army and head of the 26th of July Movement, Castro quickly became the natural leader of the revolutionary government when Batista fled the country on December 31, 1958. In its first post-Batista edition, the private, popular weekly magazine *Bohemia* described him as a "national hero."[19]

A seeming upwardly mobile lawyer, Castro was a graduate of the elite Belén high school, which educated Cuba's upper classes, and his father was a plantation owner, though not a rich one. His first wife, Mirta Díaz-Balart, was the daughter of Rafael José Díaz-Balart, a wealthy and prominent conservative lawyer who was transportation minister in Batista's cabinet from 1952 to 1954. Yet Castro also had been a leader of the activist student movement at the University of Havana, a member of the leftist Ortodoxo Party, and an ardent supporter of the party's charismatic leader, Eduardo Chibás. The 1956 platform of the 26th of July Movement could have been interpreted as either a radical manifesto or a list of modest changes aimed at "national affirmation, human dignity, and democratic order," goals that earlier reformers historically had promised.[20] With this profile, it is no wonder that U.S. intelligence analysts were uncertain at first whether Castro would try to radically transform the system or institute only modest reforms, which would not fundamentally alter the structure of power on the island or with the United States.

The answer came quickly, as the new government initiated major changes in 1959 and 1960. The May 1959 Agrarian Reform Law reduced the maximum landholding size to 1,000 acres, and the excess property was largely distributed to landless farmworkers. Forty percent of Cuba's rural property was nationalized. The Urban Reform Law cut rents substantially. Cubans with more than two pieces of property were obliged to hand over the excess to the government, which then reclassified them as social property, transforming houses, for example, into day care centers.

These reforms produced little new wealth. Instead, they entailed a massive redistribution from rich to poor. The wealthiest 10 percent of the population lost much of its property, privileges, and political power. They were forced to pay new luxury taxes, their private schools and clubs were closed, private beaches were opened to the public, and private clinics were forced to treat indigent patients. At the same time, the lower classes—especially urban Afro-Cubans and all those in rural areas—received immediate benefits because historically they had suffered the greatest unemployment and had received the fewest public services. More than 40 percent of the Cuban workforce in 1958 was either underemployed or unemployed. Sugarcane workers, who made up approximately 25 percent of the national labor force, averaged less than four months of work a year, and Cuba's official unemployment rate in 1958 was 16 percent.

In addition to tangible relief, the revolutionary government set in motion processes that would create new opportunities for the previously dispossessed. It passed new laws banning discrimination on the basis of race or gender, it began to train doctors so that good health care would be universal, and it set out to strengthen the education system. The 1961 literacy campaign engaged a large number of young educated Cubans in the revolutionary process, sparking their idealism and opening their eyes to the vast inequalities in the country. University classes were suspended as students and professors went throughout the country over a nine-month period to teach adults how to read. They succeeded in reducing illiteracy from 23.6 percent of the population to 3.9 percent.

Blacks and mulattoes constitute a much higher proportion of the population in Cuba than in the United States. The 1953 census recorded 26.9 percent of Cuba as black or mulatto; in the 1981 census, it was 34 percent.[21] Racial discrimination before 1959 may have been less a result of interpersonal prejudice than in the United States, but it was entrenched in the way Cuban institutions functioned. Lourdes Casal, a seminal scholar on the subject of racism in Cuba, points out that several factors softened the expression of racism. "The most important leaders of the Cuban independence struggle such as José Martí (white) and Antonio Maceo (black)," she wrote, placed great emphasis on "racial unity and integration."[22] Still, schools for darker-skinned Cubans—when they were available—were vastly inferior than those for whites. Afro-Cubans had the worst living conditions and held the lowest-paid jobs. There was some social mobility for nonwhite Cubans, and Cubans elected Fulgencio Batista, a light-skinned mulatto, as president in 1940. But the white, upper-class Havana Yacht Club even denied membership to Batista while he was in office from 1940 to 1944.

Polarization Emerges

As the pace of change accelerated, an ideological gulf emerged between moderate and radical reformers. The struggle against Batista had brought together groups with diverse agendas. Without the common enemy, their differences came to the forefront. Some moderates joined the campaign because they were appalled by Batista's violent repression and disregard for human rights; others had focused on his regime's corruption and willingness to give the *mafia* effective carte blanche over part of Cuba's tourist industry. Some genuinely believed that the enormous gap between the country's rich and poor could be closed significantly through liberal democratic reforms. To these moderate Cubans, Castro was "betraying" the goals that led them to join the Revolution. On the other hand, some so-called moderates invoked "democracy" merely to protect their property and privilege. Saul Landau comments that they

> had little interest in ending the state of dependency with the United States, and absolutely no inclination to channel their wealth to the services of the majority. This was the essence of the class war that confronted Castro and the revolutionaries by spring 1959.[23]

In fact, the class war was only the first of three simultaneous conflicts that Castro expected the Revolution would need to fight. The second would be against the alliance of Cuban property owners and U.S. corporations that had made extensive investments in Cuba. These were the very bonds the radical nationalists aimed to cut in the hope that decisions about Cuba's economy could be made in Havana, not New York or Washington. The United States had almost never allowed a country in its sphere of influence to act so independently. The revolutionary leadership viewed the 1954 U.S.-engineered coup in Guatemala, which overthrew the democratically elected government of Jacobo Arbenz, as the model of what to expect. Castro made some attempt to blunt the negative U.S. reaction he expected. On a goodwill trip to the United States in April 1959, he offered to repay owners of confiscated lands a price that was greater than their assessed values in tax records and promised to deliver 8 million tons of sugar to the United States at below-market price. But many of his speeches in 1959 and 1960 were rife with derisive and insulting remarks that were seemingly intended to taunt the United States.

The third conflict was cultural. It involved overcoming sixty years of neocolonial acculturation to U.S. values that implicitly denigrated Cuban identity and Cubans themselves. This struggle was the most difficult because it occurred at an ideological, unconscious level, where the enemy was ingrained in each person's conception of the Cuban character. Most often the clash manifested itself as a contest over the meaning of civilization. Defenders of the old order argued that the extent to which Cuba has become civilized could be ascertained by the availability of modern technology and even "luxuries" that would enable a person to live comfortably. In contrast, Castro argued, the level of civilization should be evaluated by the percentage of people who were illiterate and unemployed and by the number of children with parasites. In effect, Louis Pérez points out, the revolutionaries sought "to rearrange in usable form the standards by which to measure civilization and in the process summon a vision of an alternative moral order."[24]

Victory in all three conflicts entailed sacrifices. It cost the middle and upper classes wealth, privileges, and status. Workers and peasants were deprived of normalcy: their values were challenged, and demands for their nonpaid "social labor" disrupted routines of daily life. Clashes with the United States involved the loss of life and caused the economy to suffer. Anticipating these costs, the revolutionary leadership reasoned that victories would require Cubans to sustain great leaps of faith that could be undermined if there were disunity and dissent.

The determination to create and maintain unity led the revolutionary government to close down newspapers, nationalize television and radio stations, and cancel promised elections. Efforts to develop a disciplined party apparatus led to the arrest of some who had fought against Batista but did not want to accept Castro's leadership. Ultimately, these measures left an indelible imprint on the Cuban Revolution. Justified at first by the necessity to galvanize the mass of Cubans and enable them to develop a revolutionary consciousness, repression became routinized by the alleged demands of national security.

To be sure, the Cuban Revolution had serious enemies. Counterrevolutionaries, centered in the Escambray Mountains and located throughout the country, fought tenaciously from 1960 to 1966. In that period, more than 2,000 insurgents and 500 Cuban soldiers were killed in battle. One counterrevolutionary veteran, Lino Fernández, told a conference in 1996 that the insurgency was essentially a military operation, not a political one, because the fighters believed that the Cuban government could be overthrown only by force, not by political means.[25] The United States began to support the counterrevolutionaries in late 1959 and attempted to overthrow the regime by mounting the April 1961 Bay of Pigs invasion. The Central Intelligence Agency (CIA) then waged a multifaceted "low-intensity" war against Cuba, code-named Operation Mongoose, which included plans for an invasion by the U.S. Marines.[26] The possibility of a U.S. attack has been ever present since then because even today the United States designates Cuba as one of four "state sponsors of terrorism" and several U.S. laws stipulate that Cuba is an "enemy" of the United States. A small country like Cuba, adjacent to the world's most powerful nation, does not have the luxury to view such designations casually, as if they had no meaning. Ricardo Alarcón de Quesada, president of Cuba's National Assembly, remarked to two of us in a 2006 interview that he "awakes every day anticipating a U.S. attack on the horizon."

Yet over time, as national security came to eclipse other priorities, some threats became exaggerated, fear replaced hope, and petty officials were given license to engage in spiteful acts of cruelty. The height of repression came in the early 1960s. Following the Bay of Pigs invasion, the Cuban government rounded up and arrested "tens of thousands of people." While most were released quickly, in 1965 Castro acknowledged that 20,000 political prisoners continued to be incarcerated.[27] Late in that year, the military began to "draft" thousands of people whom the regime designated as "socially deviant": homosexuals, vagrants, and Jehovah's Witnesses and other religious missionaries. They were placed in prisonlike camps named "Military Units to Aid Production" (UMAP)—ostensibly to be reeducated—and ordered to do nonremunerated labor. The UMAP program lasted for two years. Castro disbanded it in 1967 after the Cuban National Union of Writers and Artists protested the incarceration of many writers and university professors.[28]

Still, the early years of the Revolution produced an enormous outpouring of vibrant cultural expression. For example, the official newspaper of the 26th of July Movement, *Revolución*, included a literary supplement every Monday, *Lunes de Revolución*, which quickly gained international acclaim from the world's leading avant-garde authors. *Lunes* focused on all of the arts. In addition to the magazine, *Lunes* created a record company, it started a publishing house that emphasized works by new Cuban writers that broke with traditional themes, and it produced a weekly television program that featured modern plays, jazz, and experimental films.[29] In effect, *Lunes* became the forum for debates about Cuban culture.

The explosion of creativity inevitably ran the risk of challenging the government's plan for unity. In June 1961, Castro made clear that the limits of tolerance had been reached. In the course of a three-day meeting with "intellectuals," he laid down a new dictum. The Revolution, he said, must give an opportunity to all writers and artists, even to those who were not "genuine revolutionaries," to express themselves freely and to use of their "creative spirit." But this freedom would be available only if their creative work was consistent with the Revolution. Castro tersely summarized the rule by declaring, "Within the revolution, everything; against the revolution, nothing."[30] The trouble was that he did not provide clear parameters as to what lay "within" and what strayed outside the borders of permissible dissent. Without guidelines, enforcement became arbitrary. Writers and artists feared that the pronouncement was intended to stifle not to endorse freedom of expression, and their interpretation was reinforced in November, when Castro shut down *Lunes de Revolución*.

As the Cuban revolutionaries implemented their plans, disaffected Cubans voted with their feet and left Cuba. The first wave of émigrés (1959–1962) consisted largely of landowners, wealthy business people, former Batista government officials, managers, small proprietors, and professionals, such as doctors, engineers, and skilled technicians. Many went to the United States, where those with professional training were especially welcomed as part of a U.S. strategy to undermine the Cuban Revolution by depleting the island of people who had technical expertise. By November 1965, when Castro opened the door to unrestricted emigration, 211,000 Cubans had departed. In the next six years, an additional 277,000 emigrated from Cuba.[31]

Debate over the "New" Cuban Man (Material versus Moral Incentives)

At its core, the Cuban Revolution included a socialist humanist vision that contributed to its international appeal. The vision was based on an Enlightenment belief that human beings are "perfectible" and that their institutions make them imperfect. Simply stated, socialist humanists contend that people become alienated from their full potential when a society's institutions—and its consequent relationships—lead them to pursue self-gratification and individual survival. They assert that humans are capable of transcending individualism and selfishness and of acting with a social conscience for the benefit of the whole society.

Scholars have tended to identify Ernesto Che Guevara as the main proponent of the socialist humanist vision among the founding leaders of the Revolution. Indeed, Guevara did call for the development of new Cuban citizens—the term he used was "new man"—who would eschew "the satisfaction of their personal ambitions" and "become more aware every day of the need to incorporate themselves into society."[32] Guevara's "ultimate aim," economist Bertram Silverman explains, was "to consciously use the process of socialist development as a force to create a new morality."[33] The transition, Guevara asserted, involved reeducation that should take place not only in schools but also through extensive processes of socialization, politicization, and acculturation, implemented by revolutionary leadership and sustained by nationwide citizen participation. People needed to learn the meaning and practice of the new morality gradually through their daily activities and relationships. This would require, in Guevara's view, the use of "moral incentives" to motivate people rather than "material incentives," which would tend to reinforce individualism.

In practice, the use of moral incentives is usually accompanied by inefficiency. Appeals to a common purpose are less likely to engender consistent hard work than differentiated rewards to individuals. For a poor country like Cuba, reduced production affects the availability of basic necessities, so it could tend to undermine popular support for the Revolution itself. The dilemma—posed by the debate over the reliance on material or moral incentives—is one that continues to frame Cuban development decisions even today.

Those on one side of the debate focus on the goal of meeting Cubans' basic needs. They argue that the use of material incentives is necessary in order to produce enough wealth so that all Cubans receive adequate food, health care, education, transportation, and social services. Those on the other side emphasize the goal of instilling Cubans with a new morality based on egalitarianism and social consciousness. They argue that cradle-to-grave welfare socialism, without the concurrent or prior development of the new morality, reinforces individualism and inevitably generates inequalities that make realization of the egalitarian goal impossible.

Notably, the latter position did not lose its potency when Guevara left Cuba in 1965. Fidel Castro continued to be a forceful advocate for a new Cuban morality, often invoking Guevara's name to rail against evidence of greed and selfishness. Indeed, at key junctures, he implemented significant changes in Cuba's economy in order to restore what he viewed as a balance between material and moral incentives. In March 1968, following a January purge of "old" Communist Party members who favored material incentives, he nationalized 55,000 small businesses and called for a "revolutionary offensive" to "complete the job of making our people fully revolutionary." Cubans had to learn to develop their revolutionary consciousness from "each event . . . each new experience."[34]

The experiment with moral incentives in the late 1960s contributed to serious economic problems and the failure of Castro's heralded plan to produce 10 million tons of sugar in the 1970s. For the next decade and a half, under pressure from the Soviet Union and dependent on Soviet aid, Cuba returned to a reliance on material incentives. In 1986, however, Castro once again reacted against what he regarded as the evils of the market. He shut down private farmers' markets and denounced the distributors of agricultural produce who earned sums far greater than those of ordinary workers. At the same time, he criticized managers of state enterprises for applying capitalist principles—favoring the production of higher-priced goods that earned more money for their firms over the production of goods needed for social projects—and "people who confuse income earned through work with what can be got through speculation." These practices had to be "rectified," Castro asserted, by returning to the fundamental principles of the Cuban Revolution. "There are some," he said, "who think that socialism can be brought about without political work. . . . I believe that the problems must be resolved morally, honorably and with principles."[35]

To some extent, Cuba was able to reconcile the first goal—providing universal and quality health care and education, food for everyone, and universal access to basic necessities, such as electricity and clean water—with the second goal—developing a new Cuban morality when its economy was productive and the Soviet Union provided large subsidies. Within twenty years of overthrowing the Batista regime, the revolutionary government had eradicated epidemic diseases and lowered the rate of infant mortality to the level in the United States. Rural poverty essentially had been eliminated, in part because of a conscious effort to locate new production facilities in previously downtrodden areas and to increase wages of agrarian workers and provide them with housing, roads, schools, health clinics, and electricity.[36] At the same time, in what was ultimately a failed project, the government attempted to instill a new morality by creating free boarding schools in the countryside. Students at these schools spent part of each day cultivating and harvesting crops. The intention was twofold: to break down urban prejudices about *campesinos* by integrating urban children into rural locales and by inducing a sense of responsibility for the common good through engagement in nonremunerated "social labor."[37]

The 1986 rectification campaign began as the Soviet Union introduced perestroika, a restructuring of its economic planning process to place greater reliance on market mechanisms. Rectification was a pointed rejection of the Soviet model and implicitly of Soviet leadership. Cuba's Communist Party leaders blamed the stagnation of Cuba's economy in the late 1970s and early 1980s on their own blind adherence to Soviet practices.[38]

Four factors mainly accounted for the early 1970s growth spurt. First, a new generation of Cuban specialists had graduated from universities and were able to do the work of the professionals who departed in the early 1960s. Second, the world price for sugar jumped to historic levels—$0.70 per pound briefly in 1974—enabling Cuba to earn hard currency from surplus sugar and to buy modern technology from European firms. Third, material incentives were introduced to spur productivity. Workers could increase their salaries by working overtime at higher wage rates, and more productive workers could earn the right to buy refrigerators, air conditioners, and other consumer durables. Fourth, in 1972, Cuba joined the Council for Mutual Economic Assistance (CMEA), the socialist trading bloc headed by the Soviet Union. Cuba was designated as a commodity producer for the CMEA countries, providing sugar, citrus, nickel, and cobalt to its new partners. In turn, it was able to import petroleum, machinery, and manufactured goods from them at subsidized prices, defer loan repayments, and obtain new loans with low rates. Although the products from the Soviet Union and Eastern European countries tended to be of low quality, they provided Cuban leaders with the means to begin an effort at diversifying the economy.

In both the 1968 and the 1986 cases, Cuba's economic decisions were in part a reaction to pressures from the Soviet Union, and they reflected Castro's determination to maintain as much independence for Cuba as possible. But just as Cuba's special relationship with the United States from 1903 to 1959 created conditions that influenced the course of the Cuban Revolution, so its relationship with the Soviet Union from 1960 to 1991 reduced Castro's options.

FOREIGN RELATIONS AFTER 1959

Testing the Limits of Soviet Tolerance

Despite his reputation for rashness and braggadocio, Soviet Premier Nikita Khrushchev was quite wary about disturbing the United States in the Western Hemisphere. In the 1950s, the Soviet Communist Party had ordered its affiliated parties in Latin America to distance themselves from any attempts to forcibly overthrow or destabilize their governments. Most Cuban communists, who were organized as the Popular Socialist Party (PSP), also followed this Moscow line and had little if any contact with the revolutionaries during the struggle against Batista. The Soviets thus did not know much about Fidel Castro and the 26th of July Movement, and they were not anxious to support rebels who neither would take orders from Moscow nor were likely to survive U.S. hostility. It took until February 1960 for a Soviet trade delegation to arrive in Havana, though it was a prominent one, headed by Deputy Premier Anastas Mikoyan. Shortly afterward, the two countries reestablished diplomatic relations, which had been broken in 1952.

In the spring of 1960, the Soviets began to supply Cuba with a few light arms, artillery and mortars, tanks, antiaircraft rockets, and technical assistance. But only after the 1961 Bay of

Pigs invasion, when it was clear that the revolutionary government had popular support and staying power, did the Soviets promise to send more sophisticated weapons.[39] Of greater importance, when President Dwight Eisenhower barred any further U.S. importation of Cuban sugar in July 1960, the Soviet Union purchased the sugar that Cuba had expected to export to the United States. This began a trading relationship in which Cuba remained dependent largely on its production of sugar. By the 1980s, sugar export earnings from sales to the Soviet Union and Eastern European countries accounted for a larger percentage of total exports than sugar exports to the United States in the 1950s.[40] In addition, Soviet sales of petroleum to Cuba at below-market prices were a form of foreign assistance on which Cuba came to depend.

Still, Cuba's relations with the Soviet Union were never as congenial as U.S. officials and the Western media portrayed them. In fact, tension between the two countries was so great in 1968 that Raúl Castro publicly charged Aníbal Escalante with treason for conspiring with Soviet officials to replace Fidel Castro as first secretary of the Cuban Communist Party. Escalante had been in the PSP leadership prior to 1959 and had maintained close ties to Moscow party officials in the 1960s.

The bitterness that Cuba's leaders felt toward the Soviet Union can be traced to October 28, 1962, the day on which the Cuban missile crisis is commonly said to have ended with an understanding between the U.S. and Soviet heads of state. (The so-called Kennedy-Khrushchev agreement stipulated that the Soviets would withdraw all offensive weapons from Cuba, and the United States would pledge not to invade or support an invasion of Cuba.) The Cubans interpreted the agreement as a Soviet capitulation to U.S. threats and judged that the Soviet Union would be unwilling in the future to put itself at risk to protect Cuba. "We realized how alone we would be in the event of a war," Castro remarked in a speech to the first full meeting of the Communist Party's Central Committee in January 1968. From the Cuban perspective, the Soviet Union had made Cuba even more vulnerable than before the missile crisis. Not only had the Soviets signaled to the United States that its guarantee of protecting Cuba was hollow, but Khrushchev also was asking Cuba to return weapons to the Soviets that the Cubans believed were necessary for their defense. Castro's palpable contempt was evident in 1968 as he characterized the Soviet leaders as "feeble-minded bureaucrats."[41]

After the missile crisis, the two countries locked horns on several issues as Castro tried to demonstrate that Cuba could not be controlled by a domineering Soviet Union. In 1963, despite Soviet requests, Cuba refused to sign both the Limited Test Ban Treaty and the Tlatelolco Treaty, which declared Latin America as a nuclear-free zone. Guevara, speaking on behalf of the Cuban government at a 1965 conference in Algeria, castigated the Soviets for their regressive ideological views and for their immorality in not adequately supporting liberation movements.[42] In January 1966, Cuba frontally challenged the Soviet Union's claim to be the natural leader of the Third World. It brought together 500 delegates from Africa, Asia, and Latin America at the first Tricontinental Conference to initiate an organization that would be dedicated to promoting and supporting armed liberation struggles on the three continents. Soviet leaders had repeatedly admonished Castro to back away from supporting armed struggle. As retribution for the imperious Soviet warning, Castro did not invite any communist parties to be represented at the conference. Then in October 1967, Guevara was killed fighting against the Bolivian government. It was a terrible blow to Castro, who blamed his comrade's death on the Bolivian Communist Party and, by implication, on their Soviet puppet masters.[43]

Cuba Joins the Socialist Camp

Cuba and the Soviet Union had come close to a breaking point. Castro knew he had no other options but to reduce the tension and cease his open challenges to Soviet leadership. This was underscored by a Soviet decision to provide Cuba with less oil in 1968 than it was expecting to receive. On January 2, 1968, Castro reported that troublesome news to the Cuban people. In the first instance, he said, the shortfall would require new controls on the use of gasoline, great efforts to conserve oil, and a reliance on alternative sources of fuel to run sugar mills. But he held out the hope that the hardships would be temporary, lasting for at most three years. By achieving the goal of a 10-million-ton sugar harvest in 1970, he asserted, Cuba would earn enough hard currency to be self-reliant. It would no longer need to make undignified, "incessant requests" for advance shipments of oil. The 10-million-ton harvest thus embodied a political goal as well as an economic one. Cuba could truly be independent if the plan were successful.[44]

As a consequence, virtually the entire economy was subordinated to the task of meeting this unprecedented target. Ultimately, some 8.5 million tons were gathered. Although that set a record, it represented a pyrrhic victory. Other sectors of the economy suffered major losses because so many resources and so many workers had been diverted to the sugar harvest. The failure of the 10-million-ton campaign led directly to Cuba's decision to become a junior partner in the CMEA.

As Cuba tied its economic planning more closely to the Soviet Union, it also began to link its armed forces and intelligence services to the corresponding Soviet agencies. Despite such integration, though, Cuba took its own counsel on foreign policy. Most scholars have concluded that Cuba was neither a puppet of nor a stalking horse for the Soviet Union. While Cuba's choices often coincided with Soviet interests, there were several notable disagreements in the 1970s. In early November 1975, Cuba sent the first contingent of what would be a 35,000-soldier deployment to Angola to support the Popular Movement for the Liberation of Angola (MPLA), one of the three parties already engaged in a civil war to determine who would rule the country after independence. Castro did not inform Soviet leaders about the Cuban troop movement, fearing that they were likely to oppose it. Indeed, the Soviets were not pleased because their first priority was advancing détente with the United States. Soviet-Cuban engagement in the Angolan civil war was likely to upend delicate negotiations with the United States, which was backing the forces opposed to the MPLA. Nevertheless, Moscow agreed to provide Cuban troops with the military equipment they needed to turn back a South African invasion of Angola.[45]

In contrast, Third World countries—especially those in Africa—lavished praise on the Cubans. Cuba's support for the MPLA and its willingness to fight against the apartheid regime in South Africa was a key reason that the Non-Aligned Movement (NAM) selected Cuba to be the location for its 1979 summit. The host country also serves as chair of the NAM until the next summit, and Castro saw this as an opportunity to forge unity among poorer countries of the world. He planned to encourage oil-rich countries in the "South" to use their resources for South-South cooperative programs, which he viewed as an essential step to reduce their dependency on the advanced industrial nations.

Cuba's Internationalism

The divergent Soviet and Cuban perspectives—one from the vantage point of a small nation and the other from the vantage point of a superpower—were painfully evident to Castro in December 1979, when the Soviet Union invaded Afghanistan. The invasion vitiated Cuba's ability to serve as an effective NAM leader because Afghanistan was a NAM member and nonintervention was a core NAM principle. Castro had not even been informed in advance about the intervention. But he felt constrained to support the Soviet action by not condemning it, which was a position exactly opposite the one that NAM countries expected their chair to take. The asymmetry between Cuba and the Soviet Union, which had contributed to their friction in the 1960s, continued to generate tension for the next twelve years until the Soviet Union collapsed.[46] In particular, disagreements over support for liberation struggles in Central America and southern Africa during the 1980s led to public displays of hostility. For example, Castro did not attend the 1985 funeral of Soviet President Konstantin Chernenko to show his displeasure with the low level of support the Soviet Union was providing the Sandinista government in Nicaragua.[47]

Cuba's commitments to the MPLA's victory in Angola, to the success of the Southwest Africa People's Organization in its struggle for Namibia's independence, and to the consolidation of Sandinista rule in Nicaragua were not based on expedient short-term calculations or spontaneous bursts of revolutionary zeal.[48] They developed slowly, starting in the 1960s, and were deeply rooted in the Cuban revolutionaries' belief that internationalism served Cuba's immediate and long-term interests. In the short term, Cuba's military contributions to liberation struggles, technical assistance to newly independent states, and education and health care to people from the Third World would generate goodwill and needed allies. Ultimately, as more countries shared Cuba's views, its internationalism would have contributed to their ability to forge South-South coalitions.

Internationalism also brought ordinary Cubans into contact with the deep poverty many Third World people suffer, and new generations of Cubans who had no memory of the 1950s could gain an appreciation for the achievements of the Revolution. By the mid-1980s, approximately 15,000 Cubans—one out of every 625—were working in civilian foreign aid missions in more than thirty countries. At the same time, 24,000 students from eighty-two countries were enrolled in Cuban high schools and universities.[49]

Challenging the United States

It may be impossible now to disentangle the different ideological underpinnings of U.S. policy toward the Cuban Revolution in the early years. One strand hearkened to the U.S. patronizing attitude evidenced by General Wood in 1899. At a February 1959 meeting of the National Security Council, CIA Director Allen Dulles counseled that "the new Cuban officials had to be treated more or less like children."[50] Similarly, Secretary of State Christian Herter described Fidel Castro as "immature and irrational," and labor attaché John Correll remarked that "everybody thought he [Castro] was going to be a very good boy," but "he wasn't a good boy at all."[51]

Alternately, conventional wisdom holds that Cold War ideology shaped U.S. policy. Washington was in the grip of a mind-set that framed foreign policy decisions in terms of a bipolar, zero-sum view of the world: a country was either for the United States or for its enemy, the Soviet Union. There was no room for an independent country of the sort Cuba hoped to be. Cuba did not even establish diplomatic relations with the Soviet Union during the first year after the Revolution. But U.S. policymakers still were worried about the revolutionary government, in part because of its charismatic chief, Fidel Castro. Vice President Richard Nixon reported in a confidential memo, after his April 1959 meeting with Castro, that the Cuban leader "has those indefinable qualities which make him a leader of men. Whatever we may think of him he is going to be a great factor in the development of Cuba and very possibly in Latin American affairs generally."[52]

By the end of the year, the CIA was developing schemes to assassinate Castro and overthrow the Cuban government.[53] In a November 1959 memo to President Dwight Eisenhower, Secretary of State Herter provided the justification for the subversive plans. Cuba threatened the United States, he observed, because Castro "has veered towards a 'neutralist' anti-

American foreign policy for Cuba which, if emulated by other Latin American countries, would have serious adverse effects on Free World support of our leadership."[54]

In effect, Cuba's stance challenged the legitimacy of what Abraham Lowenthal has called the U.S. hegemonic presumption in the Western Hemisphere—a third ideological strand.[55] Castro made his opposition to U.S. "leadership" explicit in September 1960, openly proclaiming Cuba's duty to make revolution in the hemisphere. But his "First Declaration of Havana" came four days after the Organization of American States (OAS) approved the Declaration of San Jose (August 28, 1960), in which the hemisphere's foreign ministers implicitly condemned Cuba for permitting Soviet and Chinese "extra-continental intervention" that "endangers American solidarity and security."[56]

Whether the initial U.S. concern was over the apparent threat to U.S. hemispheric hegemony or was in fact the so-called Soviet threat, Cold War assumptions had gained full rein over U.S. policy by mid-1960. There was no longer any question as to whether Cuba was in the Soviet camp because the two countries had negotiated a trade agreement in February and reestablished diplomatic relations in the spring. At this point, Cuba was not yet ruled by a Communist Party. Castro first declared the character of the Cuban Revolution to be "socialist" only on the eve of the April 17, 1961, Bay of Pigs invasion.

Within months of the failed U.S.-sponsored attack, Kennedy authorized the CIA to undertake a more ambitious effort to overthrow the revolutionary regime. Code-named Operation Mongoose, the project had four components: (1) terrorism—CIA agents and assets based in Florida conducted raids in Cuba to sabotage factory equipment, burned sugarcane fields, contaminated processed sugar, and provided weapons to counterrevolutionaries who undertook their own "military" actions; (2) political isolation—the United States was able to pressure enough OAS members in January 1962 to gain the necessary votes to suspend Cuba from the organization; (3) economic strangulation—in February 1962, Kennedy instituted a full embargo on all transactions between Cuba and the United States, including food and medicine; (4) military intimidation—the U.S. Navy conducted several unusually large exercises in the Caribbean in 1962, including one that involved the practice invasion of an island named "Ortsac," that is, "Castro" spelled backward. There was also an associated project that ran concurrently with Mongoose to assassinate Castro and the other Cuban leaders.[57] Castro interpreted all of this activity as prelude to a U.S. invasion. He sought Soviet assistance to defend Cuba, and Khrushchev offered ballistic missiles. The October 1962 missile crisis confirmed the Kennedy administration's worst fears about how the Soviet-Cuban connection could undermine U.S. security. Subsequently, Cuba's supposed threat to the United States, because of its close ties to the other superpower, remained a core assumption of U.S. policy until the Soviet Union imploded in 1991.[58]

Still, there were three brief periods during the Cold War when the glimmerings of a U.S.-Cuban modus vivendi surfaced. In 1963, Kennedy used unofficial emissaries to probe the possibility of restoring relations between the two countries. But these efforts ended shortly after Johnson became president. In 1974, Secretary of State Henry Kissinger initiated secret negotiations between U.S. and Cuban officials aimed at normalizing relations. The next year, as a signal of good faith, the United States voted with a majority of members in the OAS to lift the 1964 hemisphere-wide embargo against Cuba. President Gerald Ford then relaxed the U.S. embargo to permit subsidiaries of U.S. corporations in third countries to trade with Cuba.[59] Cuba's response to the conciliatory U.S. moves, Kissinger believed, was decidedly hostile. He viewed its support for the MPLA in Angola later that year as an assault on U.S.-Soviet détente. In December 1975, President Gerald Ford announced that Cuba's Angola operation "destroys any opportunity for improvement of relations with the United States."[60]

The third opening occurred during the first two years of the Carter administration. Shortly after his inauguration, President Jimmy Carter expressed a hope to alleviate tensions between Cuba and the United States.[61] A few weeks later, Carter announced that he would not renew the ban on travel to Cuba by U.S. citizens and that U.S. citizens would be permitted to spend money in Cuba related to their travel. He also approved negotiations with Cuba over maritime boundaries and fishing rights, and an agreement was finalized in April 1977. In September, the two countries opened diplomatic missions in each other's capitals.

However, by 1978, the Cold War had intruded once again. Cuba had deployed more than 20,000 troops to Ethiopia to support its conflict with Somalia over the Ogaden Desert. While not enamored of Somalia, U.S. officials were concerned that the Cuban presence in Ethiopia would provide a foothold for the Soviet Union on the horn of Africa. Moreover, Carter's national security adviser, Zbigniew Brzezinski, relentlessly urged the president to interpret Cuban behavior in terms of the Cold War because he believed that the Soviets were using the Cubans as a "military proxy" in Africa to serve their own expansionist aims.[62] Carter acknowledged in his memoir the influence Brzezinski had on his thinking: "Originally from Poland, he [Brzezinski] had made a special study of the Soviet Union and Eastern Europe. . . . I was an eager student, and took full advantage of what Brzezinski had to offer."[63]

As the president began to adopt Brzezinski's worldview, he painted himself into rhetorical corners, quickly responding to each new Cuban "challenge" with a tough stance even when the reality turned out to contradict his allegations. Wayne Smith, who was in charge of the State Department's Cuba desk at the time, recalls that in 1978 and 1979, Cuba made sincere efforts to be cooperative, but these were rebuffed.[64] On October 4, 1979, Carter issued PD-52, a presidential directive that ordered key national security agencies to devise ways "to contain Cuba as a source of violent revolutionary change."

Thus, when President Ronald Reagan took office, the U.S. hostility toward Cuba that already was in place provided firm ground from which to launch a more threatening policy. Secretary of State Alexander Haig established the tougher orientation in February 1981, asserting that the United States must "deal with the immediate source of the problem [in El Salvador]—and that is Cuba."[65] Cuba took the threat seriously. It responded by creating a 1.5-million-person "Territorial Troop Militia" to defend the island with a Swiss-like strategy of a "people in arms."[66] In fact, the Reagan policy offered more continuity than change. The U.S. president tightened the embargo; launched *Radio Martí*, a station that transmitted propaganda broadcasts to the island; and generally closed the door to any discussions with Cuban officials. However, the United States did engage in negotiations with Cuba about migration issues in 1984, and it acceded to Cuba's presence at multiparty talks in 1988 that ended the fighting in Namibia.

After the collapse of the Soviet Union, Cuba's threat to U.S. national security largely disappeared. With the danger gone, the rationale for U.S. policy toward Cuba evaporated. To President George H. W. Bush, the change meant that Cuba was no longer a significant foreign policy issue. Instead, domestic political considerations took center stage. Before the 1980s, the Cuban exile community played only a small role in shaping U.S. policy. Anti-Castro Cubans did not have an organization that operated in the commonly accepted manner of other ethnic lobbies until 1981, when the Cuban American National Foundation (CANF) was founded with the assistance and encouragement of Reagan administration officials.[67] Structured much like the effective American Israel Public Affairs Committee (AIPAC), CANF received guidance from AIPAC to broaden its focus beyond Cuba. At the time, there were just over 1 million people in the United States who were born in Cuba or were of Cuban descent. Concentrated largely in South Florida and northern New Jersey, they could not hope to influence policy merely by the power of their votes in a few congressional districts. Moreover, even then the Cuban American community did not have a monolithic position on U.S. policy toward Cuba. Notably, in 1978, a group of Cuban Americans formed the Committee of 75 to engage in a "dialogue" with Cuban officials on behalf of Cubans in exile. The committee focused on humanitarian issues, such as the release of political prisoners and the right of Cubans outside of the country to return for family visits. Beginning in 1979, the Cuban government granted visas to people entering Cuba to see families; more than 100,000 Cuban Americans visited the island in 1979–1980.[68]

Beyond Cuban Americans' votes, CANF relied on campaign contributions shrewdly spent by its political action committee and the power of a few well-placed senators and representatives who valued CANF's support to influence Congress. As the "Special Period" in Cuba started, CANF had effectively gained control of U.S. policy and was determined to restructure the policy in order to push the revolutionary regime into the abyss toward which it seemed to be tipping.

REINVENTING THE CUBAN REVOLUTION

By 1990, Cuba had developed to the point where infectious diseases had been eradicated and its rate of infant mortality was comparable to that of advanced industrial nations, where there were more doctors per capita than in any other country and free universal health care was available throughout the island, and where universities had been established in every province, education through graduate school was free, and racial and gender disparities were disappearing because of educational opportunities. Although Cuba was still a poor country by standard measures of gross domestic product (GDP), it was an egalitarian society where most people considered themselves to be middle class and could reasonably hope that their children's lives would be better than their own. In the first thirty-two years of the Revolution, the great majority of Cubans also had gained an intangible but discernible sense of dignity, in part because of Cuba's prowess in international sports competitions; the worldwide recognition of Cuban artists, writers, dancers, and filmmakers; and the respect that other Third World countries accorded to this small nation that had repeatedly and successfully defied the hovering giant ninety miles away.

However, the collapse of the Soviet Union in 1991 made clear the continuing weakness of Cuba's monocultural export economy and its vulnerability to the United States. Cuba's adaptation to its new circumstances altered the very nature of the Cuban Revolution, significantly impacting the economic and political organization of the country, Cuba's culture and daily life, and its foreign relations. In effect, Cuba had to abandon the former revolutionary order and invent a new one.

Economics and Politics during the Special Period

Imagine your reaction if you had to substitute sugar water for food every third day for a year and as a result you lost your eyesight because of a vitamin deficiency (as happened to 50,000 Cubans temporarily) and twenty to twenty-five pounds (the average for Cubans in 1993–1994).[69] Suppose that you could not drive your car, buses ran infrequently because of gasoline shortages, and blackouts meant that food you hoped to preserve in your refrigerator was rotting because oil imports dropped by 70 percent over a four-year period as they did in Cuba from 1989 to 1993. Picture yourself undergoing an operation at a formerly reliable hospital where now several doctors and nurses were absent because of transportation problems and there were hardly any anesthetics, medicines, or bandages. In 1990, few Cubans believed that they would ever live this kind of life, even when Cuban President Fidel Castro announced that the country was entering a "Special Period in a Time of Peace."

The collapse of the CMEA, the Eastern bloc's trading system through which Cuba had conducted 85 percent of its international commerce, forced it to find new trading partners who demanded that Cuba pay market prices in an internationally convertible (i.e., "hard") currency for the goods it imported. When the Soviet Union collapsed, Cuba lost an estimated $3 billion to $4 billion in annual economic aid. As its international trade plummeted between 1990 and 1993, Cuba's GDP declined by 30 percent.[70] A further blow came in 1993, when the United States began to implement the Cuban Democracy Act, which banned sales to Cuba by subsidiaries of U.S. corporations abroad, thereby increasing the cost of food and medicine that Cuba imported.[71]

The Search for Hard Currency

Cuban leaders understood that the economic crisis was also "a crisis in the way of conceiving of socialism, a crisis of values, a moral crisis, a crisis of society," as political scientist Rafael Hernández observes.[72] They believed that solving the economic crisis was essential to the political survival of the Revolution. While they gave some attention to long-term implications of their decisions, they focused on "a relatively narrow agenda" of immediate solutions.[73] In practical terms, the new reality meant that Cuba had to abandon its economic model of import-substitution industrialization and to insert itself into the international capitalist economy. It had to find new ways quickly to earn hard currency, though there were few options available. The export of sugar and nickel had been Cuba's main source of convertible funds. But production in both industries was inefficient and depended on imported oil that Cuba could no longer afford. Backed into a corner, Cuba's leaders opted for three strategies they had eschewed previously.

First, they sought to attract large amounts of foreign investment capital. This required removing bureaucratic obstacles, creating new Cuban companies to interact with foreigners, and approving new laws that would enable foreign enterprises to own more than 49 percent of a joint venture with a Cuban entity. The new quasi-private enterprises became staffed largely by former members of the Cuban armed forces (*Fuerzas Armadas Revolucionarias* [FAR]).[74] In 1995, the government permitted 100 percent foreign ownership in a few specified industries. There were 392 foreign joint ventures in Cuba by 2001.[75]

Hotels became the largest kind of foreign investment, coinciding with Cuba's second strategy for acquiring hard currency: building up its tourist industry. But the decision was not taken lightly. As Marguerite Jiménez explains, "Fidel Castro's reluctance to promote tourism was rooted in memories of pre-1959 Cuba, as an all-inclusive hedonist playground for affluent North American tourists, accompanied by prostitution, corruption, and gambling casinos run by organized crime syndicates."[76] By 2005, more than 2 million visitors were arriving on the island annually, and Cuba had become one of the top ten tourist locations in the Western Hemisphere. Tourism replaced sugar as the country's most important source of hard currency.

The government turned to its third strategy in 1993, legalizing the use of U.S. dollars on the island and opening dollar stores (*Tiendas de Recuperación de Divisas*) at which Cubans could purchase imported goods. The goal was to discourage the illegal black market, to capture dollars that could be used for the importation of necessities, and to encourage Cubans abroad to send even more money to their families. The policy succeeded; over the next decade, remittances sent by relatives rose to over $1 billion annually. At the same time, however, the purchasing power of the Cuban peso receded, exacerbating inequality among

Cubans by creating a two-class system of consumption: one for those with access to dollars (e.g., from remittances or tips in the tourist sector) and one for those without.

Cuban officials also sought to reduce the need for hard currency by reorganizing the system of food production. Large state farms had required imported equipment, fertilizer, and petroleum. They were replaced by small producer cooperatives called Basic Units of Cooperative Production (*Unidades Básicas de Producción* [UBPC]), in which individual families had land use rights. The government also reintroduced free farmers' markets, in which both private farmers and UBPCs could sell produce to the public at market prices. These reforms only marginally increased food production; at the turn of the century, Cuba still had to import 70 percent of its food.

Perhaps the most difficult decision concerned sugar. Cuban identity had been entwined with sugar for nearly two centuries, and Cuba had long been the world's leading producer of the sweetener. But the production of sugar became unsustainable by the end of the twentieth century.[77] At times, Cuba spent more to harvest and process the cane than it earned in hard currency. For several years, the government subsidized sugar production for political, not economic, reasons to avoid dislocations in rural areas where sugar constituted the only source of employment. The day of reckoning arrived in May 2002, when the government announced that half the island's mills would be closed down.

Rafter Exodus

In 1994, the economic calamity clearly had become a political one as emigration pressures mounted. The number of people trying to leave the island illegally every month rose from dozens to hundreds and then thousands. The deep impact of the economy's decline was evident in the desperation of those who used makeshift rafts—inner tubes, wood slats, anything that would float—to traverse the Florida Straits, one of the world's most dangerous waterways. By some estimates, three-fourths of those who attempted the trip did not survive.[78]

In 1984, as a result of the 1980 Mariel exodus, the United States and Cuba signed an immigration accord under which "up to" 20,000 would be granted immigrant visas. However, just as economic conditions got worse, the United States issued fewer and fewer visas—only 2,003 in 1993 despite more than ten times that number of applicants—leaving illegal departure as the only way out. In 1990, the US Coast Guard rescued 467 rafters; the number grew to 2,565 and 3,656 in 1992 and 1993, respectively. The 1993 yearly total was surpassed by June 1994, a month when 1,173 rafters arrived safely in the United States.[79] In July, as one group attempted to hijack a ferry, the Cuban coast guard attacked the boat with high-pressure fire hoses and sank it; forty-one people died. The ferry incident set off a series of spontaneous street riots not seen in Havana since 1959. Fidel Castro charged that the United States was encouraging the exodus by granting asylum to rafters, and early in August he announced that Cuba would not constrain anyone from trying to leave Cuba.[80] Thousands began flocking to the shore.

Significantly, most of these emigrants were Cubans who had grown up during the Revolution. They were younger than the wave in the 1960s. Two-thirds of those whose occupations could be identified had been in low-skilled jobs.[81] While it was evident that their principal motive for leaving Cuba was economic, there also was some evidence that they had become alienated from a system that seemed unresponsive to their needs, had given them little possibility for engagement in shaping their lives, and had offered little hope for the future. The exodus ended with a U.S.-Cuban accord under which the United States would grant at least 20,000 visas annually to Cubans and would house rafters whom it picked up on the high seas at the Guantánamo naval base. In 1995, the agreement was amended: the United States allowed the 23,000 Guantánamo detainees to apply for visas and committed itself to return to Cuba any illegal émigrés found on the high seas. This became known as the "wet-foot, dry-foot" policy; Cubans picked up at sea were returned to Cuba, but those who made it to the United States or a U.S. territory such as Puerto Rico were allowed to stay.

In a sense the rafter exodus represented a failure of the most important political institution in the Cuban political system, the Cuban Communist Party (*Partido Comunista de Cuba* [PCC]). In the early 1990s, the PCC was the principal venue for elite debate over strategies to survive the collapse of the Soviet Union and the CMEA, as William LeoGrande's chapter in this volume explains. However, Fidel Castro soon opted for maintaining political control. As the decade wore on, he allowed the PCC to atrophy, preferring to govern through directives conveyed by the *Grupo de Apoyo*, a small team of his intimate advisers. This group also was seen as the source of Cuba's future leaders. For example, Carlos Lage Dávila had become the Cuban vice president responsible for economic affairs and the executive secretary of the Council of Ministers; Felipe Pérez Roque had been Castro's chief of staff for a decade when the president named the thirty-four-year-old as foreign minister in 1999.

Civil Society

As the government's ability to provide employment and a social safety net for everyone diminished, it became more tolerant of religious institutions and allowed nongovernmental organizations to form. While some of the organizations continued to have links to the state and thus might not be indicative of an truly emergent civil society, there is little doubt that conditions during the Special Period fostered new networks and groups that provided some opening for the expression of independent views. The churches were the most significant element of the new Cuban civil society, in part because they had an islandwide organizational infrastructure and a mass base of members. They have had an important role at the community level delivering relief supplies from sister churches abroad. The Catholic Church, in particular, developed magazines and newsletters that circulate widely.

The Catholic Church had opposed the Revolution in the 1960s, and until the Special Period, active participation as a congregant was an obstacle for anyone who wanted to move ahead professionally or politically. But as the Church accommodated itself to the Revolution, the state softened its stance against religion. In 1991, the Fourth PCC Congress voted to allow members of any religious group to gain Communist Party membership. Three years later, the Vatican named Havana Archbishop Jaime Ortega y Alamino as a cardinal. Historian Margaret Crahan highlights his statement in which he affirmed the Catholic Church's support for the Revolution's social justice accomplishments. But she notes that he also stipulated that "the Church had an obligation to help the Cuban people transcend the revolution's limitations . . . through intensifying evangelization so that the laity would be better prepared to act through a mobilized civil society."[82]

The church's potential for expanding civil society received a boost in January 1998, when Pope John Paul II made the first papal visit ever to the island. Tumultuous crowds welcomed him, and throughout the country, Cubans placed signs in their windows proclaiming "No tengo miedo" (I have no fear). During the five-day trip across Cuba, the pope called both for more freedom of speech and religious education and for an end to the U.S. embargo. Still, the church's attempts to strengthen faith-based communities and to encourage civic engagement were hampered in the 1990s by insufficient resources and limited popular support.

One of the most prominent examples of civic engagement emerged from the work of a lay Catholic activist, Oswaldo Payá Sardiñas. In the late 1990s, he organized the Varela Project, which had the goal of collecting a sufficient number of signatures on a petition to trigger a national referendum to promote freedom of speech and assembly, the right to own a business, and the end of one-party rule. Although the 11,000 signatures he submitted to the National Assembly in 2002 exceeded constitutional requirements, the petition was denied.

While the success of the petition drive was not anticipated, the Varela Project also lacked the resources and critical mass to sustain a serious challenge to the government. Indeed, none of the small groups of "dissidents" who had been supported and/or promoted by U.S. governmental and nongovernmental organizations were able to build an effective network of opposition during the Special Period. In part, this was a consequence of state repression.[83] They also were discredited by working too closely with the U.S. government. In addition, Cubans found nontraditional ways to express their views through media such as film, the plastic arts, and music.

Culture and Society during the Special Period

Shortages during the Special Period initially took a heavy toll on all forms of Cuban culture. Money for films was scarce, as was paper for newspapers and books. Baseball games were played only during the daytime in order to avoid using stadium lights. To survive, Cuban writers and artists turned abroad to publish their works, host dance performances, curate art exhibits, and coproduce films. For example, the Academy Award–nominated 1993 film by Tomás Gutiérrez Alea and Juan Carlos Tabío, *Fresa y chocolate* (Strawberry and Chocolate), was produced as a Cuban-Spanish-Mexican venture. The film is also an example of how the new forms of financing for the arts broadened the possibilities for expression. *Fresa y chocolate* probes several previously taboo subjects: homosexuality, ideological rigidity, and even patriotism.

The 1984 Havana Art Biennial was one of the first of its kind. As it grew in popularity and drew international crowds to purchase the works on display, artists pushed the boundaries of what had been acceptable.[84] In part, this was possible because they were backed by Abel Prieto Jiménez, the creative and iconoclastic minister of culture from 1997 to 2012. (Prieto had shoulder-length hair and was an avowed Beatles fan even in the days when the band was regarded as an example of bourgeois decadence.) But Cuban leaders also bowed to the inevitable as the international market gave Cuban artists new sources of financial support.

As the Special Period persisted, musicians found ever-greater freedom to criticize not only shortages but also the shortcomings of the Revolution. Carlos Varela, a popular folksinger, carried on the *nueva trova* tradition made famous by Silvio Rodríguez and Pablo Milanés. But his songs went right to the edge, in effect calling for major reforms. For example, in "William Tell," he sings that the archer

> didn't understand his son . . .
> William Tell, your son has grown up . . .
> William Tell failed to understand his son—
> Who one day got tired of having the apple placed on his head.[85]

Resolver (to find a solution) was the catchword of the Special Period for coping with shortages in order to handle mundane tasks of daily life or carry on a profession. For musicians, the cost of equipment that could replicate the kind of rap music they wanted to play was prohibitive. "Rap was originally an import," sociologist Sujatha Fernandes explains, but "Cuban rap soon took on a life of its own." Without samplers, mixers, and albums, she notes, Cuban rappers by the mid-1990s re-created

> the rhythmic pulse of hip-hop with instruments like the melodic Batá drums, typically used in ceremonies of the Afro-Cuban Santería religion. In the tradition of Cuban a cappella groups. . . .

Cuban rappers made up for the lack of digital technology by developing the human beat box, mimicking not just drum machines but congas, trumpets and even song samples. [86]

As Cuban hip-hop evolved independently of U.S. influence, its lyrics and themes became a distinctive contrast to the American genre. Instead of promoting sexual exploitation and consumption, Cuban artists focused on the problems of daily life and the way that governmental decisions during the Special Period undermined achievements of the Revolution, such as racial equality.

As noted earlier, overcoming the racial discrimination that had been entrenched in Cuban institutions prior to 1959 was one of the Revolution's goals and successes. Historian Alejandro de la Fuente reports that "by the early 1980s Cuban society had made remarkable progress in the reduction of racial inequality in a number of crucial areas, including education, indicators of health care, and the occupational structure. Racial inequality persisted in some areas, but the trend was unequivocally towards equality."[87] He adds that even in leadership positions, "inequality had decreased significantly."[88]

But the Special Period undermined these advances, many of which depended on government spending that declined after 1990. While several market reforms engendered inequalities across the races, some had their greatest negative impact on blacks, who had less access to hard currency from remittances because whites constituted the largest portion of exiles abroad.[89] Moreover, discrimination against darker-skinned Cubans in the tourist sector limited their access to the second source of hard currency. The consequence was that while "all Cubans were equal before the law," those able to *resolver* more successfully during the Special Period tended to be lighter-skinned Cubans.[90]

Not surprisingly, Cubans' health and the quality of their education suffered during the first years of the Special Period. As noted earlier, this was due largely to an inadequate diet and the increased cost of food and medicine as a result of the U.S. embargo. Many old problems began to reappear. For example, as Robin Williams reports, diarrhea became the second most frequent condition that sent Cubans to a doctor, largely because the incidence of waterborne diseases doubled. In addition, he notes, "The country's mammography program [was] crippled by a shortage of film and spare parts."[91]

Similarly, basic teaching materials were no longer available, though the greatest impact on education came from two different effects of the Special Period. First, teachers' salaries were so low that many left the profession, and there were few replacements. Second, young people began to devalue education, as it no longer was "the main route to a higher standard of living, nor an essential mechanism for achieving social status."[92] A taxi driver could earn in three days what a teacher earned in a month.

Still, the negative impact of the economic crisis on Cubans' health and education was less than expected. The rate of infant mortality did not rise, and life expectancy did not decrease. Illiteracy did not return. Despite the economic conditions, throughout the 1990s the Cuban government continued to allocate scarce funds to health care, education, social security, and assistance to the poor at a relatively constant percentage of GDP—and at times at a higher percentage. By the end of the decade, teachers gained a 30 percent increase in their wages. Cuban inventiveness led to new forms of volunteerism in staffing day care centers, much as Cuba had relied on volunteers to work in the 1961 literacy campaign. Indeed, Cuba looked to the new millennium with a renewed confidence, in part because changing international circumstances gave it several new allies.

Foreign Policy during the Special Period

Throughout 1991, Fidel Castro repeatedly invoked the 1962 missile crisis, reminding Cubans that they had faced seemingly insurmountable challenges before without flinching and that they had successfully fought enemies with valor, salvaging "the honor of Latin America."[93] Indeed, the Cuban leader perceived that his country was utterly "alone" in the world, much as he did at the end of the missile crisis when it seemed that the Soviet Union had abandoned Cuba and that the United States remained an even greater threat.[94] On December 27, 1991, two days after the Soviet Union formally "dissolved" itself, he declared that Cuba was unique in the Western Hemisphere. "What is Latin America today?" Castro asked contemptuously. "A collection of balkanized and underdeveloped states. . . . In Latin America we have the fragmentation of Latin Americans and, within each country . . . fragmentation, ideal conditions for imperialist domination over all these countries."[95]

As in the 1960s, Cuba was not content merely to react to the isolating circumstances in which it found itself. After the missile crisis, it pursued a policy of trying to create Third World allies by supporting liberation movements in Asia and Africa and insurgencies in Latin America. Although Cuba's strategy changed in the 1990s, survival remained the leaders' primary foreign policy goal. In pursuing it, political scientist Jorge Domínguez explains, they were characteristically proactive and relied on "some pre-1990 legacies" to achieve their objective, including intense engagement in multilateral institutions and the development of new defensive economic ties with emerging powers, such as China.[96]

Building New Alliances

Cuba had built a deep well of appreciation in the Third World because of its assistance programs and sustained military commitment in Angola against the apartheid South African regime. This was highlighted by Nelson Mandela during a 1991 trip to Cuba, the year after he was released from prison. In a speech on July 26, with Fidel Castro at his side, Mandela declared,

> The Cuban people hold a special place in the hearts of the people of Africa. The Cuban internationalists have made a contribution to African independence, freedom, and justice, unparalleled for its principled and selfless character. . . . We admire the sacrifices of the Cuban people in maintaining their independence and sovereignty. . . . We too want to control our own destiny. . . . There are many things we learn from your experience. . . . But the most important lesson that you have for us is that no matter what the odds, no matter under what difficulties you have had to struggle, there can be no surrender! It is a case of freedom or death![97]

After President George H. W. Bush signed the 1992 Cuban Democracy Act into law, tightening the U.S. embargo and including extraterritorial provisions that affected how other countries might trade with Cuba, the UN General Assembly voted to condemn the U.S. sanctions. While initially more countries abstained than approved the measure, in subsequent years the number of yeas grew so that by 2005 more than 180 countries voted affirmatively. (In 2013, the vote was 188–2–3; only Israel voted with the United States against the resolution, and the Marshall Islands, Palau and Micronesia abstained.)

In its search for foreign investment, Cuba turned to Europe at the start of the Special Period. The initial response was tepid, but European investors saw new opportunities when Cuba revised its laws on foreign ownership. In part, the 1996 Helms-Burton Act was intended to scare these Europeans away by targeting investment capital for penalties. But the law had only a limited effect, as U.S. allies demanded that President Bill Clinton waive a key provision that could have been costly to several European corporations. It was the emergence of the conservative José María Aznar government in Spain, which had a greater impact on Cuba's relations with Europe. Spain's efforts to condition loans and aid to Cuba on human rights criteria led to a series of angry exchanges that reduced aid that Cuba received from the European Union (EU) and curtailed some trade. Castro viewed the EU demands as a renewed form of neocolonial intervention and bluntly asserted in 2003 that "Cuba does not need the aid of the European Union to survive."[98]

While tinged with bravado, his statement also marked a turning point in Cuban foreign policy. Cuba would no longer concentrate on its relations with the United States, Russia, or Europe. It would devote its foreign policy more intently toward the Third World, toward countries with which it could relate on the basis of mutual respect, not asymmetric requirements. Notably, in 2003, Third World countries again acknowledged Cuba as a global leader by naming it as the host of the 2006 Summit of the Non-Aligned Movement (NAM) and consequently the organization's chair for the following three years. The NAM's 118-member states include most of the Third World, and its selection was a striking indication of Cuba's standing because Havana had been the venue of a summit once before, in 1979.

In this regard, Cuban leaders have tended to view China—despite its size, wealth, military power, and potential for domination—differently than countries that previously had dominated Cuba. To be sure, until the late 1980s, China had little capacity to provide much support to Cuba, and it had little incentive to do so given Cuba's relationship with the Soviet Union. But as the Soviet Union dissolved, China began a historic spurt in the growth of its economy. In the 1990s, China also started to invest in Latin America as it searched for raw materials to fuel its fast-growing industries.

Cuba was not high on China's target list. China did ship 500,000 bicycles to Cuba in 1992 and 1993, and in 1997 it funded and provided technical assistance for the start of a small Cuban bicycle industry. But it was not until 2001 that China began to allocate large sums to Cuba. That year, it provided nearly $400 million in long-term loans and credits to upgrade Cuba's telecommunication infrastructure and to enable Cuba to purchase Chinese televisions, washing machines, and air conditioners. In 2006, Cuba signed contracts worth more than $2 billion, using Chinese lines of credit, for transportation infrastructure development.[99]

The most important international development for Cuba occurred in 1998, when Hugo Chávez was elected Venezuela's president. Chávez looked to Fidel Castro as his spiritual mentor and once in office turned to the Cuba leader for advice. Together, they began to implement an ambitious project, as Castro described it in October 2000, "to unite the Latin American and Caribbean nations and to struggle for a world economic order that brings more justice to all peoples."[100] That month, Venezuela began to sell oil to some South American countries and Cuba at a price that was not only one-third less than the world market price but also could be purchased with a loan payable after fifteen years at a 2 percent interest rate.

By 2001, Cuba was importing more oil from Venezuela than it had imported from the Soviet Union in 1990. Cuba paid for oil by sending teachers and doctors to Venezuela. The teachers contributed to the eradication of illiteracy in Venezuela, and the doctors helped Venezuela establish a medical program for the poor, *Barrio Adentro* (Inside the Neighborhood). By 2006, more than 20,000 Cuban doctors were serving in Venezuela. In 2013, 30,000 Cuban doctors were there, and Venezuela had become Cuba's major trading partner, accounting for nearly 22 percent of Cuba's imports and exports.[101]

Late in 2004, Cuba and Venezuela launched a new organization intended to achieve their common hemispheric goals: the Bolivarian Alternative for the Peoples of Our America (ALBA in the Spanish acronym).[102] Initially aimed at economically integrating Latin

American and Caribbean countries, in competition with the U.S.-proposed Free Trade Area of the Americas, ALBA also created a development bank and served as a coordinating mechanism for development projects. In January 2006, following the inauguration of Evo Morales as president, Bolivia joined ALBA.

Engagement and Disengagement with the United States

In 1991, Cuba ceased being an important foreign policy issue for the United States. The small country no longer supported revolutionary movements in Latin America and had withdrawn its forces from Africa. Meanwhile, the Soviet Union had pulled its troops out of Cuba, the Sandinistas lost the 1990 presidential election in Nicaragua, and the civil war in El Salvador ended with a conservative government in power. In this context, President Bush turned the policy over to Congress, where Cuban American legislators and others whom the CANF supported were eager to push the Cuban government over the brink. In 1992, the House and Senate approved the Cuban Democracy Act (CDA), and when presidential candidate Bill Clinton endorsed the bill, President Bush felt compelled to sign it despite his misgivings. Cuba had become a U.S. domestic political issue. As noted earlier, the CDA prohibited foreign subsidiaries of U.S. firms from trading with Cuba, and it stipulated that vessels entering Cuban ports would not be able to enter a U.S. port for the purpose of trade during the subsequent 180 days, which raised shipping costs for Cuban imports.

Cuba's tactical response was to go beyond trade by attracting new foreign investors. As the plan began to work, hard-liners in Congress sought to scare off investors with legislation that would enable former Cuban property owners, such as Bacardi, to sue the investors in a U.S. court and obtain compensation by seizing their U.S.-based properties. Officially titled the Cuban Liberty and Democratic Solidarity (LIBERTAD) Act, the bill became popularly known as Helms-Burton after its two principal sponsors, Senator Jesse Helms (R-NC) and Representative Dan Burton (R-IN). Cubans viewed the act as a challenge to its national sovereignty, much like the Platt Amendment.[103] They argued that it arrogated to the United States the right to determine whether there has been an appropriate transition to democracy, that is, whether the Cubans have established a government that the United States can trust to rule the island.[104]

Attorney General Janet Reno reportedly recommended that President Clinton veto the Helms-Burton bill because it undermined supposed constitutional prerogatives of the president. But Clinton's political advisers were more concerned about the effect that a veto would have on the president's reelection after Cuba shot down two civilian aircraft manned by Brothers-to-the-Rescue pilots in February 1996.[105] However, despite the seeming restrictions that Helms-Burton seemed to pose on a president's authority, President Clinton relaxed the embargo in 1999. His executive orders permitted an increase in cultural exchanges (including two baseball games between the Baltimore Orioles and Cuba's national team) and eased travel regulations, stimulating several new "people-to-people" educational programs by universities and organizations such as the National Geographic Society.

Meanwhile, the weakening of the anti-Castro lobby and the growing interest by U.S. agricultural interests in selling products to Cuba led to the 2000 Trade Sanctions Reform and Export Enhancement Act (TSRA), which authorized the direct commercial export of food and agricultural products from the United States to Cuban government-operated entities on a cash basis. Despite its financing hurdles, the TSRA provided the mechanism to open trade significantly. In 2008 U.S. sales of agricultural goods reached a high point of $711.5 million, though they declined to half that annual level by the end of 2013.[106]

But Bush owed right-wing Cuban Americans for the various kinds of contributions they made to his election in 2000. Based on the report of his presidential Commission for Assistance to a Free Cuba (CAFC), in May 2004, Bush issued a series of harsh regulations intended to hasten "Cuba's transition from Stalinist rule."[107] Fidel Castro responded by asserting that Cuba viewed the new U.S. policy as an attempt "to intimidate, to terrorize this country and eventually to destroy its socio-economic system and independence."[108] On the eve of Fidel Castro's illness, in July 2006, Secretary of State Condoleezza Rice and Cuban American Commerce Secretary Carlos Gutiérrez released the commission's second report, which proposed new regulations to ensure that "the Castro regime's succession strategy does not succeed."[109] The report included detailed plans for a U.S. occupation, from reorganizing the economy and the educational system to the holding of multiparty elections.

In short, as Raúl Castro took over the reins of leadership, Cuba was at a high point in its relations with the rest of the world and at a nadir in its relations with United States. The Cuban government had weathered a Special Period that might have destabilized most other countries, but it was clear that political and economic reforms were necessary if the Cuban Revolution was going to be sustainable. The Cuban people had demonstrated a remarkable resilience and ability to adapt, but in 2006 no one could be certain how much longer they would be patient.

NOTES

1. Pablo Bachelet, "U.S. Policy Gives the Bush Administration Few Options in Cuba, Critics Say," McClatchy Newspapers, August 2, 2006.

2. Julia E. Sweig, "Fidel's Final Victory," *Foreign Affairs*, January/February 2007.

3. Nelson P. Valdés, "The Revolutionary and Political Content of Fidel Castro's Charismatic Authority," in *A Contemporary Cuba Reader: Reinventing the Revolution*, ed. Philip Brenner, Marguerite Rose Jiménez, John M. Kirk, and William M. LeoGrande (Lanham, MD: Rowman & Littlefield, 2007), 27.

4. Max Weber, *The Theory of Social and Economic Organization* (New York: Oxford University Press, 1947), pp. 328ff.

5. The period from 1829 to 1860 also experienced significant political turmoil, especially around the question of how much authority the national government had in relation to the states. In effect, the national government's legal-institutional legitimacy—as a replacement for legitimacy based on tradition—was solidified only by the North's victory in the Civil War and the passage of the Fourteenth Amendment to the Constitution. Arthur M. Schlesinger Jr., *The Age of Jackson* (Boston: Little, Brown, 1945); David S. Reynolds, *Waking Giant: America in the Age of Jackson* (New York: HarperCollins, 2008).

6. Carlos Alzugaray Treto, "Continuity and Change in Cuba at Fifty: The Revolution at a Crossroads," in this volume. See also "Speech Delivered by Raúl Castro Ruz, President of the Councils of State and Ministers, at the Close of the Inaugural Session of the Seventh Legislature of the National Assembly of People's Power," Havana, February 24, 2008, http://www.cuba.cu/gobierno/rauldiscursos/2008/esp/r240208e.html (accessed August 20, 2013).

7. There were an estimated 112,000 Indians on the island in 1492 and fewer than 3,000 by the mid-1550s. See Eduardo Torres-Cuevas and Oscar Loyala Vega, *Historia de Cuba 1492–1898*, 3rd ed. (Havana: Editorial Pueblo y Educación, 2006), 25, 50–58; Irving Rouse, *The Tainos: Rise and Decline of the People Who Greeted Columbus* (New Haven, CT: Yale University Press, 1992), 157.

8. For example, see "Discursos pronunciados en el Acto Solemne, el 20 de junio del 2002 Intervención de Ricardo Alarcón de Quesada, Presidente de la Asamblea Nacional del Poder Popular," June 20, 2002, http://www.cuba.cu/gobierno/documentos/2002/esp/a200602e.html (accessed August 18, 2013).

9. Louis A. Pérez Jr., *Cuba and the United States: Ties of Singular Intimacy* (Athens: University of Georgia Press, 1990), 80–81.

10. Jules Robert Benjamin, *The United States and Cuba: Hegemony and Dependent Development, 1880–1934* (Pittsburgh: University of Pittsburgh Press, 1977), 4–5; Pérez, *Cuba and the United States*, 61.

11. Lars Schoultz, *That Infernal Little Republic: The United States and the Cuban Revolution* (Chapel Hill: University of North Carolina Press, 2009), 22.

12. Louis A. Pérez Jr., *Cuba: Between Reform and Revolution*, 4th ed. (New York: Oxford University Press, 2011), 137–38.

13. Lars Schoultz, *Beneath the United States: A History of U.S. Policy toward Latin America* (Cambridge, MA: Harvard University Press, 1998), 145.

14. Schoultz, *Beneath the United States*, 148.

15. Leland Hamilton Jenks, *Our Cuban Colony: A Study in Sugar* (New York: Vanguard Press, 1928), 286.

16. Thomas G. Paterson, *Contesting Castro: The United States and the Triumph of the Cuban Revolution* (New York: Oxford University Press, 1994), 35; Leland Johnson, "U.S. Business Interests in Cuba and the Rise of Castro,"

World Politics 17, no. 3 (1965): 443, 453; Robin Blackburn, "Prologue to the Cuban Revolution," *New Left Review*, no. 21, October 1963, 59–60.

17. Louis A. Pérez Jr., *On Becoming Cuban: Identity, Nationality and Culture* (Chapel Hill: University of North Carolina Press, 1999), 7, 157.

18. As quoted in Luis E. Aguilar, *Cuba 1933: Prologue to Revolution* (New York: Norton, 1972), 163–64.

19. Julia E. Sweig, *Inside the Cuban Revolution* (Cambridge, MA: Harvard University Press, 2002), 165–82.

20. "Program Manifesto of the 26th of July Movement," in *Cuba in Revolution*, ed. Rolando E. Bonachea and Nelson P. Valdés (Garden City, NY: Anchor Books, 1972), 113–40.

21. Lourdes Casal, "Race Relations in Contemporary Cuba," in *The Cuba Reader: The Making of a Revolutionary Society*, ed. Philip Brenner, William M. LeoGrande, Donna Rich, and Daniel Siegel (New York: Grove Press, 1989), 475; Alejandro de la Fuente, "Recreating Racism: Race and Discrimination in Cuba's Special Period," *Socialism and Democracy* 15, no. 1 (Spring 2001).

22. Casal, "Race Relations in Contemporary Cuba," 477.

23. Saul Landau, "Asking the Right Questions about Cuba," in Brenner et al., *The Cuba Reader*, xxiii.

24. Pérez, *On Becoming Cuban*, 482.

25. James G. Blight and Peter Kornbluh, eds., *The Politics of Illusion: The Bay of Pigs Invasion Reexamined* (Boulder, CO: Lynne Rienner, 1998), 10–13; Jorge I. Domínguez, *Cuba: Order and Revolution* (Cambridge, MA: Harvard University Press, 1978), 345–46.

26. Brig. Gen. Lansdale, "Review of Operation Mongoose," memorandum for the Special Group (Augmented), July 25, 1962, Office of the Secretary of Defense, declassified January 5, 1989, 8, in *The Cuban Missile Crisis 1962: A National Security Archive Documents Reader*, ed. Laurence Chang and Peter Kornbluh (New York: New Press, 1992), 47.

27. Domínguez, *Cuba*, 253.

28. Domínguez, *Cuba*, 356–57.

29. William Luis, "Exhuming *Lunes de Revolución*," *CR: The New Centennial Review* 2, no. 2 (Summer 2002): 254–57.

30. "Discurso Pronunciado por el Comandante Fidel Castro Ruz, Primer Ministro del Gobierno Revolucionario y Secretario del PURSC, Como Conclusion de las Reuniones con los Intelectuales Cubanos, Efectuadas en la Biblioteca Nacional el 16, 23 y 30 de Junio de 1961," http://www.cuba.cu/gobierno/discursos/1961/esp/f300661e.html (accessed August 18, 2013).

31. Susan Eva Eckstein, *The Immigrant Divide: How Cuban Americans Changed the US and Their Homeland* (New York: Routledge, 2009), 10–12; Felix Roberto Masud-Piloto, *From Welcomed Exiles to Illegal Immigrants: Cuban Migration to the U.S., 1959–1995* (Lanham, MD: Rowman & Littlefield, 1996), 58–59.

32. Ernesto Che Guevara, "Man and Socialism in Cuba," in *Man and Socialism in Cuba: The Great Debate*, ed. Bertram Silverman (New York: Atheneum, 1971), 343–44.

33. Bertram Silverman, "Introduction: The Great Debate in Retrospect: Economic Rationality and the Ethics of Revolution," in Silverman, *Man and Socialism in Cuba*, 15.

34. Fidel Castro, "Speech Delivered on March 13, 1968, at Ceremonies Marking the 11th Anniversary of the Attack on the Presidential Palace, at the University of Havana," in *Fidel Castro Speaks*, ed. Martin Kenner and James Petras (New York: Grove Press, 1969), 271, 283.

35. Fidel Castro, "Speech Delivered on the 25th Anniversary of the Bay of Pigs Victory, April 19, 1986," in *Cuban Revolution Reader: A Documentary History*, ed. Julio García Luis (Melbourne: Ocean Press, 2001), 243–45.

36. Susan Eva Eckstein, *Back from the Future: Cuba under Castro* (Princeton, NJ: Princeton University Press, 1994), 129–37, 151–54.

37. Marvin Leiner, "Cuba's Schools: Twenty-Five Years Later," in *Cuba: Twenty-Five Years of Revolution, 1959–1984*, ed. Sandor Halebsky and John M. Kirk (New York: Praeger, 1985), 28–29, 32–36.

38. Max Azicri, *Cuba Today and Tomorrow: Reinventing Socialism* (Gainesville: University Press of Florida, 2000), 24–31, 55–59; Eckstein, *Back from the Future*, 41–47.

39. Carlos Lechuga, *In the Eye of the Storm: Castro, Khrushchev, Kennedy and the Missile Crisis*, trans. Mary Todd (Melbourne: Ocean Press, 1995), 18; Aleksandr Fursenko and Timothy Naftali, *One Hell of a Gamble: Khrushchev, Castro, and Kennedy, 1958–1964* (New York: Norton, 1997), 146.

40. Marifeli Pérez-Stable, *The Cuban Revolution: Origins, Course, and Legacy*, 2nd ed. (New York: Oxford University Press, 1999), 88.

41. James G. Blight and Philip Brenner, *Sad and Luminous Days: Cuba's Struggle with the Superpowers after the Missile Crisis* (Lanham, MD: Rowman & Littlefield, 2007), 36, 60.

42. Ernesto (Che) Guevara, "Speech in Algiers to the Second Seminar of the Organization of Afro-Asian Solidarity, February 25, 1965," in *Che Guevara Speaks*, ed. George Lavan (New York: Pathfinder Press, 1967), 107–8.

43. Fidel Castro, "A Necessary Introduction," in *El Diario del Che en Bolivia* (Havana: Editora Política, 1987), xvii–xviii.

44. "Discurso Pronunciado por el Comandante Fidel Castro Ruz, al Conmemorarse el IX Aniversario del Triunfo de la Revolución, en la Plaza de la Revolución, el 2 de Enero de 1968," http://www.cuba.cu/gobierno/discursos/1968/esp/f020168e.html (accessed August 18, 2013).

45. Piero Gleijeses, *Conflicting Missions: Havana, Washington, and Africa, 1959–1976* (Chapel Hill: University of North Carolina Press, 2002), 260, 305–7.

46. Mervyn J. Bain, "Cuba-Soviet Relations in the Gorbachev Era," *Journal of Latin American Studies* 37 (2005): 773–76.

47. William M. LeoGrande, "Cuba," in *Confronting Revolution: Security through Diplomacy in Central America*, ed. Morris Blachman, William M. LeoGrande, and Kenneth Sharpe (New York: Pantheon, 1986), 253.

48. William M. LeoGrande, *Our Own Backyard: The United States in Central America, 1977–1992* (Chapel Hill: University of North Carolina Press, 1998), 15, 24–25; Eckstein, *Back from the Future*, 186–88.

49. H. Michael Erisman, *Cuba's Foreign Relations in a Post-Soviet World* (Gainesville: University Press of Florida, 2000), 98–99; Jorge I. Domínguez, *To Make a World Safe for Revolution: Cuban Foreign Policy* (Cambridge, MA: Harvard University Press, 1989), 171–75.

50. As quoted in Schoultz, *That Infernal Little Republic*, 90.

51. Quoted in Louis A. Pérez Jr., *Cuba in the American Imagination: Metaphor and the Imperial Ethos* (Chapel Hill: University of North Carolina Press, 2008), 241.

52. Richard M. Nixon, "Rough Draft of Summary of Conversation between the Vice-President and Fidel Castro," April 25, 1959, reprinted in Jeffrey J. Safford, "The Nixon-Castro Meeting of 19 April 1959," *Diplomatic History* 4, no. 4 (Fall 1980): 431.

53. Peter Kornbluh, "Introduction: History Held Hostage," in *Bay of Pigs Declassified*, ed. Peter Kornbluh (New York: New Press, 1998), 9; Paterson, *Contesting Castro*, 258.

54. "Memorandum from the Secretary of State to the President: Current Basic United States Policy toward Cuba," in U.S. Department of State, *Foreign Relations of the United States, 1958–1960*, vol. 6, *Cuba* (Washington, DC: Government Printing Office, 1991), doc. no. 387, 657.

55. Abraham F. Lowenthal, "The United States and Latin America: Ending the Hegemonic Presumption," *Foreign Affairs* 55, no. 1 (October 1976).

56. "First Declaration of Havana," September 2, 1960, in *Cuban Revolution Reader: A Documentary History of 40 Key Moments of the Cuban Revolution*, ed. Julio García Luis (Melbourne: Ocean Press, 2001), 45–51.

57. U.S. Central Intelligence Agency, Inspector General, "Report on Plots to Assassinate Fidel Castro," May 23, 1967, National Archives and Records Administration, JFK Assassination System, Record Series: JFK, record no. 104-10213-10101, agency file no. 80TO1357A (released June 23, 1998).

58. McGeorge Bundy, "Memorandum for the Record," November 12, 1963, in U.S. Department of State, *Foreign Relations of the United States, 1961–1963*, vol. 11, *Cuban Missile Crisis and Aftermath* (Washington, DC: Government Printing Office, 1997), doc. no. 377, 889; Gregory F. Treverton, "Cuba in U.S. Security Perspective," in *U.S.-Cuban Relations in the 1990s*, ed. Jorge I. Domínguez and Rafael Hernández (Boulder, CO: Westview Press, 1989), 71.

59. Peter Kornbluh and William M. LeoGrande, "Talking with Castro," *Cigar Aficionado*, January/February 2009, 6–7; Peter Kornbluh and James G. Blight, "Dialogue with Castro: A Hidden History," *New York Review of Books*, October 6, 1994; William M. LeoGrande and Peter Kornbluh, *Back Channel to Cuba: The Hidden History of Negotiations Between Washington and Havana* (Chapel Hill: University of North Carolina Press, 2014).

60. Henry Kissinger, *Years of Renewal* (New York: Simon & Schuster, 1999), 785–87; "Ford Says Angola Acts Hurt Detente, Cuba Tie," *New York Times*, December 21, 1975, 3.

61. Austin Scott, "Carter Outlines Basis for Better Ties with Cuba," *Washington Post*, February 17, 1977.

62. Zbigniew Brzezinksi, *Power and Principle: Memoirs of the National Security Adviser, 1977–1981*, rev. ed. (New York: Farrar, Straus and Giroux, 1985), 180–90.

63. Jimmy Carter, *Keeping Faith: Memoirs of a President* (New York: Bantam Books, 1982), 51.

64. Wayne S. Smith, *The Closest of Enemies: A Personal and Diplomatic Account of U.S.-Cuban Relations since 1957* (New York: Norton, 1987), 128–40, 141–42.

65. Richard Halloran, "From Washington and El Salvador, Differing Views on Fighting Rebels," *New York Times*, February 21, 1981.

66. Philip Brenner, "Change and Continuity in Cuban Foreign Policy," in Brenner et al., *The Cuban Reader*, 263–65.

67. Patrick J. Haney and Walt Vanderbush, *The Cuban Embargo: The Domestic Politics of an American Foreign Policy* (Pittsburgh: University of Pittsburgh Press, 2005), 32–36.

68. Masud-Piloto, *From Welcomed Exiles to Illegal Immigrants*, 73–78.

69. Diane Kuntz, "The Politics of Suffering: The Impact of the U.S. Embargo on the Health of the Cuban People" (report to the American Public Health Association of a fact-finding trip to Cuba, June 6–11, 1993), *Journal of Public Health Policy* 15, no. 1 (Spring 1994); Katherine Tucker and Thomas R. Hedges, "Food Shortages and an Epidemic of Optic and Peripheral Neuropathy in Cuba," *Nutrition Reviews* 51, no. 12 (1993): 349–57. By 1993, the average daily caloric intake in Cuba had fallen below the World Health Organization standard. Diet insufficiency led to outbreaks of disorders that had long vanished from Cuba, such as neuropathy (damage to nerves that can produce sharp pains in the fingers and feet), loss of a sense of touch, an inability to control muscle movement, and even temporary blindness.

70. Jorge I. Domínguez, "Cuba's Economic Transition: Successes, Deficiencies, and Challenges," in *The Cuban Economy at the Start of the Twenty-First Century*, ed. Jorge I. Domínguez, Omar Everleny Pérez Villanueva, and Lorena Barberia (Cambridge, MA: Harvard University Press, 2004), 19.

71. The 1992 Cuban Democracy Act bars subsidiaries of U.S. corporations in third countries from selling goods to Cuba. Food and medicine made up more than 90 percent of Cuba's imports from these subsidiaries in 1991.

Donna Rich Kaplowitz and Michael Kaplowitz, *New Opportunities for U.S.-Cuban Trade* (Washington, DC: Paul H. Nitze School of Advanced International Studies, Johns Hopkins University, 1992), 57–64.

72. Rafael Hernández, "The Collapse of Socialism Is beyond the Present Horizon," in this volume.

73. Pedro Monreal, "Development as an Unfinished Affair: Cuba after the 'Great Adjustment' of the 1990s," in Brenner et al., *A Contemporary Cuba Reader*, 117–18.

74. Hal Klepak, "The Revolutionary Armed Forces: Loyalty and Efficiency in the Face of Old and New Challenges," in this volume. The military's involvement in the economy served two purposes. First, it provided jobs to the FAR, which suffered a reduction in its size from 300,000 to 100,000 members during the Special Period. Without work, the newly unemployed soldiers and officers might have been a source of instability. Second, the discipline instilled in the FAR reduced the possibility for corruption by those working in the new companies.

75. William M. LeoGrande, "The United States and Cuba: Strained Engagement," in *Cuba, the United States, and the Post-Cold War World: The International Dimension of the Washington-Havana Relationship*, ed. Morris Morley and Chris McGillion (Gainesville: University Press of Florida, 2005), 18.

76. Marguerite Rose Jiménez, "The Political Economy of Leisure," in this volume.

77. Philip Peters, "Cutting Losses: Cuba Downsizes Its Sugar Industry" (Arlington, VA: Lexington Institute, December 2003), 3. In 1989, the price of sugar on the world market was $0.13 per pound and barely $0.06 per pound in 2002, while Cuba's rank in world production dropped from third to tenth.

78. Holly Ackerman, "The 'Balsero' Phenomenon, 1991–1994," *Cuban Studies* 26 (1996): 173.

79. Schoultz, *That Infernal Little Republic*, 466–67; "137 Cubans Land in Florida; Largest Boatload since 1980," *New York Times*, July 2, 1994, 6.

80. Under the 1966 Cuban Adjustment Act, a Cuban who remained on U.S. territory for one year and one day could become a U.S. permanent legal resident, receiving enhanced benefits not available to refugees from any other country. Until 1994, the United States also had the practice of nearly automatically allowing Cubans who arrived on U.S. territory to claim asylum and to stay in the United States while their claims were investigated, a process that invariably took more than one year. In addition, *Radio Martí* regularly broadcast detailed weather conditions for the Florida Straits as a guide for rafters.

81. U.S. Immigration and Naturalization Service, *Statistical Yearbook of the Immigration and Naturalization Service, 1996* (Washington, DC: Government Printing Office, October 1997), table 21, http://www.dhs.gov/archives (accessed August 20, 2013). See also Susan Eckstein and Lorena Barberia, "Cuban Americans and Their Transnational Ties," in Brenner et al., *A Contemporary Cuba Reader*, 269.

82. Margaret E. Crahan, "Civil Society and Religion in Cuba: Past, Present, and Future," in Brenner et al., *A Contemporary Cuba Reader*, 331–32.

83. In 2003, seventy-five so-called dissidents were arrested, tried, and sentenced (some to long prison terms) for accepting U.S. assistance in violation of Cuban law. However, more than one dozen turned out to be double agents working for state security agencies.

84. Sandra Levinson, "Nationhood and Identity in Contemporary Cuban Art," in this volume.

85. Carlos Varela, "William Tell," in this volume.

86. Sujatha Fernandes, "Straight Outta Havana," *New York Times*, August 6, 2011.

87. de la Fuente, "Recreating Racism," 68.

88. de la Fuente, "Recreating Racism," 69–71.

89. According to a study by the Pew Hispanic Center, about 86 percent of Cubans in the United States self-identified as "white" in 2004. "Cubans in the United States," Pew Hispanic Center Fact Sheet no. 23 (accessed August 22, 2013).

90. Esteban Morales, "Notes on the Race Question in Cuba Today," in this volume.

91. Robin C. Williams, "In the Shadow of Plenty, Cuba Copes with a Crippled Health Care System," in Brenner et al., *A Contemporary Cuba Reader*, 282.

92. María Isabel Domínguez, "Cuban Youth: Aspirations, Social Perceptions, and Identity," in Brenner et al., *A Contemporary Cuba Reader*, 294.

93. Fidel Castro Ruz, "Discurso en el acto central conmemorativo del XXX aniversario de la victoria de Playa Girón, efectuado en el teatro 'Carlos Marx,' el 19 de abril de 1991," http://www.cuba.cu/gobierno/discursos/1991/esp/f190491e.html (accessed August 24, 2013). See also Fidel Castro Ruz, "Discurso en el acto estudiantil con motivo del xxxiv aniversario del asalto al Palacio Presidencial y a Radio Reloj, efectuado en el antiguo Palacio Presidencial, el 13 de marzo de 1991," http://www.cuba.cu/gobierno/discursos/1991/esp/f130391e.html (accessed August 24, 2013).

94. Blight and Brenner, *Sad and Luminous Days*, 60.

95. Fidel Castro Ruz, "Discurso en la clausura del x período ordinario de sesiones de la tercera legislatura de la Asamblea Nacional del Poder Popular, efectuada en el Palacio de las Convenciones, el 27 de diciembre de 1991," http://www.cuba.cu/gobierno/discursos/1991/esp/f271291e.html (accessed August 24, 2013).

96. Jorge I. Domínguez, "Cuba and the *Pax Americana*," in Brenner et al., *A Contemporary Cuba Reader*, 205.

97. Nelson Mandela, "Speech at the Rally in Cuba," July 26, 1991, http://db.nelsonmandela.org/speeches/pub_view.asp?pg=item&ItemID=NMS1526&txtstr=Matanzas (accessed August 24, 2013); Richard Boudreaux, "Mandela Lauds Castro as Visit to Cuba Ends," *Los Angeles Times*, July 28, 1991.

98. Fidel Castro, "Speech at the Ceremony Commemorating the 50th Anniversary of the Attack on the Moncada and Carlos Manuel de Cespedes Garrisons," Santiago de Cuba, July 26, 2003, http://www.cuba.cu/gobierno/discursos/2003/ing/f260703i.html (accessed August 24, 2013).

99. Adrian H. Hearn, "China and the Future of Cuba," in this volume.

100. Fidel Castro Ruz, "Key Address to a Solemn Session of the National Assembly," Caraças, Venezuela, October 27, 2000, http://www.cuba.cu/gobierno/discursos/2000/ing/f271000i.html (accessed August 25, 2013).

101. John M. Kirk, "Cuban Medical Internationalism under Raúl Castro," in this volume; Cory Fischer-Hoffman and Greg Rosenthal, " Cuba and Venezuela: A Bolivarian Partnership," *Monthly Review*, January 13, 2006, http://mrzine.monthlyreview.org/2006/fhr130106.html (accessed August 25, 2013); *Anuario Estadístico de Cuba 2011*, http://www.one.cu/aec2011/esp/08_tabla_cuadro.htm (accessed August 25, 2013).

102. In 2009, the name was changed to the Bolivarian Alliance for the Peoples of Our America.

103. Jorge I. Domínguez, "U.S. Cuban Relations: From the Cold War to the Colder War," *Journal of Interamerican Studies and World Affairs* 39, no. 3 (1997): 58.

104. Philip Brenner and Soraya M. Castro Mariño, "David and Gulliver: Fifty Years of Competing Metaphors in the Cuban-U.S. Relationship," *Diplomacy and Statecraft*, no. 20, 2009, 247.

105. Richard A. Nuccio, "Cuba: A U.S. Perspective," in *Transatlantic Tension: The United States, Europe, and Problem Countries*, ed. Richard N. Haass (Washington, DC: Brookings Institution Press), 27 n. 9. Brothers-to-the-Rescue was created in 1991 by José Basulto, a self-described terrorist against Cuba in the 1960s, to provide search and rescue for Cubans fleeing on rafts. The 1994 and 1995 immigration accords angered Basulto, and he reportedly believed that the Clinton administration intended to normalize relations with Cuba. To prevent a rapprochement, he sought to provoke Cuba into a hostile act and did so by repeatedly flying small planes over Havana, dropping leaflets and trinkets. After repeated warnings by the United States were ignored, the Cuban military believed that the provocations presented a real threat, though the Cuban air force mistakenly shot down the planes while they were over international waters, after having left Cuban airspace.

106. U.S. Census Bureau, Foreign Trade Statistics, "Trade in Goods with Cuba," http://www.census.gov/foreign-trade/balance/c2390.html (accessed April 10, 2014).

107. U.S. Commission for Assistance to a Free Cuba, *Report to the President, May 2004* (Washington, DC: U.S. Department of State, 2004), xi, http://pdf.usaid.gov/pdf_docs/PCAAB192.pdf (accessed August 25, 2013). The new measures included a reduction in trips to the island by Cuban Americans from once a year to once in three years and a requirement that university programs in Cuba be a minimum of ten weeks. The number of programs dropped within months from more than 300 to six.

108. Fidel Castro Ruz, "Proclamation by an Adversary of the U.S. Government," May 14, 2004, http://www.cuba.cu/gobierno/discursos/2004/ing/f140504i.html (accessed August 25, 2013).

109. Condoleezza Rice and Carlos Gutiérrez, *Report to the President: Commission for Assistance to a Free Cuba*, July 2006, http://www.cfr.org/content/publications/attachments/68166.pdf (accessed August 25, 2013).

I

Politics

Cuban politics before 1959 was always circumscribed by the predominant power of the United States. From the intervention in 1898 to the imposition of the Platt Amendment in 1903 to repeated interventions in the first two decades of the century to the coup that short-circuited the 1933 revolution and installed Fulgencio Batista in power, Cubans were never truly masters in their own house. As U.S. Ambassador Earl E. T. Smith was fond of declaiming, Washington's emissary in Cuba was "the second most important man in Cuba; sometimes even more important than the president." Throughout the first half of the twentieth century, Cuba's nominally democratic institutions repeatedly failed to deliver responsive, honest government. Politicians campaigned for office promising the sky, then delivered corruption and repression. By the 1950s, Cuban political institutions had scant legitimacy.

Fidel Castro did not invent the anti-American strain in Cuban nationalism, but he reflected it, amplified it, and made it a core tenet of his political appeal. Fidel's charismatic authority derived as much from the policies he championed as the style of his leadership. The Revolution of 1959 swept away all the old institutions of government, including the Constitution of 1940 and the electoral institutions it created. The Revolution was, nevertheless, extraordinarily popular. Its initial legitimacy came from overthrowing the hated dictator Batista, who engaged in indiscriminate repression as the revolutionary wave rose against him. That legitimacy was reinforced by early policies that redistributed income from rich to poor, raising the standard of living of a majority of Cubans, and by rhetoric that defied the United States, in effect declaring Cuba's second independence.

The revolutionary government's radicalism was not universally popular. Fidel Castro was never one to tolerate dissent: "All criticism is opposition," he told compatriot Carlos Franqui early on. "All opposition is counterrevolutionary." Moderates who had opposed Batista were initially included in the new government, but their pro-capitalist, pro-U.S. instincts were not in keeping with the vision the Fidelistas had for Cuba's future. By the end of 1959, most had been eased out. Independent institutions, from unions to newspapers and radio stations, were brought under state control. By Castro's own admission, thousands of opponents were imprisoned in the early years of the Revolution for opposing its socialist trajectory, and organized opposition has been sparse since the mid-1960s. The efficiency of state security and the ease of migrating to the United States made it more attractive to oppose Castro from Miami than from Havana.

During the first decade of revolutionary government, Cuban politics had a chaotic quality. Government agencies were created, merged, divided, and abolished routinely. Most of the ministries inherited from the old regime were dissolved. As the government nationalized the economy, a whole new government bureaucracy sprang from the initial seed of the National Institute of Agrarian Reform. Key decisions were made by Fidel Castro and his "revolutionary family," a small group of trusted advisers, most of whom fought together in the mountains during the insurrection. Fidel roamed the country, stopping in on government operations far and wide, as if he could manage the whole country personally. In power, the veterans of the insurrection tried to run the country the way they had fought the war. "Guerrilla administration" was ad hoc, pragmatic, flexible, and somewhat disorganized.

In the 1970s, under the influence of the Soviet Union, Cuban political institutions began to take on the familiar shape of established Marxist-Leninist polities. The Cuban Communist Party, founded in 1965 through the merger of groups that had fought against Batista, was a small and ineffectual institution in the late 1960s. By the late 1970s, however, it had grown in size and maturity to take on the leading role in politics. Cuba adopted a new constitution in 1976, providing more permanence to state institutions and creating for the first time elected legislative assemblies at the local, provincial, and national levels—the Organs of People's Power.

The decade of the 1980s was one of gathering storms for Cuba's political system. It began with the 1980 Mariel boatlift. Propelled by deteriorating economic conditions on the island, 125,000 Cubans opted to flee to the United States. A series of corruption scandals marked the decade, culminating with the 1989 trial and execution of several senior military and security officials for drug smuggling. In the Soviet Union, the 1980s was a decade of transition. Mikhail Gorbachev's policies of perestroika and glasnost struck a chord among some Cubans. Cuba had, after all, been following the Soviet model in both political organization and economic management. If these policies were now under critical scrutiny in the homeland of socialism, why should they remain above criticism in Cuba? The collapse of European communism, first in Eastern Europe and then in the Soviet Union, intensified the urgency of Cuba's internal debate.

When European socialism collapsed, many prognosticators foresaw the imminent demise of Castro's Cuba. One key reason the Cuban regime survived was simply that Fidel Castro did not repeat Mikhail Gorbachev's mistake of combining the disruptions of economic transformation with a political opening. Even Cuba's modest economic reforms took place within the context of unremittingly tough political controls. Washington lent Castro an unintended helping hand by ratcheting up the pressure, hoping to speed up his demise. Instead, it once again gave Castro a convenient external enemy to rally Cuban patriotism. The "Special Period" of the 1990s spawned greater discontent among ordinary Cubans than ever before, but they had few opportunities to mobilize opposition.

The two most important institutions in the Cuban political system have been the Cuban Communist Party (*Partido Comunista de Cuba* [PCC]) and the Revolutionary Armed Forces (*Fuerzas Armadas Revolucionarias* [FAR]). LeoGrande describes how the PCC developed from a small, disorganized organization with a fractious leadership in the 1960s to the dominant decision-making institution in the 1970s and 1980s. In the early 1990s, the Party was the principal venue for elite debate over how to survive the collapse of the Soviet Union. After a brief flurry of debate, however, Castro opted for maintaining political control during the ensuing economic crisis. As the decade wore on, Castro allowed the Party to atrophy, preferring to govern through directives conveyed by a small team of intimate advisers.

The Party faced its toughest test in 2006, when Fidel Castro's illness forced him to turn over the reins of power to his brother. Raúl Castro's leadership style stands in sharp contrast to his brother's. He trusts and relies on established institutions in a way Fidel never did. His speeches are short and to the point, but a recurrent theme is the need to strengthen Cuba's political institutions, foremost among them the Communist Party, as the only way to guarantee the Revolution's survival when the founding generation finally passes from the scene. As Raúl gradually replaced Fidel's senior appointees, he consistently chose people with well-established, successful careers who have come up through the ranks—in contrast to Fidel's penchant of plucking young, largely untested leaders from the Union of Young Communists and catapulting them into positions of authority.

The Sixth Congress of the Communist Party in 2011 set in motion the most far-reaching program of economic reforms—or "updating" of the model, as Cubans prefer to call it—since 1959. Rapid economic and social change put new pressures on the Communist Party to rally the regime's base of support at a time when it was preparing for the imminent leadership succession from the historical leaders who made the Revolution (*los históricos*) to a new generation. Carlos Alzugaray, in his tour d'horizon of contemporary Cuban politics, emphasizes that Raúl and the next generation of Cuban leaders necessarily have to adopt new modes of governing, replacing the hypercentralized, top-down politics of the past with a polity more open to debate and even disagreement.

Rafael Hernández talks about how the Special Period was not just an economic crisis but a social and political one as well, undermining socialist values of community and equality and weakening regime legitimacy. Raúl Castro's new economic model puts economic issues front and center, but it also includes the elements of a new political model—one in which decision making is more decentralized, the state plays a less intrusive role in everyday life, and the space available for political debate is substantially wider than it has been historically. He also notes that the new policies face opposition—on the one hand from bureaucrats who are used to being in charge of the centralized Cuban economic and political model and, on the other, from ordinary Cubans fearful of the uncertainty that the elimination of "Papa state" implies.

Camila Piñeiro Harnecker describes the debate within the Cuban elite over Raúl's new economic policy as coalescing around three camps: the "statist" group, the "economicist" group, and the "self-management" group. The statists regard centralized state direction of the economy as essential to socialism and therefore are the most skeptical of and potentially resistant to Raúl's reform program—especially its call to decentralize decision making and reduce the state's role in the economy. Not surprisingly, the members of this camp tend to be the state and party bureaucrats who heretofore have been in charge and stand to see their authority (and privileges) reduced by the changes proposed. The economicist camp authored most of the current reforms, believing that greater reliance on market incentives and decentralized political control are necessary to boost economic productivity and combat a sclerotic, stifling bureaucracy. Many of them are, in fact, economists by training who have argued for these sorts of reforms for years, to no avail. Now, however, they have Raúl Castro on their side. Finally, the self-management camp—with which Harnecker clearly sympathizes—favors a highly decentralized, democratic polity in which workers have the political power to cushion the inequalities that markets inevitably produce.

The FAR has been Cuba's most stable and reliable institution—not because the military has played an independent political role but rather because, as Hal Klepak explains, it has been Cuba's best-organized, most efficient, and most respected revolutionary institution. Since the earliest years, the military has been a source of skilled managers, staffing many agencies of the civilian bureaucracy. In the 1970s, it won accolades at home and abroad for its role in Africa, defending Angola from South Africa's intervention and defending Ethiopia from Somalia's invasion. Most important, of course, the armed forces successfully carried out its central mission—defending the Revolution from the subversive efforts of the United States.

Since the late 1980s, the armed forces have also been a bellwether of economic change. Even before the collapse of European socialism and the advent of the Special Period, the armed forces had begun experimenting with Western management and accounting methods, hoping to improve the productivity of military industries. In the 1990s, these methods began to be applied throughout the state sector of the economy under the "business improvement" plan (*Perfeccionamiento Empresarial*), and they became a central feature of the new economic policies adopted at the Sixth Congress of the Communist Party.

Raúl Castro led the FAR from 1959 until he became president, and the loyalty of its top officers to him and to the present government is unquestioned. The respect with which the military is regarded by ordinary Cubans, its effectiveness as the defender of the *patria*, and the fact that it holds a monopoly of arms all make it centrally important. As president, Raúl Castro has tapped a number of officers to take new responsibilities running civilian ministries and tried to apply to the wider government the management principles that have made the FAR so successful.

The government's shrinking capacity to provide resources to Cuban society during the Special Period led to a flowering of civil society. Nongovernmental organizations were allowed to organize, new social networks developed out of market reforms in the economy, and religious institutions enjoyed a resurgence in the spiritual vacuum created by communism's collapse. The nature of civil society in Cuba has become the focus of much debate. Some scholars take a relatively pessimistic view of these developments, seeing in them at best the emergence of a protocivil society, existing at the sufferance of the state, and unlikely to pose any challenge to it. Margaret Crahan, however, describes the complexity of Cuban civil society and the absence of clear boundaries between it and the state. Some civil society institutions are completely autonomous and some semiautonomous, but even some, such as the mass organizations that are directed by the state, nevertheless play an independent role, at times representing the interests of their members to state authorities.

The churches are, by far, the most significant element of Cuban civil society. They alone have an organizational infrastructure that covers the island and a mass base of members. Since the 1990s, churches have played an important role at the community level, delivering relief supplies from sister churches abroad. The Catholic Church, in particular, has developed magazines and newsletters that circulate widely and express critical, if not oppositional, viewpoints. In 2010, the government entered into an unprecedented dialogue with Cardinal Jaime Ortega, leading to the release of 127 political prisoners, thereby recognizing the church as a legitimate interlocutor between the state and civil society.

In contrast, Armando Chaguaceda offers a stinging critique of how the Cuban state has constrained political participation. Elites have limited it to mobilization to carry out state policies and periodic consultation on major decisions. The consultations, however, are fragmented, with elites free to choose which suggestions to accept and which to ignore. The result has been a depoliticized citizenry ruled over by a huge state bureaucracy with no mechanisms for citizens outside the state to hold elites accountable. At the local level, citizens have some avenues for more authentic participation, but these are constrained by both their local scope and their limited resources. Nevertheless, Cuba experienced a flowering of independent, grassroots voluntary associations organized around a plethora of social and cultural issues during the 1990s. Despite the state's hostility, the terrain of public space occupied by the growing variety of grassroots voluntary associations continues to expand, and in them Chaguaceda sees the seeds of renewed citizen participation and elite accountability.

As civil society expanded during the 1980s, openly dissident organizations began to appear, and, though beset by harassment and arrests, they have managed to persist. Conventional wisdom held that these small, isolated groups had little capacity to reach beyond their own ranks with a message of opposition. In 2002, however, a Christian activist, Oswaldo Payá, surprised everyone by collecting more than 11,000 signatures on the Varela Project's petition demanding democratic reform. The dissidents' ability to work together and mobilize people far beyond their own numbers suggested strength greater than any opposition the Cuban government had faced before. In 2003, seventy-five dissidents, many who had worked on the Varela Project, were arrested, tried, and sentenced to long prison terms for accepting U.S. assistance in violation of Cuban law.

Under Raúl Castro's leadership, the government's treatment of dissidents has changed. Dissidents are no longer sentenced to long prison terms but continue to be harassed by police, who detain them for a few hours or a few days and then release them without charges. According to U.S. diplomats in Havana, Cuban officials are less concerned about the "old guard" dissidents, with whom they have been sparring for decades, than they are about the challenge posed by a new generation of dissidents, adept at the use of social media and linked by the Internet to one another and audiences abroad. The most famous is Yoani Sánchez, whose *Generación Y* blog offers an acerbic look at daily life in Cuba, winning Sánchez international acclaim—and the hostility of Cuban officialdom, which she regularly lampoons.

As Henken and van de Voort show, the "blogosphere" in Cuba is just as complex as the rest of civil society. Bloggers run the gamut from avid supporters of the regime to critical supporters to outright opponents. Limitations on Internet access in Cuba, both technical and political, prevent bloggers from reaching a mass audience on the island, where only a small percentage of the population has regular Internet access. Almost all the bloggers are better known abroad than they are at home. But blogs and social media represent a new venue for expression by a new generation of Cubans—one that will be increasingly difficult for the state to control as access expands. Experiences in Iran, Tunisia, and Egypt demonstrate that social media, because it is a channel of two-way communication, has the potential to be a mechanism of social and political mobilization.

Fidel Castro's immense personal authority at the dawn of the revolutionary government was rooted in his personal courage, political savvy, and heroic achievements as the leader who made the Revolution. Historically, the revolutionary regime has drawn legitimacy from Fidel Castro, not the other way around. For the next generation of leaders, this situation will be reversed. Their right to govern will derive from the legitimacy of the institutions over which they preside, not from their personal virtues, which can appear only weak and pallid in comparison to Fidel's. To meet the challenge of legitimacy, Raúl Castro is focusing on improving economic performance while at the same time appealing to culturally resonant themes, especially nationalism. As Raúl told the National Party Conference in 2012, the political requisite for economic success was "to strengthen national unity around the Party and the Revolution . . . and to consolidate the conviction of preserving the Cuban nation and socioeconomic achievements, on the basis of the idea that homeland, revolution and socialism are indissolubly fused." For half a century, this nationalist appeal has had sufficient resonance for Cubans that they have not demanded a more open politics. Time will tell whether it will retain that resonance once the generation that founded the revolutionary government has passed from the scene.

Chapter One

Continuity and Change in Cuba at Fifty

The Revolution at a Crossroads

Carlos Alzugaray Treto

Fifty years after the successful rebellion against Fulgencio Batista's dictatorship and the start of the transformation process generally referred to as "the Revolution," Cuba finds itself once again at a momentous crossroads. On the eve of his eightieth birthday, having governed for almost half a century, Fidel Castro temporarily transferred his duties as head of state to his constitutional successor, General Raúl Castro, on July 31, 2006, because of a serious illness. What was originally projected as a difficult and painful recovery process requiring several weeks of absence resulted in a definitive retirement. Some nineteen months later, on February 24, 2008, the newly elected Seventh Session of the National Assembly of People's Power appointed a new government, led up to that point by the interim president. This has opened an uncharted phase in recent Cuban history in which Fidel Castro has ceased to be the head of state and/or government for the first time since February 1959, when he assumed the role of prime minister, later becoming "Compañero Fidel." This historic moment for Cubans raises the prospect of inevitable changes and associated uncertainty.

THE CROSSROADS: CONTINUITY AND CHANGE

This chapter is an attempt to reflect and meditate on continuity and political changes—on the challenges and opportunities of this period and their significance. My intention is not to pontificate or point to inevitable paths. Nor do I wish to propose fixed alternatives because the issue requires reflection that is open to dialogue, debate, and deliberation.[1]

The chapter's point of departure is that a predictable process of evolution toward new ways of governing Cuban society has begun. It is not what current political science has called a "transition" (giving rise to a whole school of "transitology"), although the need for adjustments, transformations, and changes within continuity may correspond to a broad sense of this notion. Paradoxically, the concept of political and social transition appeared well before the current trend, being used in the Marxist literature to refer to the evolution of socialist society from an initial to a more advanced stage (Marcuse 1967, 37–54). Today, however, the concept is too "loaded" and presumes "regime change" and, more important, the enthronement of political systems that Atilio Borón (2000, 135–211) has called "democratic capitalism" in societies previously governed by regimes labeled "authoritarian" or "totalitarian." Cuba's situation does not fit this description; neither its starting point nor its ending point matches those of the political transitions most frequently analyzed in the current literature.

The fact is that Fidel Castro has governed Cuba in a way that for obvious reasons cannot be replicated. Some leadership sectors in Cuba have affirmed on more than one occasion that Fidel's absence will change nothing, to the point of including in the Cuban Constitution the idea that socialism is irrevocable.[2] This is a reaction that can be logically explained by the need to emphasize the continuity of the project begun on January 1, 1959, as a counterweight to attempts to reverse it from the outside, precisely by the superpower that has most interfered in internal Cuban affairs, the United States (Alzugaray 2007). This caution notwithstanding, it is obvious that changes must be made in politics and governance, although these changes will be a response to an internal dynamic rather than to demands coming from outside, as has happened throughout Cuban history. This principled position, for which popular support is evident, was advanced on July 11, 2008, by President Raúl Castro (2008c): "I reiterate that we will never make a decision—not even the smallest one!—on the basis of pressure or black-mail, no matter what its origin, from a powerful country or a continent."

FIDEL CASTRO, THE REVOLUTION, AND THEIR PLACE IN HISTORY

The Cuban Revolution, creator of the political regime currently governing events on the island, was a necessary and original process. The need for it, in historical terms, was born of what could be called the four great national aspirations thwarted since the nineteenth century: sovereignty, social justice, sustainable economic development, and autonomous democratic government. The triumph of the Revolution in 1959 was the result of specific internal circum-stances and not, as with socialism in Eastern Europe (with the exception of the Soviet Union), of foreign imposition.

After 400 years of Spanish colonial oppression and sixty years of U.S. domination, the Cuban people and the country's progressive political and social sectors had long demanded a truly free and sovereign nation. The recovery of national self-determination was therefore one of several driving forces—perhaps the leading one—in the process of radical change initiated in 1959. By that time, it was clear that the principal obstacle to self-determination and national sovereignty was U.S. imperialism's hegemonic designs on Cuba (Pérez 2008).

Another vital demand of Cuban society in the nineteenth and twentieth centuries was social justice—the country, "including everyone and for the good of all," that José Martí demanded. The nation was ill; it suffered from unbearable inequalities and inequities that the ruling oligarchy happily ignored.

Moreover, the political system created in the shadow of U.S. hegemony had demonstrated not only its total inoperativeness but also a perverse tendency toward venality and corruption. Throughout Cuba's brief postcolonial and prerevolutionary history, between 1902 and 1959, three dictatorships (those of Gerardo Machado from 1925 to 1933, Fulgencio Batista [behind the scenes] from 1933 to 1940, and Batista again [now openly] from 1952 to 1959) had revealed the total inability of Cuba's political class to generate a sustainable democratic capitalism. Worse yet, government amounted largely to political dishonesty and immorality. The few administrations produced by elections, rarely free and fair, were known for theft and embezzlement of the public treasury.

Finally, and above all at the middle-income and professional levels, there was a need to transform the national economy. Although cold statistics reflected a relatively high level of economic development compared with the rest of Latin America and the Caribbean, three factors were worrisome. Cuba was a monoproducing and monoexporting country whose wealth depended almost exclusively on one item, sugar, and one market, the United States. Martí (1991) had warned against such a situation, arguing that "the nation that purchases rules." The great disparities in income and well-being dissolved any satisfaction over the gross domestic product, and, as a result of the intimate ties with the neighbor to the north, Cubans did not compare themselves with the rest of the region. Their reference point was the highly sweetened image of the "average American" conveyed to the island by the constant cultural and ideological presence of U.S. consumption models. The outstanding political success of Fidel Castro during his forty-seven years of governance was precisely his ability to lead the nation toward achieving these four historical aims. While not all of these demands have been met in optimal form and degree, there is no question that Cuba's situation today reflects a radical change from that of 1958. There is also no doubt that this change took place in the direction desired by the populace and its political vanguards despite the obstacles placed in its way, especially the constant hostility of its powerful neighbor, the United States, whose policy of "regime change" toward Cuba is almost a half a century old.

It is highly improbable and indeed implausible that the Cuban people and its leadership would voluntarily and consciously abandon and renounce the achievements of these fifty years. Nevertheless, Fidel Castro's successors face serious challenges in reproducing the system without him. The reversibility of the Cuban revolutionary process as a result of internal mistakes and not from outside pressure was dramatically presented by Fidel Castro himself in his speech at the University of Havana on November 17, 2005 (F. Castro 2005; Guanche 2007).

Among the strengths of the Cuban political regime in its current structure is, first of all, its high degree of internal and external legitimacy. Externally, this legitimacy stems from the well-known Cuban activism in the international arena and the broad network of foreign relations that has allowed the country to head the Non-Aligned Movement (NAM) twice and to achieve a series of successes in the UN General Assembly on a resolution condemning and calling for an end to the U.S. blockade against Cuba. Having neutralized the policy of international and diplomatic isolation of Cuba begun by the Eisenhower administration and continued through the recent Bush administration has been one of the most important victories of the Cuban revolutionary leadership.

Internally, in addition to the majority recognition of what have been called the "conquests of the revolution," legitimacy is conferred by an institutional framework upheld by two basic pillars: the Communist Party of Cuba and the Revolutionary Armed Forces (*Fuerzas Armadas Revolucionarias* [FAR]). It is a very common error in foreign spheres, especially among political scientists and analysts, to assume that the Cuban Communist Party is copied from similar ones in the Eastern European socialist countries. Despite the fact that the party's leadership has committed widely acknowledged and/or rectified errors and that some methods and work styles—such as excessive centralism—that bear the mark of their origins in the Soviet political model persist, in reality the Cuban revolutionary leadership has concerned itself, among other things, with two central aspects: its role as political vanguard of the activists who must be and have been at the forefront of any sociopolitical initiative and the struggle against any instance of corruption in its ranks. The honesty, simplicity, and sacrifice promoted by Che Guevara and not the privileges and benefits of a nomenklatura, as in the Soviet Union and Eastern Europe during the socialist years, have been the paradigm of Cuban communist behavior.

Nevertheless—and this is an important challenge—we are still far from achieving a truly democratic culture. In too many leaders, there seems to be a common perception that the only purpose of debate is to convince the population that the course of action designed by the higher authorities at any given time is the only truly revolutionary one. "Bold attempts at analysis outside official discourse are stigmatized as immature, naïve, gullible, or simply provocative" (Fernández 2007). According to the political discourse of many leadership ca- dres, those who dare to do so "are not adequately informed," but the required information is unavailable because "disseminating it might be useful to the enemy." Sometimes the paterna- listic reproach is heard that anyone who disagrees or dissents is "naive." In addition, Cuba has lacked a real culture of debate, dialogue, and deliberation (Arencibia Lorenzo 2007).

Finally, the need to defend the achievements of the Revolution from imperialism's increas- ing aggressiveness and the practices of property nationalization and centralization of the decision-making process over the years have led to what Mayra Espina (2007) has called the "hypernationalization" of social relations: "centralization, verticalism, paternalism/authoritar- ianism, distributive homogenization with insufficient sensitivity in dealing with the diversity of needs and heterogeneous interests (of groups, territories, localities, etc.)." On occasion, one perceives a transformation of the relation between average citizens and those officials, also ordinary citizens, who hold some position in the state apparatus. These bureaucrats act more like bosses giving instructions on what can or cannot be done and enjoying that role than like persons at the service of the people and subordinate to them. As early as 1964, Raúl Roa García (1964, 590) identified bureaucracy as "one of socialism's worst stumbling blocks."

NEED FOR ECONOMIC AND POLITICAL CHANGE

In the absence of Fidel Castro's power to mobilize and to build consensus, the need for a mind-set of respect for dialogue, debate, and deliberation will increase. It will entail strength- ening real collective participation and the construction of what could be a democracy that is both participatory and deliberative. Some form of debate was not completely absent in the past, but it was always subject to the ultimate authority of Fidel Castro, who frequently circumvented it in order to create a consensus that often became unanimity.

The FAR and its important sister institution the Interior Ministry (responsible for the country's internal security but closely linked in its origin and composition to the Rebel Army, predecessor of the FAR) constitute the most effective and prestigious of the institutions creat- ed by the country's historical leadership. Their popular origin, continual involvement in peo- ple's problems, historic contribution to the country's defense and the liberation of other peoples, and economic pragmatism, demonstrated by the introduction of "business perfection" into their industries, allow them to enjoy the trust of broad sectors of the population. The upper echelons of the armed services have amassed a tradition of heroism, pragmatism, reli- ability, and professionalism not often seen in Latin America and the Caribbean or in the world.

Cohesion between these two institutions, which must be constantly nourished, will depend on the prevailing tendencies in other important sectors in Cuban society. On the one hand, we have the important business sector, composed in part of high-level FAR officers but also of a young generation of economists and administrators. One might presume that there is a desire in this sector to maintain consensus, but within it we find demands for the flexibilization of economic policy also present in the upper-echelon military although for different reasons. Among the former, it arises from concerns about administrative effectiveness; among the latter, it is also due to the need to maintain social stability. It is not a question of establishing a market economy but rather one of adopting initiatives that grant more autonomy to administra- tors, as set forth in the business-perfection program begun in the military-industrial sector. The ultimate goal is to stimulate production and develop the productive forces. It also has to do with more opportunities for individual initiative, a concern dating to the reforms that lifted the country out of the "Special Period" in the mid-1990s. These demands have begun to be expressed publicly in several scientific works (Monreal 2008; Sánchez Egozcue, Mario, and Cordoví 2008; Pérez Villanueva 2008).

Traditionally, youth, especially students, have had a central role in Cuban politics. Almost all of the high-level leaders in the country were members of and had their first schooling in public participation in the University Student Federation (*Federación Estudiantil Universitaria* [FEU]). In recent years, this organization, along with the Union of Communist Youth (*Unión de Jóvenes Comunistas*), has been among the pillars of the social programs promoted by Fidel Castro. Its role in the transformation period, which will inevitably affect Cuban society despite growing demands for greater leadership opportunities, will have to take the policies articulated by the leaders in other sectors into account. The difficulties of this process are not lost on the various social actors, as Carlos Lage Codorniú, former FEU president, noted in a symposium sponsored by the magazine *Temas*: "It is not about lack of communication, but there are many new ideas that must be allowed to be expressed. And ultimately, it is we young people who are responsible for this shortcoming. In order to strengthen the weight of the young generation we must push, be more visible. Some sectors have recognized the need for young people to take part, but others still have great reservations" (Hernández and Pañellas 2007, 160).

The organizations that serve the working class and *campesinos* will tend to seek new positions within the structure. Under Raúl Castro, they will foreseeably be afforded more leadership precisely because of the need to develop a new national consensus. Such is the case of the recently initiated process of granting lands in usufruct with a view to increasing food production, in which the National Association of Small Farmers (*Asociación Nacional de Agricultores Pequeños*) has been playing an important role (Lacey 2008). For its part, the growing role of the Federation of Cuban Workers (*Central de Trabajadores de Cuba*) was demonstrated by the yearlong national consultation on the new social security law that preceded its approval by the National Assembly in its final session of that year (Valdés Mesa 2008). While there is no doubt that this process provided the opportunity for broad debate, the unanimous adoption by the Assembly was not a true reflection of the divergent opinions that existed.

Finally, the Cuban intelligentsia, recently affected by the memory of the "gray quinquennium" (the phase in which the Soviet Union's cultural policy of the early 1970s was copied), will seek greater levels of autonomy and freedom while defending its commitment to the core objectives of Cuban society.

ECONOMIC CHALLENGES

The most important internal challenge that the leadership headed by Raúl Castro will face will be to resolve the increasing demand for salaries and legal income that are sufficient to permit all Cubans to cover their most important daily necessities. As a result of the crisis of the 1990s and the economic policies adopted, two significant equilibriums prevailing until 1989 were shattered. One was the balance between people's incomes and the prices of basic goods, in some cases rationed and in others subsidized by the state budget. The disappearance of the mutually advantageous relations with the Soviet Union and the socialist camp knocked this plan out the window.

The other equilibrium that unraveled during the Special Period was the one existing among the various sectors of the population. Although Cuba abandoned its egalitarian policies in the late 1970s and early 1980s, a healthy tendency not to allow excessive inequality persisted.

With the reforms introduced in 1993–1994, this balance disappeared; inequities arose that were the more unbearable because of the previous disparities between salaries and their purchasing power and the fact that many of these disparities were the result of illegal and corrupt practices.

Most Cubans aspire to maintain current levels of social security but would like to see Marx's formula "from each according to his ability and to each according to his needs" applied. This precept is not being fulfilled today. Although it is very difficult to determine the degree of national agreement on the issue, it can be said that Cubans, while maintaining an essentially socialist economy, would like to see more opportunities for prosperity, even at the cost of privatizing certain sectors.

The situation described has led many Cubans to supplement their salaries with activities in the so-called informal sector of the economy. This and none other is the root of the growing corruption at the lower and middle levels of business and services. Cuban leaders have only recently understood that this is the most serious threat to the sustainability of the Cuban project, as Fidel Castro himself acknowledged in his speech at the University of Havana on November 17, 2005 (F. Castro 2005). Nevertheless, despite some salary increases and other measures, the impression is that government responses are insufficient. The ideological consequences of the persistence and expansion of this phenomenon are the system's greatest weakness.

In sum, in order to understand the need to deal with corruption and lawlessness and to preserve the Revolution, we should recall an admonition of José Martí (1991): "Being good is the only way to be fortunate. Being learned is the only way to be free. *But, most often in human nature, one must be prosperous to be good*" (1991, 289, emphasis added).

The events of the past years since Fidel Castro's illness and convalescence show that modest but solid changes are occurring in politics and in the search for solutions to the above-mentioned challenges. It is not just that Raúl Castro prefers to stress collective leadership rather than Fidel Castro's high level of public and discursive leadership. Rather, as Cuba's highest official, he has been developing and promoting a series of policies that go to the heart of the problems being faced by the country.

A smooth succession has been possible despite U.S. efforts to derail it for a number of reasons. The first and most important of these is, of course, the level of support and consensus that exists in Cuba around Fidel Castro and the strategic objectives of the Revolution he has led. The second is the painstaking preparation displayed by the president to achieve it. This should dispel any doubts about the sustainability of the Cuban Revolution beyond Fidel Castro and his companions, the "historical leadership." But there is another factor worth noting. The way in which this transfer of power took place, in which Raúl Castro established his own style and his own priorities with Fidel Castro still alive, indicates complete identification between them within diversity. We can surmise that there is a mutual recognition and acceptance of the respective roles they must play. While the first was the visionary who founded and designed the policies for creating an independent and sovereign Cuba, the second has been the guardian who has faithfully fulfilled his role as what he once called the "protector of the rearguard." At the same time, by knowing when to withdraw and let his successor take the necessary measures based on his own nature, style, and tendencies, Fidel Castro has guaranteed the continuity of the project under the new conditions and the success of his heir in being what he must be, the transitional figure who will facilitate the transformation of politics and governance in Cuba.

POLITICAL CHALLENGES

On a strictly political level, what has characterized President Raúl Castro's major pronouncements has been the continual call to deepen democracy, dialogue, debate, and deliberation as irreplaceable tools for creating the consensus necessary for clarifying and advancing national policy, beginning with his speech on July 26, 2008, in Camagüey: "We should not fear discrepancies in a society like ours, which by its nature does not contain antagonistic contradictions because the social classes composing it are not like that. *The best solutions come out of the intensive exchange of diverging opinions* if it is guided by sound intentions and handled responsibly" (R. Castro 2008b, emphasis added).

In his view, not even a proposal manipulated by imperialism's propaganda machine should be excluded from consideration: "We are not going to refuse to listen to anyone's honest opinion, which is so useful and necessary, because of the ridiculous ruckus it kicks up every time a citizen of our country says something to which those making the scene would not pay the slightest attention if they heard it anywhere else on the planet" (R. Castro 2008d).

He thus invited every citizen to discuss even the issue of socialism and the ways of constructing it. In February 2008, he recalled that in his speech at the University of Havana, Fidel had made the following self-criticism: "One conclusion that I have reached after many years: of the many errors we have all committed, the most significant mistake was to believe that anyone knew anything about socialism or that anyone knew how to build socialism" (Guanche 2007, 42).

In his reflection on the need for ever-more democratic processes during his inaugural speech as president, Raúl did not exclude the Party: "If the people are firmly united *around a single party, it must be more democratic than any other*, and along with it society as a whole, which of course, like any human work, can be perfected. But without a doubt, it is just and *all its members have the opportunity to express their views* and, even more important, work to realize what we agree on in each case" (R. Castro 2008d, emphasis added). Shortly before that, in December 2007, in summarizing the conclusions of the national deliberation process around his July 26 speech that year, he had emphasized the need for all Party or government leaders to stimulate the broadest debate and consultation among their subordinates (R. Castro 2007).

Another issue that has received special emphasis in Raúl Castro's speeches and statements since taking on the top leadership of the country is the institutionalization and efficiency of government bodies. This is a particularly important matter because of the distress created by bureaucracy, inefficiency, and corruption. In this vein, he has requested and obtained from the National Assembly authorization to modify the structure of the central government:

> Institutionalism, let me repeat the term: institutionalism, is an important mainstay of this decisive proposal and one of the pillars of invulnerability of the revolution in the political realm, which is why we must constantly work to perfect it. We should never think that what we've done is perfect. Our democracy is participatory as are few others, but we must realize that the operation of the state and government institutions has not yet reached the degree of effectiveness rightfully demanded by our people. This is an issue that we should all think about. (R. Castro 2008d)

These assertions on the importance of the institutions and their effectiveness (which is an essential part of their legitimacy) stand in contrast to a fairly widespread view that the best way to fight bureaucracy is to subvert the institutions and replace them with more informal mechanisms for making and implementing decisions. The truth is that undermining the institutions inevitably leads to the loss of legitimacy of the entire system. This would suggest that the correct policy would be to oblige those who direct and participate in institutions to act within the law and with accountability.

IN CONCLUSION

Cuba finds itself at a crossroads in which changes must be made within continuity. These changes have already begun and are reflected in measures and declarations by the new administration led by Raúl Castro. They will inevitably mean a transformation of Cuban society, both economically and politically. The Sixth Congress of the Cuban Communist Party will be obliged to give a definitive response to the collection of problems afflicting the country. This is not a matter of denying the achievements made under the leadership of Fidel Castro but rather one of making the necessary adjustments and transformations. The next party congress will have to make decisions on key issues reflected in the following questions:

1. What are the bases for building a just society that reflect the ideals once clearly identified as socialism? We must resolve the discrepancies between the different forms of ownership, between centralization and decentralization, between moral and material incentives, and between the development of the productive forces and the development of a revolutionary consciousness. What the history of Cuba and other models has demonstrated is that hypercentralization, underestimation of the laws of the market, inappropriate handling of the relationship between the different forms of incentives, and underrating of the efficiency and development of the productive forces lead to dead ends and are not conducive to the formation of "the new man." While there are clear dangers in the unrestricted use of market mechanisms, ignoring people's need for progress and prosperity, collectively and individually, is not a solution to the problem. As Martí would say, "one must be prosperous to be good."

2. How is democracy to be strengthened and perfected? Cuban society needs to develop the democratic forms it has created. The absence of Fidel requires a search for new ways to create consensus. Introducing the concept of deliberative democracy, in which leaders are obliged to discuss the reasons for their decisions and citizens participate in decision making in an informed and rational way, will correct some of the system's current shortcomings, but this will require more and better information for the citizenry and the creation and promotion of public spaces in the press and other media.

NOTES

Excerpted from Carlos Alzugaray Treto, "Continuity and Political Change in Cuba at Fifty: The Revolution at a Crossroads," *Latin American Perspectives* 36, no. 3 (2009): 8–26. Republished by permission of the publisher. A version of this article was previously published in Spanish as "Cuba cincuenta años después: Continuidad y cambio político" by the journal *TEMAS*, no. 60 (October–December 2009): 37–47; this chapter was a Prize Essay Topic for 2008 in the Social Sciences category.

1. In Cuba, the absence of a "culture of debate" has been much criticized, along with the tendency to seek unanimity at all costs under the pretext of defending the necessary unity in the face of internal and external challenges. This matter warrants profound reflection on the means of creating public space for the analysis of the nation's problems based on the unity of its strategic objectives. It has been suggested that the solution is promoting debate, but I believe that we must also encourage "cultures of dialogue and deliberation" in which participants are obliged to come to a decision or solution for the problem that is the subject of the exchange.

2. The addition to Article 3 of the Cuban Constitution by the Constitutional Reform Law of June 26, 2002, reads as follows: "Socialism and the revolutionary political and social system established in this Constitution, tested by years of heroic resistance in the face of all types of aggressions and economic warfare by the administrations of the most powerful imperialist nation that has existed and having demonstrated its capacity to transform the country and

create an entirely new and just society, is irrevocable, and Cuba will never return to capitalism" (*Granma*, June 27, 2002, http://granma.co.cu).

REFERENCES

Alzugaray, Carlos. 2007. "La política de Estados Unidos hacia Cuba durante la segunda administración Bush: Continuidad y cambio." In *Estados Unidos—América Latina, los nuevos desafíos: ¿Unión o desunión?*, edited by Víctor López Villafañe and Soraya Castro Mariño. Mexico City: Joralé Editores y Orfila.

Arencibia Lorenzo, Jesús. 2007. "Debates en la beca: El ensueño y los ladrillos." Alma Mater: Revista Digital de los Universitarios Cubanos. http://www.almamater.cu/sitio%20nuevo/sitio%20viejo/webalmamater/2007/univers%2007/agosto/debate.html.

Borón, Atilio. 2000. *Tras el búho de Minerva: Mercado contra democracia en el capitalismo de fin de siglo*. Mexico City: Fondo de Cultura Económica.

Castro Ruz, Fidel. 2005. "Speech Delivered by Fidel Castro Ruz, President of the Republic of Cuba, in the Ceremony Marking the Sixtieth Anniversary of His Entry into University, Held in the Aula Magna of the Universidad de La Habana, November 17, 2005." http://www.cuba.cu/gobierno/discursos/2005/esp/f171105e.html.

Castro Ruz, Raúl. 2007. "¡Y a trabajar duro!: Declaration by Army General Raúl Castro Ruz, First Vice President of the Councils of State and Ministers, before the National Assembly of People's Power, on December 28, 2007, Año 49 de la Revolución."

———. 2008a. "Continuar perfeccionado la labor del Partido y su autoridad ante las masas": Intervention of the Second Secretary of the Central Committee of the Cuban Communist Party at the Close of the Sixth Plenum of the Central Committee of the PCC, Held in the Palacio de la Revolución, Havana, April 28, 2008, Año 50 de la Revolución." *Granma*, April 29.

———. 2008b. "Nuestra batalla de hoy es la misma iniciada el 26 de julio de 1953: Speech on the Fifty-Fifth Anniversary of the Assault on the Moncada and Carlos Manuel de Céspedes Garrisons, in Santiago de Cuba, July 26, 2008." *Granma*, July 27. http://granma.co.cu/2008/07/27/nacional/artic18.html.

———. 2008c. "Socialismo significa justicia social e igualdad, pero igualdad no es igualitarismo: Speech Delivered at the Close of the First Ordinary Session of the Seventh Legislature of the National Assembly of People's Power, Palacio de las Convenciones, Havana, July 11, 2008, Año 50 de la Revolución. *Granma*, July 12. http://www.granma.cubaweb.cu/2008/07/12/nacional/artic06.html.

———. 2008d. "Speech Delivered by Raúl Castro Ruz, President of the Councils of State and Ministers, at the Close of the Inaugural Session of the Seventh Legislature of the National Assembly of People's Power, Palacio de las Convenciones, Havana, February 24, 2008, Año 50 de la Revolución." http://www.cuba.cu/gobierno/rauldiscursos/2008/esp/r240208e.html.

Espina, Mayra. 2007. "Mirar a Cuba hoy: Cuatro supuestos para la observación y cinco problemas—Nudos." Paper presented at the seminar "Por una cultura revolucionaria de la política," Havana, November.

Fernández, Julio. 2007. Paper presented at the seminar "Por una cultura revolucionaria de la políticas," Havana, November.

Guanche, Julio César, ed. 2007. *En el borde de todo: El hoy y el mañana de la revolución en Cuba*. Bogotá: Ocean Sur.

Gutmann, Amy, and Dennis Thompson. 2004. *Why Deliberative Democracy?* Princeton, NJ: Princeton University Press.

Hernández, Rafael, and Daybel Pañellas. 2007. "Sobre la transición socialista en Cuba: Un simposio." *Temas*, no. 50–51.

Lacey, Mark. 2008. "Cuba to Grant Private Farmers Access to Land." *New York Times*, July 19. http://www.nytimes.com.

Marcuse, Herbert. 1967. *El Marxismo soviético*. Madrid: Ediciones de la Revista de Occidente.

Martí, José. [1884] 1991. "Maestros ambulantes." In *Obras completas*, vol. 8, *Nuestra América*. Havana: Editorial de Ciencias Sociales.

Monreal, Pedro. 2008. "El problema económico de Cuba." *Espacio Laical*, no. 28. http://www.espaciolaical.net.

Pérez, Louis A., Jr. 2008. *Cuba in the American Imagination: Metaphor and the Imperial Ethos*. Chapel Hill: University of North Carolina Press.

Pérez Villanueva, Omar Everleny. 2008. "La economía en Cuba: Un balance necesario y algunas propuestas de cambio." *Nueva Sociedad*, no. 216.

Roa García, Raúl. 1964. *Retorno a la alborada*. Santa Clara: Universidad Central de las Villas.

Sánchez Egozcue, Jorge Mario, and Juan Triana Cordoví. 2008. *Un panorama actual de la economía cubana, las transformaciones en curso y sus retos perspectivos*. Working Document 31/2008. Madrid: Real Instituto Elcano de Estudios Estratégicos e Internacionales.

Valdés Mesa, Salvador. 2008. "Las asambleas mostraron, una vez más, el apoyo de la clase obrera a la Revolución y a su dirección: Intervention by Salvador Valdés Mesa, General Secretary of the CTC, on the Outcome of the Workers' Discussion Process of the Draft Bill of the Social Security Law, December 27, 2008." *Granma*, December 29.

Chapter Two

Cuba's New Socialism

Different Visions Shaping Current Changes

Camila Piñeiro Harnecker

The shape of Cuba's "reformed," "updated," or "renewed" socialism depends on the relative influence of fundamentally different ways of understanding socialism and envisioning Cuba's future. These visions coincide largely in maintaining that Cuba's main long-term goal should be a more just society, liberated from economic hardship, but they differ markedly in the way they understand justice and freedom and thus socialism. Consequently, different Cubans tend to set different short- and medium-term goals and to propose different means for reaching them. I start with a brief contextualization of recent developments in Cuba and then examine three currents of opinion that I call the "statist" (*estatista*), the "economicist" (*economicista*), and the "self-managementist" (*autogestionaria*). No more than analytical tools, these terms are used to characterize different approaches to what should be done to save Cuba's socialist project.[1]

This study is based on an examination of public discourse (manifested in formal and informal debates and official declarations) and publications (academic, journalistic, and opinion) in Cuba. Whereas in the past there was concern that public debate would undermine national unity and make it easier for the U.S. government to implement its destabilization programs, now Cubans are called on to criticize problems openly and defend diverse solutions, and many are doing precisely that. Despite Cubans' known passionate extraversion and inclination to exaggerate, there is a surprisingly friendly confrontation of different positions. This is reflected in a rich exchange about theoretical concepts and interpretations of reality that is taking place not only among policymakers and academics but also in newspaper letters to the editor, books and magazine articles, public workshops, Internet articles, blogs, films, and radio and television programs.

While a few government officials, academics, journalists, and bloggers have made their visions of Cuba's future explicit or made statements that roughly correspond to one of the three positions, most people express aspects of all three. This chapter seeks not to classify Cubans by position—which could result in polarization—but to contribute to a more productive and thus respectful and nonpersonalized debate that will facilitate achieving a new consensus about the society in which they all want to live.

RECENT CHANGES IN CUBA

The current changes on the island can be traced back to a speech given by former president Fidel Castro on November 17, 2005, in which he warned for the first time publicly that the Revolution could be reversed. In contrast to the situation in the past, when the main causes of most economic problems in Cuba were attributed to U.S. economic sanctions and geopolitical warfare against Cuba, Castro said that the Revolution's major enemies were Cubans' own mistakes, especially unfair income inequality, vices such as theft, and lack of control and poor management decisions at high levels (F. Castro 2005). Less than a year later, in July 2006, he became ill, and before undergoing surgery, he ceded power to his legal successor and brother, Raúl Castro. Soon after, Raúl Castro began preparing for the deeper transformations that were needed to tackle those problems.

In a speech on July 26, 2007, Raúl Castro (2007) referred to the need for "conceptual and structural changes" and proposed a national debate to identify the main problems besetting Cuban society. More than 5 million people participated in more than 215,000 meetings between September and November 2007, and more than 1.6 million criticized the shortcomings of daily life, the underperformance of state institutions, and the behavior of public servants in bureaucratic posts.

The 2007 debate served as a prelude to the Sixth Congress of the Cuban Communist Party, but the only official information that immediately resulted from it was what everyone knew: that low salaries and inadequate food, transportation, and housing were Cubans' main sources of concern and that people were tired of prohibitions regarding their daily lives. Only a few of the measures that were expected to follow materialized in 2008–2009: the ability to buy certain goods and services previously limited to foreigners, the turning over of idle agricultural land to individuals and cooperatives, the elimination of committees in charge of approving the use of hard currency by state institutions (known as the *Comités de Aprobación de Divisas*), the creation of a national supervisory institution (*Contraloría de la República*), and initial steps toward reducing the size of ministries. Efforts were concentrated on dealing with the difficult financial situation that resulted from a series of costly hurricanes in 2008 and the international economic crisis.

Since 2010, Raúl Castro has more emphatically warned about the importance of overcoming serious economic obstacles. The preservation and sustainability of Cuba's socioeconomic system lies in the balance.[2] Reflecting the need to solve long-standing problems with the management of the Cuban economy, the Sixth Party Congress was scheduled for April 2011 for the purpose of approving general guidelines to improve economic performance, including some social policies and other areas closely related to the economic sphere.

The congress was preceded by debates in workplaces, neighborhoods, and social organizations over a document titled *2010 Draft Economic and Social Policy Guidelines of the 6th Congress of the Communist Party of Cuba* (*Partido Comunista de Cuba* [PCC] 2010). People were encouraged to propose changes, express concerns, or simply make comments on it. Cubans were called on to reach consensus on the "what," not the "how." It was suggested that the more complex discussion about how to reach the goals agreed on would occur later as institutions prepared new legislation and policies.

However, even before the debates in preparation for the congress began in December 2010, some measures were adopted and some experiments carried out with the idea of later applying them on a wider scale. The most consequential economic measure, which has been equated with another agrarian reform, had been in place since 2008. From 2008 to mid-2011, nearly 15 percent of agricultural land (1.13 million hectares) had been given in usufruct to 146,000 individual farmers (70,000 new ones) and, to a lesser degree, to worker cooperatives while recognizing that permanent (not only seasonal) wage labor was used by both. [3] This process is redistributing land from ineffective state farms and cooperatives, mostly to private farmers.

Resolution 9 of the Ministry of Labor and Social Security was passed in 2008 to link state workers' wages with productivity, following criteria approved by the ministry. These rules eliminated the cap on the amount that workers could earn beyond their base salary, thus allowing for greater wage differentials. But their implementation has stagnated because, among many factors, the Labor Ministry has ended up imposing productivity-tied pay schedules that are not attractive to either workers or managers.

In early 2010, several municipalities had begun to allow some barbers, beauticians, and transportation workers to lease barbers' chairs and taxis, respectively, from the state enterprises that previously employed them. Under the terms, the former state employees were obliged to cover all the costs of operation that the state had previously assumed but could freely set prices and keep the profits after taxes, whereas before they had in effect set prices higher than the regulated ones and kept the difference (in addition to their salaries). [4]

On October 25, 2010, a number of regulations were made public with regard to the process of "availability" (*disponibilidad*), in which state institutions were expected to relocate "excess" workers who reduced productivity. Excess workers were estimated at over 1 million, or 20 percent of total employment, averaging 30 percent of state enterprises' payrolls. These workers were to be offered alternative state jobs where there were openings, and if they decided to reject the offer, they were to be laid off with only a few months' pay, depending on how much time they had worked. The process was soon suspended because it was impossible to fulfill Raúl Castro's commitment that no one would be "abandoned to his fate" (Martínez and Meneses 2011). [5]

Other rules were passed that made independent work (*cuentapropismo*) more flexible, including the possibility of hiring wage laborers on a permanent basis. Independent workers are now able to rent spaces, establish economic transactions with state institutions, and receive lines of credit in Cuban banks. The number of licenses for independent work more than doubled in less than a year, [6] ten of these in part because many simply legalized their status. In spite of high taxes, many have seen benefits from legalizing their activities, such as access to retirement, security for disabilities and maternity, bank credit, and state contracts (Piñeiro 2011, 68–69).

There was massive participation in the discussion of the *Draft Guidelines*. From December 2010 to February 2011, a significant part of the Cuban population (9 million of a total population of about 11 million, but since most participated in more than one meeting, they were counted more than once) discussed the document in their places of work and study, their neighborhoods, and their social organizations. About 68 percent of the more than 200 guidelines were modified. Nevertheless, only a few of the changes, such as those related to market planning and prices, were substantial. One of the most important goals incorporated into the *Guidelines*—in addition to the expansion of nonstate enterprises (private and cooperative), greater autonomy for state enterprises, and greater weight for market relations—is that local governments should play a guiding role in state and nonstate economic activities, creating new enterprises, collecting taxes, and handling funds earmarked for local development.

Socialism, which was referred to only twice in the draft document, was defined in the final document as "equality of rights and opportunities" (PCC 2010, 5). Nevertheless, there are plans for the executive commission that oversees implementation of the *Guidelines* to define the "integral theoretical conceptualization of the Cuban socialist economy" (R. Castro 2011b). Now that Fidel and Raúl Castro have acknowledged the unsustainability of Cuba's current "socialist model" and the need to update or change it, it is important to fill in this "ideological vacuum" so that socially minded Cubans can be less fearful about the future and help shape the new social pact that will emerge. There is also dissatisfaction with the way in which various statements from the debate process were synthesized by PCC functionaries and with the failure to establish a horizontal exchange of ideas among PCC nuclei, workplaces, and neighborhoods (see, e.g., Campos 2011a; D'Angelo 2011). Despite these shortcomings, however, many have argued that the congress served to articulate long-recognized problems in the internal organization and management of the country and to craft a national consensus in favor of reforming Cuban socialism.

Moreover, although some argue that the root causes of the inefficiency and ineffectiveness of the Cuban state have yet to be identified, this reform period can be distinguished from others in that self-criticism by government and state functionaries is more blunt and profound. There is an acknowledgment that the historic generation is obliged to rectify its errors and hand over a country in better shape to the next generation. Recent statements made by Raúl Castro and opinions published in *Granma* have addressed concerns that it is not realistic to expect changes from the same people who put the current rules and practices in place and have argued that bureaucrats who create obstacles to change should be forced to resign.

THE STATISTS: PERFECT STATE SOCIALISM

The main socialist goal for the "statists" is a well-managed, representative state in control of society—a stronger state, not necessarily a bigger one but one that functions properly and ensures that subordinates perform their assigned tasks. They stress that such a state differs from a capitalist one in that it responds to the interests of working people, not private capital. In the statists' view, a centralized state with a vertical structure is best suited to providing all citizens with goods and services to satisfy their basic needs. Faced with the shortcomings of top-down planning, however, some statists have accepted a degree of market relations as inevitable. In their vision of socialism, horizontal coordination of autonomous individual or collective actors is impossible and will only generate chaos; democratically managed organizations are inefficient and conducive to social conflict and disintegration.

At the center of the statists' strategy is bringing control to the Cuban economy, and the reduction of fiscal and commercial deficits. This thinking has sometimes been translated into the cutting of services, closing of enterprises, and levying of taxes that are too high for both state and nonstate enterprises. The statists deny that major changes are needed. They believe that with more control by state managers and the Party, along with some decentralization and consultation with the people, the current institutions can work properly. However, some accept that the state should withdraw from the management of small enterprises and that local governments should have their own resources to solve problems. They repeat Raúl Castro's call for a "change of methods" but do not recognize a need to allow institutions to be more autonomous and democratic or to guarantee transparency by means of, for instance, the publication of information on the budgets of local governments and state enterprises.[7]

The main problems of Cuban society according to the statists are lack of discipline; insufficient control; the low standards set by managers, ministry functionaries, and party members, which have led to low productivity; disorganization; widespread petty theft; and corruption, which, although substantially less serious than in other countries, is still considered unacceptable. Indeed, an unproductive informal agreement between workers and managers has been established: "We pretend to work, and you pretend to pay us." Control, discipline, and consistency are necessary for any project to be successful, and they have not been common among Cuban workers and administrators for decades.

Although advocates of all three positions recognize a harmful lack of control in Cuban institutions, they differ in what they see as its root causes and therefore in the type of control methods they consider effective and fair. Statists stress the cultural nature of the problem and maintain that it could be solved with education by traditional means. A "change of minds/thinking" is presented as the key solution. In contrast, the economicists point to low wages and defend the need for adequate material incentives, while the self-managementists propose changing the way in which Cuban institutions are organized in favor of more democratic, less alienated forms of social relations.

In short, the solution for statists is more control and supervision in the vertical structure along with a modicum of autonomy and a wider scope of legal responsibility for managers. External supervisory bodies are expected to keep state institutions in check, with directors making sure that subordinates fulfill their responsibilities. There is little recognition of the limits of external and vertical supervision, the advantages of social control and self-monitoring by workers' collectives, or the importance of transparency and true accountability in public institutions.

The statist position is well represented in state bureaucracies among those who fear losing their posts—not an unfounded concern since state institutions are being reduced or "rationalized." This position is also supported by many ordinary Cubans who are tired of the social disorder that has arisen in recent decades. They want to restore order, and they reject more substantive changes because they are afraid of losing the social achievements of the Revolution. In addition, some intellectuals educated in Soviet-style Marxism reject any kind of decentralization and opening to any organization—whether private or collective—that is not directly and closely controlled by a heavily centralized state. Some officers in the Cuban military may be close to statism because of their preference for order and control.

ECONOMICISTS: MARKET SOCIALISM

According to the economicists, the main goal of socialism should be to develop society's productive forces in order to create more material wealth; thus, they focus on productive capacity and overlook social relations. For them, economic growth generates an increase in purchasing power and, in turn, an improvement in the material conditions of people. They argue that socialism implies redistribution of wealth and that if there is no wealth, there is nothing to distribute (Márquez 2011).

For those who support this position, current changes in Cuba should aim, above all, at improving the performance of the Cuban economy in order to satisfy the "ever-increasing material needs of the people." They argue that, with effective redistribution of wealth, all institutional arrangements that are efficient and productive are useful for building socialism. Economicists attribute the serious underperformance of the Cuban economy to centralization, state monopoly of commerce and production of goods and services, soft-budget constraints, and lack of private entrepreneurship and market relations. Although it may not be publicly acknowledged, economicists believe that the private capitalist management model (based on autonomous, nondemocratic managers responsive to private interests) is the most effective way to run an enterprise and that markets are the most efficient form of coordinating enterprise activity, allocating resources, and promoting efficiency and innovation.

Economicists defend the notion that if economic actors are to behave optimally and, specifically, managers are to make the right decisions and workers are to increase productivity, material incentives and the "discipline of the market" are unavoidable. They add that producers should pay the consequences of their poor performance even if it is due to market changes or events beyond their control. They argue against paternalistic relations between Cubans and state institutions in which the former expect to have all their problems solved by the latter.

The economicists play down warnings that their policies would aggravate inequality, the marginalization of social groups, the exploitation of employees in the private sector and in more autonomous state enterprises, and the deterioration of the environment. These social concerns are to be dealt with at a future date and meanwhile should not be allowed to interfere with the advance of privatization and marketization. They point out that significant inequality in non–wage-related income is already a reality (see Lambert 2011; Márquez 2011, 6). The economicists predict that their policies will produce "winners" and "losers" depending on their ability to adapt to market imperatives, but they point out that some measures can be taken to limit the "collateral" consequences of the reforms.

As a means to achieve accelerated economic growth, the economicists propose the incorporation of Cuba into international production chains and policies to attract foreign investment. They point to the success of China and Vietnam in promoting growth by attracting direct foreign investment and Cuba's need for external financing. In the process, however, they fail to mention the negative impacts of market reforms in those countries, such as increasing signs of inequality, corruption, social unrest, environmental degradation, spiritual emptiness, and the dismantling of social programs. They offer no suggestions for avoiding these consequences. The economicists ignore core Marxist arguments about labor exploitation and alienation. Their line of reasoning has influenced officials at the Ministry of Labor who fail to recognize that hired workers are in a subordinate position to the person who hires them even if he or she also works (Rodríguez 2011) and that this uneven relationship will increase as the availability of state jobs decreases. Denying the unequal and largely antagonistic relationship between business owners and employees allows technocrats to ignore the need to protect the latter with a labor code or some rules that guarantee their minimum rights and the complicated topic of allowing unions that represent workers in relation to management rather than to the state.

The most fervent economicists tend to be enterprise administrators who hope that they will be left to manage a state enterprise as they see fit, avoiding all the barriers and restrictions that centralized planning currently creates. Achieving more autonomy and less supervision, less job security, and only formal worker participation appears to them an almost perfect arrangement. At the same time, economicism characterizes the thinking of many ordinary Cubans influenced by the discourse that favors efficiency over social goals and attributes China's and Vietnam's economic growth to privatization and marketization. Some academics, speaking the language of mainstream scholarly circles, are the most outspoken defenders of economicist views.

SELF-MANAGEMENTISTS: DEMOCRATIC SOCIALISM

The self-managementists defend the need for a social order that is more just and sustainable than capitalism. However, they envision a different path both from the state-centered socialism that has strongly marked the Cuban version of the system and that the statists are now trying to refashion and from the market-guided socialism that the economicists present as the only feasible model. Self-managementists argue that there can be no real socialism without solidarity, equality, and substantive democratic participation of the people in decision making in all spheres of life (political, economic, cultural, and so on). The essence of socialism is instituting the social relations of self-management or self-government from communities and workplaces up to the national—and eventually global—level, that is, a democratic social control of society, the state, the economy, and all social institutions.[8]

For self-managementists, the goal of Cuban socialism should be not to satisfy the ever-increasing material needs of its citizens but to create conditions that allow them to fully develop their capacities as human beings and thus satisfy their material and spiritual needs, assuming that material needs will change under a more liberating daily life (Piñeiro 2011, 70–76).

The main problem of Cuban socialism for self-managementists has been the lack of substantive participation of workers and citizens in the administration of their lives and society. Decisions at the central state level and all the way down to local governments and enterprises have too often been made without the true participation of the people, and therefore the benefits of participatory democracy have been lost (see Campos 2011b; *Espacio Laical* 2011a, 20–21; Espina 2008, 137).

The self-managementists attribute the underperformance of state institutions to the insufficient sense of true ownership (which is not the same as legal property) by workers and even managers. It is low democratic participation and insufficient democratic control of management and executive bodies that, in addition to insufficient incomes, result in low motivation to work, mistaken management decisions, and corruption (Campos 2011b). Without true ownership by workers and citizens in general, it is argued, there will be no motivation to ensure that resources are used properly (*Espacio Laical* 2011b, 19). While for self-managementists workplace democracy is indispensable, both statists and economicists view it as a utopian concept that challenges the necessary role of their vanguard cadres and experts or entrepreneurs and would result in underperformance and chaos.

The self-managementist position highlights the need not only to redistribute wealth but also to change the way it is created by establishing relations of freely associated labor and thus achieving the principle of true socialist property, which in turn would stimulate productivity (Rafael Hernández in *Espacio Laical* 2011b, 43; Espina 2008, 134–35; Martínez 2009, 33–34; Perera and Martín 2011). Democratization at the point of production is what Marx identified as the basis of a society that has truly transcended the capitalist order (Campos 2006). The self-managementists note that these changes, not only higher wages or greater autonomy for managers, are a source of important incentives for productivity and efficiency and at the same time promote the development of the "new" socialist men and women (see Espina 2008, 135–37; Tablada 2009, 141–45, 148–49).

Those who identify with this position warn of the risks of decentralization of government and enterprises without democratization and without taking into consideration the interests of workers and all those affected by their activities. Some defend the need to establish—in addition to a sound regulatory framework—spaces for democratic coordination between producers, consumers, and other social groups (environmentalists, feminists, minorities, and so on) so that the local economy will respond to social interests rather than profit maximization and market laws.[9]

FINAL CONSIDERATIONS

Cuban society is currently engaged in defining its future direction, whether toward a better-organized state-led society, a more market-based one, a more democratic one, or—more likely—a combination of the three. Without a doubt, the economicist position is the one that currently dominates both within the central government and among a majority of Cubans. After more than twenty years of hardship, Cubans are first and foremost interested in increasing their incomes in order to satisfy basic needs. Heavily exposed to the hegemonic worldview that private enterprise and markets work best, many believe that privatization and marketization represent the best path to sustained economic growth. Faced with the failure of state enterprises and top-down planning and largely unaware of other ways of socializing the economy, they see no alternative.

At the same time, however, Cubans generally do not consider private enterprise and markets natural and hope to prevent their inequalities and other negative side effects, such as price differentials and higher profits for commerce over production. Statist positions are openly recognized as representing the status quo and what Cuba needs to move away from and are thus rejected by the vast majority of the population. The statist position, however, still enjoys significant support within the state and among Cubans who place a premium on social services. In fact, some argue that the final version of the Sixth Congress's *Guidelines* is less economicist and more statist than the initial draft.[10]

There is very little of the self-managementist vision in the *Guidelines*. The document fails to incorporate the self-managementists' main goals (satisfaction of people's broader needs, such as human development) and means (participatory democracy and democratic control of social institutions) (see Rafael Hernández in *Espacio Laical* 2011b, 29). Although President Raúl Castro had made reference to the importance of "participation,"[11] the *Guidelines* mention it only three times and mostly in the sense of "consultation" (PCC 2011, 21, 22, 38).

Nevertheless, the social imagery of social justice and emancipation is still present. Although the grandchildren of the historic generation are less familiar with socialist and revolutionary ideals, they generally grasp the importance of dignity and justice and reject subordination.[12] A culture of solidarity cultivated by the Revolution still endures, making inequality seem particularly unacceptable. Moreover, some have warned that without participation and social control of autonomous local governments and enterprises, Cuba is paving the way for the restoration of capitalism. Signs of the increasing weight of the self-managementist position have emerged recently in the form of articles in official newspapers defending the need for workers to participate fully in management decisions and thus begin to resemble true owners.[13]

However, the defenders of self-management have not yet put forward detailed, realistic propositions that appear feasible. They—as well as the economicists—need to deal with the fact that more autonomous private or even collective enterprises are already resulting in an increase in prices, especially of basic goods and services, thus further reducing the real income of Cuban workers. The three main visions analyzed in this chapter (state socialism, market socialism, and democratic socialism based on self-management) cannot be reduced to "good" or "bad" choices. All sides make legitimate points that need to be considered in the strategic decisions that are made. However, the desirability of democracy—not the formal, liberal representative one but the substantive, "participatory" one—is now widely accepted throughout the world. From a normative perspective, pursuing more democracy would appear more desirable than conferring inordinate power on state functionaries who pledge to represent the interests of society or on resourceful economic actors who direct from the shadows an "invisible hand" that affects all of us.

To the extent to which economic growth fundamentally comes not from democratically managed enterprises and socially controlled markets but from privatization and marketization, as in capitalist and market-oriented "socialist" countries, the interests of the new capitalists are inevitably going to move farther away from social interests, and they will find ways to contribute less in taxes,[14] charge higher prices, externalize as many of their costs as possible to society, and eventually make sure that the state responds to their private interests. Similarly, to the extent to which state managers are given greater autonomy without democratizing political and economic institutions, abuses of power and inequalities will become increasingly common. The ones who will suffer the most from such reforms are the staunchest supporters of the Revolution today and would be less inclined to sustain a project that does not address their needs and expectations of fairness. If the goal is to create the fairest society possible, more space needs to be opened up for the discussion of self-managementist proposals in the public media, and public discourse should center on the values of equality, justice, and solidarity.

The important role that direct, participatory democracy has played in other revolutionary processes currently under way in Latin America should influence the Cuban debate. In this way, the principles and social cohesion that have sustained the Revolution could be advanced rather than weakened.

NOTES

Excerpted from Camila Piñeiro Harnecker, "Cuba's New Socialism: Different Visions Shaping Current Changes," previously published in *Latin American Perspectives* 40, no. 3 (2003): 107–25. Republished by permission of the publisher.

1. None of the names have been used by groups to identify themselves.

2. "If we do not fix it we will fall into an abyss" because "we cannot spend more than we produce forever" (R. Castro 2010).

3. According to Pedro Olivera, a director of the Land Control Center of the Ministry of Agriculture (Ravsberg 2011), and Lugo Fonte, president of Asociación Nacional de Agricultores Pequeños (González 2011).

4. On December 1, 2011, these experiments were expanded to include all salons with up to three chairs (*Gaceta Oficial* 36, November 11, 2011), while other services, such as repairs, photography, and laundry, will be governed by similar arrangements in six provinces and will subsequently be expanded to the entire nation (*Gaceta Oficial* 46, December 23, 2011).

5. Informal estimates set the number of workers that have been declared "available" at around 150,000 (Reuters, October 5, 2011).

6. From 152,000 in October 2010 to more than 350,000 in October 2011. More than 1.8 million workers are expected to join the nonstate sector by 2015 (Pedraza 2010), representing 35 percent of total employment.

7. See Anneris Ivette Leyva's "El derecho a la información," *Granma*, July 8, 2011, and Pagola Bérger's, López Díaz's, and E. González's letters to the editor in *Granma*, April 2, 2010, February 12, 2010, and July 15, 2011.

8. Ricardo Ronquillo (2011) says that socialism "is possible only when transparent, democratic, and real control by workers predominates." Fernando Martínez Heredia (2009, 37) argues that socialism leads to human liberation but requires conscious action by the people. The social scientist Juan Luis Martín (Perera and Martín 2011) agrees with Martínez that socialism does not result automatically from the development of productive forces and that real participation "conditions" the emergence of "social subjectivity." See Campos (2011b) and Guanche (2009, 227–36).

9. Arturo López-Levy (in *Espacio Laical* 2011a, 30, 32) warns of the limitations inherent in real—as opposed to textbook—markets. He argues against "economicist conceptions" and states that the goal of sustainable development with social and environmental goals should be prioritized over economic growth. See also Piñeiro (2011).

10. Instead of combining planning and markets, it stressed planning as the central tool while taking into account market conditions. Where originally state enterprises would have set prices freely, in the final version the pricing system is to be "revised" but without specifying how this will be done. Finally, there is no full opening to foreign investment, which is restricted largely to strategic sectors.

11. For example, "The excessively centralized model that currently characterizes our economy will have to transit, with order and discipline and the participation of workers, toward a decentralized system in which planning will predominate, as a key feature of socialist management, but will not ignore market tendencies" (R. Castro 2011a).

12. For the complaints of an employee that her boss in the private sector (where wages are two to four times the average state wage) sets her schedule and abuses her verbally, see Reuters, "Cubans Look to Private Sector to Make Ends Meet," October 5, 2011. See also *Espacio Laical*'s editor Lenier González (*Espacio Laical* 2011a, 22–23).

13. Castañeda and Gonzalo (2011) propose "co-ownership" or comanagement in state enterprises. Many letters to the editor in *Granma* also suggest allowing for the creation of cooperatives that lease state businesses.

14. See Pastor Batista Valdés, "Prestos para el disfrute, escurridizos en el aporte" (*Granma*, October 4, 2011), on private businesses that pay no taxes.

REFERENCES

Campos, Pedro. 2006. "¿Qué es el socialismo?" September 29. http://www.oocities.org/es/amigos_pedroc/Socialismo-1.htm (accessed January 15, 2012).

———. 2008. "Cooperativa, cooperativismo y autogestión socialista." July 21. http://www.kaosenlared.net/noticia/cooperativa-cooperativismo-autogestion-socialista (accessed January 15, 2012).

———. 2011a. "La Conferencia del PCC puede ser la última oportunidad: Hay que acabar de hacer la revolución social pendiente." November 30. http://www.havanatimes.org/sp/?p=53606 (accessed January 15, 2012).

———. 2011b. "Democracia, para controlar la burocracia." July 6. http://www.kaosenlared.net/noticia/democracia-para-controlar-burocracia (accessed January 15, 2012).

Castañeda, Isabel D., and Rubio Gonzalo. 2011. "Una opinión: Mirar adelante con sentido crítico y con ciencia." September 2. http://www.granma.cubaweb.cu/2011/09/02/nacional/artic07.html (accessed January 22, 2012).

Castro Ruz, Fidel. 2005. "Speech at the University of Havana." November 17. http://www.cuba.cu/gobierno/discursos/2005/ing/f171105i.html (accessed January 15, 2012).

Castro Ruz, Raúl. 2007. "Speech at the 26th of July Anniversary." http://www.walterlippmann.com/rc-07-26-2007.html (accessed January 15, 2012).

———. 2010. "Speech at the Ninth Congress of the Cuban Communist Youth." April 4. http://www.cuba.cu/gobierno/rauldiscursos/2010/ing/r030410i.html (accessed January 15, 2012).

———. 2011a. "Informe central al VI Congreso del Partido Comunista de Cuba." http://www.cubadebate.cu/opinion/2011/04/16/texto-integro-del-informe-central-al-vi-congreso-del-pcc/ (accessed January 15, 2012).

———. 2011b. "Speech at the National Assembly of Popular Power." August 1. http://www.cubadebate.cu/raul-castro-ruz/2011/08/01/discurso-de-raul-en-la-asamblea-nacional/ (accessed January 15, 2012).

D'Angelo Hernández, Ovidio. 2011. "¿Qué conferencia y lineamientos necesitamos?: Conferencia del pueblo para la nueva sociedad." Compendio de la Red Protagónica Observatorio Crítico. July 12. http://observatoriocriticodesdecuba.wordpress.com (accessed January 15, 2012).

Espacio Laical. 2011a. "Cuba: ¿Hacia un nuevo pacto social?" 7, no. 2: 13–32.

———. 2011b. "¿Hacia dónde va el modelo cubano?" 7, no. 1: 23–47.

Espina Prieto, Mayra. 2008. "Mirar a Cuba hoy: Cuatro supuestos para la observación y seis problemas-nudos." *Temas*, no. 56, 132–141.

González, Ana Margarita. 2011. "Cincuenta razones para quitarnos el sombrero: 50 aniversario de la ANAP." *Trabajadores*, May 16.

Guanche, Julio César. 2009. "Todo que existe merece perecer (o una pregunta distinta sobre la democracia)." In *Un dialogo al interior de la tradición socialista*, edited by Julio César Guanche, 203–45. Havana: Ruth Casa Editorial.

Hernández Porto, Yahily. 2011. "El turismo, pilar del desarrollo local." *Juventud Rebelde*, August 28.

Lambert, Renaud. 2011. "Cuba's New Socialism." May 6. http://mondediplo.com/2011/05/06cuba (accessed January 23, 2012).

Márquez, Orlando. 2011. "Sin miedo a la riqueza." *Palabra Nueva* 19, no. 203: 6–7.

Martínez Heredia, Fernando. 2009. "Socialismo." In *Autocríticas: Un diálogo al interior de la tradición socialista,* edited by Julio César Guanche, 15–43. Havana: Ruth Casa Editorial.

Martínez Hernández, Leticia, and Yaima Puig Meneses. 2011. "Sesionó reunión ampliada del Consejo de Ministros." *Granma*, March 1.

Partido Comunista de Cuba. 2010. *2010 Draft Economic and Social Policy Guidelines of the 6th Congress of the Communist Party of Cuba*. Havana: Partido Comunista de Cuba.

———. 2011. *Economic and Social Policy Guidelines of the Party and the Revolution*. Havana: Partido Comunista de Cuba.

Pedraza, Lina. 2010. "Intervención en el Sexto Período Ordinario de Sesiones de la Séptima Legislatura de la Asamblea del Poder Popular, La Habana, December 15, 2010." http://www.granma.cu/espanol/cuba/16diciem-resultados.html (accessed January 23, 2012).

Perera, Alina, and Marianela Martín. 2011. "La fuerza invisible que modela el mundo." *Juventud Rebelde*, September 25.

Piñeiro Harnecker, Camila. 2011. "Empresas no estatales en la economía cubana: ¿Construyendo el socialismo?" *Temas*, no. 67, 68–77.

Ravsberg, Fernando. 2011. "Agricultura y tenencia de tierras en Cuba." BBC, September 29.

Rodríguez, José Alejandro. 2011. "Casi se duplican los trabajadores por cuenta propia." *Juventud Rebelde*, March 4.

Ronquillo Bello, Ricardo. 2011. "Decido, luego existo." *Juventud Rebelde*, September 24.

Tablada, Carlos. 2009. "El socialismo del Ché." In *Autocríticas: Un diálogo al interior de la tradición socialista*, edited by Julio César Guanche, 132–62. Havana: Ruth Casa Editorial.

Chapter Three

After Fidel

The Communist Party of Cuba on the Brink of Generational Change

William M. LeoGrande

"Men Die, but the Party Is Immortal," read the banner headline in *Granma*, the official organ of the Communist Party of Cuba. As suggested by this 1973 article, the Communist Party was intended to be the organizational guarantor of the continuity of Cuba's socialist system.[1] When Raúl Castro assumed leadership of the state and Party as a result of Fidel's 2006 illness, he emphasized the need to build national unity around the Party both to enlist popular support for his new economic policy and to lay the groundwork for generational succession. *Los históricos*, the founding generation of the Revolution, were gradually passing from the political scene. Their successors will face unprecedented challenges in the years to come as the Party tries to adapt its leadership to the island's rapidly changing economic and social reality.

ORIGINS

Inaugurated in 1965, the Communist Party of Cuba (*Partido Comunista de Cuba* [PCC]) was created *after* the triumph of the Revolution it was intended to lead. Built during the 1960s among veterans of three revolutionary organizations that fought against Batista's dictatorship, the PCC did not preside over Cuba's transition to socialism or direct the new political system that followed.[2] During the Revolution's critical early years, it was the Rebel Army (later, the *Fuerzas Armadas Revolucionarias*) that provided the political apparatus through which Fidel Castro and his closest compatriots governed the nation.

Creation of the new party followed Castro's declaration of the socialist character of the Revolution in 1961. Domestically, Castro sought to forge a political instrument that would unify the fractious revolutionary family and mobilize supporters. Internationally, he sought to demonstrate to the Soviet Union that Cuba was a member in good standing of the socialist camp, worthy of support. But the party-building process got off to a rocky start. The first effort, the Integrated Revolutionary Organizations (*Organizaciones Integradas Revolucionarias* [ORI]), was dismantled in early 1962 after a faction of old communists from the Popular Socialist Party tried to capture control of it by excluding veterans of Castro's 26th of July Movement.[3] The second attempt, the United Party of the Socialist Revolution (*Partido Unido de la Revolución Socialista*), was shaken by another crisis in 1964 when two leading members were implicated in the infamous 1957 murder of revolutionary students by Batista's police at 7

Humboldt Street. Only Castro's intervention prevented the revolutionary leadership from shattering into warring factions.[4] Yet another crisis erupted in 1968, when a small group of party members (a "microfaction") was caught soliciting Soviet diplomats to replace Castro because of his unorthodox economic views.[5]

As a result of this turmoil, the leaders of the Revolution were reluctant to turn over too much power to the new party apparatus for fear that their efforts to institutionalize Fidel Castro's charismatic authority might dissipate it instead. Major policy decisions continued to be made by Castro and a small circle of trusted lieutenants, most of whom had fought together in the Sierra Maestra. When the new Communist Party was finally launched in 1965, this inner circle was formally installed as the Party's Political Bureau, but the change was more a matter of name than process. The more elaborate decision-making machinery of the Party, including the 100-member Central Committee, remained unused for most of the next decade. The PCC did not convene its First Congress until 1975, before which it had neither a program nor statutes. Its small size (just 55,000 members in 1969, or 0.6 percent of the population) made it the smallest ruling communist party in the world by a wide margin, and it had cells in only 16 percent of the nation's work centers covering less than half the labor force.[6]

Only in the 1970s did the PCC develop into an organization strong enough to assert real direction over the Cuban political system. By the time of the PCC's founding Congress in 1975, it had grown to 202,807 members (2.2 percent of the population).[7] During the ten years (1975–1986) from the First to the Third Party Congresses, membership grew to 434,143 in 1980 and to 523,639 in 1985. Party bodies met regularly, and the apparatus developed a system for controlling the appointment of cadres to all major posts in the government and mass organizations.[8] The dominant theme at the PCC's Second Congress in 1980 was continuity. The bulk of the congress's discussion focused on social and economic development rather than political issues.[9]

In the mid-1980s, Mikhail Gorbachev's perestroika and glasnost stimulated debate throughout the communist bloc, and Cuba was no exception. Party ideological chief Carlos Aldana would later confess to being among those smitten by Gorbachev's ideas until he was set straight by Fidel.[10] Castro, too, saw the economic failings of the Soviet model—the inefficiency, the tendency to produce corruption, and the erosion of ideology by the individualism of material incentives. But where Gorbachev saw the need for more radical economic restructuring to give fuller scope to the market, Castro saw market reforms as the source of the problem. Thus, the Cuban version of perestroika was to reverse course, scaling back the use of market mechanisms and reemphasizing, once again, the political-ideological element of economic command.

The Third Party Congress in 1986 marked the launch of the Campaign to Rectify Errors and Negative Tendencies, a major retreat from the Soviet-sponsored economic management system installed in the mid-1970s and praised during the Second Congress. Criticizing the Soviet system for fostering inefficiency, corruption, and profit-minded selfishness, Castro called for the "rectification of errors and negative tendencies" in economic management. Cuba recentralized economic planning and dismantled material incentives and market mechanisms.[11] The private farmers' markets launched in 1980 were closed, wage inequalities were narrowed, and voluntary labor was touted once again.

By putting politics in command over economic policy, the Rectification Campaign implicitly meant a more assertive role for the PCC. Principal responsibility for economic policy moved from the Central Planning Board (*Junta Central de Planificación*) to a special "Central Group" of the PCC's Political Bureau.[12] At the Third Congress, 37 percent of the full members and 47 percent of the alternates on the Central Committee were replaced—the largest turnover in the party's elite bodies since its founding. The people promoted to the Political Bureau included the leaders of mass organizations and provincial PCC secretaries, in line with the Rectification theme of focusing on ideological work.[13]

THE COMMUNIST PARTY IN THE "SPECIAL PERIOD"

The sudden collapse of European communism between 1989 and 1991 triggered an economic cataclysm in Cuba, prompting an uncharacteristically vigorous debate over the future of the Revolution. Held at the beginning of Cuba's "Special Period in Time of Peace," the PCC's Fourth Congress endorsed a series of economic and political reforms designed to bring Cuba safely through the trauma of the demise of socialist bloc. From the outset, however, the basic strategy was to undertake only the reforms absolutely necessary to guarantee the survival of the existing order, although the leadership was not always in agreement about how extensive the requisite reforms needed to be. Socialism (i.e., state control of the commanding heights of the economy) and Leninism (one-party rule with limited freedoms of expression and association) were never in question, however, as symbolized by Castro's slogan of the time, "Socialism or death!"[14]

Starting in late 1993, the government adopted a series of structural economic reforms, including the reintroduction of farmers' markets, the transformation of most state farms into cooperatives, the legalization of self-employment in many occupations, the reduction of subsidies to state enterprises, the reduction of price subsidies on nonessential consumer goods, and the legalization of dollars. These measures successfully reversed the slide in gross domestic product, allowing Cuba to forgo more drastic changes. By the late 1990s, even these reforms were being scaled back.

In the political realm, reforms were fewer still. Fidel Castro's political diagnosis was that Cuba had copied the European socialist state model too closely, reproducing a form of socialism that was highly bureaucratized and apolitical.[15] To counter the ideological weaknesses they saw in Europe, Cuban leaders sought to reform their political institutions by making them more responsive. For the PCC, the first wave of change was the introduction of secret ballot elections for party leaders at the base (in the workplace "nuclei") in early 1990. Prior to that, elections had been by open nomination and a show of hands. Subsequently, new municipal and provincial leaders were elected (in the usual way, from slates of preselected nominees), producing a 50 percent turnover in municipal leaders and the replacement of two of the fourteen provincial secretaries.[16]

Next came a major downsizing of the party bureaucracy. The number of departments in the Central Committee staff organization was reduced from nineteen to nine, and the staff was cut by 50 percent. The Party Secretariat was abolished as a separate organization (reinstated in 2006), with its organizational responsibilities distributed to individual members of the Political Bureau. Provincial committee staffs were cut as well, and overall some two-thirds of the positions in the PCC's paid apparatus were abolished. In the posts that remained, a significant number of the incumbents were replaced.[17]

The March 1990 call for the Fourth Party Congress promoted unprecedented openness in debate, not only among party members but also among the entire populace, so as to build "the necessary consensus" for the government's policy response to the Special Period.[18] But the call was so extraordinary that people did not know how to respond, and the leadership halted the discussions after just a few weeks because the grassroots meetings were producing little more than hortatory praise for the Party and the Revolution. "We're just not used to debating," explained Party ideological chief Carlos Aldana.[19] In June, debate resumed under the guidance of a new Political Bureau statement emphasizing the virtues of open discussion. But the revised call set limits, noting that the discussions were intended to provide "political clarification" and that the socialist character of the Cuban system and leading role of the party were not open to debate.[20] Party conservatives thought that the debate process, despite its limitations, was still too vigorous.[21]

Eventually, some 3 million people participated in the pre-Congress discussion, producing over a million suggestions.[22] There was sharp debate on issues such as whether to allow religious believers to join the Communist Party and on whether free farmers' markets, abolished during Rectification, ought to be resumed.[23] One of the more popular suggestions was to have provincial assembly and National Assembly delegates directly elected rather than picked by the municipal assembly delegates.[24] Debate continued at the congress itself when it opened in October 1991, and for the first time, some votes on proposed resolutions were not unanimous. The Party statutes were amended to redefine the PCC as the party of the "Cuban nation" rather than the party of the working class, and the new statutes emphasized its ideological roots in the ideas of José Martí as well as Marx and Lenin.[25] The prohibition on Party membership for religious believers was lifted, and the process for choosing new party members was simplified so that more members could be drawn from work centers based on a vote of their coworkers (rather than requiring sponsorship by existing PCC members or prior membership in the Union of Young Communists).[26] Over the next five years, these changes produced a flood of new members as the PCC's ranks grew from 611,627 at the Fourth Congress to 780,000 in 1997 on the eve of the Fifth Congress. By 1997, 232,000 people, or one-third of the PCC's total membership, had joined the Party since the beginning of the Special Period.[27]

The Fourth Congress also adopted the proposal that all delegates to Cuba's legislative assemblies be directly elected.[28] But it rejected proposals made in the precongress meetings that candidates be allowed to campaign and thereby present contrasting policy views. Nor did it endorse the idea of allowing competing policy views in the state media.[29] On the economic front, the congress endorsed a liberalization of rules governing foreign direct investment and the legalization of self-employment, but it rejected reopening farmers' markets (though as the economic crisis deepened, that decision would be reversed).[30]

The limited reforms produced by the Fourth Congress were the result of an internal struggle in the PCC between a reform faction, led by Carlos Aldana, and a conservative faction ("*los duros*," or hard-liners, as they were known in Cuba), led by José Ramón Machado Ventura and José Ramón Balaguer. The reformers pushed for the use of market mechanisms to speed economic recovery and greater political space for dissenting views that were not manifestly counterrevolutionary. The conservatives argued that rapid economic change would undercut the Party's political control and that any political opening in the midst of economic crisis risked setting off a torrent of criticism that might sweep away the regime, as happened in Eastern Europe and the Soviet Union.[31] A delay of several months in convening the Fourth Congress was attributed to the unresolved internal debate between reformers and conservatives. "There is a major struggle between the forces represented by Aldana and those of Machado Ventura, and Fidel hasn't decided between them," explained an unnamed Cuban government official.[32] When the congress did convene, radical reform proposals, particularly creating a prime minister position separate from the first secretary of the Party and thereby devolving some of Castro's authority to other decision makers, were not on the agenda. The leadership had decided that major political changes were too risky in the midst of Cuba's economic problems.[33]

The Fifth Party Congress held in 1997 reviewed the effectiveness of the leadership's response to the crisis of the Special Period, approving two main resolutions. The economic resolution called for greater efficiency and continued growth of the tourist sector as the leading source of hard currency; it offered no new reforms.[34] The political resolution, titled "The Party of Unity, Democracy and the Human Rights We Defend," argued in defense of Cuba's one-party system led by the Communist Party, in favor of socialist democracy based on mass participation rather than the bourgeois "liberalism" of contention among diverse interests, and for a conception of human rights based on social justice rather than unfettered political liberties. In short, it presented a brief for the political status quo. The document portrayed the Revolution of 1959 as a direct continuation of the struggle for independence and national sovereignty stretching back to 1868 and the PCC as the "legitimate heir" of José Martí's Cuban Revolutionary Party. Disunity among the revolutionary forces had led to defeat in 1878, to U.S. domination after 1898, and to the collapse of the 1933 Revolution. Unity required, as in the time of Martí, a single party to prevent the United States from reimposing neocolonial capitalism on Cuba.[35]

The Fifth Congress elected a new Central Committee of only 150 members, far below the 225 elected at the Fourth Congress. The downsizing was intended to make the body more efficient and to prevent it from being infected with any "ideological viruses," explained Raúl Castro, who apparently had a major role in the selection process. "What happened to the socialist countries of Eastern Europe and the Soviet Union is not going to happen here," he added.[36] The status quo quality of the Fifth Party Congress suggested that Castro and his top lieutenants were generally convinced that they had weathered the worst of the economic and political maelstrom following the Soviet Union's collapse. The gradual recovery of the economy and the absence of further outbreaks of public disorder after 1994 served as evidence of their strategy's apparent success.

"THIS REVOLUTION CAN DESTROY ITSELF"

Despite the triumphal tone of the Fifth Congress, the PCC faced serious political problems as it entered the twenty-first century. A decade of deep austerity during the Special Period had taken a toll on regime legitimacy. Young people who came of age during the Special Period did not remember the hardships of prerevolutionary Cuba or the relatively good years of the 1970s. To them, the Revolution meant privation.[37]

Cubans of African descent, once core supporters of the Revolution because it did away with juridical discrimination and provided them with unprecedented upward mobility, suffered disproportionately during the Special Period. Few had family abroad to send them remittances. Because they lived in poor neighborhoods, few had opportunities to earn hard currency by opening *paladares* (private restaurants) or *casas particulares* (rented rooms) for tourists. And because of lingering racism, they were less likely to be employed in the tourist industry, where workers received hard-currency tips. The alienation of Afro-Cuban youth was apparent in the caustically critical lyrics of popular rap and hip-hop music.[38]

The dual currency system put in place during the Special Period to attract remittances from Cubans abroad created a dual society—those with access to hard currency and those without. As the availability of goods at subsidized prices on the ration card shrank, the rationing system ceased to provide an adequate floor for basic consumption. State sector salaries—even good ones—were not sufficient to buy many goods priced in hard currency. The unskilled, the elderly on fixed incomes, and people living in rural areas that saw few tourists all suffered enormously. At the same time, a new entrepreneurial class of self-employed—both legal and illegal—emerged, some of them earning previously unimaginable incomes—"the new rich," Fidel Castro called them.[39]

The regime's political infrastructure also suffered. The scarcity of consumer goods forced Cubans to spend hours scouring stores for food and other staples. Members of the various mass organizations had no time for meetings and little patience for revolutionary exhortations in the face of such material hardships. The Committees for the Defense of the Revolution, charged with "revolutionary vigilance" against counterrevolution and crime, largely ceased to function in most urban areas.[40] Although Communist Party membership grew to some 820,000, it faced similar problems.[41] The downsizing of the Party bureaucracy in 1991 and 1997 impaired its organizational capacity, and leadership at the provincial level struggled, not always effectively, to cope with the economic, social, and political strains of the Special Period. In 1995 alone, six of the fourteen Party first secretaries in the provinces were replaced.[42]

Another vulnerability that plagued the Party was Fidel Castro's style of governance. From the earliest days of the Revolution, Fidel harbored a deep distrust of institutions. During the Special Period, he came to rely more and more on his personal staff, the *Equipo de Coordinación y Apoyo al Comandante en Jefe* (also known as the *Grupo de Apoyo*), composed of young acolytes whom Fidel had plucked from the ranks of the Union of Young Communists (UJC). The *Grupo* evolved into a kind of shadow cabinet, operating at Fidel's behest outside the normal lines of authority of party and state. The *Grupo* had a reputation for conservatism—being more Fidelista than Fidel—and Cubans dubbed them "*los Talibanes*" for their rigid ideological orthodoxy. Meanwhile, the formal Party languished; although its statutes stipulated that a congress be held every five years to set policy and renovate the leadership, the 2002 deadline came and went with no new congress.

The erosion of the regime's capacity for social and political control contributed to the spread of corruption. Corruption was not a new problem, but it was exacerbated during the Special Period by economic hardship and the state's concessions to the market. To supplement inadequate state salaries, workers stole goods from work and sold them on the black market. A three-part investigative report by the Cuban newspaper *Juventude Rebelde*, titled "The Big Old Swindle," found that half the state-run retail enterprises visited by reporters were cheating customers by short-weighting purchases.[43] At the highest levels, managers of import/export businesses and joint enterprises were corrupted by the easy availability of hard currency through expense accounts and bribes by foreigners seeking preferred access to the Cuban market. When nationwide audits in 2003 discovered irregularities in the accounts of 36 percent of the 5,917 state enterprises examined, the leadership launched a campaign against corruption by public officials.[44]

In November 2005, speaking at the University of Havana, Fidel Castro gave a four-hour speech warning that the Revolution was in peril not from the United States but from its own internal weaknesses.[45] "This Revolution can destroy itself," he said. "We can destroy ourselves, and it would be our fault." His fears reached well beyond corruption. He worried about the handoff of power from the Revolution's founding generation to its successors. He worried about the inequality created during the Special Period, and he railed against the "new rich," including not only small businessmen but also recipients of remittances. Most of all, he worried that concessions to the market were corroding revolutionary values. "Some thought that socialism could be constructed with capitalist methods," he observed. "That is one of the great historical errors." The so-called progressive reforms of the Special Period were actually "robbery" and would have to change. In the future, Fidel hinted, there would be no more *paladares*, no more private taxis, and no more private business.

SUCCESSION

On July 31, 2006, Cuban television informed a stunned nation that illness had required Fidel Castro to temporarily hand power to his brother Raúl and a leadership team of six others. In the forty-seven years since the triumph of the Revolution, Fidel had never before surrendered the mantle of leadership. He would never resume his responsibilities as Cuba's "maximum leader." Across the island, reaction to the announcement was muted. His age and health problems had put the issue of succession on the public agenda, but faced with the possibility of losing the only leader whom 70 percent of Cubans had ever known, the public's dominant emotion was quiet concern and uncertainty about the future.

From the outset, it was clear that Raúl's leadership style would be very different. He had no intention of trying to imitate his brother, he explained. "Those who imitate fail." He would not be making all the speeches on major occasions but instead would share the opportunities with other leaders, a signal of his commitment to collective leadership.[46] When Raúl did give public speeches, they were short and to the point, not the long, rambling, didactic excursions for which his brother was famous. During the first year or so, Raúl was careful to always quote Fidel, thereby invoking his brother's legitimacy and emphasizing the continuity of policy. Even when Fidel formally bowed out of the presidency in 2008 and the National Assembly elected Raúl, the younger Castro asked the Assembly's permission to consult Fidel on "decisions of special transcendence for the future of our nation." No one person could replace the maximum leader. "Fidel is irreplaceable," Raúl affirmed. "The Communist Party, a sure guarantee of the unity of the Cuban nation, is the sole worthy heir to our people's confidence in its leader."[47]

This emphasis on the importance of institutions would prove to be a hallmark of Raúl Castro's presidency. "Institutionalization is . . . one of the pillars of the Revolution's invulnerability in the political field," Raúl said in his first inaugural speech to the National Assembly.[48] Two months later, he repeated this message to the Party's Central Committee, saying, "It is vitally necessary to reinforce the country's institutions." Strengthening the Party in particular, he reminded them, was essential "to ensure the continuity of the Revolution when its historic leaders are gone."[49]

Unlike Fidel, who worried that institutions might constrain his freedom of action, Raúl was the quintessential organization man, valuing careful management, sound administrative processes, and institution building.[50] Under his leadership, the Revolutionary Armed Forces became the most organized, efficient, and respected institution in the country. Over the years, a great many senior officers were exported into the civilian sector to try to bring some order to the relative chaos of the government bureaucracy. It came as no surprise, then, that as president, Raúl sought to imbue the rest of the government with the same managerial principles that worked so well in the armed forces. "Improvisation," he explained on more than one occasion, had led to "expensive irrationalities."[51]

Raúl's faith in institutions was also reflected in his cadre policy; he believed that people ought to work their way up through established institutions, gaining experience along the way. He was no fan of Fidel's practice of picking promising youth from the UJC to serve on his personal staff and then appointing them to top positions in the national government and provincial party apparatus. Before Fidel's illness, political influence was directly correlated with proximity to him, so it was no accident that the principal path to power for an aspiring young politician led through Castro's personal staff. But the track record of such appointees was not good; many fell into disgrace and obscurity as quickly as they rose. Their meteoric rise deprived them of the political savvy that only experience could provide and imbued them with the hubris of Icarus.

Not surprisingly, the role of the *Equipo de Coordinación y Apoyo* diminished dramatically under Raúl. Fidel's chief of staff, Carlos Valenciaga, was removed in 2008, and Cubans began referring to the *Grupo* as "*los huerfanitos*"—the little orphans. When the National Assembly elected Raúl president in 2008, his choice for vice president was not Carlos Lage (a former member of the *Equipo de Coordinación y Apoyo*), as many people, including Lage himself, expected, but José Machado Ventura, a member of the old guard. Importantly, Machado Ventura's chief responsibility since the 1970s had been building the organizational apparatus of the Communist Party.[52] Choosing him underscored Raúl's determination to strengthen Cuba's political institutions, the Party first among them.

In March 2009, Raúl abruptly fired Lage and Felipe Pérez-Roque, both of whom were frequently mentioned as possible successors to the Castro brothers. Pérez-Roque had served as Fidel's personal assistant for a decade before being appointed, at age thirty-four, to succeed Roberto Robaina (another of Fidel's young protégés) at the Foreign Ministry. Lage and Pérez-Roque were removed for criticizing *los históricos* behind their backs and being too eager to push the older generation offstage. They were, as Fidel wrote, "seduced by the honey of power for which they had not sacrificed at all."[53]

UPDATING THE ECONOMIC MODEL

As soon as Raúl assumed the presidency, he launched a barrage of candid criticism blaming Cuba's economic failures on its own policies rather than the U.S. embargo. In a speech to a closed session of the National Assembly in December 2006, he was blunt. Public transport was "on the verge of total collapse" after years of neglect. The state was 550 million pesos in arrears on its payments to small farmers, and Raúl found it "inexplicable" that "bureaucratic red tape" was holding up these payments when small farmers provided 65 percent of the nation's domestic food production. "We are tired of excuses in this Revolution," he declared.[54]

Seven months later, on July 26, 2007, Raúl extended his criticism of economic performance, acknowledging that state sector salaries were not adequate to cover basic consumption and that this shortfall was at the root of corruption. The only way to raise the standard of living was to raise productivity. "No one, no individual or country, can afford to spend more than what they have," he reminded his audience. "It seems elementary, but we do not always think and act in accordance with this inescapable reality." Cuba needed to "untie the knots holding back the development of the productive forces."[55]

Over the next several years, Raúl introduced a sweeping program of economic reform—or "updating" of the economic model, as the Cubans preferred to call it—including a wider use of market mechanisms to boost Cuba's anemic productivity. Although Raúl often invoked Fidel's November 2005 speech at the University of Havana as the inspiration for this new economic policy, their diagnoses of Cuba's problems—and thus their prescriptions—were profoundly different. To Fidel, corruption and low productivity resulted from people's character defects, exacerbated by the material incentives of the market. The solution was to increase social control and decrease the scope of market activity. To Raúl, Cuba's problems originated with defects in the hypercentralized model of socialism they had been pursuing. The solution was to honestly reexamine that model, making "the needed structural and conceptual changes."[56]

On assuming the presidency in his own right in 2008, Raúl accelerated the pace of reform. The state encouraged the growth of small private businesses and cooperatives and distributed fallow state lands to cooperatives and private farmers willing to cultivate them. State sector salaries were raised and salary caps eliminated to link wages more directly to productivity. The Office of the Comptroller was created in 2009 to improve financial management and audit state enterprises—and to curb corruption.[57] A number of early reforms involved simply eliminating prohibitions that Cubans found especially exasperating. In 2008, the government legalized the sale of computers and cell phones and eliminated rules against Cubans staying in tourist hotels or renting cars. In 2011, the government legalized private real estate and automobile markets, allowing Cubans to buy and sell directly to one another. In 2013, the government eliminated the "*tarjeta blanca*," the exit permit required for travel abroad, allowing Cubans with a valid passport to travel whenever and wherever they liked. The popularity of these changes built political capital for the government to carry out a much more profound reorganization of the Cuban economy, with its attendant social disruption.

Raúl's grand strategy for the economy was unveiled in conjunction with the Sixth Congress of the Communist Party. In the months preceding the congress, local Party branches convened more than 163,000 meetings of members and nonmembers alike, with almost 9 million participants, to discuss the leadership's strategy for economic renovation, embodied in the "Guidelines of the Economic and Social Policy of the Party and the Revolution."[58] The "Guidelines" presented the basic framework of an economic model in which the state played a much less dominant role. This new model was less centralized, was more reliant on market mechanisms to boost efficiency and productivity, and envisioned a greater role for both foreign direct investment and the domestic private enterprise. The "nonstate sector"—private enterprises and cooperatives—were treated as a permanent and dynamic part of the economy, not simply a barely tolerated appendage.[59]

In addition, the state would no longer serve as the paternalistic provider of all forms of consumption. "People cannot expect that 'Papa State' is going to solve their problems for them," declared *Comandante* Ramiro Valdés.[60] The ration card, which since 1962 had subsidized basic goods for everyone, whether they needed it or not, would be replaced by income support for the poor. Cuba could no longer afford to provide goods at what Raúl called "ridiculous prices." It had become "an intolerable burden on the economy and discouraged work," not to mention fueling the black market.[61]

In short, the new model aimed to reconnect people's standard of living to their productivity. "Socialism means social justice and equality, but equality of rights and opportunities, not salaries," Raúl told the National Assembly in July 2008. "Equality does not mean egalitarianism."[62] At the same time, Raúl repeatedly reassured people that no one would be left behind. "In Cuba, under socialism, there will never be space for 'shock therapies' that go against the neediest, who have traditionally been the staunchest supporters of the Revolution. . . . The Revolution will not leave any Cuban helpless."[63]

In January 2012, nine months after the Party Congress adjourned, 811 of the congress delegates reconvened for the First National Party Conference. Their purpose was, first and foremost, to develop a plan of political work to support implementation of the new economic guidelines. Additionally, the leadership sought to revitalize the Party by repairing the weaknesses that had developed over the preceding decade. The Party had been drawn into the administration of state agencies, interfering with the role of the government bureaucracy, and thereby neglecting its political work. Its endless meetings had degenerated into "formalism," in which no real criticism was ever voiced and little was accomplished, thereby "spreading dissatisfaction and apathy" among the membership. Its cadres too often lacked creativity, failed to take the initiative in problem solving, and took a lax attitude toward corruption. The Party's "rapid promotion of immature and inexperienced cadres"—what Raúl called "test-tube leaders"—had produced serious policy errors and failures.[64]

Finally, the Party had "lacked the political will" to promote women, Afro-Cubans, and youth into leadership positions based on their merits. "It's really embarrassing that we have not solved this problem in more than half a century," Raúl told the Sixth Party Congress. [65] The new Central Committee was significantly more diverse than its predecessors. Among its 115 members, forty-eight were women (42 percent, up from 13 percent previously), and thirty-six were of African descent (31 percent, up from 10 percent). Although no data on the Committee's average age were released, Castro noted that a large number of young professionals had been added to its ranks. [66]

To hasten the transition to a new generation of leaders, the Party adopted term limits: senior leaders would could serve no more than two consecutive five-year terms. In his speech to the National Assembly on February 24, 2013, Raúl Castro formally announced that he would retire in 2018, at the end of his current presidential term, his second. [67] He also announced the immediate retirement of several elderly comrades in arms, including First Vice President José Machado Ventura. In his place, the Assembly elected fifty-two-year-old Miguel Díaz-Canel, putting a leader born after the triumph of the Revolution in the direct line of political succession for the first time.

UPDATING THE POLITICAL MODEL

While the immediate challenge facing Cuban leaders is updating the economic model, another task, no less complex and important in the long run, is to update the political model. Cuba's governing elite faces a polity in flux. Among many Cubans, the economic reforms have generated a new feeling of hope and expectations for a better standard of living. If the reforms stall or fail, popular disillusionment will be enormous, dealing a severe blow to the regime's legitimacy just as new, untested leaders are taking over.

The risk of failure is real; the new economic policy faces significant opposition from entrenched bureaucrats in the government and Party. The turn toward the market and decentralized decision making threatens bureaucrats' control over the economy. No doubt some have resisted the "Guidelines" out of ideological commitment to the Marxist-Leninist orthodoxy and a fear that reliance on the market is a step down the slippery slope toward restoring capitalism. [68] Others, however, are defending their self-interest; along with administrative power over the economy has come access to various privileges, both legal and illegal.

But even success will bring a new set of political challenges. In an economy driven as much by the market's demand for efficiency as by the ideals of the Revolution's founders, can Cuba maintain the values of social justice that have been at the Revolution's ideological core since 1959? Some of the reforms put vulnerable populations at risk. Demanding efficiency of state enterprises meant that as many as a million state sector workers—20 percent of the labor force—would be laid off. Few of those employees have the skills or capital to launch a small business. An initial plan in 2010 to lay off 500,000 in only six months was indefinitely postponed because there was no place for them to go. Castro promised that he would not subject Cuba to "shock therapy," but if market forces are given free rein, Cuba's income disparities are sure to increase even more than they did during the Special Period. Those who are well educated, live in cities where economic development is more dynamic, and have access to hard currency are well positioned to thrive in a freer economic environment. Those who are low skilled or elderly, live in rural areas, have no relatives abroad to send remittances, or suffer from racial discrimination are all at risk.

Economic change is already reshaping the political terrain. As market reforms weaken the Communist Party's control over the economy, its political monopoly becomes frayed as well.

Emergent entrepreneurs, both farmers and small businessmen, depend less and less on the state for their well-being. As they accumulate wealth and grow increasingly indispensable to the health of the economy, their desire for less government interference is certain to take a more explicitly political direction. Concomitantly, as income disparities grow, disadvantaged Cubans are unlikely to remain silent, as the surge in Afro-Cuban cultural and political complaints about lingering racism demonstrates.

As Cubans interact with populations abroad, through tourism, family visits, professional cooperation, and the Internet, the danger of "ideological contamination" increases. Intellectuals are already pushing the bounds of legitimate debate, demanding a more inclusive definition of what counts as "within the Revolution." Nongovernmental organizations have proliferated, creating new social networks independent of state supervision and control. The vital social and spiritual role played by the Catholic Church—the only significant institution outside the government's direction—has given it a major social presence and influence. The spread of the Internet is putting a new generation of Cubans in touch with each other and the wider world in ways the government cannot fully control.

The government can try to quell these stirrings, but it cannot eliminate them because they are the unavoidable by-product of the economic changes now under way. They have created what an observer of Eastern Europe called "islands of autonomy" in civil society within which people forge new social relationships and communication networks, acquire consciousness of their common interests, and develop the capacity for politics outside the regime. This complex political panorama will not be easy for Cuba's leaders to manage, and they have fewer levers of power than ever before. The future of the revolutionary regime that Fidel and Raúl Castro founded in 1959 will depend on whether it can adapt to these emergent social and political forces or is swept aside by them.

NOTES

1. Castro first used the phrase in his July 26, 1973, speech commemorating the attack on the Moncada barracks (which produced the headline quoted in *Granma Weekly Review*, August 5, 1973).

2. The three organizations were Fidel Castro's 26th of July Movement, the student-based Revolutionary Directorate, and the old communists of the Popular Socialist Party.

3. Castro's denunciation of the ORI was delivered in three speeches, on March 13, March 18, and March 22, 1962, reprinted in Fidel Castro, *Fidel Castro Denounces Sectarianism* (Havana: Ministry of Foreign Relations, 1962).

4. Fidel Castro, "Declaración del Primer Ministro . . . en el jucio contra el delator de los mártires de Humboldt 7," *Obra Revolucionaria* 7 (March 24, 1964): 5–47.

5. Raúl Castro, "Report to the Central Committee on the Activities of the Microfaction," *Granma Weekly Review*, February 11, 1968.

6. For a more detailed discussion of the PCC's weakness in the 1960s and early 1970s, see William M. LeoGrande, "Party Development in Revolutionary Cuba," *Journal of Interamerican Studies and World Affairs* 21, no. 4 (November 1979): 457–80.

7. William M. LeoGrande, "The Communist Party of Cuba since the First Congress," *Journal of Latin American Studies* 12, no. 2 (November 1980): 397–419.

8. Communist Party of Cuba, *Second Congress of the Communist Party of Cuba: Documents and Speeches* (Havana: Political Publishers, 1981), 77–84; Marifeli Pérez-Stable, "'We Are the Only Ones and There Is No Alternative': Vanguard Party Politics in Cuba, 1975–1991," in *Conflict and Change in Cuba*, ed. Enrique A. Baloyra and James A. Morris (Albuquerque: University of New Mexico Press, 1993), 67–85.

9. Almost half of Fidel Castro's "Main Report" to the congress focuses on economic and social development plans, and the congress resolution on this subject is 123 pages long. Communist Party of Cuba, *Second Congress of the Communist Party of Cuba*.

10. Mimi Whitefield and Andres Oppenheimer, "No. 3 Man in Cuba Is Booted," *Miami Herald*, September 24, 1992; Howard W. French, "Cuban's Exit Hints at Trouble at Top," *New York Times*, September 27, 1992.

11. Sergio Roca, "The Comandante in His Economic Labyrinth," in Baloyra and Morris, *Conflict and Change in Cuba*, 86–109.

12. Fidel Castro, *Main Report: Third Congress of the Communist Party of Cuba* (Havana: Editor Politica, 1986), 38–39.

13. Jorge I. Domínguez, "Blaming Itself, Not Himself: Cuba's Political Regime after the Third Party Congress," in *Socialist Cuba: Past Interpretations and Future Challenges*, ed. Sergio Roca (Boulder, CO: Westview Press, 1988), 3–10; Rhoda Rabkin, "Cuba: The Aging of a Revolution," in Roca, *Socialist Cuba*, 33–56.

14. Castro first used the slogan in January 1989 in two speeches commemorating the triumph of the Revolution, but it became a routine closing to his speeches only in December after the collapse of the Eastern European communist regimes.

15. According to the "Resolution on the Program of the Communist Party of Cuba," adopted at the Fourth Party Congress in 1991, under the SDPE, "the political work and the actions of the revolutionary vanguard were reduced to mere formalities." The text of the resolution is in Gail Reed, *Island in the Storm: The Cuban Communist Party's Fourth Congress* (Melbourne: Ocean Press, 1992), 101–10.

16. "Asambleas de balance en las organizaciones de base del Partido," *Granma*, January 6, 1990; Marifeli Pérez-Stable, *The Cuban Revolution: Origins, Course, and Legacy* (New York: Oxford University Press, 1999), 169.

17. Susan Eckstein, *Back from the Future: Cuba under Castro* (Princeton, NJ: Princeton University Press, 1994), 114.

18. Pérez-Stable, "'We Are the Only Ones and There Is No Alternative,'" 81; "Llamamiento del Partido," *Granma Resumen Semanal*, March 25, 1990.

19. "Se require una participacíon consciente y activa," *Granma*, April 13, 1990; Reed, *Island in the Storm*, 14–15.

20. "Acuerdo del Buro Politico sobre el proceso de discussion del llamamiento al IV Congreso," *Granma*, June 23, 1990.

21. Roca, "The Comandante in His Economic Labyrinth," in Baloyra and Morris, *Conflict and Change in Cuba*, 102.

22. Reed, *Island in the Storm*, 17.

23. Eckstein, *Back from the Future*, 115.

24. Reed, *Island in the Storm*, 17.

25. Compare "Statutes of the Communist Party of Cuba," in *Second Congress of the Communist Party of Cuba*, 128, to the "Resolution on the Rules of the Cuban Communist Party," in Reed, *Island in the Storm*, 88.

26. "Resolution on the Rules of the Cuban Communist Party," in Reed, *Island in the Storm*, 88, 89, 94.

27. Max Azicri, *Cuba Today and Tomorrow: Reinventing Socialism* (Gainesville: University Press of Florida, 2001), 338 n 18; Fidel Castro Ruz, *Informe Central, Discurso de Clausura: V Congreso del Partido Comunista de Cuba* (Havana: Editora Politica 1997), 68.

28. "Resolution on Improving the Organization and Functioning of People's Power," in Reed, *Island in the Storm*, 122.

29. Jorge I. Domínguez, "Leadership Strategies and Mass Support: Cuban Politics before and after the 1991 Party Congress," in Jorge F. Pérez-López, *Cuba at a Crossroads: Politics and Economics after the Fourth Party Congress* (Gainesville: University of Florida Press, 1994), 1–18.

30. Domínguez, "Leadership Strategies and Mass Support," in Pérez-López, *Cuba at a Crossroads*.

31. A number of analysts have described the factional cleavages in the PCC: Eckstein, *Back from the Future*, 257–58; Reed, *Island in the Storm*, 21; Andres Oppenheimer, *Castro's Final Hour* (New York: Simon & Schuster, 1992), 379–80; and Edward Gonzalez, *Cuba: Clearing Perilous Waters?* (Santa Monica, CA: RAND Corporation, 1996), 39–42.

32. Pablo Alfonso, "Dispute Delays Party Session, Official Says," *Miami Herald*, March 29, 1991.

33. Oppenheimer, *Castro's Final Hour*, 383–99.

34. "Resolución Económica del V Congreso del Partido Comunista de Cuba," http://congresopcc.cip.cu/wp-content/uploads/2011/03/Resoluci%C3%B3n-Econ%C3%B3mica-V-Congreso.pdf.

35. "The Party of Unity, Democracy and the Human Rights We Defend," *Granma International*, May 1997.

36. Serge F. Kovaleski, "Castro Appears Strong, Cuban Economy Weak," *Washington Post*, October 11, 1997; Juan O. Tamayo, "Raúl Castro Takes on a Higher Profile," *Miami Herald*, December 17, 1997.

37. Katrin Hansing, "Changes from Below: New Dynamics, Spaces, and Attitudes in Cuban Society," *NACLA Report on the Americas* 44, no. 4 (July/August 2011): 16–19, 42.

38. Alejandro de la Fuente, "The Resurgence of Racism in Cuba," *NACLA Report on the Americas* 34, no. 6 (May–June): 29–34; Esteban Morales Domínguez, *Race in Cuba: Essays on the Revolution and Racial Inequality* (New York: Monthly Review Press, 2013).

39. Fidel Castro, "Speech at the University of Havana," November 17, 2005, http://www.cuba.cu/gobierno/discursos/2005/ing/f171105i.html.

40. Tim Golden, "Guardians of Castro's Cuba Have Fallen on Hard Times," *New York Times*, November 7, 1994; Roberto Suro, "With Cubans Desperate for Change, Castro Takes New Look at U.S.," *Washington Post*, August 28, 1994.

41. Marc Frank, "Cuban Communists to Hold Congress after 11 Years," Reuters, April 29, 2008.

42. "Party First Secretaries Replaced in Three Provinces," Radio Rebelde (Havana), July 4, 1995, as reported in BBC Summary of World Broadcasts, July 6, 1995.

43. Yailin Orta Rivera, Norge Martínez Montero, and Roberto Suárez, "La vieja gran estafa," *Juventude Rebelde*, October 1, 15, and 22, 2006.

44. "Irregularidades llevan a mayor control en empresas cubanas," EFE, February 21, 2004; Marc Frank, "Anti-Corruption Drive Signals Change in Cuba," *Financial Times* (London), July 6, 2004.

45. Fidel Castro, "Speech at the University of Havana," November 17, 2005.

46. "Fidel es insustituible, salvo que lo sustituyamos todos juntos," *Juventude Rebelde*, December 21, 2006.

47. "Key Address by Comrade Raúl Castro Ruz . . . at the Closing Session of the First Session of the Seventh Legislature of the National Assembly of People's Power," *Granma International*, February 24, 2008.

48. "Key Address by Comrade Raúl Castro Ruz . . . at the Closing Session of the First Session of the Seventh Legislature of the National Assembly of People's Power," *Granma International*, February 24, 2008.

49. "Continuing to Perfect the Work of the Party and Its Authority before the Masses," *Granma International*, April 29, 2008.

50. Hal Klepak, *Raúl Castro and Cuba: A Military History* (New York: Palgrave Macmillan, 2012), 91–138.

51. "The Greatest Obstacle That We Face in Fulfilling the Agreements of the 6th Congress Is the Psychological Barrier Created by Inertia," *Granma International*, August 2, 2011.

52. Nelson P. Valdés, "Cuba after Fidel," *Counterpunch*, March 1–3, 2008.

53. Fidel Castro, "Healthy Changes in the Council of Ministers," http://www.cuba.cu/gobierno/reflexiones/reflexiones.html.

54. Gerardo Arreola, "Reprocha Raúl Castro el burocratismo y el maquillaje de cifras en la agricultura cubana," *La Jornada* (Mexico City), December 24, 2006; María Julia Mayoral, "Reclama Raúl más rigor y transparencia," *Granma*, December 23, 2006.

55. "The Revolution's Most Important Weapon: The People," *Granma International*, July 27, 2007.

56. "The Revolution's Most Important Weapon."

57. Philip Peters, "A Chronology of Cuba's 'Updating of the Socialist Model,'" *International Journal of Cuban Studies* 4, nos. 3 and 4 (Autumn/Winter 2012): 385–402.

58. "Introduction to the Presentation of the Reports by Commissions," *Granma International*, April 19, 2011; Partido Comunista de Cuba, *Lineamientos de la Política Económica y Social del Partido y la Revolución*, April 18, 2011.

59. "National Conference Convocation," *Granma International*, April 21, 2011.

60. Agence France Presse, "Gobierno pide a cubanos no esperar que 'papá Estado' les resuelva todo," September 27, 2009. Author's translation.

61. "Central Report to the 6th Congress of the Communist Party of Cuba," *Granma International*, April 16, 2011.

62. "Socialism Signifies Social Justice and Equality, but Equality Is Not Egalitarianism," *Granma International*, July 15, 2008.

63. "Central Report to the 6th Congress of the Communist Party of Cuba."

64. Partido Comunista de Cuba, *Objetivos de Trabajo del Partido Comunista de Cuba Aprobados por la Primera Conferencia*, January 29, 2012.

65. "Central Report to the 6th Congress of the Communist Party of Cuba."

66. Dalia Acosta, "Raúl Castro Proposes Change from within Socialist System," Inter Press Service, April 19, 2011.

67. "Our Greatest Satisfaction Is the Tranquility and Calm Confidence We Feel Handing over the Responsibility of Continuing to Build Socialism to New Generations," *Granma International*, February 26, 2013.

68. Camila Piñeiro Harnecker, "Cuba's New Socialism: Different Visions Shaping Current Changes," *Latin American Perspectives* 40, no. 3 (May 2013): 107–25.

Chapter Four

The Revolutionary Armed Forces

Loyalty and Efficiency in the Face of Old and New Challenges

Hal Klepak

Few would doubt that Cuba's *Fuerzas Armadas Revolucionarias* (FAR) have been or still are an essential element of the state apparatus of the government of Raúl Castro, as they had been for his elder brother. But the nature of that utility is rarely addressed. Instead, often rather glib analyses make comments on the vital role they play in propping up the state in its difficult moments or suggest that the FAR are evolving in this way or that but without looking more deeply into the organization's role in support of that state and government.

This chapter looks at the nature of the internal role they have played and are currently playing in the service of the state and the Revolution. While they have always been a linchpin of both, especially when, as at the present, things continue to be rocky, they remain first and foremost Cuban national armed forces and may well survive as such through any transition. We begin with a brief look backward at the uses to which the FAR have been put since the "triumph" of the Revolution in January 1959, emphasizing their remarkable flexibility in responding to President Fidel Castro's requirements of them over the period 1959–1990. Then we discuss the particular challenges of the "Special Period," declared in the summer of 1990 and still with us in some ways to this day, again with a view to analyzing the FAR's ability to respond to even more varied and, arguably, more difficult demands over that period. We will then be able to ask the question as to what extent they can play or are playing a key role in any transition, whatever form it is taking under the direction of Raúl, as a result of their remarkable utility in the present stage of the Revolution and Cuba's history.

THE FAR FROM 1959 UNTIL 1990

The Cuban revolutionary armed forces date their official existence from the arrival of the yacht *Granma*, carrying just over eighty insurgents from exile in Mexico, to the coast of Oriente Province in the east of Cuba, in November 1956. This was the real beginning of the continuous and organized armed struggle that was to topple the Batista government in the first week of January 1959 and bring to power that of the commander of the expedition, Fidel Castro Ruz.

After impressive growth and increasingly effective fighting, this armed force was by the summer of 1958 able to advance in two columns down the length of Cuba while other columns continued the struggle in and around the eastern hills of the Sierra Maestra, the island's highest mountain range near where the 1956 landing had taken place. Besting the corrupt Batista army in battle after battle, it was a hardened and intensely loyal force that moved on to capture the capital of Havana in the first two days of the New Year, 1959.

Since the Batista army (and his police and secret police) had been disbanded and entirely replaced by the *Ejército Rebelde* (Rebel Army), the latter became the only armed force available to defend the regime and the country. Not surprisingly and following firm Latin American custom, Fidel appointed in October 1959 his own brother Raúl as minister of the FAR (the Ministry of the Armed Forces was named MINFAR) and retained the post of commander in chief (always termed *comandante* in Cuba, the title by which people refer to Fidel even now).

Over those same early months of the Castro government, the armed forces were tasked with a bewildering number of jobs within the new structures of the state. Castro needed people he could trust in positions of importance, especially those such as agrarian reform, where U.S. and local opposition was soon strong and always vocal. But elsewhere in the political reorganization of the government and for the increasingly state-administered economy, it was military personnel, on whom Fidel felt he could rely, who were called in. Given the small size of the force—only a few thousand in January 1959—these demands were hard to fill, and very young men indeed took over portfolios for which they often had little or no training. Loyalty to the *comandante* and to his revolutionary program counted for more than efficiency in these trying but heady days. Under these conditions, the Communist Party (the Popular Socialist Party), for some months growing in its influence on the Cuban state, began obviously to take an even greater role in the running of the island. The military were soon to be asked to take on the task of building a real professional army capable of deterring a U.S. attack but in its event either defeating it or at least making it an undertaking of such cost that Washington would rue the day it took it on. In this, they would soon be able to count on steadily increasing Soviet assistance in the form of advisers, training, doctrine, equipment, and weapons. In this professionalization process, slowly but surely the FAR's personnel moved out of most nonmilitary tasks.

It is important to note, however, that this transformation was never completed. Military officers still held many posts of a not strictly military nature in later years, and the FAR could be asked at any time to undertake tasks normally done by civilian authorities. Indeed, in the great but ill-starred 10-million-ton sugar harvest planned for 1970, the FAR returned to national prominence as an essential element of the agricultural program, and it was rare throughout all these years when there was not some element of the military forces engaged in activities of a nonmilitary nature, at least in the traditional sense.

Cuba's militarized status in the Americas, facing an overwhelming grouping of states led by the United States and anxious to overthrow the Revolution and reverse its program, was occasioned as well by the "export of revolution" phase of Cuban foreign policy, when the FAR trained and otherwise assisted any number of insurgent movements in Latin America and even farther afield. While the number of personnel actually sent overseas at this stage was very small indeed, the number of other Latin American insurgents trained in Cuba was impressive. The real expansion of the forces yielding large and professional regular forces and vast reserves took place in stages, perhaps the most impressive of which was the adoption of the *Guerra de Todo el Pueblo* (War of All the People) strategy in the very early 1980s.

In the wake of President Reagan's electoral victory in the 1980 elections, combined with ever clearer indications that the Soviet Union was not going to actually fight for Cuba in the case of a crisis with the United States but also was not going to continue with its lavish defense handouts to the Cubans, Havana had to find a deterrent strategy more in keeping with the country's own capabilities. This required a new strategy and the expansion of the regular force to almost 300,000 strength, with reserves in all their categories to several times that figure. Thus, Cuba became an even more vastly militarized society, more so than even in the years of highest direct threat just after the Revolution came to power.

The last years of the Cold War saw many changes for the FAR, again demonstrating their exceptional flexibility in serving the Castro government in a variety of fields. If the early 1980s were already showing that the Soviet connection was becoming, if not a weak reed, certainly a weaker reed, Cuba's economic conditions were requiring new thinking as well. In the mid- to late 1980s, Cuba entered a period of economic "rectification" brought on by increasing problems of inefficiency, absenteeism, and excessive centralization. Fidel was apparently losing confidence in Soviet-style management techniques and gave Raúl the go-ahead to implement his own thinking in restructuring the military industries of the country.

If he succeeded, the intention was that these methods applied in military industries would be employed more globally in addressing Cuba's economic woes. Deemed the "System of Enterprise Perfection" (or "Improvement"), the new approach emphasized decentralization, streamlined and effective modern management techniques, flexibility, discipline, hierarchy, a chain of command along military lines, dedication, and competitiveness as an openly desirable goal. Officers were sent abroad, mainly to Latin America, to study modern management techniques. Many of these and other officers were placed in charge not only of military industries but increasingly of civilian ones as well. More dramatic change still was on its way, and the armed forces were to be called, perhaps in as striking a fashion as ever in their history, to lead the way in the struggle to save the Revolution from circumstances as dangerous as any it had ever known.

THE SPECIAL PERIOD

In June 1990, Fidel Castro announced the "Special Period in Time of Peace." The defense plan for a "Special Period in Time of War," a national planning document related to the conduct of a spirited and long-term defense of the island, was thus amended for a peacetime effort. Belt tightening as never before would become the rule as the nation reeled from the economic crisis detailed in other chapters of this book.

The FAR had of course been something of the spoiled child of the Soviet and Warsaw Pact connection. Although Cuba had never joined the Pact, a policy decision which might well have brought U.S. direct intervention, the island's military forces benefited enormously from its special status with Moscow and several other Pact members. Over some thirty years, the armed forces had enjoyed a generosity on the part of the Soviets that left the FAR almost completely in the Soviet style of armed forces. Cuban divisions were organized along Soviet lines, and the FAR's tactical and strategic doctrine was closely modeled on the Soviet equivalents, always given that the island's strategic situation was of course vastly different from its European friends. Equipment had long since become almost entirely Soviet, and not only was training along Soviet lines, but its senior and more complicated elements were usually conducted in the Soviet Union itself. And while Cubans were careful not to allow the Soviet instructors in Cuba to have excessive access to the rank and file of the FAR, their policy of "training the trainers" left deep marks on the Cuban military from which even now they have not moved very far.

Virtually overnight, this connection was broken with the new Gorbachev policy of "cash and carry," meaning that Cuba could not even obtain vital spare parts for its equipment and weapons, never mind purchase anything new. Senior training in key tactical fields was abandoned or done with minimal resources. Fuel consumption took a nosedive with perhaps only a third of the 1980s levels available in the first years after the rupture with Moscow. Exchanges of officers evaporated, as did plum postings for FAR personnel abroad. While Cuba had long since abandoned its previous policy in support of insurrections in Latin America and Africa, it now could not afford to do anything significant at all on the regional or international stage.

With little fuel, virtually no new spare parts, a nearly collapsed training system, poor availability of ammunition especially for training purposes, no new equipment or weapons, and a shattered world intelligence network formerly considered the best in the Third World, Cuba's forces had little to look forward to. Attaché offices were cut to less than a dozen for a force, the former envy of many developed countries for its widespread relations with armed forces almost everywhere.

The forces over the next three years were cut massively, and career bottlenecks appeared at almost all ranks. From nearly 300,000 in full-time service, the FAR were soon reduced to a mere fraction of that figure, well under 100,000 and still falling. The defense budget, expressed even in the rapidly devaluing national currency, gave the lie to a serious effort to keep defense as a priority. The security and defense budget (called "defense and internal order" in national budgeting) received $1.149 billion in 1990. But in the very first year of the Special Period, it suffered a dramatic cut to $882.2 million massively devalued pesos. This sharp decline was to continue, and in 1992 the sector received a mere $736.4 million. In 1993, perhaps the deepest moment of the Special Period, some $712.8 million were given over to this sphere.

Significantly, the defense and security sector did not experience the recovery after these years that one could see in community services. The year 1994 saw a continued decline to $651.2 million, and even in 1995, usually seen as the beginning of real recovery from the worst of the Special Period, a further fall in the defense and security budget brought the figure to $610.1 million. Indeed, even in 1996, with the recovery under way, the security forces saw their portion of the national budget lose another quarter of its total, ending up with some $496.7 million. While almost all other sectors were by this time on the mend (especially education, public health, social security, and housing), the defense sector, far from being the darling of the government, was being asked to sacrifice the most and the longest.

The trend was reversed only in part in 1997, when the security sector received its first increase in the Special Period, reaching $637.5 million. But this was only some 55 percent of its pre–Special Period budget and in a peso worth only a small fraction of its 1990 value. Even so, for 1998, the figure fell back to $537.1 million, recovering only a bit more seriously in 1999 with $752.3 million. In 2000, the last year for which "proper" figures are available, the total was $879.6 million, ten years after the beginning of the Special Period and still a mere 75 percent of the 1990 figure and, again, expressed in devalued pesos.[1]

With these vastly reduced resources in manpower, equipment, weapons, skills, and money, the FAR were asked to shoulder more, not fewer, burdens within the Cuban recovery and survival plan as designed in the months and years after 1990. We now look at their extraordinary utility, flexibility, loyalty, and discipline in more than two decades of the Special Period and its sequels.

THE ARMED FORCES AS MANAGER OF THE ECONOMY

The armed forces, as we have seen, were no strangers to a role in managing the national economy. From 1959 into the early 1990s, their role evolved, but they were never entirely out of the field. As revolutionary armed forces accustomed to nontraditional roles, they quickly adapted to the tasks they received from their *"comandante."* And from the mid-1980s, that role was again expanding.

Thus, the FAR cannot have been entirely surprised when they learned that they would have a special role again in the 1990s as a result of the vastly reduced circumstances of the Cuban state. But surely nothing prepared them for the scope of the jobs they were given. Essentially, they were asked to do four things to contribute to the national effort of the Special Period:

- Continue to deter attack and, in the event it came, defeat it or at least inflict heavy losses on the aggressor but do so with greatly reduced resources
- Feed themselves from their own resources
- Take over the management of many key industries of the state, especially those with foreign exchange earning potential, bringing to them military discipline and efficiency
- Maintain emergency services in the light of the increasing strains faced by Cuban society[2]

Feeding themselves turned out to be rather easier than many expected. The forces had for long been involved in agriculture, especially at harvest time. The *Ejército Juvenil de Trabajo*, a specially established conscript force set up in 1973 that does basic training but then turns its efforts to the economy rather than strictly national defense roles, was reinforced, given better leadership and resources, and set to work even harder in the fields. Soon the armed forces were not only feeding themselves but also sending excess production into the agricultural markets of the towns and cities.

Even more striking than the agricultural role was that in businesses earning foreign exchange. The military moved into control of even more of these industries than those where it had a foothold since the late 1980s or before. While tourism is the best known of these, there are others, such as telecommunications, real estate assistance, hunting lodge management, dredging, taxi companies, hotel construction and management, internal airline service, discotheques, restaurants, shopping centers, metallurgy, vehicle production, general construction, and, of course, arms and ammunition production.

In addition, in recent years, military officers have been ministers of government departments as diverse as Fisheries and Merchant Marine, Communications, Transport, Sugar, and many others. This practice has only been heightened with the new government of Raúl. Joint ventures with foreign capital became common with the military deeply involved in them. Only firms dealing with the direct production of defense material were excluded from such deals.

Through all these directly economic roles, the FAR have acquired enormous influence on the day-to-day running of the state and its economy. Vital for earning foreign exchange, without which the crisis that the Revolution is currently facing would be immeasurably more serious, the forces are now inextricably linked with that economy and the national recovery plan as a whole.

THE POLITICAL ROLE

The Cuban armed forces are hierarchically organized, disciplined, and present in regular or reserve form throughout the island. They are mobile, flexible, accustomed to planning and in particular to "worst-case planning," constantly updating themselves as individual members and as an institution, *available* to the state, and *armed*. Their loyalty is unquestioned, and they have never failed the Revolution despite some ups and downs, such as in Grenada and with the

Ochoa crisis of 1989. This list of highly useful characteristics is the exclusive preserve of the FAR matched by no other institution in Cuba.

Only the Communist Party could in the past have made the assertion that it was in the same league in terms of influence in the country. And it no longer can do that, for the armed forces enjoy not only these otherwise unheard-of advantages but many others as well. For a start, and as mentioned, they feed themselves and part of the rest of the population as well. In addition, they enjoy prestige in the country that the Party simply cannot match. They are not closely associated with the political ideology that much of the country, especially the young, challenge. Instead, they are a source of pride for many Cubans qua Cubans as having a splendid reputation gained at home in events such as the Bay of Pigs and abroad in places such as southern Africa, where their exploits in war have brought much credit to the institution.

In addition, they are probably the most important institution in earning foreign exchange, and therefore they probably come close to paying for themselves. The other side of the drop in defense budgets during the Special Period is the fact that, to a considerable extent, the FAR paid for their own operating costs. Only this ability made the FAR able to weather the current storm without collapse. The Party does not pay for itself. MINFAR does. In a country as financially strapped as Cuba, this translates into real power and influence.

This is not to say that the Party is altogether a spent force in Cuba. This is not the case, and events such as the hurricanes of the early autumn of 2004 and those of late in that decade, where the Party on at least one occasion did arguably a better job coming to the assistance of the public than did the FAR (far from the case normally where the forces do a superb job at disaster relief and bringing succor to the public), show that there is life in the old institution still. And Raúl clearly goes out of his way to ensure that for him the Party still has a real role. But compared to the armed forces, the Party is increasingly less central to decisions taken on the future of the country.

The Party's actual role in the control of the forces has been likewise significantly weakened in recent years. It should be said that this control has been exaggerated by many analysts with a determination to make the FAR appear more like their Warsaw Pact former comrades than is warranted by the facts. For example, the political officers of the "commissar" type that ruled in that alliance's members, following the early Soviet pattern of the post-1917 era, never existed in Cuba. There is no parallel chain of command in the FAR as was common elsewhere. The commanding officer of a unit is the unquestioned *commander*, although there is an officer responsible for political training. In the early struggle for power between the FAR and the Party, the former had much the better of it.

In recent years, the independence of the forces has grown apace. Fidel's turning to the FAR once again in time of crisis and the growth of its already immense national role have made controlling it from the Party a virtual impossibility. This of course must always be analyzed with the point in mind that there is in Cuba no automatic division between Party and army with so many senior officers being also Party members (and loyal ones) and with the links between the two so generalized in the state apparatus.

THE DOMESTIC DETERRENT ROLE

The role of the FAR in deterring foreign aggression is well known. Less considered is the nonetheless equally obvious role the armed forces have in deterring internal disorder. In Cuba, the overwhelmingly key player in keeping the lid on any popular discontent is the MININT, the Interior Ministry, tasked directly with this responsibility. But the armed forces have a highly important if more indirect role in the job as well.

This is as a result of two factors. The Interior Ministry is not an entirely independent element of the state but exists in many ways as a junior partner of the armed forces proper. The uniform may be slightly different. Procedures and priorities most certainly are. But administratively and in much more than that sense, the MININT almost belongs to the FAR despite its being a separate ministry. In addition, since the shocking revelations or political maneuvers of the 1989 Ochoa scandal, that subordination has become more evident than ever.[3] Several trusted senior generals of the FAR were transferred directly into the MININT, and the purge they conducted left a weakened institution under greater military influence than ever.

Be that as it may, the useful fiction of a division between the two ministries is all to the FAR's benefit, expressing the military institution's self-image. The FAR have been raised believing deeply that they are the nation in arms, a revolutionary army in a real sense, expressing the belief of the people in the Revolution's aims and far from the Latin American model of a repressive force at the service of a corrupt and exploitative state. The FAR take as an article of faith that "el ejército no tira contra el pueblo" (the army does not fire on the people), as happened so often in Latin America. Such behavior was left behind when the Batista government fell and its army was disbanded. The FAR are keen to be seen to be as far away from any repressive role as possible, and the observation of this author is that this desire has been largely achieved. Respect for the armed forces is widespread and obvious. Pride in the FAR's achievements is important, and everyone has members of his or her family serving in the FAR or its reserve components. By now, a huge percentage of the population has done so itself.

Nevertheless, Cubans, like citizens of most states, know very well that the armed forces are the last bulwark of the state and that if that state were about to collapse, they would act to save it. This is reinforced by the FAR's constantly reiterated public posture of absolute loyalty and devotion to the present government, its leaders (especially Raúl), and its objectives and ideals. The ability of this force to mobilize, even under the difficult circumstances of the Special Period, vast numbers of people for everything from disaster relief operations to reserve forces exercises of a more traditional kind means that the FAR have an absolutely vital political role in the maintenance of domestic order and peace. No Cuban whom this author has ever interviewed believes that the FAR would not act to defend the Revolution. And the knowledge of this, generalized to the population as a whole, must be a central feature of domestic order in the long run.

THE TRANSITION

The potential role of the FAR in any transition scenario must be seen in this context. We have described the vast advantages the armed forces have over other elements of the state when it comes to staying power in difficult situations. In any transition, they are also the element of the state, apart from the MINREX (the Foreign Ministry), that has the closest ties with the other key potential actor, the United States, and specifically with U.S. military forces.

Quietly but ever so surely, the FAR has established some limited relations with the U.S. security forces almost across the board.[4] While this is obviously of political utility to the Cuban government's foreign relations, its implications for internal order in a transition make it important internally as well. Specifically, the FAR and the MININT have established reasonably close relations with their U.S. counterparts, given the attitudes of their two governments as a whole, at a number of levels—relations that may well make their cooperation in time of crisis not only possible but also potentially palatable to other key political actors.

The MINFAR has close links with the U.S. military through the requirement to handle any number of delicate issues along the border between the U.S. base at Guantánamo Bay and Cuban territory proper. There are constant communications between the two local commanders in situ, and a crisis management arrangement of some sophistication is in place. In addition, U.S. Coast Guard and occasionally naval forces work with their Cuban counterparts in key areas of U.S. security concern, especially the "war" on drugs and anti–illegal immigration operations. There is a Coast Guard officer attached to the U.S. Interests Section in Havana. And the U.S. Drug Enforcement Agency has tried to influence U.S. opinion and government policy by suggesting, not always subtly, that Washington has vastly more to gain from close counternarcotics cooperation with Cuba than it has to lose. Given the FAR's institutional advantages within the Cuban state and this special potential to act as a bridge to the United States (an inconceivable role for the Party or any other element of the Cuban state), the armed forces will surely have a central role in any transition.

The FAR are a revolutionary force beyond doubt, loyal to the Revolution without question but deeply exposed to the realities of the present world and its evolution. There is little doubt that many of the reforms of recent years, especially in the economy, originated from the ranks of the senior officer corps. Equally, Raúl Castro has proven dramatically over the years since 2006 that he can think "out of the box" when he needs to. It is also important to keep in mind that the FAR has the usual institutional desire to continue to exist. While not lacking in a desire to see the *logros* (achievements) of the Revolution survive, the armed forces are willing to make compromises in conformity with the realities around them on both the global and the domestic level.

Without doubt, the FAR is deeply committed to the Revolution and strongly revolutionary in its ideals. It will not happily part with the achievements of the Revolution, and it is worth mentioning that from its perspective, the chief of those is the national sovereignty and dignity that was obtained through the revolutionary process. In a transitional period, they will wish to ensure the survival of the best elements of the revolutionary government and be keen to ensure their own institutional future. They are extremely unlikely to "give away the shop." National sovereignty, general access to education and health services, and racial equality would not likely be on the bargaining table unless disorder were widespread and the situation close to desperate.

RECENT TRENDS

In the context of the present strategic situation of Cuba, the question on many Cuban lips, perhaps underscored by the North Korean ship affair, is the chief utility presented as the raison d'être of the FAR, that is, its ability to deter attack. The perceived likelihood of an actual military attack on Cuba was in decline over many years, especially among the nation's young, but it became exceptional again with the Bush presidency. The Cuban people then appeared more united than they had been for many years in their determination to defend the island—and even the Revolution—against any attack that might come. The Castro brothers no longer needed to do much to convince the public of the excesses of the government in Washington. The perception of the Bush administration as "inhuman" or even "fascist" and capable of anything was widespread indeed.

This greater acceptance of the national assessment of the threat was put to the test in the great national mobilization test of November–December 2004 known as "Bastión 2004" and in later versions of that exercise in 2004 and 2009 and as planned for late 2013. Air raid alarms have sounded, long-disused underground shelters were reopened, live-fire exercises have taken place, vehicles have been repaired, militia "fan-outs" (networks of calls to arms) have been dusted off and tried out, firing ranges have been made more active than in decades past, noncombat units have been tested on their often-aged skills in the field, naval craft have been put to sea, and old uniforms have been put on again and new ones issued—all in an attempt to see if the FAR's long-famed ability to turn out the people as a nation in arms was still a reality. The results in these exercises have been that the forces were indeed able to get the troops out and test them, although the decline in capabilities, linked to smaller numbers, very obsolete equipment and weapons, insufficient tactical training, and so on, cannot have escaped the senior leadership any more than it has the defense attaché community. This can only reassure the government that it still has a striking ability to mobilize the nation in time of crisis while also underscoring the grave problems at hand.[5]

Other problems of course also remain. With the Obama government, there is no longer much of a shared perception of a real possibility of U.S. aggression. Low-level corruption in the FAR is widespread, as it is elsewhere but perhaps to a lesser degree. This is only too evident to the high command, itself often accused of being prone to corruption as a result of the temptations arising from its control of the tourism and other profitable industries. Although sentences for yielding to this temptation are severe indeed, the leadership has not been able to stamp out the phenomenon by any means. Anticorruption courses, given to both military and civilian personnel, likewise are not a panacea for this almost universal challenge. There are generational problems as well, with younger officers on occasion frustrated by the slowness of change, the delays in promotion brought about by the massive cuts of recent decades, the slow but steady decline of equipment and weaponry, the age of senior leadership, and many other factors. Officers of higher rank know only too well that while the FAR still have punch, their proud capability, proven so often in the past, is eroding.

Morale, however, is surprisingly high. The explosion of roles coming with the 1990s challenged the institution, but it has not been found wanting. Plenty of young people still think seriously of a military career. The increasing role of the military in the economy, through influence or direct control over the most profitable parts of it, brings advantages as well as problems to the FAR. Raúl is, of course, a military man and shows great interest in the institution even now that he is no longer its minister. He has counted on them, as did his brother in previous periods of great challenges, but he has also prepared them for their roles in the wider state and economy. Their loyalty is not questioned, but now neither is their knowledge of their tasks. Little wonder that he turns to them, as with the cabinet changes of 2009 and later, with frequency and does so in so many fields and at so many levels of state administration.

FINAL THOUGHTS

The Cuban armed forces are the inheritors of proud traditions by any standards. They are loyal to the regime and to the country. They are vital to both. While doubtless not as able to deter attack as in the halcyon days of the Soviet alliance, with hundreds of thousands of serving personnel, not to mention modern weapons and equipment, they are still a strong force at many levels, especially in their ability to mobilize. They would surely give a good account of themselves in case of invasion in terms of courage and discipline, although the state of their weaponry is cause for real alarm.

In the absence of a real threat of invasion, however, the issues are less stark. Many senior officers now know a great deal about business as well as soldiering. They have had to adjust many times to the demands of the real and nasty world of the Special Period and the present moment. The armed forces they command, while still central, are infinitely smaller than they have been at any time since the early 1960s. They are likewise, as the North Korean repair shipment scandal of mid-2013 showed starkly, much worse equipped and much less up to date than in the past. It is interesting then that despite all this, their political influence is not less but more than in recent decades.

These forces have an absolutely proven record of loyalty and usefulness to the Cuban state since before they took Havana nearly five decades ago and at every stage of those passing years. Their flexibility in responding to their commander in chief's evolving and highly varied orders has been their hallmark and has been impressive indeed. In the future, that flexibility may be tested again. It is virtually certain that their loyalty will be. There is little reason to think that this flexibility will not stand them in good stead in any circumstances. Their usefulness to the government of Raúl Castro is as great as ever. But they will want to look to the future as well. Proper handling of this key institution will be essential to providing a peaceful transition. Holding the ring while the politicians sort things out is, alas, a long-standing Latin American military role. The FAR have shed most of the traditions of the region's militaries. Perhaps that may prove to be their most useful contribution to Cuba and to the *logros* of the Revolution.

NOTES

1. All the data for the state budget come from the 1995–2001 annual reports produced by Cuba, Oficina Nacional de Estadística, *Anuario Estadístico de Cuba*. They are given here with the caveat that like so many official state figures in Latin American countries, especially those related to defense, they should not be taken at full face value. They do, however, suggest trends of great importance.

2. The formal structuring to achieve these ends came into being with Law No. 75 of National Defense of 1995, but it rather more confirmed things already done than added new ones. See *Gaceta Oficial de la República de Cuba*, Havana, January 13, 1995, 1–14, and the interview with General Orlando Almaguel Vidal in Luis Báez, *Secretos de generales* (Barcelona: Losada, 1997), 234–47, esp. 244–46.

3. The Ochoa affair refers to the arrest and subsequent execution by firing squad of General Arnaldo Ochoa, a hero of the war in Angola, and of members of the MININT who were charged with illegal narcotics trade at a time when Castro was deeply concerned that the United States would be using that involvement as a justification for harsh action against the island.

4. This author elaborated on these linkages in "Confidence-Building Measures and the Cuba–United States Confrontation," International Security Research Paper, Department of Foreign Affairs and International Trade, Ottawa, March 2000.

5. See the special edition of *Granma*, December 20, 2004, especially the article "Se ha demostrado nuestra capacidad de combate," 3–6.

Chapter Five

The Collapse of Socialism Is beyond the Present Horizon

Rafael Hernández, Interviewed by Edmundo García

Rafael Hernández is a Cuban social scientist and the editor of the magazine *Temas*, a quarterly publication dedicated to theory and analysis of the problems of culture, ideology, and society. This December 20, 2011, exchange with journalist Edmundo García is from the program "La tarde se mueve," which is broadcast by an alternative radio station in Miami.

Edmundo García: Professor Rafael Hernández, this year, in November, you gave a presentation at the Inter-American Dialogue together with other Cuba specialists. In this meeting the current Cuban political process was described as an "updating" of socialism, and it was made clear that Cuba was not on track to replicate the so-called Arab Spring. I'd like you to explain to our audience your own view of why Cuba did not follow the path of the USSR and the Eastern European countries when they renounced [socialism] and the USSR disintegrated, and why Cuba today is not like Egypt, Libya or Tunisia, which just last weekend marked the first anniversary of their "democratic spring." Why not Cuba, and how is the "update" of socialism going?

Rafael Hernández: Well, I think that the change that took place in the European countries and the Soviet Union had a different character than that which has taken place in Cuba during the past 20 years, and which is advancing today on the basis of policies and legislation that are contributing to the emergence of a new socialist model. In the case of the Soviet Union, perestroika and glasnost began as reform policies, but it's very clear that they gave rise to profoundly anti-socialist sectors and to the expression of great evils that had been installed during the Stalinist epoch. The Soviet Union, despite the renovation period under Khrushchev during the 1950s and 60s, despite the attempts to modernize the economic model, despite the undoubted successes of the Soviet conquest of space, their immense military power, the Soviet Union as a political system could never overcome the evils that dragged it down from the times of Stalin onwards.

Traces of them remained there. The Soviet party and leadership were increasingly out of touch with their bases. Many Soviet citizens were genuinely socialist, but they didn't feel that their ideas and sentiments were reflected in the policies of the leadership. In the complex situation of the Eastern European countries, it's obvious that socialism never sunk deep roots, that it never had deep roots. This was above all due to the fact that the Red Army occupied their [countries] after the Second World War and to the [Roosevelt-Churchill-Stalin] Yalta Pact, etc. All this is understood.

In the case of Cuba, as everyone knows, the socialist process has its origins in Cuba's circumstances at the close of the 1950s. It's the accumulated result of a struggle for freedom and independence that began in the 19th century. You can't understand the socialist revolution without grasping that it's the culmination of a preceding historical process. I say culmination not because it's the end point, because there is never "the" end point, only a bridge to advancement, and this is what is happening now. What's happening now is that during the past two decades—and not only because of the end of the socialist bloc, of Cuba's disconnection from the international system thanks to its ties to the Soviet Union and the Eastern European countries, but also as a result of the deficiencies of its own socialist model—this model, which was adopted in 1976, exhausted itself. It showed signs of exhaustion during the mid-1980s, and in the 90s it entered, together with and catalyzed by the collapse of the socialist camp, a clear process of crisis. This is what we call in Cuba the "Special Period."

The Special Period is not only an economic crisis, it's a crisis in the way of conceiving of socialism, a crisis of values, a moral crisis, a crisis of society. Given this, the transformation didn't begin six years ago when Raúl Castro became acting president, nor some months ago when the PCC Congress adopted economic and social measures.

The transformation of Cuban society began much earlier, with the appearance of problems that were accompanied by the opening up of spaces in which public opinion could express itself, of a greater space for debate in the midst of the crisis. The decline in living standards gave rise to an expansion of the spaces for freedom of expression in Cuba. This is clear to anyone who visited Cuba 20 years ago and returns to visit the country today, they'd see that this public debate has greatly expanded even though it isn't reflected in the Cuban media. This has nothing to do with what happened, with what was the status quo, in the North African countries, in the Arab countries. It has nothing to do with what has happened in Egypt, Morocco, or Libya.

It has nothing in common with these countries because neither the culture, nor the political regime, nor the historical process that led to this were comparable. Certain analysts make far-fetched comparisons in which they credit mobile phones, Facebook and Twitter with the possibility of subversion, of them being tools of subversion. This is absolutely ridiculous, it's like thinking that revolutions were produced by the telephone and the telegraph. It's to invest these devices, this technology, with a muscular quality, with motive and causation in the outbreak of a process of social and political transformation.

These processes took place in the Arab world where some very authoritarian regimes, that were ever-more distant from the interests of the population, crumbled. In Cuba, during these past two decades of serious economic difficulties, of discontent and even of a crisis of values, throughout all these years there haven't been any significant signs of political instability. This is not because Cuban policies are more effective than any others [at quelling dissent]. Cuban politics does not utilize violence, does not use the repressive measures that are so common almost everywhere, including in the U.S., to suppress demonstrations. The alternative would be to think that faced with a decisive situation in which protest would be the best option, the Cuban people wouldn't have the courage to do it because they're scared of the police. That's ridiculous.

What has happened is that the political consensus that was re-forged in the context of the 1990s and 2000s is a political consensus that demands a more decentralized system, a system that gives more space to the non-state sector, that downsizes the bureaucratic apparatus and implements a series of measures to raise the living standards of the population to what had been achieved by the end of the 1980s. This was the fruit of socialism, of a socialist model that over time lost the capacity to sustain these high living standards and not only, I repeat, because of the collapse of the Soviet Union. So what is happening now is that this re-forged consensus includes agreement on the need to avoid civil unrest, disturbances, the use of force to resolve this problem [of the exhaustion of the model].

Very few people in Cuba really think—including those who are part of the opposition to the government—that the best way to resolve this situation we're in is to resort to violence, insurgency, civil unrest. This is very clear to anyone who visits Cuba and obviously it's even clearer to those who live in Cuba. The solutions have to be gradual, without delays so that we don't stop moving forward, so that we don't stop transforming and creating a space in which the citizens can find dignified employment so that they can earn enough to buy the products [they need] on the market, and of course to have a space for critical discourse.

The government has called for disagreement, for the expression of different viewpoints, it has called for the critical discussion of policies. There are very few governments—I'm not aware of any [others]—that before launching a policy of adjustment, before launching a policy for the transformation of the economic model, submit this document to a discussion by millions of citizens, yet this is what has happened. Indeed, the public debate in Cuba constitutes a form of appropriation by the citizens of the political changes, because the expression of people's views, of the opinions of the ordinary citizens, has been a fundamental step. It has been as fundamental as the measures that have been approved and those that have yet to be approved and which must be approved. Just as important as the policies themselves are the debates that have been conducted on these policies. It's a fundamentally democratic debate, and consequently the space for a Cuban Arab Spring, for a collapse, for chaos, for the implosion of socialism, is beyond the present horizon.

Edmundo García: Continuing with the theme of the reform process in Cuba, I'd like to ask you to clarify something for us. When referring to the changes on the island, most specialists, almost everybody, prefaces their comments by saying that the reforms have enemies, that there are revolutionaries who are against the reforms in Cuba. Now, can we identify some of these adversaries beyond general terms such as "the bureaucracy"?

Rafael Hernández: I think there are expressions of resistance to change that I would describe as opposition that is not negative, but constructive; and other expressions of opposition that are frankly negative. Among the constructive I'd point to those groups that are obviously not going to benefit immediately and directly because they don't participate in the spaces and the new opportunities that are opening up for self-employment and for the expansion of the non-state [i.e., small business and cooperative] sector. Among them are people whose age does not allow them to join the workforce or initiate a new life project, those who are defined as living below the poverty line, the numbers of which have increased during the crisis period—some sociologists estimate about 20 percent of the population. These people do not necessarily have the resources to be able to take advantage of the changes that are now underway, and this means we have to have a social policy that takes advantage of economic growth and directs it towards supporting those who are disadvantaged by the reforms, by the changes; those who face these changes with a degree of uncertainty, considerable uncertainty, because they don't provide them with a clear opportunity to recover their standard of living. Such people don't necessarily view the reform process with the expectations, desires and enthusiasm of others.

There is also a negative resistance which government leaders have explicitly called the bureaucracy. The bureaucracy doesn't oppose through speeches, it doesn't oppose the reforms with a document. It opposes in its slowness to implement the measures already adopted, already approved. Raúl Castro describes this as an old mentality towards change, as a hindrance, the ineptitude of an antiquated work style that is seen, for example, in the media that is an insult to the education level, and is even seen as such by party militants. This inertia that is criticized, in which the bureaucratic apparatus drags its feet in adopting the new rules, the new arrangements, in working in harmony with the new perspectives and approaches, is perhaps the most difficult thing to change, to transform. In my opinion this is one the key issues the PCC Conference will have to grapple with.

It's very logical that the old mindset, which sees the emergence of capitalism in every expression of the market and in every segment of small-scale private property, exists. Because for a long time we had a way of coping with the changes that involved stigmatizing the emergence of these new [economic] actors and new spaces for the market. Socialism [i.e., the socialist-oriented society—translator's note] was defined in absolute terms as state-centric socialism, which is what had prevailed throughout all these years.

Or rather, it's logical that there be these expressions of the mentality that says, OK, these are necessary evils. But it's clear, and this is one of the most important aspects of the present moment, that for the past year the Cuban government's position has been to not only to legalize, but to legitimize the presence of these new economic sectors in Cuban society as part of the socialist family. They, the self-employed workers, the members of cooperatives, the people that work in the small [private] enterprise sector, are not emissaries of capitalism, they're part of the socialist family, part of the revolutionary family, and this has been reiterated by the top government leadership.

Edmundo García: Let's move on now to the Cuban Communist Party (PCC) National Conference in January 2012. There are analysts, the so-called Cubanologists and Cuba observers, who take it as a given that the Economic and Social Policy Guidelines adopted by the Sixth PCC Congress is the key document that sets out the transformations, the updating of socialism, and that its proposals are sufficient for the updating of the socialist model. However, they are more critical of the [draft] National Conference document; some say the proposals are not similar. My specific questions are, do you perceive a distance between the two documents, between the Congress document and the Guidelines? Do you think the PCC is advancing in its own democratization process? And finally, what do you anticipate will be the outcome of the PCC Conference in January?

Rafael Hernández: I think that, naturally, there are things missing in the content of the Guidelines as adopted by the Congress, there are empty spaces, and these gaps sparked discussion during the debates on the Guidelines that several million people participated in over a number of weeks. I don't think you can understand what is projected in the Guidelines unless you read them together with the Main Report to the Sixth PCC Congress delivered by Raúl Castro, who made it clear that without a change in the style of political work, without a change in the conception of the Party's role, in participation, in the style of Party work in relation to the population, unless we change all this then the reforms won't succeed.

This, obviously, draws attention to the fact that—to use a mathematical analogy—the axes that these economic and social Guidelines cross are political axes. Most analysts take the view that they deal with a series of strictly economic measures, as if in a country like Cuba, with the kind of political and social system we have, one can make far-reaching economic changes that structurally modify the existing order in the economic sphere, without changing the others.

If you read the Guidelines closely, you'll find the themes of decentralization, de-statiziation, de-bureaucratization and the rule of law—the use of legality a tool of change, as a framework within which the changes are not only adopted but are consolidated and made permanent, which is very important. These changes, then, are political changes. They are obviously political changes, changes that have to do with the redistribution of power, with taking power away from the central structures and giving the base structures, the local bodies, more power. This is related to the democratization of the system.

Perhaps many of those who criticize the PCC Conference document hoped that this issue of democratization—or the gaps, the omissions in the Guidelines, such as the role of the trade unions, the role of the workers in the workplaces, in workplace decision-making, etc.—would be the key axis of the document. Given this, I think the PCC Conference can take up and elaborate on these problems that we have, which are at the very heart of the Cuban political problematic. I say this because one of the things that was truly admirable about the Party Congress is that it was a real congress, there was a debate; we saw it on TV, Cubans and non-Cubans could see in the telecast that there was a real debate on the draft Guidelines, which had previously been subjected to a popular debate.

The Congress had content, it was not simply a ritualistic exercise to rubber-stamp a policy that had already been decided. Real decisions were made by the Congress, changes were adopted that were not in the draft Guidelines. It is to be hoped that the Party Conference will make changes likewise, that it responds to the expectations of the population and that it changes, of course, what I said a moment ago would be the most difficult thing to change, perhaps the greatest challenge, which is to change the political style [of the PCC's work].

The political style, and I don't mean style in the sense of a way of doing things, it has to with the whole conception of what politics is, with what is meant by the participation of the citizens, and what is the relationship between what Che Guevara called the vanguard and the mass. Today, this is more about the relationship between the leaders and the led, between the institutions of political representation of the population, it's about the interests and desires of the population and the responses of the political institutions to these interests and desires; the ability to engage in a dialogue, to govern in a way that responds to the people, not with a package of policies that must be implemented regardless of what people think.

A measure was adopted [in the 1960s], that of nationalization, of employment [in the state sector], and there are a million surplus workers according to an economic analysis. However, the delay in implementing [the rationalization of state sector employment] has obviously been the result of the realization that the population was anxious, that there was anxiety among the people in relation to the issue of unemployment; an understandable anxiety, an understandable concern.

I think the government itself, in delaying the implementation of these measures, has displayed a great deal of political sensitivity. One thing that distinguishes the Cuban leadership is its political sensitivity regarding what the population thinks and feels. It's hard to believe, though there are those who do believe it, that the top Cuban leadership is not aware of what the person in the street thinks and feels. At a time like the present, when Cubans are expressing themselves in different spaces, putting forward their ideas, interests and opinions which are obviously not homogeneous—we're talking about debate, and whenever we talk about a space for expressing interests and ideas we're talking about differences, disagreements, but listening to them and reflecting on them and taking on board, in a responsible way, these interests and desires of the population—I think this is at the heart of the current Cuban government's concerns.

What will be implemented, including the Guidelines adopted by the Congress, is not a magic wand, it's not going to be a straight-jacket, a plan that's going to be carried out as if it were a little book, a Bible. It's a working tool that's going to be modified to the degree to which it is implemented in the months ahead, without haste, without rashness, but without pause.

NOTE

Excerpted from Rafael Hernández, "The Collapse of Socialism Is beyond the Present Horizon," Interviewed by Edmundo García, December 20, 2011, and posted by Cubadebate, http://www.cubadebate.com. Translation by Marce Cameron, from "Cuba's Socialist Renewal," http://www.cubasocialistrenewal.blogspot.com.

Chapter Six

Religion and Civil Society in Cuba, 1959–2013

Margaret E. Crahan

Amphibians are proliferating in Cuba. This is not, however, a reference to frogs or others of their species. Rather, it means individuals and groups who transcend or, perhaps more accurately, transgress the boundaries between the state and nonstate sectors. In order to better understand the nature of civil society in Cuba and how it functions, it is necessary to redefine its parameters. In short, the functions of civil society in Cuba—that is, imposing demands and accountability on the state—are exercised largely by a society incorporated into mass organizations that contain within them sectors that generate occasional alternative discourses to that of the state as well as help modify public policies and programs. The all-encompassing mass organizations have increasingly lost their capacity to impose orthodoxy on their members as well as to mobilize a civil society that is rife with complaints about the incapacities of the state.

In addition, there are networks of individuals within the core state apparatus that consult regularly concerning state policies and programs with those who are fully or partially outside it. These networks include some individuals who have been pushed out of the state sector due to their heterodoxy and others who have left to explore options in the nonstate sector. Interestingly, a fair number have ended up in the research centers and universities that are part of the state apparatus but that allow more divergence from the predominant ideology of the state. Hence, one finds "on the state payroll" scholars and other experts, together with filmmakers, painters, composers, dancers, and others, who produce alternative discourses.

Young people are emerging as an important civil society voice calling for expanded government services and employment. In addition, there is a long tradition in Cuba of religious and ethnically based networks, some of which overlap, that increasingly serve to represent community interests, particularly in view of the failure of the state to fully meet the basic needs of all Cubans.[1]

Historically, Cubans have identified themselves, in part, according to their racial and geographic backgrounds, together with their religious beliefs. Afro-Cubans, for example, have used spiritist-based religions to organize to resist exploitation and demand their rights going back to the earliest importation of Africans as slaves. Among the most pervasive networks in Cuba today are those based on spiritist beliefs, as communities increasingly have to meet their own needs in the face of the limitations of the state in providing public services. In addition, religious institutions, including the Catholic and Protestant churches, together with the Jewish community—all of which can tap into international resources—have assumed more active civil society roles, particularly regarding meeting basic needs with respect to food and medical supplies. While attendance at services continues to be relatively low, as it was historically, religious organizations or institutions provide the most extensive national networks within civil society. Recent surveys indicate that approximately 75 to 85 percent of all Cubans believe in the divine, even after more than fifty years of atheist materialism, giving religions considerable potential to exercise influence within civil society. [2]

The concept of civil society refers to a complex network of individuals and groups through which people participate in community and polity. It includes not only civic associations and institutions but also informal networks linked horizontally with one another and, at times, vertically to political elites and the state. In the Cuban case, such networks regularly transcend the boundaries of the state and nonstate sectors. If one of the defining attributes of civil society is its clear-cut differentiation from the state, then the conclusion must be that civil society is narrow and limited in Cuba. But if one recognizes the degree to which associations in Cuba, including those initially organized by the government, but subsequently "semi–spun off," have carved out expanding autonomous spaces in which to operate in recent years, then Cuban civil society appears much more vibrant.

A critical question is how much space the Cuban government is willing to accord a nonoppositional civil society that is not mobilizing for regime change but is increasingly critical of socioeconomic and political conditions. Furthermore, it is hard not only for experts but also for the Cuban leadership to disentangle oppositional, dissident, and nonoppositional sectors of Cuban civil society. Among those actors are a wide variety of religious groups that constitute the most broad-based sector with a national reach. A better understanding of the role of religious institutions in the evolution of Cuban civil society can help establish the dynamics of citizen participation, nuances in the relationship between state and society, and, to some extent, the future of Cuban civil society.

CUBAN CIVIL SOCIETY AND RELIGIONS: HOW STRONG?

Civic and other organizations were common in Cuba as early as the nineteenth century, and they continued to proliferate throughout the twentieth century. By 1959, Cuban civil society had developed into one of the most advanced in Latin America in spite of periodic prerevolutionary government attempts to regulate it both legally and through repression. [3]

The tendency for religion to be regarded as relatively weak in Cuba flows essentially from a focus on such factors as formal participation, levels of activism, and direct political influence. It is true that attendance at services and participation in religious groups was historically relatively low in Cuba and that political influence waxed and waned. What has been insufficiently studied is the very real penetration of Cuban society by indigenous, Judeo-Christian, and spiritist religions that have made the vast majority of Cubans believers, normative religious values prevalent, and popular religiosity widespread. Historically, religious beliefs have permeated Cuban culture and molded societal attitudes. At the same time, the very multiplicity of religions and the weak presence of religious institutions, especially in rural areas, contributed to low levels of practice and a high level of syncretism and the permeability of religious and secular belief systems. [4]

Catholic, Protestant, and Afro-Cuban religious beliefs were all used in the legitimization of the 1868–1898 independence movement, although the institutional Catholic Church maintained its identification with continued Spanish control. Sectors of the revolutionary movements of the 1930s and 1950s also used religious beliefs and networks to legitimate their objectives and mobilize resources and collaborators. Protestant and Catholic university students were active in both movements, while some church groups and leaders served to generate monies for their efforts. Reformist movements, including Catholic Action (*Acción Católica*) and the Catholic Association (*Agrupación Católica*), grew, particularly in the 1950s.[5] Religious beliefs and generalized identification with religious norms were common and, at times, coexisted with interest in socialism. The latter was stimulated by interpretations of the social doctrines of the churches, which increasingly emphasized socioeconomic justice and, in particular, workers' rights. This helped justify movements in support of regime change or at least less governmental corruption and abuse of power. Hence, while the percentage of Cubans actually engaging in regular religious practice was not high, religiously informed values were historically widely held and influenced concepts of polity and society as well as Cubans' involvement in civil society.

Since 1959, the revolutionary government has tried, largely through executive orders, to limit the autonomy and development of associative organizations. Nevertheless, in recent years, there has been a revitalization and expansion of civic and other organizations not dominated by the government, together with increased autonomy on the part of government-organized associations. While networking among sectors is somewhat limited, there is a positive disposition among influential sectors, such as intellectuals, artists, labor, community, and church leaders, toward the strengthening of civil society. As a result, they are increasingly assuming roles as community organizers and leaders, providers of food and medicine to those in need, and molders of public opinion. That is, they are occupying more and more public space.

DOES CIVIL SOCIETY LACK AUTONOMY IN CUBA?

Legally, citizen organizations in Cuba must be under the supervision of state agencies, and many comply.[6] However, a closer look reveals a high degree of complexity along a continuum that includes fully autonomous groups with or without government licenses, state-initiated organizations that operate somewhat autonomously, and government mass organizations that contain within them sectors that generate counter-discourses to those of the state. In terms of political attitudes and behavior, the spectrum comprises sharp opposition to the government and Cuban socialism, criticism of the Castro regime but not necessarily of socialism, dissidence within not only the state's mass organizations but also the government bureaucracy, and strong support for the government. Cuban civil society, then, can be said to incorporate opponents of the present government, dissident groups that range along a reformist spectrum, and critical and heterodox individuals within the state who participate in civil society networks. Given the increasing level of alternative discourses, it is not surprising that a growing number of organizations have carved out a certain degree of autonomy that allows them to function as a source of new ideas, debate, and citizen action.

Religious publications, in particular *Espacio Laical*, have been in the forefront in occupying political space and exploring alternatives to government policies.[7] Such developments have the potential to create spaces for debates over power, claims to authority and policymaking, and norms and practices in society.[8] Of course, the level of civic engagement and debate in Cuba is limited when compared to some other societies, but it is crucial to recognize the existence of an expanding public sphere constituted by an increasing number of minispheres within the country and sustained by higher levels of voluntary associational activity. Some of the discourses that circulate in the public sphere concern models of socialism and economic reform, nonpolitical descriptors that shape the identity of youth (particularly rap music and fashion), and the responsibilities of religious believers in a society that until the early 1990s was described in the Cuban Constitution as a materialist, atheist one. The expansion of associational autonomy in Cuba is a result, in large measure, of the interaction between two processes: first, society's increased capacity, skills, and motivation to organize outside the realm of the state, and, second, the decreased capacity of the state to control and regulate society as well as provide governmental services and ensure basic needs.[9] The provision of the latter is at the core of the Cuban government's claim to legitimacy and adherence to socialism. Its failure to do so is a result, in part, of the vast economic transformations that took place following the collapse of the Soviet Union and the Eastern European communist regimes, the ongoing U.S. embargo and the global financial crisis of 2008–2009, and repeated natural disasters.

One stimulus of civil society has been the proliferation of informal sector enterprises employing anywhere from two or three to twenty to thirty workers and contributing to an expanded labor sector that defines its agendas somewhat differently from those directly employed by the government.[10] The Catholic Church has been in the forefront of providing assistance to the growing number of private entrepreneurs, called *cuenta propistas*, who occupy much of the nonstate sector. Local churches are providing courses in business management, leadership training, and basics, such as accounting. Together with the University of Murcia in Spain, the Archdiocese of Havana initiated in 2011 a Master's in Business Administration program and in June 2012 *Cuba Emprende*, short-term immersion courses aimed at establishing a small business.

Civil society networks that have emerged, particularly since the 1990s, have taken advantage of the expansion of political and social space. Some Cubans who have left the country fund networks and contribute to more heterodox opinions both on the island and abroad. These individuals sometimes maintain contacts within their former institutions and belong to interlocking networks that exchange information and ideas about Cuba's present and future. The extent and weight of such networks should not be underestimated. They help create spaces for analysis and debate about the course of the Cuban polity and society and undercut the state's monopoly of information relating to current problems. Traditional channels for informing the citizenry—that is, the mass organizations and mass media—have been joined by expanding networks that not only transmit information but also analyze it and offer policy recommendations. Some of these find their way into the independent press and blogs and almost always are circulated among both governmental and nongovernmental elites.

In addition, a more autonomous sector of Cuban civil society has been developing. This sector includes organizations such as the Catholic Center for Civic and Religious Formation (*Centro de Formación Cívica y Religiosa* [CFCR]) in Pinar del Río, the Protestant Christian Center for Reflection and Dialogue (*Centro Cristiano de Reflexión y Diálogo* [CCRD]) in Cardenas, the Father Félix Varela Cultural Center (*Centro Cultural Father Félix Varela*) in Havana, and a plethora of Afro-Cuban groups that span the entire country.[11] Not infrequently, they have undertaken social welfare functions previously exercised by the state. For example, the CCRD in Cardenas is a major provider of socioeconomic assistance through its meals-on-wheels program, community gardens, educational and recreational groups for youth and the elderly, and environmental work.[12] The Center cooperates with government and party officials and receives most of its financial support from church organizations in Europe.[13] It has initiated an ecumenical project to promote reconciliation among Cubans both on the island and abroad. In Pinar del Río, the CFCR, through its former publication *Vitral*, was a prime outlet for the expression of critical opinions by ordinary citizens about government policies and programs.[14] In 2008, a new publication titled *CONVIVENCIA* was created by some former *Vitral* associates after some Catholic and Communist Party leaders expressed discomfort with the extent of the criticism.[15] Among autonomous international humanitarian organizations, the

Catholic Relief Service (CARITAS) has developed a national distribution network in Cuba to help provide for nutritional and health care needs in cooperation with the government. Cuban Masons and B'nai B'rith serve similar functions with assistance from their foreign counterparts.

At the local level, government officials, hospitals, convents, and churches frequently work together. Such efforts have served to increase nongovernmental input into governmental operations as well as increase the dependence of the state on nonstate actors. Considerable emphasis has been placed on strengthening civil society as well as developing mechanisms for conflict resolution and reconciliation with a view toward the future. In the past few years, there has been a proliferation of political parties, human rights groups, independent journalists, blogs, youth groups, and community groups, among others. Networking among them has increased substantially, suggesting that associationalism in Cuba is today stronger than in any period since the 1960s. This cannot but help increase public space and perhaps erode somewhat the government's ideological and political hegemony.

Government-organized nongovernmental organizations sometimes express alternative opinions and advance new policies by using traditional channels and the strength of their expertise as well as their informal networks. For those groups without large constituencies—including those that are clearly oppositional—the margins for operating are limited. The decline in the state's capacity to maintain ideological and political consensus in Cuban society has led to the use of coercion against some groups, including both those fully autonomous and those operating under the supervision of the state. The Catholic Church, however, has in recent years been somewhat exempt from close monitoring.

WHAT IS THE ROLE OF RELIGION IN A CHANGING CUBA?

In Cuba, the government appears to view the Catholic Church as a useful instrument in providing services as well as a facilitator in resolving vexing problems, such as the release in 2010–2011 of dissidents detained in 2003 and earlier. Although the Catholic Church in Cuba does not have extraordinary institutional weight and popular support, it has been able to occupy increasing political and social space without substantial governmental push-back. Competition among human rights, reformist, dissident, and opposition groups in Cuba is high and impedes attempts to achieve a common agenda. Efforts such as *Consenso Cubano*, *Principios Arcos*, and *Diálogo Nacional* to build a consensual agenda appear to have drawn more support abroad than from the island, revealing additional cleavages between internal and external civil society groups.[16] Nevertheless, a consistent plea on the part of all religions has been for reconciliation and consensus for the common good.

The nature of Cuban civil society does not, as a result, lend itself to the building of a single mobilizing agenda largely because of its multicentrism. There is in Cuba some continued support for socialism, albeit reformed, as well as a deep-seated resistance to outside interference rooted in an extended colonial past and infringed sovereignty that helped give rise to nationalist sentiments that continue to cut across the political spectrum. Hence, some critics of the current government, as well as opponents, agree on the desirability of retaining aspects of socialism, particularly in view of the poverty of some neighboring countries with free market capitalist systems. In Cuba itself, the increase in inequality and the emergence of new socioeconomic strata suggest the utility of examining Cuban civil society as an intense arena of contestation over policies, particularly those related to resource distribution. It is thus important to distinguish between the characterization of civil society coming from the government.

Despite the government's characterization of civil society as either exclusively "socialist" or as a "fifth column" on behalf of the United States, the reality of civic activity on the island is more complex. Civil society in Cuba is neither an exclusive space for the maintenance of the existing order nor an exclusive space for political opposition to the regime. At the same time, the symbolic apparatus of the state still gives it an important source of power to stimulate consensus in society, especially in terms of the defensive project of the state in relation to the historical hostility of the U.S. toward the revolutionary regime, which many Cubans, including dissidents, identify as a threat to Cuban sovereignty. Religious groups have also repeatedly warned against outside intervention in Cuba. Beyond domestic realities in Cuba, the global criticism of neoliberalism has also helped the Castro regime retain some legitimacy, particularly in Latin America. Thus, it is not accurate to pose a clear-cut division between civil society and the dominant state project. While horizontal links within civil society are still somewhat limited, there is a complex set of networks that connect civil society and the state, creating a scenario that cannot be reduced to a model of "civil society against the state."

Failure of the government's economic model to fully meet the basic socioeconomic needs of Cubans has been linked by some religious leaders, in part, to a lack of effective citizen participation in determining public policies and securing governmental accountability. In a 1999 visit to Rome, the Cardinal of Havana, Monsignor Jaime Ortega y Alamino, stated that given that the Revolution had raised the hopes of so many and mobilized Cubans to create a more just society, the Catholic Church had a duty to help preserve the achievements of the Revolution. At the same time, he argued, the church had an obligation to help the Cuban people transcend the Revolution's limitations, particularly through increased popular participation in government decision making. The latter, he posited, could best be achieved through intensifying evangelization so that the laity would be better prepared to act through a mobilized civil society.[17]

In order to facilitate this, the Catholic Church adopted Global Pastoral Plans for 1997–2000, 2000–2005, 2006–2010, and 2011–2016. The stated objective was to promote evangelization via prophetic and enculturated communities that would disseminate the gospel message in order to promote human dignity, reconciliation, and the construction of a society characterized by love and justice. This would require the strengthening of faith-based communities in which all individuals would be regarded as children of God and therefore treated justly.[18] This required substantial resources, in terms of both monies and personnel, which were in short supply.

Some clerical and lay leaders felt that the 1997–2000 Plan was too general and not sufficiently proactive. A group of priests issued a public critique arguing that a basic prerequisite had to be overcoming the profound passivity of citizens inculcated by the political system. In addition, they felt that calls by both the Catholic and other churches for a national dialogue were flawed because they were premised on the government's willingness to dialogue. Some priests proposed that what the Catholic Church should do instead was create a national dialogue that included a broad coalition of civil society sectors, including other churches, fraternal organizations, and autonomous groups.[19] Others, including Christian Democratic groups, have called for a dialogue among all Cubans. To date, there has not been the necessary strength and unity of purpose within the religious sphere or within civil society more generally to realize such an effort.

There are additional impediments to the religious community mobilizing civil society. Virtually all religions in Cuba suffer from a scarcity of resources and face increasing demands for humanitarian assistance from the Cuban populace. Most of the material resources available come from abroad and are subject to government regulation and control, thereby encouraging caution on the part of churches and other religious organizations. They, as well as foreign religious donors, have been careful not to become identified with some of the dissident or oppositional sectors of civil society. Even so, the increased role of religious groups in responding to the socioeconomic needs of the population has expanded the credibility and influence of most religions within civil society.

Overall, while religious groups are emerging as critical elements of a slowly revitalizing civil society, there is an understandable desire on their part not to precipitate serious conflicts with the government. While religious leaders, by and large, may have become more publicly critical of the government, this has not translated into substantial efforts on their parts to mobilize civil society. The 1998 visit of Pope John Paul II raised hopes that religion would occupy substantially more political space than it had previously. Such hopes were not realized, in part because religions in Cuba have never exercised power comparable to that of their counterparts in Poland, Chile, or Spain. The visit was, in fact, the pragmatic result of the conjunction of limited agendas on the part of the Vatican and the Cuban government.

The Vatican and the Cuban episcopacy aimed at consolidating the revitalization of the Catholic Church and thereby facilitating the reevangelization of the island. Preaching the gospel and disseminating Catholic social doctrine with its emphasis on socioeconomic justice has been a principal goal not only of the Cuban episcopacy but also of the Vatican. Transforming societies was to be achieved through the conversion of hearts and minds. Indeed, the Cuban Catholic Church appears to be committed to positioning itself to stabilize the country as it experiences considerable change. This objective was affirmed by the statements of Pope Benedict XVI during his March 2012 visit to Cuba. Pursuit of this agenda requires more public space than resulted from the popes' visits, leaving the Catholic, as well as Protestant leadership, frustrated but not to the extent of allying themselves with strongly oppositional sectors of civil society in Cuba or outside.

Since 1998, church-state relations in Cuba have been characterized by a degree of cooperation, albeit with some discomfort on both sides. The Catholic bishops have been increasingly publicly critical of the government. The latter has responded occasionally by questioning the motives of the episcopacy and alleging that they are giving support to Cuba's enemies. Protestant and Jewish leaders have been less publicly critical of the government, focusing more on consolidating gains in membership and securing resources to tend to the needs of their members and the broader community. Spiritist leaders range across the spectrum in terms of their positions, with many focusing on meeting the socioeconomic needs of their communities, including through cultivating government sources. Horizontal links among the various religious communities are not strong because of historical rivalries, residual prejudices, and differing agendas.

Nevertheless, there is currently a "ripening" of civil society under way in Cuba, and religions are prime actors in the process. Citizens are occupying new spaces outside government control and gradually reshaping the everyday experience of state-society and citizen-citizen interaction. While widespread societal discontent (and hence pressure) exists, it has not been transformed into substantial civil society mobilization. There clearly is a growing level of organization and pressure on the government to respond more effectively to citizen needs, but this inchoate movement lacks a recognized national leadership and a broad-based consensual agenda. The development of a national leadership requires increased construction of horizontal links and interaction among proactive citizens and associations. Can religious groups facilitate the development of such leadership? There have been some efforts by various religions to train community leaders, professionals, youths, and others to take a more active role in civil society, but there has not been a coalescing of such individuals around a consensual agenda.

Can the principles and norms that sustain a strong civil society be a basis for the incorporation of self-organized groups into a socialist system, thus making it more pluralistic and participatory? If a pluralistic civil society were deemed compatible with Cuban socialism, then a program of reforms would have to focus on expanding structures of participation in such a way that they would not be totally subsumed by centralized political or economic structures.[20] Some analysts posit that Cuba could deepen the autonomy of mass organizations as a way of allowing civil society to help rebuild social and political consensus. Thus far, however, the Cuban political class has restricted the debate about civil society and limited the broadening of the public sphere, arguing that civil society could become a "fifth column" on behalf of the United States.

At the same time, globalization has resulted in the penetration of Cuba by nonsocialist norms and behaviors, including those transmitted by tourists, businesses, and religious actors.[21] One of the most notable developments is the intensification of international exchanges between religious organizations at both the macro and the micro level. This has been stimulated by a variety of humanitarian efforts as well as the natural impulse to build community with one's counterparts.[22] It has resulted in more discussion of the need for religious groups to formally undertake a role in promoting reconciliation, including developing a theology of reconciliation, among Cubans on the island and with Cubans abroad. Such a development could help increase the likelihood of a consensual civil society agenda.

Given that religions in Cuba are increasingly playing an intermediary role (both formally and informally) between state and society in meeting the latter's needs, can religious actors gradually assume a mediating role? Does increasing governmental and societal dependence on religious actors—national and international—provide a real opportunity for religions to influence the direction of society? The indications to date are that the government would be uncomfortable with such a development. Furthermore, given the broad spectrum of opinions within the religious sector over the island's future and the extent of the restructuring under way, would there be a consensus that goes much beyond the need for change? In the 1950s, the vast majority of Cubans supported an end to the Batista regime, but there was no overall agreement on what precisely should replace it, thereby providing Fidel Castro with the opportunity to introduce his own ideas. To what degree will a civil society with strong strains of secularism be willing to accept a substantial leadership role by religions even if the latter have the most extensive institutional presence and networks? In short, what is the disposition of Cuban citizens to accept the leadership of religions in building the Cuban society of the future?

In recent years, religious groups have often served as a stimulus for the growth of activism in civil societies, particularly in countries experiencing substantial pressures for change. In Cuba, where the revolutionary government initially attempted to subsume organized civil society into the state and marginalize religions, the possibilities for religions to assume a major leadership role in determining Cuba's future are unclear. Not only are there obstacles resulting from the limits imposed by the state, but there are also signs that religions in Cuba are not decisively disposed to work for such incorporation, though there is, at present, considerable difference of opinion on this point. While there has been an upsurge in church attendance and involvement in religious groups in recent years, it is possible that if there were more secular associational alternatives, the current popularity of religious involvement might decline. On the other hand, it is a misperception to assume that the current attraction of religion in Cuba is solely for the material resources provided. High levels of anomie and alienation in

Cuba, as well as loss of faith in the Revolution by a good number of Cubans, especially young people, have fueled a fairly generalized search for spiritual and psychological consolation through religion.

In short, although Cuba has a strong history of associational activity, with deep historical roots and a society permeated with religious beliefs, these historical legacies have not succeeded in coalescing civil society. The state continues to maintain considerable political hegemony in the face of a variety of counterdiscourses that have had limited impact over society in general, in large measure given historical cleavages and sectoralism that have been exacerbated by tensions among Cubans within and without the island. As a result, while Cubans have a history of strong associationalism, together with a tradition of religious beliefs informing civil society, neither appears to have sufficient strength at present to guarantee that a religiously informed civil society could determine the outcome of the process that is currently under way in Cuba.

NOTES

This essay is an elaboration of ideas initially presented in Margaret E. Crahan, ed., *Religion, Culture, and Society: The Case of Cuba* (Washington, DC: Woodrow Wilson International Center for Scholars, 2003), and is an update of Margaret E. Crahan and Ariel C. Armony, "Rethinking Civil Society and Religion in Cuba," in *Debating Cuban Exceptionalism*, ed. Bert Hoffman and Laurence Whitehead (New York: Palgrave Macmillan, 2007), 139–63. The author wishes to acknowledge the substantial contributions of Ariel Armony. In addition, the author is grateful for the support of the Rockefeller Foundation's Bellagio Study and Conference Center, the Center for Philanthropy and Civil Society of the City University of New York, and City University's Collaborative Grant #80209-02-12.

1. The UN Development Program ranks Cuba fifty-first among the nations of the world in terms of its Human Development Index based on a variety of socioeconomic indicators. UN Development Program, *Human Development Report 2007/2008*, http://hdr.undp.org/en.

2. In 1960, nominal Catholics constituted approximately 70 to 75 percent of the total population of 7,500,000, while Protestants amounted to 3 to 6 percent. The Jewish community numbered approximately 12,000 in the 1950s, while spiritists were estimated at about 65 percent of the total population, overlapping with other religions. In the late 1980s, the *Centro de Investigaciones Psicológicas y Sociológicas* estimated that 65 to 85 percent of Cubans believed in the supernatural, while 13.6 percent did not. In the mid-1990s, believers were estimated to constitute approximately 85 percent of the population. Currently, regular practitioners are estimated by various religious sources to be around 1 to 3 percent. For an examination of Cuban religious statistics, see Margaret E. Crahan, "Cuba," in *Religious Freedom and Evangelization in Latin America: The Challenge of Religious Pluralism*, ed. Paul E. Sigmund (Maryknoll, NY: Orbis Books, 1999), 297–98, and Margaret E. Crahan, "The Church of the Past and the Church of the Future," in *Cuban Socialism in a New Century: Adversity, Survival, and Renewal*, ed. Max Azicri and Elsie Deal (Gainesville: University Press of Florida, 2004), 123–46.

3. Alfonso Quiroz, "The Evolution of Laws Regulating Associations and Civil Society in Cuba," in Margaret E. Crahan, ed., *Religion, Culture, and Society: The Case of Cuba* (Washington, DC: Woodrow Wilson International Center for Scholars, 2003), 59–63.

4. A 1957 survey of 4,000 agricultural workers in Cuba revealed that while 96.5 percent believed in God, 41.4 percent claimed no religious affiliation. In addition, although 52.1 percent claimed to be Catholic, more than half of them (53.5 percent) stated that they had never laid eyes on a priest, and only 7.8 percent ever had any contact with one. Oscar A. Echevarría Salvat, *La Agricultura Cubana, 1934–1966: Régimen social, productividad y nivel de vida del sector agrícola* (Miami: Ediciones Universal, 1971), 14–15.

5. Catholic Action, which originated in Europe in the 1920s and championed political and economic reforms that could undercut the appeal of socialism, was identified with Christian Democratic parties and movements. *Agrupación Católica* members tended to be identified with social democracy.

6. Quiróz, "The Evolution of Laws Regulating Associations and Civil Society in Cuba," 63–64.

7. The most active religious publication in contributing to a broader debate on current problems in Cuba is *Espacio Laical* established by the Archdiocese of Havana. For a survey of all religious publications in Cuba, see Margaret E. Crahan, "Expansion of the Religious Media in Contemporary Cuba," in *Handbook of Contemporary Cuba*, ed. Mauricio Font (Boulder, CO: Paradigm Publishers, 2013).

8. See Mary P. Ryan, "Civil Society as Democratic Practice: North American Cities during the Nineteenth Century," in *Patterns of Social Capital: Stability and Change in Historical Perspective*, ed. Robert I. Rotberg (Cambridge: Cambridge University Press, 2001), 242; Mark E. Warren, *Democracy and Association* (Princeton, NJ: Princeton University Press, 2001), 162–81; and Iris Marion Young, "State, Civil Society, and Social Justice," in

Democracy's Value, ed. Ian Shapiro and Casiano Hacker-Cordón (Cambridge: Cambridge University Press, 1999), 157.

9. See Adrian H. Hearn, *Cuba: Religion, Social Capital, and Development* (Durham, NC: Duke University Press, 2008).

10. On recent Cuban economic developments, including the evolution of the informal sector, see Jorge Mario Sánchez, "Challenges of Economic Restructuring in Cuba," *Socialism and Democracy* 26, no. 3 (November 2012): 139–61; Richard E. Feinberg, *Reaching Out: Cuba's New Economy and the International Response* (Washington, DC: Brookings Institution Press, 2011); Philip Peters, *A Viewer's Guide to Cuba's Economic Reforms* (Arlington, VA: Lexington Institute, 2012); and Philip Peters, *Cuba's Entrepreneurs: Foundation of a New Private Sector* (Arlington, VA: Lexington Institute, 2012).

11. Adrian Hearn's *Cuba* describes in detail the role of Afro-Cuban religious groups in a variety of community development projects.

12. For the breadth of the Center's work, see its website at http://www.ccrd.org.

13. Religious groups in Cuba have expanded ties to their counterparts, particularly in Europe and the United States, including congregation to congregation as well as between national religious organizations, such as the national councils of churches of Cuba and the United States. Katrin Hansing and Sarah J. Mahler, "God Knows No Borders: Transnational Religious Ties Linking Miami and Cuba," in Crahan, *Religion, Culture, and Society*, 123–29.

14. http://www.vitral.org.

15. http://www.convivenciacuba.com.

16. Consenso Cubano, http://www.consensocubano.org/eng/whatiscc.htm;cubafacts.com; "New Dissident Initiatives," http://www.cubafacts.com/Humanrights/HRPers99/hrpers99p.5.htm.

17. Jaime Ortega y Alamino, "Discurso de Mons. Jaime Ortega y Alamino: Visita Ad Limina de los Obispos de Cuba, 25.VI.94," Rome, June 25, 1994.

18. Conferencia de Obispos Católicos de Cuba, *Plan Global Pastoral, 1997–2000* (Havana: Secretariado General de la COCC, 1996), 2–4; Obispos Católicos de Cuba, *Plan Global de Pastoral, 2006–2010*, April 19, 2009, http://www.iglesiacubana.org/contens/ind_4doc.htm.

19. "Cuba, Its People and Its Church," *LADOC* 30 (July/August 2000): 11–17.

20. Ariel C. Armony, "Civil Society in Cuba: A Conceptual Approach," in Crahan, *Religion, Culture, and Society*, 26.

21. Armony, "Civil Society in Cuba: A Conceptual Approach," 17–36.

22. Hansing and Mahler, "God Knows No Borders," 123–30.

Chapter Seven

From Cyberspace to Public Space?

The Emergent Blogosphere and Cuban Civil Society

Ted A. Henken and Sjamme van de Voort

Today, with the development of information technologies, . . . social networks, . . . computers and the Internet, to prohibit something is nearly an impossible chimera. It makes no sense.
—Miguel Díaz-Canel, first vice president of Cuba, closing speech of the National Preparatory Seminar, May 6, 2013 (Ravsberg 2013b)

While there are hundreds, perhaps more than a thousand individual Cuban blogs, this chapter focuses on the four most active and prominent blogger "collectives" to have formed on the island over the past six years (2008–2013): *Voces Cubanas*, *Havana Times*, *Bloggers Cuba*, and *La Joven Cuba*.[1] We seek to examine the extent to which they have both influenced and become an important part of Cuba's expanding public sphere. Although distinct from one another, they share a common four-front battle to: (1) establish their legitimacy and authenticity, (2) maintain a degree of independence while preserving their access to the Internet, (3) increase their visibility and accessibility to the national and international public, and (4) reach out to dialogue, debate, and collaborate with one another. These efforts take place in a polarized political context where pioneering users of social media are routinely dismissed as either "*oficialistas*" (Cuban government propagandists) or "*mercenarios*" (U.S. government lackeys).

We seek to understand Cuban bloggers' strategies dealing with the following challenges:

- How do they resolve the conflict between self-preservation and self-censorship—that is, how do they deal with the dilemma of the *doble moral* (duplicity)?
- How do they preserve an independent and critical posture toward Cuban reality in a context where the mass media are under government control and where nearly all Internet access points are mediated (and likely monitored) by institutions, by money, or by some other kind of influence or control?
- How do they access the Internet, who can revoke that access, and under what conditions?
- Who is their audience, and how do they maintain an interactive relationship with them in such a disconnected environment?
- What have been the biggest obstacles to engaging in dialogue, debate, and collaboration with other bloggers both within and outside Cuba?

In meeting the challenges of legitimacy, independence, access, and visibility, Cuba's bloggers have gradually pushed the limits of critical debate beyond relatively safe private and cyberspaces into more risky public spaces. By taking advantage of the less mediated space that is the Internet, they have challenged the unwritten rule that has long regulated critical expression in Cuba: *"bajo techo, todo; en la calle, nada"* (under the roof [i.e., in private], everything; in the street [i.e., in public], nothing) (Hoffmann 2011). In other words, the use of cyberspace has allowed them to test the silent understanding that criticisms "should be voiced inside state institutions and directly to the authorities in charge, . . . not . . . voiced publicly" (Geoffray 2013, 11).

CUBAN CIVIL SOCIETY AND THE PUBLIC SPHERE IN THE INTERNET AGE

The weakening of political hegemony in Cuba since the turn of the century has allowed elements of civil society to gradually occupy new spheres as the state draws back from various economic and social spaces that it previously monopolized. Cuba's many religious institutions, together with the various publications they sponsor, are also an important and increasingly dynamic element of Cuban civil society. This is especially true of the Catholic Church and its semi-independent publications *Espacio Laical* and *Palabra Nueva*. One might also include Cuba's many state-sanctioned mass organizations themselves, given their embeddedness in many people's lives. However, their limited autonomy prevents them from resisting subordination to the state except in rare instances. In practice, they normally function as mere consultation and "transmission belts" for top-down state policies.

Haroldo Dilla and Phillip Oxhorn (2002, 11) define civil society in Cuba as "the social fabric formed by a multiplicity of self-constituted, territorially based units which peacefully coexist and collectively *resist subordination* to the state, at the same time that they *demand inclusion* into national political structures" (emphasis in the original). By this definition, institutions of civil society need not be absolutely independent from the state or have an antistate agenda. However, they must exercise significant autonomy from the state; have some organic, sui generis base; appeal to or derive from elements within the national territory; seek to impact national issues; and accept nonviolent coexistence with other civil and political organizations.

Although many conditions for the development of a civil society and a singular yet pluralistic public sphere are present in Cuba, what existed until the mid-2000s were multiple, parallel, but largely segmented spheres of debate (Chaguaceda 2011a, 2011b; Chaguaceda and Cilano 2009; Geoffray 2013)—most of them not truly "public" given their limited visibility and accessibility. Some of these are clearly captured and controlled by the political leadership, others are defiantly independent (sometimes with outside support), and still others strive to maintain a modicum of independence without being considered outside of and thus opposed to the Revolution. Geoffray (2013) argues that by the mid-2000s, a variety of small, closed spaces, or "micro-arenas" had developed, including (1) a *dissident* arena, (2) a *critical* arena (often inside state institutions and elite intellectual publications, such as the journals *Temas* and *Criterios*), (3) a *contentious* arena (led by self-educated artists and marginalized intellectuals), and (4) a *diasporic* arena that consciously engaged with island publics (best exemplified by the now defunct literary journal *Encuentro de la Cultura Cubana*).

Since 2007, many of these formerly isolated contentious voices[2] have begun to make critical use of new information and communication technologies in order to overcome these obstacles and begin to stitch together a more intricate and integrated public sphere (Díaz 2013; Geoffray 2013). While nearly all the Cuban bloggers who make up the collectives that we profile here are "territorially based" in Cuba, they simultaneously inhabit a complex transnational space, often relying on hosting, servers, administrators, webmasters, translators, and even some financing from outside of Cuba, not to mention drawing the bulk of their readers, commentators, and critics from abroad as well.

FROM *NADA* TO *"NAUTA"*: INTERNET PENETRATION AND ACCESS IN CUBA

The most recent official Cuban statistics indicate that 23.2 percent of the island's population has access to the Internet (*Oficina Nacional de Estadísticas* 2012). However, this refers only to people with access to e-mail and the island's limited domestic *Red Cuba*, or national *"intranet."* Estimates are that only 5 percent of the population has access to the Internet proper, some at their workplaces and schools, others at hotels, and still others via the black market (Freedom House 2012). Although some professionals and government officials are provided legal household access, it remains impossible for the Cuban public to legally contract a home-based connection. In spite of the recent legalization of the sale of mobile phones, it remains virtually impossible to access the Web via a smart phone in Cuba as Wi-Fi "hot spots" are exceedingly rare and costly, intended mainly for foreign tourists.

Because of the U.S. embargo, since the mid-1990s when Cuba came online, its Internet connection was exclusively via satellite. However, after years of delays, a fiber-optic cable from Venezuela reached Cuba in February 2011, a development that was expected to increase the connection speed by a factor of 3,000. However, more than two years passed before the cable became operational in early 2013. Ongoing financial and infrastructural obstacles, as well as a lack of political will, have so far prevented major improvement in public access to the Web—effectively making the cable a "strong link in a weak chain" (Miroff 2013; Press 2012). Most recently, 118 cybercafés finally began providing Internet service to the public across the island on June 4, 2013 (Del Valle 2013).

While a positive step toward greater access, the new service remains a monopoly of the Cuban state telecom company ETECSA and is available only to those able to pay in hard currency. Current prices remain far out of reach for most Cubans. The $5 (4.50 CUC) cost for one hour of "full" access to international Internet at one of these cybercafés is equal to a full week's average Cuban salary (Díaz Moreno 2013). Additionally, there will be only 334 of these public access computers in the country's 118 cybercafés (Ravsberg 2013a). Furthermore, Internet access will be provided through a tightly controlled "walled garden" format via ETECSA's local server, *"Nauta,"* allowing the government the ability to engage in surveillance and filtering of all content. For example, all "inter-nauts" are required to sign a contract that all but declares that they will be under surveillance, stating that the government reserves the right to block those who engage in activities that "undermine public safety or the country's integrity, economy, independence and sovereignty" (*Café Fuerte* 2013; Sánchez 2013).

NAVIGATING BETWEEN SIRENS: *VOCES CUBANAS, HAVANA TIMES, BLOGGERS CUBA,* AND *LA JOVEN CUBA*[3]

Government policies of the United States and Cuba transform the Cuban Internet into a rough and inaccessible space where it is nearly impossible to navigate without being co-opted by the Scylla of state capture or beholden to the Charibdis of foreign support. Indeed, both governments employ tactics that treat the Internet as a tool for achieving their strategic and geopolitical goals, creating an atmosphere of extreme suspicion and polarization. This means that anyone who wishes to join the Cuban blogosphere while maintaining a degree of independence from the designs and dogmatism of these two camps must go to great lengths to establish and defend their legitimacy as part of a nascent Cuban civil society.

What is now known as *Voces Cubanas* began in December 2004 as a digital magazine named *Consenso desde Cuba*. It then had the format of a traditional magazine and was hosted at the portal *Desdecuba.com*. It was jointly run by Reinaldo Escobar, Yoani Sánchez, Miriam Celaya, Dimas Castellanos, Marta Cortizas, and Eugenio Leal, who made up its editorial board. Since its inception, *Consenso* was established as a virtual space for the development of "citizen journalism" and gave visibility to points of view not found in Cuba's official media or in other publications "conditioned by political requirements." In its first editorial in December 2004, the magazine declared its intention to maintain a moderate tone, distinguishing itself from the intransigence of both the right and the left.

In early 2007, after a little more than two years of existence, *Consenso* was renamed *Contodos* and took on a profile more resembling a blog than that of a traditional magazine. In fact, it included a space for various "portfolios" where a growing number of personal blogs began to appear, starting with Sánchez's own blog, *Generación Y*, in April 2007. The spark that set fire to Sánchez as a blogger was her frustrating participation in the previously described e-mail debate in January and February 2007 known as the *polémica intelectual*. Since then, Sánchez and her husband Escobar, along with a growing group of more than sixty independent cyberactivists, have gone beyond the limited world of e-mail by taking advantage of the interactive social networks that define Web 2.0. Focusing initially on the use of blogs and Twitter, their aim has been to use citizen journalism to expand the space for serious, respectful, and pluralistic debate within Cuba.

Founded in October 2008, *Havana Times* is an independent media experiment begun by the American expatriate Circles Robinson. Invited to work in Cuba in 2001 after seventeen years of residence in Nicaragua, Robinson began working in Cuba as a translator-corrector first for *Prensa Latina* and later for the state translation agency, ESTI, translating articles for the official Cuban media. However, Robinson felt a growing sense of frustration with the poor quality of the work he had to translate. In response, he began to look for a medium that could reflect the many Cuban voices that he was hearing around him every day but that never seemed to be included in the official press. His answer was *Havana Times*, which he launched in October 2008 with the help of a Cuban residing in Spain, a handful of U.S.-based translators, and a small group of young Cuban writers on the island who provided most of the content.

From the beginning, the project was intended to be an alternative to the official media while avoiding falling into the twin traps of implacable criticism or uncritical praise. The site proudly declares itself "an independent source of news and opinion about and from Cuba." When asked the meaning of the word "independent," Robinson replied, "Independent of both the Cuban government and the U.S. government and Cuban exile groups in Miami and all programs that they fund directly or indirectly. Independent of any political party, organization, or movement." Maintaining this independence has been a challenge given that Robinson has had to recruit writers "in a country where working for an independent digital medium is considered taboo by the government and most citizens." He explained that all those interested in participating had to be "willing to take the risk of possible persecution in their personal and professional lives." Robinson insists that he never asked anyone's permission to start *Havana Times* and that no one from the Communist Party or the government has censored it directly.

Bloggers Cuba was born in fits and starts between June and September 2008. Its original Web presence lasted until December 2009, when it inexplicably went offline. After a year and a half in the dark, the *Bloggers Cuba* community reappeared on July 8, 2011, back at its original domain http://www.bloggerscuba.com.[4] This time around, the group made more explicit its purpose by including a declaration of principles on its renovated site. The most interesting aspect of this new statement is its criticism not only of Cuba's "national media" for its failure to reflect Cuban reality but also of the foreign media for presenting a distorted image of that reality. Likewise, the group is at pains to clarify that it believes in pluralism, diversity, and inclusiveness on the one hand and "the right to self determination and sovereignty, social justice and equality" on the other. That is, *Bloggers Cuba* attempts to establish its independence and credibility by taking both the domestic state media and the foreign corporate media to task and by trying to simultaneously reconcile the goals of democracy, nationalism, and socialism.

The group's best-known blogger is Elaine Díaz, University of Havana professor of communications, whose blog is titled *La Polémica Digital*. Also active are the race and gender activists Sandra Álvarez (whose personal blog carries the provocative name *Negra cubana tenía que ser*—"It must've been a black Cuban woman") and Yasmín Portales as well as Portales's husband, Rogelio Díaz Moreno. The majority of the members of *Bloggers Cuba* work as educators, researchers, or writers in the state sector and enjoy institutional access to the Internet, a reason for them to moderate their critical language. Still, they have been sharply critical of various aspects of Cuba's current social and political reality and especially dismissive of certain officials and journalists whom they see as decidedly opportunistic or demagogic. At the same time, in their criticisms they always attempt to remain clearly "within the Revolution," justifying their arguments with references to socialist principles and the various reform-minded statements from government leaders starting with President Raúl Castro. Most members of *Bloggers Cuba* share a profound belief in the ideals of socialism, mixed with a growing frustration over the often insurmountable state bureaucracy, the opportunism of many party and government officials, and the limited means available for open, honest debate.

In essence, *La Joven Cuba* is a project that defends socialism and Cuba's national sovereignty while roundly criticizing many self-described "independent bloggers," such as Yoani Sánchez and Miriam Celaya (of *Voces Cubanas*) based on their supposed lack of independence. The site's creators are three graduate students and professors at the University of Matanzas (Harold Cárdenas, Roberto Peralo, and Osmany Sánchez). Founded in April 2010 with the conscious purpose of not only "defending the Revolution but also [of facilitating] an internal debate about its present and future," the site aims to push back against what its creators saw as the "unjust manipulation of the facts about the Internet in Cuba" both in the international press and on dissident blogs.

La Joven Cuba's blog roll references a group of the most staunchly official, proregime blogs and news sources. In contrast, one of the richest sections of *La Joven Cuba* is the normally diverse and extensive chain of comments that quickly appears after each of their posts. Often growing to more than fifty entries, these exchanges sometimes become real debates that extend far beyond the content of the original post and include a group of quite faithful visitors. Indeed, many of their visitors are Cuban exiles. For example, statistics published on the portal indicate that of the 107,000 total unique visitors to the site in its first eighteen months of existence, almost 95 percent are from outside Cuba with the largest number being from the United States (23,533, or 22 percent of the total). Thus, while both *Generación Y* and *Voces Cubanas* are often criticized for having no following in Cuba and catering to an exclusively international audience, *La Joven Cuba*—like *Havana Times* and *Bloggers Cuba*—also has far more international than domestic readers. The majority of these visitors clearly do not share the progovernment orientation of the blog's administrators, often openly and eloquently critiquing their arguments. However, they engage with the authors of each post in a respectful tone and a spirit of free debate. Still, as we will chronicle below, it was likely their tolerance of frank debate, combined with the sharp, critical tone of some of their most popular posts from the early summer of 2012, that led to the blog's being temporarily blocked (Ulloa 2013).

BLOGAZO POR CUBA AND THE CLICK FESTIVAL: FROM CYBERSPACE TO PUBLIC SPACE

On November 8, 2011, Cuba's Twittosphere welcomed a new user with the handle @CastroEspinM. Mariela Castro Espín, the daughter of Cuban President Raúl Castro, and his late wife Vilma Espín, longtime president of the Federation of Cuban Women, had joined Twitter. Apart from her illustrious revolutionary pedigree, Mariela Castro's entry into Cuban cyberspace was notable given her role as a trailblazer directing Cuba's National Center for Sexual Education, an organization that has fought for equal rights for sexual minorities on the island. Castro subsequently used Twitter to announce her plans to participate in Cuba's first official gathering of self-described "revolutionary" bloggers organized at the University of Matanzas by *La Joven Cuba* at the end of April 2012, calling the event "an opportunity to socialize with protagonists of the Cuban blogosphere." She followed up this initial mention of the planned *Blogazo*, more properly named "*Encuentro de Blogueros Cubanos en Revolución*" (Gathering of Cuban Bloggers in Revolution), with a series of messages that clearly communicated her belief in the "revolutionary" power of social media. "New technologies can be vehicles of revolutionary methods of social participation," she wrote. "The blogosphere [provides] spaces of revolutionary debate." Finally, while attending the event itself at the end of April, Castro engaged in a bit of public criticism of the Cuban press, just as her father Raúl himself had already done in a series of speeches. "The best journalism in Cuba today," she claimed, "is in the blogosphere, as Cuban as the palm trees."

Mariela Castro's and Yoani Sánchez's competing use of social media has laid bare two competing notions of Cuban civil society. On the one hand, Sánchez celebrates Twitter and other similar technologies because she believes that they enable Cuba's citizen journalists like her to challenge the state monopoly over mass media. One need not obtain the permission of a gatekeeping institution of Cuba's socialist civil society in order to *demand inclusion* into national political structures," in the words of Dilla and Oxhorn (2002, 11). On the other hand, Castro believes that there is no legitimate participation in Cuban civil society outside of socialism or the Revolution. She considers those who attempt to do so illegitimate since they are supposedly supported and controlled by extraterritorial entities. At the same time, however, she clearly believes that blogs, Twitter, and other forms of social media can be harnessed by revolutionaries not only to defend socialism but also to strengthen the Revolution and make it more inclusive.

This was exactly the goal of the late April *Blogazo*: to convene a group of critical yet revolutionary bloggers to use their blogs to "defend and perfect socialism." However, while they intended to celebrate diversity and respect the individuality of and differences among the more than fifty bloggers invited to the event, the bloggers explicitly acknowledged that they write "within" or in support of the Cuban Revolution (Biddle 2012; Ravsberg 2012). At the conclusion of the event, the bloggers even pledged to improve the collaboration of bloggers "in Revolution" and to blog in the spirit of Cuban leaders of the past, such as Che Guevara. In fact, their declaration invoked Fidel Castro's own 1961 "Words to the Intellectuals," when he addressed the censorship fears of a group of Cuban intellectuals at the dawn of the Revolution. "We respect and promote critical thinking," they wrote, "which is necessary . . . in preserving our revolutionary condition, based on the premise that it is not possible to be revolutionary outside of the Revolution" (Biddle 2012; *Blogazo por Cuba* 2012).

This prompted *Bloggers Cuba* member Yasmín Portales, who was not invited to the event, to ask, "And who conducts the 'revolutionary' exam in order to access the Internet in Cuba?" (Portales 2012). Indeed, following the meeting, bitter controversy unfolded around this new iteration of a decades-old question: does the expression of criticism automatically put one "outside" the Revolution, especially when the criticism is happening online? *Bloggers Cuba* blogger Elaine Díaz declined an invitation to the meeting and later criticized it, noting the limited value in convening a group of bloggers who "basically think the same way." She pointed out that bloggers from *Observatorio Crítico* and *Havana Times*, both sites whose authors favor the socialist model (but are often directly critical of the government), were not invited at all. She then added pointedly, "The heterogeneous, diverse, irreverent, highly participatory, generous, and controversial space . . . has been cruelly caricatured [by this meeting]" (Díaz 2012).

An apt postscript to the *Blogazo* appeared in a post by an anonymous *Observatorio Crítico* author, envisioning a world "where public space is the patrimony of all people, not a minority in power." It also pushed back against the idea that either the cyberspace of the emerging Cuban blogosphere or the country's public space should be the exclusive province of revolutionaries, adding, "One must not fear the participation of a person who thinks differently. . . . Indeed, the stimulation of diversity and alternative approaches to the problems and action is what leads to opportunities for the creative enrichment of reality." Finally, responding to those who would claim a right for themselves while denying it to others, the post concluded with a pointed quote from the revolutionary socialist Rosa Luxemburg. "Freedom only for supporters of the government, only for members of one party—no matter how large its membership—is not freedom at all. Freedom is only freedom if it applies to the one who thinks differently" (*Observatorio Crítico* 2012).

Two months after the *Blogazo* event in Matanzas, Havana saw its own public and equally controversial gathering of cyberactivists. This meet-up, however, which called itself the "Click Festival," was distinguished by being open to all comers and co-organized by three independent, nongovernmental entities: *Voces Cubanas*'s Blogger Academy, EBE (a Spanish blogging collective), and *Estado de SATS*. Since none of these groups had access to a large public space in which to hold such an event (a total estimated 300 people attended during the three-day, June 21–23 event), *SATS* founder Antonio Rodiles converted his Miramar home into the event's headquarters. Festival organizers were careful to highlight its independent, pluralistic, and nonideological character. For example, Yoani Sánchez underlined the fact that there would be no "political segregation" or "ideological screen" in the selection of participants, adding pointedly that "the Click Festival will not have a final declaration insulting anyone or engaging in character assassination, much less will it consider the web to be a battlefield against any other group, event or tendency" (Sánchez 2012).

Sánchez also anticipated the obligatory attacks in the state media and tried to preempt the tired claim that such independent civil society activities are illegitimate since they are supposedly paid for by Cuba's foreign enemies, categorically stating, "The resources . . . will come from the organizers and the participants themselves. No party, government, or institution has funded the event, participated in the design of the program, or influenced the initial idea of holding it" (Sánchez 2012). Nevertheless, the day before the festival was to kick off, the hardline Cuban state media website *Cubadebate* included an unsigned editorial titled "The Impossible Innocence of the Click Festival." To drive the point home, the bombastic headline carried the capitalized initials "*CIA*" as part of the Spanish word for innocence, "*inocenCIA*" (*Cubad-*

ebate 2012). The editorial did not mince words in openly linking the supposedly "counterrevolutionary" meeting with the organizers' "unconcealed intention of turning this scenario into a spearhead for their much yearned for construction of a Cuban 'civil society' in the service of Washington" (*Cubadebate* 2012).

In his own commentary on the festival and *Cubadebate*'s response to it, Haroldo Dilla refers to the mortal danger that the creation of an independent public sphere and horizontal social networks represent for a state predicated on a vertical, command-and-control relationship with society. "The problem is a matter of unauthorized social contacts," writes Dilla (2012), "of people who have decided not to ask for permission, of several dozen people who are looking to the sides and not up." In other words, *Cubadebate*'s vociferous reaction to the festival arises from the event's conscious and unapologetic attempt to develop independent, unauthorized social networks that are the building blocks of civil society. Thus, the demagogic message from the official media following the Click Festival was unmistakable. Either you are a blogger "*en revolución*" or you are mercenary (Chaguaceda 2012; Prieto 2012; Robinson 2012). However, even the revolutionary bloggers who hosted the *Blogazo* and trumpeted their loyalty decidedly *within* the parameters set by Fidel Castro's "Words to the Intellectuals" were not immune to suspicion.

THE CUBAN BLOGOSPHERE: ¿TAN CUBANA COMO LAS PALMAS?

Despite the fact that Mariela Castro had celebrated the Cuban blogosphere on her Twitter feed in April 2012 as "the best journalism in Cuba today," calling it "as Cuban as the palm trees," one of the most significant developments in Cuban cyberspace during 2012–2013 was the ten-month "blockade" (July 2012–April 2013) imposed by the University of Matanzas on the proudly revolutionary but also staunchly independent blog of *La Joven Cuba*. In fact, after their original claims that they were only taking a summer "rest" proved spurious, in December 2012, after months of silent frustration, they resorted to posting a bold denunciation on the masthead of the blog that read,

> BLOCKADED: The blog continues blockaded for its administrators and we cannot access it to comment or read its contents, but we will continue publishing thanks to the solidarity of our friends. We are confident that common sense will break the virtual barrier and that we will be able to return to normal in the near future. (Ulloa 2013)

This statement was combined with a chorus of frustrated posts published on other blogs with self-explanatory titles, such as "Am I a counterrevolutionary?" (Cruz 2012b), "Will history absolve them?" (Cruz 2012a), "While Raúl Castro calls for criticism, there are those who stop it" (Manzaneda 2012), and "Blockade of *La Joven Cuba*: Why don't they show their faces?" (Padilla 2013). A few exasperated bloggers even fumed at the supreme irony that the *La Joven Cuba* blog was inaccessible at the University of Matanzas while Yoani Sánchez's much more critical blog was just a click away (Alfonzo 2013; Pérez 2013).

What is new here, of course, is not that a state institution blocked the independent blog of a group of its students but that the blog being blocked turns out to be the very same one administered by the young people who had convened the prorevolutionary *Blogazo* not three months earlier. While the reasons for the closure have never been clarified, it seems that the problems began during May and June 2012 when *La Joven Cuba* published a series of openly critical posts tilting against the mediocrity of the Party newspaper *Granma* and complaining about the slow implementation of the accords agreed to at the January 2012 Party Conference (*Café Fuerte* 2012; Peralo 2012a, 2012b). In fact, in a sign of things to come, their post criticizing the government for not implementing the Party accords quickly enough actually disappeared from the blog a few days after it had been posted, along with the more than 250 comments it had already generated. Then, at the beginning of July, just two days after reaching the 1-million-visitor milestone (Ulloa 2013), an elliptical entry appeared on the blog under the title "*La Joven Cuba* takes a rest," followed by the brief declaration "For many reasons it is very difficult for us to maintain a blog as complex as *La Joven Cuba*. We will take a rest. We hope to be able to continue in the future" (*La Joven Cuba* 2012).

In the case of the closure of *La Joven Cuba*, a key lesson is that even the most revolution-ary voices—and blogs—can be silenced if they insist on editorial independence, if they lodge criticisms that cross over the invisible line separating what is considered "within" from what is "against" the Revolution, and if they depend on a state institution for Internet access. Never-theless, at the end of April 2013, following an unprecedented personal meeting between the blog's young administrators and Cuba's new, fifty-three-year-old First Vice President Miguel Díaz-Canel, "common sense" prevailed (*La Joven Cuba* 2013). In fact, instead of detailing the reasons behind the forced closure or offering an explanation for their reversal of fortune, *La Joven Cuba* came back online by simply posting a smiling group photo with Díaz-Canel (flanked by large portraits of both Fidel and Raúl Castro in the background) under the title "Common sense." As if to drive the point home that the Revolution was now under new, more tolerant and intelligent management, less than two weeks later, on May 6, Díaz-Canel de-livered the speech quoted in the opening epigraph, stating in part that "to prohibit something is nearly an impossible chimera. It makes no sense" (Basile 2013; Ravsberg 2013b).

DISCUSSION: "THE MEDIUM IS THE MESSAGE"

Despite the limited reach of the Internet in Cuba, social media's disruptive potential arises there from the same "leveling" process that it exhibits in other contexts. It blurs the traditional distinction between the public and the private, the real and the virtual, the professional and the amateur, and formal one-to-many broadcasting and informal one-to-one communication. It can also undermine the authority and hegemony of dominant telecom institutions by placing inexpensive broadcast technology in the hands of "the people formerly known as the audi-ence." Furthermore, it allows for greater independent and horizontal communication, sharing of information, convening of publics, crowd-sourcing, "peer production," and creative non-proprietary collaboration through harnessing Cuba's collective surplus time and energy, all abilities that can undermine the power of traditional media (Mandiberg 2012).

The emergent character of social media in Cuba combined with at least an initial hubris on the part of the government has allowed its denizens to begin to share spontaneous critical commentary in what is still an uncharted, ambiguous space, granting them a modicum of safety. That is, while "the street" may still belong to Fidel ("*la calle es de Fidel*" being a typical revolutionary slogan), it is much less clear who Cuban cyberspace belongs to, if anyone (Gámez 2013). Moreover, Cuba's cyberactivists have not been content to remain "in the cloud," forever isolated from one another. Instead, they have sought to turn their visibil-ity—long understood as a dangerous liability—into an asset (Geoffray 2013, 14–16), harness-ing their transnational digital presence (as "the whole world watches") to serve as a protective shield when they dare to occupy the public sphere.

The heated but revelatory debates in the Cuban blogosphere have resulted in opening cracks in the wall of separation (Rojas 2013) that had kept bloggers largely isolated, suspi-cious, and ignorant of one another. In fact, bloggers from different groups have begun to interview, profile, and debate one another, even if those interactions have so far been restricted largely to cyberspace (Calzadilla 2013; Sautié 2013; Rodríguez 2012a, 2012b, 2013). Moreover, the very fact that the members of these various blogging collectives have turned to social media as the platform where they seek to establish their legitimacy, preserve their independence, and engage in a dialogue both with the public and with one another is noteworthy. The horizontal, many-to-many architecture of social media is inherently at odds with the top-down architectural logic of traditional, vertical, one-to-many broadcast media. Indeed, while Cuba's bloggers are diverse, we would do well to remember Marshall McLuhan's now famous dictum that "the medium is the message" (Hoffmann 2011).

While early blogger debates have been largely been restricted to cyberspace—making them all but invisible to the Cuban public, we have chronicled a number of increasingly bold and confident attempts on the part of some of Cuba's bloggers to claim a *public space* for their debates. "These virtual and real activities," writes Geoffray (2013, 28) perceptively, "have played a crucial role for the convergence of micro-arenas that used to be segmented from one another." The convergence of these "allies of convenience" does not necessarily make them political allies. In fact, their lack of any political alliance makes these contentious interactions all the more important in establishing "a more plural and connected public arena" where "protagonists [can] recognize one another as legitimate opponents" (Geoffray 2013, 28). Indeed, in her November 2012 post "Something in common," *Voces Cubanas* blogger Regina Coyula lamented the closure of her sometime nemesis *La Joven Cuba*, with which she had sustained a series of vigorous online debates. "In the country that I envision," she reasoned, "diverse antagonistic ideological currents will coexist, but not as enemies" (Coyula 2012).

NOTES

1. Cuban researcher and blogger Elaine Díaz (2013) has identified three other blogging groups, including *Cuba Blogs Club*, *Blogcip*, and *Observatorio Crítico*. To this we add the site *Cubano1erPlano* run by Alejandro Cruz, which aggregates posts from a variety of Cuban bloggers, journalists, and intellectuals.

2. Apart from the blogger collectives we profile here, three other prominent civil society groups to have emerged since 2007 are *Omni Zona-Franca*, a communitarian poetry and performance group based in Alamar in eastern Havana; *Observatorio Crítico*, a progressive group of young critical socialists who jointly host a blog and periodically carry out independent public activities; and *Estado de Sats*, a forum for civic dialogue with videos posted on the Web founded by Antonio Rodiles.

3. This section is a condensed and slightly updated version of articles that previously appeared in *Cuba in Transition* (Henken 2008, 2011a), *Buena Vista Social Blog* (Henken 2010), and *Nueva Sociedad* (Henken 2011b).

4. In the fall of 2012, however, *Bloggers Cuba* went dark again because of the inability to pay for the hosting cost on a foreign server. Still, many former members of the collective continue to blog, including Elaine Díaz, Sandra Álvarez, Yasmín Portales, and Rogelio Díaz Moreno.

REFERENCES

Alfonzo, Lilith. 2013. "¿Yo extraño a la Joven Cuba, y tú?" *La Joven Cuba*, April 12.
Basile, Vincenzo. 2013. "La prensa cubana silencia la 'crítica al silencio' de Miguel Díaz-Canel." Cubano1erplano.com, May 7.
Biddle, Ellery Roberts. 2012. "Cuba: Questioning Digital Expression within the Revolution." *Global Voices*, May 18. http://globalvoicesonline.org/2012/05/18/cuba-questioning-digital-expression-within-the-cuban-revolution.
Blogazo por Cuba. 2012. "Declaración Final del 'Encuentro de Blogueros Cubanos en Revolución,'" April 28.
Café Fuerte. 2012. "La misteriosa desaparación de *La Joven Cuba* o los hijos de Saturno," July 9. http://cafefuerte. com/cuba/noticias-de-cuba/sociedad/1988-la-misteriosa-desaparicion-de-la-joven-cuba-o-los-hijos-de-saturno.
———. 2013. "Cuba amplía acceso público a internet en moneda convertible," May 28. http://cafefuerte.com/cuba/noticias-de-cuba/sociedad/2882-cuba-ampliara-acceso-publico-a-internet-en-moneda-convertible.
Calzadilla, Erasmo. 2013. "Welcome Home Yoani Sánchez the 'Tube Worm.'" *Havana Times*, June 3. http://www.havanatimes.org/?p=94012.
Chaguaceda, Armando. 2011a. "Medios y esfera(s) pública(s) en Cuba: Entre los malestares y los sueños." *Espacio Laical*, no. 147. http://espaciolaical.org/contens/28/6265.pdf.

————. 2011b. "The Promise Besieged: Participation and Autonomy in Cuba." NACLA Report on the Americas, July/August, 20–25. https://nacla.org/sites/default/files/A04404022_6.pdf.

————. 2012. "Los conspiranoicos y la agresión a *Havana Times.*" *Havana Times*, July 14. http://www.havanatimes.org/sp/?p=67354.

Chaguaceda, Armando, and Johanna Cilano. 2009. "Entre la innovación y el inmovilismo: Espacio asociativo, estado y participación en Cuba." *Pensamiento Propio* 14, no. 29 (January–July).

Coyula, Regina. 2012. "Algo en común." *Penúltimos Días*, November 29.

Cruz, Alejandro. 2012a. "¿La historia los absolverá?" *Observatorio Crítico*, December 11.

————. 2012b. "Soy contrarrevolucionario?" Cubano1erplano.com, November 6.

Cubadebate. 2012. "La inocenCIA imposible del Festival Clic." Editorial, June 20. http://www.cubadebate.cu/especiales/2012/06/20/editorial-la-inocencia-imposible-del-festival-clic.

Del Valle, Amaury. 2013. "Cuba amplía el servicio público de acceso a Internet." *Juventud Rebelde*, May 27. http://www.juventudrebelde.cu/cuba/2013-05-27/cuba-amplia-el-servicio-publico-de-acceso-a-internet.

Díaz, Elaine. 2012. "¿Por quién doblan las campanas?" *La Polémica Digital*, April 29.

————. 2013. "Deliberar en red: Consenso y disenso en la blogosfera cubana." Paper presented at the 32nd International Congress of the Latin American Studies Association, Washington, DC, May 30–June 1.

Díaz Morneo, Rogelio. 2013. "Por sus precios los conoceréis." *Bubusopia Blog*, May 31. http://bubusopia.blogspot.com/2013/05/por-sus-precios-los-conocereis.html.

Dilla, Haroldo. 2012. "Cuba's 'Festival CLIC' and the Vast Majority." *Havana Times*, June 25.

Dilla, Haroldo, and Philip Oxhorn. 2002. "The Virtues and Misfortunes of Civil Society in Cuba." *Latin American Perspectives* 29, no. 4 (July): 11–30.

Freedom House. 2012. "Freedom on the Net, 2012: Cuba." http://www.freedomhouse.org/sites/default/files/Cuba%202012.pdf.

Gámez, Nora. 2013."Technology Domestication, Cultural Public Sphere, and Popular Music in Contemporary Cuba." Paper presented at the 32nd International Congress of the Latin American Studies Association, Washington, DC, May 30–June 1.

Geoffray, Marie Laure. 2013. "Internet, Public Space, and Contention in Cuba: Bridging Asymmetries of Access to Public Space through Transnational Dynamics of Contention." Working Paper No. 42, Desigualdades.net, Research Network on Interdependent Inequities in Latin America. http://www.desigualdades.net/bilder/Working_Paper/42_WP_Geoffray_Online.pdf.

Henken, Ted. 2008. "Desde Cuba con Yoani Sánchez: Animando al periodismo ciudadano digital y desafiando a la violencia verbal." *Cuba in Transition* 18: 83–95. http://www.ascecuba.org/publications/proceedings/volume18/pdfs/henken.pdf.

————. 2010. "En busca de la *Generación Y*: Yoani Sánchez, la blogosfera emergente y el periodismo ciudadano de la Cuba de hoy." In *Buena Vista Social Blog: Internet y libertad de expresión en Cuba*, edited by Beatriz Calvo Peña, 201–42. Valencia: Aduana Vieja.

————. 2011a. "A Bloggers' Polemic: Debating Independent Cuban Blogger Projects in a Polarized Political Context." *Cuba in Transition* 21: 171–85. http://www.ascecuba.org/publications/proceedings/volume21/pdfs/henken.pdf.

————. 2011b. "Una cartografía de la blogósfera cubana: Entre 'oficialistas' y 'mercenarios.'" *Nueva Sociedad*, no. 235, September–October, 90–109. http://www.nuso.org/upload/articulos/3799_1.pdf.

Hoffmann, Bert. 2011. "Civil Society 2.0?: How the Internet Changes State-Society Relations in Authoritarian Regimes: The Case of Cuba." German Institute of Global and Area Studies (GIGA) Working Papers, no. 156, January. http://www.giga-hamburg.de/dl/download.php?d=/content/publikationen/pdf/wp156_hoffmann.pdf.

La Joven Cuba. 2012. "La Joven Cuba se toma un descanso," July 6.

————. 2013. "Sentido Común," April 24.

Mandiberg, Michael, ed. 2012. *The Social Media Reader*. New York: New York University Press. http://digitalrights.net/wp-content/uploads/books/Mandiberg-theSocialMediaReader-cc-by-sa-nc.pdf.

Manzaneda, José. 2012. "Blog *La Joven Cuba*: 'En Cuba, mientras nuestro presidente Raúl Castro fomenta la crítica, hay personas que la frenan.'" Cubainformacion.com, December 12.

Miroff, Nick. 2013. "Cuba Internet: Wired, but Not Connected." *Global Post*, January 25. http://www.globalpost.com/dispatch/news/regions/americas/cuba/130124/cuban-undersea-internet-cable-web-connection.

Observatorio Crítico. 2012. "El espacio público es patrimonio de toda la nación," April 4.

Oficina Nacional de Estadísticas. 2012. "Tecnología de la información y las comunicaciones (TIC) en cifras, Cuba." June.http://www.one.cu/publicaciones/06turismoycomercio/TIC%20en%20Cifras%20Cuba%202011/TIC%20en%20Cifras%20Cuba%202011.pdf.

Padilla, Alexei. 2013. "Bloqueo a *La Joven Cuba*: ¿Por qué no muestran el rostro?" *La Chiringa de Cuba*, April 12.

Peralo, Roberto. 2012a. "Los incumplimientos a lo acordado en la Conferencia del PCC." *La Joven Cuba*, May 28.

————. 2012b. "Some Cadres Are Square: A Reply to *Granma.*" *Progreso Weekly*, July 4.

Pérez, Carlos Alberto. 2013. "*Generación Y* Sí, *La Joven Cuba* No." *La Joven Cuba*, April 10.

Portales Machado, Yasmín S. 2012. "Estoy suspensa." *Blog En 2310 y 8225*, April 29. http://yasminsilvia.blogspot.com/2012/04/estoy-suspensa.html.

Press, Larry. 2012. "Pasado, presente y futuro de Internet en Cuba." *Voces* 15: 7–11. http://vocescuba.files.wordpress.com/2012/06/voces15.pdf.

Prieto Samsónov, Dimitri. 2012. "Recordatorio: La difamación en Cuba es un delito." *Observatorio Crítico*, June 20. http://observatoriocriticodesdecuba.wordpress.com/2012/06/20/recordatorio-la-difamacion-en-cuba-es-un-delito.

Ravsberg, Fernando. 2012. "Blogósfera sí . . . pero organizada." *Cartas desde Cuba*, May 3. http://www.bbc.co.uk/blogs/mundo/cartas_desde_cuba/2012/05/blogosfera_si_pero_organizada.html.

———. 2013a. "Cuba's New Cybercafés: A Piecemeal Strategy." *Havana Times*, May 30. http://www.havanatimes.org/?p=93834

———. 2013b. "El tiro por la culata." *Cartas desde Cuba*, May 16.

Robinson, Circles. 2012. "*Havana Times* and Some Low Blows." *Havana Times*, July 5.

Rodríguez, Yusimi. 2012a. "Dimas Castellanos: Cuba Needs a Market Economy with Social Justice." *Havana Times*, May 25. http://www.havanatimes.org/?p=71229.

———. 2012b. "Miriam Celaya, una disidente por naturaleza." *Havana Times*, January 10. http://www.havanatimes.org/sp/?p=55621.

———. 2013. "Cuba: Interview with Reinaldo Escobar, an Independent Citizen." *Havana Times*, February 27 and March 1. http://www.havanatimes.org/?p=88473 and http://www.havanatimes.org/?p=88614.

Rojas, Rafael. 2013. "Reforma y reacción en Cuba." *El País*, May 2. http://elpais.com/elpais/2013/04/22/opinion/1366657694_292595.html.

Sánchez, Yoani. 2012. "A CLICK from Afar." *Generation Y*, June 24. http://www.desdecuba.com/generationy/?p=3037.

———. 2013. "Playa Siboney: La punta del cable de fibra óptica." *Generación Y*, June 10. http://lageneraciony.com/?p=7640.

Sautié Mederos, Félix. 2013. "Entrevista Dimas Decilio Castellaos Martí, historiador y periodista." *Observatorio Crítico*, June 16. http://observatoriocriticodesdecuba.wordpress.com/2013/06/16/entrevista-a-dimas-cecilio-castellanos-marti-historiador-y-periodista.

Ulloa, Alejandro. 2013. "Breve cronología de *La Joven Cuba* (¿o qué revolucionarios hoy para qué Cuba mañana?)." *Esquinas de Cuba*, April 9.

Chapter Eight

The Promise Besieged

Participation and Autonomy in Cuba

Armando Chaguaceda

After the triumph of Cuba's 1959 Revolution, the country established a state socialist regime based on the Soviet model. This model's features are by now well known: state-party fusion, the control and colonization of society by the state, and the systematic obstruction of society's self-organizing capabilities. It has fostered a kind of militant citizenship that identifies state order with the nation, favors unanimity as a way of expressing identities and views, and encourages the social redistribution of wealth and the rejection of exclusion based on gender and race. However, the new revolutionary order established after 1959 also deemed alternative, non-"revolutionary" collectivities and identities—such as homosexuals, religious groups, and some artistic movements—as suspicious (and punishable) even if they did not necessarily oppose the Revolution.

Given this legacy, exploring the contemporary relationship between the Cuban state's policies of citizen participation on the one hand and the practices of autonomy that emerge organically from society on the other can help us assess the current state of affairs in Cuba and explore the potential for greater citizen empowerment in the future.

The current model of participation in Cuba emerged in the 1960s, when the counterrevolutionary opposition ended up in exile and defeat. The subsequent revolutionary process socialized millions of people who participated in social, economic, and political tasks directed by the state: literacy campaigns, agricultural plans, and large public assemblies. As prerevolutionary forms of association disappeared, these gaps were filled by new mass organizations, such as the Committees for the Defense of the Revolution and the Federation of Cuban Women, both organized at the local level. With time, these were joined by other professional and civil associations of, for example, farmers, lawyers, and environmentalists. Social rights to health, education, social security, and employment, together with cultural rights, such as access to artistic training and recreation, became preeminent in the collective imagery. Civil and political rights, meanwhile, were to be conceived and realized only within state institutions and according to the new regime's policies.

By the 1970s, dysfunctions in this scheme began to reveal themselves. Voluntaristic notions of political leadership and social development that appealed to human will, embodied in charismatic leaders and enthusiastic masses, came to obviate institutional mediation and popular deliberation. State-sponsored planning, investment, and production accelerated, generating administrative chaos (most dramatically in the failed 10 Million Ton Harvest of 1967–1970, when the Cuban state launched a campaign to produce a record amount of sugarcane). As a result, the institutional order was restructured more closely along Soviet lines. Despite popular enthusiasm and creativity, both the personalism and the institutionalization of the political regime and its rituals gained strength in subsequent years to the detriment of more autonomous forms of participation. Following the state socialist model, a system of assemblies was formed, called Popular Power, and established at the local, provincial, and national levels, along with centralized ministries. An enormous, more or less professional bureaucracy was put in charge of this system, planning and managing public policy and distributing the economic surplus generated by workers.

The Cuban state has demonstrated its role as the defender of national sovereignty, sponsor of development, and guarantor of social justice through the redistribution of goods and services. But it has also proved its inability to satisfy a great number of Cuban society's expectations for participation, with its vertical model of central management, in which top management positions in the state and in the Communist Party overlap and are occupied by the so-called historical leadership (i.e., Fidel Castro's generation of leaders). At the lower levels, there is usually a similar overlap among party leaders serving as government leaders; this is particularly visible in the provinces and the countryside.

Genuine popular participation would require that people who are not formally part of the state evaluate and correct public policies, a role not currently played by the press or neighborhood associations, human rights defenders, consumers, or parents' associations. Their participation would presuppose the state's respect for and promotion of societal autonomy, which is under siege in contemporary Cuba. Without such participation, institutional performance has become symptomatically precarious, as centralization, administrative discretion, and personalism, from national bodies to local ones, have put a halt on collective dynamism and deliberation. In this system of organizing collective life, social spaces, whether organized or informal, tend to be subsumed or simply controlled by the state within an asymmetrical power structure.

The Cuban press constantly defines the country's regime as a "participatory democracy," while the citizen and the act of participating are viewed in a trivialized and restricted way, bearing the imprint of a state-centric system that weakens the civic commitment required to successfully implement changes. Since 2007, the government has employed classic administrative and technocratic solutions to address demands for improving institutional performance; these solutions include installing new officials to oversee other officials and shrinking the bureaucracy. But there has been no effort to expand citizen participation based either on the socialist traditions of bottom-up collectivities (workers' councils, self-managed businesses, and popular assemblies) or on contemporary democratic innovations that continue to emerge in many parts of Latin America (management boards, social auditing, and roundtables). In preparation for the Communist Party's various congresses, the state has sponsored National Debates that call for a broad discussion of national issues and prioritize consultative forms of participation, but they are territorially fragmented and thematically parochial.

Participation, as it is defined in practice, has a consultative bias in the sense that citizens' discussions take place on courses of action that have already been outlined or determined at higher institutional levels, such as the State Council and Politburo. Thus, the possibilities for participation are minimized to individual voices and the limited aggregation of demands; shaping the agenda and its execution and control is off limits. Policy corrections are exclusively up to the leadership, which operates with total discretion. This has been the experience in the debates ahead of party congresses (1991 and 2010) and discussions of legislative initiatives, such as that of Labor and Social Security (2009), which had great social impact.

This fragmented way of exercising "participatory democracy" and the media's failure to communicate the results of these debates to society prevented the differentiation between personal and social expectations. It also inhibited the formation of collectives capable of advocating policies—in an organized manner and in accordance with existing legislation—with key political caucuses, such as the Communist Party congresses or National Assembly sessions. This is how the socialization and political participation of the citizenry is repressed.

Participation is thematically parochial because in the so-called neighborhood accountability assemblies of Popular Power, the democratic potential is limited almost exclusively to summoning low- and middle-level officials for evaluation. The issues raised almost always deal with unmet demands for goods and services rather than procedural questions or other broader matters. In the end, although removing representatives by grassroots voters is rare, citizen protagonism in this forum, as well as the relatively greater transparency in institutional performance associated with it, is real. But they are limited by a vertical subordination of local organisms according to a conventional approach to the role of the Communist Party as a driving force for the community and the persistence of traditional models of leadership that are authoritarian and personalist. Meanwhile, participation is narrowly viewed as a means of mobilizing.

The Popular Councils, as territorial entities, gather people at the level of neighborhood streets and blocks, serving as channels for local participation. But their effectiveness is limited, and they have even fewer resources, which is why their promising expansion during the 1990s did not produce the expected results, as they were inserted within a vertical, centralized order (even when Popular Council Law 91 formally provides power to these entities for the promotion and stimulation of citizen initiatives). The weakness of the popular economy, the inexistence of urban cooperatives for anything other than agricultural production, the weakness of local and national association, and the absence of legislation and policies for (and from) municipalities have lessened the Popular Councils' role as spaces for participation. As seems to be the case in various Latin American nations with, for example, Citizen Power in Nicaragua and Communal Councils in Venezuela, Cuba seems to now have a "sea of participation that is only an inch deep."

If we add the accumulated material and symbolic exhaustion of the Cuban population after twenty years of socioeconomic crisis and the debilitating effects of a vertical system (which so far has limited the resources and powers available to local authorities), one can understand that many people identify participation (and accountability) with traditional practices, thus limiting potentially emancipatory discourses. In this vein, the Cuban experience with popular education, beyond its attractive rhetoric, has not been able to become the generating principle of a liberating pedagogy because it is confined to work spaces and praxis in small communities—with limited impact on the dynamics of national life—and the evasion of an analysis of the structural factors that reproduce authoritarianism. [1]

Furthermore, social autonomy and the development of policies of participation are inseparable from the quality of political representation and the performance of accountability. Understanding participation as a process that stems from individual action by citizens and reaches collective forms that constitute practices and spaces of representation (managing and electoral councils, participatory budgeting, and so on), the relationship between participation and representation is complementary, given that the legitimacy and effectiveness of the two processes are presupposed. And social autonomy must be strengthened through policies of accountability that allow social actors to determine the responsibility and sanction governmental performance. This would presuppose interaction between social and state agents.

Pernicious consequences, both economic (crushing productive initiatives and self-management) and political (general demobilization), result from channeling "citizen initiative"
through state and party structures and the "mass organizations." Groups that are independent
of the state, including those that are legally registered or recognized (including nongovernmental organizations (NGOs), cultural organizations, and neighborhood movements), are
made invisible by the establishment and by conservative sectors of the academy. While such
groups are recognized as playing subsidiary roles in social functioning, their nongovernmental
character is a cause of apprehension, and they are sanctioned when they contest the government's decisions.

In the 1990s, a group of new civil organizations appeared: centers for training and services
(some of them religious), foundations, fraternities, and Masonic lodges. These more professional entities had operating expenses and a membership that included some paid staff. The
most powerful of them developed complex programs and projects in diverse areas and maintained a formal, stable leadership. They often functioned as mediators between governments,
international groups, and various grassroots organizations, and they generally depended on
external funding (private or governmental or from foundations). Within this segment, there
were entities concerned with various themes, including sexual diversity, environmentalism,
and popular education.[2]

In those years, various neighborhood movements also emerged, many of them associated
with initiatives such as the Workshops for the Integral Transformation of the Neighborhood
(TTIB) and other community projects supported by Cuban associations and their foreign
counterparts. They were essentially local, with almost no connection among them, and tended
to be informal and territorial and had limited access to economic resources. Depending on
external sources, they functioned with neighborhood participation and prevalent women's
leadership. The TTIB were launched in the 1990s when multidisciplinary teams of planners,
psychologists, and cultural activists expanded into twenty Havana neighborhoods with the
purpose of working with neighbors' participation on community issues. Their work was assisted by the Group for Integral Development of the Capital, an entity for metropolitan planning, and they were closely linked to Popular Councils, which generated some conflict because of the latter's traditional authoritarian leadership style and attempts to interfere with the
TTIB's work. Despite the group's proven success, the group's expansion to other neighborhoods in Havana and other provinces was limited by governmental decision.

Faced with these experiences, the state played a contradictory role, providing material
resources and support to the personnel while blocking legal recognition and the consolidation
of self-management in the popular economy and trying to co-opt local productive initiatives.[3]
Even so, these experiences demonstrated reciprocal relations in the form of neighborhood
cooperation, food distribution, and donations and prompted communal benefits for self-employed workers as well as cooperative arrangements to contract their services for projects
supported by civil associations.

Beginning in 1996, the state began restricting the expansion of new associations. They
were excluded from the official Association Registry, new controls were imposed on existing
organizations, and surveillance on external financing was reinforced. Ever since, rather than
grow, the Cuban NGO community has shrunk. In spite of this, citizen interest in self-management and organization allows different participatory frameworks to enter state institutions and
new associations or spaces of contact between both—for example, through sociocultural projects—developing activities and performances that occasionally go beyond their formal objectives.[4]

The usual justification for these new measures is the increase in destabilizing U.S. policy, expressed in the approval of the Helms-Burton Act and its Title II, which proposed work with "civil society organizations in Cuba" as its main axis and identified them as antisystemic organizations: opposition movements and parties, human rights groups, independent journalists, and so on. Consequently, many associations were reduced to very discreet roles (paying the price of near invisibility); others were shut down under the criteria that their functions would be assumed by the state (e.g., the participatory urban planning project Habitat Cuba). Some organizations were partly able to avoid these results because they enjoy special political protection or because of the importance of their international contacts (e.g., the Martin Luther King Memorial Center), which allow them to maintain some impact within Cuban society and to benefit from foreign financial support.

Truncated experiences such as those of the post- and neo-Marxist intellectual group Paideia (closed in 1990), the feminist collective Magín (closed in 1996), the leftist student space Che Vive (closed in 1997), Habitat-Cuba (closed in 1998), and the environmentalist collective Sibarimar (closed in 2005) are a sign of the Cuban bureaucracy's profound and instinctive rejection of autonomous social practices (known as *autonomofobia*). These groups, as well as other, lesser-known ones, suffered official repression and sanctions that led to authentic personal dramas of their members and founders, who were in many cases leading militants of the Revolution. Although they have not received the study and notice that they deserve, their greatest value resides in building initiatives for participation and activism outside the bureaucratic logic of Cuban institutions. These institutions, in turn, reacted apprehensively, seeing the autonomous groups as a threat to the symbolic monopoly through which they have always tried to simplify and represent the Cuban left in its entirety.

Fed up with this, alternative social groups have emerged in Cuba, born at the margins of institutionalism and inclined toward self-management and participatory leadership. They seek cultural experimentation and activism by creating spaces of autonomy and articulation, confronting the state and authoritarian mercantilist threats (be they internal or external). The initiatives include environmentalist and peace groups, art workshops and groups, community intervention forums, and workshops, among others. Notwithstanding this progress, these groups find it difficult to connect with each other, and they have organizational weaknesses, lack resources, and face institutional pressures. Their political culture and praxis is dominated by a form of "self-limited radicalism," as the Polish dissident intellectual Adam Michnik put it, which supports the creation of autonomous islets within a society governed by a state-centric order.[5] This is a valuable strategy for its civic potential and setting a precedent, but it is constrained by the disarmament and disarticulation that prevail at a social scale.

Through their interactions, these collectives develop a particular way of being that comes from the intertwining of knowledge, affection, and shared values that evolve daily. With a more or less coherent discourse, they attempt to transform their communities through testimony and practice. There are still authoritarian positions and internal tensions, but they resolve these tensions and become aware of the nature of these conflicts in substantially different ways than those of traditional institutionalism: words prevail over sticks.

It is difficult to provide a short summary of the current Cuban situation with regard to participation and autonomy. However, I am convinced that any proposal for a democratic and participative reform (not merely technocratic) of Cuban institutionalism has to learn from the structural crisis of the current socioeconomic and political model. It must consider the strength that the global crisis provides some sectors of the bureaucracy that are eager to extend the militarized logic of the "country camp" or to make a pact with transnational capital in obscure and predatory ways.

Cuba needs to preserve national sovereignty and guarantee the development of a heterodox process of non-neoliberal economic reforms (with the participation of workers' collectives, democratic planning, and regulated markets) and an expanded form of governance with citizen participation. It must also establish a popular control of the elites, control that can derail both bureaucratic counterreforms and the privatization of national resources in order to advance toward a true socialist democracy.

NOTES

Excerpted from Armando Chaguaceda, "The Promise Besieged: Participation and Autonomy in Cuba," *NACLA Report on the Americas* 44, no. 4 (July/August 2011): 20–25, 42. Copyright 2012 by the North American Congress on Latin America, 53 Washington Square South, Floor 4W, New York, NY 10012. Reprinted by permission of the publisher.

1. See VOCES: Comunicación Alternativa, "Educación popular: Participación ciudadana," 2010, http://www.cubaalamano.net/voces/index.php?option=com_debate&task=debate&id=17.

2. Chaguaceda and Cilano, "Entre Ia innovación y el inmovilismo."

3. Dilla, Fernández, and Castro, "Movimientos barriales en Cuba."

4. Chaguaceda and Cilano, "Entre Ia innovación y el inmovilismo."

5. Cited in and developed by Andrew Arato and Jean Cohén, *Sociedad civil y teoría política* (Mexico City: Fondo de Cultura Econòmica, 2002).

II

Economics

For 200 years, Cuba was the paradigmatic case of a monocultural export economy, dependent on the production of one primary commodity—sugar—for sale to one principal trade partner—Spain during the early colonial period, the United States during the nineteenth and early twentieth centuries, and the Soviet Union after 1960. Overcoming dependency was high on the agenda of economic reforms pledged by the leaders of the 1959 Revolution. Yet despite a promising start in the 1960s and early 1970s, Cuba could not easily escape the twin afflictions of sugar dependence and a dominant trade partner. Only the collapse of European communism freed Cuba from dependent trade relations with the Soviet Union and its Eastern European allies—albeit at the cost of enormous economic disruption.

In the late eighteenth century, sugar displaced tobacco as Cuba's principal crop, and comparative advantage soon made the island the dominant producer in the world market. For over a century, sugar brought Cuba prosperity, dulling the economic conflicts that fueled the wars of independence in Spain's other New World colonies. The rise of sugar also linked Cuba to the United States. When a collapse in international sugar prices in 1884 pushed many Cuban sugar mills into bankruptcy, capital from the United States poured into the island, consolidating and modernizing the sugar sector. In 1898, Washington's desire to protect these new economic interests contributed to the decision to intervene in Cuba's war of independence. The subsequent U.S. occupation of the island tied its economy ever closer to the United States by giving U.S. firms concessionary access to the Cuban market. By the late 1920s, U.S. firms controlled 75 percent of the sugar industry and most of the mines, railroads, and public utilities.

The Revolution of 1959 was animated in part by a nationalist desire to reduce Cuba's dependency on the United States. By 1960, Cuba's revolutionary leaders had concluded that the path to economic independence and development was a socialist one, and before the year was out, $1 billion of U.S. direct investment had been nationalized. Cuba's revolutionary government could not have survived Washington's declaration of economic war without external assistance. With the help of the Soviet Union, Cuba's international economic relations were radically transformed. By 1962, trade with the United States had fallen to zero, and trade with the Soviet Union, negligible before 1959, had jumped to half of all Cuban trade.

Having ended Cuba's dependency on the United States, the revolutionary leadership next took aim at sugar. Their first development strategy, pursued until 1963, planned for balanced growth based on agricultural diversification and rapid development of both light and heavy industry. By 1961, bottlenecks associated with the shift from the market to central planning began to appear. Reduced sugar production (as called for in the diversification plan) led to a severe balance-of-payments crisis. Rapid industrial growth was beyond the capital-generating capacity of the Cuban economy, and the Soviet Union was unwilling to finance consistently huge deficits. In mid-1963, returning from a trip to the Soviet Union, Fidel Castro announced a return to specialization in sugar. By the turn of the decade, Castro pledged, Cuba would produce 10 million tons of sugar annually and use the proceeds to develop the rest of the economy. Meeting the target of 10 million tons of sugar in 1970 became enshrined as a matter of political prestige and regime legitimacy. Economic rationality took a backseat. Despite herculean efforts that disrupted every other sector of the economy, only 8.5 million tons of sugar were produced.

The economic reforms that followed this failure marked the beginning of a deeper economic relationship with the Soviet Union. A more rational planning process modeled on the Soviet system was installed in exchange for increased economic aid. To reduce Cuba's perennial bilateral trade deficit, the Soviets agreed to pay higher preferential prices for Cuban sugar and nickel. Future trade credits were extended interest free, and the repayment of Cuba's existing debt was deferred for thirteen years. In 1972, Cuba was admitted to the Council of Mutual Economic Assistance (CMEA), becoming one of the main sugar suppliers to the trade bloc.

The attractiveness of these arrangements was undeniable. Cuba was assured a reliable market for its exports, favorable terms of trade, significant development assistance, and an expansive line of credit, allowing it to live beyond its means. Cheap oil reinforced the disincentive for Cuba to diversify its exports or to develop energy-efficient production. The combination of low oil prices and high sugar prices hid the real costs of sugar production, making it seem more lucrative than it was. These structural weaknesses in the Cuban economy would become apparent only when the system of subsidized prices disappeared in the 1990s.

Overall, Soviet aid and the concomitant changes in Cuba's domestic economic policy had a salutary effect in the early 1970s. The economy enjoyed a robust recovery, with double-digit average annual growth through 1974. In the late 1970s, however, a new economic crisis was precipitated by Cuba's attempt to expand its trade with the West. In 1974, an upward spike in the world market price for sugar gave Cuba an unexpected hard-currency windfall, enabling it to expand imports from the West. Anticipating that higher sugar prices would last and enticed (as were many Third World countries) by the easy availability of credit due to the global glut of petrodollars, Cuba took on $4 billion of debt. By 1978, however, the world market price for sugar had declined to more traditional levels, and by 1982, Cuba could no longer maintain regular debt service. In 1986, after several restructurings, it declared a moratorium on payments.

Cuba's hard-currency crisis forced it back into an even more exclusive economic relationship with the Soviet bloc. With little hard currency and no credit, Cuba could not buy much from the West. Trade with the Soviet Union ballooned from just 41 percent of total trade in 1974 to 69 percent in 1978 and remained at or above 60 percent until the Soviet Union collapsed. Cuba's trade dependence on the Soviet bloc also reinforced its dependence on sugar. Under the socialist division of labor that characterized relations within the CMEA, Cuba was designated as the group's primary sugar provider in 1981.

By the mid-1980s, Cuba's economic situation had become precarious. Despite the preferential prices that Cuba received from the Soviet bloc, the balance-of-trade deficit expanded as domestic production of exports fell short of planning targets. In early 1986, Fidel Castro announced a new direction in economic policy. Criticizing the Soviet-sponsored socialist management system (SDPE) for fostering inefficiency, corruption, and profit-minded selfishness, he called for the "rectification of errors and negative tendencies." The rectification campaign focused on recentralizing economic planning authority, dismantling material incentives and market mechanisms, abolishing the free farmers' markets launched in 1980, and combating corruption. The rectification campaign did not solve Cuba's economic problems; if anything, it compounded them. The retreat from market-based material incentives hurt productivity just as it had in the 1960s, so much so that Cuba's trade deficit grew despite the austerity measures aimed at controlling it.

Thus, Cuba's economy was already vulnerable when it was hit by the shock of European communism's collapse. The postcommunist regimes insisted on trading at world market prices, refused to tolerate Cuba's trade deficits, and shut down their aid programs. The preferential prices and aid that Cuba had enjoyed amounted to several billion dollars annually. Without the subsidies, Cuba's capacity to import shrank by 75 percent, causing severe shortages of energy, raw materials, and food. The resulting depression slashed gross domestic product by at least 35 percent, closed hundreds of factories, and left tens of thousands of Cubans unemployed. By one estimate, real wages shrank 80 percent between 1989 and 1995.

Faced with the worst economic crisis in the history of the Revolution, Castro announced the beginning of the "Special Period in a Time of Peace" in 1990. Its central goals were, first, to reorient trade relations toward the West, attracting foreign investment capital to substitute for the lost subsidies, and, second, to produce enough food to avert serious malnutrition. The strategy included a series of market-oriented reforms, including the reestablishment of free farmers' markets, the devolution of many state farms to cooperatives, reductions in subsidies to state enterprises, the legalization of self-employment, and, most significant, the legalization of dollars.

A key element in sustaining the ability of ordinary Cubans to get through the "Special Period" was support from abroad in the form of remittances. In 1993, in hopes of increasing the flow, the Cuban government legalized the possession of dollars and opened dollar stores (*Tiendas de Recuperación de Divisas*) for Cubans to purchase imported goods. The policy succeeded; over the next decade, the remittances sent to relatives by Cubans abroad rose to over $1 billion annually. At the same time, however, the purchasing power of the Cuban peso receded, creating a two-class system of consumption: those with access to dollars (from remittances, work in the tourist sector, or the black market) and those without.

Another major concession to the market was the decision in 1993 to legalize self-employment (*trabajo por cuenta propia*). Energy shortages after 1991 forced the closure of many factories, producing significant unemployment for the first time since 1959. Unable to provide jobs, the state was forced to recognize the reality that many Cubans had begun working in the informal sector to make ends meet. Legalizing self-employment gave the government an opportunity to license, regulate, and tax the activity. However, confiscatory taxes and intricate regulations were so stultifying that many prospective *cuentapropistas* either operated without a licensing or quit altogether; by the end of the decade, there were fewer licensed self-employed than when self-employment was first legalized.

Cuba's large state farms were dependent on expensive imported equipment, fertilizer, and petroleum, which became unaffordable after the loss of Soviet assistance. They were replaced by small producer cooperatives called Basic Units of Cooperative Production (*Unidades Básicas de Producción Cooperativa* [UBPC]), in which individual families had land use rights. Moreover, the government reintroduced free farmers' markets, in which both private farmers and UBPCs could sell produce to the public at market prices. This increased food production but only marginally. At the turn of the century, Cuba still had to import 70 percent of its food.

Once Cuba had to pay world market prices for the petroleum to run its sugar industry and had to sell its sugar abroad at world prices, the obsolescence of a large part of the industry became unavoidably clear. For several years, Cuba continued subsidizing sugar production in many rural areas where sugar constituted the only source of employment and income. But in 2002, the day of reckoning arrived, and half the island's mills closed down. Cuba's infrastructure, especially housing and public transportation, decayed dramatically during the Special Period for want of domestic reinvestment. Foreign investment lagged because of the political and bureaucratic maze that investors still had to navigate. But the economy stabilized in 1994 and began a slow recovery. By the end of the 1990s, the government had begun to scale back some of the market-oriented reforms, suggesting a degree of official complacency about prospects for future growth.

As sugar declined in importance, tourism rose to takes its place. Marguerite Jiménez describes not only the economic logic that drove the tourist boom but also the negative social consequences that accompanied it. Tourism was second only to sugar before 1959, but in the 1960s, the revolutionary government neglected tourism because of its association with the social ills of prerevolutionary Cuba, especially gambling, prostitution, and foreign domination. In need of hard currency during the Special Period, the Cuban leadership revived the tourism sector because it was attractive to foreign investors and had the potential for rapid growth. It became a critical component of economic recovery.

By the turn of the century, the export of medical services—principally to Venezuela—had become as important as tourism. Economic cooperation between Venezuela and Cuba dates to 2000, when the two signed their first economic cooperation agreement, and the relationship has been expanding ever since. By 2013, Venezuela was providing Cuba with some 110,000 barrels of oil daily at subsidized prices, worth $4 billion annually and representing two-thirds of Cuba's domestic oil consumption. In exchange, Cuba provided some 40,000 skilled professionals, working mostly in health.

Fidel Castro was always uncomfortable with the market-oriented reforms his government was forced to adopt in the early 1990s at the depth of the Special Period. Speaking on August 6, 1995, he explained to Cubans why it was necessary to "introduce elements of capitalism into our system." It was not, he assured them, because he wanted to unleash market mechanisms in the Cuban economy. "We have gone down this road basically because it was the only alternative for saving the revolution," he said. Over the next few years, the limited reforms of the 1990s were gradually constrained, and Fidel intensified his criticism of the social inequality they had produced.

UPDATING CUBA'S ECONOMIC MODEL

When Raúl Castro assumed the presidency in July 2006 because of Fidel's sudden illness, the Cuban economy had yet to fully recover from the Special Period. Although it had been growing gradually since the 1990s, the gains were concentrated in tourism and medical services for export. The actual production of goods on the island still lagged behind 1989 levels, and many state enterprises operated at a loss. Agricultural production was so poor that this agriculturally well-endowed island had to import 70 percent of its food at a cost of $1.5 billion every year.

Almost immediately, Raúl Castro began a crusade to bring the Cuban economy into the twenty-first century. The hypercentralized model imported from the Soviet Union in the 1960s "doesn't even work for us anymore," Fidel admitted in 2010. The central problem, Raúl bluntly pointed out, was low productivity. "No country or person can spend more than they have," he reminded the Communist Party Congress in April 2011. "Two plus two is four. Never five, much less six or seven, as we have sometimes pretended." Cuba needed to "untie the knots holding back the development of the productive forces," starting with excessive regulations.

One of the fetters holding back Cuba's forces of production was corruption. As Archibald R. M. Ritter recounts, the economic hardship of the Special Period led to widespread corruption, especially the pilfering of goods from state enterprises for sale on the black market. Since state sector salaries alone were inadequate for subsistence, people were forced to seek other sources of income wherever they could in order to get by (*resolver*).

In 2008, the government began eliminating prohibitions that Cubans found especially exasperating, legalizing the sale of computers and cell phones, for example, and eliminating rules against Cubans staying in tourist hotels. In 2011, the government legalized private real estate and automobile markets, allowing Cubans to buy and sell directly to one another without a state intermediary. And in 2013, the government eliminated the "*tarjeta blanca*," the exit permit required for travel abroad; now, Cubans with a passport can travel whenever and wherever they like.

Raúl's grand strategy for economic reform—or "updating" the economic model, as Cubans prefer to call it—was unveiled in November 2010 with the distribution of the "Guidelines of the Economic and Social Policy of the Party and the Revolution," which outlined 291 proposals. After popular discussion, a revised version was approved at the 2011 Communist Party Congress, and since then the National Assembly has been hard at work on implementing legislation.

Cuban economists Jorge Mario Sánchez and Omar Everleny Pérez provide overviews of both the persistent problems that led to the new economic policy and its key components. The most important change in the "Guidelines" is philosophical: the "nonstate sector"—private enterprise and cooperatives—is treated as a permanent and dynamic part of the economy, not as a barely tolerated appendage. In fact, the reform process began in agriculture even before the "Guidelines" were drawn up, as Armando Nova describes. In a 2008 bid to boost agricultural production, the state decentralized the distribution system so that local produce could be sold locally, adjusted the prices it pays to private farmers, and started leasing idle state land to them. By the end of 2012, 3.5 million acres had been distributed. Cooperative farms divided their lands into family farms. Farmers' markets have proliferated across the country, from huge covered marketplaces in Havana to roadside stands in Oriente province, with prices set by supply and demand.

Restrictions that constrained small business growth in the 1990s have been relaxed. Philip Peters, who has chronicled the evolution of Cuba's incipient private sector since its appearance in the 1990s, reviews the recent measures aimed at revitalizing it. A confiscatory tax code was revised, and the prohibition on employing nonfamily members was eliminated. Size restrictions, such as one limiting private restaurants ("*paladares*") to twelve chairs, have also been eased, so there is no longer any preordained limit on how large a "small" business can grow. The government has also legalized nonagricultural cooperatives, which, along with private businesses, are allowed to contract with state enterprises, opening a huge potential market for them. Before the reform process began, only 15 percent of the labor force was employed in the nonstate sector, almost exclusively by private farms; by the end of 2012, that had risen to 23 percent, and Cuban economists predict that by 2016, it will be as much as 40 percent.

Among the obstacles to small business growth have been the lack of wholesale markets and credit. The "Guidelines" promised to remedy both problems, and banks began providing small business loans. Remittances from the United States provide an alternative source of capital. Orozco and Hansing's survey of Cuban remittance recipients indicates that while most are still using remittances to augment consumption, others have begun to invest as small business opportunities have opened up. Prior to 2009, the U.S. government limited remittances to $1,200 per year, and recipients used the money to supplement consumption rather than saving or investing it. Since U.S. President Barack Obama lifted the limits in 2009, remittances have jumped from an estimated $1.4 billion to $2.6 billion annually. Miami has become both the banker and the wholesale market for Cuban small businesses, the embargo notwithstanding.

Cuba has also revised its laws on foreign direct investment (FDI), offering investors more favorable terms in hopes of attracting more outside capital. Because of the history of U.S. economic domination of the island, the revolutionary government had little interest in foreign investment before the Special Period. Several revisions of the foreign investment laws since then have opened most of the economy to FDI, but as Richard Feinberg explains, bureaucratic obstacles still discourage most potential investors, depriving Cuba of an important source of capital.

As a package, Cuba's reforms look very much like the early stages of Vietnam's "Doi Moi" (renovation) reforms, begun in 1986, aimed at creating a "socialist-oriented market economy," and Deng Xiaoping's 1978 reforms aimed at building "socialism with Chinese characteristics." With a smile, a retired Cuban official described the Cuban model as "socialism with Cuban characteristics." But that is as far as it will go, Raúl insists. "I was not elected president to restore capitalism in Cuba nor to surrender the Revolution," he has said. "I was elected to defend, maintain and continue improving socialism, not to destroy it."

To do so, however, he faces a number of challenges. The real test of the reform process will come in the state sector, which still employs most of the Cuban labor force and produces more than 80 percent of the gross domestic product. The government's goal is not to privatize the state sector but to modernize it so that it produces efficiently. The *"perfeccionamiento empresarial"* (business improvement) model is the same one Raúl Castro introduced in defense industries in the 1980s. Enterprises will have to adopt standard accounting practices and become profitable. Control over business decisions will devolve from central ministries to enterprise managers who will have the power to lay off unnecessary labor. By the government's own estimate, as many as a million workers in the state sector hold jobs that should be eliminated. State enterprises that fail to become profitable will be at risk of closure.

Castro has promised that he will not subject Cuba to "shock therapy" and that "no one will be left behind." But if market forces are given free rein, Cuba's income disparities are sure to increase even more than they have in the past two decades. There will be winners and losers. Those who are well educated, live in cities where economic development is more dynamic, and have access to hard currency will be well positioned to thrive in a freer economic environment. Those who are low skilled or elderly, live in rural areas, have no relatives abroad to send remittances, and suffer from racial discrimination are at risk, as María del Carmen Zabala Argüelles's study of poverty and vulnerability recounts.

The government pledges to maintain the collective welfare system of which the Revolution is most proud, including free health care, free education, and social security. But other state subsidies for consumers are already being phased out, including the ration card, which Raúl called "an unbearable burden" on state finances. Instead of subsidizing everyone's consumption, the government plans to subsidize only the poor.

Concern about the social dislocation that will inevitably accompany such a radical economic shift is clearly on the minds of Cuba's leaders. The pace of change will be slow and steady "in order not to err," Raúl has said. "To those [who] are encouraging us to move faster, we say that we will continue without haste, but in a measured way, with our feet planted firmly on the ground."

Chapter Nine

Challenges of Economic Restructuring in Cuba

Jorge Mario Sánchez Egozcue

Once again, Cuba is in the midst of structural change.[1] Unlike the adjustments made in the 1990s (required by the reinsertion in the international economy that resulted from the collapse of the socialist bloc), this time the catalysts are accumulated internal pressures and an inability to deal with them within the framework of the "prevailing rules."

For the first time in the history of the Revolution, what is involved is a restructuring of the social contract between state and society. Among the most important aspects in the economic realm is that this restructuring will gradually leave behind the model of massive social coverage based on subsidies and administrative transfers of profits, to move instead toward more targeted policies of social protection, administrative decentralization, and a reduction of the state's exaggerated presence in economic life so as to make more room for cooperative associations and the private sector.

No less important is the recognition that in the sociopolitical realm, the current panorama is quite different from that of only a few years ago. The state's traditional hegemony is becoming more porous as new actors and spaces of opinion formation emerge, rendering internal political dialogue more complex. Critical internal debate is gradually reemerging, as is legitimization of differences by way of an explicit rejection of "false unanimity." Cuba is moving toward term limits—a maximum of two five-year periods—for those holding the highest offices. The January 2012 Communist Party Conference agreed to "rejuvenate the cadre rolls and avoid immobilism and inertia."

Even before the Conference, there were calls for a change of mentality among leaders and administrators, including a call to listen to the population, at the same time that the press began to publish letters and articles exposing wrong or arbitrary decisions in state enterprises and ministries to public scrutiny. Similar measures have included a national program to "recycle" officials through professional development schools focusing on economic issues. Insofar as internal mechanisms of Party work are concerned, there have been calls to reject imitative theories and submissive mentalities and to forge its own path free of "immobilism based on dogmas and empty slogans."

In essence, what is involved is not so much a reconfiguration of actors and rules as a change in the basis of government, on a new and irreversible scale, so as to eliminate once and for all the complacency, false triumphalism, and social apathy—a change that would constitute, in fact, a negation of the culture and thinking that have been years in the making. At the same time, there is an attempt to introduce forms of economic management that will counter deep accumulated deterioration.

It is true that some very important restrictions on the country's activity derive from external factors. These include the global economic crisis; the U.S. policy of international harassment and sanctions affecting investors, banks, and other commercial entities; the complex effects of growing international economic interdependence; and the severe effects of climatic events, such as hurricanes and droughts.[2] However, it is also true that today's domestic Cuban society displays many symptoms that are not attributable to these factors, and these symptoms must be addressed. Unless there are changes, the viability of the system has clearly been compromised by increasing erosion of its capacity to achieve economic sustainability on efficient and stable bases.

Among the factors provoking internal strains are an overgrown public sector, an unbelievable overabundance of quasi-juridical rules and restrictions that have strangled enterprise-level initiatives (both public and private), institutional structures and incentives that are distorted or inherited from other circumstances that no longer apply, a powerful state bureaucracy that is resistant to change and to public scrutiny, inertia, corruption, a culture resistant to critical discussion, low productivity, decapitalization of productive structures and industry, and severe demographic pressure resulting from an aging population conjoined with a human resource drain tied to emigration. Some of these characteristics have manifested themselves most sharply in a serious deterioration of the country's capacity to feed itself (by way of high percentages of idle land and an accelerated accumulation of foreign debt due to food imports).

These are the conditions surrounding the initiation of the program of reforms contained in the "Economic and Social Policy Guidelines"—a program that seeks to gradually meet the challenges of reviving the economy and introducing new ideas and mechanisms that will equip the country's institutional and political life for the future. The changes whose implementation has begun imply a "loss of habitat" for the bureaucracy that has, until now, benefited from the status quo. Therefore, it is natural for the bureaucracy to respond by obstructing these changes. Such obstruction, in turn, leads in one way or another to discontent in a population that already resents limitations and shortages that result from not-always-justifiable flaws (high losses in the channels of food distribution, artificially high prices inflated by inefficient quality control, and so on) that cause significant losses that could sometimes be resolved without much additional spending. All of this erodes the credibility of institutions.

Thus, a consensus finally emerged among decision makers that partial improvements were not enough. Without radical modification of the economic bases and of the policymaking process in general, there could be no development model that would succeed in breaking the vicious circle in which widespread social coverage and control of poverty also implied massive subsidies that piled up increasing debt, losses from deteriorating efficiency, and low international competitiveness.

THE CUBAN CHANGE AGENDA: THE "GUIDELINES"

The formal initiation of this process came in November 2010 with the issuance of a document called "Proposed Guidelines of the Economic and Social Policy." This document was to be discussed in public meetings in order to collect proposals for modification, preparatory to the April 2011 Communist Party Congress. The "Guidelines," as they are generally called, were at once the response to public opinion's growing demands for change and the strategic platform that would define the transformations to be promoted by the government after consensus had been reached.

The consultation process had three stages. In the first, between December 2010 and February 2011, the public received a first draft with 291 articles (or guidelines). This phase included discussions in the Sixth Ordinary Sessions of the Seventh National Assembly of People's Power. The result was an expansion of the "Guidelines" to 311 articles on the basis of the 395,000 statements of opinion that were accepted. The next stage, in April 2011, moved the scene of discussion to the provinces and into the hands of delegates and other invited figures who would shortly attend the Sixth Party Congress. In the last phase, at the end of April, the final discussions took place within five commissions at the Party Congress itself, from which emerged the final version of the "Guidelines" containing many modifications and a total of 313 articles.

With respect to the speed at which the changes listed in the document would be implemented, Raúl Castro warned in his speech against sowing false hopes among the population; he said that successful implementation would require at least five years. Once they were approved, the "Guidelines" became the policy outline for the transformations to be promoted. The major changes being introduced or to be introduced in the economy, institutional structures, and (by extension) the society are thus partially codified in a process officially termed "updating of the socialist economic model." Past measures have been placed in the context of this new and broader perspective, whose ultimate goal has been explicitly defined as adjusting the system, not dismantling it.

The document contains a diagnosis of the causes of Cuba's economic problems, which it attributes to a lack of integration in the planning process that stemmed from overprioritizing the foreign sector and the short-term balance of payments. The main consequences are noted as disproportionate overemployment by the state, decapitalization of industries, significant expanses of idle farmland, unsustainable levels of state subsidies, a high dependence on imports, a predominance of egalitarianism without attention to social and geographic differences, paternalism, a need to strengthen local and regional development, and a need to eliminate the dual currency (gradually and to the degree that necessary conditions are present).

Major identified priorities are sustainability (nutritional, economic, energy, environmental, and social), more institutional flexibility, promoting international competitiveness, and restructuring the relations between state and society in a way that retains a dominant role for state planning and a commitment to preserve equality of rights and opportunities.

The document also points out that two different approaches must be reconciled. One has to do with short-term solutions: eliminating the balance-of-payments deficit, promoting export earnings, and substituting domestic production for imports; facing the biggest immediate problems affecting economic efficiency, worker motivation, and income distribution; and creating the necessary conditions for transition to a later era of deeper changes. The other, longer term, has to do with promoting sustainable development, which will allow for food and energy self-sufficiency, efficient use of human resources, improved competitiveness of traditional products, and new product lines in high-value-added goods and services.

In sum, the context envisioned for the coming years is framed by the challenge of how quickly and effectively the change from a vertical administrative structure to a flexible decentralization of the state can be achieved alongside a reconfiguration of institutions and incorporation of new, nonstate actors (the private and cooperative sectors) in a relationship of complementarity and competition that will have to be built almost from scratch and will surely lead to some degree of social restratification. This "structural migration" will be achieved through coordinating incentives to promote autonomy of state-owned enterprises along with parallel development of the private and cooperative sectors.

CHANGE IN PRIORITIES: FROM FOREIGN THREAT TO INTERNAL VULNERABILITY

The change in focus from foreign pressures to accumulated domestic problems constitutes an explicit recognition that the most immediate threat to the continuity of the Cuban political system does not emanate from the effects of the international crisis or from U.S. government policy. New policies to address adverse changes in the domestic and international environments began to be implemented in 2003. Among the most important were reorganizing the structure and functions of the State and the Government by combining some and simplifying others while seeking a better distribution of tasks among them.

Other measures included reorienting investments with a priority on short-range objectives so as to help relieve the effect of debt on the balance of payments, decentralizing the use of hard currency so as to promote exports, rescheduling debt payments, granting usufruct rights on state lands to private farmers and cooperatives, energy-saving initiatives, selective experimental elimination of state services (in the areas of transportation and food), and renting out space or equipment to individuals in some small-scale activities (taxis and local services).

More and more prohibitions were eliminated but without this being publicized through the big media campaigns that marked previous eras. This is another of the distinguishing traits of Raúl Castro's presidency. His style is more pragmatic and directed toward solving the problems that have been identified, making a clear distinction between immediate- and medium-term goals. There is also a notable tendency toward increasing delegation of responsibilities. The modification of prohibitions began in 2006 with the elimination of restrictions on Cubans buying goods and services with convertible currency (household appliances, cellular phones, car rentals, and tourist services in international hotels). Land grants to individual farmers to stimulate domestic food production began at this same time. Also, the artificially low prices paid to farmers for their output were raised, and almost all their debts to the state were written off, some of many years' duration. The year 2007 saw liberalization of the granting of licenses to private *transportistas* (drivers of taxis and other service vehicles), and more recently people have been encouraged to legally build and repair houses. (Relieving the housing deficit is one of the most important demands, and its potential for job creation has been harnessed very little.)

Other important changes have come in the area of government spending. Excessive subsidies and other "gratuities" have gradually been eliminated. For example, state-funded foreign travel by officials and managers has been cut by more than 50 percent, and an incentive program for outstanding officials, leaders, and workers costing more than $60 million a year was dropped. The budgeting of resources for some cultural, health, and sports services has been modified, cigarettes have been removed from the ration book, and provision of subsidized meals in workplace cafeterias has been gradually reduced or in some cases eliminated. Finally, the system of supplying rationed goods to households through the nationwide ration book is in the process of being dismantled, with the products (coffee, beans, oil, cleaning products, and so on) being gradually shifted into other markets whose prices include profit margins. Other changes include updating the tax system and raising electricity prices (in response to the worldwide growth in petroleum prices).

None of these measures is by itself very complex or is particularly disruptive for social development as a whole, but taken as a group, they show a will to implement, step-by-step, concrete actions that represent a profound change in the national environment, one occurring without large-scale trauma.

In a speech closing the National Assembly sessions of 2008, Raúl Castro noted that these transformations should be carried out "without hurry and without excess of idealism, in accordance with available resources." Soon afterward, there was a temporary postponement of the process due to the urgent tasks of recovery from the hurricanes that hit the island that year.

Action resumed in mid-2009, and in late 2010 there began a new stage, going beyond piecemeal changes to the presentation of the structured ensemble of changes embodied in the "Guidelines." In practice, the steps taken from 2003 to 2008 pointed in the right direction but were insufficient to deal with the roots of dysfunctionality.

This period gave rise to steady deceleration of economic growth while at the same time food imports were growing—a result of evident failures in the way in which agriculture was being managed[3] —and distortions in the ratio of income to consumption deepened[4] in the context of an environment made more difficult by unresolved issues, such as market segmentation and the dual currency. Thus, the steps taken up to that point clearly represented only a small portion of those truly needed.[5]

The need for a reform of the Cuban economic system grew ever more evident—a reform that would assign new roles to the state and the market, to various forms of property, and to enterprise organization.[6] More than a few studies were devoted to putting forward proposals regarding these issues,[7] but several years passed before these received the attention they deserved.

In December 2010, the office of the president declared a commitment to these transformations in dramatic terms. In his key National Assembly speech, President Raúl Castro said, "Either we will rectify [our course], or we will run out of time perched on the edge of disaster, and we'll sink, dooming . . . the efforts of whole generations."

To comply over the medium term with the needed changes in the role of the state, the directives included reducing excess spending; making more rational use of existing infrastructure to increase the quality of social programs in health care, education, culture, and sports; supporting export growth; and concentrating investment in the activities that can be revived most quickly.

Proposals for immediate action included ending overspending of state budgets and underfulfillment of economic plans. The speech called for eradicating "all types of excuses, extending to vagueness and lies, whether intentional or not, when stated goals are not reached," because supplying false data, even without fraudulent intent, can lead to wrong decisions with greater or lesser effects on the nation.

The same speech pointed out the importance of open discussion of the "Guidelines" in order to shape a democratic consensus (not excluding divergent opinions) on the necessity and urgency of introducing strategic changes in the functioning of the economy, including the legitimization and stimulus of private initiative and of cooperative associations as "irreversible" components—while also making clear that accumulation of capital by the new owners would not be permitted and that the plan would have primacy over the market.

A DECISIVE TRANSFORMATION IN THE RELATIONSHIP BETWEEN STATE AND SOCIETY

One of the key immediate challenges is a short-term transition from a vertical administrative culture to a flexible decentralization of the state. This involves granting a more active role to local and provincial government while reshaping the institutional fabric and incorporating new, nonstate actors from the private and cooperative sectors, which will doubtless have important effects on future social restratification.

This dual structural shift will require coordinating incentives for promoting state-enterprise autonomy with a parallel development of the private and cooperative sector based on economic and financial criteria so as to eliminate massive dependence on state subsidies while removing artificial barriers from the areas in which self-sustainability might be achieved. This process requires innovations that include shutting down enterprises that become bankrupt, forming second-level cooperatives (cooperatives made up of other cooperatives), and allowing competition between private and state suppliers (which has already begun in farm-product sales to hotels).

Part of the Cuban adjustment requires a realignment of the visions and proposals emanating from intellectuals and technocrats. Many of the measures now being implemented had been discussed and suggested for years within these circles of thinking, without having much impact on decision making. Two of the most active intellectual forums—the journals *Temas* and *Espacio Laical*—provide clear examples of how spaces for discussion and the content of discussion have been evolving. New digital communication technologies have given rise to an unprecedented variety of actors and subjects in a sort of "parallel atomization" that has gone beyond the formal institutional framework and has also made room for the opinions of Cuban emigrants with a wide range of perspectives.

These new dynamics drive a transformation that is taking place in the culture of discussion to which state and party structures must adapt. In the Cuban state-run press and communications media, the syndrome of "captive information" and homogenization of thought continues to prevail. Although some relatively more critical analyses suggesting a moderate change of attitude have begun to appear, we are still a long way from a press that would adequately represent today's society in all its complexity and conflicts. Raúl Castro himself has remarked on how, to get an article published that severely criticized the management of a state entity, he had to personally intervene in order to overcome resistance that hid behind the argument that we "cannot reveal our internal weaknesses to the enemy."

The challenges associated with the transformations now beginning may be viewed in three general dimensions. The first is connected with the results of the process now under way, particularly its effects on the underlying social contract (equal opportunity, preservation of full access to social services, and state protection against vulnerability and poverty). This approach recognizes that the social changes that will necessarily occur (restratification of socioeconomic sectors, greater polarization of incomes, and so on) are still in process, and it is still too early to know how far they will go.

In this dimension, it is equally important to see that if an economistic vision of the changes prevails, that would carry the latent danger that social impacts would be minimized and that the need to provide parallel supports that absorb some of the social costs would be undervalued. (Such supports include increased retiree pensions, retraining and placement of workers, protections for vulnerable low income families, and so on.) Although it has been stated that no one will be left out in the cold by this transition (the transition from the traditional massive state subsidy of products to a more focused subsidization of low-income individuals and families), adjustments in income levels will not necessarily keep up with spontaneous changes in prices that will occur when private supply mechanisms increase in a context of scarcity. In fact, the polarization of incomes will continue to widen the gap between state employees and private sector workers no matter how aggressively the latter are taxed given that so far the problem of the immense parallel underground economy has not been resolved.

A second dimension of analysis is associated with the political consequences potentially implied over the longer term by an expansion of the private and cooperative sector in the midst of an environment in which other problems, such as corruption and growing polarization, have not been resolved. The decision to promote a larger self-employed (private) sector constitutes an important transformation reflecting the emergence of a different way of thinking that does not assume a dichotomy between state and market in which one side or the other must prevail (as was assumed under the conception of socialism prevailing for the previous fifty years).

The socialist implosion of the 1990s and the changes it brought to Cuban society and economy allowed for the emergence of a private sector—"permitted but not desired or promoted"—without any "facilitating" legislation or a policy of state protection or recognition that would include incentives, links to state entities, and so on. In that decade, what dominated was the notion that allowing room for a private sector was an ad hoc, temporary phenomenon (i.e., one lasting only until conditions improved and there could be a return to the state-owned property and employment of the 1980s). This position was clearly linked to fear or rejection of the possible increase in social inequality that would result. Thus, what emerged was an eminently urban private sector engaged in small-scale activities of providing prepared foods, lodging, transportation, repairs, and so on that excluded any interaction or links between the state and the private sector. The regulatory environment was primarily fiscal (taxation) and restrictive concession of licenses.

In spite of this relatively hostile environment, these limited actors created a sector of self-employment for economic survival—a peculiar development in which small private businesses took advantage of the market niches allowed by the state but without much hope for future success. (Research has shown that at least 50 percent of small private business shared this perception.[8])

As the idea of an eventual reversion of the private sector has explicitly disappeared, the rationale underlying that model—which saw coexistence of such a sector with a socialist economy as impossible—has been subverted. Now, the state has become the main promoter of the private sector's formally institutionalized relation to the market and its independence of action. In principle, this reconsideration also allows for that sector to compete with the traditional state dominance in areas not considered essential.

Some of the changes now under way are truly new in their conception and proportions. What has attracted most attention is the downsizing of state employment through reduction of inflated payrolls. At first, it was announced that 500,000 jobs were to be eliminated in stages, primarily those linked to bureaucratic and service tasks in state enterprises and organizations. These workers were expected to move to other productive jobs both in state enterprises and in the private and cooperative sector. A complementary measure was broadening the categories of licensed self-employment to 178 economic activities, many of which would be permitted to subcontract workers. (Paradoxically, none of these categories included professionals, who are one of the most important labor reserves created by years of mass access to education.)

The original announced goal was to relocate around a million state employees (nearly a quarter of the country's economically active population), something that would substantially reduce the enormous and costly bureaucratic apparatus. The word "layoff" (*despido*) was never used. Rather, commissions created in the various work centers would propose which employees should be deemed "available," and they could take advantage of temporary benefits that would be offered on the basis of seniority, qualification, and so on in the form of payments over a period of one to three months, according to what was deemed necessary.

The secretary-general of the Cuban Workers' Union, Salvador Valdés, declared repeatedly that this plan of workforce adjustment would "not leave anyone unprotected." In spite of this and other similar pronouncements, the fact is that after nearly fifty years during which several generations grew up with the idea of job security and stability as an unquestionable right, a change of this sort gives rise to natural uncertainty that cannot be satisfied until reality confirms that the promised alternative spaces will effectively replace lost family incomes.

The sectors chosen to initiate this gradual "labor reorganization" were five ministries: Sugar, Agriculture, Construction, Public Health, and Tourism. However, the process was soon apparently postponed, possibly to provide a margin of time for introducing and consolidating new legal regulations and systems of credit to aid in the formation of cooperatives and private businesses that would create alternative jobs. More than 300,000 licenses for self-employed work have been granted in record time, but it has been announced that the process of reducing state employment will continue albeit "in accord with circumstances and with flexibility as to deadlines."

This workforce reform is absolutely necessary. If the sizable losses caused by artificial overemployment are not eliminated, efforts to put other economic activities on a sound footing will remain permanently at risk.

Finally, the third dimension or level—no less important—to be considered is the positioning of key countries in Cuban foreign relations with regard to these new developments. This involves issues of multilateral exchanges and assistance, including support for the development of local and small businesses (*microempresas*)—primarily through international organizations—as well as bilateral mechanisms of trade, investment, and aid, and (indirectly) probable scenarios of trade with and/or assistance from the United States and other, broader, collateral influences.

The current changes are more significant than those of the 1990s. Even before the collapse of the socialist bloc, the Cuban economy was showing clear signs of stagnation due to its own structural problems, such as low levels of productivity and competitiveness, a limited ability to generate internal savings, an international position based on low-value-added exports and financial and commercial dependence on a single market (the Soviet Union) and a single product (sugar), a weak industrial fabric, and mounting fiscal disequilibrium.

The adjustments introduced in the 1990s represented a change unprecedented in the history of the Cuban Revolution. Several major transformations occurred during that decade. Sugar, for the first time in Cuban history, ceased to be the economic engine of the country; it was replaced by tourism and the export of medical services. There was an opening to foreign banks and foreign investment. State agricultural property was redistributed to the cooperative sector, and licenses for small private urban businesses were granted. The dollar became a legal currency, and markets were segmented into different circuits using different currencies, generating a permanent tension that affected efficiency, salaries, and prices, reinforced in turn by remittances from abroad that became a significant source of income.

As a consequence of these changes and their mutual interactions, social impacts soon followed. Problems of poverty, growing inequality, and geographic stratification appeared, along with increased migration from countryside to cities. New challenges demanded responses on an unprecedented scale. It should not be surprising, therefore, to find these phenomena reflected in the realm of ideas and values. Nearly twenty years later, the main negative macroeconomic effects of the shock have been reversed, while others persist and are accompanied by new challenges. The current era has neither the pressure nor the sense of urgency of those earlier days, which were marked by a crisis of reinsertion in the global economy and reshaping of the economic system in response to an external shock. Today's challenge is a political-institutional transformation that responds to new internal realities, a process that extends farther than the generational changeover to which many observers reduce it.

As one Cuban intellectual has pointed out, the main challenge now is how to remodel the system without creating greater problems[9]—not to repair an exhausted and dysfunctional model still bearing the marks of European "really existing socialism" but rather to gradually develop a different one, according to the logic of current Cuban society's problems and needs.[10]

At both the subjective and the practical level, conditions have reached a point of no return. What distinguishes this moment and today's transformations from what was done in the 1990s is that the current process began with a public admission that things were not going well domestically, with a real political will to make the changes, and with an acceptance of these changes as irreversible. Within a few years, Cuban society will be different from what it has been. It is quite possible that the normal process of trial and error will give rise to still-unforeseen alternatives, as those who govern and those who are governed will learn how to reform what can be salvaged and discard what is not viable. What is beyond doubt is that the society will never again be the same as it was in the previous decades.

The specific steps that are being taken, such as the tightening of state employment and subsidies, mean that this time the responses will be deeper, going beyond the limits of the reforms of the 1990s, when the level of public spending and the policy of full employment were maintained in the midst of the crisis that followed the socialist collapse. Thus, this time there is a frank acceptance of the need to do away, once and for all, with the vicious circle of low wages and low productivity.[11]

The changed conception of the role of the state has left behind the 1990s model of vertical subordination in which the upper levels laid out the plans for every other stratum, moving instead in the opposite direction toward a separation of government from enterprises. The key sectors remain in the hands of the state, and administrative decisions are based on economic and financial criteria, while unprecedented powers are granted to enterprises within the context of a general policy. Now, enterprises decide for themselves who will make up their management teams, and they may choose alternative means of financing their operations, eliminating their traditional dependence on the national budget. Similarly, they have autonomy in investment decisions, hiring, and pricing. When enterprises make profits, they may devote these to creating development funds, to new investments, or to employee bonuses.

RESISTANCE FROM WITHIN

The transformations described above face internal resistance that is expressed in multiple ways. On the one hand, there are the inherited bureaucratic culture and the vertical, rigid institutional structures. On the other, there are a lack of practical experience with the new mechanisms, a pressing and immediate scarcity of resources (financing, equipment, inputs, tools, and so on), and the multiple layers of rules and regulations generated at different levels and by various institutions that must be adjusted to make application of the new directives faster and more efficient.

In his speech at the opening of the Party Congress, Raúl Castro referred to the role of state institutions and enterprises in moving from a centralized economic model to a decentralized system, emphasizing the need to eradicate the widespread attitude of waiting for decisions to be made at higher levels so as to avoid the risks of taking one's own positions. This mentality of inertia must be definitively uprooted, he said, and he stressed a need to insist on fulfillment of contracts between parties as a way to spread responsibility. He noted that it was necessary to increase political sensitivity, to confront violations, and to demand discipline of everyone, especially leadership cadre. Over the years, many resolutions aimed at solving practical problems had become empty words. What we approve at this congress, he urged, cannot suffer the same fate as previous accords that were not fulfilled.

To these factors must be added a lack of legal instruments and services. Both the farmers and the new urban cooperative members and private workers have had, literally, no other options if the established mechanisms for supplying financing, transport, packing materials, and other inputs fail to work. Although new legal regulations covering the private and cooperative sector have now been presented (a review of more than 180 existing laws is now under way), some of the old mechanisms are still partially in effect—and these either do not recognize the new forms of property and economic action or even penalize them. In this area, the first steps have barely been taken. Implementation and monitoring of the new measures also run up against the interests of socioeconomic groups that have enjoyed powers and access to resources that are now threatened by new competitors, structures, and priorities. It is natural that, instead of facilitating the changes, these groups put up resistance in a variety of ways.

Perhaps the most illustrative example of practical barriers to the transformations is the food production sector. Cuba has been spending more than $1.5 billion per year on food imports (which supply 80 percent of demand), a financially unsustainable burden that is totally irrational given that 40 percent of arable land on the island remains idle [12] for lack of incentives and because of bureaucratic restraints. Paradoxically, harvested crops frequently go to waste because of lack of transport. The solution—recognized or not—requires dismantling the whole scaffolding of regulations and prohibitions that block any alternative methods (whether state or private) when the established mechanisms fail to work. Otherwise, the adaptive response by the farmers is to prioritize harvesting in order to be able to collect payment, whether or not the food ever makes it to market. Since September 2008, with the goal of increasing food production, 1.18 million hectares of idle land have been awarded as usufruct holdings to 128,435 new proprietors. However, two and a half years later, 30 percent of these parcels are not yet ready to produce food because of bureaucratic delays in making the actual grants, delays in training new proprietors, an insufficient provision of necessary tools and inputs, and the above-mentioned shortfalls in the systems of transportation and commercialization.

CONTINUITY AND CHANGE: OLD HABITS DIE HARD

It may seem that the repeated emphasis on restoring control and discipline is the slogan that best expresses the vision behind the changes. In reality, however, the determining factor is the dismantling of obsolete ideas, practices, and structures. There is no doubt that restoring the role of the law is a necessary strategy in a society that became accustomed to living with the breaking of rules and with ad hoc improvisation as a means of survival in the face of accumulated prohibitions and recurrent scarcity. That context generated a culture of permanent subversion of the law that now must be reversed. However, the vision behind the changes has been declared to rest on the priority of state management, gradual implementation so as to avoid improvisation, the preservation of consensus, and keeping the social costs of the changes under control.

Right now, the delicate balance between elements of continuity and of change is substantially evident in the field of economic management, in the restructuring of the institutional apparatus, and in policymaking (methods and styles of work). However, it would be illusory or reductionist to assume that the success or failure of the process is limited to these dimensions. The collateral improvements needed in other areas—such as updating legislation; restructuring institutions; changing the vision of the role of the Communist Party and its methods of coordination and oversight; broadening and empowering new actors, such as local government and the cooperative and private sector; and the multiplying interactions in various forums in civil society—point toward a necessary process of decentralization (not only destatization) that must, progressively, lead to greater transparency and relative transfer of governance toward intermediate levels.

While building consensus out of various visions of the changes is of the most visible importance, still the challenge facing Cuba in the current circumstances is not only about whether the reforms can be put into practice but also about their effectiveness in truly replacing the inherited culture that has viewed change more as a threat than as an opportunity. That culture, as noted, expresses itself in many and varied forms of resistance. The importance accorded to this issue is demonstrated by Raúl Castro's declaration that "we will be both patient and persistent with respect to resistance to change" but that "any and all bureaucratic resistance to the strict fulfillment of the Congress's accords, which are massively supported by the people, will be useless."

This directive took concrete form in the National Conference of the Cuban Communist Party, where the importance of changing Party members' mentality was cited as a necessary condition for carrying out the transformations. Also singled out was the need to separate the Party's activities from those of the government and administrative entities so as to eliminate interference and arrogation of functions. [13] Every two or three months, there are press reports of some prohibition being made more flexible, of the introduction of a new mechanism with that same goal, or of the experimental application of some new regulation or incentive (which later becomes generalized). This illustrates the way in which some of the reforms are being introduced without great fanfare or national campaigns.

In the case of housing, channels for supplying materials were decentralized, and permission to subcontract the work to private tradesmen was reintroduced. Prohibitions that limited citizens' ability to build houses were lifted, as was the ban on buying and selling houses. Another change was an end to the practice of confiscating the homes of citizens who emigrate; the emigrants can now sell or give them to others. The state soon began to issue bank loans for housing construction or repair (and, in parallel fashion, subsidies to poor families to repair their homes). All this has led to a visible, short-term reactivation of microenterprise in housing repair and construction, which now does not depend on public programs that for years were overwhelmed by the demand. In the case of large state entities, two ministries (Sugar and Telecommunications) were restructured and were converted into state-owned enterprises, thus noticeably reducing their numbers of employees and saving considerable artificial management costs.

As far as the speed and content of the reforms are concerned, reference has been made on various occasions to a strategic plan containing projections as far ahead as 2016. This plan has not yet been made public, but evidently the procedure is one of a sequence preceded by studies of alternatives and evaluation of impacts (for perhaps as long as two years) followed by small-scale implementation and then by the full-scale one, which will only occur after the minimal conditions to avoid additional problems are in place.

SOME CONCLUSIONS

The process of change in Cuba is inevitable and irreversible. Whether or not one agrees with the proposed content or the pace of implementation, there can be no doubt that a transition that allows for an institutionalized reshaping of the economy (and the resulting interactions), one that guarantees stability and at least a minimum of coherence about priorities, is preferable to a situation of ad hoc and uncoordinated responses. Decentralization of state administration, the emergence of new forms of property, and the creation of new legal frameworks will cause the conventional actors and mechanisms to be reshaped and progressively displaced by new dynamics.

The immediate tasks identified in the "Guidelines" point unambiguously to a need to shake off the accumulated obstacles and deformations that led to a generalized loss of economic efficiency. They similarly point to a need to review and revise institutional structures and policies while creating the conditions for transition to a later period of deeper transformations. In practice, what is under way is a dual process involving both a learning curve and a shift in the limits of what is permissible and appropriate. This perception will be reinforced to the degree that the changes that are introduced succeed in generating the expected results. There is no process of rupture associated with these transformations or one of dismantling government structures. To mechanistically equate an economic reform with drastic political change would constitute an oversimplification of the complex internal dynamic that is taking place in Cuba and a failure to understand the priority being assigned to the governability of the process and the management of its effects.

Cuba's major challenge today does not lie in determining the speed or depth of the transformations or in improving the quality of methods and oversight, although all of these are clearly needed. Nor is the key issue which particular leaders will be at the head of the country in a few years, though this is also an important issue. What will be decisive to the viability of the transformations has been clearly stated by Graziella Pogolotti: "Without a doubt, what is crucial to the viability of the Cuban project is a rearticulation of a vision of the future, one which links the personal life projects of the country's citizens with the transformations being implemented. This alone, not the institutional aspects, is the key to sustainability."[14]

NOTES

Excerpted from Jorge Mario Sánchez, "Challenges of Economic Restructuring in Cuba," *Socialism and Democracy* 26, no. 3 (2012): 139–61. Reprinted by permission of the publisher.

1. Some of the subjects discussed here were partially treated in my chapter "Cuba, el cambio interno y la política norteamericana, en busca de la racionalidad perdida," in Luis Fernando Ayerbe, ed., *Cuba, Estados Unidos, y América Latina en el cuadro actual de las relaciones Hemisféricas* (Barcelona: Editorial ICARIA; Buenos Aires: Ediciones CRIES; São Paulo: IEEI-UNESP, 2011), 11–46.

2. Over the course of ten years, sixteen hurricanes caused damages in the range of $20.5 billion. In 2008 alone, the losses due to hurricanes represented 20 percent of gross domestic product. Between 2003 and 2005, damages due to drought totaled $1 billion.

3. Armando Nova González, "El papel estratégico de la agricultura: Problemas y medidas," *Temas*, April 2010.

4. Mayra Espina Prieto, "Looking at Cuba Today: Four Assumptions and Six Intertwined Problems," *Socialism and Democracy*, no. 52, March 2011, 95–107.

5. Omar Everleny Pérez Villanueva, "Notas recientes sobre la economía en Cuba," paper presented at the Tenth "Semana Social Católica," *Espacio Laical*, June 2010, http://www.espaciolaical.net.

6. Jorge M. Sánchez Egozcue and Juan Triana Cordoví, "Panorama de la economía cubana, transformaciones y retos futuros," in *Cincuenta Años de la Economía Cubana*, ed. Omar E. Pérez (Havana: Editorial Ciencias Sociales, 2010), 83–152.

7. Carlos Alzugaray, Arturo López-Levy, Alexis Pestano, and Lenier González, "Cuba: ¿Hacia un nuevo Pacto Social?" *Espacio Laical*, Suplemento Digital no. 125, April 2011, http://www.espaciolaical.org.

8. Aymara Hernández Morales, "Estado y sector privado en Cuba: Políticas, relaciones y conflictos de un manejo restrictivo," paper presented at the Taller Internacional Centro de Investigaciones Psicológicas y Sociológicas, Havana, 2006.

9. Aurelio Alonso, "Salir del caos sin caer en la ley de la selva," in *Cuba desde el período especial hasta la elección de Raúl Castro*, May 2008, http://www.pensamientocritico.info/articulos/otros-autores/139-salir-del-caos-sin-caer-bajo-la-ley-de-la-selva.html.

10. Rafael Hernández, "Cuba, políticas en la transición," *La Vanguardia*, March 2008, http://www.almendron.com/tribuna/index.php/19322/cuba-politicas-en-latransicion.

11. Gerardo Arreola, "Más allá de las reformas de los 90," *La Jornada*, November 10, 2010, 36.

12. Pedro Olivera (director of the Agriculture Ministry's National Center for Land Control), in a statement to the official daily *Granma*, cited in *El Universal*, January 25, 2011.

13. Alina Perera Robbio and Francisco Rodríguez Cruz, "Ser parte, no observador," First National Conference of the CCP, Commission no. 1, on functioning, methods, and style of work, *Cubaweb*, January 30, 2012, http://www.granma.cubaweb.cu/2012/01/30/nacional/artic04.html.

14. Graziella Pogolotti, "Para dialogar con los jóvenes," *Juventud Rebelde*, March 3, 2010.

Chapter Ten

Updating the Cuban Economic Model

Omar Everleny Pérez Villanueva

Cuban authorities have stressed since 2007 that the structural problems facing the country need to be solved in the shortest amount of time possible because they are handicapping economic development. It is precisely this argument, alongside other objective and subjective economic factors, that have been behind the "updating" of Cuba's economic model. However, we should not forget that in the 1990s, there was already prolific academic work on the subject, and many proposals were put forth that underlined the necessity of enacting significant reforms of the Cuban economy.

In other words, structural economic problems have been strongly debated, at least in academic circles, for the past fifteen years. What are some of these structural problems that have contributed to the worsening of the majority of the country's economic indicators?

- The current configuration of gross domestic product (GDP), with a high expansion of services (particularly professional ones), while agriculture and industry remain backward and of lesser importance
- Excessive economic centralization
- Little diversity in foreign trade, where the balance of payments relies on the export of professional services, particularly medical personnel, and the carryover effects on the rest of the economy are still low
- Low productivity in a large part of the state-enterprise sector, contributing to low economic efficiency overall with a high consumption of energy and other resources
- An unsustainable relationship between the earnings of workers and the high cost of goods and services in both private and state markets
- Strict prohibitions for citizens, such as on the acquisition of certain goods and services
- Complex demographic structure, with low birthrates, a sizable segment of the population over the age of sixty, and rates of emigration that exceed 35,000 persons per year

These problems are interrelated, and they have spread throughout an economy that has a small internal market, is extremely dependent on imports, and must face an economic embargo enacted by the United States.

The time and effort devoted to the socialist project, combined with the experiences of socialist countries in Asia, place the Cuban government in the position of needing to update the country's economic model. The market needs to have an increasingly larger role in Cuba's economy, even if the country maintains a planned economy.

Thus, it is necessary to implement changes in Cuba's economic structure. However, not just any change will suffice, at least in the medium term. Rather, any effective change needs to reach sectors of the economy with the highest productivity or aggregate value.

It has already been accepted that the state does not have to control nonstrategic sectors that are capable of absorbing the large number of workers who will become available in the coming years as part of the reorganization of businesses and other economic units. The number of workers who will have to be reassigned to a new sector in the first phase is between 1 million and 1.3 million. However, this first phase began in 2011, when there were 500,000 state workers who needed to be relocated.

With an increasing number of calls to update Cuba's economic model, it was necessary to convene a Party Congress (the Sixth), which had not been held for more than thirteen years. For the congress, a document titled "Guidelines of the Economic and Social Policy" was prepared, and its recommendations and proposals were debated throughout the country.

In the analysis of Cuba's principal economic indicators, it is possible to understand the sagacity and need of the Cuban government when it began to update the economic model. Cuban authorities have highlighted, nonetheless, the resistance to the economic changes from both current party leaders and the larger population, which has grown accustomed to a paternalistic state and is interested more in state spending than in state revenue.

A close analysis of Cuba's current economic situation shows some disheartening trends: these are discussed in the following sections.

EVOLUTION OF GDP

In 2010, the Cuban economy halted the trend of negative economic growth of past years and grew by 2.1 percent. The growth rate between 2000 and 2006 was significant in that it reached an annual average rate of 6.2 percent of GDP (at 1997 price levels), but this rate is still low when compared to the untapped potential of the so-called "real economy" of industry and agriculture and the accumulated needs of both the general population and the government.

STRUCTURE OF GDP

In the structure of GDP, there is a downward trend in the relative weight of the goods sector (agriculture and industry) and of basic services, such as construction and transportation. Additionally, there has been a significant increase in the "other services" category, especially in health, commerce, and other areas, such that services contributed nearly 80 percent of the country's GDP in 2010. Therefore, it is necessary to consider whether it is possible to attempt development on the basis of service sectors with low productivity, such as health, commerce, education, and others.

Even though areas in which the country should prioritize economic growth have been identified, the sectors that are most likely to propel the economy forward have yet to be identified. That is, the country is working toward economic stabilization, but this does not mean that the routes to economic development have been defined, and the country still does not know with which products it will insert itself into the globalized economy.

The so-called real sector of the economy, such as industry and agriculture, have a weak role in contributing to GDP growth, and in 2008, 2009, and 2010, they actually stagnated.

LOW EFFICIENCY IN INVESTMENTS

In the past decade, as well as in previous years, there was a strong immobilization of financial resources in Cuba since there were fewer new investments than those that were already in place. From 2000 to 2009, the approved investment plan was never put into practice, demonstrating either an inadequate elaboration of the plan alongside low interest among the persons tasked with executing the plan or a lack of construction materials and other equipment. This derives from the fact that the country lacked the external financing that investors were seeking, resulting in the immobilization of material and financial resources. Thus, the state lost financial resources and opportunities because of these shortcomings.

AGING AND LOW RATES OF POPULATION GROWTH

As a result of low fertility among Cuban women, the percentage of the national population between the ages of zero and fourteen has fallen, whereas the percentage of Cubans aged sixty and over has increased. Nearly 1.9 million Cubans were between the ages of zero and fourteen in 2010, while an equal number was over the age of sixty.

The aging of the population is one of the most neuralgic effects of the demographic transition in the country and will demand the efforts of all the institutions and elements of society to address this issue. The first stage of this trend in Cuba began in the 1970s, and already by the end of that decade the country was registering a negative birthrate, and citizens over the age of sixty represented more than 10 percent of the national population. In 2010, the aging of the population stood at 17.4 percent.

UNFAVORABLE RELATIONSHIP BETWEEN PRODUCTIVITY GROWTH AND AVERAGE SALARIES

An analysis of the relationship between productivity growth and average salaries until 2009 reveals a near total imbalance, as salaries were rising faster than productivity. Evidently, in a country with "inflated payrolls" and nearly a million underemployed workers, it is possible to think that this relationship was never viable. This is a challenge that the government must solve, or at least this is what Cuban authorities have expressed.

A sectorial analysis of employment structure clearly shows that there would likely be available workers in the "other services" sector, which is where the number of jobs has increased in recent years. This increase was accompanied by a decrease in persons employed in the goods sector.

Since 2010, the government has accelerated its analysis of jobs that could become available as well as those that were created in health, education, public administration, and other sectors as a result of programs associated with the "Battle of Ideas."

COMPLETED DWELLINGS PER YEAR

In 2006, Cuba implemented a special program for the construction, conservation, and rehabilitation of the housing stock, and 100,000 dwellings were ordered to be constructed starting in that same year. This program was only fulfilled in 2011 because priority was given to clearing a backlog of houses requiring small actions to be completed—a backlog that has been around since the beginning of the "Special Period." Current policy has been geared toward favoring the construction of dwellings, where Resolution No. 40/2010 of the Institute of Housing, published in the *Official Gazette of the Republic of Cuba* on February 17, 2010, allows for incentivizing the building of dwellings by independent actions through granting construction licenses.

In Resolution No. 40/2010, there is a special mention of the "Third Special Disposition," which authorizes municipal units that invest in housing to approve without prior selection applications for building permits by persons from these units for new works, remodeling, rehabilitation, and a variety of other modifications. The license will be granted on presentation of proof of ownership of the land or the right to use the roof.

FOREIGN TRADE IN GOODS

The commercial imbalance of goods continues to characterize Cuba's foreign trade. Exports are not growing with the necessary dynamism because of decreases in sugar production, a stagnation of mining operations, and a decrease in the export of shellfish, citrus fruits, and other goods. Additionally, imports are very high despite official policies aiming to reduce them.

Stemming from an increase in imports in 2008 and previous commitments, Cuba has experienced increased pressure on its balance of payments and even began to withhold foreign payments, especially in 2009. This has contributed to an extraordinary increase in debt related to both the export of goods and the export of both goods and services together.

FOREIGN TRADE IN GOODS AND SERVICES

The service sector has been one of the largest earners for the state since 2004, and several changes have taken place as knowledge-intensive services have replaced the tourism industry as the main generator of revenue for the state. It is estimated that more than 50 percent of exports of services are in the form of medical services. It is these types of services that contributed to a surplus in the commercial balance of goods and services in 2009 and 2010.

After analyzing these selected economic indicators, we will look at the content of the proposals outlined in the "Guidelines of the Economic and Social Policy of the Party and the Revolution," which were approved at the Sixth Congress of the Communist Party on April 18, 2011, and approved in the National Assembly of People's Power on August 1, 2011.

The main proposals and adjustments approved during the Party Congress are the following:

- Adjustments in budgetary spending, especially in education, health, sports, and culture
- Adjustments in employment in the state sector through the elimination of inflated payrolls
- Handing over idle land in usufruct
- Reorganization of the state apparatus, ministries, and large state-owned businesses
- Incentives for nonstate employment, such as self-employment
- Proposals for the creation of nonagricultural cooperatives
- Ability to hire employees
- Proposals to eliminate restrictions on the buying and selling of houses, automobiles, other goods and services, and so on
- Greater entrepreneurial autonomy
- Development of local projects and greater autonomy for local government
- Equality of opportunity for all but not "egalitarianism"
- Search for self-sufficiency in food production and the gradual elimination of rationing

- Ability to rent state installations, including ones relating to gastronomy
- Separation of state and business functions
- Updating tax policy
- Strategies to reorganize external debt
- Promotion of the creation of Special Development Zones

Updating Cuba's economic model requires an analysis of the so-called small and medium-size businesses (*pequeñas y medianas empresas*, PYMES), whose possible implementation was first mentioned in the mid-1990s but ultimately never came to fruition for various reasons. These businesses fall within proposals for the expansion of self-employment that were put forth by the National Assembly of People's Power in August 2010 and published in the *Official Gazette of the Republic of Cuba* in the extraordinary Edition Nos. 11 and 12 on October 1 and 8, 2010, respectively.

The advantages of the PYMES are numerous. They are an alternative form of work that is necessary in Cuba's economic climate; they contribute to higher standards of living and personal income, facilitate the decentralization of certain production processes and services, and allow for a greater output of goods and services.

Perhaps most interesting is that the PYMES are not derived from Cuba's economic situation. Instead, they are part of a global trend to structure economic production based on small and medium-size businesses, with flexibility, a highly skilled workforce (one of Cuba's strongest assets at the moment), and a high degree of competitiveness. The Cuban government is currently analyzing the need to implement some variant of the so-called PYMES, especially "cooperatives" for the socialization of production and the benefits from this production style.

It is also possible to study other ways to foment economic development, such as businesses that can be composed of self-employed and state workers or individual laborers and cooperatives. It is widely known that many of these entities exist, and there is an effort to make this type of labor relations more explicit and open, setting their corresponding social responsibilities and organizing and controlling these activities on behalf of the state.

There exists a group of activities that were proposed on one occasion but did not appear in the manual of approved self-employment in the mid-1990s. Others worked for a while and then disappeared, but their revival could be worthwhile in the government's plan to update the country's economic model.

Additionally, given the highly skilled labor force and the high percentage of youths who do not work, the type of businesses that require a higher use of skilled knowledge should be studied. This will prevent skilled youths from leaving these fields for higher-paying jobs that require less intellectual input and can also stem emigration. These types of jobs can be found in consulting, auditing, architecture, design, and other fields that may even have been proposed by the citizens themselves.

This new process should overcome the insufficiencies that harmed self-employed workers in the past, which have included difficulties in purchasing supplies, contractive fiscal policies, virtually nonexistent financial aid mechanisms (microcredits), lack of state controls, and regulations concerning the hiring of workers, among other challenges.

The experiences of China and Vietnam should be taken into account in this process, especially as Cuba reflects on its economy, society, politics, and ideology. The Chinese and Vietnamese cases are part of broader discussions in Cuba about contemporary socialism, largely because socialism has been the reference point for the country's transformation ever since the breakdown of "real socialism" in Europe. China and Vietnam, as socialist countries, have the potential to be a good model for Cuba.

For Cuban economists, one of the principal areas of focus in the analysis of the experiences of China and Vietnam is the study of broader and more radical market reforms enacted by the Chinese Communist Party, which has been very successful in economic affairs, relatively far reaching and beneficial (although controversial and contradictory) in social matters, and legitimizing in the political realm. It could be argued that Vietnam is a similar case, and it likely is.

China always offers an economic image limited to only a few aspects: very high economic growth, a magnet for foreign investment, and a formidable export capacity. However, the ability to experience directly the Chinese and Vietnamese realities may have the effect of downgrading these aspects to second class and may instead highlight the important role of the *internal market*. In other words, the dominant image of China today is of a country with an enormous internal market and dizzying economic growth.

The central role that has been conceded to the internal market in the context of the Chinese reform is a result of agricultural reforms and has been reinforced as time goes by. This has been reflected in favoring policies aimed at diversifying forms of property with a high bias toward the generation of income, supported in the extension of private economic activity.

This leads us to reflect on the fact that even though Cuba is an "open economy" (an export economy) very different from China, the expansion of the internal market is an essential condition for the development of any type of economy and therefore must have a prominent role in any development strategy. This has obviously been an element that has been absent from Cuban economic policy in recent years, and I believe that it should be *the* priority of development plans in the update of Cuba's economic policy.

Updating the Cuban model is an essential step in the design of a model for medium-term development. It is necessary to tackle some of the structural distortions that we have mentioned. Of course, the development of the internal market must be one of the essential components of this project. The transformation of this model, keeping in mind the new economic variables that have been introduced, will permit annual growth of 5 percent. It is forecast that in 2015, 35 percent of the jobs in Cuba will not be in the state sector. In other words, the stimulus to production that hopefully will occur—the strengthening of industrial growth in addition to infrastructure and industrial megaprojects already in place, such as the development of the port of Mariel, the petrochemical plant in Cienfuegos, the development of nickel (among others), and the incentive to develop nonstate forms of production both in agriculture and in the service sector—can contribute to the growth of the country's principal economic indicators.

For this, it is necessary to "open the minds" of decision makers and utilize the word "autonomy" conclusively, break myths from the past, and understand that current and future generations cannot remain tied down to the recent past.

NOTE

Excerpted from Omar Everleny Pérez, "La Actualización del Modelo Económico Cubano," October 2011, Desde la Isla website (Cuba Study Group), translated by Kevin Gatter. Reprinted by permission of the publisher.

Chapter Eleven

Cuba's Entrepreneurs

Foundation of a New Private Sector

Philip Peters

After years of stagnation, Cuban entrepreneurship has changed and grown dramatically. Regulations governing entrepreneurship were liberalized significantly in October 2010, notably allowing the hiring of employees. Official attitudes about it changed from indifference to encouragement. The number of Cubans employed in this sector increased 145 percent, from 157,371 in October 2010 to 385,775 in July 2012, representing about one in thirteen workers.

Most important, the purpose has changed. In the past, when no thought was being given to changing the socialist model, entrepreneurship seemed to be viewed as a necessary evil, of marginal importance to the economy. It is now viewed as a strategic necessity for a government that is determined to cut costs and boost economic output by reducing government payrolls and expanding the private sector. For every new person employed as an entrepreneur, the government counts one more job created, one more stream of tax revenue, one more household with higher income, and one less household in need of the universal food subsidies that it aims to eliminate.

Entrepreneurship, in Cuba called *trabajo por cuenta propia* (self-employment), is the most visible manifestation of economic reforms undertaken by President Raúl Castro since he took office in 2008. The entrepreneurs, called *cuentapropistas*, are operating their new businesses on the streets of every city and town. State media are covering this sector amply and, in a new twist, favorably.

But the new entrepreneurs are only part of the reform plan, which is being developed and implemented according to a blueprint approved by the Communist Party in 2011. To reach major economic objectives involving job growth, productivity increases, improved government finances, and reduced incentives for young Cubans to emigrate, a larger "nonstate" sector of the economy has to develop, one that will need to include larger and more complex businesses than those that today's entrepreneurs are creating.

THE EVOLUTION OF CUBA'S PRIVATE SECTOR

When Cuba's socialist government came to power in 1959, it did not set out immediately to eliminate small private enterprise. The first years of the socialist revolution saw the nationalization of large and foreign enterprises, the agrarian reform that redistributed agricultural lands, and the urban reform that did the same for residential property.

It was in 1968, the year of the "Revolutionary Offensive," that the small business sector came to be targeted. In a speech in March of that year, President Fidel Castro stated, "If this Revolution can be reproached for anything it is not in the least for being extremist, but rather for having been insufficiently radical. And we should not miss the opportunity or let the hour or moment pass to radicalize this Revolution even more. And we have to finish making a revolutionary people. . . . If many are asking what kind of Revolution this is, that still permits such a class of parasites [small business owners] after nine years, they would be perfectly right to ask." With words like that, the small and medium-size business sector that predated the socialist revolution was put on the chopping block. Restaurants, bars (Fidel noted in his speech that Havana had 955), and service operations of all kinds were "intervened," or taken over by the state.

Cuba's future soon became one with only slight vestiges of private entrepreneurship, mainly barbers and beauticians, numbering 10,000 to 15,000. The economy, from farm to factory to retail services, came to be dominated by state enterprises. It all ran under a Soviet-style model where the state attempted to plan nearly all economic activity, including production levels, employment, allocation of resources, pricing, and trade and investment with Soviet bloc partners.

The aversion to private entrepreneurship continued until the early 1990s, when the dissolution of the entire Soviet bloc provoked a sharp economic crisis in Cuba. Responding to that crisis, Cuba legalized the circulation of hard currency, built up its tourism sector, opened to foreign investment, promoted incentive-based agriculture, and undertook a limited opening to small-scale entrepreneurship.

The entrepreneurial sector, like the other reforms, was carefully circumscribed. Private entrepreneurship was permitted only by license, it was limited to 158 specific lines of work, and employees were not permitted except in the case of family "assistants" in cafeterias, lunch stands, and small restaurants. The sector peaked in 1996 at 209,000 *cuentapropistas* operating restaurants and lunch stands, bed-and-breakfasts for tourists, and home repair and service operations of all kinds all across the island.

The government's attitude toward entrepreneurship ranged from neutral to wary and never expressed a policy goal of encouraging its growth. A June 1998 document from the Cuban labor federation expressed concern about increasing corruption, including theft of state supplies, and partially blamed the economic reforms that the government had been "obliged" to make. It lamented inequality arising from the parallel hard-currency economy, which allegedly produces "egotism, the cult of capitalist fetishes, and the mentality of the small property owner."

A typical official view was stated by Economy Minister José Luis Rodríguez in February 2001: "We don't see that our country's development rests on self-employment or small private property holders." In March 2001, he said, "We believe there is no reason for the self-employed sector not to exist if it follows certain regulations, but we don't stimulate it because we don't think it is the solution to our economic problems."

Come 2004, Cuba's economy had improved from its condition a decade earlier but had by no means fully recovered. With a new and beneficial economic relationship with Venezuela maturing, the government decided to pull back from some of the previous decade's reforms. On October 1, 2004, as part of the general retrenchment in economic policy, the Ministry of Labor and Social Security issued new regulations governing self-employment, noting in a statement that "self-employment, in the current economic revival that our country is experiencing, acts as a complement to some state activity in the production of goods and the supply of services of value to the public, and is an alternative source of employment." However, it continued, some private economic activities might "be assimilated . . . by the central state administration."

The regulations provided that no new licenses would be granted in forty categories of self-employment, but those working in the remaining 118 lines of work could continue to work and have their licenses renewed. In those, an "annual analysis" by municipal authorities would determine whether any licenses at all were necessary. No new licenses were to be granted for private family restaurants, cafeterias, and lunch stands, and the numbers of these businesses dropped noticeably while the government expanded its own retail food services. The result was that the number of entrepreneurs declined beginning in 1997 and stabilized at about 150,000 during the decade 2000–2010. The causes were many. An income tax was introduced in 1996. Some businesses fell victim to competition from the state or from other entrepreneurs down the street. Others were affected by regulatory enforcement that was in many instances normal, such as health inspections of food establishments, and in many other instances seemed punitive. Given all this, many thousands of Cubans risked working without a license, engaging in occasional, part-time, or full-time business activity. This is the situation that would remain until 2010, when a new political leadership produced a new economic diagnosis and a new plan to revamp Cuba's socialist economic model.

ENTREPRENEURSHIP IN A CHANGING SOCIALIST ECONOMIC MODEL

In the 1990s, an expansion of *trabajo por cuenta propia* was undertaken to make a modest contribution to economic recovery in a context in which Cuba's economic model was being adjusted but not changed in fundamental ways. By contrast, today's expansion of entrepreneurship is part of a major overhaul of the economic model, and its role in that change is of central importance. When Raúl Castro assumed Cuba's presidency on an interim basis in 2006 and fully in 2008, he led a process of analysis, debate, and reform in economic policy that, while not yet complete, is more consequential than any economic policy change in Cuba since the early 1990s. His actions are based on assessments made by him—and earlier by his brother Fidel in his last major policy speech as president in 2005—that economic failings constitute a threat to the survival of Cuba's socialist system itself. Among its main features are the following:

- Blunt assessments, in official statements and in state media, of the shortcomings of Cuba's economic performance.
- A critique of "paternalism" in the form of excessive social benefits, an oversized government role in economic activity, and a need "to erase forever the notion that Cuba is the only country in the world where one can live without working," in Raúl Castro's words.
- A recognition that strategic goals for the economy—preserving essential social benefits, ending the dual currency system and creating a unified currency, improving government finances and Cuba's external balances, addressing income inequality by raising state sector wages for doctors and others—can be met only if the economy as a whole becomes more productive.
- A recognition that greater output will not be achieved through the state sector; rather, the state must shed unprofitable enterprises and unnecessary activities, substantially reduce its payroll, and allow a larger private sector to operate within the socialist economy.

Any doubts about government intentions to reduce its own payrolls were set aside in September 2010, when this headline appeared on the front page of the Communist Party daily *Granma*: "Announcement of the Central de Trabajadores de Cuba." The announcement, by Cuba's labor union federation, was that 500,000 state sector jobs would be eliminated by the following May, with a "parallel increase in the non-state sector."

For laid-off workers, the announcement explained, there would be a "broadened and diversified" set of job opportunities, including "renting, usufruct, cooperatives, and self-employment, toward which hundreds of thousands of workers will move in the coming years." Those are all private sector options: "renting" refers to the leasing of state installations, such as barber shops, beauty shops, and taxis, where the workers now operate as small entrepreneurs; "usufruct" refers to long-term leasing of land or other facilities, as in farm cooperatives; "cooperatives" suggests nonagricultural uses of that formula; and "self-employment" means entrepreneurship. The announcement stated that "it is known" that the state sector has more than 1 million excess workers. It noted that opportunities for reemployment in the government and its enterprises would be limited to agriculture, construction, teachers, police, and industrial workers.

SIGNS OF THE TIMES

Also in September 2010, a briefing document that explains these layoffs was made public. It quotes Raúl Castro saying that if Cuba continues to maintain "inflated payrolls in almost all areas" and to "pay salaries with no link to results," prices will continue to rise, purchasing power will continue to erode, and pay increases for productive workers will remain impossible. The document anticipated that 64,546 new private jobs would be created in Havana, 85 percent in small entrepreneurship. It lists dozens of ideas for businesses that can be performed by private cooperatives outside the farm sector, although policies to establish such cooperatives have not yet been issued.

In practice, the layoffs proceeded more slowly than planned, but they have proceeded. State payrolls were reduced by 140,000 in 2011, and a 500,000 reduction is expected by 2015, according to a Cuban labor federation official and published economic plans. In other contexts, the stated estimates have been higher; for example, the finance minister projected that 1.8 million workers will join the "nonstate" sector by 2015. Vice President Esteban Lazo predicted in April 2012 that the private sector's share of gross domestic product would grow from 5 to 45 to 50 percent within five years.

In this context, job generation in the private sector—combining the *cuentapropistas*, private sector agriculture, future private cooperatives, and other private entities—is an essential enabler of various elements of the reform process. Stronger private sector job creation allows the government to proceed faster with layoffs and to reap their budget savings. As more entrepreneurs pay taxes, they boost government revenues, hastening the day when the government can afford to attack the pernicious disparities in Cubans' purchasing power by, for example, raising the pay of doctors and others in the health sector. And each time a household income improves because of a private sector job, it becomes easier for the government to end universal benefits, such as food rations, and to direct them to the needy only.

OCTOBER 2010: THE POLICY LIBERALIZATION

Shortly after the announcements about state sector layoffs, the government followed with announcements about new regulations that would permit an expansion in Cuba's entrepreneurial sector. A September 2010 *Granma* article previewed the new policies and stated, almost apologetically, that they would aim to "distance ourselves from those conceptions that condemned self-employment almost to extinction and stigmatized those who decided to join it, legally, in the 1990s." The new regulations themselves were published in October. Soon thereafter, the reality of new policies became clear on Cuban streets when the Labor Ministry started opening special municipal offices to process applications for business licenses.

Public response to the new policies was strong because of the government's new disposition to issue new licenses again and because they in fact expanded opportunities for entrepreneurship:

- Licenses are now available in 181 lines of work.
- To bring entrepreneurs in from the black market, licenses may be granted to those without a *vínculo laboral*, that is, those with no current workplace.
- Previously, only restaurants and small food service operations, such as sandwich stands, were permitted to employ assistants. The new regulations permitted employees to be hired in eighty-three lines of work, and later they were changed to allow employees to be hired in any line of work.
- In private restaurants, the seating limit was increased from twelve to twenty and later to fifty. Prohibitions on serving beef and shellfish were ended.
- "Housing, rooms, and spaces" may be rented to entrepreneurs for use as places of business.
- Entrepreneurs may now have licenses for more than one line of work.
- Unlike before, entrepreneurs may work anywhere, not just in the municipality in which they were licensed.
- Instead of being restricted to selling to individuals, they may now sell goods and services to state entities, foreign companies, and cooperatives.
- Entrepreneurs must pay income tax. The first 10,000 pesos of income, an amount that equals approximately twice the average salary paid in the state sector, is tax exempt. The top marginal rate is 50 percent. Expenses totaling up to 40 percent of gross income may be deducted from taxable income (the previous limit on deductions was 10 percent). In addition, there is a sales tax, a public service tax, and a tax per employee hired, all deductible from income tax. The tax on hired labor is explained as necessary "to avoid concentrations of wealth."
- Finally, there is a contribution to social security, which entitles entrepreneurs to disability and maternity benefits and monthly payments on retirement. Taxpayers can vary the amount they contribute, and benefits will depend on the amount contributed.
- In May 2011, these policies were eased to favor job creation over tax collection. The tax per employee was suspended for businesses with fewer than six employees, taxes were reduced and deductions increased in some occupations, and businesses were allowed to close for repairs more easily and for longer periods, suspending their licenses and their tax obligations.

Beyond the new regulatory treatment, other government actions evidence a change in attitude toward entrepreneurs and a desire to see the sector grow rather than simply subsist. The Cuban media's treatment of the sector has changed dramatically. In the past, coverage of entrepreneurs was sparse and fell mainly into three categories: stories about pilferage of state resources to supply private businesses, stories about food service establishments that violate health codes, and stories about entrepreneurs profiting from deeply subsidized public services, such as electricity.

Since late 2011, there has been much more coverage of entrepreneurs, and much of it is positive. Cuban media encouraged people to apply for licenses and explained how to do so. In November 2011, an article in *Granma* detailed the new regulations governing home rental and the ways in which they "considerably broaden" the possibilities for this line of work. It explained that entire houses may now be rented in the Cuban peso or convertible currency, space can be rented for lodging or for use by other entrepreneurs (e.g., a room for a hairdresser or a front porch for a sandwich stand), those who rent out their homes can now get licenses for additional lines of work, and they may hire employees.

In December 2010, with new licensing processes in effect barely one month, *Granma* ran a 1,300-word article on the necessity "to untie the bureaucratic knots that slow down the expeditious issuing of licenses to small entrepreneurs." With the new policies governing entrepreneurship, a retiree in rural Pinar del Rio province said, "The only people not working are those that don't want to." That is an exaggeration but an easy one to make given the appearance of so many new businesses across Cuba.

ASSESSMENTS

The growth of small enterprise has been strong and positive in several respects. After hovering around the 150,000 level for more than a decade, the addition of 228,000 to this sector, counting both entrepreneurs and their employees, represents very substantial growth of 145 percent in legal employment. It has demonstrated the amount of grassroots economic initiative that previous regulations had driven into the underground economy or suppressed altogether. The expansion of entrepreneurship has improved family welfare, boosted government revenues, and begun to provide a destination for workers laid off from the government's "inflated payrolls." Current regulations do not amount to an open grant of economic freedom to all who wish to start the business of their choice, but the 2010 liberalization greatly expanded space for private economic initiative and is a positive step in human rights.

Government statements that the new policies are here to stay are credible. While Cubans remember the retreats from the economic openings of the 1990s, many are watching the policies in action and the change in official discourse and are believing that there will be no turning back this time. With the reform process steadily reducing state sector employment, further expansion of private employment is essential. A reduction would disrupt other parts of the reform program and be politically problematic. Regulations continue to limit the growth of entrepreneurship and the benefits it provides the public.

The new regulatory regime is a significant progrowth improvement: it allows entrepreneurs to hire employees, to hold multiple licenses, and to sell to government entities, state enterprises, and joint ventures. Development of markets for entrepreneurs' basic supplies, especially at wholesale, will mark a further improvement.

Yet the need to choose among a list of 181 licensed lines of work is a limiting factor, preventing would-be entrepreneurs from choosing the activities that appeal to them and in which they believe they can succeed. More than small-scale entrepreneurship in its current form is needed to meet the government's goals for generating new private sector employment. An expansion of Cuba's entrepreneurial sector by more than 200,000 was unimaginable a few years ago. So was a government decision that a key to improving productivity is to expand the private sector by more than 1 million workers. But entrepreneurs alone are not likely to generate 1 million new private sector jobs under current rules. Those jobs, combined with further reductions in the public sector workforce, can potentially eliminate a fiscal deficit that has already declined from 6.9 percent of gross domestic product in 2008 to 3.8 percent last year.

In Cuban discussions of economic policy—in academic journals, public debates, Catholic Church magazines, and state media—there is no shortage of ideas for policies to spur the expansion of the private sector. When it comes to entrepreneurship, the most common suggestion is to treat the sector as an "infant industry" by reducing taxes to promote growth until the sector matures. Other suggestions are to do away with the list of 181 permitted lines of work and instead to allow entrepreneurial ventures in any line of work except those that the state may reserve to itself and to allow professionals to work as entrepreneurs in the field for which they were trained. However, the potential for far more substantial job growth lies in the creation of private nonfarm cooperatives. In this area, policies have yet to be defined except in general terms.

The economic policy blueprint adopted in 2011 by the Communist Party stated that private cooperatives will be formed "as a socialist form of collective property in different sectors . . . integrated by persons who join together contributing goods or labor . . . and assume all their expenses with their income." A policy for pilot projects for nonagricultural cooperatives in three provinces was approved in March 2012, but details were not released. Among the issues to be defined will be policies governing cooperatives that are converted from state enterprises (such as cafeterias, repair shops, and manufacturing operations that are handed over to workers) and start-up cooperatives formed by persons who affiliate for that purpose. Also to be defined are levels of taxation, the sectors in which cooperatives may do business, and whether professionals will be permitted to participate. A likely limiting factor in the policies governing cooperatives is the government's concern about "concentration of wealth," which will presumably be addressed through taxation.

The new tax system is a key variable. A primary consideration in tax policy has been fairness: charging entrepreneurs for the government services and benefits they receive. The choice of tax rates is a matter of conflicting objectives. Higher rates can potentially increase near-term government revenues, enabling expenditures on other priorities, such as attacking income inequality by raising some state sector salaries. Lower rates can encourage job creation and increase disposable income, and this, in turn, can fuel further private sector growth. The government has shown that it is weighing these considerations, and its 2011 tax reductions were a midcourse correction to encourage job creation over immediate revenue generation. To date, the impact of taxes on the entrepreneurial sector has varied. Surely, taxes are among the factors that have caused some entrepreneurs to return their licenses. It is also possible to find entrepreneurs who are not held back by the current tax burden.

An entrepreneur who runs a pizza and sandwich stand in a good Havana location said that he pays 400 pesos per month in tax—a burden that is "not very strong." He has operated since May 2011, and his gross revenues average about 2,000 pesos daily, although he says that with each passing month, he is feeling the effects of greater competition from additional private establishments. With his savings, he is starting a new cafeteria ten blocks away. Many entrepreneurs are working below their professional potential and outside the fields of their education and training.

The lack of entrepreneurial opportunities for Cubans with advanced professional and technical skills means that Cuba is failing to take full advantage of the investment made in their education and forgoing their potential contribution to economic development: innovation, competitiveness, export growth, job growth, and reduced incentives for young Cubans to emigrate. Many of the new entrepreneurs, such as those reselling housewares brought to them from relatives abroad or selling copied music and movies on disc, have created jobs and pay taxes but otherwise contribute little to development.

NOTE

Excerpted from Philip Peters, *Cuba's Entrepreneurs: Foundation of a New Private Sector* (Arlington, VA: Lexington Institute, 2012).

Chapter Twelve

Cuban Agriculture and the Current Process of Economic Transformation

Armando Nova González

The Cuban economy has begun an interesting and important process of economic transformation that has been identified as the "updating of the economic model." It covers all economic sectors, with important implications for the economic, social, and political sectors of the nation. These changes have been reflected in the "Guidelines of the Economic and Social Policy of the Party and the Revolution," adopted during the Sixth Congress of the Communist Party held in April 2011.

One may note that the most profound and important transformations have been initiated in a sector that is economically vital and strategic for the Cuban economy, as is the agricultural sector. Insufficient domestic food production (see Nova 2010) is an issue that has been prevalent during the past fifty years in the national economy, increasing the country's dependence on foreign food, making it more vulnerable, and resulting in a high expenditure of foreign currency for food imports (see table 12.1) when most of these could be produced domestically under competitive conditions.

The current issue of the agricultural sector could be summarized as follows: agricultural and livestock production is down, there are records of significant quantities of idle agricultural land, and food imports continue to grow to cover the shortfall in domestic production. This leads to obvious signs that the productive forces are still frozen and the need to transform systemically production relationships and analyze how to solve the issue of ownership of the land and the changes needed to achieve it.[1]

The current situation of dependency in the area of food products is paradoxical given the fact that the agricultural sector shows a significant number of unused areas (more than 2 million idle hectares). Results obtained from various scientific and technical institutions indicate that there is a material basis (although undercapitalized largely by years of economic crisis, but it exists and can be improved and used) and that the sector has significant human capital. All this suggests that agriculture holds an important productive potential that must be put to use.

From 2007 to date, a series of measures aimed at finding solutions to the revitalization of this important sector have been implemented, searching for solutions to increase production, the substitution of food imports, and the generation of surpluses to increase the exports of goods. These measures include an increase in the price of milk, beef, and agricultural products; decentralization of functions by identifying the municipality as the key space for the

Table 12.1.   Dynamics of Imports for 2002–2010 and Estimated for 2011 (in millions of U.S. dollars)

	Total imports	Total food imports	Food for humans	Food for animals	Food as percentage of total imports
2002	4,140.767	827.236	762.385	64.851	20.0%
2003	4,612.598	998.120	912.296	85.824	21.6%
2004	5,615.198	1,183.273	1,073.422	109.851	21.1%
2005	7,604.259	1,494.204	1,357.313	136.891	19.6%
2006	9,497.890	1,391.928	1,261.697	130.231	14.7%
2007	10,082.557	1,746.402	1,570.706	175.696	17.3%
2008	14,249.234	2,544.822	2,280.401	264.421	17.8%
2009	8,909.541	1,755.604	1,524.645	230.959	19.7%
2010	8,000.000	1,600.000	1,400.000	200.000	20.0%
2011 (est.)	8,100.000	1,700.000	1,500.000	200.000	21.0%

Source: Prepared by the author with data from the National Office of Statistics (ONE 2002–2010).

execution and decision making in agricultural activities; and simplification of the structures and functions of ministries that generate primary production and food processing (Nova 2010). Recent steps have been taken with regard to the hiring of a labor force, agricultural expansion of microloans, and the gradual decentralization of the marketing of agricultural products.

But the most important decision has been the delivery to individuals of idle (uncultivated) farmland under conditions of usufruct.[2] These deliveries are made currently under the conditions of lease for a renewable period of ten years. Decree Law 259 on the distribution of land in usufruct has been an important and decisive step, although from its inception it included a number of restrictions and limitations that caused a significant degree of uncertainty for the beneficiaries (Nova 2009). Currently, although Decree Law 259 has not been officially changed, official statements have been made promising to increase the time period of the usufruct contract, recognize the right to build housing, and increase the area of land to be delivered, as long as there is the possibility of its being cultivated.

The current distribution of idle land also leads to a new stage and agricultural model that establishes and reinforces the dominance of nongovernment producers, particularly the Cooperativas de Créditos y Servicios (Credit and Service Cooperatives [CCS]) and the private sector, which could increase from 18.5 to 51.0 percent in landownership (see table 12.2). If these producers are often the best (according to the results[3]) and the measures to be analyzed below are implemented under a systematic approach, we should expect significant increases in food production.

There is a trend toward the dominance of small and medium-size nongovernment companies, both in the possession and in the ownership of the land, in a spiral movement that involves qualitative changes. This does not represent a return to the situation observed in the late nineteenth century[4] (Nova 2011) but rather to a form that, although rooted in the dominant forms of that time, is strengthened by the collective forms of production (cooperatives), the farmer's knowledge transferred through the years from generation to generation and enriched by scientific and technical development.

Table 12.2.   Forms of Land Ownership (%)

Agricultural Area	Total	Government	Nongovernment	UBPC	CPA	CCS and Private**
2007	100	35.8	64.2	36.9	8.8	18.5
2011*	100	17.0	83.0	23.0	9.0	51.0

* Estimated.

** Includes those benefited by Decree Law 259.

UBPC: Unidades Básicas de Producción Cooperativas (Basic Units of Cooperative Production).

CPA: Cooperativas de Producción Agrícola (Agricultural Production Cooperatives).

CCS: Cooperativas de Créditos y Servicios (Credit and Service Cooperatives).

Source: Prepared by the author from the National Office of Statistics (ONE 2007–2010).

The more wealth is distributed, the less inequality there will be and a more fair model of agriculture and social-economic model will be created. This is consistent with the thoughts of José Martí: "A rich country is a country that has many small owners" (quoted in Almanza 1990, 261).

HOW IS THE AGRICULTURAL SECTOR BEHAVING?

Regardless of the measures taken since 2007, the results obtained have not been the results expected. During 2009 and 2010, agricultural production declined or, in the best case, remained stable. In 2009, total agricultural and livestock production closed at 100.5 percent, a stable level when compared to 2008, while the production of vegetable foods grew by 5.6 percent, and production of livestock fell by 4.6 percent. In 2010, the agricultural sector reported a decrease of 2.8 percent. There was a decrease in agricultural and livestock production in twelve basic items, including rice, pork, eggs, vegetables, beans, root vegetables (potato, *malanga*), citrus fruits, and poultry. At the end of 2011, there was an increase in total production (agricultural and livestock); however, the levels of food supply to the population decreased with a corresponding increase in prices. According to reports from the *Oficina Nacional de Estadísticas* (National Office of Statistics) (2002–2010), agricultural production grew 8.7 percent (11.5 percent agriculture and 6.0 percent livestock).

WHAT ARE THE FACTORS THAT HAVE A NEGATIVE INFLUENCE?

Sometimes, the reduction in agricultural and livestock production is attributed to the effects caused by drought, and to some extent this is a contributing factor, but this is a variable that must always be kept in mind. It is necessary to prepare early for this effect and reduce the current vulnerability. This requires creating the necessary food reserves during the spring, or rainy period.

However, the most important aspect is the delay in implementing reforms in the agricultural sector, formalized in the "Guidelines" adopted at the Sixth Congress of the Communist Party of Cuba and the systematic failure to apply them:

1. A delay in delivery of land to farmers under the framework of Decree Law 259 and its regulations (primarily bureaucratic aspects)

2. An insufficient offer of supplies, insufficient means of labor and production, with high prices (recent measures have been taken aimed at reducing prices) not adjusted to the demands, requirements, quality, and specifications of producers and regions and not taking into account the actual objective existence of the market and its role

3. A need to amend Decree Law 259 to eliminate the uncertainties that it contains and that do not favor the permanence of the producer

4. The failure to implement comprehensive measures for the decentralization of marketing and elimination of the government inventory system

5. The issue of prices paid to producers that are not satisfactory (despite the price increases in some categories), particularly those products that replace imports, while paying high prices for imported products and not to the local producer

6. The late delivery of loans and technical assistance

In summary, reaffirmed by the results achieved at the end of 2011, there are still three aspects that have not been settled:

- Limited rights of the owner of the property: the producers should be allowed to make their own decisions throughout the production-distribution-consumption-change cycle.
- Failure to recognize the real and objective existence of the market and its complementary role with planning.
- Lack of systemic approach in the design and implementation of measures.

Given this ongoing situation, it is evident that the productive forces of the agricultural sector are still detained, and it is necessary to remove the obstacles that hinder its development, which implies continuing as fast as possible the transformation of production relations in agriculture, which is a strategic economic sector for the Cuban economy.

NOTES

Excerpted from Armando Nova González, "Cuban Agriculture and the Current Economic Transformation Process," April 2012, Desde la Isla website (Cuba Study Group). Reprinted by permission of the publisher.

1. The right of the producer to be able to decide what to produce, how to sell it, and at what price and to be able to participate in an open market to purchase the necessary means and at the appropriate time in order to reach the successful closing of the productive cycle.

2. Uncultivated agricultural land, initially estimated at 1,868,210.84 hectares, was recently discovered to be some 500,000 hectares more.

3. The agricultural and livestock sectors are integrated by five productive entities: Unidades Básicas de Producción Cooperativas (Basic Units of Cooperative Production), Cooperativas de Producción Agrícola (Agricultural Production Cooperatives), Cooperativas de Créditos y Servicios (Credit and Service Cooperatives), private, and government. The most efficient are CCS and private. These two economic entities produce 57 percent of the total production of food in the country from only 24.4 percent of land. They also produce 63 percent of milk (the government produces 13 percent) and have more than 64 percent of milking cows and more than 57 and 60 percent of the cattle and pigs, respectively.

4. The Cuban agrarian situation in 1899 recorded the primacy of the small and medium-size companies with regards to larger enterprises.

REFERENCES

Almanza, R. 1990. *En torno al pensamiento económico de José Martí*. Havana: Editorial de Ciencias Sociales.
Nova, A. 2009. "50 años de la agricultura en Cuba, Línea de desarrollo, Resultados y Transformaciones." Seminario Científico Anual CEEC, May.

————. 2010. "La agricultura cubana medidas implementadas: Para lograr incrementos en la producción de alimentos. Análisis y valoración," Seminario Científico del Centro de Estudio de la Economía Cubana (CEEC), Universidad de La Habana, CD, June.

————. 2011. "Valoración del Impacto en Cuba de las medidas más recientes en el Sector Agropecuario y los Lineamientos de la Política Económica y Social." Seminario Científico Anual CEEC, U.H., June.

Oficina Nacional de Estadísticas. 2002–2010. *Anuarios Estadísticos de Cuba.* Havana: Oficina Nacional de Estadísticas.

Chapter Thirteen

The New Cuban Economy

What Roles for Foreign Investment?

Richard E. Feinberg

The Cuban Revolution defined itself in large measure in terms of what it was not: not a dependency of the United States, not a dominion governed by global corporations, and not a liberal, market-driven economy. As the guerrilla army made its triumphal entry into Havana and the infant revolution shifted leftward, a hallmark of its anti-imperialist ethos became the loudly proclaimed nationalizations of the U.S.-based firms that had controlled many key sectors of the Cuban economy, including hotels and gambling casinos, public utilities, oil refineries, and the rich sugar mills. In the strategic conflict with the United States, the "historic enemy," the Revolution consolidated its power through the excision of the U.S. economic presence.

For revolutionary Cuba, foreign investment has been about more than dollars and cents. It is about cultural identity and national sovereignty. It is also about a model of socialist planning, a hybrid of Marxist-Leninism and Fidelismo that has jealously guarded its domination over all aspects of the economy. During its five decades of rule, the regime's political and social goals always dominated economic policy; security of the Revolution trumped productivity.

Fidel Castro's brand of anticapitalism included a strong dose of antiglobalization. For many years, El Comandante en Jefe hosted a large international conference on globalization where he would lecture thousands of delegates with his denunciations of the many evils of multinational firms that spread brutal exploitation and dehumanizing inequality around the world.

Not surprisingly, Cuba has received remarkably small inflows of foreign investment, even taking into account the size of its economy. In the twenty-first century, the globe is awash in transborder investments by corporations large and small. Many developing countries, other than those damaged by severe civil conflicts, receive shares that significantly bolster their growth prospects.

Today's ailing Cuban economy, whose 11.2 million people yield the modest gross national product reported officially at $64 billion[1] (and possibly much less at realistic exchange rates), badly need additional external cooperation—notwithstanding heavily subsidized oil imports from Venezuela. As with any economy, domestic choices made at home and by Cubans will largely determine the country's fate. Yet as Cubans have been well aware since the arrival of

Christopher Columbus, the encroaching international economy matters greatly; it can be a source of not only harsh punishments but also great benefits.

CUBA'S SHIFTING ATTITUDES

The rise and fall in the stock of joint ventures on the island has reflected the dramatic shifts in Cuban economic policies since the Revolution. Over the past five decades, we can distinguish five periods. During the revolutionary 1960s, the regime systematically nationalized most foreign- and Cuban-owned properties, beginning with large U.S.-owned properties and eventually extending to small-scale enterprises and even mom-and-pop retail outlets. Soviet-style planning came to dominate economic policymaking. In the second phase, the sudden loss of the large Soviet subsidy occasioned an interlude of liberalization, of warm welcomes to European, Canadian, and Latin American investors, often extended by Fidel Castro himself. But once the economy showed signs of recovery, Castro reevaluated the opening to foreign capital and ordered the closure of many joint ventures, especially smaller firms, amid a more general recentralization of economic decision making. During the fourth phase, the Cubans turned toward state-backed projects involving Venezuela, China, and Brazil.

Since assuming the presidency in 2008, Raúl Castro has sent contradictory signals regarding foreign investment. In principle, Cuba's foreign investment laws offer favorable conditions, and some joint ventures are successfully navigating the Cuban economic system. But the government has been keeping many suitors waiting for the final green light. Projects for large golf and marina resorts have been pending for years. The owners of the prime commercial office space in Havana have been unable to secure authorization for next-phase construction. An international hotel chain that offered to refurbish the shabby downtown Habana Libre hotel was refused an equity share. Brazilian negotiators have been urging Cuba to allow large investments in sugar mills and associated ethanol plants, only to be frustrated by "political symbolism"[2] —lingering fears of compromising the sacred gains of the Revolution and endangering national security.

Even more alarming, major joint ventures have recently been shuttered or challenged by the authorities for failing to meet demanding performance requirements. Nevertheless, the government has been debating revisions to the foreign investment law, opening the possibility for a new, more positive phase in Cuba's treatment of foreign direct investment (FDI).

THE CUBAN ECONOMY TODAY: HOW FDI FITS IN

In recent years, Cuba has suffered from the painful external shocks of exorbitant energy costs and rising food prices. And the island has been laid siege to by its formerly dominant and geographically proximate economic partner, the United States, which has imposed punishing comprehensive economic sanctions—including prohibitions against investments—unprecedented in their scope and longevity. The sudden withdrawal of Soviet subsidies in the early 1990s precipitated a major crisis but only a partial, hesitant course correction while Cuba's Latin American neighbors made major strides forward through structural reforms and deepening engagement with the global economy. Only through such integration into the global economy can Cuba hope to modernize its factories and farms, realize economies of scale, and gain access to large markets, new technologies, and investment capital.

Tough and resilient, the Cuban economy survives and evolves—and is today opening another reform chapter, one that seems likely to be more consequential than earlier turns of the wheel. This time around, Cuba can build on its impressive investments in human capital, its quality health care, and universal education, originally undertaken by the Revolution largely for humanitarian reasons. Today's high-quality workforce is a potent building block in the race toward higher earned incomes and more lucrative integration into global markets.

THE CUBAN ECONOMY: WEAKNESSES AND STRENGTHS

By several key indicators, the Cuban economy is seriously underperforming:

- The Cuban economy has increasingly become a low-productivity service economy. Industrial production is stalled at less than 50 percent of its pre-1989 levels. Agricultural output, despite some gains, remains insufficient to feed the population, and hefty imports of food staples bite off a big share of foreign exchange earnings. By 2010, agricultural output had recovered from mid-decade droughts and hurricanes but only to regain 2000 levels.
- Merchandise exports, reported at $4.6 billion in 2010, were less than 10 percent of national output, reflecting the low international competitiveness of much of Cuba's industry and agriculture. The weak export performance opens a gaping merchandise trade deficit that Cuba struggles to finance, often by accumulating payments arrears that irritate its international partners and undermine its credit ratings. Cuba has managed to narrow its bulging foreign exchange shortfall thanks only to the largesse of Venezuela, which barters its oil for Cuban medical personnel on terms highly favorable to Cuba.
- Especially debilitating, national savings and investment rates are very low at around 10 percent of gross domestic product, half of the Latin American average and even further below the strong Asian investment rates. This results in the ongoing decapitalization of some sectors and relegating Cuba to a low-growth trap. From 1996 to 2008, the ratio of gross capital formation to gross domestic product averaged about 12.5 percent, startlingly low by international standards. In a survey of 157 countries, Cuba's investment rate was consistently below the lowest tenth percentile during the period from 1990 to 2008.[3]

The reforms of the 1990s did yield some important results as Cuba opened select sectors to foreign investment and commerce. In 2012, in partnerships with foreign hotel investors, managers, and tour operators, Cuba will host some 3 million tourists, yielding well over $2 billion in gross receipts. A Canadian nickel mining and smelter company, Sherritt International, is generating the largest single source of foreign exchange earnings, surpassing sugar. Other joint ventures with major European multinationals are successfully distributing premium Cuban rum and tobacco in international markets. These positive developments in international tourism, nickel and cobalt mining, and high-value-added agriculture (hand-rolled cigars and vintage rums) are foundations for future growth. They have not yet, however, sufficed to lift Cuba onto a strong sustainable growth path. To overcome the critical problems still confronting the Cuban economy, the Cuban government publicly recognizes that it will have to undertake more and deeper policy reforms.

REFORM GUIDELINES

In April 2011, under the leadership of Raúl Castro, the Cuban Communist Party approved the "Guidelines of the Economic and Social Policy of the Party and the Revolution." A lengthy document with 313 points, the official blueprint recognizes the economy's major shortcomings and proposes pathways forward. Just twelve of the 2011 guidelines (numbers 96 through 107) directly address foreign investment—and these table no major policy reforms. The relevant guidelines neither recognize the critical role that foreign investment is already playing in the Cuban economy nor propose that foreign investment become a central driver of growth. Nevertheless, in the internal debates during the drafting of the guidelines, the proreform factions did manage to insert some positive language recognizing the potential contributions of FDI: "access to advanced technology, the transfer of management skills, a diversification and expansion of export markets, import substitution, the generation of new employment," and access to external finance.

The more orthodox factions within the government and Communist Party seem to have gained the upper hand in drafting the section on foreign investment. The conservatives inserted language revealing their enduring distrust of foreign capital and underscored the need to carefully screen projects as well as to monitor closely those projects that are allowed to proceed:

- Foreign capital is categorized as a "supplement" to national savings. While under any likely scenario domestic savings will indeed exceed foreign capital inflows, economists in Havana interpreted the "supplemental" label as demoting FDI to playing a secondary, nonessential role in economic planning.
- Foreign investments should be carefully screened to be "consistent with the National Economic Plan" and "to make sure that the foreign capital satisfies a host of objectives."
- The guidelines suggest that foreign investments be subject to both external and domestic performance requirements. Foreign-owned firms should purchase goods and services supplied by Cuban companies.
- Approved projects should be subject to continuous and rigorous monitoring to ensure that the foreign partner is observing its commitments. Existing partnerships should face "assessment and adjustment" to ensure consistency "with the country's requirements."
- A time limit should be set for approved foreign investments to commence operations "to avoid their continued utilization of resources indefinitely with a resulting increase in inefficiency."

Amid these cautionary notes, the guidelines do contain some positive news for potential foreign investors. The guidelines call for "more expedient" assessment and approval procedures. Investments that target the domestic market rather than the high-priority export sector should nevertheless be considered where they provide "indispensable" products or substitute for imports. Special Development Zones that attract FDI and promote exports and high-tech projects should be created. The guidelines also called for an up-to-date portfolio of investment projects that might be of interest to foreign partners. After persistent expressions of interest from the diplomatic community in Havana, the Cuban Chamber of Commerce—whose leadership is appointed by the Ministry of International Commerce and Foreign Investment (MINCEX)—issued such a portfolio in December 2011. But the surprisingly short list broke little new ground and addressed a truncated number of sectors. Rather than signal a renewed interest in attracting foreign investment, the chamber's portfolio seemed to confirm that many Cuban economic planners believed that FDI was, at best, a secondary supplement to more promising sources of growth.

THE LEGAL FRAMEWORK

As part of the post-Soviet economic opening, Cuba authorized a new foreign investment law (Law 77, 1995) that combines elements commonly included in such national FDI frameworks with characteristics specific to the Cuban system. Law 77 stipulates that FDI may take the form of joint ventures with state firms or may be fully foreign owned.[4] Investors enjoy full protection against expropriation, "except for reasons in the public interest," in which case they will be indemnified, and have the right to appeal to a mutually agreed-on international investment dispute resolution entity. Litigation over other disputes between FDI and state-owned enterprises (SOEs) or government entities is referred to the jurisdiction of national courts. FDI firms pay income taxes at a 30 percent rate of net taxable income, although reinvested income can be exempt if so authorized by the government. Additional taxes of 25 percent are levied on employee wages, composed of an 11 percent wage tax and 14 percent social security contribution. Profits and dividends are freely transferable abroad in convertible currency.

All sectors of the economy are open to FDI, excluding only health and education services and the armed forces. FDI firms can import and export directly (i.e., without passing through a state wholesale company).

THE APPROVAL PROCESS

For interested investors, an especially irritating peculiarity of the Cuban FDI system is the prolonged multilayered approval process. First, the foreign investor must draw up its application with its proposed SOE partner and the relevant ministry and then present that request to MINCEX. Second, MINCEX must then consult with all the corresponding agencies and institutions, which typically include the pertinent sectoral ministry, the powerful Ministry of Economy and Planning, the influential Ministry of Finance and Prices, the central bank, and the Ministries of Labor and Environment. Third, if subsequent to these broad consultations MINCEX is favorably disposed, it makes a recommendation to the Executive Committee of the Council of Ministers (CECM), which is composed of several national vice presidents and pertinent ministers and formally chaired by President Raúl Castro. Fourth, according to legal experts familiar with these procedures, the CECM normally accepts the recommendation of MINCEX, although it is not unknown for CECM to refer a proposal back to MINCEX for further elaboration.

Law 77 requires that applications be acted on within sixty days, but in fact the FDI approval process may drag on for two years or longer or may languish unanswered altogether. Moreover, MINCEX does not feel obliged to provide a written ruling to applicants and may or may not offer an oral explanation for its ruling. This demanding screening process could be admired for its inclusiveness, but it also contains a plethora of veto points and opportunities for delay. Applicants complain that the process is a nontransparent black box, denying access to many of the decision makers or even knowledge as to which personalities are at the table.

Law 77 allows for 100 percent foreign ownership. Yet only six such wholly foreign-owned firms exist today: three in petroleum and energy, two in maritime transport, and one in the financial sector.[5] Underscoring the wide degree of bureaucratic discretion in the foreign investment regime, government functionaries have chosen to largely ignore an important option that dominates FDI in most countries that would allow foreign investments independent of Cuban SOEs. Another curious feature of the Cuban system is that FDI ventures are approved for a fixed time period—as low as fifteen years—on which time the contract is terminated unless it is renewed by joint agreement of the parties and the government. As many FDI firms have discovered, renewal is anything but automatic, and the government may seek to alter the contract terms in fundamental respects. For example, whereas in the 1990s the government often granted the foreign partner majority control, now it is seeking to revert 51 percent or more of the voting shares to the SOE partner. This revealed Cuban preference for management control discourages some investors altogether.

It also drives joint ventures to finance themselves through higher debt—rather than equity—than they might otherwise. In another escalation of conditions placed on new joint ventures or those up for renewal, the government is also pressing firms to export at least 20 percent of their production.

In principle, the Cuban authorities have honored the prohibition against expropriation without compensation guaranteed in Law 77 (chapter III, article 3). But many FDI firms have been closed through the nonrenewal of contracts or, more precipitously, by the state placing the firm in a nontenable position and forcing sale of shares to the state. The government has also seized the property of shareholders accused of corruption, as in the dramatic case of the successful fruit juice manufacturing and distribution firm Rio Zaza.

THE WORLD'S HEAVIEST TAX ON LABOR

The most unusual characteristic of the Cuban FDI regime is the labor contract system. FDI firms are not generally allowed to directly hire labor. Rather, a state employment agency—typically a dependency of the relevant sectoral ministry (e.g., Tourism or Light Industry)—hires, fires, settles labor disputes, establishes wage scales, and pays the wages directly to the workers. The FDI firm pays the wage bill to the state employment agency, which in turn pays the workers. But there is a very special twist to the Cuban system: the FDI pays wages to the employment agency in hard currency, and the employment agency turns around and compensates the workers in local currency, an effective devaluation or tax of twenty-four to one. Thus, if the firm pays the employment agency $500 a month and the employment agency pays the workers 500 pesos, over 90 percent of the wage payment disappears in the currency conversion; the effective compensation is instantly deflated to $21 per month. This could be the world's heaviest labor tax. It provoked one Cuban worker to remark to the author, "In Cuba, it's a great myth that we live off the state. In fact, it's the state that lives off of us." This labor system, which also authorizes only one national union (the Confederation of Cuban Workers, which is closely allied with the Communist Party), violates many principles of the International Labor Organization, of which Cuba is a charter member. It also freezes Cuba into a low-wage, low-productivity trap.[6]

The legal regime governing FDI has permitted broad official discretion. In the mid-1990s, the government welcomed and approved many joint ventures. But beginning in 2003, without any formal legal alterations, the government began to rigorously review existing firms and closed many that failed to meet its shifting standards, favored larger over smaller businesses, and privileged foreign SOEs over private partners.

FEW FOREIGN FIRMS, BIG CONTRIBUTIONS

Assessing foreign investment in Cuba is complicated by the scarcity of data. The Cuban government's culture of secrecy takes on extreme form when it addresses international capital flows. Spectacularly, Cuba simply does not publish a capital account. Cuba releases no numbers on capital inflows or outflows, nor is there an official accounting of foreign reserves. And offerings within the current account that record capital-related flows are presented in highly aggregate form: there is but one line for "*renta*" (income), which includes transactions (both outgoing and incoming) on interest, dividends, and profits, "among others."[7]

When pressed for an explanation, the Cuban government points to U.S. hostility, affirming that the U.S. Treasury might take advantage of greater transparency to harass Cuba's economic partners or seize Cuban assets. These fears may well be justified, demonstrating yet another example of how U.S. sanctions engender precisely the behavior pattern—in this case, extraordinary state secrecy—that the United States decries. In spaces where Cuba apparently feels less threatened, such as social indicators or even the direction and composition of merchandise trade, statistics are made more readily available.

During the brief period between 1993 and 2001, the Cuban government did publish some limited, highly aggregated data on foreign investment flows. Cumulatively, reported flows through 2001 totaled $2 billion (table 13.1).

This useful series was discontinued after 2001, when another emerging option caught Cuba's attention: the availability of state-owned capital in countries, notably Venezuela and China, which offered certain advantages from the Cuban perspective. These friendly powers were prepared to offer capital on subsidized terms and in ideologically comfortable state-to-state deals.[8] For these state-to-state deals, which are notoriously nontransparent and often not reported to the international agencies that track FDI, it is extremely difficult to estimate actual investment flows; to disentangle announcements, commitments, and on-the-ground implementation; and to decipher whether the deal is structured in the form of equity (wholly owned or joint ventures) or an arms-length service contract or as a production-sharing agreement (as is often the case in the petroleum sector). The capital flows may not qualify as FDI at all but rather as state banking loans. This has been the case with the Brazilian involvement in the Mariel port expansion and in the renovation of a sugar refinery in Cienfuegos province—projects often erroneously labeled in the media as "investments."

Perhaps the best informed estimate of the stock of Cuba FDI comes from an international financial consultant (who wished to remain anonymous) with privileged access to foreign investment data. The source noted that according to the Cuban central bank, FDI inflows as of 2001 totaled $1.9 billion (very close to the published figure of $2.02 billion in table 13.1) and estimated that by 2009 the total stock may have reached $3.5 billion. He added another telling estimate: twenty investors accounted for nearly $3 billion of the $3.5 billion; indeed, the top ten investors accounted for the lion's share. The remaining universe of some 200 joint ventures, therefore, would account for only about $500 million in investment capital, or an average of $2.5 million per project.

Table 13.1. Foreign Investment Inflows, 1993–2001 (millions of dollars)

Year	Annual Flow	Cumulative
1993	54.0	54.0
1994*	563.4	617.4
1995	4.7	622.1
1996	82.1	704.2
1997	442.0	1,146.2
1998	206.6	1,352.8
1999	178.2	1,531.0
2000	448.1	1,979.1
2001	38.9	2,018.0

* The reported flows jump in 1994, when the government decided to fold in flows from years prior to 1993.

JOINT VENTURES: NUMBERS AND SIZE OF FIRMS

As of 2011, the total number of joint projects stood at 245. These 245 projects included sixty-seven hotel administration contracts, eight production and service administration contracts, and thirteen production cooperation agreements. Moreover, not all of these joint projects included private partners; some hail from Venezuela as the source country, and presumably many of these projects engage not private investors but rather Venezuelan SOEs. Compare the number of joint ventures operating in Cuba with the number of foreign affiliates reported to be operating in other countries of roughly comparable size and development: 911 in Chile, 754 in Croatia, 5,387 in Ireland, 2,761 in Malaysia, 5,144 in Portugal, and 2,049 in Taiwan.[9]

The number of joint projects in Cuba has been in sharp decline since 2002, when they peaked at just over 400, then fell by half by 2008. This consolidation occurred for several reasons. The Cuban state closed down many joint ventures, having concluded that they were either not living up to their original promises, were not advancing Cuban economic goals, were losing money, or were behaving illegally.[10] Some firms withdrew on finding it impossible to carry on a successful business within the context of Cuban state planning; firms entering during the heady reform years of the mid-1990s were taken aback when Fidel Castro decided to halt and even roll back some of those hopeful market-oriented measures. In some cases, Cuban SOEs did not welcome competition from private firms that had certain advantages, such as superior access to foreign credit and therefore to imported inputs, and so used their access to government agencies to squeeze the joint ventures; hapless joint ventures reported that their electricity rates or real estate rents suddenly spiked, gasoline was no longer delivered on time, visas were denied to international experts, access to critical foreign exchange was blocked, and so on. Students of the political economy of state planning would not be surprised to hear of SOEs leveraging their political networks to disable private competitors.

In 1998, the Cuban government announced as a matter of principle that it preferred large-scale joint ventures to smaller ones.[11] Apparently, this preference remains in place. Yet this bigger-is-better prejudice flies against contemporary trends in international economic thought that argue the opposite: that small and medium-size firms are often more innovative, more flexible, and employ more workers per dollar invested than very large firms. Nor is it necessarily an either/or proposition, as larger firms can benefit from being surrounded by efficient, specialized smaller suppliers. The Cuban government's opposition to smaller joint ventures seems particularly odd at a time when it seeks to stimulate employment, increase the availability of consumer goods, and actively promote small-scale enterprise.

JOINT VENTURES: EMPLOYMENT, SALES, AND EXPORTS

Citing internal government documents, Cuban sociologist Mayra Espina Prieto estimated that joint ventures employed 0.7 percent of the state's 4.9-million-person workforce—about 34,000 people.[12] This rather small number seems plausible, considering that some of the larger joint ventures are located either in capital-intense mining and energy (Sherritt International) or in international marketing (Habanos and Pernod Ricard) whose sales forces are located primarily overseas and who do not directly employ the producers of tobacco or rum. Nor does this estimate take into account the large numbers of workers in hotels that are owned by Cuban SOEs but managed by foreign firms under hotel administration contracts.[13]

Some joint ventures are strategically placed in the vital export sector. According to Cuban economist Omar Everleny Pérez Villanueva (based on his access to unpublished data), joint ventures accounted for $1.9 billion in exports in goods and services in 2008. He attributed 80 percent of these exports to just seven firms.[14] Pérez Villanueva places these businesses in nickel, tobacco, citrus fruits, beverages, tourism, and communications, among others.[15] Based on our case studies and the high degree of industrial concentration, we can place names on these firms: Sherritt International (nickel), Habanos (British Imperial Tobacco, cigars), Havana Club rum (beverages), Rio Zaza and BM (citrus fruits), as well as Sol Meliá (tourism).[16]

Further relying on unpublished government statistics, Pérez Villanueva presents data indicating that total joint venture sales in the period from 2007 to 2009 averaged $4.5 billion, including both exports and domestic sales. At $4.5 billion in sales, joint ventures would account for roughly 7 percent of Cuba's total production of goods and services, reported at $62 billion (2009).[17]

DE FACTO EXCLUDED SECTORS

Law 77 (chapter IV, article 10) allows for FDI in all sectors except health, education, and "the armed forces institutions, with the exception of the latter's commercial system." In practice, joint ventures have also been largely excluded from two sectors where foreign investors could make a huge contribution: sugar and biotechnology.[18] In the case of sugar production, the obstacles appear to be rooted in revolutionary history. The expropriations of the large, often foreign-owned estates were a hallmark of the Revolution; to return the land to foreign hands might seem an inglorious retreat. There is also the unresolved question of compensation to the former owners, necessary to free the lands from potential legal challenges by claimants and U.S. sanctions. Today, as officials reconsider FDI within the context of economic reforms, there is a sharp debate over whether and to what degree to further open food processing and agroindustry, including sugar-based biomass, to external capital. In an apparent victory for more favorable treatment for FDI, in late 2012 and after lengthy negotiations, the Cuban government approved a joint venture, Biopower, S.A., with British investors to generate biomass from sugar derivatives; the roughly $50 million investment is to construct a thirty-megawatt power plant. Billed as a pilot project, the British firm Havana Power hopes that other biomass energy projects will follow.[19]

In the case of biotechnology, government officials voice fears that foreign partners will take advantage of Cuban firms and pirate their innovations. Rather than turn to the European and Japanese multinational pharmaceutical giants to assist in marketing Cuban innovations and pharmaceutical products, Cuba has preferred to seek state-to-state commercial deals with developing countries (notably Venezuela), and to attempt joint ventures abroad (notably in China), where Cuban firms are the foreign investors.[20] Cuba has had some success with these strategies but has had great difficulty accessing promising markets in Europe, Latin America, and much of Asia. Yet it is the pharmaceutical multinationals that possess the requisite knowledge of national patent regimes and distribution networks that could take the Cuban biotech sector to another level of success.

Also largely excluded are financial firms, reserving a monopoly over most financial transactions to state-owned banks. A legacy of the Soviet planning model, capital markets are severely repressed in Cuba. Those international banks allowed to open representative offices in Cuba are generally restricted to international transactions that serve client needs.

Summarizing these findings, we can conclude that FDI added about $3.5 billion to Cuban savings and investment over the past two decades or so, contributed handsomely to exports of goods and services, and accounted for roughly 7 percent of domestic output. Joint ventures currently employ about 34,000 Cuban workers, or under 1 percent of the active labor force.

The flows of FDI to Cuba compare unfavorably to the experience of other countries, whether for countries of similar size and location in the Caribbean Basin or in high-growth East Asia. Joint ventures can be successful in the Cuban context. But the Cuban government has driven a wedge—whether by directly denying business permits to operate or by indirectly discouraging investors—between Cuba and the vast ocean of savings circulating the globe and driving capital formation, technological diffusion, economic growth, and poverty reduction in developed and developing countries alike.

THE DIASPORA AS INVESTORS

The overseas Chinese and Vietnamese are two examples of diasporas that have made use of their kinship connections and cultural knowledge to help fund economic development in their home countries. Many of the 1.8 million Cuban Americans (2010 U.S. Census) have prospered and would invest in Cuba—if the two governments allowed them to do so under reasonable conditions.

According to Miami real estate lawyer Antonio Zamora, a Bay of Pigs veteran who has since traveled to Cuba dozens of times, there could be a booming condominium market for mainland investors and Cuban Americans looking to retire in a culturally comfortable environment that offers good health care and relatively inexpensive, secure living. Zamora also counts some twenty golf resort and boat marina projects on the drawing boards—of which four alone are worth more than $1 billion—waiting for the green light from Cuban authorities.[21]

The future of investments by Cuban Americans is linked to Cuba's immigration rules, which currently deprive many émigrés of the right to own property. Changes in the rules governing émigré property holdings could set the stage for the release of pent-up Cuban American demand for housing, property, and other investments on the island. Already, many Cuban Americans are pumping money into their relatives' restaurants and other small businesses now authorized as part of the regime's policies of growing the nonstate sector (private businesses, cooperatives, and private farms). Sanctions by the United States do not yet permit investments—risk capital seeking a return—on the island but do permit donations. The conditions under which these remittances occur are known only to the parties to the transfer. They may lack formal legal protection, but as some Cuban Americans assert, "trust can be a stronger bond than written contracts." One informed Cuban American businessman estimated that as many as 80 percent of the larger *paladares* (restaurants) opening in Havana benefit from expatriate funding. Thus, the imposition by the Cuban government in September 2012 of hefty taxes on gift parcels, some carrying materials for use by small businesses, was a setback to emerging private enterprises.[22]

Very few Cubans can accumulate savings from their meager salaries. Cuban state banks are accustomed to lending to medium- and large-scale enterprises, not to risky start-ups. Hence, aspiring Cuban entrepreneurs must rely on remittances or, in some cases, income earned during sojourns overseas. The financial constraint is a major obstacle to the blossoming of the small-scale private sector. The Miami-based Cuba Study Group has partnered with the Catholic Church–affiliated Félix Varela Center to offer instruction to aspiring microentrepreneurs in subjects such as accounting, marketing, and composing business plans. The project, "Cuba Emprende," could be a prototype of cooperation between businesspersons in the diaspora and the emerging private sector on the island.

Despite the numerous obstacles, many Cubans are now dreaming of starting their own businesses—and some are succeeding. For example, they are succeeding as owners of fine-dining restaurants, stands selling cream-filled churros, a beauty salon specializing in Afro-

Cuban hairstyles, a high-concept barber shop, a graphics design venture, a cell phone repair shop, and home remodeling and as managers of apartment rentals and taxicab fleets.[23] Many of these young businesses are receiving some form of assistance—remittances, supplies, or customers—from the diaspora.

The United States could do much more to bolster Cuba's emerging entrepreneurs. It could facilitate the pooling of remittances targeted at investing in nonstate firms. More boldly, the United States could lift sanctions on investment and trade with nonstate Cuban firms rigorously certified as genuine private businesses and independent cooperatives. Larger investments by Cuban Americans or by U.S.-based corporations must await changes in regulations in both nations. The outstanding claims of properties expropriated in the early years of the Revolution stand as another barrier to investment flows.[24]

As emphasized throughout this study, changes in legal frameworks by themselves will not be sufficient to unlock large-scale investment flows. Many U.S. individuals and firms will wait until they perceive a more attractive investment climate, with all that entails. Some Cuban Americans may exhibit a somewhat lower threshold, whether as the result of a "sentimental premium" or because they believe that their strong social networks reduce their risks.

LOOKING AHEAD

Cubans will decide the roles that foreign investment will play in the island's development. But it is difficult to imagine that Cuba, with only its own resources, can save enough, innovate rapidly and widely enough, and access enough distant markets to meet the rising expectations of the Cuban population. Rather, Cuba should make up for lost time, learn from its mixed experiences with joint ventures and free trade zones, and study the success stories of other developing countries in harnessing foreign capital for national development. Cuba should also recognize that far from being a threat to the social gains of the Revolution, international capital is the best hope for preserving quality social services within the context of a more productive and competitive national economy.

Cuba is richly endowed with more than enough comparative advantages to compete successfully in the global economy. The Cuba of the twenty-first century can offer deep history (a renovated Habana Vieja), attractive lifestyles (sun and surf, rum, and tobacco), quality performing arts and design, cutting-edge innovations in medicine and health care, and enduring affinities to European, Latin American, and U.S. popular cultures. A good portion of the workforce is already well educated, including in engineering, mathematics, and computer technologies.

Rather than perceiving its proximity to the United States as a danger, Cuba will sooner or later grasp the tremendous opportunities of a mass market of over 300 million consumers. At the same time, when compared to the prerevolutionary Cuba of the 1950s, today's more diversified global economy offers a plethora of competing sources of capital; a new Cuba will host a rainbow of international investors who will be more respectful of Cuban political sovereignty.

EPILOGUE: CUBA'S NEW INVESTMENT LAW; OPEN FOR BUSINESS?

Dateline Havana, April 1, 2014: The Cuban legislature has approved a new foreign direct investment law (FDI), and the detailed follow-on regulations will be issued within the next 90 days. From my informal conversations in Havana, Cubans on the street seem to accept with enthusiasm the government's *dual* message: that the new guidelines will not compromise

Cuban sovereignty—a key gain of the 1959 revolution—but will encourage badly needed inflows of foreign capital and technology.

In a shift from past practices, government messaging has emphasized the importance of foreign investment worldwide, with the Communist Party daily, *Granma* (March 31, 2014), quoting a government commission declaring that "no country today has successfully developed without foreign investment as a component of its political economy." President Raúl Castro asserted that "we must take into account the absolute necessity to stimulate and attract foreign investment, to add dynamism to our economic and social development." Experienced commentators have noted, however, that many of the more positive paragraphs in the new law could also be found in the previous 1995 FDI regulations, which were outweighed by more restrictive clauses and by a recalcitrant bureaucracy that in recent years has approved very few major new foreign ventures.

Several of the more promising sections of the new law echo recommendations in the 2012 Brookings monograph, *The New Cuban Economy: What Roles for Foreign Investment?*:

- A strong official recognition that FDI must be integral to Cuba's development strategy if the country is to depart from its sluggish economic path.
- Majority foreign ownership is an option (this was also the case, even if ignored in practice, under the 1995 regime).
- The project approval process should be streamlined and made more transparent.
- Firms should have more flexibility with regard to wage scales, such that remuneration can be a stimulus to productivity. In addition, the much anticipated currency unification will likely reduce the extraordinarily heavy tax on wages paid by foreign investors.

Other noteworthy aspects of the new law include reductions in certain taxes and the promise of just compensation in the event of expropriation. But some existing obstacles to investment appear not to have been adequately addressed. For example, the new law continues to press investors on local content requirements, even as it also notes the importance of firm integration into global value chains.

The proof will be in the pudding, and investors will be watching closely for the fine print in the new regulations and, most importantly, for the implementation of the approval process. The new law recognizes that Cuba badly needs foreign investment in many sectors of its economy, including but not limited to agriculture and sugar, energy, bio-technology, construction, and tourism. Will the government establish an investment climate that attracts foreign investments and a truly transparent bureaucratic process that vets proposals in a prompt timeframe competitive with international standards?

NOTES

Excerpted from Richard E. Feinberg, *The New Cuban Economy: What Role for Foreign Investment?* (Washington, DC: Brookings Institution Press, 2012). Reprinted by permission of the publisher.

1. *Oficina Nacional de Estadísticas* (ONE), National Accounts, table 5.2, "Global Supply and Demand," http://www.one.cu/aec2010/esp/05_tabla_cuadro.htm. Figure is for 2010.

2. Embassy of Brazil in Havana, "La industria de la caña de azúcar en Cuba," sector report, 2012.

3. Gabriel Di Bella and Andrew Wolfe, "Cuba: Economic Growth and International Linkages—Challenges for Measurement and Vulnerabilities in a Bimonetary Economy," *Cuba in Transition* 19 (2009): 354–67.

4. Law 50 of 1982 had established a ceiling of 49 percent for the participation of foreign capital in joint ventures. Law 77 opened the door to joint ventures with either majority or minority foreign ownership shares as well as to wholly foreign-owned ventures. Formally, Law 77 of 1995 allows for FDI to take one of several forms: (1) a joint venture in which one or more foreign investors participate with one or more national investors to form a Cuban commercial company that adopts the form of a nominal share corporation, (2) an international economic association

contract in which the national and foreign investors cooperate without the establishment of a legal entity distinct from each of the parties, and (3) totally foreign capital company, without the involvement of any national investor.

5. Center for the Study of the Cuban Economy, *La Inversión Extranjera y de la Unión Europea en Cuba* (Havana: European Union, 2012), 5.

6. Pavel Vidal Alejandro and Omar Everleny Pérez Villanueva, "Apertura al cuentapropismo y la microempresa, una pieza clave del ajuste estructural," in *Miradas a la economía Cubana: El proceso de actualización*, ed. Pavel Vidal Alejandro and Omar Everleny Pérez Villanueva (Havana: Editorial Caminos, 2012), 51.

7. ONE, External Sector, "Methodological Notes," http://www.one.cu/aec2010/esp/08_tabla_cuadro.htm.

8. See Richard E. Feinberg, "Cuba's Emerging Market Strategy," in *Reaching Out: Cuba's New Economy and the International Response* (Washington, DC: Brookings Institution Press, 2011), 23–44. Source: ONE, Anuario estadístico de Cuba 2002 and other issues, and Jorge F. Pérez-López, "The Rise and Fall of Foreign Investment in Cuba," *Cuban Affairs Journal* 3, no. 1 (February 2008): 25, http://www.cubanaffairsjournal.org.

9. UN Conference on Trade and Development, table 34, "Number of Parent Corporations and Foreign Affiliates, by Region and Economy," 2010, *World Investment Report 2011*. These country numbers should be treated as rough orders of magnitude, as country reporting methodologies are not uniform and may understate quantities.

10. Center for the Study of the Cuban Economy, *La Inversión Extranjera y de la Unión Europea en Cuba*; see also Emily Morris, "Cuba's New Relationship with Foreign Capital: Economic Policy-Making since 1990," *Journal of Latin American Studies* 40 (2008): 769–92, and Paolo Spadoni, "Foreign Investment in Cuba: Recent Developments and Role in the Economy," *Cuba in Transition* 12 (2002): 158–78.

11. U.S.-Cuba Trade and Economic Council, "Foreign Investment Policy Change," *Economic Eye on Cuba*, February 16–22, 1998, http://www.cubatrade.org/eyeonr.html#4; see also Economist Investment Unit, "Foreign Investment Focuses on Large Projects," *Cuba Country Briefing*, February 12, 2001.

12. Mayra Espina Prieto and Viviana Togores González, "Structural Change and Routes of Social Mobility in Today's Cuba: Patterns, Profiles, and Subjectivities," in *Cuban Economic and Social Development: Policy Reforms and Challenges in the 21st Century*, ed. Jorge I. Dominguez et al. (Cambridge, MA: Harvard University David Rockefeller Center for Latin American Studies, 2012), 267, table 8.2.

13. E-mail communication of Mayra Espina Prieto with author, June 2012.

14. Omar Everleny Pérez Villanueva, *The External Sector of the Cuban Economy* (Washington, DC: Woodrow Wilson International Center for Scholars, 2010), 4–5, http://www.wilsoncenter.org/cuba. See also Omar Everleny Pérez Villanueva, "Foreign Direct Investment in China, Vietnam, and Cuba: Pertinent Experiences for Cuba," in Dominguez, *Cuban Economic and Social Development*.

15. In 2009, mining exports were $839 million, sugar industry exports (e.g., rum) were $226 million, and tobacco exports (cigars and cigarettes) were $212 million. In each sector, brand-name joint ventures were dominant. ONE, External Sector, table 8.7, "Exports of Good per Groups of Products," http://www.one.cu/aec2010/esp/08_tabla_cuadro.htm.

16. Communications, however, has since been fully nationalized, as has Rio Zaza fruit drinks. The contribution of Sherritt to exports will vary with the market prices for nickel and cobalt. The tourism exports attributed to foreign investment would capture joint ventures but not hotels managed by service contracts with international hotel operators.

17. ONE, National Accounts, table 5.2, "Global Supply and Demand," http://www.one.cu/aec2010/esp/05_tabla_cuadro.htm.

18. Also excluded in practice have been domestic and international commerce and legal consultancy. See Rolando Anillo, "Cuban Reforms and Foreign Investment Legislation: Knowing Your Neighbor and Future Partner," *Cuba Law Update*, January 2010 (Law firm of Fowler Rodriguez Valdés-Fauli).

19. Marc Frank, "Britain's Havana Energy Sets Cuban Bioenergy Venture," Reuters, November 12, 2012.

20. On joint ventures in China, see Julio A. Díaz Vázquez, *China-Cuba: Relaciones económicas 1960–2010* (Mexico City: Universidad Nacional Autónoma de México, Cuadernos de Trabajo del CECHIMEX, 2011), 7, table 2.

21. Statement at the annual meetings of the Association for the Study of the Cuban Economy, Miami, August 2012, http://www.cubastandard.com, February 2011. However, some of the proposed golf resorts pertain to non-U.S. investors.

22. One knowledgeable observer estimated the value of remittances entering Cuba at $2.2 billion and of merchandise entering as packages at $2.0 billion to 2.5 billion in 2011. Emilio Morales, "What's behind the New Cuban Tariffs," Havana Consulting Group, July 9, 2012, http://thehavanaconsultinggroups.com/index.php?option=com_content&view=article&id=329%3Awhats-behind-the-new-cuban-tariffs&catid=47%3Aeconomy&lang=en. A former executive with the SOE CIMEX, Morales attributed the new taxes in part to pressure from state-owned firms suffering from the competition. See also Marc Frank, "Reforms and Informal Market Hit Cuban State's Retail Sales," Reuters, September 14, 2012.

23. Richard E. Feinberg and Collin Laverty, *Cuba's New Entrepreneurs: Recent Experiences and Policy Options* (in press).

24. For an expert discussion of settlement options, see Rolando Anillo-Badia, "Outstanding Claims to Expropriated Property in Cuba," in *Proceedings of the Association for the Study of the Cuban Economy* (Miami: Association for the Study of the Cuban Economy, 2011).

Chapter Fourteen

The Political Economy of Leisure

Marguerite Rose Jiménez

More than 2.9 million international tourists visited Cuba in 2012. It was the tenth year in a row that Cuba had surpassed the 2-million-arrivals mark, further solidifying Cuba's place near the top of the Caribbean tourist market in terms of total visitors annually. Cuba's return to the international tourism market has profoundly affected the Revolution in the past twenty-five years. Only 275,000 tourists—less than one-tenth the 2012 figure—came to the island in 1987, when the government approved a law allowing joint ventures with foreign investors in tourism-related projects, such as hotels.[1]

The decision to rely on tourism for hard-currency earnings was not taken easily. Cuban leader Fidel Castro's reluctance to promote tourism was rooted in memories of pre-1959 Cuba as a hedonist playground for affluent North Americans, accompanied by drugs, prostitution, corruption, and gambling casinos run by organized crime syndicates. These pathologies were largely eliminated in 1959 or shortly thereafter when the tourist industry was essentially shut down. As a result, images of Cuba's prerevolutionary past complicated the discourse on possibilities for Cuba's economic recovery. But the unwanted saviors—international tourism and dollarization of the Cuban economy—became necessities, however unpalatable, as the Cuban economy spiraled downward in the first years of the "Special Period."

During the first decades of the Revolution, tourism and foreign investment were disdained by the fiercely independent government. By the late 1980s and early 1990s, economic necessity had caused the government's previously hard-line position to soften considerably. With limited options and tourism's potential to quickly generate high returns on investment, 20 percent of total investment during the 1990s went to developing the tourist industry.[2] The government's focus on tourism paid off, and the industry has grown exponentially during the past twenty-five years. For example, between 2000 and 2005, tourism increased nearly 20 percent annually, helping Cuba break into the top ten most frequented tourist destinations in the Western Hemisphere.[3] Today, Cuba, along with Puerto Rico, the Dominican Republic, and the U.S. Virgin Islands, accounts for more than 50 percent of total arrivals in the Caribbean, even though Cuba remains closed to U.S. tourists because of the embargo.[4] With $2.6 billion in revenues generated in 2012, tourism has replaced sugar as a primary driver of the Cuban economy.

Along with the beneficial effects of tourism's rise to economic dominance on the island, there are several potentially problematic consequences as well. By jump-starting the economy with an infusion of hard currency from tourists and foreign investments, the Cuban government set off a chain reaction that has contributed to a gradual deterioration of many of the ideals on which revolutionary Cuba was founded. Prior research about Cuba's turn to tourism has focused on aspects related to its economic impact. Often excluded from the discourse on tourism, until recently, are its inherent sociopolitical consequences, such as discrimination, unequal power relations, and socioeconomic inequality. These negative effects raise questions about the viability of tourism as a means to sustain both economic development and the Revolution's sociopolitical goals. The detrimental long-term side effects of tourism result from several factors: (1) the re-creation of class conflict within the dual economy, (2) the renewed objectification of Cuban women (and men to a lesser extent), (3) the growth of race-based discrimination, (4) the commodification and marketing of Cuban culture, and (5) the loss of human capital as educated professionals seek out opportunities to earn hard currency in the tourist sector.

DUAL ECONOMY OR DUEL ECONOMY?

After the fall of the Soviet Union, tourism emerged as "the only sector of the Cuban economy with the capacity to act as a 'leading sector' for the country's development," according to Cuban economist Pedro Monreal.[5] It seemed to be an obvious choice because of Cuba's abundance of natural resources, which gave Cuba a competitive edge over its Caribbean neighbors. Cuba has more beachfront than all of the other Caribbean islands put together.[6] Other assets, as stated by Charles Suddaby, are Cuba's "geographic diversity, enormous range of existing and potential attractions, cultural and architectural history and combination of educated workforce and low incidence of crime,"[7] which makes Cuba a desirable destination for pleasure-seeking travelers.

To make Cuba attractive to foreign investors, major shifts in economic policy were required. After extensive debates during the Fourth Congress of the Cuban Communist Party in October 1991, two key reforms were enacted that were calculated to ease obstacles for foreign investors. The first came in the form of a constitutional amendment in 1992 that allowed foreign companies investing in Cuba to own a 49 percent share in joint ventures.[8] The second occurred in 1993 with Decree Law 140, which legalized the use of dollars on the island.

While the 1993 decision was necessary given the dire economic situation, Max Azicri notes, "the *dollarization* of the economy raised concerns with its social implications."[9] Dollars, which began to circulate freely, came mainly from Cubans who worked in the tourist industry or from those with family abroad who sent monthly remittances.[10] Their access to dollars enabled them to purchase material goods that were unavailable to the majority of Cubans. Thus developed the "dual economy," consisting of the *peso* economy, where *moneda nacional* (national currency, or *pesos cubanos*) is used, and the dollar economy, where only foreign currency, or *pesos convertibles* (convertible pesos, CUC), are acceptable.[11] Aside from operating with separate currencies, the two economies had their own stores, restaurants, and forms of transportation. State salaries are paid mainly in the national currency, as is social security. National currency can be used to ride a bus, pay for some state services, and buy basic foodstuffs (bread, rice, beans, vegetables, milk, and meat) and a meal in some restaurants. But it cannot, for the most part, be used to buy imported goods (toiletries, gasoline, electrical appliances, most clothing, or goods that can be exported for hard currency). The failure of the *peso* economy lies in the average Cuban's inability to buy necessities with the national currency. This inability has increased the pressure for Cubans to find ways of obtaining hard currency, although access to the tourist economy is difficult for most to acquire. The dual economy has produced several problems, the most prominent of which is the emergence of significant inequalities in the population.

ENTERTAINMENT OR EXPLOITATION: SEXUALIZING THE REVOLUTION

One of the many attractions drawing tourists to Cuba is the entertainment industry dominated by music and dance. The tourist-oriented entertainment industry has contributed to the hyper-sexualized image and objectification of Cuban women (and increasingly of Cuban men as well). The use of women in the promotion of tourism in Cuba was epitomized at the very beginning of the Special Period when *Playboy* was allowed to tour the island and run a feature on Cuban women.[12] Susan Eckstein claims, "The government's interest in hard currency led it to play on its prerevolutionary reputation and to reverse its earlier puritanical stance on such matters."[13]

Immediately after the Revolution, the government made efforts to eradicate prostitution by rehabilitating and educating former prostitutes, incorporating them back into the new Cuban society as productive workers.[14] According to Elisa Facio, "The revolutionaries aimed to free women from sexual exploitation in all sectors of society."[15] Azicri further explains, "The government enforced policies directed at women to facilitate their progress and incorporate them into the overall development programs, so their gains would be parallel to men's."[16] Cuban women experienced opportunities previously unimaginable in Cuba, in areas such as education, health care, and employment. They became full participants in the Cuban economy, increasing their economic activity by 223.9 percent between 1970 and 1990.[17] During these years, prostitution in Cuba all but disappeared.

Coincident with the start of the Special Period and the growth of tourism, prostitution, and sexual tourism reemerged.[18] Cuban authorities have tended to place a large share of the blame for the rise in prostitution directly on the women involved rather than on the men who pay them or on the economic circumstances on the island. Facio argues,

> To succeed, sex tourism requires Third World women to be economically desperate enough to enter prostitution. . . . The other side of the equation require men from affluent societies to imagine certain women, usually women of color, to be more available and submissive than the women in their own countries.[19]

There is some debate among social scientists writing on sex work in Cuba (in which both women and, increasingly men, participate) as to whether materialism or genuine necessity drives these individuals to prostitution or sex work on the island.[20] Eckstein states, "A lust for dollars, meals in dollar restaurants, and gifts from the dollar stores outweighed the social stigma, the degradation, the health risks and the fear of arrest."[21] According to the Cuban government, individuals do not have to resort to these sorts of "deviant" acts to survive because the population's most basic needs are covered. Fidel Castro remarked in 1993,

> There are no women forced to sell themselves to a man, to a foreigner, to a tourist. Those who do so, do it on their own, voluntarily, and without any need for it. We can say they are highly educated hookers and quite healthy, because we are a country with one of the lowest number of AIDS cases. . . . Therefore, there is truly no prostitution healthier than Cuba's.[22]

Sex work in Cuba is not only a problem because of the exploitation of women (and men). The rise in sex work has also exposed and perhaps exacerbated a racial divide within Cuban society. Tourists seeking sexual relations on the island are known to prefer darker-skinned and "exotic" consorts, and Afro-Cubans have a preexisting economic disadvantage. Facio explains, "The combination of foreign men seeking sexual partners who are racially and cultural-ly different, coupled with the sexual double standard's separation of women into 'good' versus 'bad' ones, reinforces the desirability of darker-skinned Cuban women as sex objects."[23]

THE COLOR-BLIND REVOLUTION

The dream of a color-blind Cuba began long before 1959. José Martí, one of the major heroes of Cuba's War of Independence, propounded the idea in the 1890s. Martí envisioned the creation of a shared Cuban identity, or *cubanidad*, where people were neither black nor white but simply Cuban. He wrote, "There is no danger of war between the races in Cuba. Man means more than just white man, mulatto or black man. The souls of white men and negroes have risen together from the battlefield where they have fought and died for Cuba."[24]

After 1959, there was a decrease in the material inequalities that had been so prominent in prerevolutionary Cuba and had disproportionately affected Afro-Cubans. Alejandro de la Fuente quotes Fidel Castro as saying, "We believe that the problem of discrimination has an economic content and basis appropriate to a class society in which man is exploited by man. . . . Discrimination disappeared when class privileges disappeared."[25] Clarence Lusane, a scholar of comparative race relations, disputes this position. "Cuba eradicated institutionalized racism," he explains, but "racial prejudice and individual discrimination continue to occur at other levels."[26] While a decrease in the material gap between the races did occur in socialist Cuba, since 1991 class inequality has once again coincided with racial inequality. The reintroduction of tourism into the Cuban economy appears to have exacerbated the racial inequality, as Afro-Cubans have significantly less access to jobs in the legal tourist industry, placing them in direct contact with visitors who tip for services rendered.[27] In the late 1990s, 60 percent of the Cubans involved in legal tourism were light skinned.[28] This phenomenon is strengthening the racial divide because Afro-Cubans have less access to hard currency with less opportunity in the tourist industry. The discrepancy in access to hard currency would be problematic on its own because of its impact on Cuba's goal of creating an egalitarian society. It is compounded by the fact that Afro-Cubans had been the most economically disadvantaged segment of prerevolutionary Cuban society and had not achieved equality when the Special Period began. As Lusane points out, the revolutionary leaders did not initiate programs targeted at overcoming the effects of racial discrimination. They assumed, he explains, "that a rising tide would lift all boats, and that a broad distribution across all of Cuban society would necessarily benefit Afro-Cubans." Their assumption was problematic in the first instance, he argues, because "it reduced racial discrimination to material relations."[29]

In spite of the disproportionately negative impact the economic crisis has had on many Afro-Cubans, race is still not commonly addressed in official discourse. De la Fuente notes that the "official silence" about racism in Cuba has enabled negative racial stereotypes to continue and to be reproduced throughout the population.[30] In fact, the tourist industry has included these in advertising that depicts Cuba as an exotic destination. Writer Eladio Secades notes, "The tourist is a type . . . who has become tired of civilization and seeks the primitive. To create the primitive where it does not exist is one of the ways to promote tourism."[31] This can be seen in the mass marketing of Afro-Cuban spirituality via reenactments of religious ceremonies, along with traditional song and dance forms packaged for tourist consumption.

PROMOTING AND PROTECTING THE "REAL" CUBA

There is perhaps no other country in the Western Hemisphere that evokes such romanticized images as Cuba. Tourists traveling to the island often come with detailed fantasies, which undoubtedly would include old cars, exotic women, cigars, rum, salsa music, the *Buena Vista Social Club*, Latin dancing, and beaches. It is easy to see how tourist promoters would begin their effort based on such preconceived notions of their potential clientele. They lay out Cuban culture (or what tourists believe is Cuban culture) for consumption. Such promotions are evident in and around the major hotels or tourist establishments. In Old Havana, for example, miraculously preserved prerevolutionary American cars, waiting for tourist passengers, line the streets in front of the high-end hotels surrounding the *Parque Central.* More than merely the pride of their owners and a source of hard currency, these cars also embody the expectations of tourists. Travel writers and movies depicting prerevolutionary Cuba create such expectations with their lyrical elegies and imagery. Cuban-born novelist Cristina García observes,

> There is a name for the gorgeous old American cars that continue to hum, rattle, and roll through the Cuban landscape: *cacharros.* Normally the word means broken-down jalopy. . . . But in the case of these Yankee beauties . . . cacharro is whispered softly, tenderly, like the name of a lost first love.[32]

The *Buena Vista Social Club,* both the documentary and the sound track, gave unprecedented exposure in North America to Cuban "traditional" music. While the group could rightly attribute its success to the breathtaking musical talents of its members, it also succeeded by resurrecting a romanticized prerevolutionary Cuban fantasy, with octogenarian musical phenoms being "rediscovered" by foreign musicians and producers. Regardless of its actual popularity (among Cubans) in Cuba today, the *Buena Vista Social Club* has come to epitomize Cuban music for many foreigners. As such, many tourists expect to hear songs featured in the documentary, sung by grandfatherly Cubans in fedoras smelling of Cuban cigars. In order to meet these expectations, Cuban musicians have committed the film's sound track to memory and regularly reproduce the tourists' desire for nostalgia on request.[33] This is consistent with a pattern that social scientist D. J. Greenwood has described:

> Culture is being packaged, priced and sold like building lots, rights-of-way, fast food, and room service, as the tourism industry promises that the world is his/hers to use. All the "natural resources," including cultural traditions, have their price, and if you have the money in hand, it is your right to see whatever you wish.[34]

One consequence of such packaging is the "commodification" of culture; that is, cultural practices are transformed into something whose value is measured by sales in the marketplace. In order to attract a steady tourist clientele, it is necessary to create and provide a desirable tourist experience.

Indeed, in Cuba as well as other tourist-dependent developing nations, local artists tend to skew their own work so that it conforms to tourists' expectations. Yet in much of the scholarly literature on tourism, the host population is rarely included in analyses about internal cultural changes or adaptation. Historian Louis Pérez's description of the way in which prerevolutionary Cubans contorted themselves indicates why Cuban leaders were so reluctant in the 1990s to embrace tourism as a solution to the Special Period's economic problems:

> The expanding tourist presence introduced changes that were both profound and permanent, transformations to which the Cuban people adjusted as a normal part of daily life. . . . This involved a complex transaction by which the North American notion of "Cuban" acted to change or otherwise modify Cuban self-representation as a means of success and advancement.[35]

People in areas where tourism is common often try to preserve their cultures and the normalcy of their daily activities by keeping much of their life hidden away from the gaze of tourists eager to explore exotica. By conducting many of their traditions and rituals or even basic aspects of their daily lives out of the tourist arena, they are able to express their culture as they choose without worrying about whether it fits the tourist's vision of how their culture ought to appear. This concept has been explored by anthropologist Laurie Medina, relating to interactions between tourists and local Mayan populations near Cancún, Mexico:

> The host population confronted with the arrival of tourists in their midst, protect and insulate their culture by dividing their lives into "backstage" areas, where they continue meaningful traditions (and go about their everyday lives) away from the gaze of tourists, and "frontstage" areas, where they perform a limited range of activities for a tourist audience. This makes available portions of host culture for guest consumption, while it protects other parts from commoditization. [36]

In this sense, official regulations limiting Cubans' interactions with tourists facilitated efforts by Cubans to preserve their culture. To be sure, another motive of these rules was to ensure that most of the tourists' hard currency went to the Cuban government, not to private individuals. A third objective was (and is) to insulate tourists from the exigencies of Cubans' daily lives. The average tourist does not spend time in the homes of Cubans, visit Cuban schools, travel by distinctly Cuban transportation, or participate in Cuban recreational activities. Few tourists thus experience blackouts, wait hours for overcrowded buses, or experience material shortages of any kind while in Cuba. Photojournalist Fred Ward noted, "Generally, living in first-class Cuban hotels is convenient and pleasant. Tourists are spared almost all the everyday problems plaguing citizens."[37]

However, there is a fine line between self-segregation and government-imposed segregation, with the latter giving rise to the term "tourist apartheid" used to describe discrimination against and exclusion of Cubans within the tourist industry on the island during the 1990s and up through 2010s.

With the resurgence of tourism in the late 1980s and early 1990s, the Cuban government grew concerned about the negative impact of tourism on the maintenance of revolutionary values such as collectivism, egalitarianism, and inclusiveness. As a consequence, the government began a campaign to root out social ills seemingly associated with tourism by limiting the opportunities for Cubans to interact with tourists. Laws focused primarily on restricting Cuban access to tourists and tourist facilities rather than on restricting the actions or behaviors of tourists. For example, there were laws that required hotel guests to pay in hard currency when Cuban possession of hard currency on the island was still illegal. Other laws prohibited Cubans from entering the residential areas of tourist hotels or other specifically designated guest areas. In practice, the restrictions were enforced inconsistently and rarely with any substantive punishment; however, domestic tourism was virtually nonexistent on the island. As a result of both legal restrictions and economic realities, Cubans were effectively excluded from participating in their country's booming tourist industry—that is, unless they were able to secure employment in it.

CUBAN TOURISM LOOKS AHEAD: PROSPECTS AND CHALLENGES

During the past five years, under the leadership of Cuban President Raúl Castro, Cuba has undergone a series of dramatic reforms intended to strengthen the Cuban economy. Tourism remains a vital part of Cuba's economic growth and development strategy. At the helm of the tourist industry is Minister of Tourism Manuel Marrero Cruz, an ally of Raúl Castro and former president of the Cuban military's prized Gaviota tourism conglomerate. Marrero, known as an effective, innovative, and disciplined leader, was appointed to his post in 2004 when the tourist industry on the island seemed on the verge of a major downturn. Marrero has deftly made the transition from directing a single albeit important tourist enterprise to overseeing the development and execution of a national tourism strategy encompassing a wide range of both state and increasingly nonstate actors. According to Marrero, in order for Cuba's tourist industry to continue serving as an engine of the Cuban economy, Cuba needs to access new markets, develop new strategies, take advantage of existing competitive edges, and attract new investors.

AUTHENTIC CUBA: PROMOTING CUBA TO THE WORLD

In May 2010, at Cuba's Thirtieth Annual International Tourism Fair, Minister Marrero announced a new campaign to promote tourism on the island.[38] As part of the "Authentic Cuba" campaign, representatives from Cuba's tourist industry would roll out a range of promotional activities in countries worldwide intended to expose potential industry executives and travelers to Cuban arts, food, culture, music, and general tourist offerings. After a slow start in 2010, by mid-2013 the campaign was in full force.

During the last two weeks of June 2013, Authentic Cuba campaigns were launched in a range of countries, with special emphasis placed on attracting visitors from nontraditional sending countries. At a kickoff event at the residence of Ernesto Plesencia, Cuba's ambassador to Qatar, guests from Middle Eastern tourist companies and other industry executives from the region enjoyed samplings of traditional Cuban food, performances of Cuban dance and music, and presentations made by Cuban Ministry of Tourism officials. While speaking to Qatari journalists covering the event, the ambassador explained that Cuba hoped to attract new visitors from the Gulf countries, noting Cuba's "historic connection" with the Arab world.[39] The event in Doha was followed several days later by a "Cuban night" hosted by the Cuban embassy in Cyprus.[40] Similar events were scheduled to take place in other Middle Eastern countries as well as Southeast Asia, China, and India.

In addition to attracting visitors from afar, the Authentic Cuba campaign has also set its sights on potential tourist markets closer to home in the Americas. Promotional efforts since May 2010 have been especially effective in the Southern Cone and Peru. Compared to the first half of 2011, visitors from the subregion grew 131.64 percent during the first six months of 2013, with a total of 94,234 tourists from the subregion visiting Cuba between January and June.[41] Efforts to promote South American tourism on the island continued in July 2013 with a series of high-profile meetings in Brazil between Cuban Minister Manuel Marrero and Brazilian Tourism Minister Gastao Dias Vieira. While in Brazil, Marrero, who arrived in the Brazilian hub by way of a Cubana Airlines flight, marking the resumption of direct flights between Cuba and Brazil,[42] signed a series of agreements with his Brazilian counterpart intended to increase collaboration in the tourist sector between the two countries.[43]

There is another important new tourist market in Cuba, one that not only is evidence of changes in economic conditions and policies on the island but that also underscores the magnitude of broader changes under way in Cuba. Once legally excluded from tourist establishments and expected to tolerate the omnipresence of tourism on the island as a necessary evil and economic savior, Cubans themselves are now active participants in the industry—not simply as servants but increasingly as those being served. Gone are the prohibitive policies restricting Cuban access to tourist facilities and hotels. Instead, during the past several years, Cuba's Ministry of Tourism has actively encouraged hard-currency-holding residents to enjoy Cuba's wide array of tourist amenities throughout the island. In 2012, roughly 1 million Cubans living on the island participated in the domestic tourist industry.[44] Of those 1 million

Cuban tourists, an estimated 570,000 paid in hard currency to stay in hotels across the country.[45]

TEEING OFF ON THE GREENS: COMMUNISM VERSUS CAPITALISM

In addition to seeking new tourist markets at home and abroad, a key aspect of Cuba's longer-term strategy involves expanding tourist options, recreational activities, and amenities on the island. One such area ripe for expansion is golf. Golf courses were once viewed as playgrounds for the rich and foreign; in 1962, Fidel Castro shut down the island's golf courses and private clubs, ordering the land to be put to less "bourgeoisie" use.[46] Several were turned into military training facilities, and one became the site of a leading art school. However, today, as part of Cuba's overall strategy of tourist sector development, golf has resurfaced as a potential draw for both tourists and investors alike.

In May 2013, several days after Antonio Castro, son of former president Fidel, won a golf tournament hosted by Esencia, a British development company, at the Varadero Golf Club, British ambassador to Cuba, Tim Cole, announced a Cuban-British joint venture to develop Cuba's first golf resort.[47] In addition to constructing only the second eighteen-hole golf course on the island, the $350 million project will feature private villas and apartments along with a country club, tennis courts, spa, yacht club, and hotel.[48] This joint venture between Esencia and the Cuban government will be the largest British investment on the island in the past decade.[49]

Beyond the novelty of being the first full-fledged resort of its kind, the Carbonera Country Club will be a novelty on the island for another, arguably more significant reason: foreigners will be allowed to purchase private property and own vacation homes on its 420-acre grounds.[50] The Carbonera website (in development) describes the facility as offering an "elegant lifestyle" and "gated community real estate" that "represents a unique investment opportunity on the island."[51] The site explains, "With great medical services, an unbeatable climate and a very friendly tax regime, the future looks bright." The question here, as with so many other aspects of the tourist industry on the island, is, bright for whom?

TOURISM: SAVIOR OR DESTROYER?

In order to survive today, the average Cuban needs access to hard currency. For many Cubans without a family abroad to send remittances or employment within Cuba's ever-expanding private sector, working with tourists is the only legal option for acquiring hard currency. Recognizing the need for some adjustment, the government has begun to offer hard-currency compensation along with worker's state salaries in certain enterprises. However, the government has found itself, once again, in a battle of moral versus material incentives.

If Cubans cannot legitimately gain access to hard currency through occupations that provide for the common good—such as medicine or education—they will have less incentive to educate themselves. This has already resulted in a serious drain (and will continue to do so) of Cuba's well-trained professional population—a group that has been one of Cuba's defining strengths throughout the Revolution thus far. Miren Uriarte describes this risk as "the 'inverted pyramid,' a phenomenon that reflects the devalued return on education and professional preparation in the new economy. The immediate result has been the exodus of public service workers into low-level service jobs in the tourism industry."[52]

Cuba cannot afford this brain drain from the professional and high-value-added sectors of its economy. Such a loss would undermine many of the progressive elements on which Cuban national identity has developed, such as health care, education, and cultural production. Of even greater concern, this loss of human capital would cripple Cuba's prospects for development beyond the tourist industry.

Regardless of the obvious economic benefits derived from the tourist industry and claims of a trickle-down effect with rising tourist tides lifting all boats, tourism will not generate greater equality or renew a spirit of egalitarianism. Tourism by its very nature creates distinctions between those who serve and those who are served, regardless of whether those being served are foreigners or hard-currency-holding Cubans—members of Cuba's new and expanding "elite." In many developing countries, it is an industry built on and fueled by the exploitation of inequality. Without greater attention to and concrete government efforts to address the inherent contradictions in the promotion of tourism, the Cuban government ignores a phenomenon that is difficult to hide: contemporary Cuba increasingly resembles prerevolutionary Cuba, with its glaring social inequalities and other trappings of dependency.

NOTES

1. Philip Peters, *International Tourism: The New Engine of the Cuban Economy* (Arlington, VA: Lexington Institute, 2002), 2.

2. Peters, *International Tourism*, 2.

3. Stanley Turkel, "Cuba: Tourism Thriving despite the U.S. Trade Embargo," *Hotel Interactive*, October 4, 2006, http://www.hotelinteractive.com/index.asp?page_id=5000&article_id=6319.

4. Caribbean Tourism Organization, "State of the Industry Report on February 15, 2012," http://www.onecaribbean.org/wp-content/uploads/StateIndustryStats15Feb2012.pdf.

5. Pedro Monreal, *Development Prospects in Cuba an Agenda in the Making* (London: Institute of Latin American Studies, University of London, 2002), 15.

6. Julio Cerviño and Maria Cubillo, "Hotel and Tourism Development in Cuba: Opportunities, Management Challenges, and Future Trends," *Cornell Hotel and Restaurant Administration Quarterly* 46, no. 2 (2005): 225.

7. Charles Suddaby, "Cuba's Tourism Industry," paper presented at the seventh annual meeting of the Association of the Study of the Cuban Economy, Miami, August 7–9, 1997.

8. William M. LeoGrande and Julie Thomas, "Cuba's Quest for Economic Independence," *Journal of Latin American Studies* 34 (2002): 344.

9. Max Azicri, *Cuba Today and Tomorrow: Reinventing Socialism* (Gainesville: University Press of Florida, 2001): 141.

10. Sending remittances to Cuba became legal during the administration of Jimmy Carter but expanded considerably during the 1990s.

11. The U.S. dollar was used in Cuba until November 8, 2004. After November 8, all dollars had to be exchanged for *pesos convertibles*, a transaction that included a minimum tax of 10 percent.

12. Susan Eckstein, *Back from the Future: Cuba under Castro* (Princeton, NJ: Princeton University Press, 1994), 105.

13. Eckstein, *Back from the Future*, 105.

14. Oscar Lewis, Ruth M. Lewis, and Susan M. Rigdon, "The 'Rehabilitation' of Prostitutes," in *The Cuba Reader: History, Culture, Politics*, ed. Aviva Chomsky, Barry Carr, and Maria Smorkaloff (Durham, NC: Duke University Press, 2003), 395.

15. Elisa Facio, "Jineterismo during the Special Period," in *Cuban Transitions at the Millennium*, ed. Eloise Linger and John Cotman (Largo, MD: International Development Options, 2000), 57.

16. Azicri, *Cuba Today and Tomorrow*, 87.

17. Azicri, *Cuba Today and Tomorrow*, 87.

18. While women made up the majority of sex workers during the 1990s and early 2000s, it has become increasingly common to see men (accompanying both women and other men) involved in sex work as well as other forms of "hustling," where there is a monetary or material transaction in return for companionship that may or may not also involve sex.

19. Facio, "Jineterismo during the Special Period," 71.

20. Facio, "Jineterismo during the Special Period," 58.

21. Eckstein, *Back from the Future*, 123.

22. Douglas Farah, "Catering to Foreigners Instead of Cubans Puts Castro on Defensive," *Washington Post*, August 9, 1992.

23. Facio, "Jineterismo during the Special Period," 69.

24. Hannah Caller, *History of Cuba: José Martí 1853—1895 and the War of Independence*, Rock around the Blockade Educational Series, http://www.rcgfrfi.esaynet.co.uk/ratb/cuba/history2/htm (accessed December 1, 2005).

25. Alejandro de la Fuente, "Race and Inequality in Cuba, 1899–1981," *Journal of Contemporary History* 30 (2005): 133.

26. Clarence Lusane, "From Black Cuban to Afro-Cuban: Issues and Problems Researching Race Consciousness and Identity in Cuban Race Relations," in Linger and Cotman, *Cuban Transitions at the Millennium*, 87.

27. Based on the author's observations while traveling throughout Cuba in 2003 and 2004.

28. Alejandro de la Fuente, "Recreating Racism: Race and Discrimination in Cuba's Special Period," *Georgetown University Cuba Briefing Paper Series* 18 (1998).

29. Lusane, "From Black Cuban to Afro-Cuban," 94.

30. de la Fuente, "Recreating Racism," 133.

31. Eladio Secades, quoted in Louis A. Pérez Jr., "Image and Identity," in *Inside Cuba: The History, Culture, and Politics of and Outlaw Nation*, ed. John Miller and Aaron Kenedi (New York: Marlowe & Company, 2003), 144.

32. Cristina García, "Cacharros," in Miller and Kenedi, *Inside Cuba*, 147.

33. Personal communications between the author and Cuban musicians in several of the "house bands" playing nightly in the hotels surrounding El Parque Central, Havana, December 2004.

34. D. J. Greenwood, "Culture by the Pound: An Anthropological Perspective on Tourism as Cultural Commoditization," in *Hosts and Guests: The Anthropology of Tourism*, ed. V. Smith (Philadelphia: University of Pennsylvania Press, 1989), 171–85.

35. Louis A. Pérez Jr., *On Becoming Cuban* (Chapel Hill: University of North Carolina Press, 1999), 395.

36. Laurie Kroshus Medina, "Commoditizing Culture Tourism and Mayan Identity," *Annals of Tourism Research* 30, no. 2 (2003): 353–68.

37. Fred Ward, "Havana, 1977: Welcome Tourists," in *The Reader's Companion to Cuba*, ed. Alan Ryan (Orlando, FL: Harcourt Brace, 1997), 252.

38. Agnerys Rodríguez Gavilán, "Authentic Cuba Campaign," Cubaweb, May 4, 2010, http://www.cubaweb.cu/en/component/content/article/226-campana-autentica-cuba.

39. Ramesh Mathew, "Cuba Woos Tourists from Qatar, Region," *Gulf Times*, June 24, 2013, http://www.gulf-times.com/qatar/178/details/357366/cuba-woos-tourists-from-qatar,-region.

40. "Cyprus Promoting Tourism to Cuba," website of the Cuban embassy in Cyprus, http://www.cubadiplomatica.cu/chipre/EN/Home/tabid/14167/ctl/Details/mid/22723/ItemID/30055/Default.aspx.

41. "Growing Number of South American Tourists Coming to Cuba," *Cuba Contemporánea*, June 26, 2013, http://www.cubacontemporanea.com/en/growing-number-south-american-tourists-coming-cuba/.

42. "Cuba Airliner Resumes Nonstop Flights to Brazil," *Cuba Contemporánea*, July 12, 2013, http://www.cubacontemporanea.com/en/cuban-airliner-resumes-nonstop-flights-brazil/.

43. "Brazil, Cuba to Collaborate in Tourism Sector," *Cuba Contemporánea*, July 17, 2003, http://www.cubacontemporanea.com/en/brazil-cuba-collaborate-tourism-sector/.

44. "Experts Address Challenges, Prospects of Cuba's Travel Industry," *Cuba Contemporánea*, June 1, 2013, http://www.cubacontemporanea.com/en/experts-address-challenges-prospects-cubas-travel-industry/.

45. Domingo Amuchastegui, "Marrero Reveals Tourism Growth Plans," *Cuba News*, June 12, 2013, http://www.cubanews.com/sections/marrero-reveals-tourism-growth-plans.

46. Sarah Rainsford, "Cuba Golf Project Gets Green Light," BBC News, May 13, 2013, http://www.bbc.co.uk/news/world-latin-america-22507776.

47. "A Tale of Politics, Corruption and Golf," *The Economist*, May 25, 2013.

48. Rainsford, "Cuba Golf Project Gets Green Light."

49. Maria Valencia, "China to Invest in Cuba Golf Courses," *Cuba Contemporánea*, June 4, 2013, http://www.cubacontemporanea.com/en/china-invest-cuba-golf-courses/.

50. Rainsford, "Cuba Golf Project Gets Green Light."

51. Carbonera Country Club website, http://www.thecarboneraclub.com/.

52. Miren Uriarte, *Cuba, Social Policy at the Crossroads, Maintaining Priorities, Transforming Practice* (Boston: Oxfam America, 2002), 27.

Chapter Fifteen

Remittance Recipients and the Present and Future of Microentrepreneurship Activities in Cuba

Manuel Orozco and Katrin Hansing

This chapter explores the extent to which Cuban remittance recipients are responding to the Cuban government's economic reforms that seek to incentivize entrepreneurial activities as an economic growth strategy and to state liberalization policy. The analysis is based on fieldwork and a survey of remittance recipients in Cuba (see the section "Appendix: Survey Methodology" for a description of the survey). The findings show that remittances continue to play an important role in the economic survival of Cubans, with money coming from the United States and other parts of the world. We find that an important proportion of recipients want to own a business and that some already have established one. The businesses that remittance recipients have established or aspire to establish are geared toward the service sector and led by microenterprises aimed at achieving self-subsistence rather than wealth generation.

In light of the reforms introduced by the Cuban government, there seems to be a mismatch between government policies and people's needs and interests. Many of the economic activities that remittance recipients would like to undertake through small businesses are not within the scope of the new reforms. Moreover, these policies may not be sufficient to enable an amenable environment for business development. In light of these shortcomings, there is an expectation among remittance recipients wanting to set up a business that remittances and families abroad will help them finance their businesses. However, given the global recession and particular socioeconomic situation of many Cuban remitters, these inflows do not constitute a formal mechanism for small business development and should rather function as a complement to possible policy and development incentives. Given the precarious position of ongoing and potential businesses and reforms that would provide limited incentives for growth, it is important to consider implementing strategies that respond to the prevailing conditions of these enterprises, such as microcredits, wholesale markets, technical advice on business development, and financial training.

CURRENT TRENDS IN REMITTANCES TO CUBA

Remittances have continued to flow into Cuba, with the flows having four characteristics (table 15.1). First, the United States continues to dominate transfers but with less presence than in earlier periods; transfers from Europe and Latin America have increased in importance. Second, despite the 2009 changes in U.S. remittance policy to Cuba, few remittance transfer operators have entered the market, and the use of informal transfer mechanisms continues. Third, the amount received has remained the same or declined, most likely a symptom of the recession. [Editors' note: Since this article was written, remittances have grown from about $2 billion annually to over $2.6 billion.] Fourth, remittances continue to represent at least one-half of the total income of recipients, who are able to save, though they tend to do so informally.

According to survey data, 68 percent of remittance recipients interviewed received money from relatives in the United States, 13 percent received remittances from Europe (primarily from Spain), and 19 percent received remittances from Latin America and other developing countries, of which 8 percent were from Cuban workers in Venezuela. This last observation can be explained by the stronger relations between Cuba and Venezuela, including labor contracts to bring Cuban doctors and nurses to Venezuela. Regarding transmission channels, informal networks continue to be prevalent. Although policy changes in the United States have liberalized previous restrictions set in 2005, few businesses have entered the remittance market to offer transfers to Cuba.

Recipients own few assets that could serve as resources in productive or commercial activities, and most do not own bank accounts (87 percent). However, all of the respondents acknowledge that they save utilizing various methods, most of which are informal. While their assets are limited, they have accumulated liquid assets (table 15.2) in the form of cash savings amounting to a reserve or stock of nearly U.S.$900. These data suggest that the characteristics of remittance recipients have not changed substantially in the past five years despite policy reforms in the United States. Informality would have been expected to decrease and the amount sent to increase as a result of the initiatives by the Obama administration.

Another important point to highlight is that income dependence on remittances invariably remains below 60 percent. Cuban remittance recipient earnings range under $100 a month. This figure is important in that it points to a few broader issues that relate to the size of the Cuban economy. Specifically, remittance recipients earn incomes above average, but even using their average income as a reference for the entire population, it would mean that national income is less than U.S.$25,000 million as opposed to the officially recorded U.S.$40,000 million. Earnings among remittance recipients also hint at the extent of the size of their financial stock—typically, remittance recipients save more than nonrecipients and in amounts

Table 15.1.   Remittances Transfers to Cuba: Some Characteristics

	2005	2010/2011
Receiving from the United States	81%	68%
Receiving from Spain	12%	7%
Number of years receiving	4	9
Amount received per month	$150	$125
Frequency receipts per year	6	9
Receiving from parents	18%	20%
Receiving from siblings	22%	35%
Receives via money transfer operators	44%	47%
Receives via *mula* (informal)	54%	50%

Table 15.2.   Savings Methods Used by Remittance Recipients and Stock of Amount Saved

	%	U.S.$
I put money aside from what is left over at the end of the month	57	$827
I invest it in a business	2	$2,000
I work extra hours	3	$1,900
Take advantage of special sales	36	$758
I buy durable goods	3	$2,600

Source: Stock of amount saved refers to the amount of money one has accumulated in savings at the moment of the interview. A stock is what one has on reserve as opposed to what one does to save yearly, for example.

between U.S.$1,000 and U.S.$2,000. Together with other assets, these funds constitute a basis for potential business investment.

CUBAN REFORMS AND SMALL BUSINESS OPERATIONS

The efforts of the Cuban government to reform its economy by encouraging small business entrepreneurship among its population has brought attention to the potential role of remittances and their recipients in triggering business development.[1] In the small business sector, the reforms authorize the establishment of business enterprises for 178 economic activities within the Cuban economy. The activities generally fall into categories of manual labor, services, artisanship, and performance, the last two possibly considered part of Cuba's important tourist industry.[2] It should be noted that the list of legal economic activities includes very few opportunities for professionals. Small businesses are to be taxed at a 25 percent rate, while businesses with employees may be taxed at a rate of up to 50 percent. Guidelines for salary levels for employees stipulate that wages must increase as the number of employees increases such that minimum salary for employees working at a firm with fifteen or more workers is three times the median monthly salary.[3]

Given the changing context for small businesses and the assumption that remittance recipients may be more prone to invest in a business, this section explores the extent to which these recipients might decide to engage in a business activity. The results show that there are three distinct groups: those who are not planning to establish a business, those who are, and those who already own a business. Forty-three percent of recipients expressed that they would not form a business in Cuba, whereas 34 percent expressed that they would, and 23 percent said that they already had a business. Here we focus on those who are interested in setting up a business as well as those who already have a business. However, it is important to mention that the large number of people who said that they would not create a business stated as their main reasons for not doing so the following: a lack of resources, a lack of entrepreneurial know-how, and an undependable, risky economic and political context. In other words, it is not that this group is per se uninterested in starting a small business but rather that its members' current situations and the wider context make it unviable for them to do so.

Moreover, among those planning to establish a business or who already have one, a general finding is that, given their economic position, this is a population whose potential and actual businesses are limited to subsistence enterprises. Those interested in establishing a business are primarily men (67 percent) and suggest that they would invest mainly in a commercial activity involving food or clothing, while a fifth would be interested in a manufacturing trade.

The activities listed as potential lines of business included the sale of food, clothing, or CDs/DVDs. These activities are a partial fit into the list of businesses that the Cuban government has announced could be allowed by the state.

When asked about the purpose of a business, the majority expressed that the business would be a complement to their current job or as a survival strategy should they lose their current job (table 15.3). Only a small group (9 percent) stated that they wanted to own a business as a matter of interest. These responses are important in that they provide clues as to the direction of possible entrepreneurial activity. Those who engage in a business out of necessity due to job loss or to add to their income are less likely to grow their enterprise substantially after achieving self-subsistence. Moreover, if the business is unable to obtain financing and strengthen its marketability through additional training, its competitive edge decreases.

When thinking about the position of a business in the market, a successful enterprise is the result of various factors, such as access to capital, linkages to the value chain, entrepreneurial skill, and support from the regulatory environment. Even when a business is created out of necessity, getting access to financing, being competitive, or enjoying government support or incentives can help these businesses grow and accumulate wealth. In turn, enterprises are able to reinvest in jobs and machinery or accumulate personal wealth.

A closer look at remittance recipients shows important features that characterize their potential for engagement and performance in the business environment as it pertains to available resources, access to financing, and expertise in the trade. Overall, 95 percent of those interested in setting up their own business consider that their investment would involve less than U.S.$5,000 and most likely less than U.S.$1,000.[4] Moreover, when asked about what resources they had available to start the business, one-quarter affirmed that they already had sufficient savings, whereas 30 percent said that they already had a locale to operate and 16 percent had working capital. Those with cash in hand and working capital held a stock of savings worth up to U.S.$1,600. In addition to their existing investment stock, remittance recipients were asked about sources of financing that could complement their initial investment, business upkeep, and available guarantees. Just over a quarter stated that their own resources served as their additional financing source, and nearly two-thirds responded that they would seek financing from relatives living abroad. This dependency or expectation of support from relatives abroad confirms similar expectations in the media about the role of the Cuban community in the United States in particular. Moreover, no one considered institutional support to finance their business, and for the most part they saw their savings or the relative abroad themselves as a guarantee to financing.

Despite their financial weakness and no formal access to the financial sector, most of these individuals have some experience in the trade in which they plan to engage. Such a condition would give them an edge were they to compete in the market, unless it is already saturated.

Table 15.3.   Purpose for Setting Up a Business among Remittance Recipients

	%
Start a new job if I lose the current one	44
Complement my current income	38
To own my own business, I like to do business	9
Support my family	8
Other	1

These responses point to individuals seeking to form relatively small, subsistence operations for which they will depend on support from families living abroad and that may be outside the scope of government intervention. In turn, they will have a limited impact on economic growth and business development.

CURRENT BUSINESSES AMONG REMITTANCE RECIPIENTS

Those who already owned a business (23 percent) share similar characteristics with those who want to start a new one, except that 60 percent of current owners are women compared to 33 percent of those interested in setting up a new business. Consider the following:

- These entrepreneurs work mainly in services and sales, in many cases in activities similar to those of persons who want to start an enterprise.
- Twenty-two percent sell food, and 4 percent own a *paladar*.
- Seventy percent have the owner him- or herself as the employee, and the rest have only one additional employee.
- Sixty-two percent have a license to operate, while 38 percent in street sales and other trades operate informally.
- The average value of monthly sales is U.S.$200 (table 15.4), an amount that may add little to their total income. Because more than half of their income is coming from remittances, these entrepreneurial activities may complement their earnings from additional work but may not represent half of all income unless 40 percent of their sales go into salaries.
- In order to keep the business running, 63 percent fund the operations from business-related sales, and 27 percent do so with remittances.
- They typically operate their businesses out of their place of residence (80 percent) or are street vendors (12 percent).

CONCLUSIONS AND OBSERVATIONS

The results of the survey show that Cuban remittance recipients continue to rely on such flows to manage their day-to-day survival. Moreover, there are indications that those interested in setting up a business or who already have one are operating mainly at a subsistence level and are not able to generate additional wealth. As Cuba promotes self-employment, it is important to consider the issues that may contribute to the development of small businesses. It is also important to understand the correspondence between the type of enterprise emerging in the Cuban context, resources needed to strengthen and develop these into successful enterprises, and the short- and long-term impacts.

In any society, small businesses are faced with striking a balance between achieving success and overcoming challenges. Depending on the type of business, the issues to deal with may vary. Their business success depends on achieving increasing profit margins, maintaining financial liquidity, covering labor costs, promoting innovation, and consistently selling quality goods or services. They also are confronted with various challenges, some inherent to a business (capital access linked to value chain) and others associated with the global economy (managerially and commercially competitive) and the motivations of entrepreneurship. Because current Cuban entrepreneurs are mainly subsistence enterprises, what is critical is to identify the instruments that can enable these businesses to develop and grow as enterprises that can generate wealth. This may mean looking at the development of their business capabilities, their insertion into the global and domestic value chains, their access to financial re-

Table 15.4. Economic Activities of Entrepreneurs and Value of Sales per Month

	%	U.S.$
Food sales	22	$123
Beauty parlor (manicure), hairdresser	19	$60
Sell, repair garments	8	$95
Rent rooms	4	$1,400
Rent and sell videos	7	$40
Artisan crafts	4	$233
Paladar	4	$500
Agriculture	3	$75
Child care	3	$110
Import/export	3	$550
Teacher	3	$100
Ponchero (tire repair)	3	$200
Other	15	$200

sources to function and expand, and the incentives they would need to operate in a formalized environment. A number of observations regarding entrepreneurial activities in Cuba are in order:

- Relying on remittances or savings accrued as a primary means to invest is not an ideal situation, as such resources are typically fungible and can be used for various other activities. Savings can serve as part of a financial guarantee for a loan but not as the primary financing source: if they are depleted before the business fully develops, the enterprise can fail, and the entrepreneur is left worse off.
- The role of microfinance is pivotal, as it can help put these businesses in a better position to expand their activities and become sustainable. Moreover, microfinance would give nonremittance recipients the opportunity to gain access to credit and enter the emerging small business sector. Because ongoing businesses do not generate annual revenues over U.S.$3,000, projecting the right amount of financing needed to help a business grow is part of a financing strategy. On that basis and assuming that about 100,000 small and microenterprise operations were created as a result of the reforms, credit portfolios may need to reach at least U.S.$300 million.
- Training to orient interested entrepreneurs toward activities that are competitive, that are directly connected to commercial value chains, and that exhibit the potential to reach economies of scale is important. Many of the respondents were interested in setting up businesses or activities that may not be competitive or that may be market saturated. Thus, assessing the marketplace for commercial and productive activities can coincide with technical advice to businesses on where to invest and establish their enterprise and how to go about it.
- There are no wholesale markets in Cuba at this time. In order to make it worthwhile for people to seriously contemplate creating a small business, the Cuban state would do well to sell goods and materials at wholesale prices.
- The current regulatory environment is not friendly to entrepreneurs. Taxation by the state is quite onerous and will strangle the capacity of businesses to operate and reinvest in busi-

ness growth; such an environment will not prolong subsistence-level businesses. Exempting new businesses from paying taxes during a certain period and gradually introducing them into the tax structure can help them grow in the short term.

APPENDIX: SURVEY METHODOLOGY

The survey in Cuba was conducted in various cities across the country. Researchers worked on a representative sample of the population's social, demographic, ethnic, regional, and social strata. However, given the Cuban political context, researchers did not do random street interviewing; instead, the sample units relied on the snowball procedure among people who could be interviewed in confidentiality. The sample size was 300 remittance recipients.

NOTES

Excerpted from Manuel Orozco and Katrin Hansing, "Remittance Recipients and the Present and Future of Micro-Entrepreneurship Activities in Cuba," in *Cuba in Transition*, Association for the Study of the Cuban Economy, 2011. Reprinted by permission of the publisher.

1. Josh Goldstein, "Cuba & Remittances: Can the 'Money in the Mail' Drive Reform?," Center for Financial Inclusion, http://centerforfinancialinclusionblog.wordpress.com/2011/02/01/remittances-a-key-driver-of-economic-reform-in-cuba/.

2. The musical group Los Mambises and dance duo Amor are examples of the surprising specificity of the regulations within the performance category. "Actividades autorizadas para el ejercicio del trabajo por cuenta propia," *Juventud Rebelde*, September 24, 2010, http://www.juventudrebelde.cu/cuba/2010-09-24/actividades-autorizadas-para-el-ejercicio-del-trabajo-por-cuenta-propia/.

3. Oscar Espinosa Chepe, *Cambios en Cuba: Pocos, Limitados, y Tardíos*, http://reconciliacioncubana.files.wordpress.com/2011/03/cambios-en-cuba.pdf.

4. U.S.$1,000 is less than the average saved and would represent the minimum start-up investment, plus the resources they say they would use to establish the business.

Chapter Sixteen

Poverty and Vulnerability in Cuba Today

María del Carmen Zabala Argüelles

Poverty and vulnerability are important human issues in any context but even more so in a society that, exactly fifty years ago, embarked on an alternative path of development—socialism—which prioritizes the emancipation of human beings and the fulfillment of their potential. This required as its point of departure a commitment to social development, justice, and equity, based on universal and multifaceted social policies. Below I reflect on current poverty and vulnerability in Cuba and their determinants and forms of expression. My thesis is that these are diverse and heterogeneous, and their analysis must be supplemented by a family and gender perspective. Finally, I outline some ideas about how to improve social policies to address these issues.

SOCIAL DEVELOPMENT, JUSTICE, AND EQUITY
IN THE CUBAN SOCIAL MODEL

When the World Summit for Social Development took place in Copenhagen in 1995, many of the world's pressing social problems had already been solved in Cuba, and several of the proposals agreed on at this important forum were already an integral part of the Cuban concept of social development that had been devised and implemented since 1959. Among them are the promotion of social integration, especially of the most disadvantaged groups; access to a quality education and basic health care; gender equality; and the eradication of poverty.

While the rest of Latin America embraces the reigning belief that economic growth will solve the problems of poverty and inequity ("trickle-down theory") and has been pursuing policies of structural adjustment and privatization, Cuba has placed its bets on universal social policies and the central role of the state to promote and achieve just and equitable human development. Cuba's concept of social development is defined by these basic principles: it is comprehensive and multidimensional in character, economic and social aspects are assumed to be interconnected, the state plays a central role in the design and implementation of social policies that ensure free and universal basic social services, there is broad public participation in social policies, individual and social consumption together ensure higher consumption standards, and differential treatment of those groups considered vulnerable (children, women, and the rural population) with appropriate policies is acknowledged as necessary. These principles give rise to multifaceted, coherent, and systematic social policies that are comprehensive and universal (Rodríguez and Carriazo 1987).

This Cuban model places special emphasis on equity, consistent with its aim of social justice. Equity does not pertain only to the distribution of income; it also includes equal opportunities and universal access to social services, with specific attention to disadvantaged groups so they can benefit from the existing structure of opportunities (Alvarez and Mattar 2004).

Cuban social policy regarding poverty attempts to eradicate it by addressing its causes, promoting equity as a means to integrate all sectors of society, fostering human development and well-being, and guaranteeing the entire population basic social protections. Above and beyond these objectives are more specific policies of direct assistance for those sectors considered vulnerable. In keeping with the ethical and humanistic principles of Cuba's social program, merely reducing, alleviating, or mitigating poverty is not enough. The aspiration is to eliminate or minimize the conditions that produce and/or reproduce poverty and to promote human development in all its aspects.

As a result of implementing this concept of development and the social policies it implies, Cuban society for nearly three decades enjoyed a trend toward a more equitable distribution of wealth, which has been documented by renowned authors and institutions[1] and advanced significantly in terms of social development, as evidenced by very favorable social indicators—some of which are even comparable to those of developed countries—at virtually the same level throughout the island. Particularly outstanding among these indicators is the Human Development Index. Cuba's rank has risen significantly since 1998, and as of 2013 it was ranked fifty-ninth (United Nations Development Program 2013). According to the Human Development and Equity Index,[2] whose goal is to measure equity in the relevant aspects of human development, Cuba ranks among the top five nations of Latin America and the Caribbean—along with Trinidad and Tobago, Colombia, and Costa Rica. It must be emphasized that these results were achieved by an underdeveloped country with limited resources and almost constantly facing adverse economic conditions.

POVERTY AND VULNERABILITY IN PRESENT-DAY CUBA

The crisis and economic reforms that occurred in Cuba during the 1990s not only severely hurt the country's economy but also seriously affected everyone's quality of life. In particular, material insecurity grew and intensified. In this complex scenario, poverty reemerged as a social problem, and, consequently, the thesis that poverty was being eradicated in Cuba (Rodríguez and Carriazo 1987), which had been widely shared in all spheres—political, social, and academic—and proven by indisputable social advances and achievements, began to be questioned.[3] Special terms are used to discuss problems connected with types of personal insecurity (*precariedad*), reflecting both the aforementioned social achievements and the specifics of the phenomenon of poverty in Cuban society. Among these terms are "social disadvantage," to describe adverse socioeconomic and familial conditions that place schoolchildren at risk (Díaz et al. 1990); "vulnerable groups," defined as groups with incomes too low to provide a minimum standard of living (Torres 1993); and "at-risk population," defined as that population in danger of not being able to meet some basic needs (Ferriol et al. 1997)—a term the authors explicitly prefer to use instead of "poverty."[4] The recognition of poverty in today's Cuba requires acknowledgment of its sui generis character. It is limited in extent and one does not find critical or extreme poverty of the sort that would produce malnutrition, poor health, illiteracy, insecurity, and social exclusion. It is also unique with regard to the social protection received by the entire population.

Even those sectors with scarce resources are guaranteed access to basic social services (Zabala 1996). It is precisely this social protection—free and accessible health care, education and social security, guarantees of employment, wages and basic foodstuffs, and indirect residential subsidies—that keeps social exclusion to a minimum. It is this social protection that accounts for Cuba's favorable ranking in terms of human development and poverty. According to the Human Poverty Index, Cuba has ranked among the top five developing countries over the past ten years, with poverty rates ranging from 4.1 percent (2002) to 5.1 percent (1997). It has ranked between second and sixth, and in every case the results have been considered very favorable.[5]

The second report prepared by the *Instituto Nacional de Investigación Económica* (National Institute of Economic Research [INIE] 2005) on the Millennium Development Goals showed that Cuba was doing very well at meeting those goals. Regarding the goal of eradicating extreme poverty and hunger, unemployment fell from 7.1 percent (1997) to 1.9 percent (2004), a rate that can be regarded as full employment, benefiting all sectors of society, especially youth, women, the disabled, and the people of the country's eastern provinces—the region where unemployment was highest during the economic crisis. Over this same period, minimum wage increased (by 125 percent, benefiting 1,657,191 workers), as did the base pay in various sectors. Social security benefits to low-income pensioners increased, benefiting 1,468,641 individuals, as did social assistance, benefiting 476,512.

In terms of the goal of reducing the rate of hunger by half between 1990 and 2015, food availability increased between 1999 and 2003, from an average of 3,007 kilocalories to 3,165 per capita per day. The proportion of the population at risk of malnutrition fell to 2 percent. The incidence of low-birth-weight babies has fallen since 1993 and is consistent throughout the country. Likewise, the percentage of children up to five years old who are moderately or severely underweight decreased to 2 percent—a very low incidence by worldwide standards—and with very little variation between the sexes. Specific programs are now being developed to ensure the proper nutrition of children, the elderly, pregnant women, and the chronically ill. Given all of this, the achievement of this millennium goal is quite possible for Cuba. Cuba has shown significant progress toward fulfilling other related goals, such as universal primary education, women's equality and independence, reduction of infant mortality, better maternal health, and combating HIV/AIDS, malaria, and other diseases.

One should add that social vulnerability has increased to a degree in Cuban society. Major contributing factors are the aforementioned economic crisis and reform, the effects of the U.S. economic blockade, and the natural disasters that frequently assault the country. Other factors are associated with the characteristics—gender, race, age, and so on—that can make individuals, households, or groups more vulnerable. In addition, the most vulnerable can be identified by looking at poor people's resources and assets—physical, financial, productive, and human and social capital—and particularly the types of strategies developed by an individual or a household (Moser 1998).

INSUFFICIENT INCOME

Most economic studies of this phenomenon—and in particular those using the income or poverty line method—have revealed insufficient income to be the essential determinant of poverty and its sole, most important and widespread form. This view of poverty places emphasis on the inputs available to individuals or households to satisfy their material needs. Those individuals or households who do not have the monetary income to satisfy their minimum needs within the historically determined norms of a society are considered to be below the poverty line. We know that the income redistribution that took place during the first two decades of the Cuban Revolution resulted in notable increases in the incomes of the poorest sectors (table 16.1).

This tendency toward equitable distribution of wealth in Cuban society is demonstrated by the Gini coefficient, which shows a continual decrease in values from 1953 to the end of the 1980s: 0.56 (1953), 0.25 (1978), and 0.22 (1986) (Baliño 1991; Zimbalist 1989). Although in later decades the value of this coefficient has increased somewhat, to 0.38 between 1996 and 1998, it still ranks among the lowest in Latin America and the Caribbean. Cuba's rank is even more significant because these calculations include only monetary income and do not include transfers, such as health care, education, and housing. Cuban experts explain these low levels of income inequality recorded until 1989 by the high employment rate—95 percent—in the state sector of the economy, the implementation of a unified salary system with a relatively narrow range of pay levels, the importance of salaries to household income, the effect of state-subsidized consumer items, and the maintenance of an overvalued exchange rate (Alvarez and Mattar 2004).

However, the crisis and the economic reforms reversed this trend in income distribution and equity. Various factors contributed to this: the declining purchasing power of salaries due to price increases; the dual currency system[6]; a segmented market system with different prices, currency, and quality of products; diversification of income sources; and the divorce of the pay scale from work effort and professional skill, among other factors. Taken together, these factors led to an increase in social inequalities and socioeconomic differentiation. Mayra Espina (1997) studied these aspects in depth and found that they are expressed in the polarization of income and the emergence of vulnerable groups who do not enjoy high levels of consumption or material well-being. In her most recent work, Espina links this tendency to the emergence of poverty: "Without producing a mechanism for restoring the relations of exploitation or of private property on a large scale, Cuban reform measures led to restratification, providing the context for the growth of poverty as a social problem, the expansion of the at-risk segments of the population, and a general trend of widening socioeconomic inequalities" (Espina 2008, 161).

Such social restratification and growth of income inequality are linked to the increased role of the market in distribution. Macroeconomic studies designed to identify sectors of the population with insufficient income have found an increase over the past two decades. A study carried out by experts at the INIE and the *Centro de Investigaciones de la Economía Mundial* (Global Economy Research Center for Study of the World Economy [CIEM]) looked at the urban population at risk and found that this sector had more than doubled, from 6.3 to 14.7 percent, between 1988 and 1996; in both years, the income of the majority of the at-risk

Table 16.1.   Income Distribution

Years	Gross Domestic Product per Capita (U.S. dollars)	Income per Capita of the Poorest 40%	Proportion of Total Income (%)	Income per Capita of the Richest 5%	Proportion of Total Income (%)
1958	866	182	6.5	5,947	26.5
1962	882	379	17.2	2,237	12.7
1973	996	506	20.3	1,892	9.5
1978	1,395	865	24.8	3,068	11.0

Source: Brundenius (1984).

population was near the poverty line. By region, although the east was most affected (21.7 percent of the population at risk), the western region and the city of Havana showed the sharpest increase in risk. The urban at-risk population includes disproportionate numbers of seniors, women, individuals with only primary and middle school education, the unemployed, state workers, and large households (Ferriol et al. 1997). As of 1999, 20 percent of the urban population was at risk. The data show that there is little variation within this group and that most of these people live close to the poverty line. Preliminary calculations for 2001 have indicated that this situation has not been reversed (Alvarez and Mattar 2004).

Insufficient income is directly associated with limited consumption of all kinds but food most of all. A study performed in the city of Havana by researchers of the INIE, the *Oficina Nacional de Estadísticas* (National Office of Statistics [ONE]), and the *Centro de Estudios de Población y Demografía* (Population and Development Studies Center [CEPDE]) highlights the insufficient food consumption of households in the two lowest-income deciles and their dependence on the rationed goods from the state markets complemented by government-subsidized meals and other forms of social protection (Ferriol et al. 2004a).[7]

Economist Viviana Togores combines the rates of dependence and salary income of households and an estimate of the basic food basket into a single index. From these, she calculates income poverty, defined as a condition in which the household is not able to meet its basic food needs. According to her estimates, 48.4 percent of the Cuban population is in this category. But at the same time, she acknowledges that the redistributive effect of social expenditures—in education, health, social assistance, and so on—while it does not compensate for the loss of purchasing power, does have a favorable effect on the population, especially those in more needy sectors (Togores 2000, 2004).

In contrast with other countries, insufficient income in Cuba is not directly related to unemployment; even during the economic crisis, workers' nominal salaries remained unchanged, and the employees affected by company closings received subsidies. Moreover, as the economy recovered, unemployment dropped significantly. In 1995, the unemployment rate was 8.3 percent; by 2000, it had dropped to 5.4 percent. In 2006, it stood at only 1.9 percent, and in 2007 just 1.8 percent, or nearly full employment. In addition, nominal wages in the state sector have been gradually increasing as a result of wage reforms. The average monthly salary in state and mixed enterprises increased from 261 pesos in 2002 to 408 in 2007 (ONE 2008).

Furthermore, the social security program ensures universal protection for workers and their families and also for sectors of the society whose essential needs are not otherwise met or who, because of life circumstances or health reasons, cannot meet their needs without social assistance.[8] Expenditures on social security and services as well as pensions have increased substantially in recent years. The costs of social assistance programs and the number of beneficiaries have also increased dramatically (table 16.2).

Insufficient income is related primarily to the decline in purchasing power of salaries and social security and assistance benefits. According to Togores (2004) and Pérez (2008), this occurs because nominal wages have not kept up with increases in the Consumer Price Index[9] so that real wages have fallen by 37 percent between 1989 and 2000 (Pérez 2008). This affects particularly those whose main income comes from the state, such as traditional state sector employees who do not receive other benefits or perks and those receiving pensions and social assistance.

Although unemployment is not the main cause of insufficient income, households with low adult employment and high rates of economic dependence are among those with the lowest income levels (Ferriol et al. 2004a; Zabala 1999). Although these estimates reflect the signifi-

Table 16.2.   Social Security and Social Assistance Data

Indicators	2002	2003	2004	2005	2006	2007
Social security expenditures (millions of national pesos CUP)	2,098.2	2,144.7	2,172.1	3,088.8	3,783.0	3,730.0
Social security beneficiaries	1,422,511	1,464,049	1,483,779	1,495,825	1,533,230	1,571,924
Average pension	112.81	119.04	120.69	179.36	191.83	194.11
Social assistance expenditure (billions CUP)	102.6	215.7	261.9	451.6	572.4	590.7
Social assistance beneficiaries	269,495	395,821	476,512	535,134	599,505	595,181

Source: ONE (2008).

cance of insufficient income in today's Cuba, they should be analyzed with caution and in the light of important qualifications. For example, free public services, such as health care and education, satisfy important needs. Furthermore, the cost of the basic goods basket is difficult to calculate because basic goods are acquired in various markets with different prices; each household has its own formula for satisfying its needs. Moreover, such estimates are themselves questionable because they do not take into account income not stemming from formal employment, such as hard-currency income and various types of worker incentives.

UNMET BASIC NEEDS

Poverty can be identified directly by examining whether individuals' or households' actual consumption of goods and services meets their basic needs (as opposed to being measured by income, which is an indirect approximation, as it represents only a portion of inputs). In order to identify the unmet basic needs, each household's success at meeting a group of specific needs—housing, water, sewage, electricity, furniture and household items, and so on—is evaluated. In each case, a minimum value is set. If the household falls below that level, the need in question is considered unmet, and an overall lack of essential services exists (Boltvinik 1992). Studies on spatial inequalities undertaken by the Center for the Study of Health and Human Welfare at the University of Havana have revealed interregional and intraregional inequalities; some of these are due to spatial inequalities inherited from before the Revolution and the new inequalities that emerged during the crisis and the economic reform. Such inequalities involve differences in housing quality, access to consumer goods and social services, and levels of socioeconomic development that give advantages to certain regions over others, the so-called luminous and opaque areas, respectively (Iñiguez and Pérez 2004; Iñiguez and Ravenet 1999).

The housing question is, without a doubt, one of the most pressing problems facing Cuban society. Despite efforts and achievements, the latest data available indicate that 26 and 15 percent of Cuban homes were considered to be in fair or poor condition, respectively (Alvarez and Mattar 2004). Estimates made in 1993 indicated that fair and poor structural conditions were more common in rural areas (Hábitat 1996); nevertheless, the city of Havana was in a particularly critical state: not only were 20 and 16 percent of units, respectively, classified as fair or poor, but in addition, 60,000 houses needed to be replaced, another 60,700 dwellings were located in tenement buildings,[10] and 2,700 units were homeless shelters that accommodate families whose housing is uninhabitable; in addition, there were sixty unhealthy districts and 114 precarious settlements with marked deterioration in the capital (Coyula 2006).

Another housing problem is the accumulated housing shortage, which the National Housing Institute has estimated at about 530,000 units (Alvarez and Mattar 2004), and the overcrowding that this causes. Currently, a do-it-yourself construction program is under way with the participation of the state. In 2007, 57.4 percent of homes were built without state involvement, and of these, 52 percent were do-it-yourself (ONE 2007); however, the construction is far from meeting expectations and existing needs.

The natural disasters endured by Cuba, steadily more frequent and intense, have had a damaging effect on the country's housing situation by destroying dwellings entirely or partially and accelerating the deterioration of the housing base.[11] Although reconstruction and rehabilitation of housing damaged by hurricanes are given priority in allocating the scarce resources available for construction, only 22 percent of the affected dwellings have been repaired (Rodríguez 2008).

In terms of safe drinking water, the coverage of households is high—95.2 percent, according to 2002 data—although in rural areas the figure is only 85.4 percent, and only 75.4 percent of covered households have direct connections. In many homes, water must be stored because water service is intermittent, affecting its quality and availability; 94.2 percent of households in 2002 have sanitation services, of which 38.4 percent are sewer connections and 55.8 percent pits and latrines. The situation is worse in rural areas, where 84.6 percent have services, only 9.8 percent of which are sewer connections. In general, the lowest levels of access to water and sanitation are found in the rural areas of the country's eastern provinces (Alvarez and Mattar 2004).

Regarding electricity, 95 percent of households have service: 100 percent in urban areas and 83 percent in rural areas (ONE 2002). The state continues working to bring electricity to the more remote areas.

SOME PERSPECTIVES OF ANALYSIS: FAMILY AND GENDER

The diversity and heterogeneity of poverty are also evident when examined by gender and family status. This investigation also brings subjective and sociocultural dimensions into the analysis. Poverty studies from the family perspective[12] have revealed the impact of poverty on family structure, dynamics, and functioning as well as on the ways in which families respond to their situation—including survival strategies. Poverty also influences the ways people interpret their family situation in plans, self-perception, self-esteem, and values, among other things. The family perspective incorporates both analysis of the immediate socioeconomic impacts specific to families and analysis, over time, of the changes that occur through the entire life cycle of a family.

Along these lines, I have conducted studies of families living in poverty based not only on their unfavorable living conditions but also on family composition: high average size, mainly young age structure, education level slightly lower than the national average, low rate of employment, overrepresentation of blacks and mixed-race individuals, and female heads of household. They are characterized mainly by extended families and single mothers, unstable relationships, predominance of the maternal role in all areas of family life, patterns of early motherhood and high fertility rates, and limited educational role of the family. In the family-society relationship, one can discern various family strategies oriented toward subsistence; a high degree of social integration, except in employment; a limited degree of social participation; and some conflicts with or alienation from social organizations. In subjective terms, one can observe the variable self-perception of families regarding their poverty, the predominance of a family-centered perspective instead of a social perspective along with short time horizons, and the importance of the family in transmitting values.

These studies reveal a reciprocal relation between the characteristics of structure, functioning, and dynamics of families living in poverty and the organization of their daily lives based on family survival via various strategies. This relation reinforces disadvantaged living conditions, family dysfunction, and the insufficient use of opportunities offered by society, thus feeding the generational reproduction of poverty and the intensification of this phenomenon at certain stages of the family life cycle. The studies also highlight the importance of the family in the reproduction of poverty, expressed in three dimensions: traditional, situational, and current. The traditional includes the lack of material wealth and other assets as well as some generationally transmitted patterns of behavior and values. The situational dimension is linked to the economic crisis and reforms. In this context, the current dimension refers to reinforcement of some traditional characteristics and behaviors.

Subsequent research reaffirms some of these findings. A study by the Center for Psychological and Sociological Research confirmed that the most disadvantaged families were extended, single parent, growing, and with female heads of households and many economically dependent family members. It also revealed that such families are most common in poor housing conditions, areas of little socioeconomic development, urban shantytowns, and resource-scarce rural areas (Díaz Tenorio 2008). Families' lack of various kinds of capital affects their poverty. According to psychologist Patricia Arés (2008), families with high educational and cultural capital and declining economic capital—professionals and technicians belonging to the traditional state sector—and particularly those with low cultural capital and declining economic capital are financially insecure.

Other studies conducted in Havana city found that with regard to income, poorer families were those headed by women and pensioners, those with more children, elderly individuals living alone, the unemployed, the chronically ill and disabled, women, full-time homemakers, the less educated, larger families, and people of color (Ferriol et al. 2004a). From the foregoing, it can be concluded that the diversity and heterogeneity of poverty are linked to specific characteristics of the family group, their living conditions, their links with society, and their subjective representations.

The gender perspective in the analysis of poverty enriches the understanding of this phenomenon. In the Cuban context, it acquires special significance because of the important achievements of women in the social sphere and the social and legal protection they enjoy. Regarding the problem of poverty, according to estimates of the at-risk population, defined as those with incomes below the poverty line, there were no significant gender differences in urban areas in 1997: females accounted for 50.7 percent of total population at risk (Ferriol et al. 1997). More recently, research on at-risk populations in Havana found that women were slightly overrepresented (57 percent) in the lowest monetary income groups—the two lowest deciles (Ferriol et al. 2004a). Although there is no occupational or wage discrimination in Cuba and although women have achieved high educational levels, their greater poverty could be due to their overrepresentation in lower-paying occupational categories, such as service and administration, even though they make up the majority of professionals and technicians (Núñez 2000); unequal access to management positions of leadership (Díaz 2004); the existence of a sector of the female population that has no economic autonomy because it engages only in homemaking; and the greater role of women as caretakers for children and the infirm.

In the realm of family, this analysis points to the possible vulnerability of households headed by women, particularly single mothers, whose numbers are steadily rising in Cuba. These households are in some cases in a state of poverty and vulnerability because of the structure, composition, and conditions in which the mothers fulfill their roles and responsibilities. Several studies have shown that households headed by unemployed, single-parent females who lack technical training or have low educational levels are vulnerable and in poverty. This analysis highlights the importance of access to and control over job opportunities, training, education, and social support networks available to women, which may be decisive in breaking the cycle of poverty.[13]

This demonstrates that women still suffer some disadvantages that are made to seem natural or justified by symbolic representations of women, families, and various social actors that are historically and culturally conditioned and that contribute in various ways to a certain level of vulnerability in women not only in the employment and social realms but also in the family environment. It is important to consider that such representations can be determinants of gender-associated poverty and thus contribute to the social exclusion of women.

CONCLUDING REMARKS

Comparative analysis shows not only that the conditions and manifestations of poverty in Cuba are unique but that that uniqueness is strongly influenced by the social policies implemented in the country and the social protection they provide. In Cuba as elsewhere, poverty is diverse and heterogeneous in expression. Considered separately, its manifestations—insufficient income and unmet basic needs—can offer only a partial and incomplete view of the phenomenon.

Other dimensions of poverty, especially the subjective and cultural, complement that diversity and are reflected when poverty is analyzed qualitatively from the perspective of family and gender. The results of such analysis reaffirm the importance of Cuba's educational and cultural policy. Poverty in rural areas remains to be studied adequately; the issue has been left unexplored in recent decades.

The goals of equity and social justice, inherent in a society that seeks to build socialism, make it essential to eradicate poverty. To that end, it is critical to maintain existing social policies and continue improving them. In the present decade, these policies have been expanded through various social programs currently under way and have assumed a more personalized character. The further development of policy should take into account the diversity and heterogeneity of the phenomenon. Addressing the problem of low incomes would require changes in employment and wage policies, while the persistence of unmet basic needs would require prioritization of housing construction and repair and improvement of related infrastructure. Policy should also recognize the more specific needs of its beneficiaries. Another positive move would be to implement social policies affecting the family as a unit, transcending the traditional sectoral approach that focuses on particular members. Finally, it is necessary to encourage families and local communications to take a more proactive approach to solving their problems.

NOTES

Excerpted from María del Carmen Zabala Argüelles, "Poverty and Vulnerability in Cuba Today," *Socialism and Democracy* 24, no. 1 (2010): 109–26. Reprinted by permission of the publisher.

1. For more information, see Baliño (1991), Brundenius (1984), and Zimbalist (1989).
2. This index was developed by a collective of Cuban researchers (CIEM 2000).
3. Evidence of conditions of insecurity was already recognized before the crisis, as in research by the Institute for Research and Orientation on Internal Demand, which revealed socioeconomic variation among households and regions in the country, including some classified as disadvantaged. Consistent with this, some researchers believe that the current situation reflects a deterioration of poverty relief mechanisms since total eradication has not been possible.
4. Subsequently, they developed the concept of poverty with protection and guarantees, characterized by insufficient income to cover the cost of the basic goods basket but with social protection in key areas—namely, food, health, education, employment, and universal social security services that are free and subsidized. This condition certainly distinguishes the Cuban situation from the destitution that characterizes poverty in the rest of the world (Ferriol et al. 2004b).
5. The Human Poverty Index includes an estimate of the number of individuals who will not survive to the age of forty, illiterate adults, individuals without access to safe drinking water, individuals without access to health care, and children under age five with moderately low or severely low weight. This index came into use in 1997. In 1996, the *Índice de Pobreza de Capacidad* was used. Cuba received a score of 7.8, placing it tenth among 101 countries. In 2001, Cuba's Human Poverty Index ranked it in fourth place among ninety developing countries.
6. Two currencies circulate in the country: Cuban pesos (*moneda nacional*) and convertible pesos. The former are used for rations, subsidized meals, social consumption, domestically produced items for domestic consumption (with prices set by the state), and farmers' markets (with prices determined by supply and demand). The latter are used in hard-currency stores. Until 2004, U.S. dollars also circulated in the hard-currency market.
7. Calculations from 1992 regarding households with low monthly incomes—50 pesos or less—showed that this amount was insufficient to meet basic needs. As mentioned earlier, Julia Torres (1993) called these sectors "vulnerable groups" because of their lack of food security.
8. Currently, the system provides social protection to those experiencing illness, maternity, work-related injury or illness, partial or total disability, or retirement and to survivors of deceased workers. It includes not only monetary provisions (direct income in the form of salaries, subsidies, and pensions) but also a range of services and in-kind benefits.
9. This is due to the high price in Cuban pesos of products in the nonregulated markets—especially farmers' markets—and the prices of food and nonfood items in the hard-currency stores, which reflect a high exchange rate.
10. These are buildings divided into residences with shared bathrooms and kitchens called *solares ciudadelas*.
11. Hurricanes Gustav, Ike, and Paloma alone damaged 530,758 dwellings (Rodríguez 2008).
12. See Zabala (1996, 1999).
13. These issues were the focus of a study I carried out as a senior fellow with CLACSO-CROP: *Jefatura femenina de hogar, pobreza urbana y exclusión social: Una perspectiva desde la subjetividad en el contexto cubano* (Zabala 2009).

REFERENCES

Alvarez, Elena, and J. Mattar, eds. 2004. *Política social y reformas estructurales: Cuba a principios del siglo XXI.* Mexico City: CEPAL/INIE/PNUD.

Arés, Patricia. 2008. "Familia como red familiar compleja." Paper presented at the Centro de Estudios Demográficos, University of Havana.

Baliño, Gerardo. 1991. *La distribución de los ingresos en Cuba.* Havana: INIE.

Boltvinik, Julio. 1992. "El método de la medición integrada de la pobreza: Una propuesta para su desarrollo." *Comercio Exterior* 42, mo. 4.

Brundenius, Claes. 1984. "Crecimiento con equidad: Cuba 1959–84." In *Cuadernos de Pensamiento Propio.* Managua: INIES-CRIES.

Centro de Investigaciones de la Economía Mundial. 2000. *Investigación sobre desarrollo humano y equidad en Cuba 1999.* Havana: Centro de Investigaciones de la Economía Mundial.

Coyula, Mario. 2006. "La Habana toda vieja." *Temas,* no. 48, October–December.

Díaz, B., I. Guasch, B. Vigaud, et al. 1990. "Caracterización del niño en riesgo por condiciones socioeconómicas y familiares adversas: Acción preventiva intraescolar y comunitaria." Research report. Havana: Ministry of Education.

Díaz, Elena. 2004. "Mujer cubana: El progresivo proceso de empoderamiento." Unpublished research report.

Díaz Tenorio, Mareelén. 2008. "Investigación sobre grupos familiares en un cuarto de siglo." In *Cuadernos del CIPS 2008: Experiencias de investigación social en Cuba,* edited by María Isabel Domínguez et al. Havana: Editorial Caminos.

Espina, Mayra. 1997. *Transformaciones recientes en la estructura socioclasista cubana.* Barcelona: Editorial Servei de Publicaciones.

———. 2008. *Políticas de atención a la pobreza y la desigualdad: Examinando el rol del estado en la experiencia cubana.* Buenos Aires: CLACSO.

Ferriol, A., G. Carriazo, O. U-Echavarría, et al. 1997. *Efectos de políticas macroeconómicas y sociales sobre los niveles de pobreza: El caso de Cuba en los años 90.* Havana: INIE/CIEM.

Ferriol, A., M. Ramos, and L. Añé. 2004a. *Reforma económica y población en riesgo en Ciudad de La Habana.* Havana: INIE/CEPDE/ONE.

Ferriol, A., G. Therborn, and R. Castiñeiras. 2004b. *Política social: El mundo contemporáneo y las experiencias de Cuba y Suecia.* Havana: INIE.

Hábitat. 1996. *Informe Nacional de Cuba para Hábitat II.* Havana: Instituto Nacional de la Vivienda.

Iñiguez, Luisa, and Omar Everleny Pérez. 2004. "Territorio y espacio en las desigualdades sociales de la provincia Ciudad de Havana." In *Colectivo de autores, 15 años Centro de Estudios de la Economía Cubana.* Havana: Editorial Félix Varela.

Iñiguez, Luisa, and M. Ravenet. 1999. *Desigualdades espaciales del bienestar en Cuba: Aproximación a los efectos de los nuevos procesos en las realidades sociales.* Havana: Centro de Estudios de Salud y Bienestar Humanos.

Moser, Carolina. 1998. "The Asset Vulnerability Framework: Reassessing Urban Poverty Reduction Strategies." *World Development* 26, no. 1.

National Institute of Economic Research (INIE). 2005. *Millennium Development Goals Cuba: Second Report.* Havana: INIE.

National Office of Statistics (ONE). 2002. *Anuario Estadístico de Cuba.* Havana: ONE.

———. 2007 and 2008. *Anuario Estadístico de Cuba.* Havana: ONE.

Núñez, Marta. 2000. "Estrategias cubanas para el empleo femenino en los noventa: Un estudio de caso con mujeres profesionales." *Caminos. Revista Cubana de Pensamiento Socioteológico*, nos. 17–18.

Pérez, Omar Everleny. 2008. "La economía en Cuba: Un balance actual y proyecciones necesarias." In *Boletín Cuatrimestral, agosto 2008.* Havana: Centro de Estudios de la Economía Cubana.

Rodríguez, José Luis. 2008. "Presentación a la Asamblea Nacional del Poder Popular del informe sobre resultados económicos del 2008 y los lineamientos del Plan Económico y Social para 2009." December 27.

Rodríguez, J. L., and G. Carriazo. 1987. *Erradicación de la pobreza en Cuba.* Havana: Editorial de Ciencias Sociales.

Togores, Viviana. 2000. *Cuba: Efectos sociales de la crisis y el ajuste estructural en los 90s.* Havana: Centro de Estudios de la Economía Cubana.

———. 2004. "Ingresos monetarios de la población, cambios en la distribución y efectos sobre el nivel de vida." In *Colectivo de autores, 15 años Centro de Estudios de la Economía Cubana.* Havana: Editorial Félix Varela.

Torres, Julia. 1993. *Pobreza. Un enfoque para Cuba.* Havana: INIE.

United Nations Development Program. 2013. *2013 Human Development Report.* New York: United Nations Development Program.

Zabala, María del Carmen. 1996. "Familia y pobreza en Cuba." Master's thesis, University of Havana.

———. 1999. "Aproximación al estudio de la relación entre familia y pobreza." Doctoral thesis, University of Havana.

———. 2009. *Jefatura femenina de hogar, pobreza urbana y exclusión social: Una perspectiva desde la subjetividad en el contexto cubano.* Buenos Aires: CLACSO.

Zimbalist, A. 1989. *The Cuban Economy: Measurement and Analysis of Socialist Performance.* Baltimore: Johns Hopkins University Press.

Chapter Seventeen

Economic Illegalities and the Underground Economy in Cuba

Archibald R. M. Ritter

Various types of economic illegalities and underground economic activities occur in all countries. In Cuba, however, public policies and structural economic forces have promoted these phenomena. Indeed, Cuba appears to be awash with economic illegalities. Many Cuban citizens insist that almost everyone is involved in economic activities that are considered illegal by the state, contributing to a pervasive culture of illegality. This perception was well expressed in a 2004 Havana street saying: "Todo se prohíbe pero todo se hace" (Everything is prohibited, but everything is done). Another street saying highlights the ineffectiveness of the myriad measures put in place by the government to address these problems: "Al tratar de controlarlo todo, termina sin controlar nada" (By trying to control everything, the government ends up controlling nothing).

Economic illegalities and the underground economy are serious problems with corrosive effects on Cuban society. This chapter analyzes the nature and scope of these problems, the forces that produce them, their consequences, the policies necessary to reduce them, and the anticorruption campaign of late 2005.

DEFINITIONS: ECONOMIC ILLEGALITIES AND THE UNDERGROUND ECONOMY

The term "informal economy" was introduced in 1972 by the International Labor Organization in the context of Kenya and was further elaborated in the Latin American context by Victor Tokman (2004), De Soto (2002), and others and by more recent analyses (Portes and Haller 2005). However, because none of these sets of definitions fit the unique institutional character of Cuba, a custom-designed set of categories was developed for this chapter. The four categories included are household economy, formal economy, underground economy, and criminal economy. The household economy is similar to the International Labor Organization's (2002) concept of "reproductive economy" and includes all nonmonetized production and exchange of goods and services within the home and between friends and neighbors. The formal economy includes the public sector, state enterprises, mixed enterprises (with joint foreign, multinational, and state ownership), and cooperative enterprises. Licensed self-employment is also included in the formal economy, as it operates within the tax and regulatory framework of the state.

The analysis in this study focuses on the underground economy and the criminal economy. The underground economy involves the production and exchange of legal goods and services and the generation of income in unlicensed enterprises or using unauthorized methods. It is complex and includes a variety of phenomena: (1) "legitimate" underground economic activities; (2) underground activities operating within registered self-employment activities; (3) underground activities operating within state firms or the public sector; (4) unrecorded and unofficial income supplements paid by foreign organizations, mixed enterprises, state firms, or the public sector to some employees; (5) unrecorded and unofficial payments from customers to employees; and (6) black markets or illegal exchanges of goods and services.

"Legitimate" underground economic activities involve the production and exchange of legal goods and services although the persons producing them are outside the control of the state. Although tolerated elsewhere, in Cuba such unauthorized activities are considered criminal. A second variety of activity would be the private or semiprivate enterprises, operated by some employees within the state sector, which require additional payments from citizens for their services. Some employees of mixed enterprises receive additional dollar incomes "under the table." Some employees of state firms and institutions use public property for private activities and may receive particular benefits such as access to foreign travel and the per diems this generates. Other observers of the Cuban reality attest that almost every single employee of a state firm and institution uses public property of any kind for private activities or sale or exchange for other desired items.[1]

The criminal economy refers to economic activities that produce illegal goods and services in clandestine circumstances outside the regulatory and fiscal purview of the state. Illicit drug manufacture and sales, prostitution, trade in endangered species, gambling in some jurisdictions, the sales of some types of firearms or explosives, smuggling, theft, and the sale of stolen property are cases in point. Bribery and overt corruption would also be part of the criminal economy.

CHARACTER AND DIMENSION

There are many varieties of economic illegalities in Cuba. The following provides a list of some of these that are known to the author. This list could probably be extended considerably:

- A butcher reserves some choice cuts of meat for "under-the-counter" sale to clients who are willing to pay more than the official rationed price.
- Cigar makers remove cigars from the cigar factory for resale.
- An official at a state institution with access to a vehicle for official purposes uses it more or less as a private vehicle and uses the chauffeur as a personal employee.
- A waiter or barman provides low-cost homemade peso-economy rum instead of official dollar-economy rum to clients. The dollar-economy rum is then sold for a dollar price.
- A doorman at a cinema permits entrance without the purchase of a ticket but instead with a small payment on the side.
- An inspector of *cuentapropista paladares* (microenterprise restaurants) disregards discrepancies in restaurant owners' input purchase and receipt records in exchange for a payment.
- A mechanic for a state sector enterprise tells a client that a placement part is not available from official sources but that he is able to locate and provide the part from outside the shop at a higher price. While this may often be legitimate, it may also involve theft and resale of the part from the enterprise.

- A gasoline tank truck provides a larger amount of gasoline at a gas station than officially recorded. The *gasolinera* provides the driver of the tank truck with a payment and then resells the gas unofficially at a higher price.
- A taxi driver provides a ride with the meter off and for a fixed fee, explaining that the meter is not working—or that he needs the money. Alternately, a taxi driver returning from a destination to home base picks up a client and requests payment without use of the meter.
- A foreign enterprise provides salary supplements in food and homemaking supplies to its employees.
- The owner of a house not licensed as a room rental facility rents a room illegally.
- The local *Comité de Defensa de la Revolución* president accepts a $10 bribe in exchange for overlooking an illegal room rental.
- A citizen pays a 5.00-convertible-peso bribe to an agent in order to secure a scarce 85-peso (*moneda nacional*, or $3.15 convertible peso) one-way airline ticket from Havana to Holguín.
- Jobs that permit the acquisition of significant foreign exchange through tips, notably in tourism, are sold to applicants by the hiring decision maker.
- A citizen sets up a satellite dish, receives foreign broadcasting, hooks up his neighbors for a 10.00 convertible peso monthly fee, and provides twenty-four-hour cable service. (This was a common practice in early 2005.)
- Some tourists are overcharged, ostensibly by mistake, for their meals in a restaurant, with an additional beer billed in some cases with a "tip" included in the bill (though this is not in the menu or in the policy of the restaurant) or with the prices for some items overstated.

There are also innumerable microenterprises in what has been labeled here legitimate underground economic activities. As noted, these activities are legal in virtually all countries producing legal goods and services. However, in Cuba, numerous policy limitations force many of these otherwise perfectly legal activities into the underground economy. These microenterprises produce every imaginable but otherwise legal product or service. A partial listing of such activities that are known to the author, directly or indirectly, includes the following:

- Personal services: barbers, hairdressers, manicurists, clothes washing, teachers, clothing repair, shoe repair, film rental, and "messengers"
- Gastronomic services: snack bars, soft-drink vending, baking, fruit vending, candy vending, seafood vending, and pizza vending
- Retailing: bicycle parts, ice vendors, jewelers, cigarettes, newspapers, and plumbing parts
- Automotive repair services: mechanics, electricians, body shops, adornments, painters, tire repair, auto upholsterers, and locksmiths
- Appliance repair: pumps, stoves, air conditioners, TV and video, water pumps, locks, and furniture upholstering and repair
- Construction trades: carpenters, plumbers, electricians, plasterers, glass workers, painters, and concrete construction
- Transportation: taxis, bicycle taxis, and carters
- Manufacturing: shoemaking, mattress making, cigarette and cigar making, soft-drink bottling, and rum making
- Primary sector activities: fishing, woodcutting and vending, charcoal burning and vending, and food growing and vending

While it is difficult to know exactly how significant the above-mentioned types of economic illegalities and underground activities may be, the scale appears to be enormous. A glimpse may be obtained from a number of examples. One report indicated that in three of the fifteen municipalities in Havana, police and customs officials raided 150 clandestine cigar-making operations, which were then shut down. A total of 11,935 boxes of cigars were confiscated (http://www.Cubanet.org, June 1, 2004). If there were 150 illicit cigar operations in three of the fifteen Havana municipalities, it is likely that there are thousands across the country because of the widely known skills, the low barriers to entry into the activity, and its profitability. Recent restrictions on the export of cigars without proper paperwork and purchase validation has perhaps impeded but certainly not blocked the illegal production and/or sale of cigars.

There also have been a variety of illicit practices in the tourist sector. In the words of a manager of a five-star hotel,

> This is a billion-dollar business where millions flow daily in a poor country of people struggling to survive. Everyone finds some way to get unearned income and a few people get greedy. Just like in many other Third World countries, people often pay to work in the industry and then kickback a proportion of what they earn to their superiors. I could give you hundreds of examples. How high up these little mafias go, and if the problem is related to the Cubanacán scandal, is anyone's guess. (Frank 2004)

This was corroborated in early 2004 when fifteen higher officials in Cubanacán were dismissed from their jobs, as was the tourism minister (Frank 2004). On February 19, 2005, Resolution 10 was enacted by the Ministry of Tourism, defining a code of conduct for the workers in the sector as well as higher-level management officials. A further revealing example occurred in October 2005 when the government ordered a change of personnel in all the gas stations on the island in order to stop the theft of gasoline that had reached alarming levels (BBC Mundo América Latina 2005).

CAUSES OF ECONOMIC ILLEGALITIES

The causes of the illegal activities are complex but are rooted mainly in the economic policies that compel citizens to act outside the letter and spirit of the law in order to survive. It is also important to bear in mind that economic illegalities of various sorts are common in most countries and that some of the forces at work in Cuba are common to most other countries as well.

To begin with, Cuban citizens' disregard for economic authority has historical roots. From the earliest colonial times, Cubans broke the enforced bilateral trade relationship with Spain. Contraband trade was common with France, Britain, and later the United States as well as with corsairs and pirates. Moreover, in the colonial era, Spain attempted significant micromanagement of the Cuban economy despite distance and slow communication. The response of many Cubans to this situation was to obey the regulations and rules from Spain only nominally while continuing their own activities illegally. The phrase summing up this widespread practice was "Obedezco, pero no cumplo" (I obey but do not comply).

While Cuba had developed a diversified range of large modern corporate business by the 1950s, large numbers of small-scale cottage industries continued to exist in many areas of the economy. This was an authentic "informal economy" that was producing legal goods and services and tolerated by the state, although it was outside the state's regulatory framework. These small enterprises evaded taxes, paid lower wages than the large firms, were nonunionized, and avoided social benefit payments. There was probably a considerable degree of continuity between underground economic activities before and after the 1959 Revolution. People already functioning "in the shadows" in 1958 could easily remain underground after 1959.

A second factor promoting economic illegalities is the character and functioning of the central planning system adopted in 1961–1963. The rationing system implemented in 1961 was designed to provide everyone with the same basic supply of foodstuffs, clothing, and household products in order to achieve a minimum level of equality. This was to be achieved by replacing individual (or family) choice, expressed through markets, with an allotment of basic goods available at prices that were low relative to the average monthly income. However, because everyone received essentially the same rations and not all necessities were covered, many people would sell the rationed items they did not want or trade them for other products they did want. In this way, the rationing system converted many people into minicapitalists, searching for opportunities to sell and to buy.

Because the central planning system could not and cannot work perfectly, especially in the context of economic turbulence, enterprise managers must often improvise to resolve unforeseen problems. To obtain required inputs, they must negotiate with other enterprises, with superior officials, or with superiors or inferiors in other sectors or ministries. Indeed, managers of state companies were more effective and successful if they had a strong net of "extraplan" sources of inputs in order to keep their enterprises functioning. This also promoted the illegal and extralegal exchange of goods.

A third factor is what appears to be a "common property problem" at work with respect to state property. A general attitude appears to be that state property belongs to no one and to everyone so that if one person does not help himself to it, someone else will instead. Public property therefore is treated as if it were firewood in a public forest or fish in the seas, belonging to no one in particular. It is "up for grabs" by whoever needs it and is in a position to take it. Similarly, public property, such as a vehicle accompanying an official position, is readily used for personal purposes with few qualms of conscience. In the words of the sociologist Juan Clark, "The majority of people believe that stealing from the state is not a crime" (cited in Pérez-López 1995, 99). Others add that such theft is seen not as a crime but as a right (Yanes, personal communication, October 2005). The standard for this type of attitude and behavior may be the Communist Party of Cuba and President Castro, who are able to use state property for partisan political purposes and often for personal purposes.

A fourth reason for the expansion of illegal economic activities in the 1990s and 2000s is the coexistence of the old-peso economy (with rationed products at very low prices) and the new economy (now with convertible pesos and previously with dollars and partly market-determined prices). The gap in prices between these two economies is enormous, creating an opportunity for arbitrage in a "black market" in which prices are determined by supply and demand. An example of the price gap between the two economies will illustrate the scope for arbitrage. The price of sugar with the ration book is 0.15 old pesos per pound. In comparison, a pound of sugar in the dollar stores costs 1.50 convertible pesos, or 39.00 old pesos (at the exchange rate relevant for Cuban citizens; that is, 1.00 convertible peso = 26 old pesos). This is 260 times higher than the ration system price. Of course, the "black market" also includes the exchange of products that are pilfered from the state sector.

A fifth factor is that policy limitations on the legal microenterprises also promote economic illegalities. For example, all legal microenterprises must be licensed, but relatively few licenses are in fact granted. In the municipality of Havana in 2001, only 23.9 percent of the 97,687 applications were in fact approved with licenses granted (Dirección Provincial de

Trabajo y Seguridad Social, Ciudad Habana 2001). Restrictive licensing means that potential legal microenterprises are pushed into the underground economy. Legislation in October 2004 banning the issue of new licenses for some forty types of microenterprise will further intensify this effect. [Editors' note: These restrictions have since been relaxed to encourage legal small enterprises.]

The tough regulatory regime for microenterprises also makes their lives difficult and leads some of those who can to the underground economy (see Government of Cuba, Decreto Ley 174 of 1997). Tough regulations regarding the inputs that can be used and where they can be purchased push some microenterprises into illegal acquisition of inputs. Restrictions on employment have a similar effect.

Basically, the more complex the regulations governing the conduct of particular economic activities, the greater the scope for illegal actions. In consequence, there are frequent violations of those rules that are thought to be unreasonable by the self-employed. Heavy taxation also leads some microenterprises to try to evade taxes in various ways. In consequence, large numbers of enterprises that would otherwise operate legally are forced into clandestinity. As noted above, there are innumerable such microenterprises or "legitimate underground economic activities" operating in the shadows of the underground economy, producing huge varieties and volumes of goods and services.

However, the most powerful force promoting economic illegalities of many sorts is necessity. Citizens earn old pesos, but their earnings are insufficient to purchase the basic foodstuffs—not to mention everything else—that they require for survival. This means that people must find additional sources of income in old pesos or convertible pesos (previously U.S. dollars). Cuban citizens often remark that their official monthly wage will buy basic foodstuffs from the rationing system and other sources that are sufficient for only about ten to fourteen days of the month. Purchases for the rest of the month must be made with funds from other sources. In addition, the number of products available through the rationing system is inadequate. Other goods and services have to be obtained from the dollar stores, from *cuentapropistas*, or from the state or private agricultural markets at high prices. (Electricity, water, and most types of health services but not telephone services were also available for low old-peso prices.)

This meant that virtually all Cubans needed additional sources of income, preferably in dollars or now in convertible pesos, simply to buy food. But people need more than food to survive. Clothing, transportation, utility payments, personal hygiene products, and so on are all necessary. Some of these—such as sanitary napkins—are available only in convertible pesos at the dollar store prices.

The inadequacy of peso incomes was confirmed in April 2005 when President Castro announced major wage, salary, and pension increases. The minimum wage was increased from 100 to 225 pesos, and the minimum pension was raised from 55 to 150 pesos (*Granma* 2005). The increased incomes will have to be spent on nonrationed products from the *mercados agropecuarios*, the state vegetable markets, and the hard-currency stores (at international prices plus a 140 percent sales tax). The latter require convertible pesos, available at 26 old pesos to 1 convertible peso. In consequence, the purchasing power of the income increases for pensioners and those on the minimum wage is not particularly significant.

However, people have in fact survived. They purchase not only their required food but also other daily requirements because they have other sources of income besides those earned from the official wage and salary system. There are a number of ways that people acquire additional incomes:

- Some receive remittances from family members or friends outside Cuba; these are estimated to total between U.S.$700 million and U.S.$1 billion annually. [Editors' note: Since President Obama relaxed restrictions on remittances in 2009, the estimated annual total has risen to more than $2 billion.]
- Some acquire convertible pesos from foreign travel for governmental, business, or academic purposes.
- Income supplements to Cubans are paid "under the table" by foreign enterprises or organizations.
- Some 140,000 Cubans earn incomes from self-employment. A large number of individuals work formally and informally with the registered *cuentapropistas*. [Editors' note: As of early 2014, the number of licensed self-employed had risen to more than 400,000.]
- Some receive additional income working abroad—in Venezuela, for example—in officially sanctioned capacities.
- Some earn tips from their work in the tourist sector. These payments make the approximately 100,000 tourist sector workers among the highest paid in the Cuban economy and provide a powerful incentive for qualified people to leave other areas of the economy, such as university teaching, for tourism.[2]
- Income supplements in kind or in cash (convertible pesos) are also provided to considerable numbers of workers in key sectors of the economy and in international or foreign organizations. Such supplements in kind also can enter the black market for resale.

However, for those citizens lacking access to any of these sources of supplementary income, the situation has been desperate. They have been below or near a minimum subsistence level of income. Necessity is therefore the primordial force pushing citizens into economic illegalities or the underground economy.

This general situation was aptly expressed by "Adrian," one of the gasoline employees expelled in the October 2005 firing of all gas station attendants in an attempt to stop the theft of gasoline: "What's most important in looking for a job is not the salary but what can be 'resolved,' meaning in good Cuban Spanish what we can steal." "Of course we rob, chico! Or does he (Fidel Castro) think that I can maintain my wife and two children with the 10 dollars per month that he pays me" (BBC Mundo América Latina 2005).

ECONOMIC AND SOCIAL CONSEQUENCES OF ECONOMIC ILLEGALITIES

The economic illegalities that are practiced in Cuba have a range of consequences. Some of these are benign and even useful, but others are socially and economically noxious. The consequences vary, depending on the specific character of the illegality.

The "legitimate" underground economic activities that produce legal goods and services have mixed impacts, but on balance, these are strongly positive. On the positive side, such enterprises consist of low-income people producing a range of goods and services for other low-income citizens. Usually, these goods and services are provided ineffectively by the state sector but are important for people's daily lives (see the list of activities that presented earlier in the chapter).

The microenterprises generate jobs and incomes for the entrepreneurs and the workers. The entrepreneurs save and invest with no access to banks, public support, or microfinance. They earn foreign exchange for Cuba by selling products to tourists, and they save foreign exchange by relying heavily on recycled and domestically available inputs. They are also valuable "schools of entrepreneurship." The owners of these enterprises work hard and utilize their resources as efficiently and carefully as possible under the circumstances of clandestinity. On the other hand, by forcing such enterprises underground, the government does not collect taxes from them. They may also be inefficient because of their small size and the "costs of clandestinity" and therefore may waste a proportion of the entrepreneurial energies of their owners. They also may rely on inputs pilfered from the state sector.

On the other hand, theft from state enterprises and institutions and the use of public property for personal purposes are at the other end of the spectrum. While these activities may help some people survive, they also have noxious effects. Theft damages the enterprises and institutions in which it occurs by impairing the capacity to provide the goods and services they are intended to provide to the general public. Theft also worsens income distribution in that those who do not steal have lower effective incomes than those who do, and it reduces the available quantity of lower-priced state goods and services. The use of state property and the abuse of power for personal purposes may be less visibly noxious, but it damages income distribution because those with privileged access gain at the ultimate expense of the broader society. Corrupt practices, such as the taking of bribes or the selling of jobs, also have harmful consequences. In such cases, strategically placed individuals are able to use their positions of privilege and trust for private gain. Those who are able to pay the bribes or purchase their jobs also gain privileged access to scarce goods and services, again damaging other people's access and thus harming the broader society.

Black markets may either enhance or diminish the welfare of society. If the black market exchange between a willing buyer and seller does not involve stolen property but, rather, only the recirculation of rationed goods, for example, then it benefits both seller and buyer. As a case in point, both buyer and seller benefit from under-the-table payments accompanying a "*permuta*," or the exchange of housing of unequal value, as indicated by their willingness to undertake the transaction. On the other hand, a good deal of black market merchandise is stolen from the state sector. Obviously, this is a negative phenomenon. Even if both buyer and seller gain, they are doing so at someone else's expense.

Finally, stealing from the state breeds attitudes and cultures of lawlessness that damage trust and the ethical foundations of the economy and society. The practice of economic illegalities could escalate further and become a sort of undeclared civil war among citizens for spoils from the economic system. So far, this has deformed the economy and society seriously. However, it has permitted people to survive an otherwise impossible situation.

REDUCING ILLEGALITIES

In view of their corrosive and perverse effects, widespread illegalities and the culture of petty corruption in time should be reduced. What measures might be effective in this regard?

The main methods used by the government of Cuba to deal with the phenomenon are preaching, policing, proscription, and punishment. The effects of this approach in the past have been transient, and the illegalities have surfaced as soon as the pressure and the campaigning subsided. If the underlying forces that generate the economic illegalities are not addressed, it is unlikely that the latter will disappear with this type of approach.

The government of Cuba often asserts that the principal source of pervasive illegalities is the existence of the licensed and therefore legal microenterprise sector and the private farmers' markets. Invariably, it then moves to further restrict their operation. But limiting legal microenterprise numbers and tightening the regulations on them merely pushes some of them into the underground economy. Those formerly self-employed legally would also have an incentive to engage in a variety of other illegal activities as well in order to make ends meet.

A frequently used approach to dealing with the more noxious economic illegalities is to monitor and police them more vigorously. A major role for the police has been to stop and question anyone traveling by foot, bicycle, or car on the street with large packages or backpacks in order to apprehend anyone engaged in the transport of black market products. However, the police themselves may overlook possible or actual infractions out of friendship for the perpetrator or empathy for his or her situation or perhaps because they have received a payoff of some sort.

Infractions may be punished by prohibitions of the relevant activities, but this may only push the activities underground. To prevent infractions, monitors or inspectors are required to police the legal self-employment activities. The role of the inspectors for the *paladares* and bed-and-breakfast operations is well known. However, it is also reported that, in some cases, the inspectors have become avaricious and require payoffs for infractions that may be real, imagined, or fabricated. In other cases, the inspectors seem to be somewhat less officious in enforcing the letter of the innumerable regulations relevant for the microenterprises.

Part of the task of monitoring people's activities in order to prevent illegalities is passed on to the *Comités de Defensa de la Revolución* (CDRs) or the neighborhood monitoring committees. In some areas, the CDRs may carry out this task effectively. However, the local officials of the CDRs also need additional income to survive. They are likely to be involved in illegal activities themselves and therefore may not be diligent in exposing and prosecuting their neighbors. Or they may acquire a small share of the benefits of such illegal activities. In other contexts, security guards are used to try to prevent theft or other illegal activities. However, these individuals also would like to survive, so they may look the other way when an infraction or theft is occurring in order to obtain a payment. They may also pilfer articles from their place of work or obtain a payment from others who may be doing the pilfering.

In other situations, the government uses a pretext to undertake house-to-house searches for illegal activities. In January 2003, for example, a campaign against drugs was used to search numerous homes and to penalize any illegal and underground economic activities encountered. This led to a cessation of some underground activities but only until the pressure was off, at which time they resumed.

Another method used to reduce economic illegalities is exhortation through speeches, statements, editorials, or articles in the media. However, it is not clear how much attention people give to the voluminous presentations of President Castro. It would be surprising if the attention paid to his words did not meet diminishing returns many years ago.

FUNDAMENTAL CHANGES REQUIRED

To sum up, as long as the basic conditions of people's lives require them to acquire additional income to survive, the various layers of inspectors, monitors, security guards, and CDR officials constitute corruptible layers in the system. Their true effectiveness in enforcing the regulations and preventing illegalities of various sorts is limited.

More fundamental policy changes will be necessary in the future. First, as argued earlier, the dual monetary and exchange rate systems generate primordial economic forces that motivate people to undertake various types of illegalities. Unifying the dual economy will be a difficult task, requiring complete realignments of internal wages and salaries on the one hand and costs and prices on the other.

A second fundamental change would be to revamp the regulatory, fiscal, and policy environment within which legal microenterprises operate in order to permit them to thrive. An appropriate approach would be to permit licensing for all microenterprises that want to establish themselves and that paid taxes and respected reasonable regulations. However, the credibility of such a change in government policy would be problematic. Underground microenterprises might not be willing to emerge aboveground if they thought that government policy would change again, jeopardizing their future existence. However, with a different government or an authentic and credible change in policy toward microenterprises, the result in time would be that most currently unlicensed microenterprises would come aboveground and come into the official tax and regulatory system.

Additionally, the government could simplify its dense regulations and establish a reasonable taxation system so that there would be less incentive to remain underground. It would also be desirable to establish normal sources of inputs for the microenterprises besides the high-priced former dollar stores. This would reduce and perhaps eliminate the tendency of some microenterprises to resort to illegal sources of inputs. Easing the regulatory burden and simplifying bureaucratic requirements would also reduce the often-abused discretionary powers wielded by officials and inspectors of all types.

State property poses a more difficult problem. In Cuba, as was also the case in Eastern Europe, a clear distinction between the public and the private use of public property has not been maintained. The result of this ambiguity is widespread pilferage and the use of public property for private purposes. To the extent that people view the economic system as hostile and one that makes it impossible for them to survive legally, theft may be viewed as necessary and legitimate. Dealing with this deeply rooted behavior will not be easy. Reducing the role of the state in running economic enterprises may reduce much of the scope for the pilfering of public property. Changing behavior at the highest political level so that there is a strong demonstration effect regarding the public use of public property would help as well. A strong economic recovery and a broad-based improvement in real incomes or living standards so that people did not have to act illegally to survive would also help greatly to reduce such illegalities.

In the longer term, the task of reducing economic illegalities will be one of changing the economic culture that has evolved. The deeply ingrained behavior of pilferage, extraction of personal benefits from positions of power and responsibility, and use of public property for personal gain will be changed. More fundamental policy changes will be necessary in the future only with changes in the objective conditions that generate it.

PROSPECTS FOR CHANGE

Some of the policies adopted in the current campaign against corruption should have a positive impact, though others are more likely to have only a transitory impact. More exhortation is also likely to be of limited and temporary benefit. Increased wages, pensions, and social security payments may result in a minor reduction in the incentive to pilfer from the state, but the impact will likely be limited, as peso incomes are still far below the level necessary for reasonable survival. If the wage and pension increases prove to be inflationary (Frank 2005), this will reduce the value of the old peso in relation to the convertible peso and drive the two currencies farther apart rather than toward unification.

It is also questionable whether current approaches to changing popular perceptions of the sanctity of public property are serious and likely to be effective. As long as the leadership, the party, and higher officials use state property for partisan and personal purposes, it will be difficult to persuade citizens not to do so as well.

Finally, economic recovery, increased real wages in the old-peso economy, and an authentic improvement in living standards should reduce the incentive of people to pilfer state property or use it for their personal purposes and undertake other types of illegality. While living standards have improved somewhat from the dark days of 1992–1994, relative material hardship continues for many—and probably the vast majority. It is unlikely that many people could survive on their peso incomes alone without additional sources of income. Until this situation changes, the economic illegalities will continue. In summary, it seems unlikely that the scope and intensity of the economic illegalities analyzed here will diminish significantly as long as some of the fundamental approaches to public policy and institutional structures remain unchanged.

NOTES

Excerpted from Archibald R. M. Ritter, "Economic Illegalities and the Underground Economy in Cuba," *Focal*, RFC-06-01, March 2006. Reprinted by permission of the author.

1. "The personal benefits of a particular position in Cuba are measured in terms of what kind of goods the individual is able to manage to take home, and not in terms of salary (which is in reality little more than symbolic). This has created a market for 'positions' or 'jobs' where access to a number of them is sold by a price determined by 'how much' the individual is going to make out of the related illegal activities. This happens not only in tourism, but elsewhere, especially in places related to food (bodegas, carnicerías, comedores obreros y escolares, almacenes de víveres), and other basic needs, like clothes, items of personal consumption or gasoline. To obtain a job as a 'bodeguero' or in a retail store, or in a garage, has a high price" (Yanes, personal communication, October 2005).

2. As of January 19, 2005, Resolution No. 10 of the Ministry of Tourism prohibited the receipt of tips by tourism sector workers from foreigners (Ministerio de Turismo, Capítulo Primero, Artículo 1). All tips actually received by tourist sector workers are to be turned over to their managers or chiefs for subsequent distribution. This regulation may be difficult or impossible to enforce. It will likely push more people into a new zone of illegalities. To the extent that it can be enforced, it may reduce the incentives for tourism workers to provide good service.

REFERENCES

BBC Mundo América Latina. 2005. "Cuba: Sorpresa en las gasolineras." October 17. http://news.bbc.co.uk/hi/spanish/latin_america/default.stm.

De Soto, Hernando. 2002. *The Other Path*. New York: Basic Books.

Dirección Provincial de Trabajo y Seguridad Social, Ciudad Habana. 2001. *Información estadística mensual*. Havana: Dirección Provincial de Trabajo y Seguridad Social, Ciudad Habana.

Frank, Marc. 2004. "Cubans Purge Hotel Trade of Bad Habits." *Financial Times*, January 7.

Granma. 2005. "Incremento salarial para los trabajadores de más bajos ingresos del país," April 22.

International Labor Organization (ILO). 2002. *Women and Men in the Informal Economy: A Statistical Picture*. Geneva: ILO.

Pérez-López, Jorge. 1995. *Cuba's Second Economy*. New Brunswick, NJ: Transaction Books.

Portes, Alejandro, and William Haller. 2005. "The Informal Economy." In *The Handbook of Economic Sociology*, edited by Neil J. Smelser and Richard Swedberg, chap. 18. Princeton, NJ: Princeton University Press.

Tokman, Victor. 2004. *Una Voz en el Camino: Empleo y Equidad en América Latina: 40 Años de Búsque da*. Santiago: Fondo de Cultura Económica. http://www.Cubanet.org.

Yanes, Ana. 2005. Personal communication, October.

III

Foreign Policy

In 1991, as the Soviet Union neared its end and Cuba began to experience the hardships of the "Special Period," a Cuban official wryly remarked to one of the editors that "history has yet to record whether Cuba suffered more from U.S. imperialism or Soviet friendship." Indeed, both countries had a significant impact on Cuba and on its foreign policies during the Cold War, and ironically Cuba's relations with both countries had the qualities of a double-edged sword.

Soviet subsidies and military assistance enabled Cuba to pursue an egalitarian program at home and a revolutionary vision abroad. But the subsidies locked Cuba into the socialist trading bloc—the Council of Mutual Economic Assistance (CMEA)—and fettered Cuban development. The CMEA designated Cuba as a producer of basic commodities within the network—sugar, citrus, and nickel—and production of these goods had to take precedence over other development possibilities. More than 85 percent of Cuba's international commerce at the end of the 1980s involved CMEA countries. As a consequence, when the Soviet Union and the CMEA disappeared, Cuba suddenly had to find new markets and pay for its imports with an internationally recognized convertible (hard) currency that it did not have in reserve.

Cuba's special relationship with the United States during the Cold War also produced benefits and ultimately costs that intensified the risks it faced. Cuba gained the admiration of Third World countries in part because it was a model of resistance to U.S. domination, and Havana was often an essential ally of progressive forces in Africa, Asia, and Latin America during direct confrontations against U.S.-supported forces or agents. Meanwhile, the ongoing U.S. threat to Cuba's fundamental security justified the maintenance of a militarized state, which gave Cuba its capability to support Third World countries. Yet each peso or person devoted to national security was one less that could be directed to economic diversification and development. In addition, each new clash with the United States undermined nascent efforts to change the policy by U.S. opponents of the embargo. As a consequence, extreme right-wing Cuban Americans had little opposition in 1991 as they developed legislation intended to topple the revolutionary regime.

The dire circumstances at the start of Special Period makes the achievements of Cuba's foreign policy during the ensuing fifteen years all the more impressive. By 2006, when Raúl Castro took over the leadership from his brother, Cuba had established new trading relationships with a broad array of countries. Spanish investments in Cuba's leisure industries gave

Cuba the capacity to accommodate more than 2 million visitors annually. Chinese financing promised to modernize Cuba's nickel industry, pay for the exploration of deep-sea oil deposits in Cuba's coastal waters, and provide a new source of hard-currency earnings. Venezuela's cooperative agreements bestowed Cuba with affordable oil and enabled Cuba to send doctors and teachers to Latin American and Caribbean countries with a resulting triple benefit.

First, they have helped to carry out Cuba's self-proclaimed internationalist mission by providing health care, education, and training to poor people who had never received such services in countries such as Bolivia and Ecuador. Second, the poor have bolstered governments in these countries opposed to neoliberalism, encouraging even moderates such as Brazil's president, Luiz Inácio Lula da Silva, or Argentina's presidents, Néstor Kirchner and Cristina Kirchner, to champion alternative development strategies intended to reduce poverty and inequality in Latin America. Finally, these missions have reduced the risk of a brain drain because they have given Cuban professionals an opportunity to earn hard currency they cannot earn in Cuba. At the same time, they alleviate the glut of highly educated Cubans who cannot find jobs on the island for which they can use their skills.

Partly in response to Cuba's foreign policy successes during the Special Period, the Non-Aligned Movement (NAM) in 2003 named Cuba for a second time as the host of it triennial summit. The meeting was held in Havana in 2006, and Cuba served as the NAM chair for the following three years. Founded in 1961 as a supposed neutralist haven for countries caught up in the East-West conflict, the NAM has been little more than a sounding board for Third World ire about unfair terms of global trade, neocolonial exploitation, apartheid, and infringements on the rights of "self-determination" by powerful countries. Still, the NAM's 120 member states make up most of what is considered the Third World, and its selection of Cuba as host was a striking indication of Cuba's standing. Also in 2003, the Latin American countries in the United Nations selected Cuba to fill one of the six seats designated for the region in the United Nations Commission on Human Rights despite vociferous objections from the United States.

It was said that during the Cold War that Cuba was a little country with a big country's foreign policy. On one hand, the depiction accurately captured a distinguishing feature of Cuba's international behavior. Small countries tend to focus narrowly on their immediate neighborhoods. Great powers act globally with a greater sense of freedom than small countries, because they perceive that only another great power can threaten or stop them. In contrast to most small countries, Cuba focused globally. Cuban leaders shared with Fidel Castro a vision that their country should lead a global revolution on behalf of the poor. This is evident in the way Cuba's controlled media, which is hardly the model of a free press, does provide broader coverage of world events than is commonly found in most U.S. media. Their international focus has encouraged ordinary Cubans to think globally and to identify with the struggles of people in other Third World countries. The subtle denigration of Cuba's foreign policy as being inappropriate for its size overlooks a key difference between Cuba's international orientation and those of most great powers. Cuba has not sought to dominate and control other countries, nor has it sought to exploit the resources of another country for Cuba's exclusive benefit. Rather, Cuba has understood that its own national interest is inextricably linked to a world order in which all small countries enjoy freedom from domination by great powers.

As anticipated, Cuba's foreign policy under Raúl Castro did not depart much from the internationalist path it had taken under Fidel Castro. After all, the new leader had been vice president and minister of the armed forces for more than forty years and consequently a partner with his brother in establishing the path. The chapters in this section provide a basis on which to analyze the continuities and changes in Cuban foreign policy under the new president's guidance. They highlight Cuba's important new relations with China and the countries in Latin America and the Caribbean, the most important of which is Venezuela; Cuba's use of "soft power" to strengthen its ties with other parts of the Third World; the country's ongoing tense relationship with the United States and the changes that occurred during the first five years of Barack Obama's presidency; and the way in which Cuban emigration affects the sustainability of the Revolution along with the potential role of the Cuban diaspora in shaping the future of the country.

One source of change has been external events. For example, the death of President Hugo Chávez in March 2013 could have created a serious hardship for Cuba because of its reliance on inexpensive oil from Venezuela, as Michael Erisman's chapter notes. In fact, Chávez's successor, Nicolás Maduro, maintained his country's oil agreement in part because Cuba provided Venezuela with needed medical personnel and teachers. Erisman further explains that Raúl Castro has continued to pursue the three goals that had long been characteristic of Cuba's foreign policy. The first is economic security, which he has attempted to achieve by expanding the number of Cuba's trading partners so that the loss of a single connection does not undermine the whole economy. In this regard, China and Venezuela have been the most important new trading partners. Second, he has enhanced Cuba's international stature by increasing the number of countries that receive Cuban assistance or with which Cuba cooperates and the number of international and regional organizations in which Cuba is actively engaged. Finally, Cuba has sought to protect its "effective sovereignty" by promoting and engaging in plans for Latin American and Caribbean integration.

Despite China's large population, military capability, and economic power, Cuba has tended to be less concerned about losing effective sovereignty to the Asian giant than it had been with the Soviet Union or the United States. As Adrian Hearn explains in his chapter, China has shown sensitivity about the matter of sovereignty, in part by emphasizing its "Five Principles." In addition, he reports,

> State-to-state cooperation has focused on building critical infrastructure as a basis for Cuban economic growth. Bilateral projects have targeted the upgrading of Cuban manufacturing, the gradual opening of markets, the coordination of industrial sectors, and more recently the controlled introduction of private entrepreneurship.

Still, Hearn notes, "Chinese enterprises have found themselves subjected to the meticulous regulations of the Cuban state." These have created some friction. But China's larger efforts to change the rules and criteria in international financial institutions may prove the most important for Cuba's future and pave the way for Cuba's reentry into these organizations.

While Cuba has been less than enthusiastic about engaging with the International Monetary Fund, it has actively pursued membership in multilateral organizations not dominated by the United States. As Monica Hirst notes in her chapter, Cuba began in 1991 to attend the Ibero-American Summit and in 2009 joined the Rio Group. In 2013, it secured the presidency of the Rio Group's successor organization, the Community of Latin American and Caribbean States (CELAC in the Spanish acronym), with the slogan "unity within diversity." She adds that "Havana has cultivated close links with the CARICOM [Caribbean Community] countries based on a broad agenda of cooperation and solidarity." Although Cuba is not a CARICOM member, it signed a Trade and Economic Cooperation Agreement with the Caribbean Community in 2000.

Cuba's engagement in regional organizations has been reinforced by its growing bilateral trade with countries in Latin America. Hirst points to the reconstruction of the Port of Mariel, which a Brazilian enterprise manages. Officially opened during the January 2014 CELAC summit, it will service supercargo ships traversing the newly widened Panama Canal. The port's terminal will have an annual capacity of 1 million containers.

Until at least 2013, the most important institution that helped to strengthen Cuba's bilateral relations in the region has been the Bolivarian Alliance for the Peoples of Our America (ALBA in the Spanish acronym). President Chávez put forward the idea of ALBA in 2001 to counter the Free Trade Area of the Americas, a plan the United States initiated in 1994 to integrate the Western Hemisphere. ALBA, which began operations in 2004, was envisioned to exclude the United States and Canada. Backed by Venezuela's oil wealth and in conjunction with ALBA, Cuba has provided medical aid—including a program to restore eyesight to more than 2 million Latin Americans since 2005, as John Kirk reports in his chapter. In addition, Cuba has sent teachers, engineers, and scientists to countries in the region.

Kirk explains that Cuba's "tradition of medical internationalism dates back to 1960," and as of 2011, the program was sending about 41,000 health workers to sixty-eight nations. Notably, many of the cooperative missions (Kirk notes that Cuba prefers to designate the programs as "cooperation" rather than use the paternalistic term "aid") involve training as well as the direct provision of health care. Cuba also has created a medical school with free tuition to train students from abroad. The commitment to medical internationalism, Kirk reports, has not diminished since Raúl Castro began to lead Cuba. But there has been an effort to make some projects self-financing by charging fees to countries that can afford them.

As noted earlier, medical internationalism serves multiple interests for Cuba. Michael Bustamante and Julia Sweig point to the program's contribution to Cuba's "soft power," a term that connotes the ability of a country to influence others by example rather than by coercion. They explain that Cuba has accumulated its soft power through several mechanisms in the past fifty years. In addition to cooperative aid programs, these include making effective use of the mass media; exporting Cuban films, music, and ballet; appealing to other Third World countries as an underdog that resists U.S. oppression; supporting solidarity groups throughout the world; and focusing on Cuba's own war against terrorism and its suffering from terrorism. These have contributed to a positive image that enables Cuba "to be seen as a trusted and valued partner in many international arenas and institutions" despite its lack of democracy.

Cuba's effort to free the "Cuban Five"—a case that the late Saul Landau describes in his chapter—has been one of the country's most ardently propagated campaigns. As Landau explains, the "Five" were Cuban agents whose mission was to monitor terrorist activities against Cuba that were organized by exiles in South Florida. Convicted of conspiracy to conduct espionage and murder by a jury working in Miami's politically charged atmosphere, the treatment of the Five contrasts with the way the United States has treated Cuban exile terrorists who live openly in South Florida.

From Cuba's perspective, the contrast highlights one reason for its continued wariness about the United States. Philip Brenner and Soraya Castro review U.S.-Cuban relations during the first five years of President Obama's presidency in considering whether the "knot of antagonism and hostility" that has been tightened over many decades can still be untied. They observe that the president who promised change did modify U.S. policy but that he failed to overcome key elements of the legacy he inherited from President George W. Bush.

However, Brenner and Castro also point to several factors that could enable the two countries to cooperate and in the process possibly reduce the antagonism and begin to develop a modicum of trust. One factor is pressure from Latin America. By 2009, all of the countries in the Western Hemisphere except the United States had established diplomatic relations with

Cuba, and many have been demanding that the United States end its embargo. Another factor is the constructive role Cuba has played in hosting and supporting negotiations between the Colombian government and the principal guerrilla organization in that country, the Revolutionary Armed Forces of Colombia, aimed at ending the civil war in Colombia, a high-priority U.S. goal. Moreover, there are several issues on which Cuba and the United States share a common interest—such as drug trafficking, environmental protection, and epidemic disease—and cooperation would benefit both countries.

Emigration from Cuba has been both a source of tension between the two countries and a basis for imagining there could be improved relations. As Antonio Aja Díaz remarks in his chapter, the 1995 migration accord "suggested the possibility of regulating the legal migratory flow of Cubans to the United States and of trying to stop illegal emigration." Since then, more than 20,000 have emigrated annually. In part, they are attracted by the benefits that go uniquely to Cuban immigrants under the 1966 Cuban Adjustment Act. These émigrés tend to be younger and better educated than those who left since between 1965 and 1995. Half were unemployed, which indicates that their motive for leaving is economic. This fact provides a source of hope for improved relations because the newer exiles do not harbor the deep animosities against the Revolution characteristic of older generations.

Jorge Domínguez, however, suggests that dialogue between Cubans and members of the diaspora has many hurdles standing in the way. He notes that family visits, made easier by the Obama administration's decision to end restrictions on travel to the island by Cuban Americans, can help overcome the obstacles, and he acknowledges that newer émigrés are more open to dialogue than previous generations. But he also points to the difficulties some members in the diaspora have in accepting any positive information about Cuban achievements. Honest dialogue, he concludes, is essential for Cuba to have a "better future" and will depend on a goodwill that is now too often missing.

Díaz explains that for Cuban leaders, the "brain drain and loss of talent" resulting from emigration have been a source of worry. As a result, permanent emigration generated pressure for developing "new legislation that takes into account the political, economic, and social importance of this issue." His chapter, which was published originally in 2011, thus provides background for understanding the Cuban government's decision in January 2013 to permit most citizens to obtain passports, to travel abroad without an exit permit, and to stay outside of the country for up to two years and return without forfeiting their property or their right to return. It was a reform many Cubans had been demanding, and it quickly increased the number applying for U.S. visas. (Notably, in July 2013, Cuba and the United States resumed talks over migration issues. These were held every six months as a result of the 1995 accord, but President George W. Bush suspended them in 2003. President Barack Obama resumed the sessions in 2009, but only for two rounds before suspending them again.)

Leonardo Padura, one of Cuba's leading contemporary writers, concludes the "Foreign Policy" section with an evocative chapter that conveys how the current Cuban-U.S. relationship and Cuban migration laws have forced Cuban baseball players to choose permanent exile. Their situation is a metaphor for the country as a whole, he suggests, a country whose heart is broken by the detachment of so many Cubans from Cuba.

In sum, as the chapters in this section explain, the continuity of Cuban foreign policy under Raúl Castro has occurred in a context of significant changes in Latin America, the increasing influence of China, reforms within Cuba, and a relatively unchanged relationship with the United States. However, changes in Cuba's migration laws and in the demography of Cuba's diaspora may influence the U.S.-Cuban relationship, which could have a profound influence on the future of Cuban foreign policy.

Chapter Eighteen

Raúlista Foreign Policy

A Macroperspective

H. Michael Erisman

Even before the transition in leadership from Fidel to Raúl Castro, international events had transformed Cuba's foreign policy in the 1990s. The disintegration of the socialist bloc destroyed a central pillar of the country's foreign policy and presented Havana with the daunting task of radically reconfiguring its network of international relations. This was most apparent with respect to trade and related economic concerns.

Yet no matter how spectacular such changes may be, the basic rule of thumb is that elements of continuity will remain part of the scene. Or, to put it in historians' terms, the present is always to some degree a product of the past. This cautionary note holds true with respect to contemporary Cuban foreign relations, for juxtaposed against the modifications that have taken place are certain important elements of the policy equation that have persisted over time. Specifically, revolutionary Havana has *always* defined its role on the world stage in terms of promoting and protecting three goals: economic security, international stature, and effective sovereignty.

Economic Security

One common conception of economic security focuses on the progress that occurs within a society toward higher levels of industrialization and modernization and the ability of the society to sustain these levels. But for smaller, lesser-developed countries, defending against potential external economic threats is often the most important dimension of this issue. For Cuba, the pursuit of economic security has been manifested in policies aimed at minimizing its vulnerability to hostile economic penetration or economic sanctions. In particular, since 1959, Havana has sought to use its international ties as a buffer against the economic war that Washington has directed at Cuba.

International Stature

Most revolutionary experiments are messianic to some degree if for no other reason than their supporters often tend to see them as having a relevance or a "mission" that goes beyond the borders of the societies from which they emerged. In this respect, the Cubans have not been markedly different from other rebels who have managed to triumph against tremendous odds, for they also have aspired to influence world affairs in a way that seemed unrealistic for a country with a modest population and limited natural resources. Yet unlike others, Cuba did attain an international influence and stature incommensurate with its size, as political scientist Jorge Domínguez observed in 1978:

> Cuba is a small country, but it has a big country's foreign policy. It has tried to carry out such a policy since the beginning of the revolution, but only in the second half of the 1970s did it have conditions . . . to become a visible and important actor actually shaping the course of events. [1]

Effective Sovereignty

Observers who are influenced by the realist school of thought tend to be pessimistic about the prospects for small countries to be able to control their destinies. They see such states as victims of global power differentials whose weaknesses often result in their incorporation into another country's sphere of influence. [2] Such observers highlight the importance of distinguishing clearly between *formal* and *effective* sovereignty. The former is in many respects symbolic, involving such things as admission to the United Nations and other similar badges of acceptance into the international community. Effective sovereignty, on the other hand, refers to circumstances where a country and its people *truly control* their own destinies; they are, in other words, exercising their right of national self-determination to the greatest extent possible. The architects of the Cuban Revolution, acutely aware of the island's tragic history of encounters with imperial Spain and a hegemonically inclined United States, embraced the proposition that their highest priority must be to maximize their country's effective sovereignty. Indeed, this pursuit represents the leitmotif underlying much of Havana's foreign policy; in other words, it long has been and remains probably the single most important consideration influencing the dynamics of the Revolution's international relations.

From a broad conceptual perspective, then, Cuba's foreign relations can be understood in terms of the various strategies that Havana has employed in its efforts to guarantee the integrity of these three key national goals. The pursuit of these goals represents a constant within the Revolution's foreign policy equation, while the methods used to try to secure them have often been "adjusted" due to such things as developments in the larger global environment within which the Revolution has had to operate (e.g., the transition from a Cold War paradigm to the post-Soviet world). More recently, the tides of change have manifested themselves in Raúl's elevation to the Revolution's top leadership position. It is the impact (or lack thereof) of this latter change on the style and substance of Cuba's foreign policy in the three key areas detailed above that are examined here.

GENERAL POLICY TRENDS IN THE POST-SOVIET ERA

In contrast to the more unitary nature of the late Cold War period, wherein practically all threads in Cuba's web of international relations were anchored in Havana's Soviet bloc connection, in the post-Soviet era Cuba has relied on two distinct strategies to pursue its foreign policy goals. First, trade restructuring has functioned primarily to promote economic security. Second, various aid/cooperation initiatives—two key examples being *Alianza Bolivariana para las Américas* (Bolívarian Alliance for the Americas [ALBA]) and Havana's massive medical aid programs [3] —have served to enhance the Revolution's international stature and influence.

Necessity rather than choice forced the issue of radically reconfiguring Cuba's economic relations in general and its trade networks in particular to the top of Havana's international agenda in the early 1990s. The catalyst for this process was the turmoil that engulfed the Soviet Union and Eastern Europe at the time. One major casualty of this chaos was the Council for Mutual Economic Assistance, which was disbanded in June 1991. With it went the privileged trade regime and developmental aid packages that had long provided Cuba with a high degree of economic security.

Such a disruption in the increasingly interdependent modern world would be a matter of serious concern for practically any government, but it represented a disaster of epic proportions for an island country like Cuba, whose economic health tends to be heavily reliant on foreign trade. Making the situation even more precarious, of course, was Washington's eagerness to intensify the crisis in yet another effort to drive a dagger through the Fidelistas' political heart. These circumstances led many observers to conclude that the Revolution was finished—it would follow the Eastern European socialist countries into oblivion. Such dire predictions were obviously erroneous, and one major factor that contributed to the Revolution's survival was Havana's ability to radically restructure its shattered web of international economic relations. Supporting the campaign to expand its trade and related ties were such major initiatives as a drive to develop new export product lines (e.g., in the biotechnology field) and efforts to attract foreign investors by further liberalizing the laws that govern joint ventures on the island.

The post-Soviet era data clearly demonstrate that Havana has been quite successful in its efforts to restructure its trade and related ties by interjecting into their basic fabric an important element of diversification. Gone is the near-monopolistic position, rooted in the Revolution's membership in the Council for Mutual Economic Assistance, that Eastern Europe once occupied. In its stead has emerged a much more complex web of economic relations, with the most important and multifaceted new threads radiating out to Western Europe and the Americas (see table 18.1), where in both cases Havana has developed a fairly varied list of trading partners. However, while such achievements can generally be seen as having a positive impact on the island's quest for greater economic security, they have contributed little directly to the Revolution's international stature and influence.

Cuba had already gained considerable international prestige during the Cold War via its high-profile involvement in Third World affairs. In the post-Soviet era, however, this dimension of Cuba's foreign policy has played itself out primarily in terms of Havana's efforts to encourage its hemispheric neighbors to embrace neo-Bolívarianism. Although this concept entails important economic integration dimensions, its total scope is much broader in the sense that neo-Bolívarianism represents the Hispanic (and Anglophone Caribbean) alternative to a hemispheric landscape dominated by the United States.

Table 18.1. Cuban Trade Profile, 1989 and 2006 (percentage of total Cuban trade)

	1989	2006
Western Europe	8.0	27.8
Eastern Europe	77.1	3.2
Americas	5.9	43.3
Asia	5.1	20.9
Africa	0.9	2.0
Other	3.0	2.8

Source: Chart created by the author from data compiled by the *Oficina Nacional de Estadísticas* (Cuban National Office of Statistics).

The key idea here is that any contemporary (developmental) cooperation schemes launched by hemispheric states should be modeled along the lines of Simón Bolívar's vision of a politically unified Latin America that would be clearly separate from and independent of the colossus to its north. As such, this approach rejects, at least for the time being, any significant involvement in the process on Washington's part. Instead, it sees the whole enterprise unfolding under Latin American (rather than U.S.) leadership, the ultimate goal being to achieve a level of cooperation that would put the hemispheric community (defined as South America and the Caribbean Basin countries) in a position where its pooled power would to a great extent be sufficient to counterbalance that of the United States.

Not surprisingly, given its desire to inject a strong South-South dimension into its international/hemispheric relations and its penchant for playing the Latin American David to the U.S. Goliath, Havana has long been an advocate of neo-Bolívarianism in one form or another. Indeed, as noted by Luis Suárez, "The Revolution has always posited the doctrine of *latinamericanismo*, adopted in the Cuban constitution of 1976, which seeks the integration of Latin American and Caribbean nations."[4] The keystone of this neo-Bolívarian coalition, at least from Havana's perspective, has been ALBA, which includes a very strong dimension of Cuba's larger, globe-girdling medical aid programs.

Cuba's post-Soviet initiatives to enhance both its economic security and its international stature have contributed to strengthening the island's effective sovereignty by providing counterweights to Washington's efforts to undermine it. In a nutshell, the essence of the U.S. strategy to replace the revolutionary government with a more acceptable (i.e., subservient) one has been to employ *isolation* as the mechanism to destabilize and ultimately destroy the Revolution. Trade sanctions have been the instrument used to pursue economic isolation, while the political side of the equation has involved attempts to convince the world community to sever all diplomatic ties with Cuba and thereby treat it as an international pariah. Thus far, however, Cuba has largely been able to frustrate and neutralize these ambitions. On the economic front, its widely diversified network of post-Soviet trade relations has replaced its Cold War communist bloc connection as an "insurance policy" against Washington's trade sanctions, while its solid international stature has translated into diplomatic recognition and strong political support across the global landscape. As such, Cuba's effective sovereignty does not currently appear to be in any serious jeopardy. Indeed, Washington's policy has served to isolate the United States rather than Cuba. Consider that the UN General Assembly voted in 2012, as it had done similarly for the previous twenty years, to condemn the U.S. embargo against Cuba. The vote was 188–3 with two abstentions.

RAÚLISTA FOREIGN POLICY: SOME GENERAL OBSERVATIONS

Whatever potential might have existed for dramatic policy transformations as Fidel withdrew into the background has not, for the most part, materialized. The substance of Cuba's foreign affairs agenda has not changed radically. There have, of course, been some minor adjustments (e.g., in the rankings of trading partners), but the overall essence/nature of the island's approach to international affairs has not changed drastically since 2006. Political scientist William LeoGrande succinctly confirmed this observation, utilizing a tripartite analytical paradigm similar to the one elaborated above, in writing,

> Since he succeeded Fidel in 2006, Raúl Castro's foreign policy has had three key components: first, to diversify Cuba's international economic relations so that the disruption of ties with any one country will not throw the economy into chaos; second, to build diplomatic support both regionally and globally through active participation in a wide range of international organizations; and third,

to pursue normal relations with the United States, reducing the threat Washington poses to Cuba's security and opening the doors to expanded trade and investment.[5]

What, then, represent some of the highlights of Raúl's efforts in the international arena to promote and protect Cuba's three key national attributes?

With regard to economic security, the record is somewhat mixed. As indicated in table 18.2, Cuba had achieved a high degree of regional diversification by 2006, when Raúl assumed leadership. A different dynamic emerges, however, when one looks at the percentage of total trade data in table 18.2. What was a fairly broad distribution in 2006 becomes much more concentrated in 2011 under Raúl's watch, with Venezuela's share nearly doubling to a point where it appears that Cuba could suffer serious economic problems if that relationship were disrupted. LeoGrande, for example, has noted that "by some estimates, Cuba would have to cut its oil imports by 20–25 percent, or else cut back on its other major import, food" if Venezuela ended preferential pricing and concessionary loans for Cuba or sent Cuban professionals home.[6]

This doomsday scenario loomed on the horizon when Hugo Chávez died of cancer in March 2013. Some feared that the main candidate opposing Nicolas Maduro, Chávez's hand-picked successor, in the April 2013 presidential election might radically downsize Venezuela's Cuban connection. Maduro's victory, though, makes it unlikely that Raúl will confront any serious crises on this foreign affairs front for the time being because the new Venezuelan president had developed close ties with Cuba while serving as foreign minister.

What is surprising in table 18.2 is the slippage in China's percentage of total Cuban trade. Beijing launched a major economic campaign in Latin America in the first decade of the twenty-first century. Its two-way trade with countries in the region jumped from U.S.$10 billion in 2000 to $183 billion in 2011.[7] One would therefore have expected to see an expanding Chinese presence in Cuba's foreign trade profile. Instead, Beijing, like Havana's other main trading partners, has increasingly been overshadowed by Venezuela during Raúl's tenure. Cuba's history has repeatedly demonstrated the danger of becoming overly reliant on a particular economic partnership that may not stand the test of time. Admittedly, Havana's current Venezuelan connection is not nearly as extensive as was previously the case with either the United States before 1959 or the Soviet bloc. Nevertheless, conventional wisdom suggests that Cuba's long-term economic security will be best served by a strong commitment to diversification.

There is, however, one tantalizing "silver bullet" that entered the picture during the Raúlista transition and that has the potential to solve many of the island's economic problems. Specifically, in 2008, reports began to circulate about the possibility of significant oil deposits north of Cuba in the island's offshore exclusive economic zone. The estimates ranged from approximately 5 billion barrels (U.S. Geological Survey) to 20 billion barrels (Cuban government). If the mid- to higher range of these estimates were proven to be correct, Cuba would enter an exclusive club as one of the top twenty nations of the world in terms of petroleum reserves. Even using the lowest estimate, Canada and Venezuela would be the only nations in the Western Hemisphere to surpass the island on the basis of per capita reserves. This potential bonanza has, however, remained elusive. By mid-2013, five test wells had been drilled by various international partners, but none proved to be commercially viable because of geological problems (e.g., hard rock, which makes it extremely difficult to extract whatever oil may be present). While oil production remains an option to be pursued, Cuba will have to employ more conventional strategies in the near future to promote Cuba's economic security.

On the international stature front, Raúl continued and expanded Havana's medical aid programs, though with some revisions in their financial arrangements. The growth in these

Table 18.2.   Cuba's Primary Trading Partners, 2006 and 2011

Country	Imports from (1000s pesos)	Exports to (1000s pesos)	Total (1000s pesos)	Percentage of Total
2006				
Venezuela	2,232,423	408,787	2,641,210	21.26
China	1,571,130	243,971	1,815,101	14.61
Spain	859,625	156,908	1,016,533	8.18
Canada	351,604	545,381	896,985	7.22
Netherlands	67,932	788,045	855,977	6.89
Brazil	428,255	24,756	453,011	3.65
Germany	618,463	21,413	639,876	5.15
United States	483,591	0	483,591	3.89
2011				
Venezuela	5,902,286	2,432,200	8,334,486	41.68
China	1,281,742	786,200	2,067,942	10.34
Spain	1,019,677	165,400	1,185,077	5.92
Canada	479,257	718,800	1,198,057	5.99
Netherlands	72,978	656,400	729,378	3.65
Brazil	643,082	82,100	725,182	3.63
Germany	286,732	40,200	326,932	1.63
United States	430,420	588	431,008	2.16

Source: *Anuario Estadístico de Cuba 2011*, available athttp://www.one.cu/aec2011/esp/08_tabla_cuadro.htm.

endeavors during his administration is summarized in table 18.3. There has been a 60 percent increase in the number of personnel deployed between 2005 and 2013. Initially, these contingents were dispatched at little or no cost to the host nations. Under Raúl, however, in some cases there have been changes in the financial arrangements. Specifically, some of the more affluent countries who receive such assistance are today being asked to pay or to pay more for it.[8] In 2013, Cuba earned nearly U.S.$6 billion from its medical services exports, which made it "the leading source of hard-currency income for the nation," according to Cuban Foreign Trade Minister Rodrigo Malmierca.[9] Whatever the financial provisions might be, it is widely recognized that Havana reaps considerable nonmonetary rewards from its medical aid programs, as illustrated by President Obama's comments in a press conference at the 2009 Summit of the Americas meeting:

> One thing that I thought was interesting—and I knew this in a more abstract way but it was interesting in very specific terms—was hearing from these leaders who when they spoke about Cuba talked very specifically about the thousands of doctors from Cuba that are dispersed all

Table 18.3.   Cuban Medical Aid Personnel Abroad

Year	Number
1999	3,600
2001	3,800
2003	15,000
2005	24,500
2006	28,664
2007	29,809
2008	36,770
2009	38,000
2010	37,000
2011	40,000
2012	38,000
2013	40,000

Source: Created by the author using data gleaned from various international governmental organization and media sources. An especially useful source of data and information about Cuban medical aid activities are the various issues of *MEDICC Review*, available at http://www.medicc.org/index.php.

throughout the region, and upon which many of these countries heavily depend. And it's a reminder for us in the United States that if our only interaction with many of these countries is drug interdiction, if our only interaction is military, then we may not be developing the connections that can, over time, increase our influence and have a beneficial effect when we need to try to move policies that are of concern to us forward in the region.[10]

Although previously Cuba's international stature had been enhanced as a result of its leadership in various Third World groups (e.g., the Non-Aligned Movement), Havana interjected a new dimension into this aspect of its twenty-first-century hemispheric policies by moving, in conjunction with and as a result of its increasingly close ties with Hugo Chávez's government in Caraças, to create a new organization designed to counteract Washington's dominance of Latin American/Caribbean affairs. On December 14, 2004, Cuba and Venezuela signed the ALBA Pact in Havana, thereby transforming neo-Bolívarianism from an abstract philosophical concept into a formal international treaty with provisions for institutionalization. Among ALBA's key objectives are to promote trade and investment between member governments based on cooperation and with the aim of improving people's lives, not making profits; for member states to cooperate to provide free health care and free education to people across the ALBA states; to integrate the ALBA member's energy sectors to meet people's needs; and to develop basic industries so that ALBA member states can become economically independent.[11] With Cuba and Venezuela playing leading roles, ALBA has evolved into a highly multifaceted undertaking that includes initiatives such as the following:

• Operation Milagro (Miracle), a vision restoration project wherein Venezuela provides most of the funding while surgeries and related care are the responsibility of Cuban medical specialists.
• The Cuban "Yo, sí puedo" literacy program, which taught approximately 1,700,000 Latin Americans to read and write through 2009, with Bolivia and Nicaragua joining Venezuela on the UN list of illiteracy-free countries in the process.

- The ALBA Oil Agreement, which is modeled on a larger Venezuelan enterprise launched in 2005 known as PetroCaribe. The agreement allows ALBA members to finance their oil purchases on a long-term, low-interest basis of which a portion can be repaid in goods and services.
- The Bank of ALBA, which was set up in 2008 to serve as a source of developmental capital for ALBA members. [12]

Cuba also expanded its influence in the region in November 2008 when it gained full membership in the Rio Group, an informal association of countries that Brazil organized in the 1980s to help broker peace in Central America. In December 2011, the Rio Group formalized itself in creating the Community of Latin American and Caribbean States (CELAC) in Caraças. With thirty-three countries (every country in the Western Hemisphere except the United States and Canada) representing roughly 600 million people, CELAC presented a major challenge to the U.S.-dominated Organization of American States as the major international organization for the region. Notably, the high esteem the region held for Cuba was demonstrated by naming it the organization's chair for 2013.

CELAC and ALBA share several similarities:

- Both view integration in more than simply economic terms, seeking also to promote political, social, economic, and cultural unity as well as sustainable development.
- Both represent a conscious and collective effort to combat U.S. economic, political, military, and cultural domination in the region.
- Both emerged as a result of efforts by Havana and Caraças, the two prime movers behind its establishment.

While it remains to be seen whether CELAC will develop into a viable, highly effective undertaking, it, along with ALBA and Havana's expanding medical aid programs, is an indicator of the high priority Raúl has given to maximizing Cuba's international stature and influence.

The litmus test for the revolutionary government's effective sovereignty has always revolved heavily around its relationship with the United States. The key issue here has been its vulnerability, both real and perceived, to Washington's hostility—the greater the vulnerability, the more severe is the threat to Havana's ability to exercise effective sovereignty over its affairs (both domestic and, especially, foreign). But as noted previously, by 2006, Havana's effective sovereignty in relation to the United States seemed secure. Indeed, it appears that Havana no longer even views Washington or relations with the United States as a major problem. As historian Julia Sweig reported in 2013 about conversations with Cuban officials,

> Cuba no longer seems to need to see the relationship with the United States improve as rapidly as it might well have, for example, when the Soviet bloc collapsed and it lost its Soviet subsidy overnight. . . . The government seems to be quite gratified by the consensus in Latin America and globally that the U.S. policy should change, but is clearly not willing to tie itself up into pretzels in order to satisfy an American demand that it reshape its politics in our image. [13]

CONCLUSION

When speculating about the transition to a post-Fidel political order in Cuba, many observers (particularly in U.S. governmental/mass media circles and especially in Miami) tended to assume that the process would somehow be extremely chaotic—Fidel would soldier on until the very last minute, and then his demise would create a power vacuum that would plunge the society into chaos. This speculation proved to be totally divorced from reality because Fidel had made provisions for an orderly changing of the guard. The Revolution had been Fidel's life work, and he was not about to put his legacy at risk by allowing a situation to develop that might endanger it.

Given the orderly transition, it should not be surprising that there has been a significant degree of policy continuity under Raúl, especially in the realm of foreign affairs. Fidel and the party/governmental leadership have always shared, along with the general population, a strong commitment to the deep currents of nationalism that have long flowed through the island's political culture. These sentiments have, from the very beginning of the Revolution, manifested themselves in an international agenda that stresses maximizing the country's economic security, its prestige in world affairs, and its effective sovereignty. Raúl, of course, has been and remains a part of this tradition. Therefore, while there has been and will continue to be some tactical policy adjustments in response to changes in the domestic or international environments, the larger strategic vision summarized here should continue to characterize the basic dynamics of Cuba's foreign relations under Raúl.

NOTES

1. Jorge Domínguez, "Cuban Foreign Policy," *Foreign Affairs*, no. 57, Fall 1978, 83.

2. See, for example, William Demas, *Consolidating Our Independence: The Major Challenge for The West Indies* (St. Augustine: Institute of International Relations, University of the West Indies, 1986), 12.

3. For more regarding Cuba's medical aid programs, see John M. Kirk and H. Michael Erisman, *Cuban Medical Internationalism: Origins, Evolution, and Goals* (New York: Palgrave Macmillan, 2009), and Julie Finesilver, *Healing the Masses: Cuban Health Politics at Home and Abroad* (Berkeley: University of California Press, 1993).

4. Luis Suárez, "Cuba's Foreign Policy and the Promise of ALBA," *NACLA Report on the Americas*, January/February 2006, 28.

5. William M. LeoGrande, "The Danger of Dependence: Cuba's Foreign Policy after Chávez," *World Politics Review*, April 2, 2013, http://www.worldpoliticsreview.com/authors /947/william-m-leogrande.

6. LeoGrande, "The Danger of Dependence."

7. Adrian H. Hearn, "China, Global Governance and the Future of Cuba," *Journal of Current Chinese Affairs*, no. 1, 2012, 156.

8. Of the sixty-six countries hosting Cuban medical aid contingents in 2013, twenty-six paid some amount for these services. The rest, mostly sub-Saharan African nations, paid nothing. For more information on this topic, see "Los 66 países donde trabajan los médicos cubanos," *El Nuevo Herald*, June 13, 2013, http://www.elnuevoherald.com/2013/06/18/1502724/los-66-paises-donde-trabajan-los.html

9. Quoted in "Cuba Nets Billions Each Year by Hiring Out Its Doctors to Asia, Africa and Latin America," Agence France-Presse, June 19, 2013, http://www.rawstory.com/rs/2013/06/19/cuba-nets-billions-each-year-by-hiring-out-its-doctors-to-asia-africa-and-latin-america/.

10. Quoted from a transcript of his April 19, 2009, press conference, available at http://www.realclearpolitics.com/articles/2009/04/19/obama_summit_americas_ press_conference_96076.html.

11. ALBA's members are Cuba, Venezuela, Antigua/Barbuda, Bolivia, Dominica, Ecuador, Nicaragua, and St. Vincent and the Grenadines. Honduras was a member but withdrew in January 2010.

12. For more information and analyses of the Cuban/Venezuelan relationship within the ALBA context, see H. Michael Erisman, "Cuba, Venezuela, and ALBA: The Neo-Bolívarian Challenge," in *Cuban-Latin American Relations in the Context of a Changing Hemisphere*, ed. Gary Prevost and Carlos Oliva Campos (Amherst, NY: Cambria Press, 2011), 101–47.

13. Julia E. Sweig, "Wariness in Cuba toward the Obama Administration," Council on Foreign Relations interview, March 9, 2009, http://www.cfr.org/cuba/wariness-cuba-toward-obama-administration/p18715.

Chapter Nineteen

China and the Future of Cuba

Adrian H. Hearn

Financial instability in the United States and Europe has intensified China's engagement with developing countries. Sino–Latin American trade skyrocketed from U.S.$10 billion in 2000 to U.S.$183 billion in 2011, and China's priorities in the region are clear: tap new sources of foodstuffs and energy to sustain domestic growth and open new markets for Chinese-manufactured products.

Literature on the resulting transpacific relationships focuses mainly on the economic and strategic implications of this process, drawing predictable conclusions. With few exceptions (e.g., Gonzalez-Vicente 2011; Hearn and León-Manríquez 2011; Kotschwar, Moran, and Muir 2011), little attention has been paid to the influence of China's rise on the coordination and development of Latin American industrial sectors and how this influence resonates—or not—with international conventions of governance. The case of Cuba is instructive, as no other country is so openly condemned by Washington and so publicly praised by Beijing. China is Cuba's second-largest trading partner, and the two countries have pursued state-led cooperation in sectors as diverse as biomedicine, tourism, industrial manufacturing, nickel and oil mining, and oil refining (UN Commodity Trade Statistics Database 2011).

This chapter argues that in spite of continuing differences between international conventions of governance and China's approach to foreign engagement, the line between the two is narrowing. The first part of the chapter traces the key points of contention to diverging evaluations of state intervention but finds that these tensions are diminishing as multilateral institutions evolve to accommodate China's influence. For instance, adjustments to fiscal reserve policies within the International Monetary Fund (IMF), as well as the gradual relaxation of the IMF's benchmark guidelines on public sector expenditure, resonate with China's vision of public-private integration as a basis for economic development.

As China becomes more integrated into the existing geopolitical architecture, its government has encouraged political outliers, most notably Cuba, to follow its example. The remainder of the chapter finds that the trajectory of Chinese cooperation with Cuba has evolved from state-centric bilateral accords to an increasing emphasis on economic liberalization. Consequently, even some of Cuba's staunchest critics have recognized that, with China's assistance, the island is headed toward rapprochement with the international economic system.

CHINA, THE STATE, AND GLOBAL GOVERNANCE

China's "peaceful rise" is complicated by the existence of an international system in which the rules of appropriate conduct have already been defined. From political transparency to commercial conditionality, the controversies that distinguish China's approach from international conventions stem from a common source: diverging views of the state. Richard Feinberg (2011) notes that the IMF's aversion to state intervention is not set in stone: "Over the years, the IMF has admitted many new members whose statist economic policies diverged greatly from free market norms" (63). Nevertheless, the IMF recommends that developing market economies should not allow their ratio of public debt to gross domestic product to exceed 25 percent (IMF 2003). Although the IMF replaced its structural performance criteria with more flexible "structural benchmarks" in 2009, the underlying ideology remains the same: macroeconomic growth should be a prerequisite for government spending (IMF 2009). Chinese analysts typically view the development process in reverse, advising partner-country governments to undertake initial investments in infrastructure and technical upgrading to enable subsequent economic growth under "the supreme guidance of the state" (Yan 2011, 12–16).

To diminish the tensions that result from conflicting visions of development, Chinese negotiators have sought to influence the policy charters of multilateral institutions, particularly the United Nations and the IMF. The transformation of the G8 into the G8+5, the subsequent creation of the G20, and the formation of informal groupings, such as the G20 Developing Nations, BRICS (Brazil, Russia, India, China, and South Africa), and BASIC (Brazil, South Africa, India, and China), have augmented China's confidence and international profile. The G20 in particular has provided a platform for President Hu Jintao to describe China's transformation into a "leadership state" (Wang 2011).

If the G20 has augmented China's diplomatic exposure, the IMF has enabled practical advances. China now holds the largest IMF voting quota after the United States and Japan, its rights having increased from 3.65 to 6.39 percent over the past two years. Prior to becoming managing director of the IMF in 2011, Christine Lagarde stated, "If the Chinese economy continues to grow and be a driver of the world economy, then clearly that percentage will have to further increase" (quoted in Hille 2011, 6). It is well known that Chinese negotiators are pushing to secure a place for the renminbi in the IMF's multicurrency reserves (Special Drawing Rights [SDRs]) and promoting SDRs as an alternative to the U.S. dollar as the world's base currency.

China's vision of state-guided development can be traced to the communist revolution of 1949, but more influential are the lessons learned from the nation's subsequent embrace of "market socialism." Since the early 1980s, centrally designed pilot programs and "experimental points" have allowed adjustments and midstream corrections as market structures moved inward from the margins of the planned system (Devlin 2008, 129). Success with public-private integration at home has conditioned the formulation of Chinese overseas development programs, which are typically managed through bilateral governmental accords and joint ventures. China's advocacy of reforms within the IMF, from securing a place for the renminbi in SDRs to building endorsement among member countries for greater public spending, aims to substantiate the legitimacy of this controversial approach.

According to Hu Jintao (2011), by the end of 2010, China had completed 632 infrastructure projects in developing countries. Across Latin America, the Caribbean, Africa, and the Asia-Pacific region, these projects (many of them related to natural resource extraction) have been criticized for their excessive state intervention and inadequate transparency (Corrales et al. 2009; Eisenman 2006; Hanson 2008; Lam 2004; Santoli, Scheidel, and Shanks 2004). China's deepening partnerships with the world's commodity exporters, writes Cynthia Sanborn, are characterized by a lack of checks and balances: "There are no incentives for Chinese leaders to take a stand on social and environmental responsibility" (quoted in Kotschwar et al. 2011). China's preference for negotiating directly with foreign governments has also attracted accusations that it is enabling undemocratic regimes, Venezuela and Cuba among them, to avoid public disclosure of ecological impact and labor conditions (Caspary 2008; Ellis 2009; King 2009). China, it is argued, is spreading the message that "discipline, not democracy, is the key to development and prosperity" (China–Latin America Task Force 2006, 21).

The Chinese Ministry of Foreign Affairs maintains that China stands ready to offer assistance within its capacity to developing countries having difficulties. Although China's aid is limited, it is provided sincerely and without any conditions attached (Ministry of Foreign Affairs of the People's Republic of China 2003). Chinese officials defend their "no-strings" approach as a commitment to political noninterference and, following domestic experience, argue that it minimizes corruption because it substitutes cash transfers with self-contained projects, such as the construction of schools, hospitals, roads, and sports stadiums.

In 2008, the Chinese government responded to international concerns by publishing its first Policy Paper on Latin America and the Caribbean. The paper refers to the Five Principles of Peaceful Coexistence—unchanged since their establishment in 1954 to resolve a border dispute with India—to define the parameters of transpacific engagement (Ministry of Foreign Affairs of the People's Republic of China 2008). The Five Principles provide a general and hence adaptable framework for international cooperation: mutual respect for territorial integrity and sovereignty, mutual nonaggression, noninterference in the internal affairs of other countries, equality and mutual benefit, and peaceful coexistence. Chinese commentators have argued that the Five Principles reflect a Confucian perspective of nationhood and statecraft, particularly through their emphasis on consensual "harmonious" development, their pursuit of "holistic" outcomes, and their implicit advocacy of state stewardship over national and international affairs (Pan 2004; Wen 2004; Yang 2008). Notwithstanding the appropriation of Confucius to legitimize contemporary policy, analysts—Chinese and Western—detect genuine traces of traditional values in Chinese policymaking. David Shambaugh (2008), for instance, argues that "for the Chinese, cooperation derives from trust—whereas Americans tend to build trust through cooperation."

In Argentina and Venezuela, Chinese enterprises have demonstrated a preference for long-term outcomes over quick returns, offering respective currency swaps and credits of U.S.$10.24 billion and U.S.$20 billion in return for natural resource concessions a decade into the future. In Brazil and Cuba, Chinese investments promote the integration of logistics, education, and manufacturing, achieving a degree of collective sectoral coordination beyond the capabilities of any individual firm-to-firm partnership. In Mexico and the Caribbean, Chinese business initiatives have relied on informal networks and *guanxi* (ethnic and family relationships) rather than official institutional channels, particularly when the latter lack local legal and public support (Haro Navejas 2011; Hearn, Smart, and Hernández 2011).

Like their Chinese counterparts, Cuban officials are often accused of excessive intervention in the economic and social lives of their citizens. Moreover, Cuba's cooperation with China, managed exclusively through state channels, has drawn criticism for its undisclosed (hence suspicious) nature. From secret arms transfers and development of biological weapons to anti-U.S. intelligence gathering, commentators perceive a sinister intergovernmental strategy underlying the bilateral relationship (Cereijo 2001, 2010; Institute for Cuban and Cuban American Studies [ICCAS] 2004).

Sino-Cuban cooperation is indeed driven by a political strategy, but it is focused less on undermining the United States than on the long-term (and less newsworthy) goal of upgrading and coordinating Cuba's industrial capacities. Although Chinese "assistance" to Cuba is managed through governmental channels, it has been accompanied by advice from Beijing about the benefits of incorporating a greater degree of private initiative into the existing state-led system. Under the leadership of Raúl Castro since 2008, the Cuban government has begun to heed this advice as it seeks to open the island's economy in a controlled manner.

CHINA AND CUBA: THE LONG MARCH TO THE MARKET

China's relations with Cuba date back to 1847, when the first of more than 150,000 Chinese indentured laborers arrived in Havana's port of Regla. These people and their descendants actively took part in Cuba's two wars of independence (1868–1878 and 1895–1898) and in the social movement that culminated in the Cuban Revolution of 1959. On September 2, 1960, Fidel Castro declared that Cuba would sever ties with Taiwan; this was done within a month, on September 28, making Cuba the first Latin American country to establish diplomatic relations with the People's Republic of China. Since their inception, Sino-Cuban economic relations have been managed exclusively through governmental channels.

State-to-state cooperation has focused on building critical infrastructure as a basis for Cuban economic growth. Bilateral projects have targeted the upgrading of Cuban manufacturing, the gradual opening of markets, the coordination of industrial sectors, and, more recently, the controlled introduction of private entrepreneurship. As Chinese enterprises become increasingly comfortable with the rules of market exchange, Cuba's slow implementation of reforms has generated bilateral tensions. However, since Raúl Castro replaced his brother as Cuba's president, the pace of change has quickened, and China's domestic experience with economic reform has assumed growing relevance for the island.

China's interest in developing Cuban manufacturing capacities and markets extends back to the collapse of the Soviet Union. Following an initial shipment of 500,000 Chinese bicycles to Cuba in the early 1990s, Mao Xianglin, a former envoy of the Central Committee of the Chinese Communist Party, visited Cuba in 1997 to assist in the establishment of a bicycle factory with Chinese capital and technical expertise. The success of the initiative led to a similar export-to-production scheme for electric fans. Mao described this as an "incremental" strategy that Chinese businesses have since employed across a range of sectors in Cuba:

> I would hesitate to say that our Cuban manufacturing operations are entirely commercial, because what we're doing is broader than that. We're trying to help Cuba to incrementally upgrade its technical ability. If our products prove popular and useful then we assist by setting up factories. . . . Using Chinese expertise, Cuba could come to produce electronic goods for sale to Latin America. (interview with Mao Xianglin, December 14, 2007)

Chinese technical and financial assistance to Cuba demonstrates the sincerity of these words. During a 2001 visit to Cuba, Chinese President Jiang Zemin offered an interest-free credit line of U.S.\$6.5 million and a loan of U.S.\$200 million to modernize local telecommunications with Chinese products and a U.S.\$150 million credit to buy Chinese televisions (Erikson and Minson 2006, 14). Following the successful sale of Chinese washing machines, televisions, air conditioners, and refrigerators to Cuba, Hu Jintao signed sixteen accords in 2004 pledging Chinese support for the domestic manufacture of these and other goods. This promise has materialized in a facility next to Havana's Lenin Park, where television sets and other light consumer products are assembled. Indicating the success of the scheme, in November 2009 the Cuban Ministry of Information and Communication's Grupo de la Electrónica entered into a joint venture with Chinese electronics giant Haier to domestically manufacture computer components and assemble household consumer goods (*Cubaencuentro* 2009). Visiting Cuba for a second time in November 2008, Hu offered extensions on the repayment of previous loans, a donation of U.S.$8 million for hurricane relief, and a credit line of U.S.$70 million for health infrastructure (*Granma* 2008, 5). The visit also cleared the way for the China National Petroleum Corporation to invest U.S.$6 billion in both the expansion of an oil refinery in Cienfuegos to produce 150,000 barrels per day and the construction of a liquefied natural gas plant on the same site (Hutchinson-Jafar 2011).

China's pursuit of industrial integration is evident in the Cuban transport sector, which in 2006 received a U.S.$1.8 billion revolving credit line backed by the China Export and Credit Insurance Corporation (Sinosure), whose repayment was renegotiated in 2010 (EFE 2010; ICCAS 2009, 47). The Cuban government also announced in 2006 that contracts totaling more than U.S.$2 billion had been signed, primarily with Chinese counterparts, to improve Cuban road and rail transport (*Nuevo Herald* 2009). Five hundred Chinese freight and passenger train carriages were ordered for Cuba's rail fleet, with twenty-one complete locomotives entering service in 2009. In 2008, the Chinese firm Yutong sold 1,000 energy efficient buses to the island, 200 of which were in circulation by midyear. According to Rosa Oliveras (interview, November 18, 2008) of the Grupo para el Desarrollo de la Capital, "The Chinese buses saved our city, and actually the whole country, from a very grave situation."

Rather than deliver complete buses to Cuba, Yutong shipped components from its factory in Zhengzhou for assembly in Havana, saving 12 to 15 percent in transportation costs (Pizarro 2009). The scheme facilitated skills transfer through the training of Cuban automobile assembly technicians by a team of thirty Chinese counterparts. As with training in Cuban electrodomestic factories, a marsh gas extraction, a sheep-rearing farm, a reservoir fishery, and three pesticide production plants, this approach is building a valuable source of specialized talent that may facilitate Cuba's entry into global production chains. The project's integration into a broader, coordinated program of development and skills training distinguishes it from private sector investments from Europe (particularly Spain) that have focused on enclave sectors, such as hotel construction and tourism services.

The integration of infrastructure upgrading with information technology and electronics training has laid the foundation for a coordinated industrial chain that supports domestic manufacturing along with the shipment of goods to markets around Cuba and potentially to neighboring Latin American and Caribbean countries. Facilitated by the refurbishment of Cuba's ports with Chinese equipment, this strategy could significantly advance both countries' regional influence (Frank 2006).

The Chinese government adopted the strategy of gradual liberalization at home in the early 1980s and has repeatedly advocated it to Cuban officials ever since Fidel Castro's 1995 meeting with Premier Li Peng in Beijing (Cheng 2007; Jiang 2009). After fifteen years of hearing their advice, Cuba's reformers—led by Raúl Castro—are now listening.

Cuba's sixth Communist Party Congress, which took place in April 2011, showed a growing acceptance of the market as a catalyst for national development. The Economic and Social Policy Guidelines approved by the congress declared that ownership of private property, long considered antithetical to socialism, is now considered acceptable on the condition that it is not "concentrated" (República de Cuba 2011, 5, 11). The critical concern has therefore become how the state might leverage its considerable institutional capacities to optimize and guide economic performance.

Effective implementation of the 2011 reforms will require a phased and coordinated approach, and in this regard China can provide some useful lessons. Among the insights that Cuba has derived from China—with varying degrees of attentiveness—are the gradual sequencing of reforms under the management of a state-appointed reform commission (Laverty 2011, 65; Lopez-Levy 2011a, 9; Lopez-Levy 2011b, 43–44), the adaptation of socialist principles to national conditions (Mao Xianglin et al. 2011, 199), the military management of commercial activities (Klepak 2010), the attraction of investment from emigrants (Ratliff 2004, 21–22), and the testing of liberalization in target territories prior to wider implementation (Heilmann 2008).

In November 2010, the president of the Cuban National Assembly, Ricardo Alarcón, visited Beijing and officially recognized the relevance of China's economic evolution to Cuba's development. Raúl Castro had already expressed this sentiment during his visits in 1997 and 2005, which focused on labor market reform and the creation of hybrid state-market economic structures. In China's experience, particularly since joining the World Trade Organization, these transformations were achieved through a blend of state oversight and privatization, an approach that Chinese officials now routinely recommend to Cuba. When Vice President Xi Jinping of China and President Jiang Jiemin of the China National Petroleum Corporation visited Havana in June 2011, they not only signed memorandums of understanding on oil and gas investments but also discussed banking and economic planning. As Feinberg (2011) notes, "Some observers opine, albeit with some exaggeration, that China has become Cuba's IMF!" (42).

Cuban leaders have rejected the notion that they intend to follow a "China model" of development. A historically accrued wariness of excessive foreign influence has long colored the character of the island's international engagement, and relations with China appear to be no exception. Spanish colonialism in the nineteenth century, along with U.S. domination in the first half of the twentieth century and Soviet micromanagement in the second half each provoked strong nationalistic responses. Chinese enterprises have found themselves subjected to the meticulous regulations of the Cuban state. Technical cooperation is carefully monitored and subsumed by central policy objectives, leading Chinese entrepreneurs to complain about missed opportunities for expanding trade and deepening investment.

Political orthodoxy has also generated headaches for Cuba. The buses purchased from Yutong under a bilateral governmental accord, for instance, arrived in bulk in 2008, but their relentless use on dilapidated roads caused many to break down simultaneously in late 2010 and early 2011. According to an official close to the project, Cuban negotiators incorrectly assumed that open-ended "political goodwill" signified that Yutong, a state enterprise, would provide the Cuban fleet with ongoing maintenance and replacement parts. Electronics manufacturing has suffered similar setbacks: in the absence of independent quality control, televisions, rice makers, and appliances assembled in Cuba under Chinese brand names have lived notoriously short lives. The extensive circulation of spare parts recovered from antique Russian and U.S. appliances has done little to service the sleek, energy-efficient, but incompatible Chinese models. Together with the progressive economic recommendations of Chinese officials, these setbacks have served to remind Cuban leaders of the point conveyed to Fidel Castro during his 1995 visit to Beijing: political ideology no longer subsumes economic pragmatism.

Since the early 1990s, state-to-state cooperation has enabled Cuba to leverage Chinese support for the development and coordination of basic industrial infrastructure. The bilateral relationship has now moved into a new phase marked by strategic planning of economic opening and controlled privatization. Tensions and disagreements are to be expected, but since Raúl Castro assumed power in 2008, Cuban authorities have shown sincere interest in learning from China's experiences with liberalization.

The Chinese government has a vested interest in the success of Cuba's reforms, reflected in the negotiation of the first Five-Year Plan for Sino-Cuban cooperation in June 2011. As a longtime financier of Cuba's development, many are looking to Beijing to underwrite the credits and loans that aspiring entrepreneurs need to grow small businesses.

As Cuba's need for capital deepens, its leaders have expressed "no principled position against relations with the IMF or World Bank" (quoted in Feinberg 2011, 67). The internal evolution of the IMF to accommodate changing global conditions, including China's deepening influence, makes engagement with Cuba more likely. Growing international reliance on the renminbi and greater provisions for public spending are important in this regard, but equally important are Cuba's domestic reforms, which are bringing the island into closer alignment with conventions of economic governance. China sits at the crossroads of these local and global developments, encouraging Cuba toward rapprochement with international norms even as it works to reform them.

CONCLUSION

The Latin American operations of Chinese state enterprises, undertaken through state-to-state channels with "no strings attached," challenge orthodox conventions of international cooperation. Alarmist reports of worst-case scenarios and potential threats, from disregard for human rights to telecommunications espionage, obscure the more encompassing and genuine challenge of building dialogue with China on Western Hemisphere affairs. As Daniel Erikson (2011, 132) has written, the energy of policymakers and publics would be better directed at leveraging China's intensifying engagement with multilateral institutions as a basis for discussing regional codes of governance and approaches to state intervention. The changing internal dynamics of the IMF, including the increase of China's voting rights, suggest that this process is now under way.

Recent changes in Cuba indicate that even in a country at diplomatic odds with the United States, Chinese initiatives are not inimical to mainstream principles of development and governance. Long-term market expansion, coordinated industrial sectors, and state oversight of private initiative are goals that drive the engineers and policy advisers behind Sino-Cuban projects. These goals also resemble the principles advocated by Latin American, European, and U.S. officials. The Cuban reforms formalized by the 2011 Communist Party Congress will support a further convergence of positions, as they propose a more balanced mix of state and market forces. Although Sino-Cuban initiatives are managed under the banner of state-to-state cooperation, Chinese support for Cuba's liberalization agenda is prompting the Western Hemisphere's only communist nation toward alignment with international norms.

NOTE

From "China, Global Governance and the Future of Cuba," *Journal of Current Chinese Affairs* 1, no. 1 (2012): 155–79. Reprinted by permission of the author.

REFERENCES

Caspary, Georg. 2008. "China Eyes Latin American Commodities." *YaleGlobal Online*, January 18. http://yaleglobal.yale.edu/content/china-eyes-latin-american-commodities(accessed June 22, 2011).

Cereijo, Manuel. 2001. "China/Cuba: A New Dangerous Axis." *Guaracabuya*. http://www.amigospais-guaracabuya.org/oagmc065.php (accessed June 22, 2011).

————. 2010. "Inside Bejucal Base in Cuba: A Real Threat." *The Americano*, August 27. http://theamericano.com/2010/08/27/bejucal-base-cuba-real-threat/ (accessed June 22, 2011).

Cheng, Yinghong. 2007. "Fidel Castro and 'China's Lessons for Cuba': A Chinese Perspective." *China Quarterly* 189, no. 40: 24–42.

China–Latin America Task Force. 2006. "Findings and Recommendations of the China–Latin America Task Force" (March–June). Miami, FL: University of Miami Center for Hemispheric Policy.

Corrales, Javier, et al. 2009. *Undermining Democracy: Twenty-First Century Authoritarians*. Washington, DC: Freedom House.

Cubaencuentro. 2009. "Más acuerdos con China-Esta vez en industria básica, transportee informática." November 16. http://cubaencuentro.com/es/cuba/noticias/mas-acuerdos-con-china-esta-vez-en-industria-basica-transporte-e-informatica-223337 (accessed June 24, 2011).

Devlin, Robert. 2008. "China's Economic Rise." In *China's Expansion into the Western Hemisphere: Implications for Latin America and the United States*, edited by Riordan Roett and Guadalupe Paz, 111–47. Washington, DC: Brookings Institution Press.

EFE. 2010. "Cuba and China Renegotiate Debt." December 21. http://latino.foxnews.com/latino/politics/2010/12/21/cuba-china-renegotiate-debt/ (accessed June 28, 2011).

Eisenman, Joshua. 2006. "More Progress in Latin America: Jitters over U.S.-Japan Strategic Cooperation." *China Reform Monitor* 613. Washington, DC: American Foreign Policy Council.

Ellis, R. Evan. 2009. *China in Latin America: The Whats and Wherefores*. Boulder, CO: Lynne Rienner.

Erikson, Daniel P. 2011. "Conflicting US Perceptions of China's Inroads in Latin America." In *China Engages Latin America: Tracing the Trajectory*, edited by Adrian H. Hearn and José Luis León-Manríquez, 117–35. Boulder, CO: Lynne Rienner.

Erikson, Daniel P., and Adam Minson. 2006. "China and Cuba: The New Face of an Old Relationship." *Hemisphere* 17 (September 22): 12–15.

Feinberg, Richard E. 2011. *Reaching Out: Cuba's New Economy and the International Response*. Washington, DC: Brookings Institution Press.

Frank, Marc. 2006. "Trade with China Primes Cuba's Engine for Change." *Financial Times*, March 29. http://yaleglobal.yale.edu/content/trade-china-primes-cuba's-engine-change (accessed June 24, 2011).

Gonzalez-Vicente, Ruben. 2011. "China's Engagement in South America and Africa's Extractive Sectors: New Perspectives for Resource Curse Theories." *Pacific Review* 24, no. 1: 65–87.

Granma. 2008. "Firmados Importantes Acuerdos." November 5, 5.

Hanson, Fergus. 2008. "The Dragon in the Pacific: More Opportunity Than Threat." Lowy Institute Analysis Series. Sydney: Lowy Institute for International Policy.

Haro Navejas, Francisco. 2011. "China's Relations with Central America and the Caribbean States: Reshaping the Region." In *China Engages Latin America: Tracing the Trajectory*, edited by Adrian H. Hearn and José Luis León-Manríquez, 203–19. Boulder, CO: Lynne Rienner.

Hearn, Adrian H., and José Luis León-Manríquez, eds. 2011. *China Engages Latin America: Tracing the Trajectory*. Boulder, CO: Lynne Rienner.

Hearn, Adrian H., Alan Smart, and Roberto H. Hernández. 2011. "China and Mexico: Trade, Migration, and Guanxi." In *China Engages Latin America: Tracing the Trajectory*, edited by Adrian H. Hearn and José Luis León-Manríquez, 139–57. Boulder, CO: Lynne Rienner.

Heilmann, Sebastian. 2008. "From Local Experiments to National Policy: The Origins of China's Distinctive Policy Process." *China Journal* 59: 1–30.

Hille, Kathrin. 2011. "Lagarde Woos China to Back IMF Bid." *Financial Times*, June 10, 6.

Hu Jintao. 2011. "Promote Growth through Win-Win Cooperation." http://news.xinhuanet.com/english2010/china/2011-11/04/c_131228470.htm (accessed January 1, 2012).

Hutchinson-Jafar, Linda. 2011. "China's CNPC in Talks for Possible Cuba Oil Block." Reuters, July 13. http://www.reuters.com/article/2011/07/13/cuba-china-oil-idUSN1E76C1S620110713 (accessed January 4, 2012).

Institute for Cuban and Cuban American Studies. 2004. "Crouching Tiger, Hidden Dragon: China in Cuba." *Focus on Cuba* 58 (September 7). http://ctp.iccas.miami.edu/FOCUS_Web/Issue58.htm (accessed June 22, 2011).

————. 2009. "Cuba's External Debt." In *Cuba Fact* 47. Havana: Institute for Cuban and Cuban American Studies.

International Monetary Fund. 2003. *World Economic Outlook*. Washington, DC: International Monetary Fund.

————. 2009. *Creating Policy Space: Responsive Design and Streamlined Conditionality in Recent Low-Income Country Programs*. Washington, DC: International Monetary Fund.

Jiang, Shixue. 2009. "Cuba's Economic Reforms in Chinese Perspective." Chinese Academy of Social Sciences. http://blog.china.com.cn/jiangshixue/art/915280.html (accessed June 21, 2011).

King, Royston. 2009. "South-South Cooperation Should Be Set in a Framework of Good Environmental Governance." *Stabroek News*, September 25.

Klepak, Hal. 2010. *Raúl Castro, Estratega de la Defensa Revolucionaria de Cuba*. Buenos Aires: Capital Intelectual.

Kotschwar, Barbara, Theodore Moran, and Julia Muir. 2011. "Do Chinese Mining Companies Exploit More?" *Americas Quarterly* (November).

Lam, Willy. 2004. "China's Encroachment on America's Backyard." *China Brief* 4, no. 23. Washington, DC: The Jamestown Foundation.

Laverty, Collin. 2011. *Cuba's New Resolve Economic Reform and Its Implications for U.S. Policy*. Washington, DC: Center for Democracy in the Americas.

Lopez-Levy, Arturo. 2011a. *"Change in Post-Fidel Cuba: Political Liberalization, Economic Reform and Lessons for U.S. Policy."* Washington, DC: New America Foundation.

———. 2011b. "Reformas Económicas y Desarrollo en el Este de Asia: ¿Una Experiencia para Cuba?" *Espacio Laical* 3: 40–44.

Mao Xianglin, Carlos Alzugaray, Weiguang Liu, and Adrian H. Hearn. 2011. "China and Cuba: Past, Present, and Future." In *China Engages Latin America: Tracing the Trajectory*, edited by Adrian H. Hearn and José Luis León-Manríquez, 187–201. Boulder, CO: Lynne Rienner.

Ministry of Foreign Affairs of the People's Republic of China. 2003. "China's Stand on South-South Cooperation." August 18. http://www.fmprc.gov.cn/eng/wjdt/wjzc/t24884.htm (accessed June 24, 2011).

———. 2008. "China's Policy Paper on Latin America and the Caribbean." http://www.fmprc.gov.cn/eng/zxxx/t521025.htm (accessed June 24, 2011).

Nuevo Herald. 2009. "Diario Oficial Señala 'Deterioro' de 90 Por Ciento de Vías Férreas Cubanas." November 7. http://www.elnuevoherald.com/noticias/america_latina/cuba/story/583269.html (accessed June 24, 2011).

Pan, Tao. 2004. "Timeless Theme of International Relations." *Beijing Review* 47, no. 23 (June 10).

Pizarro, Renato Pérez. 2009. "Chinese Buses Are Assembled in Havana." *Miami Herald*, December 4. http://miamiherald.typepad.com/cuban_colada/2008/12/chinese-buses-a.html (accessed June 24, 2011).

Ratliff, William. 2004. "China's 'Lessons' for Cuba's Transition?" Institute for Cuban and Cuban American Studies, University of Miami. http://ctp.iccas.miami.edu/Research_Studies/WRatliff.pdf (accessed September 15, 2011).

República de Cuba. 2011. *Lineamientos de la Política Económica del Partido y la Revolución*. Havana: República de Cuba.

Santoli, Al, Miki Scheidel, and Lisa Marie Shanks. 2004. "Beijing Uses a 'weiqi' Strategy in the Americas." *China Reform Monitor* 562. Washington, DC: American Foreign Policy Council.

Shambaugh, David. 2008. "China's New Foray into Latin America." *YaleGlobal*, November 17. http://yaleglobal.yale.edu/content/china%E2%80%99s-new-foray-latin-america (accessed June 24, 2011).

UN Commodity Trade Statistics Database. 2011. "Data Query Database." http://comtrade.un.org/db/default.aspx (accessed June 26, 2011).

Wang, Yong. 2011. "China in the G20: A Balancer and a Responsible Contributor." *East Asia Forum*, October 31. http://www.eastasiaforum.org/2011/10/31/china-in-the-g20-a-balancer-and-a-responsible-contributor/ (accessed January 1, 2012).

Wen, Jiabao. 2004. "Carrying Forward the Five Principles of Peaceful Coexistence in the Promotion of Peace and Development," June 28. http://www.fmprc.gov.cn/eng/topics/seminaronfiveprinciples/t140777.htm (accessed June 27, 2011).

Yan, Jirong. 2011. "El 'Modelo Chino': ¿Qué Dicen las Investigaciones?" *Temas* 66: 12–16.

Yang, Zhimin. 2008. "Technological and Cultural Exchanges: Tightening the Link between China and Latin America." Paper presented at the symposium China and Latin America: The New Face of South-South Cooperation, University of Technology, Sydney, December 3.

Chapter Twenty

Cuban–Latin American and Caribbean Relations

Challenges Beyond

Monica Hirst

As the Cuban regime celebrated its fiftieth anniversary, a wave of progressive governments unleashed a nonviolent process of change in Latin America. Holding stronger ties with Latin American countries while aiming to leave behind years of isolation and selective bilateral bonds is referred to in Cuba as a process of "normalization." In fact, Cuban–Latin American relations are not nostalgic and do not at all follow a Proustian logic of the "search for a lost time." Revolutionary processes that involve the use of violence and insurgency are no longer perceived in the region as a necessary pathway to social change and international autonomy. Widespread social inclusion policies accompanied by economic measures aiming to protect national sovereignty have been pursued with no major damage to the rule of law in various parts of the region, in certain cases maintaining and deepening the democratic foundations and preserving the rules of the market economy game.

Latin American democracy processes have contributed to restoring and deepening ties with Havana—so much so that during the past twenty years, Fidel and Raúl Castro have been invited to all Latin American presidential inaugurations of elected candidates regardless of political affiliation. "Normalization" is also used to underline the acceptance of political differences within the region and that ideology should no longer be considered the dominant criterion for intraregional relations.

THE QUESTION OF CHANGE: BETWEEN REFORM AND TRANSITION

Cubans applaud the internal process of reform, although change is not associated with a political transition, as is often speculated about by Western governments, the media, and academia. The changes made essentially aim at the liberalization of the economy through structural transformations of the Cuban statist centralized model. Among Cuban intellectuals, the main dilemma challenging current reforms is that of establishing the most appropriate economic model and what its social impact should be. Political changes, albeit viewed as inevitable, are seen as challenges to be addressed down the road. Subsequently, Latin

American experiences appear less attractive than certain Asian state–centered trajectories, especially those in Vietnam and China.

From a comparative perspective, the reforms in Cuba can be juxtaposed with three experiences: those in Eastern Europe after the fall of the Berlin Wall, the ongoing sequence of regime changes known as the Arab Spring that started in Tunisia in 2010, and the Latin American democratic transitions initiated in the late 1980s.

Cuba is unlikely to replicate the South American and especially the Southern Cone's experience of transition in which local/regional prodemocratic forces worked together based on an antiauthoritarian consensus with hardly any external pressure. This is and will not in the future be the case in Cuba. In fact, Cuba is a special—if not unique—case in which antidemocratic anachronism still endures, resisting the pressure of neocolonial interventionism. The most problematic aspect of Cuba's uniqueness is its dimension that involves the United States and the U.S.-based Cuban exile community.

The principle of nonintervention is a strong feature of Latin American foreign policies, and within the region the acceptance of political diversity has been perceived as a sign of political maturity. The region's foreign policies and domestic regional campaigns in areas of human rights or political pluralism that could influence the Cuban regime are expected to be feeble. Nonetheless, the expanded access to information on current Latin American politics within democratic contexts, thanks to the presence of global instruments of communication such as the Internet and the recent presence of TELESUR in open television broadcasting, unavoidably nurtures political questioning, particularly among younger generations. Also, the expansion of Latin American tourism on the island, together with an increase of cultural and educational programs, has renewed and extended areas of exchange and mutual knowledge between Cubans and Latin Americans.

REGIONAL PARTNERSHIPS

Latin American investment, commerce, and cooperation for development are considered more as doors of opportunity for the Cuban economy than as a source of inspiration, allowing the country to pursue sustainable growth, social equity, and political change. Cuban–Latin American trade has expanded steadily in recent years, yet when current Cuban–Latin American relations are closely observed, Venezuela and Brazil are the partners that seem to count most.

The Cuban-Venezuelan nexus was established as a natural outcome of the installation of the Hugo Chávez government in 1999. Perceived by Cuban officials and intellectuals as vital to saving the Revolution after the island had struggled through the difficult period after the fall of the Soviet Union, this relationship launched the ground ideologically for reviving Latin American leftist ideals. From the outset, Cuban-Venezuelan bilateralism has been sustained by three pillars: (1) high-level political dialogue, (2) military intelligence collaboration, and (3) compensatory trade.

Based primarily on personal friendship and deep ideological affinities, the Castro-Chávez connection was central to legitimizing the Bolivarian socialist project, promoting the ALBA group (*Alianza Bolivariana para los Pueblos de Nuestra América* [Bolivarian Alliance for the Peoples of Our America], comprising Antigua and Barbuda, Bolivia, Cuba, Dominica, Ecuador, Nicaragua, St. Vincent and the Grenadines, and Venezuela), and unblocking communications between leftist guerrilla groups and the government in Colombia. Cuban military advisers in Venezuela became crucial for local intelligence activities and involved direct participation in presidential logistics, weapons training, and shared anti-U.S. strategic planning. Cuban-Venezuela cooperation in defense has involved the presence of 500 Cuban military advisers, exchange programs between defense academies, and the repair and maintenance of warships, ports, and transportation logistics (Romero 2010).

In 2011, trade with Venezuela represented 38 percent of total Cuban exchanges, while in Latin America the partnership with Venezuela represented 81 percent of Cuba's trade with the region. The bilateral accord introduced in 2003 set preferential pricing for the export of Cuban professional services (mainly medical) in exchange for the provision of oil and joint investments in strategic areas, plus the provision of generous credit lines. Bilateral exchanges registered a large leap since 2004, jumping from $346 million to $1.487 billion in 2007 and $1.6 billion in 2012. In 2005, it was agreed that Cuba would supply Venezuela with 30,000 medical professionals, 600 clinics, 600 centers for physical therapy and rehabilitation, thirty-five centers for high-technology diagnosis, and 100,000 eye operations, besides the training of 40,000 doctors and 5,000 health workers and the provision of 10,000 scholarships. In exchange, Venezuela was to provide 53,000 barrels of oil daily at preferential rates of $27 per barrel (Benzi and Lo Brutto 2013; Feinsilver 2008; Serbin 2006).

Venezuela is the only Latin American country that could strongly affect the island, particularly if the Chavista regime were to be destabilized. The uncertainties of post-Chávez Venezuela have created uneasiness in the Cuban government in that a reconfiguration of the bond with Caraças could replicate the gap experienced in the past when the Soviet Union collapsed. After President Hugo Chávez's death in March 2013, new presidential elections were held in Venezuela in which Nicolás Maduro won by a small margin of 1.7 percent over the opposition leader Henrique Capriles. Immediately afterward, President Maduro met with Fidel and Raúl Castro in Havana, when fifty-one cooperation projects were signed for $2 billion in the areas of food supply, culture, sports, education, energy, health, and transportation. Also, recent tension between the governments of Venezuela and Colombia may also become a source of concern for Havana, as they could affect the ongoing Colombian peace talks.

An unprecedented dialogue taking place between Cuba and Brazil has brought concrete results for investment, credit, and cooperation in biofuels, health, education, culture, agriculture, and infrastructure. The Brazilian strategy has been to maximize the opportunities created by Cuba's economic reforms as an important partner of the Cuban state. For Brazil, this relationship allows access to myriad Cuban technological areas of accomplishments and human capabilities, such as those in biotechnology, in the pharmaceutical industry and public health organizations, and even in Olympic sports (Garcia 2013).

Food supply and cooperation for agriculture development are important parts of the ongoing collaboration between the Foreign Trade and International Investment Ministry in Cuba and the ABC agency in Brazil, with special attention extended to cooperative and family production. Brazilian investment has also connected with the Cuban sugar industry, an area until recently inaccessible to foreign investment since the first phase of the Cuban Revolution. Ironically, the Cuban government still holds strong ties with social movements in Brazil engaged in land struggles (such as the Movement of Landless Rural Workers), particularly in the preparation of organizational capacities and in health and education cooperation.

Brazilian-Cuban private-state joint ventures have expanded in various areas in spite of the different economic model in these countries. Instead of being perceived as an obstacle, the Cuban state is viewed by Brazilian entrepreneurs as a reliable and efficient partner that is fully responsible for sensitive issues, such as local labor contracts, environmental regulation, and foreign currency regulations. While it is true that Brazil's economic presence in Cuba benefits from the absence of the U.S., Canadian, and European private sectors, which are restrained by the U.S. embargo, it also suffers in areas of Brazilian commerce and investment that are dependent on U.S. technology and/or industrial parts.

Brazilian investment is perceived as having promising effects for the local economy. The construction of the Mariel port by the Odebrecht group, registered locally as COI, is considered the most important infrastructure project in progress in Cuba. The Mariel port is expected to be completed by 2014 with a pier of 700 meters, giving access to ships with more than forty-five feet of draft, and a terminal with an annual capacity of approximately 1 million containers. This port will also include the logistics necessary for offshore oil drilling. Its construction involves 3,500 workers, of which only 100 are Brazilian, and an investment of $900 million, of which 85 percent has been financed by BNDES and 15 percent by the Cuban government. This project allowed for the participation of more than 400 Brazilian exporters. Beyond participation in the industrial zone planned to function next to the port, COI wishes to become a central investor in the modernization and expansion of Cuba's airports. Prospects are also good if and when the U.S. trade embargo is suspended, which would give the Mariel port a privileged position in the Caribbean for trading connections with Florida and other southern U.S. states.

At first there were expectations that the Lula da Silva government would play an overall role in the Cuban process of change, but Brasilia has occupied more of an economic than political place in Cuban transformations. Furthermore, there are commonalities between the current Cuban reform process and the gradualism experienced in Brazil during democratization. (In Brazil, the first steps toward democratic transition took place in the mid-1970s, but direct elections for president were allowed only in 1990.) The refrain "without pausing but in no hurry" used by President Raúl Castro resembles the slogan "slowly and gradually" used by the Brazilian military authorities during the 1970s. Even more important is the Cuban military's control of the main economic posts and commitment to a statist production structure intertwined with local and foreign private investment.

Brazil and Cuba have coordinated their efforts and are working well in multilateral arenas. Besides shared views on global and regional matters, Cuba's closeness to other developing countries, particularly the left-wing grouping, has helped Brazil win support in Africa, Latin America, and Asia for the carrying forward of diplomatic initiatives in global governance.

CUBA'S RENEWED PRESENCE IN REGIONAL ORGANIZATIONS

Cuba's attendance at Latin American meetings started at Ibero-American summits in 1991 and was followed by participation in the Rio Group in 2009 once diplomatic ties had been reestablished with all the countries in the region (El Salvador and Costa Rica were the last two). Immediate membership of the *Comunidad de Estados Latinoamericanos y Caribeños* (Community of Latin American and Caribbean States [CELAC]) when it was created in 2011 came as a natural outcome, as did the current presidency of this organization according to its system of rotating presidencies. During the second CELAC Summit in Chile (2013), the rules were changed to allow for the appointment of a widened troika, which meant that the Cuban presidency was assisted by its predecessor, Chile, and its successor, Costa Rica, and by a Caribbean Community (CARICOM) member state (represented by its pro tempore president).

Cuba sealed the presidency of CELAC with the slogan "unity within diversity," suggesting that the political face of any individual country should not be a matter of division within the region. Havana aspired to use this post to promote the deepening of cooperation in the region according to its comparative advantages, particularly its well-known education and health capabilities.

The fact that the country presiding over CELAC should represent the Latin American and Caribbean Group in all multilateral stances has been extremely important to push for a Cuban regional-global diplomacy. This opportunity may contribute to opening new areas of interest and involvement in topics such as climate change, human rights, migration, drug-trafficking control, and nuclear technology, among others. This may also be advantageous to the facilitation of international negotiations, particularly with the European Union (EU).

Cuba's presence in CELAC has also allowed it to underline in a regional scenario its historic support for specific claims of individual countries' territorial and economic sovereignty, such as Argentina's demand to be given sovereignty over the Malvinas Islands and Bolivia's demand for access to the sea. Reciprocity has been assured by the systematic condemnation in CELAC of the U.S. economic blockade (embargo) of Cuba (CELAC 2011, 2013).

The Cuban presence in CELAC has been central to the deepening of Latin American–Caribbean relations. Havana has cultivated close links with the CARICOM countries based on a broad agenda of cooperation and solidarity and similar perceptions in terms of decolonization and nonintervention. Beyond this—and as part of its commitment to continuously assist Haiti with robust social programs—Cuba has moved significantly to keep the former under the region's spotlight.

Although CELAC's Latin Americanism has not been conceived to replace inter-Americanism, Cuba's presence in CELAC has escalated the debate on its reincorporation into inter-American multilateral schemes, particularly the Organization of American States (OAS). The fact that the Cuban regime has shown no interest in recovering its seat in this organization has not kept its intellectuals from discussing if the time is ripe to do so. Between CELAC and the OAS lies the question of Cuba's participation at the Summit of the Americas, which was raised at the 2012 Cartagena Summit. After lack of consensus on this matter prevented the approval of a final declaration, the ALBA group and countries like Argentina and Brazil conditioned their attendance at the 2015 summit, scheduled to be held in Panama, on U.S. acceptance of Cuba's official presence.

LATIN AMERICAN/CUBAN-U.S. AND CUBAN-EU BILATERALISM

For many decades, connections with Havana had inevitable implications for U.S.–Latin American relations because closeness to Washington was defined by whether governments were friends or foes of Cuba. While it is true that such rigidity no longer exists, narrow mindsets have not been completely discarded. From a Cuban perspective, closer relations with Latin America are perceived as part of a more distant and critical stance toward the United States. For the U.S. government, this is essentially a bilateral matter with long-standing ideological contents to be addressed in the context of bilaterally unsettled negotiations. For Latin American countries, the U.S. blockade represents an anachronism, and any step on Washington's part to eliminate it would be read as a positive sign toward the region. For their part, Europeans have observed the recent Cuban–Latin American rapprochement positively and are themselves about to take a first step toward opening negotiations with Cuba. [Editors' note: The first set of negotiations took place in April 2014.] Relations between European countries and Cuba have followed a dual pattern: while the EU has resisted proceeding with the negotiation of collective accords with the island, bilateral ties have been pursued by many EU members. EU-Cuba talks have been resisted by ex-members of the Soviet bloc and conservative governments, such as those of Spain and Sweden. In 2005, the Czech Republic, Slovakia, Poland, and the Netherlands took up a negative position on negotiations with Havana (Knigge 2005). Yet the recent [2013] visit of Polish representatives to Cuba to expand bilateral cooperation and trade may be a sign of change that could contribute to expediting Brussels-Havana exchanges (*Prensa Latina* 2013).

Conditions imposed by the EU are focused on expected changes on the part of the Cuban regime regarding the protection of human rights, the rule of law, and adherence to the International Court of Justice. The seventeen bilateral accords in place cover investment, trade, and cooperation initiatives. Prospects have recently emerged for the drafting of a framework to start a negotiation process with Brussels. Europe is Cuba's second-largest trading partner (after Venezuela), and relations therefore benefit from bilateral understandings and commercial preferences. The EU does not support the U.S. blockade in any way. In terms of business, European expectations are based on the "day after" the suspension of the U.S. blockade, particularly in areas such as tourism, services, and infrastructure, since European investments are affected by the limitations imposed by U.S. legislation. With the current economic crises Europeans face at home, the importance of expanding markets and foreign direct investment in Latin American and Caribbean countries has been reinforced. Even more meaningful than potentially expanding the Cuban domestic market are expectations that the island could become a regional hub to serve neighboring islands together with southeastern U.S. ports (Feinberg 2012, 15).

REGIONAL/GLOBAL PERFORMANCE AND SOFT POWER ASSETS

Cultivating a spectrum of ties with the developing world has been a relevant dimension of Cuban foreign policy, contributing to the establishment of a coherent link between regional and global politics. Cuba's activity in the Non-Aligned Movement (NAM) and at the UN General Assembly has enabled the country to expand its visibility in two relevant areas of international expertise: peace negotiations and South-South cooperation. (Cuba, Yugoslavia, and Egypt have been the only countries to twice assume the presidency of the NAM; the Cuban presidencies occurred from 1979 to 1982 and 2006 to 2009.) Cuban diplomacy has aimed at projecting itself as a broker in complex international situations (Cuba cosponsored the UN General Assembly resolution changing Palestine's status at the United Nations to that of observer), regional interstate tensions (Costa Rican–Nicaraguan and Colombian-Venezuelan tensions), and intrastate conflicts (the Colombian peace negotiations). Cuba has also downplayed the political impulses of allied countries that are aimed at challenging world powers. An illustration was the effort to stop Hugo Chávez's idea of creating a pro-Iran group in the NAM as a reaction to the sanctions approved by the UN Security Council in June 2012.

Cuba's role in the Colombian peace process, together with Norway and accompanied by Venezuela and Chile as observers, is vitally linked to the regional/global dimension of the island's foreign policy. (The peace process was launched in Norway on October 18, 2012, after which negotiating rounds took place in Havana.) This involvement is not new, and previous attempts to promote a constructive dialogue between the Colombian guerrilla forces and the Colombian government had already taken place in the 1990s (Castro Ruz 2009). The present Colombian peace talks between the Santos government and the Revolutionary Armed Forces of Colombia, which follow a single-undertaking approach, involves a five-point agenda: land reform, political participation, ending conflict, drug trafficking, and victim reparations. Havana's role in getting negotiations started was decisive, and it has continued to ensure that the guerrillas participate in ongoing talks. For the Cuban regime, apart from deepening ties with Latin America, this involvement could facilitate relations with the United States and help remove Cuba from the U.S. State Department's list of states that sponsor terrorism.

However, Cuba's performance as a peace mediator or facilitator does not imply acceptance of the current methods and prescriptions adopted or under debate in global governance arenas on conflict resolution and international intervention. Cuban foreign policy has a critical view of UN peace operations, normative innovations such as the Right to Protect, and recent NATO- and/or European-led interventions in the Arab world and Africa. These are perceived by Havana as conceptual and practical dissimulations that violate the principles of international law, perpetuate great power interests, and waste enormous amounts of resources. Accordingly, preventive action aimed at meeting the social and economic needs of poor nations should replace militarized intervention (Baró Herrera and Chailloux 2008). Cuba has been selective regarding multilateral organizations by giving preference to those dealing with the economic, social, and cultural needs of the developing world. Examples are the UN Economic and Social Council; the UN Development Program; the Food and Agriculture Organization; the Pan-American Health Organization/World Health Organization; the UN Educational, Scientific, and Cultural Organization; and, more recently, the Human Rights Council (UPR Watch 2009).

Similarly, the Cuban regime has been reluctant to expand its connections with the bilateral and multilateral donors of the Organization for Economic Cooperation and Development's Development Assistance Committee, acting much more as a southern partner than an aid recipient. Cuba proactively contributes with humanitarian assistance and as a provider of health and education cooperation in various parts of the globe, often in postconflict reconstruction scenarios in which UN-led missions operations take place. [Editors' note: See chapter 21 in this volume.] Yet because of the current constraints in the state budget, Cuba now differentiates between what it considers to be services exports of public goods that can contribute to the establishment of reciprocal trade schemes and solidarity and humanitarian assistance for vulnerable countries.

Finally, Cuba holds a discretely defensive posture toward the ongoing configuration of a multipolar world order and has kept away from the debate regarding the reform of global governance structures. Cuban foreign policy espouses the belief that respect for the norms of international law depend on the full representation of the developing world without diluting the principle of the sovereignty of national states. Inner circles that reinforce the asymmetric distribution of power are questioned and considered detrimental to a genuine democratic multilateral system. Nonetheless, Cuba's caution toward the BRICS (Brazil, Russia, India, China, and South Africa) and IBSA (India, Brazil, and South Africa) in no way affects the strong bonds with all members of these groupings.

CONCLUSION

Based on the above analysis, while Cuba and Latin America and the Caribbean have experienced a notable rapprochement, the trajectory is not conclusive because of the sensitive aspects of this process and to the challenges ahead:

- Since 2007, the Cuban government has conducted a reform process without affecting the fundamental nature of its political regime. The present restructuring, however, is not understood as a transitional trajectory similar to those experienced in Eastern Europe, Latin America, or, more recently, the Arab world. The concept of transition is not part of the Cuban official lexicon.
- The Cuban government expects that Latin America may understand and go along with its reforms by offering support in certain areas that may contribute to the ongoing reform

process, mainly in terms of specific economic needs. Along the same lines, any sort of lecturing from governments or organizations in the region regarding the appropriate political route for Cuba would be considered misplaced by the Havana regime.

- Lessons learned from the regional democratic trajectory indicate, however, that some sort of political openness can be anticipated as a natural consequence of Cuba's ongoing reforms, especially in light of their impact on younger generations. The Cuban regime is more likely to follow the Chinese and Vietnamese example in which political opening is more likely to translate into a generational renovation of political leaderships than an acceptance of a competitive political system.

- Venezuela's future could affect the island, particularly if the Chavista regime were to be destabilized. While the most recent Maduro-Castro negotiations aim to avoid more dramatic scenarios, they also indicate the magnitude of the risks involved in this bond. In this context, ties with friendly oil-exporting countries such as Angola have become crucial for the Havana regime.

- Cuba's presidency of CELAC has occurred at a beneficial time when the role played by regional institutions is tending to expand in a setting increasingly prone to moderation and pragmatism.

- When current Cuban–Latin American relations are closely observed, Venezuela and Brazil are the partners that seem to matter most. Condensed to actors, roles, and outcomes, it could be said that while the Fidel Castro–Hugo Chávez ties have been vital for the survival of Cuban socialism, those formed by Raúl Castro with Luiz Inácio Lula da Silva and Dilma Rouseff are central to the current push for economic reform. While the first relationship (Castro-Chávez) applies to an ideological framework, the second reflects the pragmatic approach that increasingly characterizes the Havana regime.

- Expanded relations with Latin America have accompanied the Cuban regime's reform process, with careful consideration of its timing and priorities. This is a major difference between the United States and EU imposing conditions on the island for advancing the rule of law, democratic practices, and economic openness.

- Latin American and Caribbean solidarity in the condemnation of the U.S. blockade hardly goes beyond rhetoric. Cubans and Americans agree on one point when addressing their complex agenda: both sides consider this a bilateral/intermestic and not a regional matter. Recent nongovernmental initiatives have suggested the formation of an ad hoc mediating regional group to push for a more flexible position on the part of the United States. Countries such as Brazil, Colombia, and Mexico that have a robust agenda in Washington and access to U.S. domestic actors would be crucial players for promoting an initiative of this kind.

- Cuban diplomacy is regarded for its soft power assets, especially South-South cooperation initiatives and brokerage expertise, to foster peaceful solutions in areas of conflict. The possibility of expanding triangular cooperation initiatives is to be maximized by northern and southern partners, multilateral agencies, and philanthropic organizations. Recent Cuban joint action in Haiti with Brazil and Norway are positive examples of this process.

- For Latin America and the Caribbean, a positive link with the Cuban process of change helps leave behind the damage caused by interventionism and ideological polarizations in regional politics. Yet if this rapprochement is to proceed, it will have to cover the bilateral/intermestic dimension of U.S.-Cuban affairs, which inevitably includes the U.S.-based exile community and involves a more ecumenical and sustainable idea of normalization.

NOTES

From "Cuban-Latin American and Caribbean Relations: Challenges Beyond," *NOREF Report*, The Norwegian Peacebuilding Resource Centre, June 2013. Reprinted by permission of the publisher.
I wish to thank Natalia Herbst for her work as my research assistant.

REFERENCES

Baró Herrera, Silvio, and Graciela Chailloux. 2008. *¿Hacia un gobierno global?* Havana: Editorial de Ciencias Sociales.

Benzi, Daniele, and Giuseppe Lo Brutto. 2013. "La cooperación Sur-Sur en América Latina a principios del siglo XXI (un enfoque menos indulgente)." In *Volver al desarrollo o salir de él: Límites y potencialidades del cambio desde América Latina,* coordinated by Liza Aceves López y Héctor Sotomayor Castilla. Mexico City: Ediciones EyC.

Castro Ruz, Fidel. 2009. *La paz en Colombia.* Havana: Editora Política.

Community of Latin American and Caribbean States. 2011. "Special Communiqué on the Need to Put an End to the Economic, Trade and Financial Embargo Imposed by the United States on Cuba." December 3. http://www.sela.org/attach/258/default/Embargo_on_Cuba.pdf.

———. 2013. "Comunicado especial sobre la necesidad de poner fin al bloqueo económico, commercial y financiero de los Estados Unidos contra Cuba." January 28. http://www.gob.cl/media/2013/01/Combloqueo-Cuba.pdf.

Feinberg, Richard E. 2012. "The New Cuban Economy: What Roles for Foreign Investment?" December. http://www.brookings.edu/~/media/research/files/papers/2012/12/cuba%20economy%20feinberg/cuba%20economy%20feinberg%209.pdf.

Feinsilver, Julie M. 2008. "Oil-for-Doctors: Cuban Medical Diplomacy Gets a Little Help from a Venezuelan Friend." *Nueva Sociedad* 216 (July/August).

Garcia, Marco Aurelio. 2013. "Dez anos de política externa." May 29. http://www.cartamaior.com.br/ templates/materiaMostrar.cfm?materia_id=22118.

Knigge, Michael. 2005. "Cuba-EU Relations Warming Up." January 5. http://www.dw.de/cuba-eu-relations-warming-up/a-1449283.

Prensa Latina. 2013. "Cuba and Poland to Expand Bilateral Cooperation." April 4. http://www.plenglish.com/index.php?option=com_content&task=view&id=1277701&Itemid=1.

Romero, Simon. 2010. "Venezuela's Military Ties with Cuba Stir Concerns." January 14. http://www.nytimes.com/2010/06/15/world/americas/15venez.html?pagewanted=all&_r=1&.

Serbin, Andres. 2006. "Cuando la limosna es grande: El Caribe, Chávez y los límites de la diplomacia petrolera." *Nueva Sociedad* 205 (September/October).

UPR Watch. 2009. "Universal Periodic Review—Cuba." February. http://upr-epu.com/ENG/country.php?id=109.

Chapter Twenty-One

Cuban Medical Internationalism under Raúl Castro

John M. Kirk

At the beginning of this decade, Cuba had more medical personnel working in the developing and underdeveloped world than all countries of the G-8 combined. In 2011, Cuba's medical internationalism program involved approximately 41,000 health workers engaged in sixty-eight nations. Indeed, the impact of five decades of Cuba's medical cooperation (a term consistently employed instead of the paternalistic "aid") has been enormous. Cuban medical personnel have "saved more than 1.6 million lives, treated over 85 million patients (of which over 19.5 million were seen on 'house calls' at patients' homes, schools, jobs, and so on), performed over 2.2 million operations, assisted 768,858 births, and vaccinated with complete dosages more than 9.2 million people" (Feinsilver 2010).

However, Cuba's ability to sustain its medical internationalism program has been called into question by the state of the country's economy and the plans proposed to improve it. Cuban President Raúl Castro suggested in a 2010 speech that all projects were up for review as he starkly articulated the problems facing his country. He added, "We are convinced that we have to reject all forms of dogma, and we assume with firmness and confidence the continuation, which has already started, of our model to reform the economy" (Castro 2010b).

In light of the pressing economic difficulties facing Cuba, a logical question arises about how this important aspect of Cuban foreign policy has fared. Moreover, what can we expect in the future in terms of Cuban commitment to medical internationalism? Will it be cut in order to focus on domestic public health concerns? For example, there have been criticisms by Cubans about some shortages of doctors in local clinics, as approximately 22 percent of them are working abroad as *internacionalistas*. Accordingly, this chapter examines the evolution of medical internationalism since 2006, analyzing the degree of changes undertaken by the revolutionary government and offering an assessment on probable future developments.

THE CONTEXT OF MEDICAL INTERNATIONALISM SINCE 1960

The tradition of medical internationalism dates back to 1960, just a year after the Batista dictatorship was overthrown—and at a time when approximately half of Cuba's 6,000 doctors were in the process of leaving the island. In other words, Cuba's first internationalist mission—to Chile in the wake of a devastating earthquake—could not have come at a worse time in terms of the island's own economic conditions and the availability of medical personnel.

Three years later, an even larger delegation of medical personnel went to newly independent Algeria to set up the bases of the national health system. The essential point to bear in mind is that, even fifty years ago, Cuban ideology and a spirit of humanitarianism trumped domestic economic challenges (Kirk and Erisman 2009).

In all, almost 130,000 Cuban medical personnel have served on such internationalist missions. In 2005, shortly after Hurricane Katrina battered Haiti, Cuba created the Henry Reeve Contingent to provide medical cooperation at times of natural catastrophes. The contingent has been sent to Guatemala, Pakistan, Bolivia, Indonesia, Belize, Peru, Mexico, Ecuador, China, El Salvador, and Chile, a phenomenon often ignored by the media.

Another key dimension of Cuba's approach is the focus on training medical personnel in poor countries—particularly people in those sectors of the population who would not normally be able to afford to study medicine. The theory is that, once they have been trained as physicians, they would have "buy-in" to their local community and would be prepared to work with those people who traditionally could not afford access to the appropriate treatment. As part of this effort, Cuba has established nine medical schools in the developing and underdeveloped world. In 2012, teachers from Cuba's twenty-two medical schools were teaching in fifteen countries around the globe. Back in Havana, the Latin American Medical School (known better by its Spanish acronym ELAM) had graduated more than 20,000 doctors from more than seventy countries between 1999 and 2013 (MEDICC 2013).

It is widely recognized that health care and education are the two jewels in the Cuban crown. It is also understood that, among the various modalities of medical internationalism, providing free medical education to students from developing countries is a long-standing facet of Cuba's most important solidarity activities with the developing and underdeveloped world. This trend began under the leadership of Fidel Castro and was developed for almost fifty years. There is no evidence that Cuba has in any way reduced its interest in training doctors for the Third World since 2006. In fact, as will be discussed later, it has become even more interested in doing so through nontraditional medical training and particularly in Cuba and Venezuela as well as in other countries—from Bolivia to East Timor. In early July 2011, for example, 115 Haitian medical graduate students graduated from the Caribbean School of Medicine based in Santiago, bringing to 731 the total of Haitian physicians trained for free in Cuba (Agencia de Información Nacional 2011). Many from earlier graduating classes joined their Cuban colleagues and fellow medical students from ELAM in January 2010, when they flew back to provide medical care to the victims of the earthquake that flattened Port au Prince. Students from scores of countries continue to study medicine in Cuba, spending the first two years at ELAM or in Santiago (a campus mainly for Francophone students) before being distributed around the island to work in clinics or hospitals while continuing their university medical education for a further four years. It is expected that, on graduation, they will return to their own countries and work with underserved communities there—or to other developing countries that need their assistance. (The latter opportunity is pursued by those students who at times encounter difficulties imposed by traditional—and conservative—medical federations in their home countries and cannot have their titles recognized. As a result, many return to Cuba for more specialized training or volunteer in other developing countries. Some, for example, joined the Cuban medical brigade in Haiti.) In this way, the traditional "brain drain" of medical personnel in developing nations in fact becomes a "brain gain."

The largest contingent of Cuban medical personnel is currently working in Venezuela (roughly some 30,000 medical personnel). But more typical is the case of Guyana, where some 200 Cuban medical staff are working—while over 400 Guyanese are studying medicine in Cuba. Under Raúl Castro, there has not been any noticeable change in terms of the numbers of Cuban medical personnel either working abroad or studying at ELAM (where there is an annual intake of some 1,400 students from approximately fifty countries, including the United States). Both programs have functioned well, are relatively cost effective, and have produced a variety of benefits for both host country and recipient.

Another of the ongoing initiatives revolves around the victims of the Chernobyl nuclear meltdown in April 1986 who have been treated in Cuba (at no charge) since 1990. By March 2010, an astonishing 25,457 patients (including 21,378 children) had been treated (Alvelo Pérez 2010), and at that time there were 160 Ukrainian patients receiving medical treatment. It is worth noting that the largest number were treated in the 1990s, just as the Soviet Union was imploding and economic aid to Cuba and trade were disappearing.

Despite the disastrous economic conditions in Cuba during the "Special Period," Cuba continued to receive patients, mainly from Ukraine. The patients are based in Tarará, some twenty kilometers east of Havana, where they are evaluated on arrival; those needing specialized medical care are then treated in the appropriate hospitals. Room, board, and all medical services are provided by Cuba at no cost to the patients, an extremely generous act because medications alone have cost approximately $350 million (Grogg 2010). With reason, former Ukrainian President Leonid Tuchman noted on a visit to Cuba in 2010 that while other, richer countries had shown pity, Cuba had supported the victims in concrete terms (Álvarez 2010). Yet again, despite dire economic circumstances, humanitarianism and medical support for those less fortunate dominated. This project for the Chernobyl victims continues, although the number of patients continues to decrease as the impact of the nuclear meltdown does likewise.

FRESH INITIATIVES IN MEDICAL INTERNATIONALISM

One of the most significant developments in recent years has to do with what is often referred to as the "new paradigm," or the "Polyclinic Project," in medical training, designed for students from nontraditional backgrounds who otherwise would probably not be able to afford a medical education. Cuba and Venezuela have stated that they will train—at no cost to students—100,000 doctors for the Third World within a decade, and they are well on their way to doing so. Dr. Juan Carrizo, president of ELAM, noted that in 2010, 24,000 students were being trained through this method in Cuba, with a further 25,000 being trained in Venezuela (Agencia de Información Nacional 2010). The complete name for the medical training program is the *Nuevo Programa de Formación de Médicos Latinoamericanos* (NPFML), although in fact it has also been employed in Africa and Asia, adapted to local conditions. It was introduced in 2005, largely in the wake of commitments made by Cuba and Venezuela in various agreements related to the *Alianza Bolivariana para las Américas* (ALBA), when Cuba offered to provide the massive training in medicine for young Latin Americans. A similar program was instituted in Venezuela, using Cuban medical personnel, called the *Programa Nacional de Formación de Medicina Integral Comunitaria en Venezuela*. The first 8,000 students of this program graduated in 2011 and are working in traditionally underserved regions of their country. The initiative was born from discussions between Fidel Castro and Hugo Chávez in 2005, the central idea being to train doctors for Latin America and in particular for those areas where medical care was either exorbitantly expensive or not available. As is the case with ELAM students, the focus was on selecting medical students from nontraditional backgrounds because it was believed that they would be more likely to return to their home communities on graduation.

The essence of the new programs is a hands-on form of medical training. The community itself becomes the "laboratory" for the training, with extensive work carried out by students in the various popular clinics, diagnostic centers, and technology and rehabilitation clinics. Between the two programs (in Cuba and Venezuela), almost 50,000 doctors were being trained in 2011. Students are taught alongside a professor (the vast majority of whom are Cuban) who is a specialist in *medicina general integral* (comprehensive general medicine). Significantly, most of these medical mentors already possess experience abroad and are familiar with conditions in the developing world. The practicum assumes far more importance in this new approach, as the student learns in the consulting room alongside the doctor and in the polyclinic. The central idea is to produce physicians who will be engaged with the community, will emphasize preventive medicine, will be prepared to work wherever they are needed, and will always place community needs before individual ones (Alvelo Pérez 2010). Clearly, this constitutes the professional formation of a radically different form of medical practitioner.

The impact of Cuban medical personnel was great in Venezuela, where the national Medical Federation was displeased with the new approach of the Cuban physicians, their ethic of hard work, their ability to provide care in chronically poor neighborhoods, and their low salaries. With the advent of a new wave every year of Venezuelan medical graduates, it is clear that there will be major tensions over the model of public health to be implemented.

One notable Cuban medical initiative has been the attention given to East Timor and other small countries in the southwestern Pacific. The initial contact dates from 2003 with East Timor, followed by ties with Kiribati, Nauru, Vanuatu, Tuvalu, and the Solomon Islands between 2006 and 2008. As Tim Anderson reported, "By 2008 there were around 350 Cuban health workers in the region, with 870 East Timorese and more than 100 Melanesians and Micronesians engaged in medical training" (Anderson 2010, 77). The first cohort of eighteen Timorese have now graduated as medical doctors following studies in Cuba (with their training being completed back home). It is worth pointing out that as late as 2002, there were only forty-seven physicians in that country.

The Cuban role in East Timor (and increasingly in the southwestern Pacific) has been multifaceted. In the first instance, it represents the major component of public health care delivery in the country. By 2008, there were some 300 Cuban health workers, and their role had been extremely important since their arrival in East Timor: more than 2.7 million consultations had taken place, and an estimated 11,400 lives had been saved because of their medical interventions (Anderson 2010, 82). Cuba is also training 658 Timorese medical students in Cuba, with a further 186 in Timor (Araújo 2009, 1). The first contingent of interns graduated in August 2010, with a total of more than 800 expected to have graduated by 2014. In other words, they will produce an astonishing seventeen times the number of physicians who were working in their country as late as 2002. There is no indication to date that this program will be curtailed or reduced by Havana.

One of the fundamental purposes of Cuban medical internationalism in 2010 was to provide the basics for recipient countries to train and replace Cuban personnel—in other words, to help them help themselves. In the case of East Timor, this can be seen in the Faculty of Medicine, established in 2005 in the National University with the support of Cuban medical professors. Until this point, Timorese students had either been trained in Cuba or in small groups by Cuban physicians working at local hospitals and district health centers, somewhat along the lines of the NPFML program noted above. Increasingly, students from the region will be trained locally instead of traveling to Cuba. Cuban medical personnel will also gradually withdraw as the need for their cooperation decreases and their role as physicians and educators is filled by Timorese—who in turn will be able to use their Faculty of Medicine to train medical students from several South Pacific islands. The multiplier effect of medical personnel is thus the goal, with the intention of gradually reducing the number of Cubans as local practitioners fill the vacuum.

As noted earlier, the first *internacionalista* medical experience came in the wake of a major earthquake in Chile in 1960. Given Cuba's rich tradition of responses to natural disasters, which is deeply rooted in the Cuban medical psyche, and with the creation of the Henry Reeve Contingent, it is most likely that Cuba will maintain its pattern of sending emergency missions abroad. This commitment to employ Cuba's medical prowess to serve people facing major challenges can be seen most clearly in the commitment to Haiti, in response to the January 2010 earthquake and a 2010–2011 cholera outbreak.

In both cases, Cuban medical personnel took the lead despite the international media ignoring their contribution. Within twenty-four hours of the earthquake, the first group of trauma specialists of the Henry Reeve Contingent arrived to support the work being carried out by the hundreds of Cubans and ELAM-trained Haitian graduates already working on the island. Cuban medical personnel had in fact been working in Haiti since the devastation of Hurricane Georges in 1998, when about 500 arrived to help there; there were still some 340 working there at the time of the earthquake. Indeed, by 2007, Cuban medical personnel were already treating almost 75 percent of the Haitian population, with corresponding decreases on a large scale of infant and maternal mortality rates (Kirk and Kirk 2010). In the case of the cholera outbreak, Cuban medical staff treated some 40 percent of the victims throughout the country.

After the worst of the earthquake emergency was over, Cuba volunteered to provide the principal support for the restructuring of the public health care system in Haiti, supported by Venezuela and Brazil. The outbreak of cholera in October 2010 posed a fresh challenge to the Cuban medical personnel, who were soon joined by reinforcements, both Cuban and ELAM graduates (from twenty-three countries). By the end of 2010, there were 1,398 members of the Cuban-led medical team, of whom 61 percent were working actively in cholera-affected areas. They had established sixty-six cholera treatment centers, treated 56,967 patients, and had a mortality rate of 0.48 percent, significantly lower than the national average (Gorry 2011; Somarriba López 2011).

MEDICAL INTERNATIONALISM IN THE FACE OF THE *LINEAMIENTOS*

In November 2010, the Communist Party of Cuba published the *Lineamientos de la política económica y social*, a thirty-two-page discussion document on the suggested plans for the restructuring of Cuba's political economy. In terms of medical internationalism, there were several key areas where government proposals might have a major impact on this policy. From a Western capitalist perspective, it would be normal to expect that, in times of financial belt-tightening, "frills" such as medical assistance abroad would be among the first cuts to be made. In the case of Cuba, this has not been necessarily so, for reasons analyzed below; in essence, it comes down to balancing a mixture of five decades of successful humanitarian solidarity with stark financial challenges. Also to be added into the analysis are factors such as the immense diplomatic value of Cuba's medical internationalism, the financial opportunities it provides to medical personnel frustrated by the inverted social pyramid in Cuba with its corresponding poor financial remuneration, the process of socialization according to which Cuban medical personnel see this as a rite of passage, and the commercial value for the Cuban state resulting from the impact of having 40,000 working abroad.

In terms of market potential for Cuban medical internationalism and the sale of pharmaceutical products, this is clearly articulated in the *Lineamientos*. Number 74, for instance, notes the desire to create a strategy for market development in terms of exporting medical services and pharmaceutical products. In terms of the latter commercial interest, it is not widely known just how advanced (or how profitable) the Cuban biotechnology industry is. The *polo científico* in Havana, where thousands of scientists work in some fifty-two research institutions, has produced valuable pharmaceutical products for export—as well as 83 percent of the medicines consumed in Cuba.

As of 2010, Cuba was producing some thirty-eight pharmaceutical products exported to forty countries (Reuters 2010). A few examples will help to illustrate this. Over 120 million doses of a hepatitis B vaccine have been exported in recent years. Vaccines against meningitis B and meningitis C, leptospirosis, and typhoid fever have long been established and exported to many developing countries. Cutting-edge work on cancer and AIDS vaccines has resulted in successful trials and may soon be commercialized. The medication known as Nimotuzumab has been used in clinical trials in twenty-five countries and has shown an ability to significantly reduce tumor sizes in patients suffering from brain and esophageal cancer. After fifteen years of research into its ability to stop tumor growth, Vidatox (based on properties of the blue scorpion) has been recently launched. Particularly promising is Herberprot-B, an invaluable find for diabetics suffering from foot ulcers (who otherwise would face amputation). In addition, two Cuban pest control products, Griselesf and Bactivec, are widely used in Africa to control the breeding of mosquitoes and thereby reduce mortality rates from dengue, malaria, and other transmittable diseases.

Significantly, transfer technology of these products has resulted, with factories in China and Argentina now producing them and several others to be opened in another six countries. Likewise, Cuba and Brazil are producing a meningitis vaccine, mainly for distribution in Africa. Finally, Cuban scientists have initiated memoranda of understanding with Syria, established joint operations in India, China, Vietnam, Iran, and Brazil, and set up agreements for further research with the governments of Algeria and Belarus. In all these cases, a combination of commercial potential and solidarity (because the pharmaceutical products are sold at substantially lower prices than those charged by transnational drug corporations) can be seen. The potential for the export of pharmaceutical products is enormous, particularly if the United States drops the economic embargo against the island. Cuba has already been extremely active in the developing and underdeveloped world, but the largest potential market is Europe and, ultimately, the United States. The sale of over $300 million of pharmaceutical products in 2009 (placing it in second place behind nickel as Cuba's most valuable exported products) illustrates this potential (Grogg 2010).

The export of Cuban professional services—particularly those in the medical and educational fields—has been generously supported by Venezuela, where some $6.6 billion in payments for professional services were disbursed in 2008. The official figures for 2009 in terms of the exportation of goods and professional services (mainly medical services) was $11.171 billion, while Reuters (2010) reported $9.9 billion resulting mainly from the contribution of medical personnel abroad. In 2010, there were approximately 39,000 Cubans working in Venezuela, of whom some 30,000 are in the health care field—roughly 75 percent of the total of Cuban medical personnel working abroad (Romero 2010, 110). There is little doubt that, as long as financial support is provided to Cuba by Venezuela in return for these professional services, Cuban medical services will continue at this rate. Once again, commercial logic, combined with a medical humanitarian spirit, has proved to be a successful model.

Cuban medical cooperation is currently being provided around the globe and in a variety of different formats. These include subsidies that Venezuela provides to Cuba for medical services in countries that belong to ALBA as well as to Haiti, where there are a dozen "triangulation cooperation" agreements from countries that pay the expenses of Cuban staff there. Norway, for example, pledged $885,000 to Cuba for supplies and medicines just ten days after the 2010 earthquake. Sub-Saharan countries typically provide a nominal contribution to Havana, while at the opposite end of the scale, Qatar and Kuwait pay full costs for the supply of Cuban medical personnel in their hospitals.

The *Lineamientos* have two clauses with a direct bearing on this situation, stressing the need to seek financial self-sufficiency while also repeating Cuba's ongoing internationalist solidarity. Article 104 emphasizes the need to seek, where possible, at least compensation for medical services rendered abroad. It is significant that the sections of the document dealing with health care in Cuba emphasize the same two basic elements: a sound financial footing and the need for humanitarian medical collaboration. This approach will be employed in the field of medical internationalism, with solidarity and economic efficiency being key goals.

CONCLUDING THOUGHTS

For over five decades, Cuba has shown a remarkably consistent record of medical collaboration with nations around the world. Significantly, in good times and bad, humanitarian needs have always been seen as more important than basic financial considerations. Under the government of Raúl Castro, the need for financial stability and sound economic planning has become of paramount importance, and at first glance there would appear to be an impossible gulf between the long-standing humanitarian tradition of the Cuban Revolution and the current financial exigency. Yet a study of events since he assumed power in 2006 shows clearly that, while all efforts will be made to cover costs of these ambitious programs, international cooperation will not be affected to any great degree. Instead, as recent practice has shown, it will remain more or less constant, ultimately diversifying in new directions.

A few examples help to illustrate this phenomenon. In the past years, the size of the Cuban medical brigade in Mozambique has been increased from 130 to 160. In June 2010, a new eye clinic was established in Botswana. Eleven Cuban medical school professors arrived in Ghana to teach in Tamale University. Early in 2010, thirty-one Cuban doctors arrived to work in Rwanda on a project financed by the government of South Africa. In Pisco, Peru, there are now three contingents of medical personnel. They had originally arrived after an earthquake in 2007, but their emergency mission has evolved into the staffing of community clinics. There has been an increase in the production of biotechnology products in joint ventures in India and China. Cuba has initiated a program of mosquito and malaria control in Ghana. In Tanzania, Malawi, Congo, and Ethiopia, sales of medical products by the Cuban company Labiofam have increased sharply in the past year. Mobile clinics have been set up in the south of Belize. Argentina has seen the rapid development of ophthalmology clinics staffed by Cuban personnel since 2005 (with over 30,000 patients treated). Likewise, the vision restoration program *Operación Milagro* (Operation Miracle) has increased its role in Jamaica (where a new ophthalmology clinic was opened in Kingston in 2010), and some 61,000 Jamaicans had been treated. In May 2011, sixteen Cuban nurses joined thirty-five others in Jamaica following the signing of a bilateral agreement. In February 2011, Cuban medical personnel initiated a new program for patients with diabetes in Algeria. In the summer of 2011, Cuba initiated the coordination of an eight-nation project to carry out research and to control the spread of dengue. Many of these projects do not provide any financial gain for the Cuban economy but are nevertheless pursued at the request of the host government and with the support of Havana.

There are several loose threads that need to be considered in seeking to appreciate the future path of this complex reality. It is clear that Cuba has no plans to expand its ambitious program abroad in any major fashion. At the same time, it is important to recognize that for the foreseeable future, it will not make any major reductions in its medical cooperation. Indeed, the Cuban medical presence in the ALBA nations, where Cuban medical personnel are subsidized by the Venezuelan government, will probably continue to grow.

Operación Milagro, for instance, continues to flourish. Funded by Venezuela and employing Cuban ophthalmology personnel, it has restored sight to over 2 million people since its inauguration in 2005. By September 2011, for example, some 600,000 patients had been operated on by Cuban doctors at twenty eye clinics in Bolivia. Of these, approximately 500,000 were Bolivians, the remainder being from Argentina, Brazil, Peru, and Paraguay who had traveled to clinics on the Bolivian border (*Granma* 2011). *Operación Milagro* will likely emerge largely unscathed from any considered cuts.

In addition, Cuba had sent in 2009 a medical brigade of 213 people to Bolivia in the *Brigada Moto Méndez* to undertake a nationwide survey of health needs there. In all, the Cuban mission visited over 3 million homes, making an inventory of people with physical and mental challenges and their needs (Elizalde 2010). Similar fact-finding health missions were also undertaken in Venezuela and Ecuador, and other similar public health initiatives are probable.

The Henry Reeve Contingent will also continue its exceptional program of relief in natural emergencies around the globe. Likewise, the Cuban role in Haiti will remain strong because of Cuba's contribution since 1998 and the trilateral financial support from a number of countries. Supported by Brazil and Venezuela, Cuba has already made a commitment to restructure Haiti's public health system and will undoubtedly maintain a large presence.

While there are no plans to develop large-scale medical faculties, it would not be surprising to see the development of the "hands-on" medical training now being employed by Cuba in several countries, such as Gambia, East Timor, and, of course, Venezuela. The first 8,000 students of *Medicina Integral Comunitaria* graduated in Venezuela in 2011, following their training by Cuban medical school teachers. Until the graduation of 50,000 in Venezuela (with a similar number in Cuba), Cuban medical faculty will remain fully engaged in this project. In East Timor, the Faculty of Medicine at the National University established by Cuba in 2005 will continue to broaden the intake of students from other South Pacific nations. During this rapid increase of medical training, the Cuban medical profile will understandably increase in the region. That said, when the mission is completed, the number of Cuban personnel will move elsewhere, leaving public health responsibilities to the local staff.

In sum, despite the many economic challenges facing the government of Raúl Castro, medical internationalism remains a major priority of the Cuban government, which views it as both a long-term investment and a necessary obligation, with a tradition stretching back to 1960. Medical cooperation abroad also brings in a substantial amount of funding—some of which is used to subsidize medical cooperation in poor, underdeveloped countries. It opens the door for the sale of Cuban pharmaceutical and surgical goods, and this has risen remarkably in recent years. In August 2011, Ecuadorean President Rafael Correa announced that his country would prioritize the purchase of Cuban medical products over those produced abroad. In all, $1.3 billion would be spent on pharmaceutical goods: they would first try to source them from local producers (but after that would look to Cuba) before seeking medicines from transnational companies. It is likely that this trend will continue to rise dramatically both through joint ventures with other developing countries and through direct exports. The quality of Cuban medical products is well known, and if the U.S. embargo is ever lifted, biotechnology will become crucially important for the Cuban economy. It is also a significant part of the profoundly rooted essence of Cuban foreign policy. Moreover, it enhances Cuba's international image, winning much goodwill in international fora. Indeed, so important is this fifty-two-year-old program that it is enshrined in the preamble of the Cuban Constitution.

Raúl Castro, presented as the quintessential pragmatist, desperate to balance the financial books in Cuba at a crucial stage in its development, has said little about medical internationalism. But he is hardly blind to the traditions and the international prestige that it has brought, the badly needed hard currency from Venezuela, or the massive needs in the developing world. In his February 2010 speech to the summit of the Latin American and Caribbean Community in Cancún, he spoke about Cuba's commitment to support the Haitian population. This speech in many ways can be taken as a symbolic declaration of the broad sweep of Cuba's program of medical internationalism:

> The solidarity of the Cuban people did not arrive in Haiti with the 2010 earthquake. It has been present for over a decade . . . can assure you that the modest efforts of Cuban medical cooperation will remain in Haiti for however many years it is needed, providing that the Government of Haiti wants this to continue. . . . Our country is the victim of a harsh blockade, and has little to spare. Quite the contrary—we are short of everything. However we are prepared to share our poverty with those nations that have even less, and especially today the country in our continent which needs it more than anybody. (Castro 2010a)

One way or another, Cuban medical internationalism is here to stay.

NOTES

From "Cuban Medical Internationalism under Raúl Castro," in *Rethinking the Cuban Revolution Nationally and Regionally: Politics, Culture and Identity*, ed. Par Kumaraswami, published by Wiley-Blackwell, 2012. Reprinted by permission of the publisher.

Funding for this research project came from the Social Sciences and Humanities Research Council of Canada. I would also like to thank Emily Kirk, a doctoral student at the University of Nottingham, for her editorial assistance.

REFERENCES

Agencia de Informacíon Nacional. 2010. "Cuba Has Trained over 8,000 Physicians from 54 Nations." August 9. http://www.granma.cubaweb.cu/2010/08/nacional/artic05.html (accessed August 18, 2010).

———. 2011. "Over 700 Haitian Physicians Graduated from Cuba's Caribbean School of Medicine." July 7. http://www.cubanews.ain.cu/2011/0707Over-Haitian-Physicians-Graduated-from-Cuba-Caribbean-School-of-Medicine.htm (accessed October 7, 2011).

Álvarez, L. E. 2010. "Leonid Kuchma: Unos mostraron lástima, pero Cuba nos ayudó." *Juventud Rebelde*, March 29. http://www.juventudrebelde.cu/internacionales/2010-03-29/leonid-kuchma-unos-mostraron-lastima-pero-cuba-nos-ayudo/ (accessed October 8, 2011).

Alvelo Pérez, D. R. 2010. "Estrategia para el desarrollo de competencias didácticas en profesores del Nuevo Programa de Formacíon de Médicos." March 27. http://www.portalesmedicos.com/publicaciones.articles/2088/1/Estrategia-parael-desarrollo-de-competencias-didacticas-en-profesores-del-Nuevo-Programa-de-Formacion-de-Medicos.html (accessed September 15, 2010).

Anderson, T. 2010. "Cuban Health Cooperation in Timor Leste and the South West Pacific." In *The Reality of Aid: Special Report on South-South Cooperation 2010*. Quezon City: IBON Books.

Araújo, R. M. de. 2009. "A Snapshot of the Medical School, Faculty of Health Sciences, National University of Timor Lorosae, Democratic Republic of Timor-Leste." Unpublished conference paper presented to the Expert Group on Finalization of Regional Guidelines on Institutional Quality Assurance Mechanism for Undergraduate Medical Education, WHO/SEARO, New Delhi, October 8–9.

Castro, R. 2010a. "Intervencíon del General de Ejército Raúl Castro Ruz, Presidente del Consejo de Estado y de Ministros en la sesión plenaria de la Cumbre de América Latina y el Caribe, el 23 de febrero de 2010." http://cuba.cu/gobierno/rauldiscursos/2010/esp/r230210e.html (accessed October 25, 2010).

———. 2010b. "Raúl Castro no teme a la mentira ni se arrodilla ante presiones." Speech delivered at the closing of the IX Congress of the Union de Jóvenes Comunistas de Cuba, April 4. http://www.cubadebate.cu/opinion/2010/04/04/cuba-no-temea-la-mentira-ni-se-arodilla-ante-pre (accessed September 26, 2010).

Elizalde, R. M. 2010. "Fidel y la brigada 'Moto Méndez': 'La felicidad de hacer el bien.'" August 18. http://www.cubadebate.cu/noticias/2010/8/18/fidel-y-la-felicidad-de-hacer (accessed September 7, 2011).

Feinsilver, J. 2010. "Cuba's Health Politics: At Home and Abroad." Report prepared for the Council on Hemispheric Affairs, March. http://www.coha.org/cuba/%e2%80%99s-health-politics-at-home-and-abroad (accessed September 20, 2010).

Gorry, C. 2011. "Haiti One Year Later: Cuban Medical Team Draws on Experience and Partnerships." *MEDICC Review* 13, no. 1.

Granma. 2011. "Destaca Evo Morales ejemplo solidario de Operacíon Milagro." September 3. http://www.granma.cu/espanol/nuestra-america/3sept-Destaca%20Evo.html (accessed October 8, 2011).

Grogg, P. 2010. "Biotecnología cubana toca las puertas del Norte." Inter Press Service, October 22.

Kirk, E., and J. M. Kirk. 2010. "Uno de los secretos mejor guardados del mundo: La cooperacíon médica cubana en Haití." April 7. http://www.cubadebate.cu/especiales/2010/04/07/la-cooperacionmedica-cubana-en-haiti (accessed February 2, 2011).

Kirk, J., and M. Erisman. 2009. *Cuban Medical Internationalism: Origins, Evolution and Goals*. New York: Palgrave Macmillan.

MEDICC. 2013. "Cuba Graduates 10,000 Cuban and International Physicians." July 23. http://medicc.org/ns/?p=840 (accessed August 4, 2013).

Reuters. 2010. "Cuba Says Its Trade Figures Improving." November 1.

Romero, C. 2010. "South–South Cooperation between Venezuela and Cuba." In *South–South Cooperation: A Challenge to the Aid System*. Quezon City: IBON Books.

Somarriba López, L. 2011. "Cuba ha salvado miles de vidas haitianas y seguiremos haciéndolo." January 16. http://www.cubadebate.cu/opinion/2011/01/16/cuba-ha-salvado-milesde-vidas-haitinas (accessed February 4, 2011).

Chapter Twenty-Two

Cuban Public Diplomacy

Michael J. Bustamante and Julia E. Sweig

Attempts to link Venezuela and Cuba as part of a common left-wing axis diminish the significant differences in the ways each country promotes its image abroad and the success with which they accomplish their goals. Although Cuba and Venezuela employ many of the same tactics, the Cuban regime has proven more successful at playing the role of the victim and using this position as a way to increase its international legitimacy. In part, this is the result of Cuba's longer experience forging links of solidarity with the Third World and serving as a symbolic center of anti-U.S. resistance on the global stage. But it is also the result of circumstance. Cuba faces a U.S. economic embargo that, according to a Zogby International (2007) poll, is opposed by 56 percent of the U.S. population. Internationally, denouncements of the embargo policy have become routine at the European Union, the Ibero-American summits, and the UN General Assembly. As a result, the cash-strapped island's international health programs, even when they earn the Cuban regime hard currency, appear all the more unselfish. Cuba has also proven to be far more sophisticated at employing cultural products to support diverse political, diplomatic, and economic ends, many of which arguably serve a market-oriented purpose rather than a strictly anti-imperialist or antiglobalization agenda.

The term "public diplomacy" traditionally refers to ways in which governments use aid, cultural, media, and exchange programs to influence the ways in which they are seen by citizens in other countries (Schneider 2005; Tuch 1990). Yet as the Cuban and Venezuelan cases demonstrate, an analysis of public diplomacy cannot be divorced from an understanding of more traditional types of state-to-state interactions. Not only is the line between the two often blurry, but the nature of traditional commercial or political diplomacy can impact the extent to which public diplomacy efforts are received positively. The Cuban and Venezuelan examples also show that successful public diplomacy is not just about what governments do to promote themselves abroad but also about how they react to, take advantage of, or benefit from external circumstances and actors. These include the activities of citizens, nongovernmental organizations, and corporations that generate ideas, culture, art, and other messages with the power to influence public perceptions (Nye 2002, 2004; Ruggie 2004).

CUBA *SOLIDARIA*

Across the world, from Argentina to Andalucía, from small clubs of fifteen members to large conferences with hundreds of attendees, private citizens seem to voice their support for the

Cuban Revolution's achievements and criticize current U.S. sanctions against the island with surprising consistency. T-shirts stamped with Che Guevara's image are ubiquitous. The Pew Global Attitudes Project (2007) found that pluralities in Bolivia, Brazil, Argentina, Peru, and even Canada thought Fidel Castro had "been good for Cuba" (75–82). Leaving aside the argument about the "gains" of the Revolution and acknowledging that many of Cuba's achievements in health and education are impressive, it seems worth examining to what extent this apparently sizable reserve of international public support is the result of concrete public diplomacy efforts on the part of the Cuban government. To what extent is it simply an expression of resistance to an apparently ineffective and widely unpopular set of U.S. policies? And to what extent do the visions of such people and groups matter politically?

From the moment they took power, Cuba's political leaders have supported left-wing movements across the globe in an effort to internationalize their own socialist and anti-imperialist goals. By the end of the 1960s, however, Cuba's attempts to directly sponsor armed insurrections had by and large failed. Particularly in the Western Hemisphere, Cuba found itself isolated diplomatically, forbidden from participating in such bodies as the Organization of American States, and threatened by U.S. intervention. As a result, seeking ideological allies beyond traditional diplomatic ties became vital to sustaining the revolutionary government's legitimacy in Latin America and preserving some semblance of independence from its increasingly dominant financial patron: the Soviet Union. The Cuban Revolution perhaps possessed a unique potential to forge lasting people-to-people ties with citizens across the globe. An uncertain and at times tense diplomatic environment in the Western Hemisphere only reinforced the strategic value of this approach (Domínguez 1989, 111–83).

Officials in Havana designed several initiatives to help Cuba achieve these goals. One prominent program was the Organization for Solidarity with the Peoples of Asia, Africa, and Latin America. Cuban officials also spent much time and energy attempting to show off the benefits of their social and economic model to foreigners. To complement these efforts, Cuba works equally hard to promote its message in the international media. Between 1959 and 1961, the still-young revolutionary government founded *Prensa Latina* and *Radio Habana Cuba*, news outlets akin in purpose (though not influence) to the Voice of America or Radio Moscow. Today, *Prensa Latina* has correspondents in twenty-two countries around the world, its own active radio station with international broadcasts, and a website that promotes the Cuban state's anti-imperialist world vision (*Prensa Latina* n.d.). The advent of the Internet has likewise allowed *Granma* and other Cuban state publications to reach a broader international public while also supporting the efforts of "alternative" media outlets elsewhere in the hemisphere. It is in these venues that Cuba most often trumpets the successes of its universal health care and education systems, key selling points for the regime. Similarly, partnerships with sympathetic publishers, such as Australia-based Ocean Press, the only foreign publisher with an office on the island, help Cuba diffuse the political thought of the Revolution's past and present leaders to the broader global public.

But a far more important element of the Cuban government's public diplomacy strategy has been the U.S. embargo itself. Without it, the narrative of victimization repeated by regime officials would lack credibility, and because of it, Cuba has received an inordinate amount of sympathy, not necessarily for the entirety of its political and economic programs but for the government's defiance in the face of all U.S. efforts to undermine its stability. In a hemisphere with a long history of U.S. interventionism, resistance to the United States possesses intrinsic political value (McPherson 2003; Sweig 2006, 2–17). And for many citizens across the Americas and the world, Fidel Castro's perseverance after years of U.S. plots to unseat him merits tremendous respect despite the Cuban government's widely recognized and continued failure to abide by fundamental international norms concerning freedom of expression and other basic political rights. Over time, Cuba's symbolic importance as the anti-U.S. rebel par excellence has gradually superseded its role as a practical revolutionary example (Norris 2006). The fall of the Soviet Union, Cuba's subsequent abrupt economic collapse, the progressive strengthening of U.S. sanctions (in 1992 and 1996 as well as several occasions under the George W. Bush administration), and the Cuban government's ability to withstand all of these obstacles have only reinforced the gradual mythologizing of the island's resistance to U.S. aggression.

In the aftermath of the Cold War, the pressures of economic recession forced Cuba to make a number of notable concessions to the global marketplace. Yet as the 1990s progressed and new voices emerged protesting the inequalities, injustices, and other inadequacies of the Washington Consensus, Cuba came on a new framework through which to sell its ideas to the broader public: the antiglobalization movement. Even as they opened the country to limited foreign investment and established joint ventures with foreign tourist enterprises, the island's leaders also embraced the language of "sustainable development" and "biodiversity" (Perez Roque 2002). They also expressed solidarity with nascent political movements, such as the *Zapatistas* in Mexico and the *cocaleros* in Bolivia. (In the case of the *Zapatistas*, it is important to note that Cuban officials let it be known that they were not providing material assistance to the rebels.) They also joined the chorus of regional actors denouncing U.S.-led free trade agreements (Harris 2003). In this context, Cuba's education and medical programs have become increasingly important as symbols (and a material demonstration) of the island's commitment to grassroots solutions for global problems. Solidarity has taken on a new meaning, and Cuba's intransigence in the face of the capitalist West has garnered a fresh wave of sympathizers (Erikson 2004).

Following the attacks of September 11, 2001, the launch of the Bush administration's campaign against global terrorism introduced yet another paradigm through which Cuba would seek to gain grassroots support abroad. Members of Fidel Castro's government have long been the targets of violence and threats from their primarily Miami-based opponents, and on several occasions, even Cuban civilians have been attacked. The most well known terrorist act was the bombing of a Cubana Airlines jet in 1976, widely suspected to be the work of Luis Posada Carriles, a former agent of the Central Intelligence Agency. Posada has routinely evaded prolonged incarceration or capture. In the early 1980s, while being tried in a Venezuelan court for his involvement in the 1976 bombing, he escaped from prison. And despite being convicted by a Panamanian court in 2000 for his role in an assassination attempt against Fidel Castro, Posada received a pardon in 2004 from the country's outgoing president, Mireya Moscoso (Bardach 2002, 171–222; Bardach 2005).

Thus, when Posada reemerged on American soil in April 2005 and was charged only with minor immigration violations, Cuba was handed the perfect pretext to publicize its very own "war on terror." After more than two years in prison, Posada was set free when a Texas judge found that he had been unlawfully interrogated by immigration authorities. In Havana, the quest to bring Posada to justice for the full extent of his crimes remains a key rallying cry promoted amply through government media outlets and in international forums (*Cuba contra el Terror* n.d.).

Closely related to this initiative is Cuba's international campaign to free five men imprisoned in 1999 for their alleged roles in *Red Avispa*, a Cuban spy network in Miami. Cuban authorities claim that the so-called Cuban Five were only seeking to obtain information about the activities of exile organizations plotting terrorist attacks on Cuban soil, acts that have been historically sheltered and abetted by U.S. authorities. [Editors' note: See chapter 23 in this volume.] The Cuban government has responded fervently to their incarceration, mounting a broad international media campaign. The wives of the imprisoned have gone on international tours to seek support, and a documentary about the case (*Misión contra el Terror* [Mission against Terror] 2004) has been heavily circulated by Cuban diplomats and independent activists. Moreover, committees to free the Cuban Five have spread throughout the globe and have staged protests in prominent locations, including Capitol Hill in Washington, DC.

Cuba's war on terror, while a clear and obvious political maneuver, has generated a considerable amount of support and even started to reap concrete rewards in more traditional diplomatic forums. For example, at the Fifteenth Ibero-American Summit held in Salamanca, Spain, in October 2005, heads of state from across Latin America denounced Washington's "selective approach" to terrorism and issued a statement demanding that Posada be tried for his crimes (Giles 2005).

In sum, Cuba's approach to the concept of solidarity has proven to be enormously adaptable to changing times and situations. We can also see strong indications that Cuba's public diplomacy is often not proactive but reactive to external conditions. In the case of the U.S. embargo, the regime actively works to disseminate a narrative of its victimization through the promotion of antiembargo campaigns, documentaries, and literature (*Cuba vs. Bloqueo* n.d.), but the opportunity to do so is sustained by factors outside of Havana's direct control. Similarly, in the case of Luis Posada Carriles and the campaign to free the Cuban Five, an external series of events (the attacks of September 11, 2001, and the beginning of the Bush administration's war on terror) provided a rhetorical space in which prior disputes gained new international relevance.

On the surface, it may seem that the political impact of Cuban public diplomacy remains somewhat limited. After all, three members of the Cuban Five are still in prison, Posada Carriles has been released from custody, and the U.S. embargo persists. Yet solidarity has mattered for Cuba. Opposition to the embargo, even within the United States and, even more remarkably, in the halls of the U.S. Congress, has grown, and the policy is condemned almost unanimously by the UN General Assembly year after year (Bachelet 2007; Mack 2005).

Other results are more indirect but no less important. Cuba remains an important symbol for many members of left-of-center parties across the hemisphere. The seeds of Cuba's early outreach efforts have thus begun to bear fruit. By gradually cultivating deeply felt bonds of loyalty among many Latin Americans, the island's leadership has successfully secured a source of sympathy within foreign electorates and thereby inoculated itself from most attempts to pursue more hard-line anti-Castro policies. For example, the notable cooling of Mexican-Cuban relations under the presidency of Vicente Fox outraged members of Mexico's former ruling party, the *Partido Revolucionario Institucional*, who for years had prided themselves on their commitment to diplomatic noninterference and relatively close ties to Havana. The backlash was so large that incoming President Felipe Calderon quickly moved to indicate his government's willingness to reopen a bilateral dialogue with Cuban officials (Bachelet and Hall 2006). In this way, links of solidarity that Cuba has fostered over time, however superficial, do indeed affect political outcomes.

PUBLIC DIPLOMACY AND THE POLITICS OF CUBAN CULTURE

Cuba has also engaged in many cultural promotion activities that are not explicitly political in their orientation or purpose. Particularly in the post–Cold War era, the promotion abroad of Cuban art, music, and film has helped the island fulfill other, equally important national interests: the attraction of tourists and hard currency, for example. Although nearly all Cuban cultural products sold or promoted abroad are channeled through state-run cultural institutions, their connection to political actors and traditional foreign policy objectives often appears indirect (Fernandes 2006, 9–16). Such state involvement in the domestic culture industry is not in and of itself politically motivated. Throughout Europe, state-sponsored film subsidies have helped directors confront Hollywood's tremendous economic and cultural power (Cowen 2002, 73–82). Yet from the early days of the Revolution, Cuban cultural authorities have heavily screened the types of narratives and messages that artists on the island are able to disseminate. As a result, painters, filmmakers, and musicians alike are by now familiar with the general parameters of what is and what is not acceptable (Aguirre 2002; Fernandes 2006, 47–51).

Still, notwithstanding notable and continuing instances of censorship, the relationship between the government and the artistic sphere is not strictly hierarchical. In other words, the themes that artists treat and the ways in which they are treated are subject to more debate and flexibility than in other realms of Cuban domestic politics. Since the end of the Cold War, Cuba has been forced by economic necessity to turn to foreign partners to help sustain domestic cultural production, a process that has naturally exposed the island to the commercial demands of the international market. The rebirth of tourism as a strategic sector of the Cuban economy has also helped introduce themes that were previously frowned on by cultural officials. In many ways, then, what we are discussing here is the flow of cultural discourses in a globalized economy and how the Cuban state attempts to influence or benefit from their diffusion. Rather than simply mandating the type of art or music to be produced, Cuban cultural authorities help reframe and orient grassroots trends to match their own objectives (Fernandes 2006, 33–41; Moore 2006, 251–65).

One of the early noteworthy cultural movements to serve a public diplomacy purpose for the Cuban government was the rise of the *nueva trova* music style in the late 1960s. Observing the growing power of protest songs throughout the hemisphere (*nueva canción*), Cuban authorities recognized that music could play a powerful role in uniting domestic and international audiences alike in the fight against U.S. imperialism. Despite their origins as underground performers viewed suspiciously by the state, artists like Pablo Milanés and Silvio Rodríguez were eventually embraced by government institutions and came to be identified with the humanitarian and selfless spirit that ostensibly guided the Revolution, writing songs dedicated to Che Guevara and other noted revolutionary figures and events. Casa de las Americas, Cuba's well-known publisher and cultural house, created the *Centro de la Canción Protesta* (Center for Protest Song) to support their efforts (Fairley 1984; Moore 2006, 135–69). As Rina Benmayor (1981) put it, even when the lyrics were not overtly political, singers of the *nueva trova* were often "seen by foreign audiences as live representations of the Revolution, and their songs [were] heard as documents of the history, struggles, loves, problems, and dreams of that social process" (11). To this day, both Milanés and Rodríguez remain important cultural figures with domestic political influence, global artistic appeal, and sizable profit potential.

Film is another arena in which Cuba has obtained notable international success. Motivated by the idea that a revolution in politics simultaneously required a revolution in culture, Fidel Castro's fledgling government established the Cuban Institute of Cinematic Arts and Industry (ICAIC), just eighty-three days after it took power. ICAIC-sponsored productions have demonstrated a striking degree of sophistication and independence over the years. In particular, the films of noted director Tomas Gutierrez Alea have challenged simplified, triumphalist depictions of the Revolution and its progress. As uncomfortable as some Cuban officials may have felt about such films as *Memorias del Subdesarollo* (Memories of Underdevelopment 1968) (a nuanced account of a young man grappling to understand the rapid changes the Revolution has brought to Cuban society) or *La Muerte de un Burócrata* (Death of a Bureaucrat 1966) (a caustic critique of the Revolution's inefficient bureaucracies), the richness of these works as compared to the social realism of other Soviet bloc countries helped sell the idea that the Cuban Revolution, despite headlines about political prisoners and repression, could be seen as a vibrant, stimulating, and intellectually creative endeavor (Schroeder 2002).

In the post–Cold War era, ICAIC has been able to survive only by partnering with international distributors and at times foreign directors. As a result, Cuban film today, though still rich in social content, also incorporates narratives that fulfill a market purpose. In line with the island's revived role as a prime tourist destination, Cuba is once again portrayed as an alluring land of music, dance, sex, and darkly pigmented skin. Yet these portrayals are often coupled with story lines that reinforce political discourses supported by the Cuban state (Soles 2000).

Take, for example, the feature *Habana Blues* (2005), written and directed by Spaniard Benito Zambrano, coproduced by a Spanish company, and widely played in commercial theaters across Europe and Latin America but filmed on the island with ICAIC's full input and a cast of well-known Cuban actors. The film tells the story of Ruy and Tito, two best friends frustrated with Havana's poverty and determined to achieve international success as rock musicians. As they had hoped, Ruy and Tito are offered a contract from a foreign record company, but the agreement includes provisions stipulating that they will be marketed abroad as antigovernment exiles, an approach with apparently more commercial potential. The quintessential dilemma between "making it big" and "selling out" is thus reconfigured as a choice between global commercialism and patriotism. Ruy eventually sides with his country and decides to stay behind. While the screenplay's frank portrayal of the problems Cubans face each day is revealing, the film's pulsating rhythms, sexually suggestive dancing, and romanticized depiction of Cuba's cultural underground reinforce common stereotypes of the island's exotic appeal and depict Cuba as a commodity to be consumed by tourist dollars. Of course, each of these narratives serves the public diplomacy interests of the Cuban state. In the end, Cuba is both a grassroots ideal that Ruy cannot abandon and a land that foreigners should visit as an escape (Del Pozo 2005).

With such active international participation and broad commercial success (most Cuban films typically travel on the international film festival circuit), *Habana Blues* (2005) stretches the definitions of "Cuban cinema." While the film may have been conceived by a foreigner, because it was produced in consultation with Cuban cultural officials at ICAIC and (more important) because it participates in creating a distinctive imaginary of contemporary Cuba, it is relevant to a discussion of Cuban public diplomacy. In fact, it is precisely this interaction of public and private actors that makes the film an apt example of the complex sources of public diplomacy in the globalized world.

Other contemporary Cuban films possess similar dualities. The critically acclaimed *La Vida Es Silbar* (Life Is to Whistle 1998), for example, confronts the alienation that many Cubans feel in an economically deprived country struggling to find itself in the post–Cold War wreckage. In the end, the film's various characters reconcile themselves to their pasts, and their faith in Cuba's future is restored. Yet at the same time, the film employs tropes of Afro-Cuban spirituality that have become highly marketable to international audiences as signs of Cuba's "otherness" (Fernandes 2006, 61–71).

Recent trends in Cuban music demonstrate many of the same contradictions and subtleties. The Buena Vista Social Club (1997), a Ry Cooder project that reunited long-forgotten musicians of traditional Cuban *son*, sold millions of records internationally in the 1990s, won a Grammy Award, and generated numerous spin-off albums. As the owner of the copyrights on each of the disc's tracks, *Editora Musical de Cuba*, a government-owned publishing company, has benefitted financially from direct sales of the disc abroad. Yet the government has arguably gained more from the project's perpetuation of discourses and imagery that drive the tourist industry. An integral part of Buena Vista's success stems from the ways in which the disc as well as the subsequent documentary directed by Wim Wenders (*Buena Vista Social Club* 1999) "represent Cuba as a nostalgic fantasy that has been preserved intact from the 1950s" (Fernandes 2006, 94). It is no casual coincidence, then, that in almost every café on Old Havana's tourist-friendly Obispo Street, small music groups dutifully replay the album's most well-known songs. In fact, the international orientation of the project was so important that the group did not give its first public performance in Cuba until 2000, a full four years after the initial recording was made (Neustadt 2002; *New York Times* 2000).

Less well known is the rise of Cuban rap music during the same period that Buena Vista achieved its success. As Sujatha Fernandes explored in her book *Cuba Represent!* (2006), rappers on the island generally fall into two categories. Commercial rappers, like the members of the hugely popular group Orishas (the members of which now reside in Europe), tend to portray Cuba as an exotic land of dance, rum, cigars, and sexuality, the ideal hedonistic tourist getaway, while shying away from explicitly political themes. The relationship of the group Orishas to the Cuban state is perplexing. With origins in the influential underground group Amenaza, Orishas formed in Paris when two of Amenaza's members were permitted to travel to France on an educational exchange trip and joined forces with other expatriate Cuban musicians. While the group has continued to reside abroad, signing major record deals, collaborating on film projects from across the world, and undoubtedly amassing a fortune from touring and disc sales, they have performed in Cuba, sampled one of the Buena Vista Social Club's most well-known songs, and even, according to their website, met personally with Fidel Castro. They continue to be promoted by the Cuban press as legitimate representatives of Cuban youth culture abroad. Yet although nationalistic displays of the Cuban flag form an integral part of their act, they have generally refrained from overt political activity and have even collaborated with popular Cuban American rapper and outspoken Fidel Castro critic Pitbull (Fernández 2005; Orishas n.d.).

On the other hand, more politicized groups, such as Anónimo Consejo and Obsesión, popular internationally via grassroots networks, echo the Cuban government's critiques of materialism, globalization, and the United States. Many of these noncommercial groups, however, have also pushed the domestic envelope, boldly inserting racial issues into public discourse and suggesting that Cuba's leaders are complicit in the growing inequalities emerging in their own society as the island is slowly inserted into the global economy. Nonetheless, as Fernandes (2006, 85–134) detailed, Cuban cultural institutions have proven to be quite effective at co-opting and containing these critiques at an acceptable level.

Cuba's government has clearly benefited internationally from the spread of certain cultural phenomena. While some of the island's cultural promotion activities took direct cues from Soviet precedents (e.g., both the Soviet Union and Cuba heavily promoted their respective national ballets abroad, and Cuba continues to do so), Cuba was and remains unique among communist nations in the degree to which it has successfully mobilized more popular art forms (Gould-Davies 2003; Nye 2004, 74). Yet analyzing Cuban cultural politics as public diplomacy presents a number of unique challenges. It remains unclear how and to what extent the symmetries between the island's cultural, economic, and foreign policy needs are coordinated across governing institutions. While different branches of the island's government receive guidance from the central organs of the Cuban Communist Party, tacit understandings also are likely to influence the criteria that cultural authorities use when assessing their approaches to the arts. On the other hand, the government is not all-powerful, especially when confronting the demands of the international market and the increasing pace at which artists themselves have pushed the thematic agenda in recent years. Nonetheless, whether by virtue of conscious manipulation, luck, or a bit of both, Cuba has successfully managed these competing imperatives in ways that both boost the government's reputation abroad and sustain primary sources of income. And despite their strong criticisms of Cuban society, films like *La Vida es Silbar* or the music of Obsesión indirectly reinforce the power of the state by suggesting that the ideals of the Cuban Revolution are constantly evolving but never entirely irrelevant.

SUCCESSES, FAILURES, AND THE SEARCH FOR SOFT POWER

If we define public diplomacy as the quest to build symbolic capital on the world stage, both Venezuela and Cuba have achieved noteworthy levels of success. Officials also frequently describe public diplomacy as an effort to build "soft power," a term coined by Joseph Nye (2004) to denote "the ability to get what you want through attraction rather than coercion or payments" (x). While Nye's work has focused largely on projections of U.S. power, Cuba demonstrates the concept's validity as clearly as any other example. With little military or economic might, especially after the disappearance of Soviet subsidies, Cuba's diplomatic successes in recent years are almost wholly attributable to the island's soft power—the gradual but persistent branding and projection of a series of intertwined discourses generating sympathy for Cuba's culture, social achievements, and revolutionary mystique. In public, Cuban officials might resist the implication that their exchange programs, humanitarian aid efforts, or cultural activities are designed to help the island accumulate "power" of any kind on the world stage. Such a suggestion undermines the carefully constructed narrative of victimization so central to the regime's public identity. However, Cuban leaders are also clearly cognizant that public diplomacy is a fundamental source of international legitimacy and influence, both of which are crucial to the preservation of the government's power at home.

Cuban and Venezuelan foreign aid programs also elucidate one of the most insightful elements of Nye's theory—namely, that the line between hard and soft power is rarely clear. The ability to provide foreign aid ultimately stems from economic resources and can therefore be considered a form of hard power. Yet Venezuelan and Cuban aid programs, marketed as more than just humanitarian gestures, are deployed to reinforce an association of each government with anti-imperialism, Third World solidarity, and social justice, thereby enhancing each country's national prestige on the global stage. A tool of hard power is thus used to pursue soft power. Conversely, in Cuba's case, elements of soft power—film and music—sustain narratives that help Cuba earn sizable quantities of cash, a form of "hard power."

When compared to the United States, another distinguishing characteristic of Cuban and Venezuelan public diplomacy is that many of the same tactics, tools, and messages used to promote each country's interests abroad are equally popular as promotional tools at home. While an average U.S. citizen has little knowledge, for example, of the activities of USAID or may be unexposed to the Voice of America, Cuban and Venezuelan officials aggressively market their social achievements, cultural products, and narratives of revolutionary solidarity in pursuit of domestic as well as international support. Tensions do exist, however. Frustrated with the quality of health care and without a public forum to voice their concerns, Cubans may privately object to the thousands of doctors being sent abroad by authorities on international missions.

Cuban public diplomacy is far from uniformly successful. The 2003 incarceration of seventy-five independent journalists elicited outrage internationally and motivated many longtime supporters of the regime to speak out in opposition to the government's repressive actions. Cuba's sustained material and human assistance programs, combined with its geopolitical success at defying the United States, may have helped the island's government earn enough clout to serve on the new UN Human Rights Council as well as its predecessor, the UN Commission on Human Rights. Yet the island's own deplorable human rights record is still regularly examined—not just by the United States but also by independent organizations, other countries, the European Union, the United Nations, and, of course, the Cuban American community.

Still, in a period where basic democratic practices remain a litmus test of a country's acceptance in the international community, it is remarkable that Cuba's one-party government continues to be seen as a trusted and valued partner in many international arenas and institutions, including the United Nations, UNESCO, the World Health Organization, the Non-Aligned Movement, and others. In the end, Cuba's public diplomacy, indeed its soft power, has been instrumental in helping Havana wield a degree of international influence far out of proportion to the size and relative strategic importance of the country.

NOTE

From Michael J. Bustamante and Julia E. Sweig, "Buena Vista Solidarity and Cuban Public Diplomacy," *Annals of the American Academy of Political and Social Science* 616, no.1 (2008): 223–56. Reprinted by permission of the publisher.

REFERENCES

Aguirre, Benigno. 2002. "Social Control in Cuba." *Latin American Politics and Society* 44, no. 2: 67–98.

Bachelet, Pablo. 2007. "Polar Opposites United against Cuba Policy." *Miami Herald*, February 5.

Bachelet, Pablo, and Kevin G. Hall. 2006. "Calderon to Set New Path, Redefine Relations with U.S." *Miami Herald*, November 15.

Bardach, Anne Louise. 2002. *Cuba Confidential: Love and Vengeance in Miami and Havana*. New York: Random House.

———. 2005. "Our Man's in Miami: Patriot or Terrorist?" *Washington Post*, April 17.

Benmayor, Rina. 1981. "La 'Nueva Trova': New Cuban Song." *Latin American Music Review* 2, no. 1: 11–44.

Buena Vista Social Club. 1997. CD. New York: Nonesuch Records.

———. 1999. DVD, directed by Wim Wenders. Berlin: Road Movies.

Cowen, Tyler. 2002. *Creative Destruction: How Globalization Is Changing the World's Cultures*. Princeton, NJ: Princeton University Press.

Cuba contra el Terror. n.d. http://www.cubacontraelterror.cubasi.cu.

Cuba vs. Bloqueo. n.d. http://www.cubavsbloqueo.cu.

Del Pozo, Diego. 2005. "Review of *Habana Blues*, Dir. Benito Zambrano." *Chasqui* 34, no. 2: 201.

Domínguez, Jorge I. 1989. *To Make a World Safe for Revolution: Cuba's Foreign Policy*. Cambridge, MA: Harvard University Press.

Erikson, Daniel P. 2004. "Castro and Latin America: A Second Wind?" *World Policy Journal* 21, no. 2: 32–40.

Fairley, Jan. 1984. "La Nueva Canción Latinoamericana." *Bulletin of Latin American Research* 3, no. 2: 107–15.

Fernandes, Sujatha. 2006. *Cuba Represent! Cuban Arts, State Power, and the Making of New Revolutionary Cultures*. Durham, NC: Duke University Press.

Fernández, Enrique. 2005. "From Afar, Orishas Carry Cuba's New Vibe. *Miami Herald*, October 28.

Giles, Ciaran. 2005. "Iberoamerican Ministers Urge End to U.S. Blockade of Cuba." Associated Press, October 13.

Gould-Davies, Nigel. 2003. "The Logic of Soviet Cultural Diplomacy." *Diplomatic History* 27, no. 2: 193–214.

Habana Blues. 2005. DVD. Directed by Benito Zambrano. Sevilla: Maestranza Films; Havana: ICAIC.

Harris, Richard L. 2003. "Popular Resistance to Globalization and Neoliberalism in Latin America." *Journal of Developing Societies* 19, nos. 2–3: 365–426.

La Muerte de un Burócrata [Death of a Bureaucrat]. 1966. DVD. Directed by Tomas Gutierrez Alea. Havana: ICAIC.

La Vida Es Silbar [Life Is to Whistle]. 1998. DVD. Directed by Fernando Perez. Havana: ICAIC, Madrid: Wanda Films.

Mack, Lauren. 2005. "U.N.: U.S. End Cuban Embargo." United Press International, November 8.

McPherson, Alan. 2003. *Yankee No! Anti-Americanism in U.S.-Latin American Relations.* Cambridge, MA: Harvard University Press.

Memorias del Subdesarollo [Memories of Underdevelopment]. 1968. DVD. Directed by Tomas Gutierrez Alea. Havana: ICAIC.

Misión Contra el Terror [Mission against Terror]. 2004. DVD. Directed by Bernie Dwyer and Roberto Ruiz. Havana: Canal Educativo de Cuba.

Moore, Robin. 2006. *Music and Revolution: Cultural Change in Socialist Cuba.* Berkeley: University of California Press.

Neustadt, Robert. 2002. "Buena Vista Social Club vs. La Charanga Habanera: The Politics of Cuban Rhythm." *Journal of Popular Music Studies* 14, no. 2: 139–62.

New York Times. 2000. "Buena Vista Social Club, Little Known in Cuba, Is Glad to Be Home." August 13.

Norris, Michelle. 2006. "Cuba's Castro an Inspiration, Not a Role Model." *All Things Considered*, National Public Radio, September 15.

Nye, Joseph, Jr. 2002. *The Paradox of American Power: Why the World's Only Superpower Can't Go It Alone.* Oxford: Oxford University Press.

———. 2004. *Soft Power: The Means to Success in World Politics.* New York: Public Affairs.

Orishas. n.d. "Biografia." http://www.orishasthebest.com/lndex2.html.

Perez Roque, Felipe. 2002. Speech given at the Global Summit on Sustainable Development, Johannesburg, South Africa, September 3.

Pew Global Attitudes Project. 2007. "Global Opinion Trends 2002–2007: A Rising Tide Lifts Mood in the Developing World." July 24. http://www.pewglobal.orglreports/display.php?ReportiD=257.

Prensa Latina. n.d. "Quienes Somos." http://www.prensalatina.com.mx/Section.asp?Section=WHO&language=ES.

Ruggie, J. G. 2004. "Reconstituting the Global Public Domain: Issues, Actors, and Practices." *European Journal of International Relations* 10, no. 4: 499–531.

Schneider, William, Jr. 2005. *The Schneider Report: A National Model of Strategic Communication.* New York: Cosima Reports.

Schroeder, Paul A. 2002. *Tomás Gutierrez Alea: Dialectics of a Filmmaker.* New York: Routledge.

Soles, Diane. 2000. "The Cuban Film Industry: Between a Rock and a Hard Place." In *Cuba Transitions at the Millennium*, edited by Eloise Linger and John Cotman, 123–35. Largo, MD: International Development Publications.

Sweig, Julia. 2006. *Friendly Fire: Losing Friends and Making Enemies in the Anti-American Century.* New York: Public Affairs.

Tuch, Hans. 1990. *Communicating with the World.* New York: Palgrave Macmillan.

Zogby International. 2007. "Poll on U.S. Familiarity with Latin America and Its Leaders." http://www.zogby.com/news/readnews.dbm?ID=1347

Chapter Twenty-Three

The Cuban Five and the U.S. War against Terror

Saul Landau

In September 1998, agents of the Federal Bureau of Investigation (FBI) in Miami arrested eighteen Cubans. Miami newspapers identified them as part of *Red Avispa*, or the Wasp Network of Cuban intelligence agents. Most of them pled to benign charges and served short sentences or fled back to Cuba. However, the U.S. attorney charged the five Cuban men who pled "not guilty" with twenty-six counts of violating U.S. laws, twenty-four of which were relatively minor and technical offenses, such as the use of false names and failure to register as foreign agents. None of the charges involved violence in the United States, the use of weapons, or property damage. The two remaining charges, conspiracy to commit espionage and conspiracy to commit murder, were not minor.

At the 2001 trial, it became clear that Cuban intelligence had sent the "Cuban Five" to the United States as a kind of early warning system to stop a wave of violence against Cubans and foreign tourists on the island. The attacks had been orchestrated by a network of terrorist groups drawn from the Florida Cuban exile community. The perpetrators whom Cuba suspected had long and bloody records.

For example, in 1978, right-wing exiles murdered Eulalio Negrin, a New Jersey–based Cuban exile who favored reconciliation with Havana. On April 28, 1979, Cuban exile hit men murdered Carlos Muñiz in San Juan, Puerto Rico, because he favored reconciliation and had started a travel agency arranging for charter flights to Cuba. On September 11, 1980, a Cuban exile gunman shot and killed Félix García, a Cuban UN diplomat, on a New York City street. Shortly afterward, the New York bomb squad defused a bomb that Cuban exiles had attached to the car of Cuba's UN chief of mission, Raúl Roa. Routinely, over five decades, Cuban authorities discovered periodic landings by armed exiles from Florida who came to the island to kill people and destroy property.

For over forty years, successive U.S. administrations had either supported or tacitly tolerated these activities and allowed the presence of most of the violent anti-Castro exile organizations in the United States. Some of the groups had received U.S. money and weapons. Numerous Cuban protests to the U.S. government and at the United Nations fell on deaf ears, though Cuba suffered significant casualties (more than 3,000 dead) and significant property destruction at the terrorists' hands. Indeed, the violent exiles held frequent fund-raisers in Miami to garner cash for their missions inside Cuba or their targeting of allegedly pro-Castro people in the United States. Their lives revolved around violence directed against Cuba. For each terrorist act they committed, they proudly assumed responsibility, which they then turned into a fund-raising technique. "You heard about what we did to the Cuban airliner right? You have a nice store here in Miami, and we could protect your store for a small contribution to our cause."

Following the demise of the Soviet Union and its Eastern European socialist bloc in the early 1990s, Cuba struggled to establish a viable tourist industry to earn foreign exchange. Some of the militant Cuban exiles in South Florida, to discourage foreigners from visiting the island, organized a campaign of violence to create a "free fire zone" in Cuba. Luis Posada Carriles, allegedly backed by his rich exile patrons in Miami, paid Salvadoran nationals posing as tourists to travel from Central America to Cuba, to plant bombs at leading tourist hotels, bars, restaurants, and clubs. Cuban authorities even discovered some of their bombs on tourist buses and at the airport.

The Salvadorans detonated bombs at the Sol Melia, Capri, and Nacional hotels. Dozens of people (mostly Cuban hotel and restaurant employees) were injured. A waiter at the popular Bodeguita del Medio was knocked out by a blast that also burned all his hair. The face of a Sol Melia hotel maid was pummeled with shrapnel. One bomb at the Hotel Copacabana killed Fabio di Celmo, an Italian tourist.

Otto René Rodríguez, one of the Salvadoran bombers, confessed to Cuban police after they caught him that Posada Carriles had masterminded his bombing plot, given him the material to make the bomb, and bought his round-trip ticket to Cuba from San Salvador. Posada Carriles paid him $1,000 plus a free tourist stay in Cuba—just for planting bombs. "Not a bad deal, huh?," said Otto René during an interview shown in the film *Will the Real Terrorist Please Stand Up?*

Five Cuban intelligence agents (part of a larger group called the Wasp Network) had been able to infiltrate several groups that Havana had designated as violent. They volunteered for their assignments, despite its inherent risks to their lives, with the intention of monitoring these groups from the inside in order to prevent future terrorist incidents. The U.S. government, however, charged that the Five were spies whose mission was to obtain U.S. military secrets. But the prosecutors marshaled no facts for their case. They relied instead on having an intimidated jury whose license plates were photographed in the court's parking lot so they could all be identified. Jury members were thus assured that an acquittal of the Five would result at best in the firebombing of their homes by militant anti-Castro exiles.

Beyond problems with an intimidated jury, the Five had to face the problem of an extremely hostile atmosphere in the trial's venue, Miami. After all, they admitted in court that as Cuban intelligence agents, their mission was to monitor and report to Cuba the planned activities of the exile terrorists. Under normal circumstances, judges would regularly permit a change of venue in light of the prejudicial nature of the publicity surrounding the trial and the community's history. But motions to change the venue were denied.

The trial exposed the hypocrisy of the U.S. government's claim to be fighting terrorism. When faced with charges against two Cuban exile terrorists, Orlando Bosch and Posada Carriles, the Justice Department faded away or was overruled by the president. The Central Intelligence Agency (CIA) and the FBI had compiled ample evidence about both men, which included their own boasts of committing terrorist acts and numerous documents that demonstrated their involvement in organizing the bombing of a Cuban civilian airliner. The Cuban plane exploded in midair in October 1976, killing all seventy-three people on board. Documents later declassified showed that the CIA had information even before the bombing that Bosch and Posada Carriles had planned the hit. In 1990, Bosch applied for legal residence in the United States. The Justice Department recommended that his application be denied, following an investigation that exposed Bosch's thirty-year history of criminality and terrorist actions, including the bombing of a Soviet freighter in Miami harbor. Its report concluded that "over the years he [Bosch] has been involved in terrorist attacks abroad and has advocated and been involved in bombings and sabotage." President George H. W. Bush, however, ignored the recommendation and official findings and granted legal residence to Bosch.

Posada Carriles had worked for the CIA in the 1960s and early 1970s. Toward the end of his tenure with the CIA, he became a high official in Venezuela's secret police, DISIP. Linked to extrajudicial murders and cases of torture, DISIP typically had intimidated judges who attempted to bring any of its agents to justice. Thus, when Venezuelan prosecutors accused Posada Carriles of masterminding the 1976 bombing of the Cuban airliner, it surprised no one that two courts declined to convict him. But prosecutors persisted, and he was still awaiting the determination of an appeals court when he "escaped" from a Venezuela prison in 1985—with a $50,000 bribe for the prison guards and warden. The warden actually escorted him out the front door. The bribe payer was Jorge Más Canosa, who directed Miami's Cuban American National Foundation.

In 1998, Posada Carriles admitted to two *New York Times* reporters, Anne Bardach and Larry Rohter, that he orchestrated a series of 1997 bombings in Havana. In 2000, a Panamanian court convicted Posada Carriles and three other Cuban exiles of "endangering public safety" by having several dozen pounds of C-4 explosives in his rental car, which he intended to detonate at a public gathering featuring Cuban President Fidel Castro at the University of Panama. Had the Panamanian police, tipped off by Cuban security officers, not prevented the explosion, it certainly would have killed Castro, along with the audience of hundreds of people, mostly students.

Despite CIA and FBI documentation about Posada Carriles's violence, he became the recipient of U.S. hospitality, like Bosch. After Panamanian President Mireya Moscoso pardoned the four Cuban exile terrorists on her last day in office, allegedly with a large payment made to her offshore bank account, Posada Carriles found his way to Miami. Although he was on an antiterrorist watch list that nominally barred him from entering the United States, his illegal presence in Little Havana became an open secret; U.S. marshals finally took him into custody but only after Posada Carriles called a televised press conference that made it impossible for U.S. officials to claim any longer that they had no knowledge of his whereabouts.

Venezuela immediately requested his extradition so that he could be tried for the prison escape and on the earlier charges of murder. The Justice Department refused the request, asserting that he would likely be tortured in Venezuela and could not receive a fair trial there. The Justice Department then charged him with the minor offense of having inappropriate immigration documents and lying on his immigration forms, crimes that could have led at worst to his deportation from the United States. At his El Paso, Texas, trial, U.S. prosecutors did show the jury evidence of Posada Carriles's terrorist activities, but they had charged him only with lying on his immigration forms, not with terrorism. The jury acquitted him.

Contrast Posada Carriles's and Bosch's treatment by U.S. authorities with the way the U.S. government dealt with the five Cubans whom they arrested without a struggle. They threw the Five into solitary confinement cells reserved as punishment for the most dangerous prisoners and held them there for seventeen months until the start of their trial, which lasted seven months.

In December 2001, in the wake of 9/11, they were sentenced to maximum prison terms: Gerardo Hernández received a double life sentence, Antonio Guerrero and Ramón Labañino were sentenced to life in prison, and Fernándo González and René González received sentences of nineteen and fifteen years, respectively.

The government separated the Five into maximum-security prisons (some of the worst in the United States), each hundreds of miles from the other, where three of them remain today.

(René González was released on parole in 2011 and was permitted to return to Cuba early in 2013. Fernándo González was released on parole in February 2014 and also was permitted to serve out his parole in Cuba.) Two have been denied visits from their wives in violation of U.S. laws and international norms. The Bush and Obama administrations rejected the validity of protests from Amnesty International and other human rights organizations about the "arbitrary arrests" and inhumane treatment of the Five.

THE LONG PURSUIT FOR JUSTICE

The Five immediately appealed their convictions and sentences to the Eleventh Circuit Court, which sits in Atlanta, Georgia. Nearly four years later, on August 9, 2005, a distinguished three-judge panel of the court reversed the convictions and sentences on the ground that the Five did not receive a fair trial in Miami. In a comprehensive ninety-three-page analysis of the trial's process and evidence, the judges found that the fundamental rights of the accused had been violated, and they ordered a new trial. Notably, for the first time in the history of American jurisprudence, a U.S. federal court acknowledged (on the basis of evidence produced by the defense) that terrorist actions emanating from Florida against Cuba had taken place. The court even cited Posada Carriles's activities and appropriately referred to him as a terrorist.

The decision stunned the Bush administration. A federal appellate court had declared that Miami—with hundreds of thousands of Cuban exiles who provided the margin of victory for George W. Bush in the 2000 presidential election—was a venue incapable of providing a fair forum for a trial of these five Cubans because of an atmosphere that was overtly hostile to the Cuban government and supportive of violence against it. Moreover, it found that the behavior of the U.S. government prosecutors, in making exaggerated and unfounded arguments to the twelve members of the jury who decided the case, reinforced the underlying prejudice, as did media reporting before and during the trial. A decade after the trial, evidence emerged that the government had paid journalists in Miami's press, television, and radio to report negative stories on the Five and on Cuba before and during the trial, thus providing a poisonous atmosphere that would infect the jury as well as the larger public. In 2012, lawyers for the Five cited this evidence in a new appeal to reverse the trial decision and called for the U.S. Supreme Court to nullify the jury's verdict.

The appeal panel's findings corroborated those of the UN Working Group on Arbitrary Detention, which had concluded that the deprivation of liberty of the Five was arbitrary. The UN Working Group also called on the U.S. government to remedy the situation.

The U.S. attorney general, Alberto Gonzales, who had been President Bush's White House counsel, responded by taking the unusual step of ordering prosecutors to file an appeal to the full twelve-judge panel of the Eleventh Circuit, asking the court to review the decision of the three-judge panel. Such an appeal is both rare and hardly ever successful, especially when all three judges are in agreement and express themselves with the kind of scholarly and lengthy opinion that the three-judge panel in Atlanta had issued. Yet a majority of the Eleventh Circuit judges agreed in October 2005 to review the panel's decision and then reinstated all of the convictions. Subsequent court rulings reduced the sentences for three of the five Cubans.

The seven-month duration of the Miami trial had made it the longest criminal trial in U.S. history until that time. More than seventy defense witnesses testified, including two retired U.S. generals, one retired admiral, and a former White House presidential adviser. The trial record consumed over 119 volumes of transcripts. In addition, there were fifteen volumes of pretrial testimony and argument. The defense introduced over 800 exhibits into evidence, some as long as forty pages. The twelve jurors, with the jury foreman openly expressing his dislike of Fidel Castro, returned verdicts of guilty on all twenty-six counts without asking a single question or requesting a rereading of any testimony, unusual in a trial of this length and complexity.

The two main charges against the Five turned on prosecution allegations ordinarily used in politically charged cases: conspiracy. A conspiracy is an agreement between two or more persons to commit a crime. The crime need not occur. Once such an agreement is established, the guilt of the accused is complete. All the prosecution need do is to demonstrate through circumstantial evidence that there must have been an agreement. In the absence of evidence that an actual crime had been committed, juries often infer agreement in political cases on the basis of the politics, minority status, or national identity of the accused. This is precisely why and how the conspiracy charge was used here. The first conspiracy charge alleged that three of the Five had agreed to commit espionage against the United States. The government argued from the outset that it did not need to prove espionage occurred but merely that there had been an agreement to commit espionage at an unspecified time in the future. The media were quick to refer to the Five as spies. However, the legal fact and actual truth was that this was a case not of spying but of an alleged agreement to spy. Thus relieved of the duty of proving actual espionage, the prosecutors set about convincing a Miami jury that these five Cuban men living in their midst must have had such an agreement.

In his opening statement to the jury, the prosecutor conceded that the Five had not possessed a single page of classified government information, even though the government had succeeded in obtaining over 20,000 pages of correspondence between the five defendants and people in Cuba. Moreover, that correspondence was reviewed by one of the highest-ranking intelligence officers in the Pentagon. General James Clapper testified that he could not recall seeing any national defense information among the papers. The law requires the presence of national defense information in order to prove the crime of espionage.

The prosecution relied chiefly on the fact that one of the Five, Antonio Guerrero, worked in a metal shop on the Boca Chica navy training base in South Florida. The base was completely open to the public and even had a special viewing area set aside to allow people to take photographs of planes on the runways. Guerrero had never applied for a security clearance, had no access to restricted areas, and had never tried to enter any. Indeed, while the FBI had him under surveillance for two years before the arrests, there was no testimony from any of the agents about a single act of wrongdoing on his part.

Far from providing damning evidence for the prosecution, the documents seized from the defendants were used by the defense because they demonstrated the noncriminal nature of Guerrero's activity at the base. His objective was to "discover and report in a timely manner the information or indications that denote the preparation of a military aggression against Cuba" on the basis of "what he could see" by observing "open public activities." The information, visible to any member of the public, included the comings and goings of aircraft. Surveillance also discovered that he had clipped articles from the local newspaper that reported on the military units stationed there. Former high-ranking U.S. military and security officials testified that Cuba presents no military threat to the United States, that there is no useful military information that could be obtained from Boca Chica, and that Cuba's interest in obtaining the kind of information presented at trial was "to find out whether indeed we are preparing to attack them."

Information that is generally available to the public cannot form the basis of an espionage prosecution. In his trial testimony, General Clapper agreed: "Open source intelligence is not espionage." Nonetheless, the prosecution repeated in three separate arguments that the five

Cubans were in this country "for the purpose of destroying the United States." The jury, swayed more by passion and fear than by the law and evidence, convicted all five defendants of the charge on the basis of this fraudulent prosecution assertion.

The second conspiracy charge was added seven months after the first. It alleged that one of the Five, Gerardo Hernández, conspired with other nonindicted Cuban officials to shoot down two aircraft flown by Cuban exiles from Miami as they entered Cuban airspace. The planes had been intercepted by the Cuban air force, which killed the four crewmen. The prosecution conceded that it had no evidence regarding any alleged agreement between Hernández and Cuban officials to shoot down planes or to determine where and how they were to be shot down. In consequence, the law's requirement that an agreement be proven beyond a reasonable doubt was not satisfied. The government subsequently filed papers in which it proposed to modify the accusation because it faced an "insurmountable obstacle" in proving the charge against Hernández. The court of appeals rejected the government's request, the doubtful charge remained, and the jury convicted him on that count.

The case of the Five stands out as a historic episode in American jurisprudence. It is similar to the Nixon administration's attempt to use the court to muzzle the *New York Times* and the *Washington Post* when the newspapers sought to publish the *Pentagon Papers*, which exposed the lies supporting the Vietnam War and the failed U.S. policy. The United States did not prosecute the Five because they violated American law or harmed the United States. They languish in prison because they attempted to expose those who actually did hurt U.S. global credibility by committing terrorist acts, which broke U.S. and international laws. Through their infiltration of the terror network, which continues to exist in Florida, the Cuban Five demonstrated the hypocrisy of America's proclaimed opposition to international terrorism.

Bosch no longer remains alive to conspire against Cuba. In 2014, Posada Carriles still lived in Miami and routinely received awards for his "heroic" efforts to destroy the Cuban Revolution, efforts he formally denies while accepting the honors.

Three of the Five remain in prison. Two will be released over the next decades. Gerardo Hernández continues to live out his two life sentences in a high-security prison in the California desert.

In 2009, Cuba arrested Alan Gross, a contract agent working for a company that agreed to provide work for the U.S. Agency for International Development, as part of a covert program to destroy the Cuban Revolution by creating networks of U.S.-recruited "dissidents." Gross provided high-tech satellite and laptop equipment to establish an impenetrable and nontrackable signal that an internal network could use for messages among its members for communications with controllers in the United States. Gross was tried and convicted of crimes designed to subvert the Cuban government. He received a fifteen-year term. Cuba has offered to engage in independent humanitarian gestures with the U.S. government as a result of which Havana would free Gross and Washington would free the remaining four members of the Five.

Thus far, the White House has not responded.

Chapter Twenty-Four

Untying the Knot

The Possibility of a Respectful Dialogue between
Cuba and the United States

Philip Brenner and Soraya M. Castro Mariño

At the height of the October 1962 missile crisis, Soviet Premier Nikita Khrushchev sent an urgent letter to U.S. President John F. Kennedy. He implored the American leader to join him to stop pulling on the ends of a rope tied in "the knot of war, because the more the two of us pull, the tighter that knot will be pulled." The Cuban-U.S. relationship today is neither as tense nor as dangerous as the 1962 confrontation. But it remains fastened in a knot of hostility and antagonism that both countries have been tightening for more than fifty years and that benefits neither of them.

This chapter starts from the assumption that it is still possible for both countries to loosen the knot of hostility and replace it with positive ties. The authors appreciate that the legacy of conflict between Cuba and the United States, whose roots may extend to the political identity of each country, creates a significant obstacle to the development of a respectful dialogue. Those who disparage the tension between the two countries as a mere vestige of outdated Cold War thinking overlook how each actually perceives the other's current behavior as a threat. For example, Cuba's commitment to hemispheric relations based on equality—as expressed through its support for the *Alianza Bolivariana para los Pueblos de Nuestra América* (Bolivarian Alliance for the Peoples of Our America) an organization developed to counter hemispheric integration under U.S. leadership—does provide a serious challenge to the role that the United States perceives is central to its core interests. On the other hand, U.S. covert programs in Cuba that fund operatives who seek to encourage or facilitate regime change carry with them an implicit promise of U.S. military support if the activities lead to violence and at the least violate Cuba's sovereignty, the maintenance of which is a core interest.

At the same time, Cuba and the United States are bound together by their propinquity, by shared elements in both cultures, and by an intimacy born from close interaction and family connections. These positive factors, along with a changing domestic and international political environment, are the basis for the possibilities we identify for improving relations between Cuba and the United States. As a prelude to examining these possibilities, we provide an overview of U.S.-Cuban relations during the first five years of President Barack Obama's presidency.

FAILING TO OVERCOME THE BUSH LEGACY

President Obama took office with little obligation to Cuban-American hard-liners. [1] Yet inertia can have an insidious effect on policy. Legacies become obstacles even for a president committed to "change." He inherited from the Bush administration a set of regulations that severely limited travel even for Cuban Americans, several projects aimed at subverting the Cuban government, and a policy based on the precondition that Cuba had to move significantly in the direction of a U.S.-style capitalist democracy before a meaningful dialogue could occur. [2]

At the start of George W. Bush's presidency, there was little overt indication that his legacy would turn out to be such a hostile Cuba policy, even though he initially appointed virulent anti-Castro officials to Latin American policy posts throughout the government. In deference to European allies, he continued President Bill Clinton's practice of waiving implementation of Title III of the Helms-Burton Law, which would allow U.S. citizens to sue in a U.S. federal court persons who "traffic in property confiscated in Cuba." Then, in November 2001, in the wake of Hurricane Michelle's devastation, President Bush also relaxed some cumbersome provisions of the Trade Sanctions Reform and Export Enhancement Act of 2000 in order to facilitate the sale of some food and medical supplies to Cuba.

However, by 2003, the relentless pressure from hard-liners compelled President Bush to pursue a more hostile policy, the heart of which emerged in two reports produced by the Presidential Commission for Assistance to a Free Cuba (CAFC). The first CAFC set of recommendations, which the president accepted in May 2004 and then implemented with executive orders, were explicitly intended to create the "means by which the United States can help the Cuban people bring about an end to the Castro dictatorship." [3] While much of the report seemed to be the stuff of fantasy, Cuban officials could not dismiss the plans so easily. President Fidel Castro asserted plainly that the Bush administration's policy was an attempt "to intimidate, to terrorize this country and eventually to destroy its socio-economic system and independence." [4] Indeed, in July 2005, when Secretary of State Condoleezza Rice appointed a Cuban transition coordinator to head the newly created Cuban Transition Office, she remarked that the goal was "to accelerate the demise of Castro's tyranny." [5] The second CAFC report, issued in July 2006, similarly proposed active measures aimed at "hastening change in Cuba . . . not succession." [6]

The CAFC restrictions on travel and remittances were not popular in the Cuban American community, especially among those who had arrived most recently and had close relatives in Cuba whom they wanted to visit or support. A 2008 poll of Cuban Americans found that two-thirds of the respondents favored both "ending current restrictions on sending money to Cuba for Cuban Americans" and "ending current restrictions on travel to Cuba for Cuban Americans." [7] Senator Barack Obama (D-IL) smartly appealed to this discontent in 2008 by vowing to loosen the restrictions if he were elected president. When he fulfilled his pledge in April 2009, he attempted to portray the changed regulations as evidence of his willingness to respond to the demands of Latin American leaders that the United States end its hostile policy toward Cuba. But the hemispheric leaders at the 2009 Summit of the Americas appeared to interpret President Obama's move much as Cuban President Raúl Castro did: as merely fulfilling a campaign promise. [8]

Had President Obama truly desired to change U.S. policy toward Cuba, he could have justified a new policy on the basis of U.S. interests and relied on many domestic and international sources of support. On winning the election, he was greeted by a flurry of proposals from several ad hoc groups made up of former U.S. government officials and members of Congress, leading scholars, and prominent public intellectuals, several of whom had previously supported harsh measures against Cuba. They shared a consensus that the policy undermined U.S. interests in the Western Hemisphere and that the stable succession in Cuba has "challenged the effectiveness of a half century of U.S. economic sanctions," as a Council on Foreign Relations task force report declared.[9]

Indeed, the hostile U.S. policy against Cuba had virtually no international support. In October 2008—for the seventeenth year in a row—the UN General Assembly supported a resolution calling for the end of "the economic, commercial and financial embargo imposed by the United States of America against Cuba." The vote was 185–3 (the three votes against being cast by the United States, Israel, and Palau), with two abstentions. At a June 2009 General Assembly meeting of the Organization of American States, the United States needed to apply significant political pressure to gain a compromise resolution that paved the way for Cuba to return to the organization.[10]

Meanwhile, President Raúl Castro made clear several times that Cuba was willing to negotiate with the United States over all issues of concern. But he insisted, as he said in a December 2009 speech to the Cuban National Assembly, that engagement with the United States had to be "based on a respectful dialogue between equals, on any matter, without prejudice to our independence, sovereignty and self-determination."[11]

The Obama administration's limited actions disappointed many of those who sought to improve Cuban-U.S. relations. Still, during President Obama's first two years, there was an evident reduction in U.S. hostility toward Cuba in four areas:

- Cuban American travel and remittances: The president went beyond his promise as a candidate to loosen restrictions on travel and remittances for Cuban Americans. He abolished all restrictions on travel, permitted Cuban Americans to send unlimited funds to families, and broadened the definition of "family" to embrace aunts, uncles, and cousins.
- Migration talks: Following the 1995 migration accord between Cuba and the United States, the two governments agreed to hold meetings every six months to review the implementation of the accord and to discuss related matters. President Bush canceled the talks in 2003. The Obama administration renewed the meetings in July 2009 and sent Craig Kelly, the principal deputy assistant secretary of state for Western Hemisphere affairs, to the second meeting in Havana. He was the highest-ranking U.S. official to have visited the island in a decade.[12]
- Increased diplomatic contact: During the Bush administration, formal contact between the two governments was limited to brief meetings between the chief of each diplomatic mission (Interests Section) and a midlevel official. This changed early in 2009 when Ambassador Jorge Bolaños Suarez began to meet with Assistant Secretary of State for Western Hemisphere Affairs Thomas Shannon. (Cuba reciprocated with similar meetings in Havana.) In September, the United States sent Bisa Williams, a deputy assistant secretary of state for Western Hemisphere affairs, to Havana for discussions with Dagoberto Rodríguez, a Cuban vice minister of foreign relations.[13]
- People-to-people engagement: U.S. and Cuban officials opened discussions about the possibility of direct postal service between the two countries. Since 1963, mail sent from one country to the other has been routed through a third country, in part because the international treaty governing postal services requires mail to be carried on regularly scheduled airlines. Both countries viewed direct mail service as a way to facilitate communication between family members. The Obama administration also moved forward on other people-to-people efforts: it eased embargo regulations so that organizations such as the Smithsonian Institution could once again apply for travel licenses to take Americans on short educational trips to Cuba[14]; the State Department began, albeit slowly, to issue more visas

to Cuban scholars to do research in the United States; and the Treasury Department removed some restrictions on telecommunications companies doing business with Cuba.

As a contrast to the continuous hostility emanating from the Bush administration, the Obama administration's actions in these four areas might be seen as a fundamental shift in approach. In fact, the Democratic administration neither offered a new framework for policy nor overcame the Bush legacy. The essential continuities from the Bush administration, at least through mid-2014, were evident in four features of the Obama policy:

- Framework of reciprocity: During his second term, President Bill Clinton reframed Cuba policy in a way that facilitated change. He moved from "calibrated response"—a framework of reciprocity that tied any U.S. initiatives to reciprocal changes on Cuba's part—to a framework of "America's interests," shaping policy in terms of what best served the United States. This enabled his administration to expand opportunities for U.S. citizens to travel to Cuba without requiring that Cuba take steps to become a Western-style democracy. The Bush administration returned to reciprocity, and as of mid-2014, the Obama administration has maintained the reciprocity framework. For example, in 2012, President Obama said at the Summit of the Americas,

  > Since I came into office, we have made changes to our Cuba policy. . . . But the fact of the matter is, is that Cuba, unlike the other countries that are participating, has not yet moved to democracy. . . . I am hopeful that a transition begins to take place inside of Cuba. . . . We haven't gotten there yet. But . . . we recognize that there may be an opportunity in the coming years, as Cuba . . . starts loosening up some of the constraints within that country.[15]

- Disparaging Cuban reforms: The president's repeated statements about Cuba's lack of meaningful political change not only ignored major reforms on the island but also limited his freedom of action within a framework of reciprocity. Similarly, U.S. officials have denigrated the significant changes in the Cuban economy that have created considerable space for nonstate enterprises.[16] For example, in an interview with *Univision* after the Cuban Communist Party had approved the "Guidelines" for economic reform, President Obama said, "For us to have the kind of normal relations we have with other countries, we've got to see significant changes from the Cuban government and we just have not seen that yet. . . . The economic system there is still far too constrained."[17]

- State sponsors of terrorism list: Despite overwhelming evidence that Cuba was not a state sponsor of terrorism, the Obama administration continued to include Cuba on the State Department's list of state sponsors of terrorism. Even the authors of the 2012 report had difficulty in making the case for including Cuba, one of four countries still on the list. For example, they observed, "There was no indication that the Cuban government provided weapons or paramilitary training to terrorist groups."[18] As former ambassadors Carlos Alzugaray and Anthony Quainton have pointed out, a country on the list suffers from "draconian . . . provisions against banking transactions," which have "created problems for the United States with allies whose embassies and companies in Cuba have run into problems because of banking restrictions."[19] Of course, the rules also adversely affect Cuba's international commerce.

- Harmful covert programs: Since 2006, the United States has encouraged Cuban doctors serving abroad to give up their citizenship and emigrate to the United States. The *Wall Street Journal* reported that as of 2011, the Cuban Medical Professional Parole (CMPP) program had enticed nearly 1,600 of them.[20] The CMPP was one reason a planned U.S.-

Cuban cooperative project to help Haiti after the devastating 2010 earthquake failed. Cuba was concerned that the U.S. Agency for International Development (USAID) would use the project to recruit Cuban doctors, and USAID refused to provide assurances it would not do so.[21]

- USAID has been the lead agency in spending funds on covert programs that Cuba considers to be subversive. Although other options were available, USAID sought appropriations for its "democracy promotion" projects under authorization from the 1996 Helms-Burton Law, which has the explicit purpose of changing the regime in Cuba. Since President Obama took office, the United States has spent at least $20 million annually on these projects.[22] Until 2014, the most notorious project involved Alan P. Gross, a subcontractor for Development Alternatives International, a USAID contractor. Arrested in December 2009, Gross and the State Department claimed that he was in Cuba merely to provide the small Jewish community with telecommunications equipment that would enable its members to access the Internet without Cuban government interference. The Jewish community had not requested such assistance. In fact, what Gross provided was sophisticated satellite communications transmitters that included a subscriber identity module (SIM) card usually available only to the U.S. military or intelligence community. The SIM card could prevent detection of signals from the transmitters for a radius of 250 miles.[23] From the Cuban government's perspective, his mission was "to establish illegal and covert communications systems . . . intended to destabilize the existing order."[24] In April 2014, the Associated Press revealed a possible purpose for the network that Gross was creating. It reported that USAID had tried to establish a secret Twitter-like project for Cuba that could have been used to incite Cubans to join flash mobs of the sort that contributed to regime changes in Tunisia and Egypt.[25]

FACTORS PROPELLING A THAW

By 2011, U.S.-Cuban relations seemed to have become frozen again, as the Obama administration refused to meet publicly with Cuban officials because of Gross's incarceration. It had even suspended the migration talks in 2010. Meanwhile, Cuba pulled back its outstretched hand because of the continuing covert U.S. programs, U.S. refusal to remove Cuba from the terrorism list, U.S. unwillingness to consider pardoning or commuting the sentences of the "Cuban Five" (intelligence agents imprisoned for monitoring terrorists in the United States who had attacked Cuba),[26] and numerous unsubstantiated allegations by the United States against Cuba, such as the claim that it was involved in human trafficking.[27] Trade with the United States in 2010 dropped to $363 million from a high in 2008 of $711 million.[28]

In reality, the two countries found ways quietly to maintain and even increase contact over some matters of shared interest. U.S. and Cuban military representatives continued their monthly meetings, begun in 1997, about issues related to the fence line at the Guantánamo naval base. Technical experts from both countries participated in multilateral talks dealing with ecological and safety problems arising from deep-water oil drilling in the Gulf of Mexico and Florida Straits. In addition, for the first time in eleven years, the State Department granted visas to more than sixty Cuban scholars to attend the 2012 Latin American Studies Association conference in San Francisco, though it did deny visas to eleven prominent academics, including one of the authors of this chapter.[29]

Then, in 2013, several events and circumstances offered renewed expectations for improved relations. In January, Cuba began to implement a new law that enables most citizens to obtain passports, to leave the country for up to two years without an exit permit, and to return without forfeiting their property.[30] President Castro viewed this reform as fulfilling his commitment to deepen an irreversible process of normalization between Cubans and the diaspora.[31] The United States had highlighted Cuba's travel restrictions in attacking its human rights record.[32] From either perspective, the new law held out the possibility of being a game changer.

In May 2013, with the concurrence of the Justice Department, a federal judge permitted René González, one of the Cuban Five, to stay in Cuba permanently after he was allowed to travel there to attend memorial services for his father. He had been released on parole in 2011 after thirteen years of imprisonment but was forced to serve out his parole in the United States. Then, in June, Obama administration officials met with their Cuban counterparts to continue negotiations over direct mail service, and the State Department agreed to resume the semiannual migration talks with Cuba.[33] It was spurred to do so, in part, by the increased number of visa applications that resulted from Cuba's new migration law.[34]

Meanwhile, negotiations between the Colombian government and the country's largest insurgent organization, the Revolutionary Armed Forces of Colombia (FARC), made significant headway in Havana in 2013.[35] Aimed at ending the fifty-year-old Colombian civil war, the peace talks were made possible as a result of Cuban efforts in February 2012. The first meeting between the negotiators took place in Oslo, Norway, and the sessions then moved to Cuba in November 2012.[36] The United States has devoted billions of dollars to ending the war in Colombia, and successful negotiations improved the possibilities for a U.S.-Cuban rapprochement.

International Factors

Cuba's importance in the FARC-Colombian government negotiations suggests one international factor propelling a thaw in Cuban-U.S. relations: Cuba's stature in the Western Hemisphere. By 2009, all of the countries in the Western Hemisphere except the United States had established diplomatic relations with Cuba. In November 2008, it had become a full member of the Rio Group, an informal association of twenty-three regional countries that formalized itself in 2011 as the Community of Latin American and Caribbean States (CELAC). As Michael Erisman explains, "With 33 countries . . . representing roughly 600 million people, CELAC presented a major challenge to the U.S.-dominated Organization of American States as the major international organization for the region."[37] Notably, CELAC selected Cuba to cochair the organization for 2013–2014.

The growing isolation of the United States in the hemisphere was evident at the 2012 Summit of the Americas. Colombian President Juan Manuel Santos pointedly spoke on behalf of the region's leaders in asserting that there would be no summit in 2015 unless Cuba were invited to participate.[38] The significance of his remarks was clear to President Obama, who reportedly replaced his national security adviser for Latin America as a result of the meeting. The United States had been spending nearly $1 billion annually on aid to Colombia, and President Santos had solid credentials as a conservative and a former minister of national defense.

It may be possible that the Obama administration did not care if there were a 2015 summit because in 2013 it seemed to be focused on developing a new plan for relating to Latin America. As an aspect of the general shift in U.S. foreign policy toward Asia, U.S. officials began to highlight the U.S. interest in gaining observer status in the "Pacific Alliance"—a group of four countries: Chile, Colombia, Mexico and Peru—and linking the group to the Trans-Pacific Partnership, a free trade network.[39] Yet the United States has far too many interests in the region to turn a blind eye on all the other countries, especially with China's increasing investments in Latin America and Brazil's rise as the sixth-richest country in the world. As the White House itself highlighted in an April 2012 fact sheet, "The Western Hemisphere is the destination for approximately 42 percent of U.S. exports, more than any other region across the globe."[40] At some point, Cuba's stature in the region is likely to be a factor the United States takes into account.

Moreover, the United States continued to be isolated internationally outside the region because of its Cuba policy. This was evident once again in October 2013, when the UN General Assembly voted 188–2 (with three abstentions) to condemn the U.S. embargo. One year earlier, the European Union decided to engage Cuba in discussions about a new framework that could open the door to improved relations in the medium term by discarding the "common position" that had created significant tension.[41] Notably, in 2013, the European Union designated CELAC as its official counterpart for Latin America, replacing the Organization of American States.[42]

Domestic Factors

President Obama's relaxation of the embargo for Cuban American travel and remittances to the island appears to have been a smart political move. In 2012, he collected a greater proportion of the diaspora's vote in Florida than any previous Democrat had won.[43] At the same time, Joe Garcia (D-FL) won his election to represent the Twenty-Sixth Congressional District, replacing Congressman Lincoln Diaz-Balart (R-FL), an anti-Castro extremist. Garcia had called for a dialogue with Cuba.

The voting results in part reflect demographic changes in Florida's Cuban community. For the grandchildren of those who emigrated in the 1960s, overthrowing the Cuban government is an issue far less salient than it was for their elders. Cubans who arrived in the United States since 1995 have an interest in improved relations with the island so that they can easily maintain family ties and send remittances. Poll data indicate that two-thirds of these émigrés favor a dialogue with Cuba.[44]

While the so-called Cuba Lobby continues to have some influence—it spent more than $3 million on political campaigns from 2008 to 2012—its greatest influence appears to come from the fear that a few Cuban American legislators instill in executive branch officials.[45] For example, Senator Robert Menendez held up passage of President Obama's stimulus package in 2009 until he received a promise that he would be consulted on any changes in Cuba policy. But such power is illusory; it seems real only until a president is willing to counter it.

If President Obama or his successor did want to pursue a cooperative, respectful policy toward Cuba, there are interest groups that could provide political cover for such a policy. Several state chambers of commerce, the U.S. Chamber of Commerce, agribusiness groups, pharmaceutical companies, tourism industry organizations, and petrochemical firms have shown an increasing interest in doing business with Cuba, especially as economic updating on the island progresses. In short, domestic factors—the changing views of the Cuban American community and interest groups—could provide the necessary political space a president would need to engage Cuba in a dialogue.

ISSUES FOR DISCUSSION

Over the past fifty years, Cuba and the United States have had a succession of negotiations leading to expectations for rapprochement that have been shattered subsequently by new sources of conflict. This pattern has frustrated Cuban officials, some of whom have worked on

Cuban-U.S. relations for decades and still have foreign policy responsibilities. It also has made U.S. officials leery of sticking out their necks too far on the Cuba issue for fear that a setback will quickly change the atmosphere and create political problems for them.[46]

Analysts have offered several explanations for why Cuban-U.S. negotiations have failed to generate better relations. These include domestic Cuban politics and the way that Cuban leaders use the U.S. "threat" to stay in power,[47] domestic U.S. politics,[48] the asymmetry between the two countries,[49] and even the metaphors that each side uses to describe the relationship, metaphors that may contribute to misperceptions and mistrust.[50]

One factor rarely considered is the process by which Cuba and the United States reach agreements. In order for negotiations to act as a spur for continued good relations, they must function as confidence-building measures. As Johan Jørgen Holst explains, diplomatic negotiations may actually undermine trust because they can "include the concealment of facts" and "the manipulation of uncertainty," both of which breed distrust.[51] Above all, negotiators must engage each other with mutual respect in order for an agreement to serve as a stepping-stone to further talks.

Confidence building is a necessary element in creating the possibility for continued successful negotiations between Cuba and the United States because both maintain deep wells of distrust of the other. For this reason, direct negotiation rather than mediation is better suited to building trust because it requires the two parties to communicate only with each other and to resolve disagreements together. When two antagonistic parties are able to achieve agreements that satisfy each of their interests, the process of positive engagement itself may challenge firmly held beliefs about the implacability or unreasonableness of an opponent. Undermining those beliefs can begin to create space for empathy, which is essential in establishing mutual respect.[52]

Consider how the following four issues might be approached to engender confidence:

- Counterterrorism: Both countries have condemned international terrorism and have been the target of terrorists, and this should make cooperation against terrorism a natural goal for the two neighbors. But each has charged the other with harboring and supporting terrorists. The issue is more pressing for Cuba because there are groups in the United States that continue to plan terrorist actions against Cuba and because the United States identifies Cuba as a state sponsor of terrorism, triggering provisions in the USA PATRIOT Act that impair Cuba's interaction with international banks. Still, U.S. officials tend to fear that once they unilaterally relinquish a bargaining chip, such as Cuba's removal from the State Department's terrorism list, Cuba will take advantage of the situation and worse outcomes will emerge. In short, an important step would be for each country to express its underlying security needs and fears in a way that the other country will listen to it. For example, as a group of former government officials and scholars close to their governments recommended in a 2013 joint report, the two governments could "undertake visits by former U.S. military officers, ambassadors, and other national security officials for the purpose of helping each government appreciate more accurately the perceptions and analytical frameworks of the other government." Further, they should "acknowledge publicly any proposals submitted by either government aimed at improving security cooperation."[53] Notably, Cuba is party to thirteen international conventions and protocols relating to terrorism and has signed thirty-five bilateral agreements on legal assistance in this field with other states. Initial cooperation in this area could be directed to exchanging all judicial and police information about individuals or groups for which there is strong evidence that they may constitute an imminent danger to humanity.

- Orderly migration and trafficking in persons: Both countries have an interest in allowing orderly migration to occur, and both experienced unsettling episodes when there was disorder. It would thus benefit Cuba and the United States for both to acknowledge to each other that Cuba's new migration law might require an update of the 1994–1995 immigration accords and to use their semiannual meetings for that purpose. As a confidence-building measure, the United States should consider terminating the 1966 Cuban Adjustment Act. It acts as a powerful magnet because it provides Cubans with benefits that migrants from no other country receive, including a shortened path to U.S. citizenship. Migration discussions also could productively take up the issue of human trafficking. As noted, the United States has used this issue to level unfounded charges against Cuba, listing it as a "Tier 3" (worst offender) country in its *2012 Trafficking in Persons Report*. Were the United States willing to reevaluate its claim, such an action could lead to a positive attitudinal turning point for Cuba. In turn, the two countries could then cooperate in protecting the security of their borders, as they have done successfully in dealing with the problem of drug trafficking.
- Drug trafficking and related crimes: In its *2013 International Narcotics Control Strategy Report (INCSR)*, the State Department acknowledged that "Cuba maintained a significant level of cooperation with U.S. counternarcotics efforts" and that "bilateral cooperation in 2012 led to multiple at-sea interdictions." But the report also notes, "In 2011 the Cuban government presented the United States with a draft bilateral accord for counternarcotics cooperation, which is still under review. Structured appropriately, such an accord could advance the counternarcotics efforts undertaken by both countries."[54] In fact, according to Cuban officials whom we have interviewed, the United States has neither responded to the Cuban proposal nor explained what it means by "structured appropriately." Among other features, Cuba's proposed bilateral agreement would establish direct communication channels for exchanging real-time information and implementing joint actions. Such interactions could go beyond interdiction by including the reciprocal exchange of databases and information about ships, individuals, and groups involved in drug trafficking. It also could include bilateral cooperation in training and be expanded to matters of port security, customs and border control, and money laundering. In short, the *2013 INCSR* is a good first half step in that it acknowledges Cuba's cooperation, but real movement will come only when the two countries actually talk to each other about an accord.
- Environmental protection: Given that Cuba and the United States share ecosystems for several species, such as migratory birds, sea turtles, and manatees, they have a common interest in marine environmental protection. Discussion of this concern could begin with noncontroversial matters, such as a review of their 1977 fisheries agreement, which focuses on the demarcation of boundaries. These talks could be broadened to include environmental concerns about managing and limiting fishing in the region. A second issue could be coral reef protection. In turn, agreements about these problems could open ways to develop cooperative environmental and wildlife conservation projects between the United States and Cuba. In Johan Galtung's joint reconstruction approach for reconciliation, he suggests that when two opposing parties approach a project "shoulder to shoulder and mind to mind," they can begin to "build moral equality around positive acts."[55]

Similarly, both countries could benefit from cooperative projects related to the prediction of and protection from severe weather events, natural disasters, and the effects of climate change as well as the prevention of and recovery from human-made disasters, such as oil tanker spills and drilling explosions. But in both cases, the seeming noncontroversial objective of protecting human life and the environment runs headlong into controversy because of the U.S. embargo. Sanctions by the United States prevent Cuba from buying meteorological technology or safety equipment, even from a non-U.S. company, as long as 10 percent of a machine is manufactured in the United States or is based on U.S.-patented technology. Such rules potentially could harm the United States more than Cuba. For example, currents would carry the oil from a leak at a deep-water Cuban well to Florida's shores, not to Cuba's. Yet when the Spanish petroleum firm Repsol sought to use U.S.-made safety caps in 2012 for drilling in Cuban coastal waters, the Treasury Department denied it a license. Ultimately, the Treasury Department agreed to allow the Federal Emergency Management Administration to use or loan safety equipment on such rigs if there were a leak.

Challenges to the embargo by Cuban and U.S. scientists and oil companies could be a wedge that would break down the embargo on related environmental issues. For example, U.S. technology could enable Cuba to develop alternative energy sources—such as wind, solar, and biomass—that would enable it to diversify its dependency on a few suppliers of oil, give U.S. companies an additional market, and reduce Cuba's contribution to greenhouse gases. Both countries might work together, then, on training scientists and engineers in the Third World.

CONCLUSION : THE ART OF THE POSSIBLE

Curiously, "politics" has become a term of derision in both Washington and Havana, used by younger generations in discussing their leaders to imply that they are engaged in a form of manipulation, obfuscation, or self-serving gamesmanship. But an older, perhaps quaint, meaning of politics is that it is action intended to achieve the "possible." The four examples of possible Cuban-U.S. engagements we have highlighted do not directly address the legacy of hostility between the countries or even some pressing current concerns, such as the release of Alan Gross from a Cuban prison and the remaining members of the Cuban Five from U.S. prisons. They involve policies that make no sense, that serve neither country's interests, and that rational actors should be able to abandon easily.

Yet politics is the art of merely the possible precisely because it attempts to direct irrationally based behavior toward rationally based goals. The policies we highlighted are not so easily abandoned because it is so difficult for policymakers in both countries to act rationally when dealing with the other country. In order for them to serve the best interests of their own countries, they need to start with problems that can be solved feasibly and with a process that encourages further engagement. We are at a moment when the dynamics of global affairs and the domestic dynamics in each country provide a supportive environment for a respectful dialogue between Cuba and the United States. There are issues ripe for discussion between the two countries. Engagement is possible.

NOTES

This chapter is based on papers presented by the authors at the XI Workshop "Cuba in the Foreign Policy of the United States of America: Projections, Trends and Perspectives of Cuba-US Relations in the Context of the 2013–2017 Presidential Mandate," December 17 and 18, 2012, Center for International Policy Research, Institute of International Relations Raúl Roa García, Havana, Cuba. Philip Brenner appreciates the support he received from American University's Center for Latin American and Latino Studies to attend the workshop.

1. Obama's margin of victory in Florida—204,600 votes—was large enough that he virtually did not need any votes from Cuban Americans, though he received approximately 35 percent of the Cuban American vote, about 10 percent more than John Kerry received in the 2004 election. See Casey Woods, "Obama First Democrat to Win Florida's Hispanic Vote," *Miami Herald*, November 6, 2008.

2. For an elaboration of the Bush administration's policy toward Cuba, see Soraya M. Castro Mariño and Philip Brenner, "The George W. Bush–Castro Years," in *Fifty Years of Revolution: Perspectives on Cuba, the United States, and the World*, ed. Soraya M. Castro Mariño and Ronald W. Pruessen (Gainesville: University Press of Florida, 2012).

3. U.S. Commission for Assistance to a Free Cuba, *Report to the President, May 2004* (Washington, DC: U.S. Department of State, 2004), 2. Notably, chapter 1 of the report is titled "Hastening Cuba's Transition," http://pdf. usaid.gov/pdf_docs/PCAAB192.pdf (accessed August 25, 2013).

4. Fidel Castro Ruz, "Proclamation by an Adversary of the U.S. Government," May 14, 2004, http://www.cuba. cu/gobierno/discursos/2004/ing/f140504i.html (official translation).

5. U.S. Department of State Archive, "Announcement of Cuba Transition Coordinator Caleb McCarry," July 28, 2005, http://2001-2009.state.gov/secretary/rm/2005/50346.htm (accessed September 3, 2013).

6. Condoleezza Rice and Carlos Gutiérrez, *Report to the President: Commission for Assistance to a Free Cuba*, July 2006, 5, http://www.cfr.org/content/publications/attachments/68166.pdf (accessed August 25, 2013).

7. Institute for Public Opinion Research, Florida International University, "2008 Cuba/U.S. Transition Poll," December 11, 2008, 7–8, http://www2.fiu.edu/~ipor/cuba-t/ (accessed September 1, 2013).

8. Ginger Thompson and Alexei Barrionuevo, "Rising Expectations on Cuba Follow Obama," *New York Times*, April 19, 2009; Associated Press, "World Briefing/The Americas; Cuba: Raúl Castro Belittles U.S. Overture," *New York Times*, April 30, 2009.

9. Charlene Barshefsky and James T. Hill, chairs, *U.S.-Latin America Relations: A New Direction for a New Reality*, Independent Task Force Report No. 60 (New York: Council on Foreign Relations, May 2008), 72, http:// www.cfr.org/mexico/us-latin-america-relations/p16279 (accessed September 1, 2013). Similarly, in an early December letter to President-elect Obama, several major business groups—including the U.S. Chamber of Commerce and the Business Roundtable—urged "the complete removal of all trade and travel restrictions on Cuba" (Doug Palmer, "Business Urges Obama to Loosen Cuba Embargo," Reuters, December 4, 2008). See also Ernesto Zedillo and Thomas R. Pickering, *Rethinking U.S.-Latin American Relations: A Hemispheric Partnership for a Turbulent World* (Washington, DC: Brookings Institution Press, November 2008).

10. Ginger Thompson, "Imposing Conditions, O.A.S. Lifts Its Suspension of Cuba," *New York Times*, June 4, 2009. Within days of the meeting, Costa Rica and El Salvador became the last two countries in the hemisphere other than the United States to establish diplomatic relations with Cuba.

11. Raúl Castro Ruz, "No tenemos derecho a equivocarnos," Intervención del Presidente Raúl Castro en la Asamblea Nacional del Poder Popular, December 20, 2009, http://www.cubadebate.cu/opinion/2009/12/20/discurso-de-raul-castro-en-la-asamblea-nacional/ (accessed August 25, 2013).

12. Paul Haven, "US, Cuba Discuss Immigration Issues in Havana," Associated Press, February 19, 2010.

13. "US and Cuba in High-Level Talks," September 30, 2009, http://news.bbc.co.uk/2/hi/8281756.stm (accessed August 25, 2013).

14. The travel regulations were announced in mid-January 2011. In addition, any U.S. citizen was permitted to send money to a Cuban (other than members of the Communist Party or government) in limited amounts. See Ginger Thompson, "Restrictions on Travel to Cuba Are Eased," *New York Times*, January 15, 2011.

15. Barack Obama, "Remarks by President Obama and President Santos of Colombia in Joint Press Conference," Cartagena, Colombia, April 15, 2012, Office of the Press Secretary, The White House, http://www.whitehouse.gov/ the-press-office/2012/04/15/remarks-president-obama-and-president-santos-colombia-joint-press-confer (accessed September 3, 2013).

16. Julia E. Sweig and Michael J. Bustamante, "Cuba after Communism: The Economic Reforms That Are Transforming the Island," *Foreign Affairs*, July/August 2013; Richard E. Feinberg, *Soft Landing in Cuba? Emerging Entrepreneurs and Middle Classes* (Washington, DC: Brookings Institution Press, November 2013); Philip Peters, "Cuba's Entrepreneurs: Foundation of a New Private Sector," chapter 11 in this volume.

17. As quoted by EFE (Spanish news agency), "Obama Sees No 'Significant Changes' in Cuba," May 14, 2011, http://latino.foxnews.com/latino/politics/2011/05/14/obama-sees-significant-changes-cuba/ (accessed September 1, 2013).

18. U.S. Department of State, Bureau of Counterterrorism, *Country Reports on Terrorism 2012*, May 30, 2013, chapter 3, http://www.state.gov/j/ct/rls/crt/2012/209985.htm (accessed August 31, 2013).

19. Carlos Alzugaray and Anthony C. E. Quainton, "Cuban-U.S. Relations: The Terrorism Dimension," *Pensamiento Propio*, no. 34, July–December 2011, 76, 80.

20. Joel Millman, "New Prize in the Cold War: Cuban Doctors," *Wall Street Journal*, January 15, 2011.

21. H. Michael Erisman, "Brain Drain Politics: The Cuban Medical Professional Parole Programme," *International Journal of Cuban Studies* 4, nos. 3/4 (Autumn/Winter 2012): 277–79, 284–85. In contrast to other Cuban refugees who must reach the United States or a U.S. territory in order to apply for asylum, under the CMPP program Cuban doctors can apply for asylum at a U.S. embassy.

22. Fulton Armstrong, "Time to Clean Up U.S. Regime-Change Programs in Cuba," *Miami Herald*, December 26, 2011. Armstrong reports that in 2009, USAID spent $45 million on the covert programs.

23. Desmond Butler, "USAID Contractor Work in Cuba Detailed," Associated Press, February 12, 2012. The communications setup that Gross established would allow a Cuban enemy to communicate with operatives inside Cuba or allow subversive groups to communicate across the island if any of its members were within a few blocks of the equipment that Gross had donated to Jewish communities in three Cuban cities.

24. Josefina Vidal Ferreiro, "Press Conference," December 5, 2012, http://www.cubaminrex.cu/en/press-conference-josefina-vidal-ferreiro-head-united-states-division-cuban-chancery-international (accessed September 6, 2013).

25. Desmond Butler, Jack Gillum, and Alberto Arce, "U.S. Secretly Created 'Cuban Twitter' to Stir Unrest," Associated Press, April 3, 2014.

26. See Saul Landau, "The Cuban Five and the U.S. War against Terror," chapter 23 in this volume.

27. U.S. Department of State, *2012 Trafficking in Persons Report*, June 2012, 133–34, http://www.state.gov/documents/organization/192594.pdf (accessed September 3, 2012).

28. U.S. Census Bureau, "Trade in Goods with Cuba," http://www.census.gov/foreign-trade/balance/c2390.html (accessed September 5, 2013). The United States was Cuba's fifth-largest trading partner in 2008. See Reuters, "World Briefing/The Americas; Cuba: U.S. Trade Rises," *New York Times*, August 15, 2008.

29. Pamela Constable, "U.S. Grants Visa to Raúl Castro's Daughter but Denies Visit by Cuban Academics," *Washington Post*, May 18, 2012; Editorial, "The Refuseniks of Cuba," *Washington Post*, May 21, 2012.

30. Consejo de Estado, Decreto-Ley No. 302, Modificativo de la Ley No. 1312, "Ley de Migración" de 20 de Septiembre de 1976, *Gaceta Oficial de la República de Cuba*, October 16, 2012, 1357–87.

31. Raúl Castro Ruz, "Discurso pronunciado en el Séptimo Período Ordinario de Sesiones de la VII Legislatura de la Asamblea Nacional del Poder Popular," August 1, 2011, http://www.cubadebate.cu/raul-castro-ruz/2011/08/01/discurso-de-raul-en-laasamblea-nacional/ (accessed September 1, 2013).

32. U.S. Department of State, *Country Reports on Human Rights Practices for 2012*, April 19, 2013,http://www.state.gov/j/drl/rls/hrrpt/humanrightsreport/index.htm?year=2012&dlid=204441(accessed September 4, 2013).

33. Associated Press, "U.S., Cuba Agree to Resume Immigration Talks," *USA Today*, June 19, 2013, http://www.usatoday.com/story/news/world/2013/06/19/cuba-immigration-talks/2439915/ (accessed September 3, 2013).

34. Fabiola Santiago, "The Endless U.S.-Cuba Chess Game, *Miami Herald*, August 18, 2013. The United States granted 79 percent more tourist visas to Cubans in the first six months of 2013 compared to the same period in 2012.

35. Chris Kraul, "Colombia, FARC Rebels OK Land Deal: The Pact on Agrarian Reform, One of Six Points in a Possible Peace Accord, Gives the President a Boost," *Los Angeles Times*, May 27, 2013; Helen Murphy, "Colombia's FARC Talks at 'Critical' Stage, Government Negotiator Says," Reuters, September 3, 2013, http://www.reuters.com/article/2013/09/03/us-colombia-rebels-farc-idUSBRE9820VS20130903 (accessed September 5, 2013).

36. William Neuman, "Rebel Group in Colombia Announces Cease-Fire," *New York Times*, November 20, 2012, http://www.nytimes.com/2012/11/20/world/americas/colombia-rebels-announce-cease-fire.html(accessed September 5, 2012); Peter Beaumont, "Revealed: How Castro and Chavez Helped Colombia Peace Talks to Begin: Meetings in Havana Paved the Way for Negotiations with FARC in Oslo This Week on Ending the Long-Running Civil War," *The Observer* (U.K.), October 14, 2012.

37. H. Michael Erisman, "Raúlista Foreign Policy: A Macroperspective," chapter 18 in this volume.

38. Andrew Cawthorne and Brian Ellsworth, "Latin America Rebels against Obama over Cuba," Reuters, April 15, 2012, http://www.reuters.com/article/2012/04/15/us-americas-summit-idUSBRE83D0E220120415 (accessed September 4, 2012).

39. Philip Brenner and Eric Hershberg, "Washington's Asia-Pacific Response to a Changing Hemispheric Order," *Pensamiento Propio*, no. 39, January–June 2014.

40. The White House, "Fact Sheet: The U.S. Economic Relationship with the Western Hemisphere," Office of the Press Secretary, April 13, 2012, http://www.whitehouse.gov/the-press-office/2012/04/13/fact-sheet-us-economic-relationship-western-hemisphere (accessed September 5, 2013).

41. Joaquin Roy, "El fin de la Posición Común de la UE sobre Cuba," *El Nuevo Herald*, November 22, 2012, A23.

42. Council of the European Union, "EU-CELAC Action Plan 2013–2015," January 27, 2013, Press Release No. 5748/13, http://www.consilium.europa.eu/uedocs/cms_Data/docs/pressdata/EN/foraff/135043.pdf (accessed September 5, 2013).

43. Data from exit polls indicated that the president won between 40 percent (Reuters) and 49 percent (NBC/Pew) of the Cuban American vote in Florida.

44. Cuban Research Institute, *2011 Cuba Poll* (Miami: Florida International University, 2011); Peter Schechter and Jason Marczak, *US-Cuba: A New Public Survey Supports Policy Change* (Washington, DC: The Atlantic Council, February 2014); Jorge I. Domínguez, "Dialogues within and between Cuba and Its Diaspora," chapter 26 in this volume.

45. William M. LeoGrande, "The Cuba Lobby," *Foreign Policy*, April 11, 2013.

46. Soraya M. Castro Mariño, "Like Sisyphus' Stone: U.S.-Cuban Relations in the Aftermath of September 11, 2001," in *A Contemporary Cuba Reader: Reinventing the Revolution*, ed. Philip Brenner, Marguerite Rose Jiménez, John M. Kirk, and William M. LeoGrande (Lanham, MD: Rowman & Littlefield, 2008).

47. Jorge Domínguez, "Secrets of Castro's Staying Power," *Foreign Affairs*, Spring 1993.

48. Patrick J. Haney and Walt Vanderbush, "The Role of Ethnic Interest Groups in U.S. Foreign Policy: The Case of the Cuban American National Foundation," *International Studies Quarterly* 43, no. 2 (June 1999); Morris Morley and Chris McGillon, *Unfinished Business: America and Cuba after the Cold War, 1989–2001* (New York: Cambridge University Press, 2002), 11–21; LeoGrande, "The Cuba Lobby."

49. Lars Schoultz, *That Infernal Little Republic: The United States and the Cuban Revolution* (Chapel Hill: University of North Carolina Press, 2009).

50. Philip Brenner and Soraya Castro, "David and Gulliver: Fifty Years of Competing Metaphors in the Cuban-U.S. Relationship," *Diplomacy and Statecraft* 20 (June 2009).

51. Johan Jørgen Holst, "Confidence-Building Measures: A Conceptual Framework," *Survival* 25, no. 1 (1983): 2.

52. Ralph K. White, "Empathizing with Saddam Hussein," *Political Psychology* 12, no. 2 (1991); Ralph K. White, "Misperception and War," *Peace and Conflict: Journal of Peace Psychology* 10, no. 4 (2004).

53. Cuba-United States Academic Workshop (TACE), "Opportunities for U.S.-Cuban Relations: Working Paper," November 2012 (Buenos Aires: CRIES, 2013), 13, http://www.cries.org/wp-content/uploads/2013/06/tace-final-web.pdf (accessed September 6, 2013).

54. U.S. State Department, Bureau of International Narcotics and Law Enforcement Affairs, *2013 International Narcotics Control Strategy Report*, March 5, 2013, http://www.state.gov/j/inl/rls/nrcrpt/2013/vol1/204049.htm#Cuba (accessed September 5, 2013).

55. Johann Galtung, "After Violence, Reconstruction, Reconciliation and Resolution," in *Reconciliation, Justice and Coexistence*, ed. Mohammed Abu-Nimer (Lanham, MD: Lexington Books, 2001), 16.

Chapter Twenty-Five

Emigration and U.S.-Cuba Bilateral Relations

Antonio Aja Díaz

Although the Cold War has ended, confrontation between the United States and Cuba has continued, as has an absence of dialogue, persistent hostility on the part of several U.S. administrations, and resistance by the Cuban Revolution. Within this context, the tendency of emigration from the island to the north continued. In the contours of the bilateral relations between the two countries, migration talks have provided almost the only concrete channel of communication.

MAIN TENDENCIES IN CUBAN EMIGRATION TO THE UNITED STATES

From 1959 until today, the United States has been the main destination of emigrants from the island, and the United States has used this pattern as part of its hostile policy toward the Cuban Revolution in different eras and in accordance with the destabilization tactics of each.[1] A new such era began in 1989, with subdivisions covering the 1990s and the first decade of the twenty-first century. The unfolding of the "Special Period in Time of Peace" under the impact of the deep economic crisis besetting the country imbues the 1990s with a special role in the following analysis, particularly because of the role that relatives abroad began to play in Cuban daily life. Their role gained new dimensions with a perception that linked having such relatives with the possibility of economic help in confronting the crisis.

In the 1990s, the flow of migrants was characterized by a mix of permanent and temporary emigration as well as significant numbers of visitors to the island (estimated at more than 100,000 between 1995 and 1996 alone). Legal emigration remained low until early 1995, while illegal departures mushroomed. In just 1994, an estimated 40,000 people were involved in the latter process, successfully or not. The composition and motivation of the emigration during this decade was different from those of earlier waves. An economic component (including one of labor mobility) dominated alongside political factors and others, such as family reunification or lack of confidence that the social project of the Revolution would provide a way out of the crisis.

Since 1959, due to the politicized and ideological atmosphere surrounding the issue of Cuba-U.S. migration, the act of emigration was seen in Cuba as "abandoning the fatherland," and therefore it acquired levels of stigmatization in accord with the historical moment of revolutionary victory. The policies of both governments serve as influences that can stimulate or retard the migratory flow. They introduce elements of regulation and deregulation, and they even affect the practical means by which the emigrants carry out their journeys. In the United States, independently of the motivations of Cubans migrating to that country, these immigrants are seen as "fleeing political persecution," "escaping from communism," or "dissidents." Although these interpretations began to be questioned in the late 1990s, they remain essentially in force up to today.

In terms of potential normalization of migratory relations, 1995 represented a turning point. The signing of a new agreement suggested the possibility of regulating the legal migratory flow of Cubans to the United States and of trying to stop illegal emigration. This possibility was formalized and raised to a potentially definitive level when, on May 2 of that year, the "Joint Communiqué" on normalizing migratory relations was issued. That document, which resolved the issue of the Cuban emigrants being held at the Guantánamo naval base, reaffirmed a joint interest in avoiding "dangerous departures." These migratory accords, in attempting to solve the serious problem created by the interruption in legal migration, offered an opportunity for preferential treatment. Applying various provisions contained in the U.S. General Law of Immigration, during 1995 more than 26,224 visas were issued to Cuban citizens who applied for them.[2]

EMIGRATION AT THE START OF THE TWENTY-FIRST CENTURY

The first six years of the twenty-first century may be classified as the second most important period of emigration since 1960–1962 because of the size of net emigration from the country—226,078 individuals, of whom 54.5 percent were female. For 1994–2006, that figure is 407,145, of whom 51.1 percent were female.[3]

To better understand this dynamic requires analyzing international migration as a variable in the context of Cuban demographic tendencies. In brief, demographic figures show insufficient population growth, low birthrates, and a clear increase in the age of the population. Emigration's impact on this situation can be seen in the above-mentioned net outflow and the slight female majority among emigrants. In addition, the most common age groups among the emigrants are those between ten and twenty-nine years of age (46.6 percent).

In Cuban emigration at the turn of the twenty-first century, the presence of young professionals can also be observed. Professionals account for 12 percent of the total in the most recent five-year period, which locates Cuba within the current of "brain drain," the loss of important human capital. Studies of a possible "return to Cuba" and the conditions that would propitiate such a return reveal that 40 percent of individuals who have considered a possible return or who had not previously thought about it say that they would go back if the country's economy improves or if they do not succeed in achieving their goals for life abroad. As far as political factors, 80 percent of subjects who do not reject the idea of returning say that possible changes in the country's political system do not play a significant role. Alongside this analysis, we may note the growth over the past four years of attempts to return from the United States and from other parts of the world. Those making such attempts are mostly elderly people and emigrants who left the country since the mid-1990s.[4]

The flow of temporary return visits by Cubans residing abroad has also been studied in the case of individuals living in the United States and Puerto Rico. The results show a sustained growth of interest in trips back to Cuba to visit and also to send remittances to relatives in Cuba. Similarly, these emigrants wanted travel restrictions lifted and travel costs lowered, more mechanisms to encourage family relations, and broader options to enjoy with their families during their stay in Cuba.[5]

Illegal departures by sea to the United States remained a component of Cuban emigration. One study shows that this phenomenon increased after 1998, especially in 1999, 2001, and 2004 and during the first nine months of 2005. These figures are based on successful departures (as indicated by arrival in and admission to the United States) and on would-be emigrants returned to Cuba by the U.S. Coast Guard or by the services of third countries where those attempting to reach U.S. territory had landed. The total of such participants between 1995 and 2004 exceeded 21,900, not counting those who may have reached other shores without being sent back.[6]

The increase in those successfully reaching U.S. soil after 1999 was due in part to the growth of human smuggling operations. Moreover, given the difficulty in reaching U.S. shores without interception by the U.S. Coast Guard, new southern routes have been used for illegal departures, such as to Honduras, directly or by way of the Cayman Islands, so as to then cross through Mexico into the United States.[7]

Those opting to leave Cuba by sea are primarily young men (68 percent of them between fifteen and thirty-five years old) with secondary or higher-secondary education, a notable level of unemployment (50 percent), and criminal records (20 percent) and 8 percent having made repeated attempts to depart illegally. Studies of the causes and motivations of the decision to emigrate point to economic elements in a context where other social and political factors vary according to individual characteristics.[8] In sum, in the early years of the twenty-first century, Cuba continued to display the traits that typify it as a country of emigrants, although Cuban emigration does not contribute greatly to overall worldwide migratory flows.

CUBAN MIGRATION POLICY

Cuban migration policy has passed through varying periods from 1959 (when there were no travel restrictions in place) to the present. A continual influence on Cuban policy has been hostility and permanent aggression on the part of the United States as well as internal situations.[9]

Since 1961, the Cuban government has viewed migration as a matter of Cuba's national security. Thus, Cuban laws and regulations reflect and are linked to the intense counterrevolutionary activity and the utilization of U.S.-Cuba migration toward such counterrevolutionary ends. The application of Cuban law has been based on a series of criteria, related mostly to security issues, such as age, professional level, occupation, political affiliation, and conduct as a citizen.

In the late 1970s and early 1980s, the main shifts in Cuba's migratory policies took shape. Since then, there have been several periods of greater flexibility involving significant changes with respect to permanent and temporary departures from the country. The differential relations with Cuban emigrants in many regions of the planet, as compared with those in the United States and especially in South Florida, reveal elements of both continuity and change.

In the first decade of the twenty-first century, there has been a process of adjustment in Cuba's policy toward migration and emigrants in accordance with the characteristics of the country of destination and domestic and international political realities. There are many challenges involved in developing and applying a policy that is modern, objective, and consonant with the demands of both citizens and national security.

U.S. POLITICAL ASYLUM POLICY

U.S. immigration policy with respect to Cuba openly declares offers of political asylum. Its effect is to build up critical pressures on the island that are then released through periodic escape valves that produce cycles related to internal situations over the past fifty years.

In November 1966, the United States enacted the Cuban Adjustment Act, which more clearly and directly reaffirmed the special treatment of Cuban emigration by offering Cubans practically automatic status as political refugees. This act affords an opportunity to change one's immigration status to permanent residence after one year and one day on U.S. soil without having to leave the United States, as regulations require all other immigrants to do. The act was approved without an expiration date and remains in force.

Beginning in 1991, when Cuba was hard hit by economic crisis, the rafter phenomenon reappeared. Illegal departures by sea (including frustrated attempts) rose to more than 60,000 between 1991 and 1994, the year of the so-called rafter crisis.[10] In the months leading up to this event, a new contradictory behavior by the U.S. government could be observed in granting or denying temporary visas for Cuban citizens to visit their families living in the United States. The number of temporary visas granted significantly declined, with allegations that many of those applying were potential immigrants. As many as 80 percent of such applications were denied, in turn stimulating illegal departures and creating an additional conflict associated with the migratory flow.

The rafter crisis generated a new wave of migration (36,900 people in the first nine months of 1994) that represented a continuation of the changes in Cuban migration patterns begun with Mariel (1980). In this new case, the economic crisis and its social effects were among the main detonators of the people explosion. Most of the rafters were young white men, with secondary or postsecondary education, motivated essentially by personal aspirations for fulfillment that they felt could not be met on the island in the short term given the situation there.

The pressures generated by the illegal departures culminated in public disorder, which led the Cuban government to decide on August 12, 1994, to eliminate the restrictions on this type of departure. Thus, the histories of the events at Camarioca[11] in 1965 and Mariel in 1980 were repeated; in those incidents, too, legal migration from Cuba to the United States had been interrupted, and illegal migration took on significant dimensions.

Faced with the new situation, the United States changed course in its immigration policy with respect to Cuba, intercepting the rafters before they could enter the United States and sending them temporarily to its naval base near Guantánamo, thereby breaking a tradition more than thirty-five years old. This U.S. naval base and Panama received nearly 30,000 people who, for the moment, had no defined migratory status. In this new situation, the dynamic of migratory relations between the United States and Cuba required a new understanding. The migratory accords signed in 1994 referred, in particular, to the control of illegal emigration by sea from Cuba to the United States; they signified a substantive change in U.S. migration policy toward the largest island in the Antilles. Both parties committed themselves to preventing the use of violence in the act of emigration. For the first time in more than thirty-six years, the United States committed itself to return any Cubans intercepted on the high seas with the intention of entering the country, and Cuba declared that it would accept these individuals without taking any action against them.

This could have been a decisive step in discouraging such departures if the United States had treated Cuban migrants the same as it did the thousands of people from all over the globe who tried to enter U.S. territory in illegal or undocumented fashion. However, for this to occur, the United States would have had to end the special immigration policy for Cubans begun in 1959 and, in particular, to rescind the Cuban Adjustment Act. This did not happen.

Still, a key factor in encouraging legal and orderly emigration from the island to the United States was broached when the figure of 20,000 annual visas, as a minimum, was considered. To fulfill this goal for 1994–1995, the accords included the application of a set of powers inherent in U.S. immigration laws for the purpose of easing the awarding of such visas. That was exactly the opposite of what had been put in practice after the migration accords of 1984.

In addition, the United States established a special lottery for Cuba separate from its annual lottery for the rest of the world—thus providing another avenue through which Cuban citizens could present their immigration requests. [12] This method of granting immigrant visas was oriented toward the population sectors of greatest interest to the United States. The visas were obtained by young emigrants, with education and professional training, the majority of them white, who presumably would not represent a burden to the United States because they could quickly enter the labor market.

Once these accords were put into effect in 1994–1995, a legal, orderly, and regular migratory flow began. However, the illegal departures were controlled only to a degree because the Cuban Adjustment Act remained in effect. From 1995 to 2008, by the author's estimation, no more than 190,000 visas were awarded to Cuban emigrants. These were granted primarily through the lottery process for family reunification, to political refugees, or to those "paroled" as household members of those who had obtained visas in one of the three primary ways.

One issue remained pending from the events of August 1994: the situation of the people interned in Guantánamo and Panama. New talks were carried out, and on May 2, 1995, it was announced that an amendment to the accords had been signed, providing for the gradual admission of those interned Cubans to the United States. The joint communiqué of May 1995 underlined the prohibition of illegal migration by sea, with the commitment to return rafters captured on the high seas to the island.

Nonetheless, the survival of the Cuban Adjustment Act provoked a different outcome. Although the application of the migration accords stopped further avalanches of rafters, it could not completely close this door because any Cuban emigrant who managed to reach U.S. territory by sea retained a high likelihood of not being returned to Cuba. The case of the boy Elián González revealed what the extreme results of the "wet-foot, dry-foot" policy could be. [13]

This problem remains unsolved. Since 1998, the problem has included the thorny and dangerous component of human smuggling, organized and financed by groups of Cuban Americans in South Florida, putting human lives at risk. Between 1997 and 2008, about 8,000 people reached the Florida coast by this means.

One of the myths that has persisted most strongly is that all Cubans migrating to the United States are members of a homogeneous group. The image remains durable largely because members of one part of the emigration define themselves as exiles. Nonetheless, the social class differences and other distinctions stemming from the sociodemographic characteristics of each migratory wave refute this. The political element is still present, but the classification of those who migrate should reflect their motivations, social affiliations, life expectations, and ties to the Cuban social system.

PERCEPTIONS OF THE INTERNAL SITUATION IN CUBA

Fidel Castro's relinquishing of his responsibilities because of illness also had repercussions for the migration issue. The first reaction by the U.S. Coast Guard was to announce that there would be no special change in its activities. Nonetheless, press reports on that announcement referred to contingency plans for a crisis in Cuba and U.S. government fears of a new exodus, or of hundreds of Florida Cuban Americans setting off in small boats in search of their families. This impression was confirmed by the governor of Florida in statements affirming the existence of a plan to prevent a massive wave of immigration that could create a great risk to human life.

Another interesting event occurred on August 2, 2006, when the Bush administration showed concern about possible departures by sea from Florida to Cuba. White House spokesperson Tony Snow declared an intention to prevent movement in either direction: "It's also important . . . to tell people stay where you are. This is not a time for people to try to be getting in the water and going either way."[14] Once again, it became clear that, when the interests of Cuban-born counterrevolutionaries occasionally fail to coincide with those of the United States, the balance tilts toward the U.S. interests. Allowing uncontrolled migration between Florida and Cuba does not fit with U.S. policy premises. President Bill Clinton's decision to send Cuban rafters to Guantánamo instead of permitting them access to Florida in 1994 indicated the same.

The first reports of a possible change in U.S. policy on Cuban immigration coincided with President George W. Bush's first public statements, after the news of the Cuban president's illness, at a Texas press conference on August 8, 2008. Although the U.S. government did not refer to possible changes, word filtered out that a "working draft" was circulating among legislators and government officials. This document contained a plan to put a brake on illegal immigration from Cuba and prevent the entrance of "regime officials who have suspicions of human rights abuses hanging over them."[15] The administration's idea, apparently, was to use the 20,000 annual visas to aid family reunification. In this way, U.S. officials may have hoped to prevent Cuban Americans from encouraging illegal entry by way of smugglers. In the award of immigrant visas, there would also be the goal of promoting the entrance of Cuban professionals, particularly doctors working in third countries who would have a right to take advantage of the 20,000-visa quota.

Changes in U.S. immigration policy announced in 2006 included an increase in the proportion of visas for family reunification, a denial of consideration for U.S. entry for those intercepted at sea who had family residents in the United States, the implementation of a system to inform relatives of the latter in the United States, the denial of migratory benefits to Cuban government officials who were "human rights violators," and the use of the power of parole for the benefit of Cuban doctors in third countries.[16]

The first of these policy changes was based on the joint communiqué of September 4, 1994, which permitted the United States to process a minimum quota of immigrants for the purpose of family reunification. Each year, a significant number of the individuals who applied for family reunification visas had failed to obtain them. The new plan sought to reduce this backlog by recognizing those individuals as a fourth category of immigrants. In addition to the lottery winners, the plan proposed to allow discretionary entrance of this category by means of parole. With this new policy, family reunification would account for approximately 60 percent of those receiving visas each year, with the rest going to lottery winners.

If family reunification benefits were denied to Cuban migrants intercepted at sea, this practice could discourage illegal departures by sea, although it would not be decisive as long as the Cuban Adjustment Act and its interpretation in the form of the "wet-foot, dry-foot" policy remained in effect. The denials could be seen as a continuation of the initial intent of the existing migration accords but still as partial, fragmentary, and not addressing the heart of the matter, which truly promotes and facilitates the arrival of Cuban rafters. Therefore, this measure seemed more a response to the U.S. immigration context, in which the subject of undocumented immigrants and smugglers occupies a central and controversial place, rather than a real attempt by the administration to definitively solve the migration problem with Cuba.

With respect to family reunification and the supposed preference offered by the new U.S. immigration measures for Cubans, these actions would not necessarily have a dissuasive effect on the approximately 55 percent of potential illegal emigrants who have no family in the United States or whose relatives are uncles, aunts, or cousins who cannot request visas for them. A process of family reunification that would allow petitions from a greater number of relatives and have a truly dissuasive role should not be limited to the closest kinship relations, as the immigration laws now require. Moreover, the implementation of procedures to inform U.S. relatives regarding Cubans intercepted at sea will increase the demand for news about those returned to Cuba and thus also for news about U.S. immigration authorities' attempts to visit those people or send representatives to do so.

CONTINUATION OF MIGRATION TALKS

On July 14, 2009, a new round of migration talks between Cuba and the United States got under way, the first since the United States broke off talks in 2003. Previously, in April 2009, the Obama administration had lifted the restrictions on travel to Cuba by Cuban Americans. Less than thirty days later, the administration proposed to Cuba a resumption of talks, and on May 31, Cuba agreed. [Editors' note: The United States suspended the immigration talks in 2010 but in 2013 agreed to resume them. The first set of renewed talks were held in Washington in July 2013.]

Although the key measure to change in U.S. immigration policy toward Cuba would be to end the Cuban Adjustment Act, this is unlikely in the short or medium term, that is, in the second term of the Obama administration. Nonetheless, this administration is faced with a set of measures and precedents favorable toward making progress in the normalization of migration relations, which would be of value given the pressures swirling from the larger immigration problem facing the United States. At the same time, such progress on migration could allow for channels of communication and dialogue with Cuba, taking advantage of the Cuban side's repeated willingness to discuss any subject on a plane of full equality.

Cuba, for its part, faces significant challenges in the area of migration, in particular toward the United States, which it has to face with objectivity and with regard to its national interests. It needs a strategy to confront an erosion of its population resulting from a combination of temporary and permanent emigration. Such a strategy must take into account profiles of age, gender, and professional-technical training in various regions of the country. There is also a need to foresee a return to previous Cuban migration patterns, including possible emigration over the next ten to fifteen years, taking into consideration (among other factors) migration currents and tendencies in the region of the Caribbean where Cuba is located; the country's traditions in this regard, especially in eastern Cuba; the economic and social situation of the region, especially in labor force terms; and Cuban perspectives on society and labor in the context of the island's economy and of globalization and interdependence among nations.

Cuba must assess the complex problem of brain drain and loss of talent, a phenomenon now present in almost every society, from a perspective that considers all professional sectors and with an eye toward policies that favor social and personal development. Cuba must perfect its legal and constitutional provisions regarding emigration, which will require new legislation that takes into account the political, economic, and social importance of this issue. The current state of such regulations indicates the need, within the Cuban legal system, for a branch of law dealing with migration rights so as to make the legal system more efficient as a means of social reform. This suggests legislative review of all the current regulations. Each of the above points implies specific effects on Cuba's migration policies and specifically its policy toward emigration, both of which involve important challenges in which national security cannot be relegated to a secondary plane. [Editors' note: Since January 2013, Decreto-Ley No. 302 has eased travel restrictions for most citizens. It enables them to depart without an exit visa, to leave the country for up to two years, and to return without losing their property.]

NOTES

From *Debating U.S.-Cuban Relations: Shall We Play Ball?*, ed. Jorge I. Domínguez, Rafael Hernández, and Lorena G. Barberia (New York: Routledge, 2011). Reprinted by permission of the publisher.

1. Antonio Aja Diaz, *Al cruzar las fronteras* (Havana: CEDEM-UNFPA, 2009), 108–10.
2. Antonio Aja Diaz, "Cuban Emigration in the 1990s," *Cuban Studies*, no. 26, 2000, 1–25.
3. Aja Diaz, *Al cruzar las fronteras*, 199–212.
4. Aja Diaz, *Al cruzar las fronteras*, 201–10.
5. Study by Consuelo Martin and Antonio Aja Diaz, investigating the temporary return of Cubans living in the United States and Puerto Rico, in *Fondos bibliográficos del Centro de Estudios de la Migración Internacional (CEMI)* (Havana: Universidad de La Habana, 2004).
6. Antonio Aja Diaz, Consuelo Martin, and Magali Martin, "Estudios de las salidas ilegales por vía marítima desde Cuba hacia los Estados Unidos: Continuidad del análisis a partir de los acuerdos migratorios de 1994–1995," in *Fondos bibliográficos del Centro de Estudios de la Migración Internacional (CEMI)* (Havana: Universidad de La Habana, 2006).
7. Aja Diaz, *Al cruzar las fronteras*, 199–212.
8. Martin and Aja Diaz, *Fondos bibliográficos del Centro de Estudios de la Migración Internacional (CEMI)*, 24–40.
9. Aja Diaz, *Al cruzar las fronteras*, 129–31.
10. Aja Diaz, *Al cruzar las fronteras*, 142.
11. The first of the three very large scale migration episodes took place in 1965, leaving from Cuba's Camaríoca harbor.
12. Ruth Ellen Wasem, *Cuban Migration to the United States: Policy and Trends*, Congressional Research Service Report R40566 (Washington, DC: Congressional Research Service, 2009).
13. This is a policy applied by the Clinton and subsequent administrations to undocumented Cuban immigrants attempting to reach the United States by sea who are captured by the U.S. Coast Guard. When captured at sea, they are regarded as "wet foot" and are returned to the Cuban government as stipulated in the U.S.-Cuba migration agreements of 1994 and 1995. If they reach U.S. soil, they are regarded as "dry foot," at which point they are not returned to Cuba and have the right to regularize their immigration status in the United States under the Cuban Adjustment Act of 1966.
14. Tony Snow, press conference, Agence France Presse, August 2, 2006.
15. "Con Castro enfermo, los Estados Unidos se preparan ante posíble ola migratoria," Reuters, August 2, 2006.
16. Snow, press conference.

Chapter Twenty-Six

Dialogues within and between Cuba and Its Diaspora

Jorge I. Domínguez

Cuba and its diaspora have never had easy relations. The reason is no mystery. The Cuban diaspora, particularly the most renowned, have been organized and consolidated in opposition to the prevailing political regime in Cuba—a regime they are attempting to overthrow and replace with another. It was so during the independence wars of the last third of the nineteenth century and the second half of the twentieth century, just as much before as after the revolutionary triumph in 1959.

Throughout two centuries, Cuba and its diaspora have enriched the vocabulary of Spanish insults and opprobrium. A single word brings to mind the resentment of those who use it and the pain it seeks to provoke in the target. That word is "treason." Treason, as many in Cuba have said for a long time, is the fundamental characteristic of the diaspora. Treason, also sometimes said in Cuba, is what characterizes all who lift up the slightest criticism against everyday circumstances. Treason, as many in the diaspora have said for a long time, characterizes all who have anything good to say about something that has been achieved in Cuba or that conflicts with the prevailing views among the more powerful social and political groups in the diaspora. In fact, the word "treason" is often the recourse of those, here or there, who lack arguments, logic, and evidence and who fear that their ignorance will be revealed if they come to a debate with people willing to respect each other.

The relationship between the diaspora and the country of origin is also complex because at various times some members of the diaspora, even when naturalized citizens of another country, manage to return to their country of origin. José Martí lived most of his adult life in the United States. The main leaders of the war-of-independence Cuban Revolutionary Party, Tomás Estrada Palma and Gonzalo de Quesada, were citizens of the United States. Similarly, generals of the Liberation Army, such as Francisco Carrillo, Pedro Betancourt, Emilio Núñez, and Carlos Roloff, among others, were U.S. citizens.[1] Diaspora members were disposed to return only in 1898 as in 1959, when the previous regime was overthrown, and in both cases after a war.

The challenge for Cuba and its diaspora today is how to explore the possibility of a different relationship that does not require violence, much less a war; that does not prolong the verbal violence that brands anyone who disagrees as a "traitor"; that does not exclude those who for many reasons became citizens of another country; that values what those who call themselves Cuban have achieved, as much in Cuba as elsewhere in the world; and that deems those achievements as part of the same national heritage, that is, a relationship that accepts that the Cuban nation is found wherever there are those who feel Cuban.

A dialogue presupposes that there are at least two opinions sufficiently distinct, reasonable, and honorable on the same subject. A dialogue necessarily begins with respect for the other people. A dialogue comes from the perspective that all can learn from the exchange and debate among those who disagree.

THE CUBAN GOVERNMENT AND THE POSSIBILITY OF DIALOGUE

During the past half century, dialogue has been uncommon among Cubans who disagree. Uninterrupted monologues have been the rhetorical norm of Cuban public expression. One laudable variant has been the instances, starting in the late 1970s and continuing from time to time to this day, in which the Cuban government has invited some people from the diaspora to participate in something that has been called a "dialogue." Even so, with the exception of sessions in the late 1970s, invitations have been extended, principally or exclusively, to those who already agree with the Cuban government on fundamental questions, addressing an agenda also controlled by the government. Also useful are actions that have improved certain aspects of the relationship between the Cuban government and part of its diaspora, including consular services. But the purpose of these meetings has been to mobilize support for the government rather than engage in dialogue with those who hold divergent views.

The obstacles to dialogue or dialogues have existed on all sides in Cuba as well as in the diaspora. However, recent changes suggest the possibility of a different future. I am referring to publicly stated views of President Raúl Castro as well as the views of Miami Cubans interviewed in public opinion surveys.

A dialogue appears to be precisely what President Raúl Castro has in mind in several statements that deserve mention. Already in his first speech on the symbolic date, the July 26 state-of-the-nation speech in 2007, Raúl Castro spoke of the importance of avoiding the alleged unanimity that is alien to dialogue: "We do not aspire to unanimity, which is often fictitious, in this or any other subject."[2]

Raúl Castro broadened and deepened these criteria at the National Assembly meeting that closed 2007. The Cuban government and Communist Party should not fear, he said, when media sources, either political or governmental, in other countries use the opinions of some Cubans for their own purposes. He invited deputies—and all citizens—to disagree even with things he says himself: "I bring these ideas primarily to encourage you to think, not only you, comrade deputies, but all compatriots, the whole country. Some are personal opinions that should not be construed as immutable. These are issues that we have a duty to study and discuss in depth objectively." Finally, in that same speech, Raúl Castro urged leaders and officials to respect free expression: "Whoever occupies a leadership position must know to listen and create the environment for others to express themselves with absolute freedom."[3]

Therefore, President Raúl Castro's statement in his February 24, 2008, inauguration speech should have been no surprise: "There is no reason to fear differences in a society like ours," adding, "From the deep interchange of divergent ideas come the best solutions."[4]

THE DIASPORA IN SOUTH FLORIDA AND THE POSSIBILITY OF DIALOGUE

The Cuban diaspora can be found in Luanda, Moscow, Madrid, Caraças, and many other parts of the world, but the largest concentration of people who insist on calling themselves Cubans, outside of Cuba, resides in South Florida. This is also the leading diaspora in conflict with the

Cuban government. That Floridian diaspora has been changing, and some of the changes are signaled by the results of public opinion polls conducted since 1991 by researchers associated with Florida International University (FIU) and its Cuban Research Institute.

The question most relevant to our topic is this: "Are you for or against a national dialogue among Cuban exiles, Cuban dissidents, and representatives of the Cuban government?" In March 1991, six out of ten people were opposed to such a dialogue. In March 2007, only one out of three was opposed to such a dialogue. In table 26.1, we see that the experience of the so-called Special Period in the early 1990s in Cuba had no impact on the views of the Cuban diaspora in South Florida with respect to this issue. The most important changes occur after 1995, suggesting that the reasons for these changes of opinion in the diaspora are endogenous to it.

One source of change was the political diversification of the diaspora in Miami, evident in the change of leadership in the Cuban American National Foundation, with Jorge Más Santos presiding since the death of his father, Jorge Más Canosa; the fracturing of this organization and the modification of its platform under its new leadership; and the emergence of new organizations sponsoring the debate instead of resorting to violence, such as the Cuba Study Group, headed by Carlos Saladrigas. Demographic changes in the diaspora were another source of renewal due to the new wave of immigrants that started arriving in 1995.

Based on a survey carried out in 2007, table 26.2 compares the opinions regarding the desirability of a national dialogue among Cubans organized by date of emigration. Note that a clear majority of what is sometimes called the historical exiles, that is, those who migrated between 1959 and 1964, remained opposed to a national dialogue in 2007, while four out of five people who migrated after 1995 were in favor of that dialogue.

On the basis of these results, one can also observe changes in opinion about related topics. For example, in 1993, half of the respondents in Miami already agreed that companies should be able to sell pharmaceuticals to Cuba. In 2007, the proportion in favor of such sales increased to seven out of ten people. In 1993, only 23 percent favored food sales to Cuba, but in 2007, the proportion favoring food sales nearly tripled, totaling 62 percent.

The proportion of Cubans and Cuban Americans in South Florida in favor of the continuation of the U.S. embargo applied to Cuba for half a century was almost unchanged in the most difficult years of the "Special Period"; it was 87 percent in favor of its continuation in 1991 and persisted at 83 percent in 1995. However, this proportion has been declining steadily since then. It was 66 percent in 2004, 58 percent in 2007, and 45 percent in 2008.[5]

An explanation for the changes of opinion in relation to the embargo, apparent since the mid-1990s, is the date of emigration. I used data from the survey carried out in 2008. While in that year 65 percent of those who emigrated before 1980 still supported the continuation of the U.S. embargo, only 29 percent of those who emigrated after 1998 were supportive.

This difference in migration period has direct political consequences. Most who were U.S. citizens and were registered to vote still favored the continuation of the embargo, while most of those who had not registered to vote opposed its continuation. Members of Congress who

Table 26.1.   Percentage in Favor of or Against a National Dialogue among Cubans

	1991	1995	2004	2007
In favor	39.8	40.5	55.6	65.0
Against	59.2	59.5	44.4	35.0

Source: Guillermo Grenier and Hugh Gladwin, "2007 FIU Cuba Poll," http://www2.fiu.edu/~ipor/Cuba8/Cuba.Comp.htm.

Table 26.2.   Percentage in 2007 in Favor of or Against a National Dialogue between Cubans by Migration Period

	Emigrated 1959–1964	Emigrated 1995–2007
In favor	43.1	79.4
Against	56.9	20.6

Source: Guillermo Grenier and Hugh Gladwin, "2007 FIU Cuba Poll," http://www2.fiu.edu/~ipor/Cuba8/Cuba.Comp.htm.

represent districts in South Florida, therefore, responded to this majority opinion among U.S. citizens of Cuban origin, who still favor the embargo. The passage of time is likely to affect these results.

It would be a mistake to think, however, that with the mere passage of time the option of dialogue will triumph over violent options, according to the opinions in Miami. The same polls have been asking whether respondents are for or against military action by the exile community to overthrow the government of Cuba. The proportion in favor of the use of force has changed little. In 1991, 76 percent of respondents supported military action by exiles against the Cuban government, and in 2007, 71 percent held the same opinion. In this case, moreover, the differences of opinion between the respondents, depending on the time of emigration, are negligible, as indicated in table 26.3. According to the survey carried out in 2007, about seven out of ten respondents who immigrated between 1959 and 1964 as well as those who emigrated since 1995 support military action by exiles against the government of Cuba.

How can we reconcile these seemingly irreconcilable data? My interpretation is that the vast majority of the Cuban diaspora in South Florida is in favor of a fundamental change in Cuba regardless of the tools necessary to achieve that goal. That is, the end justifies the means. The same thing that justifies a national dialogue, removing the embargo and sales of medicines and food, would justify military action, an option that has existed for half a century for the Florida diaspora and remains a permissible option for them. What is seen beginning in the mid-1990s is, for the first time, an alternative option that favors peaceful dialogue as an instrument and seeks to use other means to achieve the same end.

For those who are opposed to any fundamental change in Cuba, this variation in the opinions of the diaspora in Miami is irrelevant. For those who favor some or many fundamental changes in Cuba, the political transformation within the diaspora has great importance. Even for the government of Cuba, focusing on mere tactics, it should be helpful to cultivate and promote the peaceful options more than the violent ones. In any case, the option of dialogue among the Miami diaspora is contingent; that is, it prevails only in a context in which Cuba is on a path toward change.

WHO TALKS TO WHOM AND ABOUT WHAT?

The title of this work is "dialogues within and between Cuba and its diaspora." The utility or the possibility of dialogue is not the exclusive property of someone or some entity, official or private. I presume it is good to promote dialogue in Cuba, dialogues within the diaspora, and various dialogues between those residing inside and outside of Cuba. Family travel, now easier thanks to the measures taken by the U.S. government in 2009 and accepted by the Cuban government, has already generated multiple dialogues within many Cuban families.

Table 26.3.   Percentage in 2007 in Favor of or Against Military Action by Exiles to Overthrow the Cuban Government by Migration Period

	Emigrated 1959–1964	Emigrated 1995–2007
In favor	74.0	71.8
Against	26.0	28.2

Source: Guillermo Grenier and Hugh Gladwin, "2007 FIU Cuba Poll," http://www2.fiu.edu/~ipor/Cuba8/Cuba.Comp.htm.

These valuable dialogues represent a breakthrough in communications. It is equally essential, however, that multiple dialogues not confined to members of a single family be generated.

Decades passed before the first meeting took place between priests and lay Roman Catholic Cubans living inside and outside of Cuba. The first meeting, which was only for priests, was held in Santo Domingo, Dominican Republic, in 1997, partly to discuss the differences of opinion that had arisen about the role of the Roman Catholic Church in Cuba, which were heightened in the months preceding the visit of Pope John Paul II. The participation of the laity in these meetings began in 2000. These meetings, especially the first ones, have not been lacking political and ideological tension, but that is precisely the value of these dialogues—namely, that they facilitate overcoming differences.[6]

In the diaspora, there is much to learn about Cuba. It is still common to hear the denial of the possibility that Cuba has built an educated populace, with an extensive and effective public health system of outstanding quality. There remains little recognition in Miami for the social transformations that have occurred in Cuba during the past half century and the significant achievements in Cuba not yet seen in the United States. I cite only one of these, that is, in Cuba but not yet in the United States: differences by skin pigmentation are negligible in infant mortality or primary school enrollment rates. That Cuban achievement deserves recognition and applause.[7]

Similarly, it is reasonable that some Cuban diaspora members may wish to participate in some open, legal, and recognized way in the production of culture, society, economy, and other aspects of public life in the country. And they would also like to discuss these issues.

Some issues are unavoidable for any serious dialogue between Cuba and the United States or between Cubans from anywhere. One is the use of impermissible methods in relations between human beings. The shared history between Cuba and the United States and between Cubans living in both countries indicates that, unfortunately, there is much to discuss.

On April 14, 1966, *Granma* published an article on the Military Units to Aid Production (UMAP). The article said that one purpose of UMAP was to "prevent [the incarcerated] tomorrow from becoming parasites, unable to produce anything, or criminals." While the article stated that, in UMAP camps, "the goal . . . is not to punish," we know well that the most common experience of those who were sent against their will to UMAP camps was precisely punishment, many charged with being homosexuals, others for having religious faith, and some for several reasons. Many were victims of abuse and mistreatment. I cite this *Granma* article because it is the only thing I found that, even though its intention was to justify UMAP camps, also notes that "some officers . . . overreacted. For these reasons, they were court-martialed, in some cases they were demoted and in others expelled from the Armed Forces."[8] The fact that this article is the only one that I found does not indicate, unfortunately, that it was a unique event.

An important part of the dialogue must be to recognize the necessity of including not only the experiences of the UMAP camps but also the experiences in prison, particularly in the 1960s, when in 1965 then Prime Minister Fidel Castro, in answering a journalist's question about "political prisoners," indicated that in Cuba there were about 20,000 people in prison who had been convicted by revolutionary tribunals.[9] It would be desirable for the historical archives of the nation to be examined by those who wish, not only the files from the colonial era but also those relevant to the history of the past half century.

The government of Cuba and Cubans living in Cuba also have legitimate reasons to complain. Morally unacceptable methods were used by both the U.S. government and some Cuban exiles who fought, mostly though not exclusively, during the 1960s against the government of Cuba. At the beginning of that period, the U.S. government authorized a campaign against the government of Cuba that we would now call "state terrorism." While the best-known means were the various attempts to assassinate Fidel Castro and Operation Mongoose, there was indeed a vast campaign against civilian and military installations in Cuba and against other facilities that mainly generated damage to the civilian population. The Kennedy administration authorized terrorist attacks that have been documented, among others, against a railway bridge, an oil storage tank, an oil refinery, a power plant, a molasses warehouse, a sawmill, and a floating crane.[10]

In over a thousand pages of documents declassified by the U.S. State Department Office of the Historian covering the years between 1961 and 1963, I have found only one quote from a U.S. official concerned about the immorality of such a policy. In September 1963, an official of the National Security Council, Gordon Chase, criticized this policy of the U.S. government on various grounds, including that these actions "kill innocent civilians."[11]

This policy of state terrorism worked precisely because many Cuban exiles were not simply agents or instruments of that policy but also the architects and shared creators.[12] Some of these Cuban exile groups persisted in using these methods even after the U.S. government stopped sponsoring this policy of state terrorism.

Another issue of importance for dialogue, both internally and transnationally, is the matter of property ownership and U.S. economic sanctions against the government of Cuba. Some economists in Cuba, as well as the Cuban government, have attempted to estimate the extraordinary damage caused by the economic sanctions imposed by the U.S. government during the past half century. The U.S. government has done the same in relation to the expropriations carried out by the government of Cuba, mainly between 1959 and 1961. The Foreign Claims Settlement Commission determined that the value of such expropriated property in the late 1960s was U.S.$1.8 billion, of which 90 percent was for the property of companies. In 2004, the U.S. government recalculated the value of these properties, adding accrued interest, and determined that the figure was more than U.S.$7 billion.[13]

The resolution of these claims has not been discussed by the two governments. Economic disputes of this kind, however, have been a normal part of negotiations during the past century between countries located on various continents. Those differences have been resolved in multiple and complex cases. It does not seem impossible, therefore, that reasonable negotiations in the future would succeed in resolving these claims between Cuba and the United States.

Property claims that directly affect people are more complex, and among all of them, none are more painful than those affecting residences. Many have lived or live in buildings that once belonged to another person whose property was involuntarily expropriated and who now lives in the United States. It is not easy to proceed in these cases. It is not merely an economic or a property matter but also something intimately personal in which the rights of current and former residents should be taken into account.

My guide—and the conclusion of my presentation, not only on this issue—is a comment from my now deceased maternal grandmother. In honor of the end of the wars of the nineteenth century, her parents, my great-grandparents, in January 1899 gave her the name of Clara Star of Peace, and she lived in accordance with her name. Eighty years later, in January 1979, I visited Havana for the first time in nearly nineteen years, and in a spare moment I walked to the house that had been hers. At that time, the house belonged to the Federation of Cuban Women (FMC). Now I quote what I included in the first chapter of my book *Cuba Today* about the conversation with my grandmother the next time I saw her:

"My grandmother never complained when, on my return to the United States, after a kiss, I told her who occupied her house and showed her a photograph that identified it as belonging to the FMC. On the contrary, with a sigh she said she would have preferred it to remain her home but, after a third slower sigh, she told me that since it could not be so, it was not bad that it was occupied by the Federation of Cuban Women." My grandmother, "in expressing her generosity, with sweetness and elegance, had tears streaming down her face, tears that were also mine."[14]

The issues are unavoidable. The dialogues within and between Cuba and its diaspora are not impossible. They are already unpostponable. They will develop with great success if all behave with the generosity of my grandmother. And a better future for Cuba—and to all who consider themselves Cuban—depends on that success.

NOTES

From *Espacio Laical* (Havana), March 2010 [Translation from the Spanish by the editors with the assistance of Uri Lerner.] Reprinted by permission of the publisher.

1. Louis A. Pérez Jr., *On Becoming Cuban: Identity, Nationality, and Culture* (Chapel Hill: University of North Carolina Press, 1999).

2. Raúl Castro Ruz, "Trabajar con sentido crítico, creador, sin anquilosamientos ni esquematismos, Discurso en el acto central por el LIV aniversario del asalto al Cuartel Moncada, Camagüey, 26 July 2007," *Granma*, July 27, 2007.

3. Raúl Castro Ruz, "¡Y a trabajar duro!, Intervención ante la Asamblea Nacional del Poder Popular, 28 December 2007," *Granma*, December 29, 2007.

4. Raúl Castro Ruz, "Discurso en la sesión constitutiva de la VII Legislatura de la Asamblea Nacional del Poder Popular," *La Habana*, February 24, 2008, http://www.cuba.cu/gobierno/rauldiscursos/index2.html

5. Guillermo Grenier and Hugh Gladwin, "2007 FIU Cuba Poll," http://www2.fiu.edu/~ipor/Cuba8/Cuba.Comp.htm; Institute for Public Opinion Research, Florida International University, Brookings Institution, and Cuba Study Group, "2008 Cuba/US Transition Poll," http://www2.fiu.edu/~ipor/Cuba8/Cuba.Comp.htm (accessed April 19, 2010).

6. See Orlando Márquez, "10 años de encuentros eclesiales," *Palabra Nueva* 16, no. 167 (October 2007): 25–26.

7. Jacob Meerman, "Poverty and Mobility in Low-Status Minorities: The Cuban Case in International Perspective," *World Development* 29, no. 9 (2001): 1457–75.

8. *Granma*, April 14, 1966, 8.

9. Lee Lockwood, *Castro's Cuba, Cuba's Fidel* (New York: Vintage Books, 1969), 230.

10. U.S. Department of State, Office of the Historian, *Foreign Relations of the United States*, vol. 11, *1961–1963* (Washington, DC: U.S. Government Printing Office, 1996), 761, 846, 887.

11. U.S. Department of State, Office of the Historian, *Foreign Relations of the United States*, vol. 11, *1961–1963*, 864.

12. An analysis of the documentation on the full relationship between the U.S. government and the Cuban exile groups can be found in James G. Blight and Peter Kornbluh, comps., *Politics of Illusion* (Boulder, CO: Lynne Rienner, 1998).

13. U.S. Commission for Assistance to a Free Cuba, *Report to the President*, May 2004, http://www.cafc.gov/documents/organization/67963.pdf, 208.

14. Jorge I. Domínguez, *Cuba hoy: Analizando su pasado, imaginando su futuro* (Madrid: Editorial Colibrí, 2006), 13. In the original version, there was an error: the second "no" was omitted from the second quote.

Chapter Twenty-Seven

Cuba, a Country with a Broken Heart

Leonardo Padura Fuentes

For Cubans, baseball is not a sport, much less a game: it is almost a religion, and taken very seriously. Baseball was brought to Cuba around the mid-nineteenth century by young men whose families had sent them to study in cities in the United States. Back then, "el juego de pelota," as it was called in Cuba, had crucial importance in different areas of the national spirituality: as a non-conformist social activity that indicated a desire for progress (United States' modernity in contrast with the backwardness of Spain—the former colonial power); as a manifestation of national unity, because very soon it was played all over the island; and as a means of bringing together social classes and ethnic groups (because Afro-Cubans and peasants soon became devotees of the game). It was also a performance in which sport and culture came together, thanks to the entertainment provided by "orquestas de danzones" (bands playing the Cuban national dance), the design of baseball teams' uniforms, modernist pennants and graphics, and the artistic and journalistic literature devoted to commenting on and promoting the sport. For Cubans, baseball has been the most played and most beloved of sports, the one that has given rise to the most legends and has carried the greatest social weight. In recent years it has also been (as it could not avoid being) a battleground for some of the most critical political, social, and economic conflicts taking place in Cuban society. Several dozen Cuban players have taken the risk of being branded "deserters" or "traitors" by official rhetoric, deciding to depart the island to try their fortunes in other leagues (especially in U.S. Major League Baseball). This has caused a commotion in Cuban society and sport, which cling to the models and politics of amateur sports followed in the socialist countries. The departure of these players from the country has had three basic consequences. One, for sport: a drain on regional and national teams, since a "deserter" is banned from returning to represent his or her club or country at any official event. Another, economic: while athletes on the island earn the salaries of "amateurs," those doing well abroad can sign contracts worth (many) millions of dollars, and even those whose performance is less outstanding can earn at least several hundred thousand dollars a year. And third, political: the Cuban government, without essentially modifying its sports policy, has begun to allow baseball players to be contracted for professional tournaments abroad (although not for the Major Leagues). The perpetual tension of baseball politics allows this sport to express, in a quantitative way, the distance between Cubans living on the island and those who have left it in search of new horizons. Its overwhelming influence in Cuban society and spirituality transform it, together with its cultural expressions, into one of the facets of Cuban life where any moves toward reconciliation and communication have special connotations, capable of influencing every order of life, including politics. Recently a Cuban businessman living in Miami had the bold idea of holding two or three baseball games in the southern U.S. state of Florida among retired players of Cuba's most emblematic club of the last 50 years, the Havana Industriales. The novelty was that they would play on the other side of the Florida Strait and the intended participants would be former players living both within Cuba and outside the country—that is, the so-called deserters. The first step would be obtaining permission from the Cuban authorities for the players to meet and play against their former teammates. Without official confirmation, it was understood that permission had been granted, but silently, as if nothing were going on. The second step was up to the other side of the Strait: would Cuban exiles accept the presence of Cubans living in Cuba at a public event? From the outset, former players living outside of the country were favorably disposed to the idea, to the satisfaction of most of the Cuban exiles, who looked forward to seeing their old idols again. However, a small but powerful minority of the exiles were against the proposal. That is when the event promoters' tortuous ordeal began, as in addition to receiving threats of all kinds, they have had to wander the city of Miami looking for a baseball field to hold the matches in. But the promoters vow that the event will be held, "even if it is in a cane field." To lack the capacity to see the momentous social and political significance for Cuba and its future of having émigré players and those who have remained in the country fraternize on a baseball field is an attitude of political blindness. But I believe, above all, it is an expression of a fracture of the Cuban national soul that is so deep, so charged with resentment, that not even something as sacred as baseball can easily mend it. Too many years of deadlock, hatred, desire for revenge, and exchanges of insults and abuse (those who left the country are "gusanos" or worms, turncoats, traitors; those who stayed behind are communists, oppressors, Castro accomplices, etc.) have accumulated and still muddy the present and future of the different fragments of the broken heart of this Caribbean island nation. [Editors' note: The teams ultimately played each other in Tampa and Ft. Lauderdale at the end of August 2013.]

NOTE

From "Cuba, a Country with a Broken Heart," *InterPress Service*, August 5, 2013.

IV

Culture

As in several aspects of life in Cuba (from foreign policy to medical care to education to athletics), in boxing terms Cuba is like a lightweight who fights in the heavyweight class—punching way above its weight. In terms of cultural expression, this is very clearly the case and has been for decades. In the developing world, Cuba leads the way in terms of the value of its originality and credibility and also in questions of accessibility for the population at large. (By this, we are referring to the availability of culture to the vast majorities of the population at an affordable, usually subsidized price.) Most of this is not reported in Western media, and as a result, the perception remains that Cuban culture is dogmatic and state controlled. Sadly, this bias is widely held; it is also wildly incorrect.

In fact, Cuban culture is alive and well. For instance, the most prestigious literary prizes throughout Latin America and the Caribbean are those granted annually by Cuba's *Casa de las Américas* cultural organization. The leading ballet in all of Latin America (and arguably one of the best in the world) is the National Ballet of Cuba. Almost every year, Cuban musicians earn awards at the Latin Grammies. (In the 2012 version, celebrated in Las Vegas, no fewer than fifteen Cuban-born musicians and bands—living both on the island and abroad—were nominated for awards and within eleven of the nineteen categories.) The annual New Latin American Film Festival celebrated in Havana is akin to the Oscar ceremonies—except that the onus in Cuba is on mass participation in the film festival, with tens of thousands of Cubans and foreigners alike lining up to see dozens of films in cinemas throughout the capital. Likewise, the annual Book Fair, which starts in Havana and then wends its way throughout the island, brings millions of people to participate. All of this, it should be remembered, occurs in a country of just 11.2 million. Put simply, Cuban cultural production goes far beyond the pleasant music of the Buena Vista Social Club.

One of the greatest misconceptions about Cuba is that there is no freedom to criticize the government or, indeed, any official aspect of Cuba's political, economic, or social system. One of the common themes found throughout most of the chapters in this section concerns the different ways in which daily reality (and, yes, criticisms) are addressed within Cuban cultural expression. A secondary theme concerns the different adaptations that have taken place within the cultural realm in response to—or perhaps as part of—the broader changes under way on the island. If one has any doubt about the liberalization of Cuban culture in recent years, it is only necessary to listen to the lyrics of some of the country's leading rap and *reggaeton* artists (studied in this volume by Ana Ruiz), to read Leonardo Padura's searing denunciation of Stalinism (and state control in general) in his superb novel *El hombre que amaba a los perros* (The Man Who Loved Dogs, recently published in English), or to watch the hilarious zombie movie *Juan de los Muertos* (Juan of the Dead). Reference is made to these below: there are indeed fresh winds blowing in the Cuban cultural scene.

As we indicated in the earlier edition of this book, there were already clear indications that cultural life was rapidly evolving as the "Special Period" advanced. The reference there to the unveiling of the statue of John Lennon in a Havana park in December 2000 by none other than Fidel Castro (whose government four decades earlier had banned the music of the Beatles for its allegedly decadent Western influence) is a fitting symbol of this fast-paced change. We have kept just a couple of the chapters found in the early edition of the book (by writers Padura and Nancy Morejón as well as the lyrics of two songs by Carlos Varela, the Bob Dylan of Cuba).

A historical note is in order to contextualize these developments. Many changes in cultural activity have taken place, reflecting the fact that Cuba itself has changed dramatically since the implosion of the Soviet Union—a process resulting in the end of generous subsidies. By the mid-1990s, the Cuban government was faced with the sad reality that there was extremely limited funding for anything, as the Cuban Revolution literally scrambled to survive in the direst of circumstances and defying all odds. Given the extremely limited funds available, ensuring a supply of food, fuel, and medical supplies obviously took precedence over the production of books or films, and understandably financial support for the arts was decimated. Newspapers were reduced to a skeleton format, often displayed publicly across the windows of small booths (since there were not enough print copies to go around). Film production dried up, and the number of books published was savagely reduced. Evening baseball games were changed to be played during the daytime—since power for the stadiums' floodlights was deemed an unacceptable luxury.

To survive, Cuban cultural leaders turned abroad to publish their works, host dance performances, curate art exhibits, and coproduce films. While at first this adaptation to the harsh realities of post-Soviet aid was extremely challenging, eventually Cuban cultural life did rebound—and, in fact, some highly original projects resulted, as this section attests. Cuban artists, dancers, musicians, writers, and film directors dug deeply into the resilient Cuban character and their famed capacity to "*resolver*" and "*inventar*" and subsequently delivered some extraordinary cultural productions. One of the best examples of the resulting renaissance of cultural life at that time was *Fresa y chocolate* (Strawberry and Chocolate), directed by Tomás Gutiérrez Alea and Juan Carlos Tabío and released in 1993. It was produced as a Cuban-Spanish-Mexican venture and was extremely successful, receiving an Oscar nomination.

It is worth summarizing briefly the plot of the film since in many ways it broke the mold of Cuban films produced until then and set the scene for the continuing cultural liberalization seen ever since. The film pits two characters against each other—David, an introverted university student who defends a rather arid revolutionary position, and Diego, a gay artist who is extremely discouraged by the revolutionary process and longs to leave Cuba and its stagnant, official cultural milieu. Another relevant character is Miguel, a homophobic and dogmatic revolutionary who pressures David to spy on Diego so that he can be punished as an enemy of the state. The film ends with Diego leaving the country and David realizing that many of the ideological positions he had previously held—in particular, his views on the nature of being a true revolutionary and his own homophobia—were simply wrong. After the release of this film, things were never the same.

This section provides insights into the sweeping changes that have occurred in Cuban cultural life in recent years. It is difficult to understand the enormous importance of culture in Cuba—seen most clearly in the 20 percent of the nation's population who attend the annual Book Fair that starts in Havana and then sweeps for several weeks throughout the island. Daniel Salas González analyzes the phenomenon of an official policy that has as its principal goal ensuring that cultural expression is accessible to all Cubans—in many ways democratizing culture. Literature, he points out, is an important expression of national culture and not merely a commodity. Government subsidies still keep the prices low on cultural performances and on books so that they can be enjoyed by the population at large.

Mention was made earlier about the *Casa de las Américas* literary prizes being the most significant for writers in Latin America and the Caribbean. This can be judged from the high number of entries in the 2012 literary competition. In all categories, some 770 submissions were received from authors from thirty-seven nations (including 172 for that year's prize for best novel and 322 for best collection of poetry). In the end, the prize for the novel category was not awarded since none of the entries were considered to be of sufficiently high standard.

Making cinema accessible to all is particularly obvious every December for the ten-day film extravaganza that envelops the nation. In December 2012 (the thirty-fourth year for the festival), some 566 films were shown—mainly but not exclusively from Latin America. There are several categories for films—documentaries, cartoons, and the full-length features—vying for the prestigious Coral awards (twenty-one competed for this award in 2012). There were also special showings of films to honor Kenji Misumi (Japan), Michelangelo Antonioni (Italy), Chris Marker (France), and Jan Svakmajer (Czech Republic) as well as a retrospective of some forty films to commemorate the centenary of the Puerto Rican film industry. In addition, twenty-one films were shown in the *Opera Prima* section, reserved for young filmmakers. In all, films from forty-six countries were shown throughout the day and night in thirteen theaters in Havana.

To make the films accessible, the prices were reasonable—a "passport" allowing the holder to see fifteen films cost 20 Cuban pesos (the equivalent of 80 U.S. cents). The variety of the films shown is remarkable. The program for December 7, 2012, to take an example from the daily newspaper *Juventud Rebelde*, lists the titles, nationalities of the director, and locations and times they are to be shown of films from Chile, Argentina, Mexico, Venezuela, Brazil, Cuba-Panama-France, the United States, Canada, Iran-Germany, Puerto Rico, Poland-Germany-Canada, France-Canada, Russia, Ecuador-Venezuela, Japan, Italy-France, Mexico-Holland-Canada, Spain, Germany, Brazil-France, Argentina–Spain–United States, Chile–United States–Mexico, Colombia-France-Italy, Great Britain–India, United States–Palestine–Israel, Czech Republic–Slovakia–Japan, Mexico-France-Spain, Cuba–Great Britain–United States, Colombia–Bolivia–United States, France-Cuba, United States–France, Sweden, Costa Rica, Colombia, the Dominican Republic, and Cuba.

Accessibility and *masividad* (mass participation) are common themes of all manifestations of cultural expression. Robert Huish and Simon Darnell study this aspect in their chapter on the development of sport capacity on the island, a program that has brought international respect for its success in competition around the world. The same commitment is found in the annual Latin American Film Festival and the biannual art exhibits (the *bienales*), at which art is taken from the galleries to the street. As Sandra Levinson indicates, the startling and provocative use of art, as well as the imagination and use of the most varied elements (including prerevolutionary refrigerators), reveals an extraordinarily vibrant cultural reality. Artistic expression is not to be restricted to traditional formats within galleries but instead is to be challenging, lively, and available to all. As a result, public spaces are often used to engage the population, as can be seen most clearly in Fuster's decoration of the buildings in an entire section of Havana.

The question of freedom of expression is, of course, pertinent to this discussion since often the impression is given (mistakenly) that artistic liberties are totally controlled by the state. Levinson shows that art has, in fact, been in the forefront of this process of adapting a pragmatic approach since many aspects of the Communist Party's reforms (such as the need for self-employment, the freedom to travel abroad, and the necessity for a rigorous questioning of official policy) had already been well established by artists. Moreover, as is the case in other cultural expressions, artists have been in the vanguard of change since they "began to say in their work what people were saying quietly in their homes."

In their insightful chapter, Par Kumaraswami and Antoni Kapcia provide an analysis of the evolution of book publishing during the Special Period and the evolving role of writers during this time. As was the case with artists, members of the National Union of Artists and Writers of Cuba stated very clearly in 2007 (following the showing of a controversial television documentary about a purge of writers in the late 1960s and early 1970s) the need for freedom of expression. They condemned in outspoken fashion the many abuses that had been committed against this in the Revolution's name in the late 1960s and throughout the 1970s. In essence, they were sending notice that their "principal loyalty to the Revolution continued to consist precisely in their ability to critique and question it from within." It was a warning to the government of Raúl Castro that cultural figures would not allow themselves to be intimidated as they had been thirty years earlier. As will be noted below, the space to critique the revolutionary process is in fact far greater than is widely thought.

Perhaps the area of cultural expression in which there have been the most rapid changes in recent years is film. Ann Marie Stock analyzes the two focal points in which this can be seen: in the use of technology and in the subject material of the films themselves. The mastery of (increasingly accessible) digital technology as well as the ability to create websites and submit their films to international festivals or upload them on YouTube have combined to create a totally different scenario for filmmakers on the island. Now, for instance, people involved in film production have access to both receive information from abroad and send their own cultural contributions. In terms of the subjects treated in the films, Stock outlines with clarity the previously taboo topics that are now treated in films, including mental illness, underground culture, the emergence of class distinctions, and a variety of social problems (e.g., in housing, employment, and health care). Particularly worthy of note is the masterful (and, for some, irreverent) 2010 film of Cuba's leading film director, Fernando Pérez, *El Ojo del Canario* (The Eye of the Canary), about the troubled adolescence of Cuba's national hero José Martí, a film that illustrates this phenomenon well. It is worth emphasizing the enormous shadow that Martí casts over all things Cuban: Fidel Castro has referred to him as his major inspiration, his bust is found in front of all Cuban schools, his image adorns Cuban 1-peso notes, and the major airport, national library, and Revolutionary Square all bear his name. To produce a film in which this immortal figure is shown to be wracked with adolescent angst illustrates an enormous degree of freedom of expression in the Cuban context.

Common to all of these aspects of cultural expression (even before the significant migration reforms of early 2013) was the element of transculturation, with Cuban artists, musicians, dancers, writers, and film directors coming and going—mainly to the United States and Spain. During the first three decades of the Revolution, this was virtually impossible, whereas now it is common. Indeed, many leading members of the cultural elite maintain homes in Cuba and abroad and travel frequently between both. The end result is a series of cultural influences across borders on what it means to be Cuban. The fact that in 2012 almost 500,000 Cuban Americans (for many seen as "refugees") returned to Cuba to visit family members illustrates clearly the welcome dropping of barriers and increase in people-to-people contacts. Obviously, this widespread exchange must also have a direct bearing on cultural matters.

On both sides of the Florida Straits, people are now realizing that barriers have to be taken down since, despite profound differences of opinion, all are Cuban. In cultural terms, the same genetic and cultural influences have had a major impact on Cubans from Havana to Hialeah. A symbol of the cultural potential that could be channeled if common sense were to prevail in the relationship between the United States and Cuba was the March 2013 concert given in Havana by *trovador* Silvio Rodríguez and *salsero* Isaac Delgado. (Delgado had left Cuba for Miami in 2006.) On a related matter, speaking of the double standard that existed in U.S. policy toward Cuba, rapper Jay-Z noted in his "Open Letter" in April 2013 after being criticized for traveling to Cuba on a cultural exchange program with Beyoncé, "I'm in Cuba, I love Cubans / This communist talk is so confusing / When it's from China the very mic / that I'm using."

Since the first edition of this book, there have been several key developments that are in many ways symbolized by three significant examples well worth noting: the publication in December 2009 of Padura's novel, the release of the zombie film *Juan de los muertos* in 2011 (both noted above), and the impact on Cuban media of the arrival in January 2013 of the Venezuela-based Telesur television channel. All three illustrate dramatically the changing face of Cuban culture.

Padura's work deals with topics that had not been examined in Cuba before, steering clear of the rather traditional novelistic fare of the day. The plot for *El hombre que amaba a los perros* is straightforward. It is the story of a series of reflections that result from meetings on a beach near Havana between a veterinary clinic assistant and a man with two large dogs who turns out to be Ramón Mercader—the person who had assassinated Leon Trotsky in Mexico in August 1940. (After serving his prison sentence, he moved to Cuba for several years before returning to live in the Soviet Union. The book is based on five years of scrupulous historical research by Padura.) There are three stories intertwined, dealing with Mercader, Trotsky, and the veterinary assistant.

The end result of this long (600-page) novel is a strong and irreverent criticism of the abuse of power and the tragic end of utopian dreams. Communism, Mercader had always been told, was supposed to introduce the perfect society, complete with justice and equality for all. This novel shows, however, that justice was perverted under the brutal control of Stalin and, by extension, the totalitarian communist dictatorship. Unquestioning militancy in political organizations and any form of fanaticism are roundly condemned in the novel by Padura, who shows how the "true believers" (such as Mercader) end up being manipulated by those who control the organizations. The end result is the kidnapping and eventual destruction of a beautiful dream by the state bureaucracy and a central dictator. Political purges, assassination, control of the media, and the development of an "Official Truth" all result in the failure of the dreamed-of socialist utopia. Heady stuff, indeed.

Prior to the publication of this novel, Padura's fame derived largely from his hugely successful detective novels (six in all), which revolved around political crimes set in Cuba of the Special Period. In these works, he also pulled no punches, criticizing the bureaucracy, corruption, double standard in Cuban society in general, and political manipulation that he witnessed in the early 1990s. Padura is hugely popular in Cuba (and is probably the best-known contemporary Cuban writer abroad, with his works translated into two dozen languages), and his novels are by far the most sought after in Havana's bookstores—when they are available. Indeed, his peers elected him as the recipient of the National Literature Prize for 2012, which in itself is a major significant development—given his penchant for criticism of the government. He has been awarded numerous international prizes. Significantly, however, the official print media on the island have traditionally chosen to downplay and ignore his work, mainly because he chose to challenge the established parameters of what should be published and has been extremely critical of aspects of contemporary Cuba, including the role of official journalism.

Clear evidence of the fast-moving changes in the Cuban cultural scene can also be seen in an unlikely format, the zombie film *Juan de los muertos* (Juan of the Dead), which was made in 2011 by Alejandro Brugués. This is a full-length film, a Cuban-Spanish coproduction that cost just under $3 million. The film follows the activities of Juan, a slacker played by Alexis Díaz de Villegas who one day discovers that Havana is being overrun by zombies. Nobody is safe from the onslaught, as the epidemic continues to grow unabated. His solution? To use his fighting skills (learned during Cuba's military intervention in Angola) and to form a business to protect Havana citizens from being turned into zombies. The slogan he chooses for his business is quite direct: "We will kill your loved ones." This is not a typical zombie film, however, since in the process of following the development of Juan's entrepreneurial skills, a tremendous amount of in-jokes criticizing Cuban foibles (and, in particular, the revolutionary government) are encountered.

Juan, for instance, refuses to head to Miami on a raft ("Why would I want to go to Miami? I have to work there," he notes). But in addition to poking fun at the slower pace of life in revolutionary Cuba and developing his skills as a self-employed *cuentapropista*, Juan viciously skewers government propaganda. Official media are ridiculed for presenting the zombies as counterrevolutionaries, U.S.-funded political dissidents, and, in general, agents of Yankee imperialism. References to the difficulties facing the population during the Special Period after the fall of the Soviet Union abound, and even the government leadership is mentioned critically. Juan defends his call to action in the exterminating business while taking a sly poke at the longevity of the revolutionary process: "What if they go on like this for another fifty years?"

This is an extremely irreverent comedy that is replete with over-the-top humor, faux gory scenes, and some hilarious moments. It is terrific entertainment and well made, with excellent acting and first-rate digital production. The film has garnered several prizes, including in 2013 Spain's prestigious Goya Award. But it also reveals the burgeoning independence of cultural expression, maturity, and self-confidence found in Cuba. This is seen in the satirical presentation of many of the challenges facing contemporary Cuba, a topic in which Brugués is extremely direct. For, as the director himself noted in a BBC interview on January 17, 2011, in summarizing the film, "It's . . . about Cubans and how they react in the face of a crisis because we've had a lot of them over the last fifty years" (http://www.bbc.co.uk/news/world-latin-america-11867532).

Another key development in the Cuban cultural scene was the arrival in January 2013 of Telesur, the Venezuela-funded television channel shown throughout Latin America. In many ways a mirror of CNN (except that its focus is clearly left of center), it has proved an extremely important contrast to the boring, one-dimensional, pro-government state channels that have been in place for decades. It is important to note that Cuban state media are generally disappointing and superficial in their news coverage, with a clear lack of balance in their reporting. The daily newspaper *Granma* (which, in fairness, notes on its masthead that it is the "official organ of the Central Committee of the Communist Party of Cuba") and the slightly less dogmatic *Juventud Rebelde* have long been the only significant source of print media. Cuban television and radio are little better, generally providing a one-dimensional summary of the news as seen by the government. (A joke about the dogmatic tone of the Cuban media is perhaps pertinent here. It is said that if the French press during Napoleon's time had been the same as the Cuban press are today, he would never have lost any wars. Why? Because no French person would ever have found out.) The arrival of Telesur has thus provided a major challenge to official media since it has provided a useful and timely alternative to the traditionally insular (and one-dimensional) Cuban media.

On April 19, 2011, President Raúl Castro's address to the Sixth Congress of the Communist Party of Cuba was direct in its criticism of the same official media: "In this area of work it is also necessary to definitively banish the habit of describing the national reality in pretentious, strident language or with excessive formality. Instead, written materials and television and radio programs should be produced that capture the attention of the audience with their content and style while encouraging public debate which demands greater knowledge and a higher level of professionalism on the part of our journalists [and the] all too common dissemination of boring, improvised or superficial reports" (http://www.walterlippmann.com/rc-04-19-2011.html). In April 2013, Deputy Minister of Culture Fernando Rojas was even more direct, calling current blogs in Cuba "the alternative press that we need." He added, "I would like us to have an alternative press, one that was revolutionary, socialist, communist, etc. And, as we don't have one, that role is assumed by the blogs" (http://lajovencuba.wordpress.com/2013/04/29/entrevista-a-fernando-rojas). Yet, while such high-ranking officials clearly saw the need for an alternative to the bureaucratic and simplistic approach to national media, little progress has been made in Cuba. Instead, that badly needed media alternative has come from abroad.

In January 2013, Telesur started its daily twelve-hour broadcasts to Cuba. They have been a revelation in Cuba, where boring, simplistic coverage on the nation's airwaves has been in place for over five decades—until now. Instead, a multitude of different stories, images, and techniques have now been presented to the Cuban audience. The inaugural speech of U.S. President Barack Obama, interviews with opposition candidates in recent elections in Venezuela and Ecuador, parliamentary discussions from several countries in the region, reports on Major League Baseball games in the United States, and widespread access to the Internet are just some examples of these novelties. Slick global news gathering, state-of-the-art technology, and the more balanced and nuanced news reports have had a major impact in Cuba, where state control of the media is complete. Undoubtedly, the concerns expressed by Raúl Castro and Fernando Rojas are significant, expressing the need for a more dynamic level of political discourse in the Cuban media. The daily broadcast of Telesur programs has now provided an alternative window on the world, and official Cuban media coverage loses badly in any comparison. It is hoped that Cuban journalists will start to emulate the more balanced view of their Latin American counterparts.

The vibrant, questioning nature of Cuban culture is illustrated throughout this section, from the insightful analyses of Cuban cultural icons such as Nancy Morejón and Leonardo Padura and the songs of Carlos Varela to the chapters of our contributors. Readers who have been brought up to believe that cultural expression on the island is one-dimensional, state controlled, and dogmatic will be surprised at the rich and varied mosaic that is analyzed here. And while state-run news media remain one area where there is indeed limited expression, it is clear that this process has to adjust to the new reality—as both the president and the deputy minister of culture indicate. Cuban cultural expression under Raúl Castro has continued the fast pace of societal change that was initiated by his brother in the early 1990s but that has developed even more rapidly—and indeed with a greater quality.

Chapter Twenty-Eight

Living and Creating in Cuba

Risks and Challenges

Leonardo Padura Fuentes

One of the problems facing Cuban culture is that it is significantly greater than the country from which it springs. This gigantic culture, whose origins can be traced back to the nine-teenth century when national culture as such was just beginning, has been with us Cubans for so long that we scarcely notice it now.

And so, when the Revolution of Fidel Castro succeeded in 1959, Cuba was already an important cultural presence in the Western world, with its creators and protagonists receiving recognition in the most diverse artistic circles. There can be no doubt that, from that point on, this solid artistic potential and this major cultural thrust received a tremendous boost in their development in Cuba. Government support helped to multiply that potential, turning it into a clear cultural reality that spread rapidly. Moreover, because of government support, culture was now available to all levels of society (as producers and consumers of our culture) and it achieved new levels of international prestige.

Other measures taken by the government helped to support and develop this new cultural reality. The 1961 Literacy Campaign was key to cultural development in the 1960s, as were the creation of schools of art and cinema, the production of books, and the development of music and theater. That decade had as its backdrop the cultural policy drawn up by Fidel Castro: "Within the Revolution, everything is possible; against it, nothing is," he noted in October 1961. An atmosphere of genuine creativity exploded full of enthusiasm and massive participation. Its first discordant note sounded with the closing down of the weekly cultural supplement *Lunes de Revolución,* its first major schism came with the Padilla affair, and the process of officially imposed "cultural parameters" that ushered in a period of profound dogma following the 1971 Congress of Education and Culture.

If the 1960s was a decade of expansion, vitality, renovation, and open commitment with the revolutionary process on the part of Cuban artists, the 1970s have been judged as a dark, repressive period, one in which numerous cultural figures (the most notable being Lezama Lima and Virgilio Piñera) were officially marginalized. Artistic parameters similar to the inauspicious dogma of socialist realism were imposed in a more or less visible fashion. It is not by chance, for example, that out of nowhere there should appear the new genre of the "revolutionary police novel." This tendency was of dubious artistic value, presenting everything in terms of us versus them, and clearly written with the intention of defending the goals of the Revolution while ignoring general aesthetic principles.

In the second half of that dark and somber decade, the Ministry of Culture was created to redirect Cuban culture. This came in the wake of several grave political errors by the government, both in the treatment of intellectuals and in the very definition of what artistic expression should be. Just a few years later, however, these new state structures began to assimilate the need for a more profound change of policy. This was not the result of a new interpretation of the cultural phenomenon per se. Rather, it was demanded by the artists themselves, who expressed their feelings clearly in their work.

As a result, from the early 1980s on, we can see the definitive rehabilitation of so many artists who had been marginalized by Cuban officialdom for almost ten years—and for a variety of reasons (perhaps because they were practicing Christians or homosexual; because their art was more of a questioning nature than one that reaffirmed official positions; or because in their literature they included clear social criticism). It was a time when a generation of Cuban cultural figures emerged. They brought a new approach to the traditional insular reality. They also felt relatively angst-free, an important development, since many of their predecessors felt burdened with the original sin of not having fought more directly in the Revolution.

If the Cuba of the 1960s was a country in the midst of social and political effervescence, a country in which socialist institutionalization was taking its first steps in the midst of the struggle for control over the cultural apparatus, the 1970s was a period when the socialist cultural project was implemented with few concessions upon a population that had mainly shown its support for the evolutionary struggle. The result of this approach, however, wreaked havoc in cultural circles: artists were repressed, and culture was taken over by an official bureaucracy.

Despite this current, however, the internal dynamic of the country, together with its deeply rooted, potent culture, ended up showing a fair degree of independence in the 1980s. At that time painters, writers, dramatists, and even dancers and people involved in the cinema took fairly substantial risks and began opting for a less inhibited cultural expression. This decision was based more on identification with the aesthetic function of art than on any direct political expression of the content.

The maturation of this process took place during one of the most convulsive social and economic periods of Cuban history and indeed the most dynamic era of the revolutionary history since the 1960s. It constituted the first clarion call, and a dramatic one at that, of significant change in Cuba. This led to the dramatic 1989 court trials that would end in the execution of important figures of the armed forces and the Ministry of the Interior, the imprisonment of other officials, and the firing of dozens more.

As the Berlin Wall was tumbling down and the Soviet Union was collapsing, Cuba experienced a terrifying political and economic solitude. The government introduced the "Special Period in a Time of Peace," a title with which it baptized the harshest economic crisis that the country had ever lived through. Just a few years later, as the crisis worsened, the government felt obliged to introduce major economic changes—with immediate social repercussions— changes never before imagined.

Many of these benefits also brought significant social change. Prostitution and a network of pimps reappeared; some social sectors suddenly became extremely wealthy; Cuban society became divided between those holding dollars and those without; an exodus of professionals moving to work in the tourist sector became visible; Cubans moved to the far corners of the earth; and religious faith and religiosity noticeable increased, as did violence and delinquency.

Symbolic of these changes was the disappearance of the term *compañero* (denoting solidarity and classlessness) in favor of the more traditional expression *señor*. All of this occurred in a society that lacked the most basic materials and where the U.S. embargo had drastically affected the economic and social life of the country.

In such a convulsive (and truly special) period, artistic and literary productive could be no less convulsive and special—as in fact proved to be the case. As a result there was a distinctive change in the relationship between the cultural creator and the state. If I were asked to define the cultural characteristics of the 1990s, I would name three: the crisis of cultural production, the winning of space by the creators to express themselves, and the massive (voluntary) exile of Cuban artists.

The first of these factors has been analyzed on several occasions. It includes a drastic reduction in the number and types of Cuban books published, television programming and films produced, art exhibitions mounted, and plays staged. It is true that in the late 1990s these difficulties were steadily overcome. Nevertheless, we have been faced with a crisis of such magnitude, a crisis in which institutions were simply unable to respond with support to the productive demands of culture. This had a special connotation in a country like Cuba, where government support had been crucial. It provoked stagnation and a fundamental rupture of the artistic growth in quantitative, and indeed qualitative, terms in several areas of cultural expression.

Closely linked to these economic difficulties of the 1990s is perhaps the factor that had proved most important of all the cultural changes of this decade—namely, the necessary opening up of space for artistic expression. It is true that there was always a certain level of ideological support for this phenomenon, and not for reasons solely linked to the economic crisis. Institutions like the Ministry of Culture, the Union of Writers and Artists of Cuba (UNEAC), and the Cuban Film Institute (ICAIC) have traditionally supported the need for their members to have access to a greater space for reflection, analysis, and criticism of themes that previously had been either censored or treated in a superficial manner.

With the economic crisis, however, the lack of institutional support to finance their projects meant that cultural figures actually gained in independence. This allowed them greater freedom of expression, and they responded with the badly needed sounds to fill the silent void that existed before. Their situation had cried out for artists and writers, film directors and singers, to voice their feelings. Yet in the midst of the previous institutionalization, this had been impossible. Now things had changed.

As a result, several alternative projects have emerged and have dealt head-on with areas previously ignored. This is seen most clearly in the Cuban cinema. To appreciate this development, one must remember that since the historic scandal surrounding the 1961 documentary "P.M.," the cinema industry has been centralized under the auspices of ICAIC and two or three similar production houses controlled by trusted institutions such as the Ministries of Education and the Armed Forces. Now that these state institutions were unable for financial reasons to take on any further projects, this created the possible space for some initial efforts by independent filmmakers—a phenomenon that previously would have been inconceivable— to produce their work in video format. Just as important, however, is the fact that even within the traditional structures Cuban cinema has developed an aesthetic vision of reality that it has been struggling to present for many years. In short, it now dealt openly with themes that it would have been impossible to examine even a decade earlier.

One film in particular clearly revealed Cuban filmmakers' urgent need to express themselves: *Fresa y Chocolate* (Strawberry and Chocolate). This film, directed by veteran Tomás Gutiérrez Alea in collaboration with Juan Carlos Tabío and based on a script of Senel Paz, has proved to be a truly significant aesthetic benchmark. It has staked out, like no other film, the claims and possibilities of Cuban art in the 1990s, one that is very different from the epic romanticism of the 1960s, the simplistic ideological presentation of the 1970s, and the critical stammering of the 1980s.

It is around this film that several others have developed, such as the controversial "Guanta-namera" (at which Fidel Castro publicly lashed out), also made by Alea and Tabío; the most recent films by Fernando Pérez (*Madagascar* and *La Vida es Silbar* (Life Is to Whistle), both of a distinctly existentialist flavor); *Amor Vertical* (Vertical Love) by Arturo Soto; and what was without a doubt the film that generated the bitterest controversy in recent years, *Alicia en el Pueblo de Maravillas* (Alice in the Town of Wonder) by Daniel Díaz Torres. *Alicia* was condemned in the local media as a counter-revolutionary work and snatched from Cuban cinemas just three days after its premiere. Even during its limited showing, the cinemas were filled with "revolutionaries," sent there to avoid any demonstration that might support a film with such perverse political intentions.

Something similar happened with Cuban literature. Again, the lack of editorial support because of the economic crisis, changes in mentality in certain spheres of the state direction, and the need for writers to reflect upon a complex and difficult reality have all combined to mold a new form of literary production. This is particularly evident in the narrative, which has contributed to the destruction of several literary taboos, as well as to the literary treatment of several topics which previously had been totally disregarded or not "well regarded." It was thought in official circles that there was never an opportune moment to deal with such themes, including exile, narcotics, homosexuality, corruption, desperation, and suicide. What is curi-ous about many of these works is that they arrived on the Cuban scene already possessing the pedigree of recognition from several international, and occasionally national, literary competi-tions. As a result, they were well known before they were distributed on the island.

And so what in happier economic times (albeit under more rigid ideological parameters) would have caused rumors and quarrels (if not full-blown scandals and possible punishment) has now been accepted as being a natural ingredient of a more open and flexible creative environment in Cuba. Perhaps the best adjective to describe this new policy is *intelligent.* And significantly all of this has come about despite the position of political protagonists (both outside and within the so-called cultural sector) who have openly expressed their opposition to this form of reflection and cultural expression, which to a certain extent they consider alien and indeed harmful to the goals of the Cuban government.

None of this means that the traditional phenomena of censorship and self-censorship have disappeared from Cuba. The freedom for all cultural figures on the island as (Cuban novelist and dramatist) Antón Arrufat explained, is conditioned by the political and social reality of the country, which in turn imposes rules of game that those in the cultural world have learned well. That said, it is indeed true that the levels of permissiveness and the ceiling of tolerance have grown. Now, thanks to the economic crisis of the 1990s, Cuban culture has gained space: cultural workers now possess increased possibilities both to reflect and to express themselves, possibilities that simply did not exist before. These possibilities now extend as far as dealing with the thorny ideological and aesthetic challenges of working "within the Revolution," a process which for many years had been reduced to working "in favor of the Revolution"—and nothing else.

The economic context has also brought about another feature of Cuban culture that previ-ously did not exist: the possibility of commercializing Cuban cultural work. As a result, several writers now publish their manuscripts in Spain, Mexico, and Italy before they appear in Cuba. Dozens of artists hold exhibitions of their work throughout the world and sell it before foreign galleries, often without the slightest involvement of the state apparatus. And Cuban actors work abroad for international companies.

The most complicated and heartrending of these end-of-the-century problems, however, against which the only bureaucratic measure has traditionally been repression, is undoubtedly the mass exodus of members of the cultural sector. This has notably impoverished Cuban cultural life. This fact of life, which, given the significance of the numbers involved, could be perhaps compared with the 1959–1961 exodus, is really quite different. Early in the revolutionary process, several key figures in the cultural realm left Cuba, including Jorge Mañach, popular singer Celia Cruz, ethnologist Lydia Cabrera, and television magnate Goar Mestre. The political process at that time, however, produced a dynamic of such tremendous growth, supporting the development of a radically new culture, that it was possible to overcome the loss of these figures.

The exodus of the 1990s was very different, however. It was produced by people who had been formed within the revolutionary cultural tradition, and it included some of its most notable representatives (the great historian Manuel Moreno Fraginals, the novelist and film director Jesús Díaz, the extremely popular painter Tomás Sánchez, musicians like Arturo Sandoval, the journalist and writer Norberto Fuentes, almost the entire generation of plastic artists trained in the 1980s, and finally a legion of television and film actors including Reynaldo Miravalles).

It is worth noting, however, that for the first time since 1959, cultural workers have left for both economic and cultural reasons. This is also seen in the public attitude toward the revolutionary process of these intellectuals. The "economic" exiles are able to maintain links with Cuban cultural institutions, to enter and leave the country, and to exhibit their work here in Cuba, a development which has meant that they have not broken completely with Cuba, even if their work for the most part is produced and distributed outside Cuba. By contrast, their "political" counterparts, definitively distant from the Cuban system, have become the last legion of political dissidents who are officially recognized as such. A significant part of their work—if not all of it—supports this definitive rupture, since it appears irreconcilable, at least given the parameters being debated at present.

Within the island an attempt has been made to build bridges between state institutions and Cuban exiles who do not maintain political positions that are hostile to the government. An example of this happens with the so-called Cuban Americans who left the island during their childhood. On the other hand, the tension is maintained, and indeed it has sharpened, between Cuban authorities and those who could be considered political dissidents. The official position toward them is the same as it has always been: to ignore them totally and, if possible, to alienate them from their cultural roots. Such an approach goes above political affiliations or political will. Guillermo Cabrera Infante is clearly a Cuban writer, even though government officials may not admit it, publish the fact, or even recognize him in Cuba. And even though Cabrera Infante himself might state that he doesn't want to be considered a Cuban writer, or denies the fact (as he has done), he is clearly a Cuban writer.

The basic option of these dissidents, meanwhile, has been more or less the same: They increase their political opposition to the government in response to the system. In some cases, too, in works of doubtful artistic merit, they have condemned the Cuban government. This tactic is clearly the quickest way to develop an audience, and it is an approach that has led to their work being distributed widely, and to a fairly substantial income.

It is a fact that, for any nation in the world, the departure from circulation of a notable percentage of those working in the cultural sector leads to a serious loss for the country's spiritual life. And Cuba is clearly no exception. The surrounding cultural atmosphere is made up of figures who grow in that country, producing work that is inspired by daily experiences there, and leaving a legacy through their words, their work, by means of a necessary accumulation of visions and opinions. The absence of such figures, whatever their cultural stature, produces a vacuum that is combined with the other vacuum stemming from the crisis of production by national institutes. The end result is that Cuban culture is suffering from the presence of both these blows, different but at the same time complementary.

Despite the complex and dramatic features of the actual situation of Cuban culture, I believe that the country is living through a period of special creative effervescence. We see in Cuba today the flowering of the results of this small space that is now available for reflection, for creation, and for debate. If it is true that some sectors, and especially the newspapers and television, are little more than instruments of propaganda instead of information, we also need to recognize that today many people in the cultural sector are expressing themselves with greater depth within the space of "conditional freedom" that they have been winning in recent years. Doing so, of course, is not without risks (which can range from censorship to deliberately ignoring them or their work in the media). That said, risks and censorship can also be a challenge to the imagination.

Because of this complex context, it is no coincidence that Cuba has once again created a culture that is so much larger than the small insular territory from which it springs. People in several Spanish-speaking nations are increasingly speaking about the boom of the new Cuban novel, thanks to the work of a dozen or so authors from several generations whose work has received a number of prizes in international competitions. In addition, Cuban music (both traditional and modern) is at a peak in terms of creativity and financial return. This can be seen in international prizes being awarded at the highest levels, concerts given at the most desirable venues in the world, and impressive record sales, even in the United States.

The Ballet Nacional de Cuba has recently celebrated its fiftieth anniversary by touring Europe and North America, revealing in its productions its continuing vitality. The plastic arts, too, are now obligatory points of reference on the artistic and commercial circuits in Paris, Geneva, and New York, with Cuban artists increasingly winning international competitions. And finally the Cuban cinema, still badly affected by the economic crisis, continues to produce miracles, with prizes piling up in many international film festivals.

And so, in the midst of tensions and risks, with artistic expression produced both in Cuba and abroad, often with virtually no resources, Cuban culture has returned, larger in so many ways than the relatively small country that produced it. This process over the last forty years has been hard and complex. The rigors of censorship, the effects of being marginalized, and the current presence of a voracious marketplace for these talents—all have blazed the trail for today's cultural expression. Above all, however, and with so many of its talents living abroad, the cultural creativity of this small Caribbean island continues to be one of the greatest riches of the Cuban nation and, why not, of the entire world.

NOTE

Leonardo Padura Fuentes, "Living and Creating in Cuba: Risks and Challenges," in *Culture and the Cuban Revolution: Conversations in Havana,* by John M. Kirk and Leonardo Padura Fuentes (Gainesville: University Press of Florida, 2001). Reprinted with permission of the University Press of Florida.

Chapter Twenty-Nine

A Black Woman from Cuba, That's All

An Interview with Nancy Morejón

Nancy Morejón

This interview took place in Havana in 2000. The interviewer is John M. Kirk.

Kirk: Does the fact that you are a poet and a black poet mean that you have more responsibilities than a white woman?

Morejón: I am always fearful of stereotypes. Of course, the very notion of being a white writer in Cuba is an exceptionally abstract concept. To a large degree, my analysis is based on the fact that every Cuban is a person of mixed cultures and diverse racial origins. Every Cuban is a true cultural blend. I have read many books on feminist philosophy, and I think that we have to proceed with great caution when analyzing any stereotypes. At the same time, I believe that, as a black woman, yes, indeed, I do have things of value to say. Because of those origins, I come from a history of suffering, and I always have to be alert, to share that history, to have it felt by others. At the same time, I don't have to exaggerate.

Kirk: Is there still racial prejudice in Cuba?

Morejón: Yes, because eradicating it is an extremely slow process. For me, racial discrimination is the exercise of those racial prejudices. To stop that, I believe that making people aware of their conduct, developing an ideological understanding of the problem, is far more effective than resolving the abuses solely through legal means. This does not mean that there should not be laws against discrimination—only that we also need to channel the true spirit of the Revolution to all sectors. Some people here say, "Don't talk to me about the race question." But we do have to examine this again because it is an important matter here in Cuba. At times, people have been afraid to talk openly about it and have not known how to deal with it as they should. And that is why there are such gaps in our understanding, gaps which we hear more about all the time. That is why we need to reconsider so many facets of our revolutionary traditions because this problem of racism is a universal problem, one affecting all humanity and not just Cuba. For example, if we analyze what has happened since 1989 in the former socialist community, we can see how the question of ethnic identity has been revisited. The proof of this can be seen in Bosnia-Herzegovina or in Chechnya. If we don't address this factor, if we do not study it and seek to resolve it, we may ultimately face unwelcome surprises. And so I think that we should examine in more detail the question of race relations.

Kirk: Do you, as a black woman, feel any responsibility to help in this process?

Morejón: Yes, I do, and also from my perspective as a writer. But it has to be by means of a high-quality artistic expression because no matter how good the message may be, it will be useless unless it is done well, but I also need to speak with others in the cultural milieu. I have already spoken with film directors and have suggested the need to make a film about this very issue. We cannot simply forget the racial question. We also need to see black characters somewhere other than in films about slavery. We badly need something more contemporary and more pertinent.

Kirk: A question on the concept of utopia, which you describe well in your poem "Divertimento" (Amusement). In it, you refer to Cuba in the following manner: "Between the sword and the carnation / I love Utopias / I love an island which lies piercing the throat of Goliath / like a palm tree in the center of the Gulf / I love a David / I love everlasting freedom?" How do your feelings of evident nationalism react to the "pact with the devil" that the Cuban government has undertaken in order to survive? How do you feel when you are faced by the near realities of tourism, prostitution, search for the dollar, and foreign investment?

Morejón: It is a reality that in many ways is upsetting, in part because it was so unexpected. We need to be audacious if we are to function properly in this new context. We are convinced about what we need in order to survive. We also know well that the process cannot be stopped since otherwise Cuba would remain completely isolated. In essence, we have witnessed several developments over which we had no control, and as a result we had to reconsider many things. Now that tourism has returned to play such a major role in the economy, we have the opportunity to receive a fair amount of income for the national economy. At the same time, we have to be careful about the type of tourism that we seek to develop. We can't develop the form that they have in Barbados, for example. We can have, for instance, a positive kind of tourism, one that does not need to use the bodies of our women as a hook to bring in male visitors. It is fair to say that we have been surprised by the kind of tourism that has sprung up in certain sectors. It has been painful for us in many ways. At the same time, I don't believe that this situation will be resolved by repression. Rather, we need to reflect upon the whole issue of tourism in order to see how it can be useful for our country and also what we need to confront in a vigorous fashion. We have discovered a very serious phenomenon, but again it seems to me that this cannot be resolved through repressive means.

Kirk: Have you written anything about this new reality of Cuba?

Morejón: No. And that is not because I haven't wanted to because I have thought a lot about this new reality (which in many ways I dislike). Rather, I haven't written anything because I don't want any of my comments to be misinterpreted. At times, if you say something controversial, people think that you want to become some kind of famous dissident. And that is definitely not my case. I believe that I have had many opportunities to play the role of dissident, but I'm not the slightest bit interested in that game. At the same time, I do believe that it is necessary to have a space where you can air concerns. We have to encourage people to study this reality and to be honest when facing the problems that we have. If that's not the case we are in trouble.

Kirk: In your opinion, what have been the major cultural successes of the Cuban Revolution? And what have been the failures?

Morejón: Often we see errors, but we don't realize just how serious they are until later. And we regret that they were made in the first place. But let's start with the positive elements. One can note there the tremendous potential which we came to see in ourselves. The Revolution opened doors for us and allowed an enormous social mobility. Many walls that blocked communication were demolished, and taboos were cast out. At the same time, there came a certain point when the idea of massive numbers of people pursuing cultural interests became a priority of the government, often above everything else. They forgot that, in order to appreciate art, people have to have some basic ideas about the need to recover the essence of beauty. It is very true that liberating social sectors as well as progress and social mobility clearly need not be limited to the individual. Just the opposite: they have to reaffirm it. The problem was that, often, closely connected with this emphasis on such a massive approach to culture there came the accompanying practice of justifying mediocrity, often in the name of a supposed form of equality. As a result, we have often protected mediocre cultural expressions, and I believe that we should be more rigorous.

Kirk: In every society, there are absolute and limited freedoms. How would you describe the freedom that currently exists in the Cuban cultural forum?

Morejón: I think it's important to take into account our reality. We are a country that is still under siege and one that has never been alone. We must always remember the hostility to which we have been subjected. There are other limitations that need to be considered. In this "Special Period," we have had limited paper and, of course, all sorts of limitations on cultural resources. This country has a very high level of education, and much of the money that we could have used for cultural purposes has instead been used to buy textbooks. We simply don't have the resources to do both. Very often, people abroad see us talking about our free education as some sort of empty political slogan, but in fact it is a reality and a priority. This element in the midst of the Special Period has limited literary life enormously, and as a result there are fewer journals, literary competitions, publications, et cetera. We need to recover all the lost terrain in this matter. I feel that Cuban writers today are demanding things that simply cannot be conceded in a period like this since we are facing difficulties as critical as the Bay of Pigs invasion or the missile crisis. This country has to survive. Moreover, "freedom" has many facets, and many people think that they have to make demands on the state for their freedom. I think that there are, in fact, several "freedoms" and not just "freedom" in absolute terms. And freedom here has to be conditioned, or affected, by the hostility that we have encountered in the last forty years. Now it is practically a psychological phenomenon. We are all subjected to the same tensions. I personally believe that a writer has to feel a major responsibility, resulting from the nation's identity, as well as a major ethical responsibility in regards to the community. As a result of those twin factors, one needs to know that there are things that can and cannot be done because the Revolution has the right and the duty to exist. Of course, there have been many errors here, basically because we all have limited conceptions of what the Revolution should be. To give you an idea, my parents had a utopian idea of the Revolution. They would argue, for example, that a revolutionary shouldn't drink Amaretto liqueur. . . . As you can see, we have come to accept many stereotypes, and we badly need to struggle against that. We need to respect differences and diversity, and precisely because of that fact, I am certain that there were errors in cultural matters. Che, too, was a declared enemy of socialist realism, and I believe that we should respect his honesty. By all means, we should have the freedom to criticize dogma and stereotypes, but we must always bear in mind the reality of our history.

NOTE

Nancy Morejón and John M. Kirk, "A Black Woman from Cuba, That's All," in *Culture and the Cuban Revolution: Conversations in Havana,* by John M. Kirk and Leonardo Padura Fuentes (Gainesville: University Press of Florida, 2001). Reprinted with permission of the University Press of Florida.

Chapter Thirty

Two Songs

Carlos Varela

William Tell

William Tell didn't understand his son
Who one day got tired of having the apple placed on his head,
And started to run away.
His father cursed him—
How could he now prove his skill?
William Tell, your son has grown up,
And now he wants to shoot the arrow himself.
It's his turn now to show his valor with your crossbow.
Yet William Tell did not understand the challenge:
Who would ever risk having the arrow shot at them?
He became afraid when his son addressed him,
Telling William that it was now his turn
To place the apple on his own head.
William Tell, your son has grown up,
And now he wants to shoot the arrow himself.
It's his turn now to show his valor with your crossbow.
William Tell was angry at the new idea,
And refused to place the apple on his own head.
It was not that he didn't trust his son—
But what would happen if he missed?
William Tell, your son has grown up,
And now he wants to shoot the arrow himself.
It's his turn now to show his valor with your crossbow.
William Tell failed to understand his son—
Who one day got tired of having the apple placed on his head.

Tropicollage (Selection)

He left in a Havanautos rented car
Heading to the beach at Varadero,
Havana Club in the sand,
Smoking a cigar
And taking pictures,
Leaning against a palm tree.
Returning to the Habana Libre hotel,

He hired a Turistaxi to go to the Tropicana night club.
On the way to the airport,
He left believing
That he really understood Havana.
He took with him
The image they wanted him to have.
And in his Polaroids
And his head he carries
Tropicollage.
He never went to the real Habana Vieja
Nor to the barrios
Of workers and believers.
He took no photos
On the city reefs
Where a sea of people swim.
He never saw the construction workers,
Cementing the future
With bricks and cheap rum.
Nor did he meet those guys
Changing money 5 for 1.
That too is my country,
And I cannot forget it.
Anybody who denies it
Has their head full of
Tropicollage
I know that dollars
Make the economy go around—
Just like flour makes bread.
But what I don't understand
Is that they confuse people
And money.
If you go to a hotel
And are not a foreigner,
They treat you differently.
This is happening here.
And I want to change it.
And anybody who denies this
Has their head full of
Tropicollage

NOTE

The lyrics for "William Tell" and "Tropicollage" are reproduced with the permission of Carlos Varela.

Chapter Thirty-One

Culture for the Masses?

Daniel Salas González

Some in Havana still remember the unusual cry of street vendors: "¡*El Quijo*! ¡*El Quijo* for just a quarter!" This was in 1960, days after the first anniversary of the Revolution, and the *Quijo* refers to the most illustrious of Spanish novels, *The Ingenious Gentleman Don Quixote of La Mancha*, which is precisely the first book title the new government printed at the recently created National Publishing Office. The idea was the result of discussions between then Prime Minister Fidel Castro and novelist Alejo Carpentier and led to an edition of 100,000 copies that, because of its low price, were meant to reach even the most humble of readers. At first glance, it doesn't seem very rational to produce such a large number of copies of an important but difficult book in a country of somewhat under 7 million habitants at the time and with more than a million people totally illiterate (and whose population over age fifteen barely had on average a third-grade education).

However, the solution for that low level of literacy was soon to be found. The Revolution committed itself to build a huge public education system that had as its cornerstone the Literacy Campaign, which was launched in 1961. In December of that year, Cuba declared itself to be a country free of illiteracy. How could it accomplish this? The campaign was carried out in a simple yet radical way: whoever knew how to read and write taught those who did not. Teenagers and youngsters in junior high and above enlisted in massive numbers, received elementary training in teaching literacy, and set out to battle ignorance, sometimes in their neighborhood, and often in faraway areas where there never had been a school at all.

In one of his best-known phrases, the nineteenth-century Cuban intellectual and independence hero José Martí noted that being cultured was the only way to be truly free. Based on this idea, the Revolution attempted to place what Fidel Castro once called "the great heritage of mankind, culture" in the hands of the masses. In a speech in 1960, he noted, "Any worker or child of a poor family can take part in that heritage. To do so they just needed one thing to be able to achieve something that took millions of people and thousands of years to develop: to know how to read" (Castro 1960).

Over four decades later, Castro's time as a head of state was coming to an end. It was a time of far-reaching social problems that resulted from more than ten years of economic crisis after the demise of the Eastern bloc in 1989. Many students were already deciding to leave high schools and universities because of the few opportunities for making a decent living based on continuing formal studies. It was then, after 2000, that the "Battle of Ideas" unfolded. This process involved a large state and social movement in the fields of education, communication, and propaganda with the goal of turning Cuba into the most educated country in the world.

Beyond the hyperbole, the basis for this massive effort in promoting education was a fundamental goal of contradicting the principle that material conditions determine culture. Conventional wisdom says that, if you are poor, you have fewer opportunities and that those that come to you are harder to seize. But the Revolution claimed to find a way out of this vicious circle by offering a basic cultural and spiritual enrichment as a means of overcoming the scarcity of material conditions that resulted from constant difficult economic times and U.S. government hostility.

There was a fundamental ambiguity in the early government approach to cultural expression, summed up in the famous quotation of Fidel Castro, "Within the Revolution, everything goes; against the Revolution, nothing" (Castro 1961). Yet who knew where the dividing line between these two concepts was? Despite the ambiguity, it is clear that Cuban cultural policy of this time cannot be properly understood without paying attention to this mass process of providing culture to all. The democratization of culture and the stimulus to popular participation are two key factors in this process.

The basic government formula consisted of placing national cultural heritage within easy reach of the majority. In doing so, it blurred the frontiers between cultural expressions of the elite and access to the popular arts by the masses of people traditionally excluded from enjoying these. As a result, we find the development of a culture that was perceived as being new, not so much because of its contents but rather because of the radically democratic way in which it was now made accessible to the masses, and was seen as one of the pillars for reshaping society. To strengthen this process, there was a dramatic expansion of high-quality art education programs on the island. The two best-known institutes are the National Art School (founded in 1961) and the Superior Art Institute (established in 1976).

It is not an exaggeration to say that this fundamental cultural program of making cultural expression accessible to all Cubans is one of the main legacies of the Cuban revolutionary process. As Cuba becomes a more complex society and the social and ideological project faces transformation amid the reform launched by Raúl Castro, it is important to reflect on how this approach continues today. To illustrate this phenomenon, an analysis of the most important examples is provided next.

THREE EVENTS

Events such as the International Book Fair, the New Latin American Film Festival, and the Havana Biennale of visual arts, among the most relevant of the cultural schedule in today's Cuba, are useful illustrations of this process of democratizing culture while at the same time indicating contemporary challenges.

The Book Fair, which celebrated its twenty-second anniversary in 2013, attracts the largest crowds of all cultural events in Cuba. Initially, it was organized biannually, but since 2000 it has been held annually. Its main location is La Cabaña, a monumental colonial fortress opposite Havana harbor. Other spaces for sales, promotion, and panel discussions of literary topics are held in bookstores and other central locations in the city. The events last about ten days in the capital and then start a journey lasting various periods of time across the island, visiting perhaps a dozen cities and towns. The fair is usually dedicated to one or more Cuban writers and countries, a tradition that has included Mexico, Germany, Italy, Russia, and Argentina, among others. The fair also brings a noticeable number of publishers and provides meeting opportunities to many writers and intellectuals (Cuban and foreigners) and receives extensive media attention for several weeks.

In 2012, more than 2 million people attended the different activities of the fair, which also includes concerts and lecture series. This is a significant statistic considering that Cuba has a population of roughly 11 million people. At the 2012 Book Fair, readers bought more than 1.5 million books, 40 percent of that number in Havana alone.

Foreigners often regard as curious the way that events such as the Book Fair and the Film Festival become the central stage for a kind of "culture fever" on the island. "The world's newspapers speak very little, and often in negative terms, about this island, but they should know that people here flood to the Book Fair to buy sonnets—and this in the middle of a storm," noted Joaquín Sabina, a famous Spanish musician, when he introduced a book of his poetry in 2006 ("Sabina se declaró" 2006).

Maybe the underlying principle that permits such popular support for the fair is a deliberate policy by the government to present books and literature as important cultural expressions and not as commodities. Maintaining a price scale that keeps books affordable is a laudable goal that requires a substantial subsidy by the Cuban state. Even after prices have risen in recent years, most of the titles still cost the equivalent of between $1 and $2 dollars for paperbacks.

In a phenomenon related to large cultural expressions such as the Book Fair, the expansion of Cuban literature has also been benefited in the past decade by the establishment of regional publishing houses. This process consists of having about twenty modules of semi-industrial presses in several provinces that deal with the task of supporting a local literary scene and that have promoted the work of literally hundreds of authors who otherwise would not have the opportunity to have these works published.

Economic dictates are key factors in the austerity policy promoted by Raúl Castro. At the same time, the government has made clear that it will continue to support publishing but within rational limits. Book publishing is thus now largely dependent on the interests of the population, with presses adjusting their print runs according to demand. As the director of the Cuban Book Institute noted in 2011, "We can't continue producing 10,000 copies of a book that probably does not have six thousand readers" (Romay 2011).

Despite official statements of support for this wide-ranging process of Cuban cultural democratization, it is clear that economic concerns are becoming increasingly important in the publishing industry. In his inaugural speech at the Book Fair in 2012, the writer Ambrosio Fornet, to whom the event was dedicated, noted, "We are concerned that socio-economic changes, the acceptance by some of market values, and the inexorable passage of time, may well dissolve or reduce drastically this process of affirming our identity or, if you prefer, this rejection of cultural colonization—which has characterized our quest for identity in the past" (Fornet 2012). Fornet's concerns are well founded. It is true that a small but valuable number of Cuban authors have achieved considerable market success. Their work is published outside of the island, mainly in Spain. Until now, Cuba's publishing industry has remained an enclave oblivious to economic reality, but that is changing.

The New Latin American Film Festival in Havana has much in common with the success of the Book Fair. Because of its hugely popular level of participation, the festival—born in 1979 and held annually—generates a sort of winter excitement that turns the landscape of Havana into one of crowded movie theaters that lasts until late at night. The fact that a ticket is just two Cuban pesos (about ten American cents) is no doubt a key factor. Some people even take their vacations at this time in order to see some of the dozens of films being shown, mainly from Latin America. Mass participation is again very noticeable.

Initially, the festival's goal was to promote a clearly Latin American cinema movement with a distinctive social and aesthetic political commitment. With the passage of time, however, the choice of films has evolved: indeed, today, a diversity of films from all over the world is shown. What has not changed, however, is the passion of the Cuban people for the cinema. The festival, held in December every year, remains as popular as ever—with tens of thousands of fans attending the scores of film showings.

Somewhat different is the underlying principle of the visual arts Havana Biennale. This art festival relies less on the mass involvement of the public in cultural expression than on the strength of a national artistic movement supported by a vigorous system of art schools. A key factor underlying this festival is a vision based on an antihegemonic cultural policy projected from the South that pioneered a form of globalization of cultural practices of recognition and decolonization. By "South," I mean a geopolitical concept that is an alternative to the powerful and rich global "North."

Starting in 1984, there had been eleven biennales by 2012. They have included artists from Latin America, Africa, the Middle East, and Asia, and in recent years European and North American artists have also participated. Organized by the Wifredo Lam Center of Contemporary Art, the biennale has traditionally aimed to support the artistic expression of the so-called Third World. Its aim is to generate alternative legitimacy in a forum different from the main centers of art in developed countries. In recent years, the biennale has been transformed from substantive Third World–related concerns to more universal social and aesthetic issues of our time. For example, under the basic goal of supporting "artistic practices and social imaginaries," the 2012 edition of the event spilled out of museums and galleries to transform iconic spaces of Havana, such as the Malecón and the Prado Avenue.

Official support for these events results in a notable level of promotion in all media and massive public attendance. Government television channels usually publicize these activities. However, as is the case with many events in Cuba, resource support is always precarious, and as a result, the biennale has at times become in fact a triennial after being postponed because of insufficient support. They remain extremely popular, however, and although it is a challenge to become "literate" in matters of contemporary art, it is worth noting that available data indicate that 1.4 million Cubans (approximately 10 percent of the population) attended professional art exhibits in 2011.

In terms of the process of democratizing art and making people appreciate/participate in related functions, perhaps the most relevant factor is the remarkable system of finding and training talents through a "pyramid" of different art schools, ranging from the elementary to the university level (all of which is at no cost to the student). This system continues to supply professional artists to the local scene as well as to the international stage. For example, the Superior Arts Institute has graduated more than 650 in the field of visual arts since its founding in 1976, while a significantly higher number have graduated from the professional midlevel National School of Art.

All of this said, hard questions remain: Is not this laudable intention of democratizing culture a smokescreen for ideological control by the government over the creation, production, promotion, and popularization of the various forms of expression? Are cultural policy and its institutions just tools to stifle creative freedom and nullify the very condition of the artist? The truth is that the reality of Cuban culture, while not resembling a fairy tale by any standards, is also far from being a Caribbean remake of an Orwellian script. It is very clear that throughout this history, one can indeed trace the attempts by the bureaucracy to minimize, contain, silence, or discredit the social and political criticism made in the languages of art or intellectual work. At the same time, creators in all areas of cultural expression have had access to and have created spaces to legitimately develop their activity (often promoted by the official institution itself). Moreover, when they were deemed to have strayed from the revolutionary path, the "punishments" (when applied by the state) have often been caricatures of the punishments of Stalinism. In general terms, this process can be seen not as a struggle between the Revolution and members of the cultural field but rather as one between the dogmatism and censorship wielded by orthodox bureaucrats and the legitimate right of criticism—all under the umbrella of the Revolution.

Precisely because they enjoyed a fair degree of autonomy, most Cuban creators, even when clear elements of criticism or dissidence concerning the official accounts can be found in their work, remain "within the Revolution," as defined by Fidel Castro in 1961. It is inside this accommodation in the larger context that their work acquires immediate social relevance, which is one of the aspects that, in addition to its own aesthetics, seduces and magnetizes the public in the island.

WHAT IS THE FUTURE?

More than a decade after the call for the Battle of Ideas, the fire of the campaign to ensure access to culture for the masses and to make education available to all has died down. There are no longer speeches—often lasting hours— at rallies, and the corresponding discourse is much calmer. Arguably, these themes are just as essential for the survival and promotion of cultural values within the revolutionary process as they were more than half a century ago. The efficiency of institutions, the drastic reduction of the influence of the bureaucracy, and the search for self-financing are among the major issues now being discussed.

Myriad closely linked phenomena must be closely monitored to update this path for cultural democratization, especially when social inequalities are accentuated. The impact of technology on consumption, the characteristics of communities, the linkage with tourism, the cultural policy instruments with which to access the expanding private and cooperative sectors, the quality of education, and many other aspects all deserve to be taken into consideration. Instead of a vertical top-down government policy, we increasingly encounter the desire to promote horizontal coordination and greater participation based on the knowledge of the concrete reality of each place, its history, its traditions, and its needs.

If culture is the object of close attention by the government, it is not just for the sake of cultural expression per se—but also because it can foster solidarity, civility, and humanism. In his speech at the Book Fair in 2012, Fornet noted, "We are not satisfied with knowing that books are published, exhibitions are inaugurated, that plays and ballet performances take place, and that the most authentic expressions of our urban and rural societies are divulged. We also need to know to what extent machismo and homophobia have been reduced, how we are going to deal with the confusion, social problems, racial prejudice, administrative corruption, the viscous waste that the crisis of the 1990s left us" (Fornet 2012).

An unavoidable reality is that the environment that allows and encourages cultural development has an economic basis. After all, in the same article that launched the important concept that real freedom required a true and solid foundation of culture, Martí also noted (although the concept is less quoted) that in the common realm of human nature, it is also necessary to be prosperous in order to be truly good. Perhaps a key issue for the future of cultural democratization in Cuba is that we can no longer choose between these two sentiments of Martí—instead, we now need both.

334

Daniel Salas González

REFERENCES

Castro, Fidel. 1960. "Discurso por la entrega del antiguo cuartel Goicuría convertido en centro escolar Mártires del Goicuría, al Ministerio de Educación, el 29 de abril de 1960." http://www.cuba.cu/gobierno/discursos/1960/esp/f290460e.html.

———. 1961. "Speech to the Intellectuals." http://lanic.utexas.edu/project/castro/db/1961/19610630.html.

Fornet, Ambrosio. 2012. "Que los cambios se produzcan dentro de una continuidad." http://www.cubadebate.cu/especiales/2012/02/10/ambrosio-fornet-que-los-cambios-se-produzcan-dentro-de-una-continuidad/.

Romay, Zuleika. 2011. "Feria cubana del libro, un proyecto ecuménico esencialmente popular." http://www.alba-tcp.org/contenido/feria-cubana-del-libro-un-proyecto-ecum%C3%A9nico-esencialmente-popular-19-de-enero-de-2011.

"Sabina se declaró 'amante' de Cuba y presentó un libro en la Feria de La Habana." *Cubaencuentro*, February 13, 2006. http://www.cubaencuentro.com/cultura/noticias/sabina-se-declaro-amante-de-cuba-y-presento-un-libro-en-la-feria-de-la-habana-12187.

Chapter Thirty-Two

Nationhood and Identity in Contemporary Cuban Art

Sandra Levinson

This generation of Cuban artists is the most educated, the most worldly, and probably the most recognized of any generation since 1959. In many ways, the artists are Cuba's superstars, equal to musicians and sports figures. At the end of this chapter, I have listed two books and several websites and urge those of you interested enough to explore Cuban art to go to these sites: first, to see the art, and, second, to learn more about what can only be touched on here: the enormous influence that the Cuban Revolution has had on every aspect of the visual arts and the way in which the artists' search for their own identity is inextricably bound up with that of their "*patria*."

"Socialism with salsa" is what *Newsweek* once called Cuba—and that was the Cuba I first met in 1969. While Fidel Castro and his *compañeros/as* were the socialism, the artists, writers, dancers, and musicians were the *salsa*. These artists played a crucial role in the developing Revolution. Their art provided the words, sounds, and images that would explain the revolutionary process to the world. More than 300 trips later, I am still stunned by the energy, passion, and creativity of Cuba's artists.

Art lost its innocence with the Revolution. The social function of art changed. No longer was it simply an aesthetic commodity to be produced for and sold in the marketplace. Art instead had an essential role in transforming the island and transmitting the ideas of the Revolution. It became a way of teaching, of persuading, and of inspiring. It taught revolutionary ideals. It persuaded Cubans to value the community over the individual. It inspired Cubans to emulate the best among them. Socially and politically engaged art was itself revolutionary.

The flourishing of the arts in Cuba that came with the Revolution is one of its most lasting legacies and one that should not be considered "secondary" to political and economic changes. The culture of the Revolution and the forced separations from the traditional—politically, culturally, and economically—has shaped something marvelously new, with more depth and breadth, a more informed art. The revolutionary years have added special ingredients to the mix. What has captivated me about Cuban art is how deeply its themes, techniques, and imagery have been affected by aspects of the Revolution and the radical changes in society. And unlike Eastern Europe, where the communist countries demanded that art conform to realism in style and socialism in content (i.e., "socialist realism"), Cuban artists were mostly free to express themselves in their own ways. This does not mean that there have not been tensions—and strong ones—between artists and government bureaucrats over the years; that is also an effect of the Revolution to be discussed later.

The changing profile of the arts kicked in almost immediately following the revolutionary victory, and all of the traditional art forms—such as photography, graphic design, painting, and printmaking—came to be used for new purposes. The great photographer Alberto Korda, who had always shot for commerce, especially in the world of fashion, now began shooting new models, Fidel and Che. Portrait photographer Osvaldo Salas and his teenage son, Roberto, returned from living in New York City, and together with Korda and Raúl Corrales, captured the life and times of Fidel and Raúl Castro, Che Guevara, and other young leaders of the Revolution.

Photography may have changed most radically, moving quickly from its early documentation of revolutionary activities to more personal work as photographers turned their lens on ordinary people going through daily life routines. Today, a new generation of conceptual artists sees photography as one more tool in their art choices, as in the works of Carlos Garaicoa and Cirenaica Moreira. Liudmila Velasco and Nelson Ramírez de Arellano Conde (he is the director of the Fototeca, started by Marucha as a repository and exhibition space for photographic work) work together under the collective name of Liudmila & Nelson. They explore Havana in a series of layered photographs, sometimes beautiful and sometimes sad or depressing, often documenting a possible future Havana. At the Eleventh Havana Biennial in 2012, their exhibit consisted solely of a huge wall-size video that showed their photograph of the José Martí monument with a gently rolling sea covering the Plaza de la Revolución, complete with the soft sound of lapping waves. Visitors stood before the wall mesmerized— and sad.

Graphic design before the Revolution was used almost exclusively to sell cigarettes, clothing, automobiles—anything. Now, design had a new purpose: to sell ideas and the new ideals—save water, save electricity, study, struggle, and emulate while also promoting the new cultural life of the Revolution, especially in film. All of the young government offices hired their own designers to publicize their work. The new posters warned against smoking, urged recycling, taught history lessons, fought absenteeism in the workplace, and urged the shaping of a collective consciousness. Throughout the 1960s, 1970s, and 1980s, many of the best graphic designers worked on posters to show Cuba's solidarity with burgeoning revolutionary forces, from Vietnam to Chile to South Africa. Today, a new generation of poster artists has taken all of these themes and is turning out exciting, edgy posters that persuade— use condoms to prevent AIDS, for example—and posters promoting revolutionary ideals fight for space alongside those that advertise the latest theater, film, dance, music, or art production. The poster is in Cuba to stay and is recognized worldwide as a uniquely Cuban contribution to graphic design.

Raúl Martínez (1927–1995), a well-known abstract painter and photographer when the Revolution came to power, exemplifies how it affected transitional art figures. The Revolution inspired Martínez: "It was important to me that my art spoke to ordinary Cubans," he once told me, and to reach those ordinary Cubans, he started with an image familiar to everyone: painting multiple images of their greatest hero, José Martí, in a pop art style.

Martínez continued painting multiple images of heroes, including Fidel Castro, and painting historical and contemporary figures together. His 1972 painting *Rosas y Estrellas* shows Simón Bolívar, Fidel Castro, Che Guevara, Camilo Cienfuegos, Máximo Gómez, Antonio Maceo, and José Martí in blues, bright reds, and oranges. These images differed radically from the macho way these heroes were usually depicted. Che Guevara is wearing an enormous white rose boutonniere and has his arm draped around Martí, who is holding a bouquet of white roses, an allusion to Martí's famous poem.

At the same time that Martínez was creating these images of larger-than-life heroes, he began painting multiple images of ordinary Cubans whom he also portrayed as heroes owing to their dedication to creating a new society. One, simply called *Cuba*, was covered with small rectangular portraits of Cuban workers (one was himself) and, as with all of his pop images, painted in flat, bright colors. His models were his Vedado friends and neighbors. Art, which in capitalism had been private, expensive, and elitist, was now to be public and accessible to all. These goals inspired many artists to bridge the gap that had existed between high art and the larger community.

With the collapse of the Soviet Union in 1991 and the subsequent economic hardship, many artists turned their attention to collective and community endeavors—as a way to survive artistically and as a way to support one another, their families, and their communities financially.

José Rodríguez Fuster (b. 1946) turned an entire working-class town into an act of creation—paintings and ceramics splashed with vibrant oranges, reds, purples, blues, yellows, and greens cover the town. Ceramist, painter, engraver, and sculptor, Fuster lives in Jaimanitas, a seaside village outside of Havana. His life work, like that of many artists, is intertwined with the Cuban Revolution, and his community projects are financed only through the sale of his art. His fluid, linear style and Cubist-like way of incorporating a profile into a full-faced figure led "Zippy" cartoonist Bill Griffith to dub him the "Picasso of the Caribbean."

Beginning in 1994, during the worst of the "Special Period," Fuster started a community project in Jaimanitas that has completely transformed the town by extending his art works from his own home to those of neighbors and entire streets. If a neighbor needs a roof repaired, Fuster will repair it and decorate it, perhaps with an iconic rooster. If a neighbor needs a new gate, Fuster will design one with her image and a special text in ceramic. There is a permanent ceramic chess table and chairs, filled day and night with local players; a ceramic horse that every visitor feels the need to sit atop; and an entire wraparound wall of the town dedicated to Gaudí with a giant ceramic crab crawling over the wall. Fuster's neighbors have internalized his belief that his art belongs to them. In 2008, Fuster inaugurated a three-story ceramic monument to the five Cubans who have languished in U.S. prisons for fifteen years. Fuster also cajoles other well-known artists to contribute to the community. Many of them painted murals on the walls of a newly built local day care center. In September 2012, in gratitude to the hospital and doctors who saved his leg following a deadly infection, Fuster unveiled a wall-size ceramic homage to Yemayá, the *Santería orisha*, who is the protector of children. Not incidentally, the project provides employment for many of the townspeople.

Working collectively is not confined to artists in rural communities doing folk art or what the Cubans call "*arte popular*." In 2012, the curator-artist Mayito (Mario González) started a new collective in Havana on the site of an old industrial laundry. Introduced as an exhibit space in the May–June 2012 Havana Biennial, the *Lavandería*'s huge space is ideally suited to what Mayito wants: a place where serious artists can work together as a group. Occasionally, the *Lavandería* will present exhibits, but its real intention is to provide a stable and collective working environment for artists.

Mayito had engineered two previous group exhibits working with large numbers of artists that were enormously successful and inspired him to build a more stable collective. Most spectacularly, in 2006, as old American refrigerators were being turned in to the government to be replaced by energy-saving Chinese fridges, Mayito and artist Roberto Fabelo got the idea to make art of these old refrigerators and persuaded the government to give the first fifty-two turned in to Cuban artists. During the IX Havana Biennial in 2006, the fifty-two recycled refrigerators were moved into the Convent of Santa Clara, one of the most spectacular and funny group shows in recent years. The first one I saw as I entered the convent was a fridge that had been designed as a confessional.

Many of the refrigerators had become commentaries on daily life in Cuba: the contents so sacred that one fridge had become a safe; another's freezer was now an oven; artist-actor Jorge Perugorría turned the fridge named Rocco from "Strawberry and Chocolate" into a coffin, complete with a final eulogy; Kcho continued his theme of emigration by putting oars on his fridge and calling it *Objeto soñado* (Dream Object). Abel Barroso filled his fridge with woodcuts of tanks, bombs, aircraft carriers, and satellites and called it *Se acabó la guerra fría, a gozar con la globalización* (The Cold War Is Over, Now to Enjoy Globalization). Nelson Domínguez's fridge became a warehouse of Cuban cigars. Luis E. Camejo turned his fridge into a car called Fast Food. René Peña covered all four sides with photographs of his own beautiful black naked body.

In addition to strengthening the sense of community, the Revolution gave value to the importance of the African heritage in Cuba. The slave trade brought Africa to Cuba and left a huge imprint. Manuel Mendive (b. 1944) is a painter, sculptor, and performance artist who grew up in a spiritual family. Instantly recognizable, he dresses entirely in white, befitting his commitment to African religious practices, his gray hair in long tresses. He is a *santero*, and much of his art reflects the influence of both slavery itself and the cultural and religious life brought to Cuba by the slaves. The first of Mendive's paintings acquired by the *Museo de Bellas Artes* was of a finely detailed slave ship in muted colors. One of his signature styles is poetic and dreamlike, tapping into realms of the unconscious; another is graphic and primitive. His haunting works draw on symbols and ceremonies of *Santería* and the mestizo culture of the Caribbean. In exploring his Yoruba roots, he captures the vibrant richness of Cuba's African culture and his belief that it has shaped Cuban national identity.

Mendive's performance pieces involve painting dancers' naked bodies (always black) and creating theatrical backdrops and environments. His performances for the 2009 and 2012 Havana Biennials shocked audiences with their graphic display and inspired wonder and admiration too. (Invited to perform at the Kennedy Center in 1999, his dancers were not allowed to perform naked, and Mendive was forced to paint their nude bodysuits rather than their flesh.)

The best of the younger artists influenced by African culture and by Mendive work with a solid conceptualism: artists such as Kcho (b. 1970), Alberto Casado (b. 1970), and Juan Roberto Diago (b. 1972). They are strongly affected by their African heritage, but whereas Mendive created his own world using elements of that heritage, Kcho, Diago, and Casado start from there to explore the society in which they live. (Kcho, whose father was a carpenter, uses the most ordinary materials for his large sculptural works and installations.)

Casado mixes elements of the *Abakuá* religion with political imagery, commentary on the art world, and whatever else catches his fancy. He uses a popular Cuban glass-painting technique, almost unheard of for use by trained artists. Imagery drawn in black ink on the reverse side of a sheet of glass (he told me that he often uses glass from old bus windows) is placed on top of crumpled aluminum foil painted with translucent colors, creating the effect of stained glass and precious metals. His works combine painting, collage, and mixed-media techniques, exploring themes of his identity as a contemporary Cuban and as a man of African ancestry, steeped in the *Abakuá* religion. Diago says that he thinks of himself as an art "fighter," and indeed his preference for raw materials and tough subject matter make one think of a fighter—for his art and against injustice. Slavery is a theme that runs through his work, and although he loves drawing and does it every day, the lack of good art materials in the 1990s during the Special Period turned him on to a new kind of art. He makes paintings and conceptual installations with things he finds around his neighborhood—bits of wood, plastic bottles, and rusty metal. The economic hardship faced by artists and other Cubans in the early 1990s exercised an enormous influence over their work. Driven by necessity, they began using different materials and less traditional methods; they found new and creative ways of expressing themselves.

The Revolution affected the arts in another way, too. The new society made it respectable to be both worker and artist. There was a liberating effect to the Revolution; it changed people's perspectives on what their professional lives should be and none more so than those who saw themselves as artists.

The Cuban Revolution had a profound effect on the lives and work of women artists whose number grew exponentially once they began to enter San Alejandro and later ISA art schools. The Revolution itself created an atmosphere in which exploring their liberation as women became part of the natural landscape. Sexuality, feminism, identity, and sociopolitical commentary found their way into women's art. For example, they are found in the work of contemporary artists such as Alicia Leal (b. 1957), whose work combines feminist themes with Afro-Cuban mythology; Marta María Pérez-Bravo (b. 1959), whose conceptual black-and-white photography plumbs her inner being in stark self-portraits; Sandra Ramos (b. 1969), who creates an artistic identity tied to the island and its symbols and to emigration; Tania Bruguera (b. 1968), whose performances, videos, and installation art take on power and control issues, both political and personal; Cirenaica Moreira (b. 1969), a performance artist whose photographs of her own body explore her inner self in the context of her created environment; and Mabel Poblet (b. 1986), a mixed-media artist whose work closely examines her own life and is intensely personal, even emotional, but never sentimental.

Rocío García (b. 1955) startles and provokes. Her paintings are large, tough, gorgeously colored, and, to some, scary. Women are often the protagonists or men showing off their power. Rocío often depicts the human body as a sexual object and by demystifying the body strips out all the myths of sexuality. She attacks the world of sexual repression; much of her work deals with male dominance in its ugliest form. Critics sometimes find her work too strong, too intense, and too violent, but she says that "life is more intense than my art. I play around with ambiguous situations, soft lines, hedonistic, sensual, dealing with subjects that everyone practices, not taboos exactly but sexuality in general. It seems not so easy to talk about sex in other countries. In Cuba, within five minutes of starting any conversation, you are talking about sex and violence. Love is the primary focus of my work, and eventually it leads to violence. It's a thesis: love is the perfect assassin" (interview with the author).

Sandra Ceballos (b. 1961) may be the one Cuban woman artist whose work and life are most closely linked to, identified with, and affected by the Revolution, often in a provocative, even antagonistic way. She lives in a tiny house with a small separate space and a little garden in the Vedado neighborhood, surrounded by a low wall that for years was covered with words from Fidel Castro speeches in her own handwriting. She has been a thorn in the side of officialdom for years. In 2003, the Aglutinador Laboratory was born in her small space, and a group of artists began doing more experimental shows without curatorial selection. In 2008, they did one called "We Are Porno," the first show of pornographic art in Cuba. Rocío was one of the participating artists. Sandra invited anyone to participate, and "when there was no more space on the walls, that's when we turned away the artists" (interview with the author).

In 1984, the first Havana Art Biennial debuted before biennials became popular in many countries around the world. Although it has seldom been celebrated every two years, the

Havana Biennial has become a major showcase for "Third World" art, an incredible accomplishment and commitment given Cuba's financial constraints. The Eleventh Biennial took over most public and private art spaces in 2012 to exhibit every imaginable kind of Cuban art as well as the art of Latin America, Asia, and Africa.

In the 1980s and 1990s, a few provocative exhibits were censored; artists considered too outrageous were not included in important exhibits either because their erotic work was interpreted as pornographic or because their work seemed excessive in criticizing political figures or ideas/ideals. *Volumen I* was a groundbreaking 1981 show that introduced the first generation of artists completely shaped by the Revolution: eleven artists with new content and different forms—minimalist, conceptual, performance, and pop. In other words, they presented a Cuban art completely different from what had come before. Important exhibits in 1988–1989 were held, with the support of the Ministry of Culture, at the *Castillo de Real Fuerza* specifically for shows that were unwelcome in Havana's official galleries. This turned into an authentic, critical reflection on contemporary Cuba.

That series of shows turned out to be a catalyst for several of the artists. Many artists of this so-called 1980s generation chose to leave Cuba in the late 1980s and early 1990s. Their motives varied. Some have said it was because of censorship; others admitted to being unable to deal comfortably with the huge economic hardship after the collapse of the Soviet Union. They took advantage of every possible invitation abroad, made possible largely because of the growing fame of artists shown in the Havana Biennials and some foreign exhibit spaces.

In sum, the Special Period was exceptionally difficult. Materials were unavailable, it was difficult to mount exhibits, and there was growing discord between some of the feistier artists and the government. Art became more controversial, as artists began to say in their work what people were saying quietly in their homes. When so many artists started leaving, doomsday predictions were rampant: all the good artists were leaving Cuba, and there were no others to take the place of those who left. It did not take long, however, for everyone to realize that, first, most of the artists remained in Cuba and that, second, younger artists almost immediately took the places of those who left. The art scene remained as vibrant as ever, just different. Indeed, while many of the reforms introduced by Raúl Castro have been acclaimed as illustrating his pragmatism, many of these—such as self-employment and traveling abroad and a plea for a more rigorous questioning—were already established for artists.

Today, even many of the well-known 1980s-generation artists who left during that time return to Cuba to participate in exhibits or the biennial; some consider themselves residents of both Cuba and a second homeland. The government itself now takes for granted that artists will do anything for their art, and, mostly, leaving artists alone is a win-win situation. Cuban artists, whether in Cuba or abroad, are artists whose lives and work have been profoundly affected by the Revolution itself and whose art would have been considerably less interesting without the drama of the Revolution.

APPENDIX

I am most grateful to Corina Matamoros, curator of contemporary art at the Museo de Bellas Artes, for sharing with me her profound knowledge and friendship. Clearly, she is not responsible for any of my conclusions about Cuban art.

The best current book about contemporary Cuban art in English is Rachel Weiss's *To and From Utopia in the New Cuban Art* (Minneapolis: University of Minnesota Press, 2011). Luis Comnitzer's *New Art of Cuba* (Austin: University of Texas Press, 2003) is the best study of art since 1959 and especially about the 1980s generation of artists.

There are several excellent websites with information on contemporary Cuban artists. The website http://www.cubanartspace.netprovides details on galleries with dozens of recent exhibits and biographies of artists. The single best website for current news about Cuban art is http://www.cubanartnews.org, sponsored by the Howard and Patricia Farber Collection. In addition, the website of the Farber Cuba Avant Garde collection, http://www. thefarbercollection.com, allows you to browse this excellent U.S. collection and has well-written biographies of the artists in the collection. The best website for interviews with Cuban artists is http://www.havana-cultura.com. In New York, you can visit the Cuban Art Space of the Center for Cuban Studies (231 West 29th Street, fourth floor), which has more than 10,000 works of art on-site. The Shelley and Donald Rubin Collection of Cuban art can be visited on the eighth floor at 17 West 17th Street.

Chapter Thirty-Three

Questioning Authority

Cultural Expression of Contemporary Cuban Youth

Ana M. Ruiz Aguirre

Cuban youth have grown up immersed in a deeply cultural realm. While Statistics Canada reports that only 19 percent of Canadian citizens attended a culture or heritage performance during 2012 (Petri 2012), an estimated 6 million Cubans, representing approximately 60 percent of the population, attend the National Book Fair every year (Reyes 2011). Indeed, the revolutionary government of 1959 insisted on the creation of a number of programs and institutions with the objective to promote and regulate cultural production in Cuba. *Casa de las Américas*, founded on April 28, 1959, through Law 299, remains one of the most important cultural institutions on the island, playing a decisive role in the promotion of art not only in Cuba but also in the rest of Latin America and the Caribbean (Fornet et al. 2011). Also in 1959, the National Ballet of Cuba, headed by prima ballerina Alicia Alonso, was recognized, and only eighty-three days after the establishment of the new government that same year, the *Instituto Cubano del Arte e Industria Cinematográficos* (Cuban Art and Cinematographic Industry Institute [ICAIC]) was created. The formation and government support given to these cultural institutions allowed for a Cuban national culture to emerge beyond the tourist kitsch so prevalent in previous years. Most important, however, the formation of these institutions and the importance placed on national cultural production throughout the revolutionary period allowed for the creation of a propitious cultural environment in which young artists could develop and thrive.

In this context, the cultural production emerging from the island has developed greatly during the past decade. Cuban artists have made their mark internationally and are highly sought after in the realms of visual arts and performance art, music, and ballet. Indeed, Cuba has become a cultural leader in the world, a statement that can be easily supported by mentioning ballet dancers Carlos Acosta and Viengsay Valdés, jazz musician Chucho Valdés, and visual artists Los Carpinteros and Alexis Leiva Machado (Kcho). Cuban youth are immersed in this rich and easily accessible creative environment, where they can attend shows by painters auctioned at Sotheby's for free and watch world-class ballet performances for eleven Cuban pesos (less than fifty American cents).

The complete accessibility (the result of a policy of *masividad*) granted to cultural production and the population's involvement with the arts is one of the main objectives of the Cuban government, represented not only in the low admission charges for cultural events but also in the effort to educate and encourage artistic creation at the neighborhood level through organizations such as the *Asociación Hermanos Saíz*. Formal art education is also easily accessible in Cuba, where schools such as the *Instituto Superior de Arte*, the *Escuela Nacional de Arte*, and the San Alejandro Academy allow for youth to study any art discipline free of charge. In this context, Cuban youth today have virtually unlimited access to all types of cultural expression and are able to participate in the Cuban art world extensively and actively. Given the emphasis that Cuban society places on cultural production and its enjoyment, it is not surprising that during the past five years, Cuban youth have visibly adopted art in all its forms not only to enjoy themselves but also to actively engage in as a political and social statement. Indeed, young Cubans employ music, film, visual arts, and a number of other disciplines as a means to engage, portray, and challenge the society in which they live.

The art disciplines employed in the creation of cultural products by Cuban youth have been greatly influenced by the "Special Period" and the consequent opening of the Cuban economy to foreign markets. Tourism in particular has become central to youth in order to emulate, challenge, or fuse foreign aesthetic elements, themes, and modes of production with their own creations. Tourism introduced the general population—and youth in particular—to artists, images, music, and production concepts that previously had been difficult to attain (Spencer 2010). Further, the opening of the Cuban economy meant that Cuban artists could travel abroad to present their work and consequently be influenced by the aesthetic qualities and the cultural characteristics of the art they encountered. This process can be understood as one of transculturation, further enriching the *ajiaco* (cultural stew) that is Cuban culture and that was outlined by Ortiz and Barreal (1993).

Indeed, despite its drawbacks, the influence of foreign elements resulting from tourism and the opening of the Cuban economy have contributed to the enrichment of Cuban cultural traditions and allowed for the youth to engage in new forms of expression through art. For instance, the appearance of hip-hop and *reguetón* on the island, the use of independent strategies in order to produce and distribute art, and the introduction of horror films as a new Cuban film genre can all be linked to this process. Here it should be noted that, as argued by prominent cultural theorist Roberto Fernández Retamar (1989), to doubt the validity of Cuban culture is to doubt its very existence and, further, to relegate the Cuban cultural realm to a mere echo of its colonial condition. Cuban culture, as expressed by youth today and influenced by a colorful heritage of nations, including Spain, the Yoruba of Nigeria, France, China, and the United States, cannot be understood as "pure" and singular. Instead, its traits of cultural blending, or *mestizaje*, and its constant processes of transculturation are precisely what define Cuban cultural production today.

Although the exchanges established between Cuban artists and foreigners have undoubtedly enriched Cuban art, they have also created disruptions in the cultural processes of the island. The emergence of *reguetón* as one of the most popular music genres among Cuban youth is a particularly illustrative example.

Reguetón first appeared in the eastern portion of the island, specifically in the provinces of Santiago de Cuba and Guantánamo. In this area, commonly referred to as Oriente, the Caribbean airwaves playing raggamuffin, dance hall, and reggae are easily accessible to the general population and allowed youth in this portion of the island to become acquainted with this musical genre as early as the 1990s (Bello 2012). Candyman, one of the original exponents of the genre in Santiago de Cuba, argues that *reguetón*'s main function is to make the listener dance, usually through the inclusion of mildly sexual or picaresque elements in the lyrics with the objective of maintaining the public's interest (Hernández and Ventana 2008). This feature is still central to the production of *reguetón* in Cuba, although the center of production has moved from the eastern to the western provinces—particularly Havana—during the past five or six years. Indeed, with the exception of Kola Loka and a handful of less well known groups, the most popular *reguetón* artists live and produce in Havana.

These artists include Osmani García, El Chacal, and El Micha. Young *reguetón* artists use references to daily life in Cuba in their songs and, like many other musicians in Cuba—including hip-hop artists and young *trovadores*—make use of a localized language in order to engage Cuban youth and assert themselves as part of it (Lavielle-Pullés 2011). For instance, in a recent collaboration between Kola Loka and El Micha titled "Se Extraña" (Kola Loka 2010), the singers refer to the common phenomenon of a Cuban woman deciding to live abroad but missing Cuba constantly. Referring to the motives compelling Dorotea to emigrate, they sing,

> Dorotea se fue pa' la yuma a luchar su yuca . . .

While the statement translates to "Dorotea went to Yuma to fight her yucca," it means that Dorotea moved to the United States in order to make more money. The meaning is thus lost to anyone who is not immersed in the constantly evolving street language of Cuban youth, even if they are Spanish speakers. The same can be said of a number of *reguetón* artists in Puerto Rico or the Dominican Republic who use localized slang terms, such as *guasa guasa* (coward), *abayarde* (a type of annoying insect), or *corillo* (a group of friends) (Wood 2009). In the same manner, the use of local phrases and street slang is common in music performed by Cuban youth, and it can be understood as a form of rebellion: when only a specific group of people understand the meaning of the song, anything can be said.

Young Cuban *reguetón* artists are usually immersed in the same daily dilemmas as the rest of the Cuban population. Thus, this commentary and their constant reference to known spaces of association and rituals, spoken in a recognizable localized slang over danceable beats, have made them increasingly popular with youth. However, the most distinguishable trait of Cuban *reguetón* today—and one that has caused controversy—is the use of explicit sexual references both in the lyrics of songs and in the visual content of the music videos (Hernández and Ventana 2008). The use of picaresque language has been a main staple of *reguetón* since its introduction in Cuba and has been part of the discourse of *reguetón* singers elsewhere, such as Tego Calderón in Puerto Rico. However, the Cuban press and many Cuban intellectuals have recently engaged in debates regarding the sexist connotations of a number of *reguetón* songs and the objectification of women in them (Bello 2012). Indeed, the genre has been termed a "musical massacre" by a number of commentators (Lavielle-Pullés 2011). Perhaps the song that has garnered the most negative attention is "Chupi Chupi." In the song—a collaboration between a number of some of the most popular *reguetón* singers in Cuba, including Osmani García, El Chacal, and El Príncipe—the male singers demand oral sexual favors from the female listener, who is supposed to acquiesce to the demand through dance.

"Chupi Chupi" (García et al. 2011) is not the only song in which outright sexual references are made in Cuban *reguetón*, and recent examples include "El Pudín" (García et al. 2011), featuring Osmani García, El Chacal, and Kola Loka, and "El Calentico" (Kola Loka 2012), featuring Kola Loka. However, none of these songs achieved the notoriety of "Chupi Chupi" or provoked the same amount of heated debate on the island. The popularity of *reguetón* singers has also allowed for cultural exchanges between Cuban youth living on the island, such as the artists themselves, and Cuban youth living in Miami and elsewhere in the United States. Recent international tours by Osmani García, Kola Loka, and El Chacal in both the United States and Canada have been immensely popular among Cuban youth notwithstanding the quality of the music (Vazquet 2012). In Florida, for instance, they have garnered the attention of club promoters, record producers, and video producers not only from the United States but also from Canada and Italy.

Even though *reguetón* has grown in popularity among young Cubans, it is by no means the only popular musical genre on the island. Historic salsa and timba bands, such as Los Van Van and La Charanga Habanera, continue to be favorites. Further, new musical forms of expression, such as hip-hop, have transitioned from a purely entertainment-oriented realm into social and political commentary. Hip-hop initially appeared in Cuba through radio waves, received on the northern coast of Havana during the late 1990s. Early rappers and emcees in Cuba sought to copy the music they listened to and regularly used the backgrounds of Notorious B.I.G., Public Enemy, or Tupac Shakur in their songs and emulated their lyrics (Fernandes 2003). During the early 2000s, hip-hop lyrics concentrated largely on topics such as violence in the streets, themes that were not regularly experienced by Cubans but that appeared constantly in the work of U.S. hip-hop artists. Today, Cuban rappers, especially those who have adopted the *contestatario* (or critical) moniker, make the center of their discourse the challenges that Cuban youth like themselves face every day. Groups such as Free Hole Negro, for instance, debate extensively the role of Cubans of African descent in society and government institutions, while Los Aldeanos discusses Cuba's slow bureaucratic structure and the perceived competition between Cubans and tourists for access to specific spaces and economic resources (Fernandes 2003). It is important to point out that young Cuban artists are part of the general Cuban population: they do not appear in the tabloids or have above-average incomes as a rule. In fact, in many instances, they work day jobs in order to support their artistic creation. This is true of a number of musicians in the *contestatario* movement, such as Escuadrón Patriota and Los Aldeanos, but it is also true of many of the young filmmakers and visual artists that are discussed later in this chapter. Their social standing as regular youth who also engage creatively allows these artists to truly engage with their peers and, most important, reflects their concerns, social views, and political attitudes through their artistic creation.

Hip-hop *contestatario* culture and a number of other emerging musical genres and artistic disciplines have received little support and distribution from the government institutions in charge of promoting and producing Cuban cultural production. Whereas *reguetón* has been distributed widely in the media, notwithstanding the recent controversy over "Chupi Chupi" and other such songs, hip-hop, punk, and a number of experimental visual arts have not been so lucky. The reason is both cultural and economic: cultural institutions such as ICAIC and Casa work within a specific government budget and thus prioritize more established artists and genres, such as *trova* or traditional Cuban music. In recent years, the lack of institutional support has not posed a prohibitive challenge to young artists in Cuba. Abel Prieto—Cuban minister of culture from 1997 to his reappointment as adviser to the president in 2012—strongly promoted investment in Cuban cultural production, attracting a wealth of foreign producers, promoters, and artists to Cuba. Throughout the past six years, independent cultural production in Cuba has exploded, including a number of disciplines, such as film, visual arts, and musical production. Indeed, hip-hop and electronic music have been at the forefront of the independent production of art in Cuba. In the case of hip-hop, it has been pointed out by Roberto Zurbano that the lack of institutional support has allowed Cuban rappers to retain full autonomy not only in the form of their creations and their performances but also in the content of their music (Pedrero 2009). Not having to comply with the requirements of a producer (whether in Cuba or abroad) grants them the ability to overcome any boundaries in what they are able to say in their music or what language is used. Thus, the discourse can remain largely localized and relevant to the listeners and use all the curse words and slang that are part of being young in Cuba. In the same way that rappers have created their own recording studios, production houses, and distribution channels, deejays in Cuba have managed to become indispensable not only to the independent music industry but also to event organizers and independent venues presenting all sorts of cultural disciplines.

Although there are a number of independent venues and events throughout the island, the most descriptive example of the trend toward Cuban youth's independent cultural production is Festival Rotilla. Taking place in Rotilla beach in Santa Cruz del Norte, Mayabeque, from 1998 to 2011, Rotilla organizers included in their roster very few established musicians, partly because of their limited budget as an independent event without institutional support and partly because of the effort to showcase new talent and emergent artistic genres (Historia 2012). Rotilla was not only a musical festival, as it also regularly included the work of visual artists, such as Iván Lejardi, as well as social projects and performance collectives, such as Gigantería Habana and OMNI Zona Franca. Furthermore, it can be argued that beyond the neighborhood of Alamar—the cradle of hip-hop in Cuba—it was in Rotilla where Cuban hip-hop and electronic music started developing and interacting with Cuban youth. In fact, the unprecedented independence in the organization of Rotilla, as well as the large number of emerging art disciplines included in the festival, created the basis for increased attendance every year until 2011, when the organizers refused to comply with the requests for the inclusion of more established artists by Cuban institutions and decided to cancel the festival (Historia 2012).

Filmmaking is another visible and challenging cultural expression of Cuban youth today. La Muestra de Jóvenes Realizadores, organized throughout the past eleven years by ICAIC, is but one of the events in which the talent of young filmmakers is presented. The documentaries and films that are usually exhibited at La Muestra touch on subjects that, while relevant to Cuban youth, do not receive much attention in the Cuban media. Further, many of the films make fun of the official government discourse or present satires of government and society alike. This is the case for *Comité 666* by Arturo Infante (2011), a film presented during the festival's 2011 edition. The film can be seen as one example of the recent interest in the creation of horror films set in Havana, such as *Juan de los Muertos* by Alejandro Brugués. In *Comité 666*, Infante presents a satire of the *Comités de Defensa de la Revolución* (Committees for the Defense of the Revolution [CDR]) through their story of a group of people in Havana immersed in preparations for the arrival of Satan. In the film, many of the elements that are central to the functioning of the CDRs are extrapolated to fit the satanic cult. For instance, the communal cauldron in which *caldosa* (stew) is collectively cooked during national festivities becomes a witch's cauldron in the movie, and the regular meetings attended by all CDR members once a month become meetings to worship Satan and prepare for his arrival. Furthermore, the promotional poster for the movie showed a *machetero* (sugarcane cutter) unusually brandishing a bloody machete and adorned with a set of horns, undoubtedly referencing Satan. The film exhibits an explicit questioning of the authority of the CDRs in Cuba and makes a joke of their role as the neighborhood organizations in charge of the defense of the revolutionary process.

Comité 666 is not the only example of film made by young Cuban directors in which satire and questioning of the status quo appear. Recent films also include *La Segunda Muerte del Hombre Útil* by Adrian Replanski (2010) and *Revolution* by Mayckell Pedrero (2009). In *La Segunda Muerte* (New Clocks for the Wasted Hours), Replanski presents a lugubrious show of old Soviet refrigerators dancing in an abandoned warehouse. The background is provided by the voice of a man speaking in Russian (a clear allegory to the influence of the Soviet Union), while a remainder of Cuba is presented in the background through the barely noticeable images of the Cuban flag and Che Guevara painted on the wall of the warehouse. The film can be interpreted as a reference to the Cuban economy after the fall of the Soviet Union, when the hardships made a significant dent in the day-to-day activities of Cuban society.

In the case of *Revolution* by Mayckell Pedrero, the fusion of different art disciplines in Cuba is clearly outlined. The documentary was presented in the 2010 edition of *La Muestra*, causing significant debate. In it, Pedrero interviews the hip-hop duo Los Aldeanos about their daily struggles to continue creating their music. The comments made by the duo were not censored in the documentary, making clear that Los Aldeanos had nothing positive to say about the Cuban government or the cultural institutions sponsoring hip-hop and youth cultural creation in Cuba, including the *Agencia Cubana de Rap* (Cuban Rap Agency) and the *Asociación Hermanos Saíz*. Nevertheless, *Revolution* won the award for Best Documentary in the 2010 edition of *La Muestra* (Selección 10ma 2012). Furthermore, although both *Comité 666* and *New Clocks* also caused great debate both in the Cuban press and in artistic circles in Cuba, they still garnered a number of awards during the 2011 edition of *La Muestra*, including Best Animation, Best Direction, and Best Score for *New Clocks* and Best Photography for *Comité 666* (Selección 11na 2012).

Reguetón, hip-hop, independent musical and film production, and art festivals are but a few of the many examples that illustrate Cuban youth's cultural expression. Throughout these disciplines, a constant pattern of rebellion and questioning of authority can be found, from the sexual lyrics of *reguetón* to the political commentary of the hip-hop *contestatario* movement and the social satire present in the work of young filmmakers. While a number of commentators have stated that these can be seen as symptoms of the Cuban youth's disillusionment with the Cuban Revolution, it could also be argued that these forms of cultural expression are representative mainly of both the commitment of the Cuban government to the creation of a vibrant cultural environment on the island and the inherent rebellion that is characteristic of youth the world over. Notwithstanding the chosen argument, it can be concluded that young Cubans' cultural production is vibrant and challenging, and it should be recognized as such.

REFERENCES

Bello, N. G. 2012. *El reguetón en Cuba: Un análisis de sus particularidades.* http://www.hist.puc.cl/iaspm/lahabana/articulosPDF/NerisLilianayGrizel.pdf.

Fernandes, S. 2003. "Fear of a Black Nation: Local Rappers, Transnational Crossings, and State Power in Contemporary Cuba." *Anthropological Quarterly* 76, no. 4: 575–608.

Fernández Retamar, R. 1989. *Caliban and Other Essays.* Minneapolis: University of Minnesota Press.

Fornet, Jorge, Marcia Leiseica, Chiki Salamendi, and Silvia Gil. 2011. "Casa de las Américas: Fundación De Sevilla. http://www.casa.cult.cu/pdfmemo/1959-1969.pdf.

García, Osmani, Blad MC, Cholocate, William "El Magnífico," Eri White, El Principe, Patry White "La Dictadora," Yulien Oviedo, Nando Pro, DJ Conds, and El Macry. 2011. *Chupi Chupi.* Video file. http://www.youtube.com/watch?v=ywoC2damVmU.

García, Osmani, El Chacal, Jose el Pillo, Kola Loka, and Entre Dos. 2010. *El Pudin.* Video file. http://www.youtube.com/watch?v=Y0H-08QpFt4.

Hernández, T. M., and L. Ventana. 2008. "La violencia de género en la construcción social de la feminidad a partir del discurso de cantantes cubanos de timba y reguetón."

Historia. 2012. "Rotilla Festival." http://www.rotillafestival.com/history/.

Kola Loka. 2012. *El Calentico.* Video file. http://www.youtube.com/watch?v=BflxqrIot1s.

Kola Loka ft. El Micha. 2010. *Se Extraña.* Video file. http://www.youtube.com/watch?v=5oDMygjy4I4.

Lavielle-Pullés, L. 2011. *Seducidos por el Reguetón. Aproximación a un estudio del producto musical desde sus consumos en la juventud santiaguera.* Santiago de Cuba: Centro de Estudios para el Desarrollo Integral de la Cultura.

Ortiz, Fernando, and I. Barreal. 1993. *Etnia y sociedad.* Havana: Editorial de Ciencias Sociales.

Pedrero, Mayckell. 2009. *Revolution.* Video file. http://www.youtube.com/watch?v=VOzsaSmv6M4.

Petri, Inga. 2012. "Survey of the General Public: The Value of Presenting: A Study of Arts Presentation in Canada." *Statistics Canada General Social Surveys.* http://www.diffusionartspresenting.ca/wp-content/uploads/2012/04/Dance_Attendance_Supplementary_Analysis_F.pdf.

Replanski, Adrian. 2011. *New Clocks for the Wasted Hours*. Video file. http://vimeo.com/36734051.

Reyes, Franklin. 2011. "Cuban Book Festival Draws Millions of Visitors." Associated Press. http://www.ctvnews.ca/cuban-book-festival-draws-million-of-visitors-1.610112.

Selección 10ma. 2012. "Muestra Joven Concurso Jóvenes Realizadores." http://www.cubacine.cult.cu/muestrajoven/index.html.

Selección 11na. 2012. "Muestra Joven Concurso Jóvenes Realizadores." http://www.cubacine.cult.cu/muestrajoven/index.html.

Spencer, R. 2010. *Development Tourism: Lessons from Cuba*. Aldershot: Ashgate.

Vazquet, Noel. 2012. "Kola Loka." *Inside Habana*. http://www.insidehabana.com/artcls_music.php?havana=34&langa=en.

Wood, A. E. 2009. "El Reguetón: Análisis del léxico de la música de los reguetoneros puertorriqueños." *Modern & Classical Languages Theses* 6.

Chapter Thirty-Four

Zooming In

Making and Marketing Films in Twenty-First-Century Cuba

Ann Marie Stock

> The cultural creativity of this small Caribbean island continues to be one of the greatest riches of
> the Cuban nation and, why not, of the entire world.
> —Leonardo Padura Fuentes

A raft floats in a tranquil sea. On it, a man lays face up with arms outstretched as if to embrace the brilliant sun. Cut to an underwater space, where low light and turbulence occlude the raft, making it difficult to discern. This opening sequence from *Juan de los Muertos* (Juan of the Dead, 2011), the highly acclaimed zombie film directed by Alejandro Brugués, can serve as a metaphor for filmmaking in Cuba in recent years. The audiovisual scene in twenty-first-century Cuba is composed of brightly lit spaces with great potential as well as some dark tones and difficulties.

Two forces collided in the early 1990s that dramatically changed filmmaking in Cuba. When the breakup of the Soviet Union unmoored the island from its principal ally, trading partner, and symbolic model, Cubans were left to float freely. Reverberations were felt in virtually every sector in Cuba—economic, political, social, and cultural. At the same time, the forces of globalization—greater interdependence and connectivity, expanded communication networks, multinational financial structures, and new technologies—were impacting the island and posing challenges to the nation. As Leonardo Padura Fuentes asserts in chapter 27 in this volume, "In such a convulsive (and truly special) period, artistic and literary production could be no less convulsive and special." And it was arguably the world of cinema that experienced the most convulsive and special shift of all: from this moment onward, films would be made and disseminated in markedly different ways.

The history of Cuba's revolutionary cinema goes back more than half a century. The establishment in 1959 of the *Instituto Cubano del Arte e Industria Cinematográficos* (ICAIC) was key to engendering a dynamic filmmaking industry. For the next thirty years, this state organization would train and support its artists, many of whom created award-winning films and earned international recognition. All of this would change, however, with the "Special Period," when island filmmakers began telling their stories with little or no support from the Cuban government. What these artists lacked in infrastructure they made up for with ingenuity. But what these artists lacked in infrastructure they made up for with ingenuity. Adapting to their changing circumstances and taking advantage of new opportunities, these audiovisual artists began working outside of official channels—on "the streets"; they employed emerging technology and partnered with a variety of individuals and institutions so as to create and market their work. (For readers of English, this rich tradition is outlined in two key texts: in *Cuban Film*, Michael Chanan [1985] treats the first three decades of revolutionary cinema, and in *On Location in Cuba: Street Filmmaking during Times of Transition*, Ann Marie Stock [2009] focuses on more recent developments in the audiovisual sphere—the impact of the turbulent 1990s and the early twenty-first century.)

INFLUENCES, EXPERIMENTATION, AND A PLETHORA OF CREATIVE POSSIBILITIES

Cuban films made in the first decade of the twenty-first century vary greatly in style, subject matter, and technique. They include features, animation, documentaries, experimental projects, and video clips or music videos. If there is any single defining characteristic of this generation of filmmakers, it is that they are intent on pushing the limits. Today's audiovisual artists employ genres heretofore absent in Cuba. They remix and mash up a variety of cultural forms, and they address social problems as well as personal concerns. Rather than staying on the well-traveled path, they venture forth to explore new territory.

These artists often try their hand at genres that have pleased audiences far beyond Cuba. Ernesto Piña Rodríguez recasts Japanese *mana* to comment on the uniquely Cuban transportation mode, the *camello*, or camel-backed trailers, in *eMm-5* (M-5, 2004). Juan Carlos Cremata and Alfredo Ureta employ road movie conventions in their respective features, *Viva Cuba* (2005) and *La Mirada* (The Gaze, 2010). Pavel Giroud nods to the gangster movie in *Omertá* (2008). Increasingly, Cuba's young filmmakers bring to the screen mobsters, monsters, and other B-movie material. Followers and fans of world cinema and expression from distant cultures, they experiment with a variety of forms.

Some of these talented creators quote and combine material from diverse sources. By borrowing and blending, they demonstrate their mastery of digital technologies of production, their capacities to reuse, and the vastness of their cultural repertoire. Esteban Insausti crafts an innovative portrait of the musician Emiliano Salvador in *Las manos y el ángel* (The Hands and the Angel, 2002). With quotes from the pages of *Rolling Stone* magazine, archival footage of concerts by the ICAIC-hosted Grupo Experimental, and interviews filmed recently for this project, he produces a film layered like an extemporaneous, playful, intertextual jazz riff. The same filmmaker relies on remixing in another of his works, *Existen* (They Exist, 2005). By incorporating sequences from the innovative *Desde La Habana Recordar 1968* (From Havana Remembering 1968, 1969) by Nicolas Guillén Landrián, Insausti recuperates, recirculates, and reintroduces the work of his talented predecessor. Susana Barriga quotes another innovative film by Guillén Landrián, *Ociel del Toa* (Ociel of the Toa River, 1965). In structuring her critique, titled *Patria* (Homeland, 2007), she replicates the rhythm and juxtaposes image and text just as Guillén Landrián did some forty years earlier.

For Miguel Coyula, it is the work of master filmmaker Tomás Gutiérrez Alea that inspires his feature. *Memories of Development* (2010), with its collage aesthetic, draws inspiration from its precursor, *Memorias del Subdesarrollo* (Memories of Underdevelopment, 1968), both of which were scripted by Edmundo Desnoes. It bears mentioning that this mode of remixing is not new in Cuban film; Guillén Landrián, Santiago Álvarez, Marisol Trujillo, and a host of others employed pastiche to tell their stories on film. Images from *Life* and *Look* magazines and footage from U.S. television broadcasts and films made their way into early Cuban films. What distinguishes these recent efforts are the new modes of storytelling made possible via the employment of emerging technologies of participation. Whereas Cuban films once combined a sampling of a handful of images and sound bites from other sources, they now take shape within a new universe of creativity made possible by everything from high-definition cameras and mobile phones to editing software programs, permitting amateurs to generate and bend musical compositions and rearrange narratives. Even some of the cultural expression created by Cubans—particularly in the 1960s and 1970s—is now being used as raw material. These new mash-ups attest to this generation's engagement with world music, graphic arts, advertising, and audiovisual culture as well as to their appreciation of their nation's strong cinema tradition.

Increasingly, Cuban films tackle topics not widely treated in ICAIC productions before the Special Period. Recent works explore subjects once considered taboo in island cinema: mental illness (*Existen*, Esteban Insausti, 2005), censorship (*Zona de Silencio*, Karel Ducasse, 2007), underground culture (*Revolución*, Mayckell Pedrero Mariol, 2010), the emergence of class distinctions (*Habanastation*, Ian Padrón, 2011), the challenge of finding meaningful work (*Cómo Construir un Barco*, Susana Barriga, 2007), drug use and abuse (*Todo Por Ella*, Pavel Giroud, 2002), inadequate housing (*Las Camas Solas*, Sandra Gómez Jiménez, 2006), the shortcomings of public health (*Protectoras*, Daniel Vera, 2006), *la doble moral* (hypocrisy) (*Utopía*, Arturo Infante, 2004; *Monte Rouge*, Eduardo del Llano, 2005), cruelty (*La Guerra de las Canicas*, Adrián Ricardo Hartill and Wilbert Noguel, 2008; *Camionero*, 2011), and so on. In focusing on the island's disenfranchised sectors, these works illuminate Cuba's darker side. They offer a stark contrast to many—but certainly not all—of the early ICAIC films celebrating the Revolution's achievements. Films like these pose a challenge to official discourse in that they expose that which often goes unreported in the national media.

In the same way that the shortcomings of the Revolution are depicted, so, too, are the imperfections of individuals. In a poignant scene in *La Vida es Silbar* (Life Is to Whistle, Fernando Pérez, 1998), one character comments to another, "Nadie es perfecto." The fact that "nobody is perfect" has made its way into recent films; the tendency in Cuba at this juncture is to present people as they are, replete with defects, rather than as exemplary human beings. This allows filmgoers to recognize and reckon with their own imperfections.

These up-close-and-personal stories feature well-known figures as well as ordinary people. Perhaps the most notable film of this kind in recent years is Fernando Pérez's portrait of José Martí. This hero is larger than life in Cuba, where busts of him mark the entrance of every elementary school, his face graces countless billboards across the island, and monuments honoring him abound. Rather than perpetuate this heroic image, however, Pérez opted to depict Martí in more human terms. He carried out extensive research—reading Martí's writings, visiting relevant sites, and studying period photographs. Despite the filmmaker's exhaustive investigation into his subject's life, gaps remained. So Pérez decided to focus on the lacunae, creating a "fictionalized biography" of Martí's childhood and adolescence. His film *Martí: El Ojo del Canario* (Martí: The Eye of the Canary, 2010), displays the protagonist's human qualities: the young José Martí is fearful and frustrated, he urinates and masturbates, and his actions sometimes result in others being hurt. This humane portrayal renders the iconic figure accessible to present-day viewers. Eduardo del Llano has managed something similar in creating a nuanced portrait of another familiar historical figure, Leonardo da Vinci. His film *Vinci* (2011) emphasizes the legendary man's youth, including time spent in prison, rather than his widely heralded accomplishments later in life.

Many other recent films present ordinary men and women living ordinary lives. With sensitivity and subtlety, director Alfredo Ureta creates a character that is anything but exemplary. In *La Guarida del Topo* (The Mole's Den, 2011), Daniel, rendered expertly by actor

Néstor Jiménez, sips coffee, cooks and eats simple fare, and watches television before calling it a day. He is a homebody who goes about the business of living. And even when circumstances require him to give shelter to his neighbor's niece, we appreciate him as a loner in search of human warmth rather than as a Latin lover. In *Oda a la Piña* (Ode to the Pineapple, 2008), the protagonist (Limara Meneses) is a dancer whose elaborate "tropical" costume cannot cover up the fact that she's missing the proper dance moves. Director Laimir Fano deconstructs stereotypes in this exploration of what it means to lose one's rhythm, to be out of step; the film parallels the experience of many Cubans—including Fano's—during this time of accelerated change. Another film in this vein is the highly successful and exceedingly moving film *La Piscina* (The Swimming Pool, 2011). Director Carlos Quintela limits the scope of the action to one place, the swimming pool, and introduces viewers to four adolescent swimmers—each with a disability—and their coach. Works like these mark a contrast to earlier revolutionary films that celebrated the heroic and exceptional—whether adolescents combating illiteracy (*Historia de una Batalla*, 1965), athletes winning Olympic medals and international competitions (*Nuevos Hombres en el Ring*, 1974; *Juantorena*, 1978; *Mundial de la Dignidad*, 1974), or a dairy farmer breaking all records in milk production (*Pedro Cero Por Ciento*, 1980). Films in twenty-first-century Cuba reflect present-day circumstances; they probe the challenges of living in—and surviving—this moment. And they continually remind viewers that "nobody is perfect."

MIGRATION, MOVEMENT, AND THE EMERGENCE OF NEW AUDIOVISUAL SPACES

Another characteristic of this moment—one driving the narrative of films as well as the experiences of filmmaker—is the prevalence of border crossings. The phenomenon of migrancy dates back centuries, and movement characterizes the entire world in this global era. Yet the subject of emigration resonates uniquely for Cubans, for virtually all of them have had to reckon with the decision of staying or going—whether personally or through the experience of a family member or friend. Not surprisingly, recent films made by Cubans, regardless of where they make their home, explore this topic. Humberto Padrón broaches the subject in *Video de Familia* (Family Video, 2001); he effectively uses the trope of a video camera to scrutinize family dynamics and dysfunction, the latter exacerbated by a family member's desire to reside outside Cuba. *ExGeneración* (Generation X, 2009) tackles the subject from Mexico City. Aram Vidal, while pursuing a master's degree there, expanded on his earlier documentary about Cuban youth in Havana (*De Generación*, 2006) to focus on Cubans living in Mexico's capital. In *Todas Iban a Ser Reinas* (All Were Going to Be Queens, 2006), director Gustavo Pérez and writer Oneyda González treat emigration—but with a twist. They probe the experiences of six Russian women who fell in love with Cuban men visiting their native country, all of whom subsequently emigrated so as to live with their husbands on the island. Alina Rodríguez frames the issues in yet another way when she takes on internal migration to expose the plight of Cubans who move from the provinces to the island's capital; *Buscándote Havana* (Searching for You, Havana, 2006) reveals makeshift dwellings on Havana's periphery to parallel their occupants' marginal position in the country. And Esteban Insausti devotes his first feature, *Larga Distancia* (Long Distance, 2010), to the impact on those affected by remaining behind in Cuba after their family and friends have dispersed.

This theme of migration on-screen has its parallel in the creative community. In recent years, "round-trip-ticket" filmmaking has become an increasingly common practice. During the first three decades of the Revolution, to leave Cuba for an extended period (unless sponsored by the Cuban government) was to relinquish one's citizenship and lose the right to return. Film specialists who opted to live outside Cuba—editor Jorge Abello, animation artist Hernán Henríquez, and director Jesús Díaz, to name only a few—left the island with little if any hope of returning. And once outside of Cuba, they lost professional momentum. More often than not, their film careers stalled out. Today, this has changed. It is now possible for many directors, actors, editors, and other artists to come and go, working sometimes in Cuba and sometimes abroad.

Round-trip-ticket scenarios have become increasingly common as this new generation explores opportunities and seeks greater financial stability. Actress Zulema Clares debuted in "Luz Roja" directed by Esteban Insausti (a work comprising the final third of *Tres Veces Dos/ 3 X 2*). Shortly thereafter, she moved to New York in hopes of developing her acting skills in theater. All along, Clares planned on returning to Cuba to star in another film. Esteban Insausti had envisioned her playing the lead role in his first feature, *Larga Distancia* (Long Distance); the director had, in fact, scripted the part of Ana with Clares in mind. So when it came time to begin shooting, the actress relocated to Cuba until the filming was complete. Filmmaker Sandra Gómez Jiménez constitutes another example. She made *Las Camas Solas* (Lonely Beds, 2006) in Havana before moving to Europe to make her home. She returns frequently to Cuba, however, and has participated in various installments of the *Muestra Joven ICAIC*, an annual festival featuring the work of young filmmakers. Still another case is that of Miguel Coyula, who graduated from the *Escuela Internacional de Cine y Televisión* (EICTV) outside of Havana and then moved to New York, where he made *Cucarachas Rojas* (Red Cockroaches, 2003) and then *Memories of Development*. As *Memories* was beginning to circulate at international festivals, Coyula returned to Havana. From his base in his bedroom studio, in the home he shares with his parents in the El Vedado district, he travels frequently to participate in international film events and offer workshops beyond the island. The possibility of coming and going has expanded the conception of "Cuban" in the island's film world; it is not so much geopolitical locale—one's rootedness on the island—that constitutes the identities of Cuban filmmakers but rather their self-identification as such. (The renowned Cuban intellectual Ambrosio Fornet first insisted on defining Cuban culture as including the diaspora. Others, including Ana López and Juan Antonio García Borrero, have built on his formulation in their respective discussions of contemporary Cuban film.)

Although many audiovisual artists of Cuban descent have preserved their connection to the island regardless of their home base, they do not necessarily consider themselves to be part of a defined movement. Unlike their predecessors—the revolutionary filmmakers working in the ICAIC between 1960 and the late 1980s—these creators emphasize their individuality and value their autonomy. Most participate in securing funding for their projects. They have assumed responsibility for pitching their ideas and garnering the financial support necessary to make their films. They procure their equipment and learn how to use it. These artists increasingly manage multiple aspects of their projects. Jorge Perrugoría, known for his acting in *Fresa y Chocolate* (Strawberry and Chocolate), *Guantanamera*, and other award-winning films, has ventured into directing with such works as *Habana Abierta* (Open Havana, 2003) and *Afinidades* (Affinities, 2010, codirected with Vladimir Cruz). The accomplished scriptwriter Eduardo del Llano has directed numerous popular shorts—among them *Monte Rouge* (2004), *High Tech* (2005), *Photoshop* (2006), *Ache* (2010), *Pravda* (2010), and *Exit* (2011)—and more recently the feature film *Vinci*. Aram Vidal constitutes yet another case of this self-reliant filmmaking mode; his *Bubbles Beat* (2012), begun while he was serving as an audiovisual artist in residence in the United States and completed as he earned his MA degree in Mexico, engaged him in virtually all aspects of its creation and production. It premiered on

Vimeo in November 2012. New technologies and shifting production practices have permitted Cubans to engage more fully in the entire filmmaking enterprise. As a result, the auteur paradigm is being employed with greater frequency—by critics as well as by the filmmakers themselves. No longer is filmmaking in Cuba considered primarily through a national lens.

Another shift has to do with where filmmaking activity is centered on the island. Whereas Havana was once the exclusive purveyor of filmed images, new spaces have opened up for filmmakers outside the capital. The *Televisión Serrana*, founded by Daniel Diez Castrillo in 1993 in the remote region of the Sierra Maestra, has become a significant media-making site. Pockets of filmmaking activity have developed in other regions as well. In Camaguey, Juan Antonio García Borrero led efforts to establish the Taller Nacional de la Crítica, an annual event convening critics and film aficionados. From their base in this provincial capital, Gustavo Pérez and Oneyda González have teamed up to make several films, and Eliécer Jiménez developed a portfolio of work impressive enough to gain him admission to the prestigious EICTV in San Antonio de los Baños. Camaguey is also the site of the *Festival Internacional de Video Arte*, a showcase of innovative works that also foments creativity. In Santa Clara, Ivette Ávila Martín has developed her animation activity; the quality of her shorts is as impressive as her commitment to educating and empowering children through workshops. And in Santiago de Cuba, where Carlos Barba first tried his hand at making documentaries, others have followed. Working far from the urban center has not been easy, for distances are great, communication can be difficult, and shortages are widespread. There is no doubt that the impediments to creativity experienced by *habaneros* are much more pronounced in the provinces. Still, these filmmakers from across the island have become adept at *resolviendo*, or making do. They have procured support from the ICAIC and other state and nongovernmental organizations in Cuba, and they have managed to establish alliances with international partners in order to develop their projects. The expansion of filmmaking efforts has resulted in a broader depiction of the lives of Cubans. Portraits of the rural experience, as told by those living it, are augmenting the island's images.

FESTIVALS, FLASH DRIVES, AND THE CIRCULATION OF CUBAN FILMS

Shifts in the making of films in Cuba have been accompanied by an evolution in the marketing and circulation of these products. ICAIC once took sole responsibility for promoting Cuban film—making multiple copies; circulating them across the island on cinema screens, at schools, and in video clubs; creating press packets and publicity materials and submitting the most promising works to international festivals; and securing international distribution. Since 1990, the state's role in film distribution has changed due to an altered audiovisual landscape.

One of the forces driving this shift is the increasingly common practice of coproduction. Collaborative creation and distribution has become a standard the world over, particularly where local markets are too small to recoup initial investments and broader audiences are sought. The combining of currency and talent has become the norm rather than the exception in Cuba. Most of the recent ICAIC productions and many of the "street" projects have benefited from joint financing and collaborative marketing. So, for example, if Wanda Films helps produce a film by Fernando Pérez (which it has on several occasions), the Madrid-based producer will also play a significant role in the promotion and placement of the film outside of Cuba.

Another factor has to do with the development of new spaces for circulating audiovisual production. In recent years, ICAIC and various Cuba-based festivals (e.g., *Festival Internacional del Nuevo Cine Latinoamericano*, *Muestra Joven ICAIC*, *Cine Pobre*, and a host of others) disseminate opportunities and information via listservs. Cuban filmmakers can—and do—create personal websites, upload their work on YouTube, and submit their films over the Internet using festival websites and clearinghouses, such as Withoutabox. In this era of global networks, paper forms and physical copies of films have given way to electronic submission and communication. This is not to say that all obstacles have been overcome. In fact, Cuban filmmakers still struggle to develop the skills necessary to navigate the global marketplace, to access a connection fast enough to upload a film, and to pay festival application fees that are exorbitant by island standards. Yet they are managing to disseminate their work widely by activating alliances and mobilizing connections—human as well as virtual.

New festivals on the island have also played a role in moving Cuban films into the marketplace. Recent years have seen the creation of a series of events across the island that promote homegrown projects and introduce Cubans to their international counterparts. Among these are *Cine Pobre in Gibara*, the *Festival Internacional del Video Arte* in Camaguey, and the *Festival Internacional del Documental, Santiago Álvarez en Memoriam*, in Santiago. Arguably the most significant for this new generation of filmmakers is the annual *Muestra Joven ICAIC* (ICAIC's Showcase of Young Filmmakers), which had its first installment in 2002. The importance of this event, held in Havana each year and sponsored by ICAIC, cannot be overstated. Many filmmakers—whether from Havana or from the provinces—cite this space as pivotal in their formation; the *Muestra* inspired them to bring their story to the screen. The event features the work of creators under the age of thirty-five and also engages young Cubans as jurors, organizers, and critics. In a country where many state agencies are directed by individuals in their seventies and even eighties (consider the *Casa de las Américas* or the *Ballet Nacional*), opportunities for young people are all too scarce. Many state organizations and cultural institutions have resisted succession—the tendency is to retain founding directors rather than pass on leadership responsibilities. The *Muestra*, in contrast, is managed, for the most part, by individuals in their forties, thirties, and even twenties. Cuba's culture workers of the next generation are the protagonists.

Whereas the *Muestra* and other domestic festivals constitute important spaces, they are by no means the only way for circulating and consuming local films. Entrepreneurial Cubans have become unauthorized distributors of films made at home and from abroad. A few years back, the standard office of a "distributor" in Cuba looked like it occupied one corner of a room outfitted with a monitor and two VHS players, a box of blank tapes, and a backpack. Films on video could be copied, lent, and sold. Knocking on doors and teaming up with others in the trade, these bootleggers did a brisk business providing aficionados with contemporary and classic films from Cuba and around the world. A satellite dish, perhaps tucked in a water tank or camouflaged by vegetation, ensured a constant stream of new material. In the past few years, this practice has evolved along with technological innovation. Distribution has become even more streamlined as flash drives and hard drives get passed back and forth in an ongoing exchange of audiovisual offerings. Cuba's filmmakers note with amusement their own role in "pirating" their work. The goal is not so much to make money, they say, as to get their films in front of viewers.

Cubans and tourists alike have access to films on DVD. Would-be buyers can, for two Cuban convertible pesos (the equivalent of U.S.$2.50), purchase a *combo*, a DVD with four or five feature films made by Cuban directors. Sales take place outside *paladares*, at used-book stalls, and in craft markets. A cardboard box or attaché case contains new releases from Cuba along with international blockbusters. If a desired title is not among those available, the salesperson generally offers to locate the film, make a copy, and deliver it—often the next day. So pervasive is this new mode of distribution in Cuba that ICAIC officials and filmmakers alike joke about providing these entrepreneurs with good copies of their films. "If they're going to reproduce and sell the works," the pragmatic professionals say, "let's make sure they're working with high-quality copies and not some inferior version filmed using a cell phone."

Additional opportunities exist for experiencing Cuban film beyond the island. Even in the United States, where the blockade has limited the movement of goods, people, and information between the countries, there are now numerous annual events featuring Cuban films. Among these are the Havana Film Festival in New York and the New England Festival of Ibero-American Film. With increasing frequency, universities host Cuban filmmakers as part of their programs in film studies, Latin American studies, and other academic areas. In addition, partners from beyond the island have teamed up to market Cuban films. There are the coproducers, of course, but also such grassroots initiatives as Cuban Cinema Classics (http://www.cubancinemaclassics.com), Film Movement (http://www.filmmovement.com), and the Americas Media Initiative (http://www.americasmediainitiative.org)—all committed to circulating films from Cuba across the United States and beyond. These are in addition to Amazon, Netflix, and other online sources.

The contours of Cuba's audiovisual landscape continue to change. There is a great deal of uncertainty at present as Cuba's master filmmakers age and ICAIC's equipment becomes obsolete. What is certain is that the future of Cuban cinema will look decidedly different from the past. Just as thirty-five millimeter gave way to other formats and truckloads of heavy equipment were replaced by lightweight handheld cameras, so, too, have state-sponsored film practices had to shift. While change has been slow and sometimes painful, ICAIC is now positioned to accommodate a multiplicity of modes for creating and marketing films. And as new filmmakers continue to come on to the scene, their innovative ideas will help chart new directions. So while there are no guarantees, it does seem that a bright future beckons. The magical and the marvelous persist in Cuba's film world. In a 2006 interview, having just completed their first feature titled *Personal Belongings*, director Alejandro Brugués and producer Inti Herrera expressed their desire to make, of all things, a zombie film. And within the space of a few years, they had accomplished that—a first in the illustrious history of Cuban filmmaking. This is proof, it seems, that dreams can come true for Cuban filmmakers. *Juan de los Muertos* once again resonates when the protagonist, having struggled and overcome all kinds of obstacles, asserts in the final sequence, "Voy a estar bien. Sólo necesito que me den un filo." There is hope that Cuban film, too, will "be all right" if just given "a chance."

REFERENCES

Chanan, Michael. 1985. *Cuban Cinema*. Minneapolis: University of Minnesota Press.
Stock, Ann Marie. 2009. *On Location in Cuba: Street Filmmaking during Times of Transition*. Chapel Hill: University of North Carolina Press.

Chapter Thirty-Five

Recovering from Crisis?

Literature, Publishing, and Nation Building in Contemporary Cuba

Par Kumaraswami and Antoni Kapcia

The changes in Cuba that began in 2007—formalized in 2008 (with Raúl Castro's election) and 2011 (with the convening of the long-overdue Communist Party Congress)—had inevitable implications for culture. While quite draconian cuts were instituted (or at least threatened and discussed) for so many aspects of Cuban society, welfare, employment, and the public sector, it seemed inevitable that culture generally would be expected to bear its share of the burden of economic austerity and streamlining. This was especially perceived from the outside, where it has long seemed that an inordinate amount of always scarce resources have been spent on what is usually, in most Western societies, deemed a peripheral or even luxury item of expenditure.

In many Cubans' eyes, the signal for this development had already been given in 2009 when, following the traumatic and damaging experience of three successive hurricanes in 2008 and the onset of the world financial crisis, it was announced that the annual Havana Book Fair would be reduced in scope. Since 2000, this event had grown spectacularly, with the initial ten-day event in Havana being then rolled out in various forms across the island over three weeks, eventually reaching forty towns and cities and attracting about 5 million Cubans. Its sudden reduction was a shock to the cultural world. Then, in March 2012, the popular and influential minister of culture, Abel Prieto, retired from office, being replaced by one of his deputies, Rafael Bernal Alemany. Many in that cultural world had long feared the effects of a ministry without Prieto since, from the late 1990s, he had successfully argued for a high profile and substantial expenditure for culture and had ensured that Cuba's artists and writers were protected and materially rewarded, giving them an importance that they had not enjoyed since the early days of the Revolution; moreover, many had hoped that another of the deputy ministers would succeed Prieto and tended to see Bernal's appointment as something of a demotion of the ministry and thus of culture generally.

This was reinforced by traditional expectations among some of those artists and writers who saw Raúl Castro as being less sympathetic toward culture's high profile and central importance than his brother had been; they cited Raúl Castro's position as defense minister in 1966 when the armed forces magazine *Verde Olivo* launched a campaign against poet Heberto Padilla (Padilla 1989). They also pointed to the armed forces' presumed role in the creation in 1965–1968 of the notorious work and reeducation camps of the Military Units to Aid Production, where several writers had been interned, mostly for their homosexuality. Finally, in 1996, Raúl Castro had taken the lead in the public criticism and purging of the independent Center for the Study of America, many of whose members remained influential in Cuban intellectual debates (Giuliano 1998). Hence, by 2012, it seemed that all that they had feared was coming to pass and that the "good times" for culture and for artists were over.

Since 1959, culture was always seen as fundamental and not peripheral, in many ways the key to unlocking the talents, willing participation, and collective and individual self-fulfillment that national unity and progress demanded. That was precisely why so much effort was put into film (able to communicate easily with hundreds at a time), into literacy and then literature, and into all manner of cultural awareness and activity. It was also why Cuban artists were redefined as state employees—not only because they had a key role in this process of cultural liberation and nation building but also because, by receiving a steady income, they would be freed from the vagaries (and often poverty) of the market.

Hence, it was this imperative—of tying the new culture to the whole nation-building project—that drove most of the campaigns, ideas, and experiments of the first three decades of Revolution. This had led to a massive expansion of production and consumption that was subsequently seen as something of a "golden age" of high expenditure, multiple opportunities for would-be artists and writers, substantial availability of books and films—and clear-cut but occasionally resented notions of what art and artists should be like. In this renaissance, literature boasted a paramount role, seemingly privileged above all other genres.

THE CRISIS OF THE 1990S

This relatively coherent drive to create and sustain a dual notion of literary culture that could create and sustain publishing opportunities for established writers while at the same time providing greater mass access to literature in terms of writing workshops, affordable books, and literary events was severely damaged by the economic collapse of the 1990s. The impact of the "Special Period" on literature was wide ranging and profound. Along with ordinary citizens, many writers emigrated and sought their fortunes outside the island, while many of those who remained in Cuba were obliged to curtail their literary careers and seek employment in sectors that could guarantee some hard-currency income. For all Cuban citizens, including writers and artists (who were, after all, state employees), daily life entailed the search for basic goods and services, a search often undertaken with no public transportation available. In these conditions, the mental and material conditions required to write literature were rarely available (Davies 1997; Whitfield 2009). Some writers, nevertheless, drew on their writing as a form of psychological release in the midst of personal and national crisis. The publishing industry for literature was virtually paralyzed as a result of shortages of necessary commodities, such as oil and paper; any available publishing outlets prioritized the national press (*Granma*, the newspaper of the Cuban Communist Party) over other text types. And, in the absence of an effective state infrastructure for culture, many of the municipal, provincial, and national events that made up the literary calendar were simply suspended. As for readers, here too the well-established patterns of access and participation that had sustained the everyday enjoyment of literature for thirty years were largely paralyzed. Indeed, given the need for hard currency and the scarcity of commodities, many Cubans sold their books to secondhand *peso* bookshops or, more lucratively, to the hard-currency booksellers in the *Plaza de Armas* of La Habana Vieja who attracted tourists in search of well-known literary and political texts.

For the first time since 1959, then, the literary environment was closely tied to economic concerns, and the effects on literary production and consumption were experienced in often dramatic terms by those writers whose work was "scouted" by foreign publishers, and who were awarded often minimal sums of money in exchange for their manuscripts (including translation and reproduction rights). This last aspect should not be underestimated, as it created a new globalizing tendency not only in the mechanisms for publishing literature but also in the subject matter that these new texts covered, in effect constructing a canon of 1990s Cuban literature that ran alongside and sometimes in opposition to the canon for national readerships that had been developed for the previous three decades (Kumaraswami 2012). This new focus often highlighted the themes of national and personal crisis, dystopia (rather than the utopia of the Revolution), the marketization of Cuban life (including hustling and prostitution), and nostalgia for a lost era (Casamayor Cisneros 2012; Whitfield 2008).

Many texts dealt even more explicitly with the collective moral crisis of the failed revolutionary project, with sordid descriptions and scatological references and an underlying narrative structure where the individual was isolated—and often mistrustful of—the collective context. This thematic strand—known more generally as "*literatura del desencanto*" (literature of disillusionment) (Fornet 2003) or "*narrativa de la interioridad*" (narrative focusing on subjective realities)—stood in sharp contrast to the collective and constructive thrust of literary texts until 1989 and itself created an assumption among external commentators that all post-1989 Cuban literature inevitably dealt with the exotic, the erotic, the decadent, or the dissident. Indeed, a more general observation could be that the incursion of foreign publishers into the Cuban literary scene itself promoted a certain vision of life on the island, and, with the national publishing industry unable to compete in terms of offering other visions, the trend of "*realismo sucio*" (dirty realism) became a powerful new current of post-1990 Cuban literature.

As always with Cuba, however, the picture is far more complex. While it is undeniable that the Special Period presented a moment of rupture with the previous thirty years and with the largely coherent thrust of the cultural policies of the revolutionary government, it is also important to note that signs began to emerge of the gradual recovery of publishing. The mechanisms for this renaissance were complex: local communities and individual actors in the literary scene worked together to create the phenomenon of *plaquettes*, or minibooks created from the offcuts of the large printing presses still functioning to publish *Granma*; editors of literary magazines accepted financial and material help from supporters in Latin America and beyond, negotiating terms whereby their publications could appear, albeit in diminished or less frequent forms, through being printed abroad; and, similarly, publishing houses in allied countries in Latin America were able to fund modest literary prizes, such as the *Colección Pinos Nuevos*, which provided some publishing opportunities for writers on the island.

For a country whose literary production had been exclusively state sponsored for three decades, the need to seek financial backing in order to see work in print must surely have come as a rude awakening to many writers and publishers. More crucially, the generous print runs of the 1970s and 1980s now gave way to minimal runs of 500 copies, creating a situation where the reading public's access to Cuban literature was severely compromised. Also important in the early 1990s was a state-level decision to accept the Japanese government gift of hundreds of photocopiers to the Cuban government. The copy machines, known by their brand name RISO, were distributed by the Cuban government to every province in the country, thus creating a network of small-scale provincial publishers across the island. This provided opportunities for writers to publish and for readers to read and, crucially, was able to publish texts more quickly than the larger national publishing houses had been able to; in addition, and even more important, it decentralized the publishing industry, which had hitherto been based principally in Havana (with some larger publishers in Santiago de Cuba).

What is clear, then, is that, at least in terms of the production of literature, the mid- to late 1990s saw a slow and partial recovery of the publishing industry, which, combined with opportunities from abroad, provided some outlets for writers on the island. Less successful, however, was the other strand that had characterized cultural policy until 1989: the notion of cultural participation as a route to individual and collective development within the larger nation-building project of the Revolution. While many of the actors in literary culture had attempted to resurrect the notion of literature as participation through reading initiatives and literary workshops in Havana, the economic hardships and daily struggles of the Special Period, the lure of mass culture such as television, and the appeal of the cultural products and services being offered to tourists all made participation in literature seem irrelevant, especially to Cuba's youth.

RECOVERING FROM CRISIS: THE BATTLE OF IDEAS

The *Batalla de Ideas*, announced in 2000, was, like "Rectification" in 1986, a multilayered campaign with various motives designed to address a great many problems. By addressing "ideas," its scope inevitably included culture and specifically literature. Indeed, once it became clear that its main purpose was to revive ideological commitment, especially among the young, and to reinvigorate Cubans after the ravages, disillusion, and demoralization of the Special Period and against the corrosive effects of the post-1993 economic reforms, it was obvious that culture would, as in the 1960s, lie at the heart of this initiative. For, just as culture had, from the outset, been seen as central to the Revolution's underlying project of nation building, so too now, as Cuba emerged from the "darkest days" of the post-1990 crisis—buoyed up by the pope's visit in 1998 and the exciting youth mobilizations of the 2009–2010 campaign for the return to Cuba of Elián González—was it again central in this new process. This process essentially meant rebuilding not only a damaged Revolution but also a severely damaged nation. Therefore, it was inevitable that some of the same mechanisms that had worked in the early 1960s would be used now to invigorate and possibly enlist a new generation of young Cubans.

There were three basic elements to the *Batalla de Ideas*: a focus on mobilization once again (since the 1980s had seen a steady decline of what had been characteristic of the early days of a new Revolution and since the Special Period had allowed little time, energy, or resources for anything other than the most essential or cursory mass mobilization) (Kapcia 2009); an educational campaign that focused on both old Cubans (offering them the chance of lifelong learning and greater involvement) and young Cubans, especially those perhaps dangerously left on the sidelines by the 1980s shift from mass higher education to a much more selective university entrance system (Kapcia 2005); and a new campaign to emphasize reading and to expand book publishing.

The latter element, especially its focus on publishing, actually grew out of another seminal experience of the 1990s—namely, the evolution of a new "localism" as a response to the weakening and stagnation of the Cuban state during the worst days of austerity and specifically of provincial publishing, which, as we have seen, began to flourish in its scope if not ever reaching the levels of production of the 1980s. It was, however, the focus on reading that was deemed to be vital, an emphasis that probably owed much to the collaboration between Fidel Castro and Prieto and to the dynamism of the new generation of young activists then leading the Union of Communist Youth (UJC), steeled in the heady days of the Elián campaign.

That they should focus on reading was logical for two reasons. First, the material deprivations of the Special Period, coupled with the temptations of a new opening to globalization and, with it, the world of the Internet and DVDs (not to mention the effects of decades of exposure to television), had created a visible decline in young people's interest in and practice of reading, lacking the books, the time, and the disposition to do what their parents and grandparents had done with such energy in earlier decades. This was certainly lamented in the media, in the education ministries, and in political circles, where it was seen as a serious problem for a nation whose system and processes of popular involvement had been built partly on the premise that an educated and reading populace was fundamental to a "new" consciousness.

The second reason for the new focus on reading was the awareness that, just as the 1961 Literacy Campaign and the subsequent campaigns on "piracy" and writing workshops had been basic blocks in the process of building the nation after 1959—that is, all focusing on the written word and imagination through writing and reading—so too now might it be possible to repeat the impetus of those campaigns to the same effect in a new rebuilding process. The essential dilemma, however, was that it was impossible to repeat the 1961 campaign since all Cubans could now read; the problem lay in getting people to read extensively once again.

Part of that campaign therefore could be addressed by boosting the production of books, repeating the impetus of the "piracy" campaign and building on the flourishing of provincial and local publishing. The strategy employed was to repeat the scale and the dynamism of 1961 in another way: by expanding the Havana Book Fair and taking it out across the island and then following it up with a number of smaller follow-up campaigns (not unlike the post-1961 campaigns to follow up new literacy with a drive to improve the levels of reading). The fair had existed since the early 1980s but had been a small, biennial, writer-focused, and publisher-focused event; its creation at that time owed much to the 1981 UNESCO designation of Havana as a World Heritage Site and was then focused on Havana as a city and the habaneros as citizens, hoping to rebuild a city identity and collective morale through physical improvement and cultural celebration. However, relatively few people attended those events, which were held mostly in the somewhat inaccessible far west of the city suburbs in one of the convention centers located there.

From 2000, however, the Havana Book Fair became the focal point for the whole cultural campaign. It became an annual event, located near the Old City (in the vast and imposing Cabaña fortress, which dominates the eastern shore of Havana Bay), which was given over to this large event. The fair also ceased focusing so much on writers, especially overseas writers and publishers, and focused instead on Cuban publishing, national and provincial, and on publications from each year's designated "country to be honored." Everything possible was now done to attract as many Cubans as possible to the event: free buses were provided, schools and workplaces organized outings to the fair during the workweek, prices were kept low, musical and other entertainment and fast food were made available throughout (giving the event the atmosphere of a U.S. state fair), and there was a ten-day parallel program of literary activities (book launches, award ceremonies, seminars, and round-table discussions) aimed at writers but open to the public, who now had the opportunity to meet their favorite authors.

The most ambitious element of this drive to attract numbers was the decision to follow the Havana event by taking elements of the original fair to the provinces, where a smaller version would be staged in significant provincial cities. This became so integral a part of the new initiative that it soon became crucial to continue to increase the geographical reach of the fair, progressing rapidly from seventeen cities and towns visited in 2002 to thirty-nine visited in 2007. As a result, the attendance figures soared from 200,000 in 2002 to 5.6 million in 2006, spectacularly realizing its aim of reaching as many Cubans as possible with as many books as possible (Instituto Cubano del Libro 2009), and the fair soon became a fixed and long-awaited event on the social as well as cultural calendar of each locality. Moreover, the characteristic energy of this success was already being followed up by those other drives: the September "Book Night" events in Havana (when unsold fair books were again promoted in an evening-long minifair on one of Havana's main streets), the "Book in the Sierra" campaign to take books to the most isolated parts of Cuba's mountain regions, and all manner of similar drives to sustain the enthusiasm that the fair had generated.

RECENT DEBATES AND REFORMS

Despite the seemingly constant expansion of the cultural calendar for literary culture, a combi-nation of internal and external forces began to emerge that would start to exert a significant influence on the UJC-driven cultural campaigns and spending under the *Batalla de Ideas*. As already mentioned, the costs of posthurricane reconstruction and the impact of the global recession on Cuba's principal income sources were onerous. However, political factors also played a role. The ongoing illness of Fidel Castro starting in 2006 was a reason for concern on several levels: with implications for maintaining public loyalty and confidence in a clearly aging leadership and for managing a transition to a successor, the period 2006–2008 was key, when change was inevitable but potentially dangerous for the revolutionary project, not least bearing in mind the constant threat—both real and imagined—from the U.S. administration. In this context, Raúl Castro's interim role as president in 2006–2008 allowed old fears and anxieties to resurface among intellectuals and artists regarding the directions that Cuban culture would take, and soon an intellectual debate was in full swing (Kumaraswami 2009).

This debate was prompted by and crystallized around the television screening in January 2007 of the weekly cultural series *Impronta*, which appeared to be an homage to Luis Pavón Tamayo, the former president of the *Consejo Nacional de Cultura* between 1971 and 1976 and thus a central figure in that nefarious period for Cuban culture later termed the *quinquenio gris* (gray five years). The program, produced by the state broadcasting institution, the Cuban Radio and Television Institute, omitted all reference to this period of cultural repression, and within a matter of days Cuban intellectuals and artists began to articulate their fears and concerns that Cuban cultural life might once again turn gray. Initially taking place as a national (but also quickly international) electronic debate, the state cultural infrastructure, under Prieto, responded by acting quickly to organize a series of meetings where those artists and intellectuals who had personally suffered the repressive effects of the *quinquenio gris* in the 1970s (and sometimes 1980s) could be allowed an institutional and public space to recount their experiences. Under the auspices of one of Cuba's most prominent cultural theory maga-zines, *Criterios*, and at a series of locations in Havana, the meetings, or *Encuentros*, took place in the first six months of 2007.

In hindsight, the virtual and real exchanges of 2007 clearly revealed the crucial hand of Prieto in being able to defuse tensions between the fields of politics and culture, and the exchanges assumed several functions at a key moment of political change. First, they served to publicly reincorporate once-marginalized artists and intellectuals but also to remind the lead-ership more generally of the crucial role of the cultural field in maintaining and renewing the revolutionary project. Second, their effect was to send an early warning to the interim political leadership, under Raúl Castro, that Cuban intellectuals' and artists' principal loyalty to the Revolution continued to consist precisely in their ability to critique and question it from within. Finally, given the recent reputation of the armed forces in several areas of public life—in dealing effectively with the economy in the wake of the economic collapse of the 1990s but also perhaps in underestimating the value of cultural life and for intervening in open sociocultural and political debates—underlying fears resurfaced that the "good times" of the 2000s, largely under the leadership of leading UJC figures, would give way to two unwelcome new directions: first, a period of economic disinvestment in culture, and, second, a more instrumentalist understanding of the function of culture.

With Raúl Castro elected as president in 2008, and subsequently elected as first secretary of the Cuban Communist Party at its Sixth Congress in 2011 and with the inevitable change of personnel that any change of political leadership implies, the changes for culture have been far reaching. Indeed, anxieties about the implications of cultural policy changes have been felt most acutely by the generations of cultural figures who "cut their teeth" in the Revolution in the 1960s and 2000s.

Furthermore, the initial publishing of the new economic guidelines (and their relevance to political, social, and cultural life) in the summer of 2011, followed by an intense consultation process through mass organizations and labor unions and the ratification and publication of the final policy reforms, the *Lineamientos*, at the Sixth Cuban Communist Party Congress in April 2012, indicate that while the political leadership perceives change as urgent, it is also aware of the sensitivity of many of the changes proposed, not least for the future of cultural life on the island. The congress also ratified a change of cultural leadership that has similarly created suspicions and debate among cultural communities, many of those debates summarized as position pieces at http://www.cubadebate.com. Abel Prieto, having served as minister of culture since 1997, was replaced by Rafael Alemany Bernal, former minister of education but also one of Prieto's deputy ministers during the period 1997–2012. One interpretation among many for this change of cultural leadership (with Prieto being promoted to the role of adviser to the Council of State and Council of Ministers) is that the age of protection—or spoiling—of artists and intellectuals by allowing them relative autonomy to function largely outside the rules of the market has come to an end.

While the limited liberalization of the 1990s allowed artists to ply their trade outside the island (not forgetting that they were taxed accordingly), these new reforms point to a further level of financial accountability and responsibility for cultural producers. Recent changes indicate that individuals and cultural groups who had hitherto used the state infrastructure of theaters, public squares, and cultural centers to provide events such as concerts and literary readings to the public in the peso currency might now be required to generate extra peso returns in order to cover some of the costs of maintaining the infrastructure, costs previously assumed (often in hard currency) by the Ministry of Culture. It is, however, crucial to recognize that this new understanding of the cultural economy still allows substantial potential for cultural agency, introducing a new aspect of nonsubsidized activity that is still facilitated but no longer determined by state structures. Early reactions from cultural producers and promoters indicate that this new "hybrid" cultural economy is a mixed blessing, allowing for greater freedom and agency but also removing important protections from cultural projects.

Although the implications of this model for cultural production are impossible to predict with any accuracy, the indications from contemporary debates point to two specific concerns: first, culture's position within the hierarchy of policy and spending priorities is set to suffer through the leadership perceiving cultural life as peripheral to more important and urgent concerns, and, second, and equally significant, the concern is being expressed that culture will gradually transform into an activity whose value is measured largely in economic terms—in short, that culture will become commercialized and that, given the necessary continued reliance on tourism as a hard-currency income stream, cultural projects will become increasingly targeted at foreign visitors. This not only will emphasize well-established stereotypes that accentuate the exotic and the tropical but also will make culture as everyday activity inaccessible to the domestic population. Especially in light of the geographical and cultural proximity of contemporary capitalist cultural models in the United States and in globalized Latin American cities, cultural figures are keen to remind the political leadership that the hard-fought national development achieved by the sustained subsidy of culture should not be abandoned. They stress the centrality of culture to social integration—to definitions of well-being and development—and, above all, they stress that the twin aspirations behind cultural policy—to massify participation in high culture and to provide the conditions for cultural producers to work within the revolutionary project—should not be dismissed as peripheral to that project. Perhaps the most crucial question for the issues raised in this chapter is how literary culture, evidently less "marketable" than other, more popular forms of culture, such as dance or music, will both respond to and be shaped by the recent reforms.

REFERENCES

Casamayor Cisneros, Odette. 2012. "Floating in the Void: Ethical Weightlessness in Post-Soviet Cuban Narrative." In *Rethinking the Cuban Revolution Nationally and Regionally: Politics, Culture and Identity*, edited by P. Kumaraswami, 38–57. Oxford: Wiley-Blackwell.

Davies, Catherine. 1997. *A Place in the Sun? Women Writers in Twentieth-Century Cuba*. London: Zed Books.

Fornet, Jorge. 2003. "La narrativa cubana entre la utopía y el desencanto." *Hispamérica* 32, no. 95 (August 2003): 3–20.

Giuliano, Maurizio. 1998. *El Caso CEA: Intelectuales e Inquisidores en Cuba. ¿Perestroika en la Isla?* Miami: Ediciones Universal.

Instituto Cubano del Libro. 2009. *Resumen estadístico 2009*. Havana: Instituto Cubano del Libro.

Kapcia, Antoni. 2005. "Educational Revolution and Revolutionary Morality in Cuba: The 'New Man,' Youth and the New 'Battle of Ideas.'" *Journal of Moral Education* 34, no. 4 (December 2005): 399–412.

———. 2009. "Lessons of the Special Period: Learning to March Again." *Latin American Perspectives* 36, issue 164, no. 1: 30–41.

Kumaraswami, Par. 2009. "'El color del futuro': Assessing the Significance of the Encuentros of 2007." *Journal of Iberian and Latin American Research* 15, no. 2: 103–20.

———.2012. "Peripheral Visions? Literary Canon Formation in Revolutionary Cuba." In *Rethinking the Cuban Revolution Nationally and Regionally: Politics, Culture and Identity*, edited by P. Kumaraswami, 91–109. Oxford: Wiley-Blackwell.

Padilla, Heberto. 1989. *La mala memoria*. Barcelona: Plaza & Janes Editores.

Whitfield, Esther. 2008. *Cuban Currency: The Dollar and "Special Period" Fiction*. Minneapolis: University of Minnesota Press.

———. 2009. "Truths and Fictions: The Economics of Writing, 1994–1999." In *Cuba in the Special Period: Culture and Ideology in the 1990s*, edited by A. Hernández-Reguant, 21–36. New York: Palgrave Macmillan.

Chapter Thirty-Six

Cuban Sport Development

Building Capacity from el Parque *to the Podium*

Robert Huish and Simon C. Darnell

In 1991, Cuba hosted the Pan-American Games. In preparation, the Cuban government built stadiums, dug swimming pools, and constructed hotels in order to host athletes from thirty-six nations in Havana between August 1 and 18. Such investment in new sports infrastructure constituted an enormous undertaking by the standards of any low- or middle-income nation; for Cuba, it was arguably even more significant given that the country was about to face near total economic collapse. Indeed, on December 26, 1991, the Soviet Union officially dissolved. This occurred just after Cuba had committed enormous resources to the construction of sports infrastructure and to the establishment of elite sport training centers.

Yet, even though food was strictly rationed and sporting equipment scarce during the "Special Period," public sport programs continued in communities across the island, and public schools remained open, providing sport and physical education opportunities. In addition, the *Instituto Nacional de Deportes y Educación Física* (INDER) continued to offer training programs and dedicated sports schools for elite athletes that produced international results. Cuba went on to place an astounding fifth overall in the final medal count at the 1992 Olympics, even outperforming Spain, the host country. Four years later, and still deep within the worst stages of the Special Period, Cuba finished eighth in the medal table at the 1996 Summer Olympics held in Atlanta. Indeed, in every Olympics and Pan-American Games since 1992, with the exception of 2008, the only countries to outperform Cuba in total medals have had a higher total gross domestic product. Cuba clearly bucks the trend of what Bernard and Busse (2004) see as the requirement of a strong economy in order to obtain Olympic success.

In this chapter, we explore how and why Cuba, despite such obvious economic shortcomings, has invested heavily in both elite sport as a cornerstone of national pride and mass participation sport as a mode of community-based development. Cuba's continued investment in sport is grounded in history, tradition, and revolutionary values and also in the pursuit of various economic and political opportunities. In this way, the investment in sport, representative of the late Special Period, can still be seen within processes of Cuban sport development in the new millennium. Such investment in community-based sport programs and international cooperation alongside elite training aligns in many ways with trends in global sports policy and organizing, which increasingly position sport as a means of social and economic development (Darnell 2012). At the same time, given its explicit connections to revolutionary values of social development and equality, Cuba's approach to sport needs to be contrasted against the commercialization, privatization, and corporatization that remain hallmarks of the global sports-industrial complex (Maguire 2011).

THE RIGHT TO SPORT IN CUBAN SOCIETY

In 1961, the Cuban government established INDER as an overarching ministry of sport that would coordinate elite training and competition alongside public access to sport programs. Sports such as baseball were effectively nationalized, and sport became nonprofessional. Generous remuneration for top athletes disappeared, and the government introduced a system of moral incentives that adhered to revolutionary values (Huish 2011). The effects of this revolutionary ethos in Cuban sport can still be seen today. Recently, in addressing the Nineteenth UN Council on Human Rights, Cuban ambassador to Switzerland Rodolfo Reyes declared that "sport is a human right." He added that sport and, more important, access to sport stand as a fundamental human right given that sport builds "individual capabilities and enriches societies by strengthening solidarity and friendship between peoples" (*Granma* 2012).

At the same time, while Cuba clearly promotes sport as a human right and a means of securing development across a variety of contexts and geographic and political scales, the Cuban approach differs significantly from many sport-focused development projects that tend to align with and even secure the commercialization and privatization of sport. The Cuban government approaches sport as part of social and community development that is distinct from corporatization, whereas many international-development-through-sport programs offer opportunities for corporate expansion and branding (Hayhurst 2011) and/or the enactment of corporate social responsibility programs (Levermore 2010). Indeed, even though there are commercial undertones to sport and sport development in Cuba, the pursuit of moneymaking activities does not necessarily restrict participation and access to sport within the nation (Carter 2008).

In addition, rather than promoting sport as a "tool" to facilitate individual development within the structures of inequality, the Cuban government arguably encourages a more holistic approach to development through sport. Wide participation in sport is encouraged based on universal access but done so alongside other programs focused on health, education, and economic development. Cuba has thus emphasized sport not as a tool for development but as a key pillar to its own social development strategies since the 1960s, and today the place of sport remains strong as a fundamental dimension to Cuba's development initiatives both at home and abroad. In this way, the political subtext of Reyes's statement to the United Nations can be read as support for sport as a public good facilitated through universal access rather than sport as a means of producing citizens within the logic of competitive capitalism and/or offering opportunities for corporations and supranational organizations, such as the International Olympic Committee, to "give back" to the less fortunate.

Indeed, Cuba has continued to ensure access to sport alongside other sectors of social programming and resources. Within elementary schools in Cuba, sport is included within the mandatory curriculum from first grade up until twelfth grade. In addition to in-school sport programs, INDER also organizes a wide range of community-based youth sport programs in both recreational and competitive fields. The range of sport programs for youth includes but is not limited to baseball, volleyball, basketball, football, tennis, handball, boxing, tae kwon do, judo, karate, swimming, synchronized swimming, gymnastics, and chess. Such priorities have resulted in estimates that over 90 percent of Cubans have participated in some form of sport or community-based recreation (Huish 2011).

This does not mean, of course, that elite sport is no longer a priority in Cuba. In all of the sport programs listed above, there is clearly an opportunity for youth to advance to elite levels. While this is not distinct in and of itself—the development of youth sport as a feeder to elite sport is a recurring model around the world—of note is that the entire participation and training process of athletes in Cuba is handled within the public sector as a universally accessible good. While for youth in many countries in the world the pathway to elite sport performance comes with high financial costs, in Cuba these costs are absorbed largely by the state. In this regard, Cuba offers a rare case where elite sport development is not only entirely funded by the state but also directly linked through policy and structure to the promotion of sport at the community level.

GOOD FOR YOU, AND GOOD FOR ALL

Striking a balance between elite sport and development and mass participation has been and continues to be an issue of central importance for sport policymakers in many countries around the world (De Bosscher and Van Bottenburg 2011). Cuba is no different in facing this basic conundrum. In July 2011, officials from INDER explained to us that the ministry views its success in elite sport not only as a product but also as evidence of the broad participation in sport by Cuban citizens. In this sense, while not perfect, the traditional pyramid model remains largely intact in Cuba given its insularity from privatization. That is, unlike contemporary elite training programs in other countries through which youth are more easily able to develop into elite athletes given access to private resources or because they have privileged access to facilities, Cuba continues to develop its elite athletes largely from a broad pool of participants. Within elementary schools, students participate in sport activities from which teachers and INDER coaches select students who demonstrate advanced ability for elite training. Some may question the opportunity costs of such attention paid to elite training, as it potentially compromises resources that would otherwise be available for other community-based participation programs. Still, the point remains that INDER does not appear to be willing to compromise community-based participation in sport for the sake of elite development; while specialized programs exist throughout the country, so too do recreational programs for youth, adults, and seniors.

That said, although INDER clearly supports broad participation with the search for elite athletes in mind, the emphasis on universal participation does not cease once Cubans pass the age of elite performance. Indeed, the active participation of seniors in sport and recreation programs is evident throughout the country. For example, within barrios across Havana and the countryside, seniors regularly assemble in public parks and squares for morning exercise and calisthenics coordinated by INDER. For seniors, sport and recreation offer a hub for community cohesion but also an opportunity to promote health and healthy aging.

An example of such programming can be found within the Wushu Institute in Havana's *Barrio Chino* (Chinatown). This institute for tai chi, dance, martial arts, and Confucius studies was founded in 1994 at the height of the Special Period crisis with assistance from the Confucius Institute in China and INDER. The institute is open to public participation and is meant to promote and maintain traditional Chinese martial arts and dance. The institute runs daily classes with the specific mandate to promote and maintain the health of participants (Salud y Vida 2012). The school is open to anyone in Havana or across Cuba to attend daily classes beginning at 7:30 a.m. and concluding at 9:00 p.m. There are over 4,000 students enrolled in the school and more than 100 instructors. In addition, the school hosts an annual festival that is open to the public in order to demonstrate various martial arts and dance techniques.

Members of the Wushu Institute also participate in numerous INDER-organized events and rallies, such as the annual Terry Fox Run for cancer research, which takes place in Havana in March of each year. In keeping with the Cuban approach to elite performance and mass participation, even though the Wushu Institute engages in internationally recognized elite performance, it remains centered on broad community participation in sport for health and well-being, based on an understanding of the health benefits of martial arts, including tai chi. The Wushu Institute advertises its programs as having benefits for people suffering from high blood pressure, arthritis, diabetes, immunity disorders, and heart conditions (Escuela Cubana de Wushu 2012).

In many ways, the approach illustrates the Cuban approach to community-based physical activity. As it is tied directly to the health system—with physicians prescribing participation to their patients—the Wushu Institute is representative of Cuba's intersectoral approach to health and sports (Spiegel and Yassi 2004). Since the exercises are open and accessible to all, there is no prohibitive cost that restricts patients from seeking out and accessing these activities. In Cuba, through organizations such as the Wushu Institute, sport is positioned as an integrated part of the development of health, community participation, and advanced training. Perhaps most important, in this system sport is a right rather than a privilege for those able to pay or a benefit conferred on the less fortunate by advantaged organizations or charities.

CUBAN SPORT AND COOPERATION ABROAD

While Cuba's program of international medical cooperation is gradually being recognized, little is known about its sports cooperation abroad. The Cuban approach that distinguishes sport from private sector interests and that facilitates community health also connects to its approach to facilitating sport for international cooperation. Cuba has established sport cooperation partnerships with more than 100 nations, and it has offered full scholarships for students from seventy-one low-income countries to train in sport and physical education in Havana (Huish 2011). The *Escuela Internacional de Educación Física y Deporte* (EIEFD) now has over 1,000 students from sixty-eight countries studying sport and physical education under the agreement that they will return to their home countries in order to help bring sport into marginalized communities within their nations. The school's mandate is not only to train low-income students as coaches and athletes but also to "train professionals in the essential values of solidarity and humanity with the capacity to positively transform sport and physical education in their home countries" (EIEFD 2012). Such capacity building is at first glance not unusual, as many nongovernmental organizations, corporations, and charities offer programs for athlete training, coaching development, and even elite performance. However, these organizations perpetuate and solidify traditional flows of development aid from North to South. They rarely question global structures of inequality and may even tacitly encourage individual development over community needs (Darnell 2012). By contrast, EIEFD's mandate to offer training to foreign nationals from poor countries suggests a commitment to development based on South-South cooperation as well as a political use of sport to promote Cuban values of self-sufficiency and universal access.

CUBAN SPORT DEVELOPMENT: CHALLENGES AHEAD

Even though Cuba has achieved success by embracing sport as a human right and supporting universal access, significant challenges lie ahead. Chief among these is that professional sports leagues—which enjoy an increasingly global reach—are more willing and able than ever to pay astronomical salaries for top athletic talent. Indeed, in recent years, many Cuban professionals have left INDER to play professional sports in the United States, particularly in Major League Baseball. INDER recognizes these pressures as well as the need to develop clear strategies regarding how best to negotiate the tension between individuals seeking prestige and generous salaries against those willing to serve sport as public goodwill. Cuba has entered into dialogue with the United States on how to negotiate the pressures of elite players hoping to go to the U.S. major leagues (Univisión 2012b), an indication that Cuba may be changing its attitude about the place of sport against the enormous pressures of privatization and globalization of sport (Univisión 2012a). However, no forms of cooperation have emerged between INDER and the U.S. majors. As a result, Cuba has sought to tighten control of the athletic exodus from the island by requiring letters of permission for athletes to go abroad for fear of desertion to the United States (*Calgary Herald* 2012; *Nuevo Herald* 2013).

Also of note, Cuba has increasingly found opportunities to capitalize on sport to its own benefit. Before the collapse of the Soviet Union, *Cubadeportes*, INDER's for-profit wing, sold sporting equipment to other Eastern bloc countries. Today, *Cubadeportes* works with INDER to arrange contracts of Cuban coaches traveling to other nations to train elite-performance athletes. The host country is expected to pay INDER directly for their services, and these coaches also receive a higher salary in local currency than they would receive working in Cuba. The idea behind these exchanges is that the hard currency gained abroad by the some 600 coaches working in 100 countries can fund the development of sport programs within Cuba at both the elite and the recreational level. While the international cooperation of these coaches, trainers, and professionals may help to integrate Cuba into a global sports community and contribute to economic development for the state, tensions for recruitment into the professional ranks will remain, and it will be a delicate balance to find the means of ensuring the right to sport while furthering solidarity and cashing in on economic opportunities abroad.

In sum, we do not see these future challenges as fundamentally contradictory or even impossible to overcome for INDER and Cuba. In part, this is because of the Cuban record in sport, in which a progressive commitment to sport as an integrated pillar of development, even during extreme economic crisis, has resulted in levels of participation and elite success that are enviable by even the standards of rich countries. While the continued privatization and commercialization of sport on a global scale presents its own unique set of challenges to countries such as Cuba as well as to the belief in rights-based sport for development more broadly (Maguire 2011), this by no means spells the end of sport as a public good in Cuba. Indeed, as long as the Cuban government remains committed to ensuring that access to sport be secured as a human right and one to be facilitated primarily in and by the public interest, it is likely that sport will remain an important holistic element of Cuban development domestically as well as in its international solidarity and outreach.

REFERENCES

Bernard, A., and M. Busse. 2004. "Who Wins at the Olympics: Economic Resources and Medal Tables." *Review of Economics and Statistics* 86, no. 1: 413–17.

Calgary Herald. 2012. "Cuban Athletes Flee to U.S. after Vancouver Soccer Game." January 26.

Carter, T. F. 2008. *The Quality of Home Runs: The Passion, Politics and Language of Cuban Baseball.* Durham, NC: Duke University Press.

Darnell, S. C. 2012. *Sport for Development and Peace: A Critical Sociology.* London: Bloomsbury Academic Press.

De Bosscher, V., and M. Van Bottenburg. 2011. "Elite for All, All for Elite: An Assessment of the Impact of Sports Development on Elite Sport Success." In *Routledge Handbook of Sports Development*, edited by B. Houlihan and M. Green, 579–98. London: Routledge.

Escuela Cubana de Wushu. 2012. http://www.wushucuba.com/ (accessed December 2012).

Escuela Internacional de Educación Física y Deporte. 2012. http://www.eiefd.cu (accessed December 2012).

Granma. 2012. "Cuba reclama el acceso al deporte como derecho humano." February 27.

Hayhurst, L. M. C. 2011. "Corporatising Sport, Gender and Development: Postcolonial IR Feminisms, Transnational Private Governance and Global Corporate Social Engagement." *Third World Quarterly* 32, no. 3: 531–49.

Huish, R. 2011. "Punching above Its Weight: Cuba's Use of Sport for South-South Solidarity." *Third World Quarterly* 32, no. 3: 417–33.

Levermore, R. 2010. "CSR for Development through Sport: Examining Its Potential and Limitations." *Third World Quarterly* 31, no. 2: 223–41.

Maguire, J. A. 2011. "Development through Sport and the Sports-Industrial Complex: The Case for Human Development in Sports and Exercise Sciences." *Sport in Society* 14, nos. 7–8: 937–49.

Nuevo Herald. 2013. "Deportistas cubanos necesitarán permiso para salir del país, pese a reforma." January 9. http://www.elnuevoherald.com/2013/01/08/1379657/deportistas-cubanos-necesitaran.html?story_link=email_msg#storylink=cpy (accessed December 2012).

Salud y Vida. 2012. "La Escuela Wushu en la Habana." http://concursocacs.com/proyecto/salud-y-vida-escuela-cubana-de-wushu/ (accessed December 2012).

Spiegel, J., and A. Yassi. 2004. "Lessons from the Margins of Globalization: Appreciating the Cuban Health Paradox." *Journal of Public Health Policy* 25, no. 1: 85–110.

Univisión. 2012a. "Cuba cambia de mentalidad sobre deserciones en el béisbol." January 13.

———. 2012b. "Cuba dispuesta a dialogar con EEUU sobre robo de talentos en béisbol." January 13.

V

Social Change

The need for change is something on which Cuban citizens, dissidents, exiles and even the government agree. However, whatever form Cuban society takes in the future, the Millennium Goals (which have already been met in Cuba) should be protected as one of the greatest treasures of this nation.
—Fernando Ravsberg, BBC, Havana, April 4, 2013 [1]

The insightful BBC correspondent in Cuba is right. Cuba's protection of many of the Millennium Goals (education, health care, the role of women, access to food, and protection of culture among others) is exceptionally good. During Fidel Castro's many years as president, these social human rights developed faster than in any developing nation. (This can be seen in data for a variety of aspects of health and education, points that are developed later). But Fidel has now left the political scene, and his brother is in charge of an economy that is still extremely inefficient and where many of the reforms introduced have resulted in significant inequality for those unable to adapt to the rigors and fast pace of change in the new Cuba. One of the key questions to be asked in any analysis of contemporary Cuba is therefore whether the scope of the changes in the social fabric is sufficient to maintain the revolutionary process itself. This section seeks to provide a variety of elements to assist in that investigation.

The starting point for this section is our finding that there have been remarkable changes in Cuba since Raúl Castro assumed the presidency—many of which would have been inconceivable just a few years ago. In the first edition of *A Contemporary Cuba Reader*, we examined the significant evolution during the early years of the "Special Period"—especially in the early years after the implosion of the Soviet Union—and the enormous impact of these reforms on the society. We concluded that Cuba had changed more in those first four years of the Special Period than it had in the previous quarter of a century.

The impact of many of those reforms diminished as the Special Period continued through the late 1990s and into the first decade of the new millennium as the economy gradually improved. Self-employment decreased noticeably as many Cubans returned to work in state-controlled industries (in particular, the increasingly important tourist sector). Yet largely as a result of the new government policies, social differences increased, in part because the social (and racial) polarization continued to increase with an ever-wider gap in incomes. At the same time, the government continued to demand greater efficiency from those employed in state-run industries, even when the salaries were barely able to keep pace with the cost of living—and often they did not. It was clear that a fresh approach was needed since the blend of outdated socialist measures (in particular, massive subsidies to unproductive industries) and an incipient private sector (both being often connected with ties of petty corruption) badly needed to be overhauled. The impact of this complex, disturbing situation on social institutions and personal relationships was clearly becoming both untenable and embarrassing—and the government of Raúl Castro therefore embarked on a series of far-reaching measures designed to provide equality of opportunities to Cubans—without ensuring basic equality. Analyzing those dramatic changes in Cuban society, this section provides a set of totally new chapters and insights into some of the principal societal changes and challenges that have resulted.

Raúl Castro has certainly introduced a fresh approach. Gone are the earlier massive public demonstrations in favor of the "Cuban Five," the sweeping condemnations of U.S. policy, and frequent use of state-controlled media to emphasize government campaigns. Instead, a low-key business-like approach has been steadily implemented. The same emphasis on efficiency and saving, with demands for harder work from state employees, and at the same time the same appeal for popular support for the Revolution are still found. But the basic strategy has changed dramatically, as have the fundamental policies in many other areas, as this book attests.

In many ways, the social changes that have resulted in Cuba since Raúl Castro assumed the presidency have significantly reduced the unique aspects of the revolutionary approach to social development. Efficiency, massive layoffs of workers, and a decrease in subsidies for many former unproductive factories are now the new order of the day, and, as Raúl Castro often says, this is a process "without haste, but without pause." Some of the most notable programs remain with generous subsidies, and Cuban medical care undoubtedly remains the best in the developing world. Indeed, in many ways, Cuba offers better health care than countries in the developed world—infant mortality rates are lower in Cuba than in the United States, for instance. The same can be said for many aspects of education. That said, the price paid for the (badly needed) reforms has often been high, and tears in the Cuban social fabric can be seen.

A warning note was sounded in April 2011 at the Sixth Congress of the Communist Party when a series of guidelines were introduced. The document of guidelines that resulted was introduced by a quotation from Fidel Castro: "The term 'revolutionary' reflects the sense of the historical moment; it *means changing everything that should be changed*" (emphasis added). Armed with that general philosophy, the document provides 313 guidelines, a common theme of which is the need for the Cuban population to be more efficient and productive, in essence, to do more with less—even in the traditionally protected areas of health care and education. Article 143, for example, emphasizes the need to "continue improving our services in education, healthcare, culture and sports. In order to accomplish this it is absolutely necessary to reduce or eliminate excessive costs in social matters, as well as generate new sources of income" (http://www.granma.cubaweb.cu/secciones/6to-congreso-pcc/Folleto%20Lineami entos%20VI%20Cong.pdf). From the government perspective, it is clearly a time for belt tightening and, in some cases, a reduction of services. Social policy in Cuba is thus being amended drastically to fit in with Cuba's economic reality.

As a result, Cuban society has changed in many ways for better and worse. For example, the food covered by the ration book has been reduced significantly, the free lunches offered at the workplace have all but gone, and huge layoffs in the state employment sector have resulted. Subsidized water and power rates have also been reduced. Cubans can now stay at hotels previously reserved for tourists and have cell phones and computers, all of which are sensible changes. The age for retirement has been increased (to sixty for women and sixty-five for men). Bank credits have been provided to Cubans in order to increase food production, repair homes, and support self-employment. In recent times, sturdy Ladas and Moskavich cars, the mainstay of family transportation, are still on the streets of Havana, but increasingly Audis, BMWs, and Mercedes (bearing the conspicuous yellow license plates identifying private ownership) are seen (perhaps that is one of the reasons why a proposal has been introduced to standardize all license plates for cars). Beauty salons and (private) health clubs have now appeared, another novelty, as is Cuba's answer to Craig's List—Revolico.com.

Many of the changes are more dramatic, however, and respond to demands that Cubans have been making for years. For the first time in fully five decades, Cubans can now buy and sell houses and cars—a major breakthrough and one that is long overdue. While to people not familiar with Cuba this might appear remarkably normal, what needs to be remembered is that since 1959, Cuba has resolutely pursued a revolutionary socialist model designed to ensure a level playing field for all Cubans regardless of income, color, or geographical location. Prior to the Special Period, for example, Cuban law stipulated that the differential between the highest and lowest salaries in the country should be no more than five to one. That has long since disappeared, with social polarization now resulting from the reforms introduced first in the early 1990s and then strengthened under Raúl Castro. (An illustration of this is the salary of doctors—who earn approximately $30 monthly—compared with chefs in the burgeoning *paladar* industry who can now earn well over $1,000.) Despite government efforts to reverse the inverted social pyramid, this remains a major challenge. There is also an insidious racial element to the "new" Cuba since *remesas*, or family remittances (now an estimated $2 billion annually), come largely from white Cubans living abroad and go to their (mainly white) relatives, thus exacerbating socioeconomic differences based largely on race.

In many ways, we now encounter the "Latin Americanization" of Cuba. By that, we mean that Cuba is losing many of its unique characteristics as it assumes aspects of society typically found in all of Latin America. Signs of this are everywhere, from the vendors of pirated CDs and DVDs to the *pregoneros* who hawk their wares (from food and flowers to brushes and cleaning supplies) with gusto as they stroll down the streets. The large pre-1959 *almendrones*, private taxis steaming down the principal arteries packed with passengers, seem to have mushroomed overnight and for many are the principal form of transportation. Small mom-and-pop stores have sprung up all over the cities, as have the tiny snack bars (usually found in the doorways to homes). As Sinan Koont shows, there has been a major attempt to revive food production in Cuba (which still imports approximately 70–80 percent of food consumed), with land (up to sixty-seven hectares) being distributed in usufruct to 12,000 would-be small farmers by March 2013. So far, the results are mixed, but the government has clearly indicated that this is an economic priority.

Cuentapropistas, self-employed workers (almost 500,000 strong) who have started their small businesses in recent years, have their signs in front of their workshops and homes advertising their trades. By April 2013, the government had rented more than 2,000 small businesses (such as hairdressers, manicurists, and shoe and clock repair operations) to their employees, who have now started up their own operations. An amazing number of private restaurants, or *paladares*, have now been established, many of which are in exceptionally luxurious facilities offering high-quality meals. They have multiplied in the past two years, and an estimated 20 percent of self-employed are working in the food industry. Significantly, whereas they were initially limited to a maximum of twelve clients, it is now common to find larger ones catering to several dozen people. An infusion of capital from visiting Cuban

American "refugees" (some 500,000 of whom returned in 2012) to family members has understandably fueled this expansion. In February 2013, I had supper at a *paladar* in the Vedado district of Havana—and was the only foreigner among over fifty clients, a telling illustration of how Cuba has changed in recent years. Likewise, in the spring of 2013, I was struck by the large number of Cuban Americans and their island-based relatives staying at five-star tourist hotels. This was inconceivable just five years ago.

Cuba under Raúl Castro is indeed changing rapidly and mainly (but not completely) for the better as the government seeks to revamp the system, injecting a greater efficiency and vitality. This process is not without major challenges, however. Prostitution, which had largely died down in recent years, has returned, largely as the result of tourism (3 million tourists are expected in 2014) and, to a lesser extent, higher salaries for some in Cuba. Fortunately, there is a limited narcotics problem. Another major challenge is represented by the aspirations of Cuban youth, many of whom were raised during the worst of the Special Period and see only a bleak future with limited prospects. María Isabel Domínguez provides some insightful research into this complex situation. Having seen their parents scrape by during this achingly difficult period, they want something better—and the new migration policy makes leaving an enticing prospect.

More serious is the potential challenge posed by racism, exacerbated by the fact that most of the capital being invested in Cuba comes from (mainly white) exiles, thereby increasing income disparities between white and black Cubans. While 37 percent of the members of the National Assembly in 2013 are black or mulatto, there is the clear need for greater transparency in an analysis of the socioeconomic reality lived by many black and mulatto Cubans, as Esteban Morales argues convincingly. And, of course, the polarization on the basis of income constitutes a major challenge to the revolutionary ethos. In the late nineteenth century, the great Cuban writer and revolutionary José Martí spoke of what he termed the "metalificación del hombre" (literally, the "metalification of people" and the weakening of spiritual values) during his stay in the United States. This referred to the fact that many American citizens cared little for their fellow human beings, instead focusing on the accumulation of wealth. It is a challenge that now needs to be faced in revolutionary Cuba, particularly among the nouveaux riches and also among younger Cubans brought up during the worst of the Special Period—since they know only the grind of the struggle to survive in those exceptionally difficult years. As Domínguez notes in her chapter, the government seeks to encourage Cuban youth to become involved in the process and not to lose themselves in technology and the search for the CUC (the hard currency employed in Cuba).

Access to technology remains a major challenge for the government and, in particular, the underwater cable that Venezuela has provided as a means of improving the connectivity of the island—which has been traditionally hindered by the need to use satellites for Internet access. The cable from Venezuela arrived in 2011, in theory allowing Cuba to overcome its status as the country in Latin America and the Caribbean with the lowest access to the Internet. It is still not being employed fully, with government officials claiming that in keeping with the goals of the Revolution, its priority should be for "social usage" (i.e., schools, hospitals, and so on). So, while access to cell phones has increased dramatically (1.8 million were in use by late 2012), Internet connectivity remains heavily limited. (Meanwhile, opponents of the government, with free access at the U.S. Interests Section and with support from foreign diplomats, have little difficulty blogging.)

In many ways, Cuba under the *raúlista* influence is taking a major risk, trusting that the population will maintain its support for the revolutionary process as a series of liberal reforms (many of which go directly against traditional government policy) is introduced. These reforms are significant, as this section illustrates, and in many ways represent a potential open- ing of Pandora's box—in essence, allowing a minority of Cubans to become extremely wealthy while maintaining the goals of the Revolution writ large and official discourse about equality of opportunity. Perhaps the most important of these changes is the new immigration law allowing Cubans to come and go as they please, leaving the country for up to two years, a policy that has been decades in the making (and that is fraught with risks). This now means that Cubans have greater liberty to travel to the United States than most U.S. citizens do to travel in the opposite direction.

The key term to describe the "new" Cuba is pragmatism, the hallmark of Raúl Castro's management style for decades in the armed forces, whose role in many areas of Cuba's economic development—ranging from tourism to agricultural production and marketing to electronics to department stores—has been extremely important, particularly since the onset of the Special Period. It is this approach that has been well channeled into Cuban development since 2006. In addition to the reduction of free or heavily subsidized government services, taxes have also been introduced for the first time since the start of the Revolution. Cubans now pay 15 percent on income of more than 10,000 pesos annually (approximately $400), and this goes as high as 50 percent on incomes of over 50,000 pesos.

This overlying pragmatism is seen in the government's approach to education and health care, the two jewels in the crown of social reforms in Cuba since 1959. But now there are new challenges facing both social programs, and radically new approaches are being used to make them more relevant to Cuba's current needs and more efficient. The postsecondary education system is being revamped to encourage the development of graduates better able to contribute to Cuba's economic development. A significantly reduced number of graduates in the human- ities, social sciences, and law has resulted, while far greater attention is now being paid to the training of teachers, agronomists, and tradespeople, as Denise Blum illustrates. Teachers are in particularly short supply, with an estimated need of an additional 1,600. In spite of shortages, Cuba does extremely well in terms of the delivery of its education system. According to UNESCO's "Índice de Desarrollo de la Educación," it is the highest-ranking country in Latin America and the Caribbean (ranking nineteen positions above the United States). It also has the highest literacy rate in Latin America and the Caribbean and spends the highest proportion of its gross domestic product on education (13 percent). Yet Cuba is facing a major challenge as the inverted pyramid of income means that it has trouble retaining its teachers—and badly needs to train more.

Likewise in health care, while Cuba has not reduced the number of students of medicine, increasingly they are being encouraged to work abroad (thus bringing in significant funding to the government's coffers, arguably the largest single source of hard currency). In addition, medical tourism continues to grow apace, and the company *Servicios Médicos Cubanos S.A.* has been tasked with generating income in Cuba and abroad by selling medical services in a way that has not been considered before. As Conner Gorry and William Keck indicate, this restructuring of the public health care system represents a major change for the body politic of Cuba. It is worth pointing out, however, that despite this process of rationalization, Cuba still enjoys an admirable health profile, exemplified by its infant mortality rate, exceptionally low rates of communicable diseases that are common in many other Latin American countries, and life expectancy that rivals those of the most advanced industrialized countries. The same approach in terms of using the export of professional services to help the national economy can be said, to a lesser degree, of the exportation of Cuban athletic services and indeed Cuban expertise and know-how in general.

One area in which surprising (and very positive) changes have taken place in recent years and one where Cuba stands out as a positive example among its Latin American and Caribbean counterparts is in the area of LGBT (lesbian, gay, bisexual, and transgender) rights. The role of Mariela Castro, daughter of Raúl Castro and the late Vilma Espín, president for many years of the Federation of Cuban Women, has been crucially important in this campaign, as is indicated by Emily Kirk in her chapter on the contribution of CENESEX (Cuba's National Center for Sex Education). In addition to Kirk's chapter, the interview with Mariela Castro provides a useful insight into the goals of this important center as it seeks to turn back the tides of decades of homophobia. These changes and the proposal to change the Family Code (legislation in place since 1975 that outlines a series of progressive laws and responsibilities governing gender relations and issues such as marriage, divorce, and recognition of children) would have been unthinkable even five years ago and illustrate just how much Cuba has changed and is changing.

The status of women in Cuba also continues to develop, and, while the traditional "glass ceiling" preventing women from reaching the upper echelons of power still exists, it has slowly been chipped away at. As a result, it is worth noting that, in terms of political influence, 48 percent of the members of Cuba's National Assembly are women, and twelve of the thirty-one members of the influential Council of State (including two of the vice presidents) are women. Perhaps most significant of all, fully ten of the fifteen leaders of provincial assemblies are women. Women also make up 65 percent of the professional and technical workforce and represent 72 percent of the workforce in education, 69 percent in health, and 53 percent in science and technology.

The promotion of a new generation of political leaders, the commitment of the president to step down as of 2018, and the appointment of Miguel Díaz-Canel as first vice president clearly illustrate the major changing of the revolutionary guard, as is commented on in the politics section of this volume. But political change among the leadership is irrelevant if the population is not buying in to the larger social project. This section provides some insights into the kind of changes that are being introduced, allowing the reader to appreciate the fast pace of change—for which, in some cases, people have been waiting a long time. These changes are needed since Cuba's population is slowly shrinking—while its population is gradually aging (18 percent are over age sixty), and there is very little immigration.

In sum, some things in Cuba remain the same. There is the same emphasis on social networks and on access at a remarkably low cost to cultural and sports activities and at no cost to education and health care. High quality in those basic social services—fundamental human rights—remains. In its 2012 report *Nutrition in the First 1,000 Days: State of the World's Mothers*, Save the Children placed Cuba in first place among eighty developing countries as the best place to be a mother (and a child). The analysis took into consideration a number of variables, including percentage of births attended by skilled health personnel, risk of maternal death, access to modern contraception, female life expectancy, formal female schooling, percentage of women in national government, under-five mortality rate, percentage of underweight children, and school enrollment. The 2013 report on the State of Mothers in the World placed Cuba thirty-third (of 176) countries—the highest in Latin America and the Caribbean.

There are many criticisms that can be leveled at Cuban society—housing needs are enormous, problems of racism are not being dealt with quickly enough, and machismo is still deeply rooted. Yet what is undoubtedly true is that Cuba is still the country throughout the region where inequality is lower than any other, where more social programs are accessible, where women have the most significant role, where children enjoy the widest range of programs to assist their development, and where greater equality of opportunity can be found.

Sadly, this necessary comparative analysis is often lacking when criticisms of Cuba are leveled.

When we prepared the first edition of this book almost a decade ago, we did so because of the significant changes that had occurred, especially in the early 1990s. Now Cuban society has changed radically again, as this section tries to illustrate. As a result, we decided that much of the material found in the earlier edition needed to be updated—so fast has been the transformation since Raúl Castro took over. And, while political leaders in the United States commonly refer to the lack of significant developments in Cuba since that time, they are badly mistaken. It is still unclear where Cuba as a country is going as Raúl Castro seeks a major overhaul—of society, economic structure, and polity. What is absolutely obvious, however, is that change has come and will continue to do so—slowly for many and rapidly for others. The genie is indeed out of the lamp.

NOTE

1. http://www.bbc.co.uk/blogs/mundo/cartas_desde_cuba/2013/04/los_objetivos_del_milenio.html.

Chapter Thirty-Seven

Cuban Youth

From the "Special Period" to the "Updating" of the Economic and Social Model

María Isabel Domínguez

When we speak of the youth of Cuba, we refer to a segment of the population between fourteen and thirty years of age, according to the definition of the prevailing legislation, although within that definition we can distinguish three groups:

- Early youth: between fourteen and seventeen years old
- Middle youth: between eighteen and twenty-four years old (the majority in terms of numbers)
- Mature or late youth: between twenty-five and thirty years old

In spite of the considerable reduction of youth resulting from the demographic transition that is taking place in Cuba and of the aging of the population, they still represent 20.4 percent of the total population (as of the end of 2011, that meant 2,297,428 young people) (*Oficina Nacional de Estadísticas e Información*, or Office of National Statistics and Information [ONEI] 2012, 3.3). This situation is the result of increased life expectancy to 77.97 years (ONEI 2012); the sustained low birthrate over past decades, which has not changed since the end of the 1970s (the average number of live births per woman is 1.55 [ONEI 2009a, 67]); and a net negative emigration rate, which has remained between −3 and −3.5 in recent years) (ONEI 2012a, 3.21).

As is the case of the general population, youth are concentrated in urban areas but with a slightly lower ratio (74 percent for youth and 75.3 percent for the total population). In terms of gender, the ratio is 51.5 percent men and 48.5 percent women (ONEI 2012a, 3.3). These figures are important and not only in quantitative terms because of their significance for the present and the future of the nation.

This chapter seeks to analyze some of the main influences on Cuban youth as a result of the economic and social changes in recent years. The youth of today have been born or at least have been socialized during the 1990s in three basic periods, to be examined here:

1. The 1990s: the economic crisis and its aftermath, known as the "Special Period"

2. The first decade of the twenty-first century, with the influence of the "Battle of Ideas" and the "New Social Programs"
3. The current decade: the "updating" of the economic and social development model

THE SPECIAL PERIOD AND YOUTH

Two major factors had a major impact on the life of Cuban youth. One was the intense economic and social transformation experienced by Cuban society in the last decade of the twentieth century as a result of the collapse of the socialist bloc. The other was the strengthening of the U.S. blockade against a society that had initiated a process of rectification of errors in economic management that had lasted over a decade. The economic crisis and recovery had a major impact on society as a whole. Yet these experiences had an even more intense influence on young Cubans at this important formative stage of their lives, especially given the impact it would have on their future development. The crisis itself and the socioeconomic policies designed to overcome it constituted a double-edged sword for the socialization and social integration for this generation of youth in the 1990s.

It is essential to emphasize that, despite the acute economic crisis and the need to rapidly implement measures to ensure an economic and social restructuring in multiple dimensions, even in the most difficult moments there remained a clear commitment to ensure significant social programs, particularly in public health and education. Primary schooling was provided for 99.7 percent of children between six and eleven years of age, while schooling was assured for 92.3 percent of middle school students between eleven and fourteen years of age (92.3 percent) (*Oficina Nacional de Estadísticas*, or National Office of Statistics [ONE] 1996, 305). Opportunities for free higher education for youth were also protected. That said, there was a decrease in the quality of education among some segments of youth. This was the result of several factors but mainly the devaluation of the national currency. Salaries did not satisfy material needs, making it less attractive for young people to continue their studies, when at the same time other ways of obtaining higher incomes and enjoying a better standard of living emerged. Money was suddenly available through work in the tourist sector, as a self-employed worker, or simply through remittances from relatives abroad.

That combination of factors reduced the proportion of youth studying at middle or higher levels, and this decrease in enrollment strengthened the overrepresentation of women students. For example, in the period 1990–1995, 57 percent of all university students in the country were women, including programs linked to technology (different engineering fields), agricultural sciences, and other specialties, such as physics and computer science. In the 1996–1997 school year, they made up 60.2 percent of students (ONE 1996, 298). The result of this process at the education level was reflected in the increasing feminization of professionals in the labor market. By 1996, women constituted 60 percent of the total number of technicians in the country (ONE 1996, 116).

High levels of vocational training for women also had implications for the family because, among other factors, this professionalization of women has resulted in higher demands in seeking a partner and in the sharing of family responsibilities. As a result, marriage is often postponed, and the number of single women has increased, with a corresponding decrease in the number of children born. All these processes produced changes in Cuban youth in terms of both their role in society and their personal interpretation of that role.

THE NEW SOCIAL PROGRAMS

The gradual economic recovery of the country and a clear understanding of the causes of this intense crisis for both society and Cuban youth resulted in a new stage of social development from 2000 on. The objective was to increase opportunities for human potential, and as a result, strategic objectives, as well as social policies, designed to improve the quality of life for the Cuban population were implemented (Domínguez 2010). This gave rise to the New Social Programs, an important part of which sought to achieve the integrated general formation of new generations. They combined the acquisition of knowledge with a range of ethical, cultural, and political values, all of which depended on a revamped educational program.

The importance of this can be seen in the fact that education constituted the largest category of expenditures within the state budget (in 2005, it reached 25.7 percent of total expenditures) (ONE 2006, V.4), and in just five years (2001–2006), it grew by 2.5 times (ONE 2007, VI.4, 160). The main programs implemented in the education field include the following:

- Massive training for emergency primary and middle school teachers to cover the deficit of teachers in these areas.
- A reduction in the number of students per classroom, to twenty in primary education and fifteen in high school with the goal of providing more personalized attention.
- Changes in curriculum, with the introduction of computer science and audiovisual programs at all levels of education and with a guarantee of technical support through the provision of televisions, computers, and video players to all schools.
- The creation of courses to overcome youth's alienation from study and work, with payment to the students and with the opportunity to continue their studies in higher education. This resulted in the graduation, in just the first two periods, of more than 100,000 young people. Of those, a third enrolled in higher education.
- The distribution of higher education to all municipalities, with the creation of municipal or satellite university campuses. Together with seventeen universities and another fifty-eight colleges, there were also 3,150 university satellite campuses functioning (ONE 2007, XVIII.5, 351). This concept of universal higher education allowed, in just five years, university registration to grow by 3.8 times, giving rise to the largest number of university students in the country's history (ONE 2007, XVIII.19, 365).
- The creation of the municipal university campuses, as well as allowing expanded enrollment, which helped modify the social composition of the university student body, increasing educational opportunities for all sectors of society, especially for young people from social groups with limited possibilities. This was intended to counteract the reproduction of social inequalities that had been occurring in society as a result of insufficient university capacity and a lack of meritocratic mechanisms to provide access to higher education. The expansion of educational opportunities resulting from the creation of these municipal campuses permitted an increase in the number of university students who were children of laborers as well as a higher proportion of blacks and mestizos.

In addition to institutionalized education, other educational possibilities aimed at children and youth were strengthened, such as the following:

- Two new educational television channels were created ("University for All") to deliver specialized programs in different subjects, including foreign languages.
- The *Joven Club de Computación y Electrónica* (Computer and Electronics) extended its programming to all localities to help provide a computer culture to the community, with

priority given to children and young people. By 2005, there were approximately 600 of these clubs with an annual average growth of eighty-two centers since its creation in 2000, distributed in the 169 municipalities and with a graduation of more than 150,000 young people in their regular courses (ONE 2006, XIX.13).

• Editorial production dedicated to children and young people increased. Between 2000 and 2005, the publication of children's books grew ninefold and for youth eightfold (ONE 2006, XIX.2).

In general, this new stage meant the gradual recovery of the value of education and its centrality (understood as the degree of importance attached to it in a person's life) for most Cuban youth. This was accompanied by the recognition of access to education as a great opportunity provided by society, and in terms of the aspirations of Cuban youth, it once again grew in importance.

As a result of the educational programs, the number of youth alienated from social activity was significantly reduced, and many rejoined the workforce. At the same time, massive access to higher education, along with its undeniable significance as an expansion of opportunities for different social sectors, also generated contradictions regarding the quality of education with certain inequalities between traditional educational spaces in regular courses and new areas of academic interest. In addition, course offerings at the municipal level were concentrated in the humanities and social sciences, with the highest enrollment in areas such as law, social communication, sociocultural studies, sociology, and psychology. The large number of young graduates in these disciplines did not find sufficient employment, so it has subsequently been necessary for them to specialize further.

THE UPDATING OF THE ECONOMIC AND SOCIAL DEVELOPMENT MODEL

Since 2010, Cuba has seen the modernization of the economic and social model, which has as its objectives "to guarantee the continuity and irreversibility of socialism, the economic development of the country and the improvement of the quality of life of the population, combined with the necessary development of ethical and political values of our citizens" (*Partido Comunista de Cuba* [Communist Party of Cuba] 2011, 10). The economic and social guidelines approved at the beginning of 2011 impact the life of society as a whole but have a particular impact on youth and without doubt will provide a challenge to society.

One of the most significant elements of the current process is the expansion of forms of nonstate management of the economy. In the 1990s, for example, the state sector dominated the employment scene. By contrast, in 2010, before the updating of the economic model began, the percentage of workers in the nonstate sector was over 16 percent of the national workforce but just a year later was over 22 percent. In less than a year, the number of self-employed workers grew by 2.7 times, while for women the rate was greater, increasing by 3.3 times (ONEI 2012, 7.2). This growth, which is expected to continue, implies a substantial modification of the occupational and social structure of the Cuban population, although this is not the same throughout the country. For example, 65 percent of self-employed workers are grouped in six of the fifteen provinces of the country—those with the largest cities, such as Havana, Matanzas, Villa Clara, Camagüey, Holguín, and Santiago de Cuba (*Trabajadores* 2012).

Another challenge for Cuban youth is that the available self-employment work opportunities often do not satisfy their professional expectations because they do not match their qualifications—and they are often overqualified. The recent economic changes introduced by the government thus imply the need for changes in the education system (particularly in terms of technical/professional training) and in particular with the need to restructure university enrollment in order to adapt it to the productive needs of the country. This implies the need for a reduction in enrollment in the humanities and social sciences and an increase in technical and agricultural sciences. For Cuban youth, the combination of these changes in educational opportunities, together with general changes in social dynamics and in economic reforms, may well mean that they will not pursue further education at the university level but instead will train for positions as skilled workers. It will be necessary to watch this process carefully since otherwise it could result in a situation similar to that of the 1990s, when there were divisions based on class and race.

Another important factor that is having a great impact on Cuban youth is the increasing role of socializing processes that occur outside the family and school environment. Among these, there is an important role played by mass media and new technologies of information communication, all of which are reference points for people to develop their concepts of the world. In Cuban society, the mass media belong to the state and are governed by a common communication policy. This makes clearly explicit all regulations over information provided to the people, according to the interests of society. As a result, they have clear guidelines for cultural and educational functions, supporting the set of values that they seek to support. For their part, these new technologies of information communication have entered Cuban social life rather late compared with other parts of the world, and their access has been designed mostly for collective, social uses. Recent studies show that while across Cuba people are in favor of access to these technologies through the technology available in work and educational centers, as well as through the *Joven Club de Computación* (to provide access to the majority who have no private access), there is a great difference in accessibility to this technology. There is also a digital gap between the capital and other areas of the country in young people being able to access equipment such as DVDs, personal computers, and cell phones.

A final point that is needed in order to have a general overview of Cuban youth today is an analysis of their participation in social activities. It is important to take into account that they are socialized individuals who live within a highly politicized society in which there is a strong network of social and political organizations and associations all of which have huge numbers involved. In other words, they live in a cultural matrix where the sociopolitical component has had a great impact on their worldview and on the way in which they interact within society. Currently, sociopolitical concerns continue to support organizations, preserve their role in terms of public authority and social regulation, and have high rates of participation, but younger generations have been losing interest in them. For example, in studies conducted early in the present century, youth groups identified a set of social opportunities in their lives in Cuba. Among these, sociopolitical participation was listed among the major opportunities offered by the model of society to youth but was not seen as being particularly important in both Havana and the country as a whole.

In Cuba, young people are seen not only as the adults of tomorrow but also as important members of today's society with their own characteristics: citizens of the present who have influence on others and in a natural, cultural context in which they develop. Therefore, their participation is promoted in and from their own scenarios of social inclusion, especially at school and in the community since it is felt that youth participation is an educational and development tool that will result in benefits not only for themselves but also for the broader context in which they participate. Through this participation, social networks, youth-society relations, and processes of inclusion are developed. This in turn strengthens the possibilities

Table 37.1.   Youth Perceptions about Opportunities Provided by Society

Cuba	Havana
1. Study	1. Study
2. Work	2. Work
3. Health	3. Tranquillity
4. Tranquillity	4. Health access
5. Fun, participation in activities	5. Social justice
6. Development of spiritual values	6. Sociopolitical participation
7. Sociopolitical participation	7. Recreation
8. Lack of discrimination	

Source: Domínguez and Castilla (2011).

for social connection that participatory practices can create and that also acts as a space for the formulation of youth demands and the promotion of social change.

Youth participation goes beyond the individual level and is organized against the background of a collective society, as part of a whole in which they have roles and functions and a certain degree of commitment. It takes the form of a network of organizations in which social and political activity is carried on within the framework of daily living. The shared objectives are to contribute to an integrated development, a love of country and nature, and to promote participation in cultural movements, sports, recreation, the environment, social work, research, and vocational training and to contribute to economic and social development.

The main school organizations in which young people participate are the *Federación de Estudiantes de la Enseñanza Media* and the *Federación Estudiantil Universitaria*. The first includes high school students (grades 10 through 12) who apply to join as well as students in polytechnics and trade schools, so it covers a range of ages between about fifteen years and seventeen to eighteen years. The second includes young people in the university who usually enter at seventeen to eighteen years of age and during the course of their studies participate in activities with other youth with greater experience. This encourages a broad participatory process not only in student tasks but also in broader social and political tasks. In addition to participating in student organizations, from the age of fourteen years, young people participate in various organizations, along with adults, as is the case with the *Comités de Defensa de la Revolución* (CDR) and the *Federación de Mujeres Cubanas* (FMC) for females. The latter has played an important role both in educational tasks to support the involvement of adolescents and young people and in encouraging their participation in gender-related activities within the community.

For example, the FMC supported the creation of the *Grupo de Educación Sexual* (Sex Education Group), which in 1977 joined the *Comisión Permanente para la Atención a la Infancia, la Juventud, and Igualdad de Derechos de la Mujer* (Permanent Commission for Infancy, Youth, and Equal Rights for Women) of the National Assembly, which in 1989 became the *Centro Nacional de Educación Sexual* (National Center for Sex Education). They have been involved in matters of sex education, sexual health, and reproduction among Cuban youth (Trujillo 2010, 63) and in recent years have performed extensive work to promote respect for sexual diversity and to combat sexism and homophobia. In 1987, the FMC also supported the formation of the *Comisión de Prevención y Atención Social* (Commission to Ensure Attention to Social Problems) to provide specialized support for adolescents and young people living in poor social and family conditions as well as those responsible for antisocial behavior (Trujillo 2010, 64).

The experience of youth participation at the local level both in educational tasks and in significant tasks in their neighborhoods and communities has over the years proved to be a contribution to the social integration of their communities. Whereas interaction in student or youth organizations is limited to people of their own age, working in these other organizations encourages intergenerational relationships that extend opportunities for socializing or developing young people's ways of thinking. In addition to participating in student and community organizations, Cuban youth also participate in a political organization, the *Unión de Jóvenes Comunistas* (Union of Young Communists [UJC]). Youth can join from the age of fifteen and participate until they are thirty-two. Membership is voluntary and selective. The projection of the work of the UJC goes beyond the interests of its members and focuses on the interests of all young people. Its main objective is the integral and multifaceted formation of the younger generations (Somos Jóvenes 2011) and the promotion of training for political participation.

In addition to student and youth organizations that all young people can join, there are others with more specialized interests. Such is the case of cultural organizations such as the *Asociación "Hermanos Saiz,"* which is for young people with interests in cultural matters, and the *Brigadas Técnicas Juveniles* (Young Technical Brigades), which young technicians join in order to develop their creative and innovative capacities and promote their work. In a study conducted in 2009 (Domínguez and Castilla 2010) in four of the fifteen municipalities in Havana (Centro Habana, Plaza, Marianao, and Guanabacoa), all with different socioeconomic and sociocultural levels, 55 percent of those who were studying at various levels belonged to student organizations, and 27.2 percent overall belonged to the UJC. In addition, while most young people spent their time mainly in student and labor centers, most (64.6 percent) also participated in various activities in their communities. These activities are shown in figure 37.1.

Community activities mentioned included voluntary work to clean up the neighborhood and to participate in the meetings of neighborhood organizations (CDR and FMC), where topics of interest to residents are discussed. Cultural activities included a wide range of activities linked to music, festivals, dancing, street theater, folk music, and so on. Political activities included participation in marches, elections, commemorative events, discussions of current affairs, and other activities, mainly games and sporting events, carried out in the communities. The majority of young people identified the existence of opportunities for cultural and political participation in their communities, such as their own social and political organizations and the *Casas de Cultura* (cultural centers), which include places for amateur

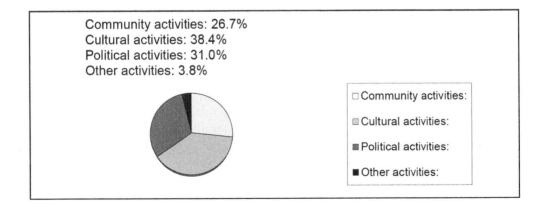

Community activities: 26.7%
Cultural activities: 38.4%
Political activities: 31.0%
Other activities: 3.8%

☐ Community activities:

▨ Cultural activities:

■ Political activities:

■ Other activities:

Figure 37.1. Principal Activities in Communities. Source: Domínguez and Castilla (2010).

musicians to practice and workshops for artistic and literary creation and for improving the neighborhood in general (known in Spanish as *talleres de transformación integral del barrio*).

In summary, in the Cuban context, there is a dense network of formal organizations that encourage the participation of youth and favor their inclusion and contribution to social and political goals. However, the sociodemographic characteristics of the population and, in particular, the aging of society constitute one of the major challenges in terms of intergenerational relationships and continuity of the sociopolitical project. In addition, the economic changes that are taking place and the growth in communities of self-employed workers create a new scenario for youth participation at the local level and require changes in the organizations that operate there.

CONCLUDING THOUGHTS: CHALLENGES FOR CUBAN SOCIETY

One of the major challenges facing Cuban society today—and one of the elements that should guide the design model for the future—is the need to continue to evaluate the impact of the recent changes on Cuban society. In particular, we need to analyze the repercussions of these changes on young people in key areas, such as education, the workplace, access to the new technologies, and participation in social and political matters. We also need to study the way in which this impacts them as individuals and as a generation both to understand the values they share and to guarantee the continuity of this commitment of young people with the construction of a better present and future for the country—including the necessary rupture with the past in order to adapt to the new circumstances.

REFERENCES

Domínguez, María Isabel. 2010. "Juventud cubana: Procesos educativos e integración social." In *Cuadernos del CIPS 2009: Experiencias de investigación social en Cuba*, edited by Claudia Castilla, Carmen L. Rodríguez, and Yuliet Cruz, 110–27. Havana: Editorial Acuario.

Domínguez, M. I., and Claudia Castilla. 2011. "Prácticas participativas en grupos juveniles de Ciudad de la Habana." In *Revista Latinoamericana de Ciencias Sociales, Niñez y Juventud* 1, no. 9. Centro de Estudios Avanzados en Niñez y Juventud (CINDE), Universidad de Manizales, Colombia.

Oficina Nacional de Estadísticas. 1996. *Anuario Estadístico de Cuba*. Havana: Oficina Nacional de Estadísticas.

———. 2006. *Anuario Estadístico de Cuba*. Havana: Oficina Nacional de Estadísticas.

———. 2007. *Anuario Estadístico de Cuba*. Havana: Oficina Nacional de Estadísticas.

Oficina Nacional de Estadísticas e Información. 2009a. *Proyecciones de la Población Cubana 2010–2030*. http://www.onei.cu.

———. 2009b. *Informe de la Encuesta Nacional de Fecundidad*. http://www.onei.cu.

———. 2012a. *Anuario Demográfico de Cuba*. http://www.onei.cu.

———. 2012b. *Anuario Estadístico de Cuba*. http://www.onei.cu.

Partido Comunista de Cuba. 2011. *Lineamientos de la política económica y social del Partido y la Revolución*. Havana: Partido Comunista de Cuba.

Somos Jóvenes. 2011. "Unión de Jóvenes Comunistas (UJC). Semana 28 julio al 4 de agosto." July 29. http://www.somosjovenes.cu.

Trabajadores. 2012. "Ejercen trabajo por cuenta propia más de 387 mil 200 cubanos." June 28.

Trujillo, Ligia. 2010. *Vilma Espín: La flor más universal de la Revolución Cubana*. Coyoacán, Mexico: Ocean Sur.

Chapter Thirty-Eight

Notes on the Race Question in Cuba Today

Esteban Morales

In Cuba today, people often think about the question of race. Unfortunately, it is a fact of life. The two issues—both reflecting about race and the very reality of the situation—feed on each other. As a result, it is absolutely necessary to work on these two levels—to understand them and then eliminate racism. Eliminating the physical reality of racism will of course always be easier than uprooting it from people's thoughts.

This is complicated by the fact that since 1959 the reality we have lived has not contributed to the development of racial stereotypes, discrimination, and racism. The predominant social climate was one in which our society exhibited the characteristics of a society with a new form of production and, along with this new model, different ways of social cooperation. The social project, together with a profound sense of justice, contributed to the development of a national identity that we had recovered, as well as a revitalized cultural identity, strengthened and inclusive. This brought educational and cultural attainments to levels that we had never thought possible. And it succeeded in making us believe that the sins of the past would disappear.

The social impact of the crisis [following the implosion of the Soviet Union] helped us to realize that we are like any other country. Social differences were accentuated, prostitution reappeared, some drugs also appeared, corruption and delinquency grew, the standard of living dropped—and in that context black and mulatto [note that the Spanish original used the term "mestizos"] Cubans began to realize that, even though they had made significant progress, they had not managed to build a society that was sustainable and balanced. Racism reemerged. It had never fully disappeared, nor was it disappearing at the rate that we thought it was. Rather, it had gone into hiding, waiting for the right circumstances to reappear—just like other challenges that occurred with the economic crisis.

In terms of the race question, Cuba had been developing into a model for the world. No other country in the hemisphere had changed as much as Cuba had since the Revolution. In no other place like Cuba had such a policy of social justice developed, nor had racism been dealt with so harshly as was the case in revolutionary Cuba. And yet it now became abundantly clear that it had not been sufficient.

Today all Cubans are equal before the law, but in terms of race we continue to live in conditions that are not equal, unable to take advantage of the opportunities that social policy puts at our disposal. Blacks and mulattoes live in worse conditions, receive the least in terms of remittances from abroad, are the most represented in prison, and have the least opportunities in the new economy and, until recently, were least represented in the political structures of the country.

Some ideas to improve this situation, especially affecting young Cubans, are the following:

1. Racism and racial discrimination are the result of the limited attention paid to these problems for many years. It was only in the mid-1980s that our leadership realized that we had to make significant changes to the social policies that we had followed until then. It was now important to consider the color of one's skin and to see it for what it was—a key social variable.

2. It is necessary to strengthen the cultural and racial identity of the Cuban people, within our national identity.

3. It is necessary to make changes in our education system at all levels and to strengthen the teaching of history. Education has to be all-encompassing and not just limited to school. In addition, it has to permeate all our media, the family, and indeed all forms of cultural expression.

4. The study of racial issues should be taught at all levels in our schools. We also need to strengthen the teaching of ethnoracial studies at our universities. In this way we will be able to deal critically with the negative aspects, which continue to encourage racism, as well as racial stereotyping, the "whitening" tendency in our society, and the existing racial discrimination in our country. It is not just a case of providing our students with cultural training; instead, we need to give them cultural training that combats discrimination and racism.

5. Our system of gathering statistics should be considerably improved so that the color of one's skin can be taken into account in the socioeconomic data collected. It is not sufficient for us to merely count our population. We also need to register all aspects about their role since one's color is a significant social variable in a country like Cuba. If we do not take into account this variable, we ignore an important series of indicators that are necessary to provide a true portrait of socioeconomic conditions of Cuba.

    Taking into account the color of the respondents' skin, we need to gather data on matters such as the level of unemployment, the type of employment, income levels, salary, condition of housing, level of marginality, history of family violence, remittance income, access to higher education, internal and external migration, life expectancy, infant and maternal mortality, as well as general mortality rates, retirement rates, access to recreation facilities, domestic facilities, and so on.

Not all Cubans enjoy to the same degree the advantages that are available through the social policy of our system. This can be seen with great clarity in terms of education since it is not the same to come from a family of university graduates as it is from a family of workers or peasants who have no experience with intellectual pursuits. Unfortunately, it is not the same to live in [the pleasant suburbs of] Nuevo Vedado as it is Párraga or Pogolotti [suburbs of Havana with large Afro-Cuban populations].

The idea that "we are all equal" was a slogan used by republican politicians. No, all of us Cubans are not equal. We need to recognize that even though we are all—white, mulatto, black—equal before the law and with the same opportunities in an extraordinarily humanitarian system, we all come from very different historical contexts. These are passed along from generation to generation since in many ways we still are influenced by a colonial and neocolonial history of 500 years. As a result, the only way of eradicating this complex reality is to base our social and political reality on an acknowledgment of the lack of equality that still is found here. As a result, we need to characterize, locate, and provide quantitative data for these inequalities. In this way we will be able to attack them at their very roots.

Cuba is not Sweden or Holland. We are a nation of the Caribbean and with a very particular history. This analysis is not based on a simple desire. Rather, the point to be remembered is that, when we do not faithfully analyze the question of color and racial identity, we are throwing into the wastepaper basket centuries of history. In this way we are in effect ignoring the (ongoing) heritage of colonialism, the effect of which all of us still suffer from.

(Taken from the blog entry by Esteban Morales of September 18, 2011, "Notas sobre el tema racial en la realidad cubana de hoy," http://www.estebanmoralesdominguez.blogspot.ca/search?updated-min=2011-01-01T00:0... [accessed November 7, 2012].)

In a blog entry found the same month, "Cuba: Raza después de 1959," Esteban Morales noted, "The principal challenge is to eliminate the ignorance that still exists about racism in Cuba: it is necessary to include more black leaders in our history books, to emphasize the role of key black figures, and to study in depth the history of Africa, Asia and the Middle East. . . . We need to deepen the racial awareness, which is still badly lacking in Cuban society, to stimulate the self-respect of black Cubans, and to ensure that the topic of race occupies the place it rightfully deserves in all levels of Cuban education" (http://www.estebanmoralesdominguez.blogspot.ca [accessed November 7, 2012]).

NOTE

Previously published in *TEMAS* 56 (2008). Reprinted by permission of the author.

Chapter Thirty-Nine

Memorable Characters of Cuba

Tracey Eaton

When Agusto González didn't have money to buy a television antenna, he improvised, making one out of sticks, a tree branch, a rubber tube, aluminum, and wire. "It may not look like much, but it works," said González, forty-eight, a coffee grower in Santo Domingo, a village at the foot of the Sierra Maestra, Cuba's largest mountain range.

Fidel Castro hid out in the Sierra Maestra in the 1950s while planning his revolt against then dictator Fulgencio Batista. I hiked through the same rugged hills to reach La Plata, Castro's once-secret command post, hidden in the forest. I met González along the way.

His ranch was filled with Robinson Crusoe–style devices. One contraption—made with a bicycle rim, a pulley, nylon string, and a bucket—fetched water from the river, down an embankment about twenty yards away.

"You need something, you invent it," González said. "That's how we do things."

I lived in Cuba from 2000 to early 2005 while working as a correspondent for the *Dallas Morning News*. And when I think back to those years, it's the remarkable people I remember the most, not the politics or anything else.

González and his neighbors lived off the land. They cooked over open fires. They farmed their land with oxen because they didn't have fuel for tractors. They used sticks and branches to make pigpens. They turned old coffee bags into curtains.

Stories of González and other characters endure even as Cuba evolves and changes, moving into the post-Castro era. Some of the people I met while covering Cuba are described below.

THE POULTRY KING

Sergio García Macías runs one of Cuba's most popular eateries, featuring roast chicken that has drawn the likes of Hollywood star Jack Nicholson and former president Jimmy Carter.

In the capitalist world, García would probably be a millionaire, maybe even chicken czar of the Caribbean. But he shrugs at the thought and says he isn't bitter that the socialist government nationalized his family business decades ago.

"My biggest satisfaction isn't money. It's seeing that a customer is satisfied," he said from his restaurant, El Aljibe, in Havana's Miramar neighborhood. El Aljibe is among the many Cuban institutions that faded away soon after the Revolution, only to be rescued years later to help prop up the ailing economy. A chicken meal when I met García fetched $12, then the monthly wage for the average Cuban.

García, seventy-three, said he never dreamed his roast chicken would become such a smash. He and his older brother, Pepe, eighty-two, opened their first restaurant, El Aljibe's predecessor, in 1947. Located in the countryside west of Havana, it was called Rancho Luna.

Their late mother, Toña Macías, came up with the chicken recipe, still secret after all these years. García revealed just two of the ingredients: garlic and bitter orange, which softens the meat. "We started with nothing and did no advertising," he said. "I was just seventeen. We were very poor. But clients came and the business grew and grew." Customers soon included Hollywood stars Errol Flynn and Ava Gardner, undefeated boxer Rocky Marciano, and baseball great Stan Musial.

The original Rancho Luna closed in 1961. The elder García went from job to job in the government, handling administrative duties for state-run restaurants. In 1993, a government restaurant chain asked if he would help revive Rancho Luna. He agreed, and it opened as El Aljibe. Word of the famed roast chicken spread, and soon El Aljibe was again drawing crowds, including everyone from director Steven Spielberg to actor Danny Glover. Said García, "This restaurant is my life."

THE OUTFIELDER

Baseball is played in 104 countries on six continents, but Cuba is probably the most baseball-crazed nation on the planet. More than a national sport, baseball—or *pelota*, as it is called—is a religion on the island, and just about everyone is a believer.

To better understand the phenomenon, I went to Havana's Latinoamericano Stadium.

One of the first people I noticed was a thin, twenty-something woman wearing jeans.

Mileisi Esquijarosa was on the edge of her seat. Then suddenly she stood, and it happened.

She started crowing like a rooster.

"Kikiri ki! Kikiri ki!" she cried as her favorite baseball team, the Sancti Spíritus Roosters, scored against the home team, the Industriales. Esquijarosa wasn't just a fan. She was a baseball fanatic who took voice lessons to master her ear-piercing call.

I realized it was going to take some time to understand this religion known as baseball. The people at Cuba's National Institute of Sport, Physical Education, and Recreation hadn't been much help. Baseball was a delicate topic. Dozens of players had defected to the United States, among them a top-ranked pitching ace, lured by the promise of lucrative contracts. Cuban baseball was slipping into decline, some fans complained. Players endured grueling schedules, crushing economic deprivation, and isolation from the rest of the baseball-playing world.

"The lack of international competition has caused our players' development to stall," said Ismael Sené, seventy-three, a former Cuban diplomat and one of the island's top baseball authorities.

I worried I wouldn't be able to find players willing to talk to me. Then I found Carlos Tabares, a gregarious, five-foot-seven outfielder. He was captain of the Industriales. He introduced me to other players and invited me to their homes, where I met their mothers, wives, and girlfriends. Tabares told me that players who defected were the exception, not the rule. "We play because we love the sport. We have nothing to do with 'rented baseball,' playing just for money. Besides, the government gives us everything we need—a salary, bats, gloves, lodging while we're on the road, meals. A full buffet."

THE SPY

Rodolfo Frómeta, head of a militant anti-Castro group in Miami, boasted that would-be assassins shot a former Cuban spy during a 2:00 a.m. gun battle.

I tracked down the ex-spy in Havana to find out if it was true. Juan Pablo Roque showed no signs of injury when I talked to him outside his home in 2003. I asked if he'd been attacked.

"I'm fine," he said. "Can't you see?"

That made me suspect the assassination attempt never occurred. But there certainly were people who wanted to do harm to Roque. He had been a spy in Miami and was a key figure in the Cuban military's shoot-down of two civilian aircraft in 1996. Roque declined to talk about any of that in 2003. He said he didn't want to somehow hurt the case of five Cuban spies who had been jailed in the United States on espionage-related charges.

I caught up with Roque again in 2012. This time he agreed to an interview.

Roque, a former fighter pilot with Hollywood good looks, didn't appear desperate but conceded he needed money. He said he was selling his house and a prized possession, a GMT Master II Rolex he bought with money the Federal Bureau of Investigation gave him while he was an informant in Florida.

Roque had staged his defection from Cuba in 1992, swimming to the U.S. naval base at Guantánamo Bay and declaring opposition to Fidel Castro. He became a pilot for Brothers to the Rescue, a group dedicated to searching for rafters in the Florida Straits. But then he stunned everyone in 1996, slipping back into Cuba the day before Cuban MiGs shot down two civilian aircraft flown by members of the exile group.

Now fifty-seven and living with his girlfriend in a cramped Havana apartment, Roque said he was sorry four people were killed in the February 24, 1996, incident. "If I could travel in a time machine," he said, "I'd get those boys off the planes that were shot down." The four dead were Carlos Costa, Mario de la Peña, Pablo Morales, and Armando Alejandre Jr.

Alejandre's sister, Maggie Khuly, said justice was never done. "Speaking for the families, my family in particular, we're looking forward to the day when Roque faces U.S. courts on his outstanding indictment," said Khuly, a Miami architect.

A federal indictment charged Roque with failing to register as a foreign agent and conspiring to defraud the United States in May 1999.

Asked about the charges, Roque sighed. He said he believes that the Cuban government was justified in defending its airspace but that he should not be held responsible for the deaths. "I am not to blame. I didn't do anything wrong. I didn't order anyone killed. The decision to shoot down the planes was a decision of the sovereign Cuban government. The decision to shoot down the planes was taken because of the constant air incursions, violating airspace."

Asked if he had any regrets, Roque said he wishes he had done more to stop the shootdown. "Perhaps now . . . I'd try to play a much stronger role in the things that happened. I'd try to play a better role. If I played it bad or good, let the people decide. Let those who want to judge me, judge me."

THE HOMEMAKER

Ana del Rosario Pérez was suddenly in trouble. Her friends had asked her to feed an entire beach party, but she had little more than two eggs and some puffed wheat. So she got creative. "I stirred up the eggs and added salt. I put oil in a pan and started to cook the eggs. Then I started tossing in the puffed wheat. When that was all done . . . I added garlic, peppers, onion, and tomato paste."

Result: Enough scrambled eggs for eighteen people. And no one knew that wheat was the key to stretching the two eggs, the forty-year-old homemaker said.

Across the island, Cubans routinely whip up culinary concoctions to ward off hunger and make ends meet. They turn potatoes into mayonnaise, peas into desserts, and green plantains into casseroles. "We don't eat meat every day in Cuba, but no one goes to bed without something to eat," said Juan José León, a spokesman for Cuba's Ministry of Agriculture.

The food situation has been critical in Cuba since the fall of the island's chief sponsor, the former Soviet Union. But many Cubans can't afford to shop in the stores, where a box of cereal fetches as much as $9.65 and a can of Pringle's potato chips goes for $3.50. So they work their magic in the kitchen, inventing recipes and turning leftovers into meals.

Variety is the key, said Cristina Ortega, a fifty-two-year-old retiree. "I can't stand eating the same thing every day." Among her favorite inventions: cupcake-size casseroles made from plantains. "You peel a green plantain and slice it. Then you fry it, mash it with a glass, and mold it into a little cup with your hands." She said she fills the cups with whatever she has—ground meat or canned ham, if possible—and tops them with grated cheese. Then she heats them for five minutes, and presto—they're done.

THE DIVORCÉE

When Yanet Vázquez finally decided to end her marriage, she and her soon-to-be ex-husband strolled into a notary public's office, plunked down $4, and were blissfully divorced in twenty minutes. "It was quick and easy," said Vázquez, thirty-one, a cashier.

Indeed, getting unhitched in Cuba is about as cheap and effortless as it gets. The country's liberal divorce laws also fuel one of the world's highest divorce rates. "For every 100 marriages in Cuba, there are almost seventy divorces. It's alarming," said María Benítez, a demographics specialist and author of the book *The Cuban Family*.

The island's severe housing shortage forces many people to live with their in-laws and other relatives, straining even the best of marriages. Economic conditions also create tension that drives many couples apart, Benítez said. "We have First World health and schooling levels but seventeenth- and eighteenth-century marriage habits," she said. Some Cubans change spouses every few years. "I've split up three times already," said José Rivero, forty, a musician. "I spent seven years with the first woman, five with the second, and eight with the third."

Cuba legalized divorce in 1869 and introduced divorces by notary public in 1994. "No other country in the world has this kind of divorce," said Ayiadna María Verrier, a notary public in Old Havana. Many divorces are not only quick but remarkably civilized. Maricel Acebo, thirty-nine, and her ex-husband, Wilfrido, continued living under the same roof despite their divorce less than a year earlier. "I'm not going to tell him, 'I want you living out on the street,'" she said. "That wouldn't be fair."

THE WORDSMITH

One day I decided to write a story about Cuban names. The idea occurred to me while having lunch with Cuban writer Senel Paz and a few other friends. Paz wrote the screenplay for the acclaimed movie *Fresa y Chocolate* (Strawberry and Chocolate). Over rice, shrimp, and salad, we somehow got onto the topic of names. Paz said his own name is an invention of sorts. His mother named him Senel but probably meant Senen, an established name. But like a lot of Cubans who automatically replace the letter "n" with "l" in their rapid-fire Caribbean speech, she made it Senel. "I don't know of any other Senels except some of my relatives—and they're named after me," Paz said.

"We invent names because we're looking for originality. I think some Cubans started inventing names to imitate the sound of Russian. People are drawn to exotic sounds." Indeed, I found Cubans named everything from Yusimi and Yanko to Yusmeli and Yasnara. One Cuban mother named her boy Yesdasi—Yes-da-si—yes in English, Russian, and Spanish. Another came up with Yotuiel. That translates roughly from Spanish as "me, you, and him."

Cubans sometimes pick names simply because they like the look of them. Scores of children living near Guantánamo, an American military base on the eastern tip of Cuba, are named Usnavy, taken from U.S. Navy. Others are Usmail, from U.S. Mail.

One woman named her son William Guillermo over the protests of her relatives. In English, that's William William.

Given such combinations, the Cuban government sometimes refuses to allow certain names. But meddling can have unintended consequences, as it did in the case of the mother who wanted to call her daughter María José. María is fine, Cuban officials said, but not José because that's a boy's name. Okay, said the mother, who finally opted for Esoj Airam—María José spelled backward. Officials accepted that.

Taking ordinary names and spelling them backward isn't uncommon in Cuba. Examples include Odraude, from Eduardo; Orgen, from Negro; Leinad, from Daniel; and Susej, from Jesus. One mother toyed with calling her daughter Vivian, but that had no pizazz, no imagination. So she settled on her own creation: Naiviv. "It's Vivian in reverse," said Naiviv Trasancos, a travel agent. "I like it. It's different, distinctive."

Some parents choose names with a revolutionary flair. "I was named in honor of Fidel," said Ana Fidelia Quirot, a Cuban track star and Olympic athlete. "I'm very proud of it." Other Cubans name their children after esoteric military institutions. One couple named their son Dampar, which stands for *Defensa Anti-Aerea de las Fuerzas Armadas Revolucionarias* (Anti-Air Defense of the Revolutionary Armed Forces). Evidently caught up in revolutionary fervor, the same couple named their daughter Sempi, for *Sociedad de Educación Patriótico-Militar* (Society of Patrotic Military Education).

Other Cubans have such names as Inra, for the *Instituto Nacional de la Reforma Agraria* (National Institute of Agrarian Reform); Init, for the *Instituto Nacional de la Industria Turística* (National Institute of the Tourist Industry); and Pursia, for the *Partido Unido de la Revolución Socialista* (United Party of the Socialist Revolution).

Devout Catholics sometimes name their children after saints. A calendar showing the saint of the day helps them pick. But things don't always go right. Some Cuban children, with humble parents still trying to figure out which side of the paper holds the saint's name, have actually been named Santoral al Dorso: "Saint on Reverse."

Félix Savón, Cuba's two-time Olympic heavyweight boxing champion, ultimately went with something safe: He named four of his five children after himself. His two sets of twins are named Félix Mario and María Félix and Félix Félix and Félix Ignacio.

Still other Cubans insist on the unusual. Take the case of Cuban actor Jorge Perugorría and his wife, Elsa. He had always wanted a daughter but got three sons instead. He persuaded her to try one last time, and she had yet another son. Thankful that childbearing was over, she named him Amén.

Chapter Forty

Cuba's Recent Embrace of Agroecology

Urban and Suburban Agriculture

Sinan Koont

One of the most interesting and important developments in Cuba in the past two decades has occurred in its food production and distribution systems. The results of this development include one of the world's shortest producer-to-consumer chains in fresh produce and the general introduction of agroecological production technologies throughout the island. (Among other characteristics, agroecological practices attempt to minimize the use of fossil fuels, including petroleum, and their derivatives, such as chemical pesticides and fertilizers, in production and transportation.)

Before discussing the reasons for this remarkable and far-reaching transformation and its evolution and consequences, it makes sense to place it in its historical and geographical context. Cuba is an island (albeit the largest) in the Caribbean region and was colonized by the Spanish Empire beginning in the early sixteenth century. After 1958, the new revolutionary government of Cuba, with the help of two Agrarian Reform Laws of 1959 and 1963, nationalized most of the cultivable land in Cuba, until then mainly in the hands of large landowners, both Cuban and foreign. Cuba eventually established an industrial agricultural system based on extremely large state farms active, among other lines, in cattle raising, sugarcane, rice, and citric crops production. The export crop production model was modified but not abandoned.

The state farms were generally unproductive, however. The monoculture cultivation in these large state farms led (as in the Soviet Union) to reduced efficiency and productivity, resulting in smaller outputs and lessened returns on agricultural investment. It was also causing increasing damage to the soil as well as to the environment in general. In addition, industrial agriculture in Cuba was completely dependent on the importation of petroleum (and machinery) from the Soviet Union and socialist Eastern Europe. And since the 1960s, the island had been caught in the cross fire of the Cold War between the United States and the Soviet Union. Cuba's national defense and security organizations could not ignore the possibility of the complete cutoff of the imports of petroleum, machinery, and petroleum derivatives, such as chemical fertilizers and pesticides, making industrial agriculture impossible.

Thus, it is not surprising that in the late 1980s a new agroecological focus started making its presence felt in Cuban agriculture. This is the foundation of the model now widely used in the twenty-first century in Cuba. Agroecology is a field of study that came into being as a counterpoint to industrial agriculture. It attempts to apply ecological theory to plant-animal communities managed by humans to produce food, fuel, and fiber. The approach is holistic and pays full attention to environmental concerns and to the human participants in their political, economic, social, and cultural settings. The management techniques it advances include the elimination of the use of agrochemicals to reduce toxicity, the enhancement of biodiversity leading to increased natural pest resistance, the practice of intercropping and crop rotation, and improvements in the quality of soils by increasing organic materials and biological activity in the soils being cultivated. The stress is on making agroecosystems more productive with fewer external inputs—ideally in a self-sustaining manner—and fewer damaging environmental and social outcomes.

With support from the government and as early as 1987, the *Asociación Cubana de Técnicos Forestales y Agrícolas* (Cuban Association of Forestry and Agricultural Technicians) was officially registered as a Cuban nongovernmental organization with an agroecological orientation. It consists of dues-paying members, by 2010 numbering over 20,000, who are active promoters of and proselytizers for agroecological practices in Cuba. Also in the late 1980s, Raúl Castro started to take an active interest in sustainable agriculture. The national security concern of weaning the provisioning of foodstuffs for the Cuban armed forces away from dependence on industrial agriculture and imported oil was also addressed. During a visit to the Armed Forces Horticultural Enterprise on December 27, 1987, then Defense Minister Castro told of an encounter with an agricultural engineer named Ana Luisa Pérez, who had carried out some successful experiments growing vegetables without using petrochemicals in plantain pregerminators. Castro suggested the desirability of generalizing this method of cultivation, a comment that led to the introduction of the *organopónico* technology later widely employed in urban agriculture. As a result, from December 1987, armed forces facilities began installing *organopónicos* (raised cultivation beds containing a mixture of soil and organic material, such as compost) to grow vegetables to meet their needs.

Although these incipient moves toward agroecology began in the 1980s, it was not until the early 1990s that Cuba faced a forced turn toward embracing agroecology in its food production system. The implosion in 1991 of the Soviet Union and its socialist allies in Eastern Europe abruptly and severely reduced Cuba's external trade. The industrial agricultural system Cuba had built up over the previous thirty years simply ceased to function due to the lack of required inputs of petroleum, pesticides, chemical fertilizers, agricultural machinery, fuel and trucks used in transportation, and spare parts. The severe reduction in the capacity to grow or import foodstuffs had by 1993 led to a situation where Cubans on average were consuming only 1,863 calories per person per day, an amount well below subsistence needs.

Almost overnight, Cuba had to adopt technologies in the production and distribution of foodstuffs that minimized the use of imported inputs. An alternative that almost naturally suggested itself was urban agriculture, the production of foodstuffs in and near cities. In urban agriculture, the proximity of large population concentrations precluded the general use of toxic pesticides and polluting fertilizers—even if they had been available—to avoid harming these populations. Moreover, the existing demand by local consumers minimized the need for fuel and trucks to transport the food to distant customers. In its forced turn to agroecology, Cuba faced various formidable challenges. These included finding appropriate spaces in and near cities to be used for food production; learning about, generating, and disseminating new agroecological technologies; and recruiting, training, and retaining (once employed) urban agricultural workers from city populations who are, for the most part, agricultural novices. In addition, all of this had to be done in the midst of the worst economic crisis in the history of the Cuban Revolution, precipitated by the collapse of the Soviet Union.

In this effort, Cuba could count on a strong central government capable of making society-wide decisions to implement new policies and create new institutions. There were also some historical legacies of thirty years of revolutionary development that would stand Cuba in good stead in confronting the challenges it faced:

- The universally and well-educated population, very capable of further learning and innovation
- A strong and coherent gender- ,work-, and territorially based social organization comprising labor unions, the Federation of Cuban Women, student organizations, neighborhood committees, and small farmers' associations

These two factors certainly facilitated the large-scale changes in food production technologies and institutions by making rapid policy innovation and implementation possible.

The real enablers, however, of the large-scale introduction of urban agriculture in Cuba's cities were similarly massive efforts in the following:

- Organization of guidance and administration through the Ministry of Agriculture
- Scientific research and technological development in agroecology at universities and specialized governmental research centers
- Creating incentives, both material and moral, to attract and retain a workforce
- Constructing support networks for generating and disseminating agroecological technologies
- Building supply networks for needed inputs for agroecological production, such as compost and worm humus, seeds, and biological pest control materials
- Education in agroecology in primary schools, in agricultural technical schools at the secondary school level, and in universities
- On-the-job training programs in the production units

In 1991, the first civilian *organopónico* was installed in the Miramar district of the city of Havana. By the end of 1993, both the Ministry of Agriculture and the provincial government of the City of Havana were strongly supporting extension efforts to spread the new technology throughout the city. The first organizational push at the national level came in May 1994 at the First National Plenary of Organopónicos in Santa Clara. At this meeting, initial steps were taken that would eventually lead in 1997 to the formal organization of the *Grupo Nacional de Agricultura Urbana* (GNAU). The GNAU was constituted as a leadership body consisting of some three dozen members to provide guidance to a burgeoning urban agriculture campaign. It was headquartered at NIFAT, a major national agricultural research center located near Havana. Its membership included PhD-level agricultural scientists, specialists from various participating ministries, and prominent leaders from agronomy research institutions.

Once in place as "supervisor" of all urban agriculture efforts in Cuba, GNAU found itself facing a complex panorama of new and old economic participants active in this area using different production modalities and organized into various land tenancy structures. The old industrial state farms had been broken up into smaller units, even when they retained their status as state enterprises. In 1993, as part of the process of dismantling the huge and now dysfunctional state farms, a law was adopted creating a new institution in land tenancy: the *Unidad Básica de Producción Cooperativa* (Basic Unit of Cooperative Production). These were new cooperative structures in which groups of former state workers were brought together in voluntary associations to work the land. They received the land from the state in usufruct. That is, the land did not become their private property, but all the crops they produced did belong to the co-op members, as did all the implements of production utilized. Individuals were also eligible to apply for usufruct plots on which they could produce food for their families and also for the market. Individual usufruct tenants were encouraged to seek membership in already existing or newly created cooperative structures called *Cooperativas de Créditos y Servicios* (Credit and Services Cooperatives) uniting usufruct tenants with individual plots and owners of (previously existing) private small farms and plots. The cooperatives had been organized as early as the 1970s to facilitate marketing and contracting on the output side and the provision of credit and other services, inputs such as seeds and fertilizers, training, and extension on the input side.

Joining these mostly new economic actors were over a million Cuban households, who had traditionally raised vegetables and planted fruit trees in the backyards of their homes. They now turned to backyard (patio) production much more seriously. In a manner reminiscent of the "victory gardens" in the United States and Britain during the two world wars of the twentieth century, the urban populations of Cuba sought sustenance through production in their home gardens.

Thus, from 1993 on, the urban agricultural landscape in Cuba contained four different modalities in the production of vegetables in and near cities: *organopónicos*, *huertas intensivas* (essentially *organopónicos* whose raised beds are not walled), *parcelas*, and plots and patios. Although, as we shall see, vegetable production has achieved most success in urban agriculture, the scope of the latter is much broader. GNAU has organized urban agriculture into twenty-eight subprograms, of which the vegetables and fresh condiments subprogram is but one. There are twelve subprograms in crop cultivation (ranging from medicinal plants and dried herbs to fruit trees to semiprotected *organopónico* production), seven in animal raising (ranging from rabbit raising to fish farming to sheep/goat raising), and nine in support areas (ranging from organic fertilizers to agroecological integration to irrigation and drainage).

These programs are not limited to a few big cities but are spread rather uniformly throughout the fifteen provinces and 169 *municipios* (municipalities) into which Cuba is divided administratively. GNAU's role is to provide guidance, information, and supervision. It acts as a tireless promoter, inspector, and evaluator of urban agriculture and is in overall control of all urban agricultural activity. The inspections and evaluations take place during tours organized by GNAU on a quarterly basis. During these inspection visits, GNAU experts give presentations on technical aspects of agroecological production, essentially providing extension services. The team also evaluates local production units, classifying them following guidelines established for each subprogram. Outstanding units are singled out for special recognition and become centers of dissemination of successful practices, often receiving visits from other units eager to learn from them.

The Ministry of Agriculture has organized a parallel track to these activities of GNAU, providing logistical support to practitioners of urban agriculture. Beginning in 1995, so-called *granjas urbanas* were established to provide operational, administrative, and executive coverage for the urban agriculture movement. These are institutions, at least one in each district, that are affiliated with the leading state agricultural enterprise in the municipality. Among other tasks and responsibilities, they buy produce from the production units (if these do not market directly to the population from their own stands); they organize marketing through municipally approved points of sale; they sell inputs, such as seeds, compost, worm humus, and biological pest control materials through a network of agricultural supply and extension stores called *Consultorio/Tienda del Agricultor*; and they contribute to production by directly operating their own production units. In short, they see to it that the GNAU guidelines for each of the twenty-eight subprograms are carried out on the ground. They are meant to be profit-making businesses, and in 2006, 135 out of 196 *granjas* were. In their efforts, the *granjas urbanas* are accompanied in each local district by an urban agricultural representative of the Ministry of Agriculture.

The twin chains of central state oversight—first, the supervisory, evaluative, and guiding chain of GNAU and its extensions at the local level, and, second, the administration, supply, and distribution chain from the Ministry of Agriculture to the business (or *empresa*) and then to the *granja urbana* and finally to the urban agriculture representative of the Ministry of Agriculture—constitute a unique organizational structure. This structure is well suited to the task of overseeing an urban food production system that has as its guiding principle the need to decentralize food production without losing control and to centralize only to a degree that does not kill local initiative.

Cuba proved itself to be quite capable of taking advantage of these formidable historical legacies and organizational innovations enabling a strong performance in urban agriculture. The first fifteen years of the "Special Period" saw outstanding results in significant aspects of urban agriculture. Among these, the increase in food production and distribution addressed the most pressing concern that led to urban agriculture in Cuba in the first place: the lack of food. The subprogram in vegetables and fresh condiments stands out as the most successful food-producing subprogram. In this subprogram, production volume went up 1,000-fold between 1994 and 2004, increasing from 4,000 tons to over 4 million tons of output, reaching a plateau that has been maintained since then (with minor fluctuations). These increases reflected improvements in yields as well as expansion in the areas cultivated.

Yields increased rapidly, especially in the early years of the Special Period with the introduction of new technologies. The new *organopónico* technology yielded about three times more output per square meter each year than the typical backyard garden or patio. The area under cultivation also expanded with large increases in the number of patios and plots incorporated into urban agriculture after 2001. These yielded less per square meter than the *organopónicos* but needed much less investment (in irrigation systems, walled beds, and so on) and thus could be expanded at a much lower cost. As a result of this performance in this subprogram, Cuba is now (in 2012) basically self-sufficient in fresh produce, with production levels well above the guidelines of the UN Food and Agriculture Organization for per capita consumption.

Although Havana played a major role in the early stages of the development of urban agriculture, the program is currently quite evenly distributed not only across major urban areas but also throughout the island's fifteen provinces. In fact, whereas the population ratio (in 2006) of the largest to the smallest province was five to four, the corresponding ratio between the maximum and minimum provincial production levels in the subprogram of vegetables and fresh condiments was only two to two. In addition, there is more modest progress in all nineteen crop- and animal-raising subprograms of urban agriculture. Thus, it can be asserted that urban agriculture has played a crucial role in restoring (by 2006) per capita food consumption to more-than-adequate levels, with significant contributions in healthy fresh foods in the daily diet of Cubans. It has eliminated the import dependence in fresh produce and reduced it, more or less significantly, in some other areas. That said, Cuba still remains heavily dependent on imports, especially in proteins (meat, dairy, and beans), fats, and grains (rice and wheat).

Besides its role in foodstuff production, urban agriculture has three other positive consequences for Cuban society. First, it has created urban employment to make up for the losses of the Special Period, when fossil fuel–using urban activities (such as industry and transportation) simply ground to a halt. By 2012, nearly 400,000 urban workers (more than 7 percent of the civilian Cuban workforce) had found relatively well paying employment in urban agriculture. Thus, by the end of the first decade of the twenty-first century, the high urban unemployment of the Special Period had been largely eliminated, thanks in no small part to the new urban agricultural paradigm. Second, there are significant environmental consequences. Urban agriculture has shifted food production away from reliance on fossil fuels and petrochemicals. Conventional industrial agriculture emits large quantities of carbon dioxide (associated with global warming). It also degrades soil and water resources and has toxic effects on human beings, all harmful consequences avoided by urban agriculture. In addition, urban agriculture is part of urban reforestation efforts, creating carbon dioxide–consuming and oxygen-producing "islands" throughout the cities.

Not to be ignored are secondary environmental benefits, such as urban beautification, as well as the physical and psychological well-being of the population, the reduction of urban stress, and increased privacy for households. Other positive consequences include the screening (or, better, the replacing of urban eyesores), the enhancement of biodiversity, and a reduction in air and noise pollution through the filtering action of plants. And finally, urban agriculture has strengthened local communities. The shift to urban agriculture in Cuba has both necessitated and enabled community building and organization. The small-scale, local, labor-intensive techniques employed in urban agriculture involved the community members not only as consumers but also as producers. Dietary changes to include more vegetables, some previously barely known in Cuba, contributed to community health but also required community education in nutrition.

When vacant lots that have turned into garbage dumps are reconstituted as green spaces full of trees, flowers, and vegetables, the results are not just aesthetic. These spaces become focal points for community involvement where people get together to buy vegetables and interact with their neighbors. The difference such a change makes in the sense of community well-being is bound to be substantial. However, after more than a decade of development and despite all of these positive accomplishments, there was still a glaring difficulty faced by the urban agriculture program—much of the land available was not being cultivated. In 2006, for example, of the officially designated 1.2 million hectares of urban agricultural land in and near cities, only about 50,000 hectares, or less than 5 percent, were being cultivated in the highly touted vegetables and fresh condiments subprogram. Altogether, more than 75 percent of the available land, lying in the periurban areas, had remained unutilized. These lands, mostly abandoned by state enterprises, were in large part infested with marabou, a highly invasive, hard-to-eradicate "weed" bush that had been brought to Cuba at the end of the nineteenth century as an ornamental plant and had become a nightmare for the Cuban countryside in the Special Period. These areas, although in the ambit of urban agriculture, were proving difficult to bring into agroecological production under the existing conditions and programs of urban agriculture. The reasons for this were twofold: the lack of a local workforce and the absence of customers within walking distance of production units.

In July 2008, to address the first problem, the State Council of Cuba passed Decree Law 259 on Turning over Possession in Usufruct of Idle Lands, which authorized the awarding in usufruct of up to thirteen hectares of land to individuals (or cooperatives) soliciting land from the state for the purpose of rational and sustainable use of these lands for food production. Already existing farms with proven track records could expand their holdings up to forty hectares. To organize and facilitate the operation of these new, or expanded, farms (*fincas*), a new program of Suburban Agriculture (related to but different from Urban Agriculture) was established and announced by President Raúl Castro on August 1, 2009, in an address to the National Assembly. Castro noted that a pilot program had been in process since 2008 in the municipality of Camaguey and stressed the continuing commitment to agroecological technologies in the new program: "In this new program, let us forget about using tractors and fuel, even if we had them in sufficient quantities. The idea is to carry out this program essentially with oxen—these are small farms—as a growing number of producers are already doing with excellent results. I have visited a few and can attest that they have converted their lands into true gardens where every inch of land is utilized" (author's translation; speech published in *Granma*, August 1, 2009). In the same speech, the mandate of the GNAU (now rechristened GNAUS with the addition of "*y Suburbana*" to its name) was extended to include the new program. And the program was soon under way in eighteen pilot municipalities, at least one in each province, which were judged to be the most ready to start implementing the Suburban Agriculture program immediately.

The program of Suburban Agriculture was set up with unprecedented and lofty goals. Each municipality's agricultural leaders had to draw up plans by first assessing the potential of the region to feed itself. Then, taking stock of the local resource base (land, water, climate, and so on) and the size of the population that had to be fed, they were to come up with a long-term project to achieve eventual local self-sufficiency (if possible). The larger farm size and the suburban setting freed from urban constraints would mean the possibility of introducing activities favoring a transition to self-sufficiency: raising livestock as well as developing pastures and animal feed crops, fruit orchards, a commercial forestry, and so on.

A municipality's participation in the new program was not automatic. The municipal project, once formulated, had to be presented before a panel of experts at the GNAUS headquarters for acceptance or rejection, with the Ministry of Agriculture having the final say in approving the participation of the municipality in the Suburban Agriculture program. Besides establishing general guidelines for the organization and development of Suburban Agriculture, the Ministry of Agriculture and GNAUS had to find practical solutions for problems that they had not encountered in the Urban Agriculture program. First, a family farm of forty acres with just a few adult workers could not be managed and maintained using only human labor. The Cuban agroecological solution to this problem has been the reintroduction of animal traction in the form of teams of oxen, which replace fossil fuel–using, soil-compacting tractors found in industrial agriculture. Second, the problem of distribution is much more complex than in urban agriculture, where much of the produce can be harvested and then carried in baskets to stands at the curbside next to the fields for direct sale to consumers who live across the street. The usufruct farmers of suburban agriculture do not have motorized vehicles to transport their production to distant locations. The solution being implemented by the Ministry of Agriculture is the establishment in each municipality of networks of points of purchase and points of sale: the former at locations convenient to the producers and the latter at locations convenient to consumers. The points of purchase buy the produce from the farmer. They are located throughout the municipality so that no farm is more than a few kilometers from a point of purchase. The farmers have to deliver their output to one of these points or to a point of sale, if more convenient, using nonmotorized means of transportation: oxcarts, bicycles, wheelbarrows, and so on. A municipal enterprise with a fleet of trucks then immediately distributes the produce to points of sale in the municipality for direct sale to the consumers. Admittedly, this requires some fossil fuel use, although this use is minimal, as there is no long-distance transport, refrigeration, or warehousing of produce, even overnight. The shortness of the producer-consumer chain is maintained albeit in a somewhat less spectacular fashion than in urban agriculture.

The Suburban Agriculture program is still very young, and its eventual success cannot yet be evaluated; however, it is developing rapidly. Camagüey, the initial pilot municipality, started in 2008 with seventy-five farms and is scheduled to establish over 1,400 farms by 2015 (including 750 in cattle raising and 450 in diversified crops). In the meantime, after reaching thirty-nine participating municipalities in 2010, the program now includes all 156 eligible for consideration. (Eight of the 168 cannot participate because they lack suitable suburban lands.) By the end of 2012, over 1.5 million hectares had been distributed in usufruct to nearly 175,000 beneficiaries, and 100,000 farms had been started. Of these, 21,000 have been approved in terms of fulfilling all eight criteria for starting production, ranging from being free of marabou to having a municipally approved plan of production to having a responsible person in charge. The hard work of clearing the land of marabou had been completed on 167,000 hectares.

Despite these advances following the adoption of Decree Law 259, sizable amounts of land remain to be distributed and made productive. In order to speed up the usufruct distribution of idle lands, a new law (Decree Law 300) was passed in October 2012. Its main provisions include an increase in the farm size upper limit (now sixty-seven hectares), enhanced tenure security for the family of the lease owner, permission to build structures (including houses) on the farm with the assurance that any value added will be retained in case of termination, and some additional measures that provide increased flexibility in the process of acquiring land.

As can be seen, the experiment by Cuba of producing locally food in an agroecological fashion and for local use is a compelling and exemplary one. It is also occurring in a world where the practice of industrial agriculture is beginning to generate opposition. This opposition is based on two principal factors: the unsustainability of fossil fuel–based production technologies and the undesirable environmental consequences of industrial agriculture, ranging from global warming to toxic pollution. Cuba may be uniquely positioned as a trailblazer in agroecological practice. For an increasing number of people in the world, including small farmers, peasants, and consumers, agroecological production of foodstuffs is already a desirable goal. The real-life experience of Cuba provides an example of a viable alternative to industrial agriculture and a new paradigm of labor-intensive, agroecological production of foodstuffs. The advances that Cuba makes and the challenges that it faces in this context (and the creative responses it makes to them) will undoubtedly continue generating new lessons and objects of study for the rest of the world.

NOTE

This chapter is based on the author's book *Sustainable Urban Agriculture in Cuba* (Gainesville: University Press of Florida, 2011) and a paper, "Urban Agriculture in Cuba: Advances and Challenges" (also by the author), presented at the LASA International Congress of 2010 held in Toronto.

Chapter Forty-One

The Cuban Health System

In Search of Quality, Efficiency, and Sustainability

Conner Gorry and C. William Keck

Provision of universal health care does not result from happenstance or circumstance but rather occurs when governing authorities exercise the political will to implement policies not only recognizing but also mandating health care as a human right. The provenance and trajectory of Cuba's universal system guaranteeing free, accessible care—set out in article 50 of the Cuban Constitution (1976), which states that all people "have the right to medical attention and health protection. The state is the guarantor of this right"—illustrate this commitment. Since 1959, the Cuban health system has undergone a series of radical transformations that have resulted in health outcomes on par with or surpassing those of developed countries. Despite periodic economic crises and over half a century of a crippling U.S. embargo, Cuba's experience illustrates how policy and practice can work together to improve the population's health. But Cuba is changing. Unprecedented economic reforms are continuing apace, and the health system is currently being reorganized to improve quality, efficiency, and sustainability. This chapter examines how Cuba has been able to achieve such enviable outcomes despite scarce resources and discusses the current challenges to maintaining quality health services in the country's changing landscape.

BLUEPRINT FOR HEALTH

The seeds of Cuba's universal health system were sown by Dr. Ernesto "Che" Guevara and his colleagues as they attended patients in their mountain encampment from where the Cuban Revolution was fought. What Che and the troops lived and learned in the mountains is that too many Cubans were dying of preventable diseases and that the principal social determinants of health included decrepit housing, unsafe drinking water, poor diet, and lack of education. Understanding health strategies in contemporary Cuba necessitates an appreciation of such historic antecedents given how formative early experiences proved in shaping the development of the country's philosophy of and political will toward "health for all" (Declaration of Alma-Ata 1978; World Health Organization [WHO] 2011b). Forged in the rebels' mountain stronghold, the pillars of Cuba's health system include the following:

- Emphasizing a preventive, integrated approach
- Prioritizing vulnerable populations, including the elderly, children, expectant mothers, and rural communities
- Providing and maintaining equitable access to services
- Improving social determinants affecting health, including housing, diet, and education
- Stimulating intersectoral action among media, housing, sports, education, and other authorities to improve social determinants
- Encouraging rational use of scarce resources

Global organizations, including UNICEF (2004), the World Bank (2001), and the WHO (2011a), have long recognized the above-mentioned factors as essential to improving population health. Indeed, mechanisms such as the UN Millennium Development Goals were developed to set targets and measure countries' progress toward better health, education, and well-being; as of 2010, Cuba ranked among the top twenty countries in achieving those goals (Overseas Development Institute 2010). This is the result of the Cuban state's recognition of its responsibility for protecting and improving the nation's health (i.e., political will) and the capacity to change and evolve those policies as the health picture evolves. It has not always been easy or successful: outside forces, including massive post-Revolution emigration of doctors, the U.S. embargo, emerging diseases like HIV, and economic crises—including the current one—have combined with a changing health picture to impel periodic shifts in the Cuban approach.

The basis of the Cuban system is the primary care system provided by the team of family doctor and nurse, which attends to up to 1,500 people in the community. This team is supported by local polyclinics offering comprehensive specialized and personalized services, including pediatrics; obstetrics; medical genetics screening, diagnoses, and counseling; advanced laboratory testing; diagnostic procedures; rehabilitation services; and dentistry. Each polyclinic serves between 15,000 and 60,000 people and is tailored to offer the services most needed by the community where it is located as determined by ongoing health analysis tools known as the Neighborhood Health Diagnosis and Continuous Assessment and Risk Evaluation. Together, these tools provide a "health picture" of individual communities by documenting disease, risk factors, and environmental influences on the health of the catchment area and classifying residents by disease and risk factors. Other primary care–level services, such as the national network of maternity homes for at-risk pregnant women, senior day care centers, old-age homes, and other facilities designed for vulnerable groups, support the doctor-and-nurse team and the local polyclinic. The next level of the health system, where surgical procedures and more complex conditions are treated, is composed of municipal hospitals, followed by specialty hospitals in provincial capitals and thirteen national research institutes, many of which provide clinical care in their given field. All of these services are provided free of charge to patients.

The pillars (i.e., policy) of the Cuban health system discussed above, combined with how that system attends to the population (i.e., practice), have rendered Cubans as healthy—and in some cases more so—as citizens of developed countries (see tables 41.1 to 41.3), including the United States. These indicators have been achieved despite periodic economic crises—some profound—and strengthening of the embargo against the island nation. What is perhaps most surprising about Cuba's enviable health outcomes is that the country has been able to maintain and, in some cases, improve on past work in the face of extreme resource scarcity. For instance, Cuba has the lowest incidence of HIV/AIDS in the Caribbean. Such success testifies to the sound nature of Cuba's integrated strategy and the capacity to implement change when problems and challenges emerge.

SURVIVING THE "SPECIAL PERIOD"

The first real test of the integrated, community-based approach came in the early 1990s when Cuba abruptly lost its trading partners and foreign aid with the collapse of the Soviet Union and the Eastern bloc. Between 1989 and 1993, the U.S. embargo, combined with the loss of trade resulted in a 70 percent reduction in hard-currency reserves for medicines, equipment, and supplies; a drop of 33 and 39 percent in the average daily caloric and protein intake of the average Cuban, respectively; a 50 percent decline in food imports; and a 35 percent drop in Cuban gross domestic product. The devastation that this prolonged economic crisis, known as the "Special Period in a Time of Peace," wrought is hard to overstate. Among the most dramatic effects on health was a neuropathy epidemic affecting more than 50,000 people. Therapeutic protocols focusing on vitamin therapy, combined with comprehensive follow-up by family doctors, resulted in the illness being controlled in 86 percent of patients. New cases were controlled by distributing vitamin supplements door-to-door so that by the end of 1993 the epidemic had been virtually eliminated.

With an economic crisis severe enough to cause a nutritional-related epidemic, it stands to reason that other indicators and the overall health picture of the nation should have been adversely affected during the Special Period. On the whole, however, that was not the case due to the policies and practices that were in place at the time the Cuban economy crashed and the proactive measures that were enacted once health problems arose. First, the health of every Cuban remained a top priority for the government. By increasing the health care budget throughout the Special Period (which went from 7.4 percent of the national budget in 1990 to 13.1 percent in 1998) and carrying out weekly assessments of available medicines and equipment throughout the system to determine what was needed and which resources could be relocated or acquired—always prioritizing vulnerable groups and lifesaving therapies—health outcomes largely held the line.

Second, the preventive approach and general health of the population established over the previous three decades proved fundamental in maintaining the population in relatively good

Table 41.1. Major Health Indicators, Select Countries

Country	Life Expectancy	Infant Mortality (per 1,000 live births)	Under-Five Mortality (per 1,000 births)	Maternal Mortality (per 100,000 live births)	Low Birth Weight (%)
Australia	82	4	5	—	—
Brazil	73	17	19	75	8
Canada	81	5	6	—	8
China	73	16	18	32	3
Cuba	**78**	**5**	**6**	**41**	**5**
Ireland	80	3	4	—	—
Japan	83	2	3	—	—
Mexico	77	14	17	54	7
United Kingdom	80	5	5	—	—
United States	78	7	8	13	8

Data for all countries from 2007, from Anuario de Estadísticas de Salud (2011) and Ministerio de Salud Pública (2012).

Table 41.2.   Major Health Indicators in Cuba

Indicator	Value
Life expectancy	77.9
Infant mortality per 1,000 live births	4.6
Survival to five years (%)	99.4
Maternal mortality (per 100,000 live births)	22.5
Low birth weight (%)*	5.4
In-hospital births (%)*	99.9
Vaccination of children under one year (%)*	99.6
Five leading causes of death (account for 72 percent of all deaths)*	Heart disease; malignant tumors; cerebrovascular disease; influenza and pneumonia; and accidents
HIV prevalence, ages fifteen to forty-nine	0.1
Infectious disease mortality (per 100,000 inhabitants)*	58.1
Organ/tissue donation rate (per 1 million inhabitants)	11.4

Unless indicated, all data are through October 12, 2012, from Morales (2012).

* Data through December 31, 2011, from Anuario de Estadísticas de Salud (2011) and Ministerio de Salud Pública (2012).

health. By the mid-1990s, more than 95 percent of the Cuban population was attended by teams of family doctors and nurses (Reed 2008). Having a dedicated, community-based network of health professionals proactively screening for diseases and monitoring vulnerable populations allowed for early warning, diagnosis, and action: for instance, a 23 percent rise in low-birth-weight infants (from 7.3 to 9 percent) between 1989 and 1993 sounded the alarm and spurred the implementation of supplemental, high-nutrition food rations for pregnant women; the trend began to decline by 1994 as a result. Likewise, access to potable water supplies fell from 98 percent in 1998 to 26 percent in 1994, leading to more than a twofold increase in diarrheal disease mortality rates, from 2.7 per 100,000 people in 1989 to 6.8 in 1993. In response, the government sought out chlorine donations and imports for municipal water supplies; by 1995, 87 percent of municipal water supplies were purified. Finally, the general educational level of the population—99.8 percent of Cubans are literate, 90 percent of Cuban youth are enrolled in high school, and all education in Cuba, including postgraduate, is free—worked in favor of health promotion, education, and hygiene measures.

The Special Period, therefore, reinforced lessons that helped build Cuba's universal health system, including the importance of prevention, the prioritization of vulnerable populations, and the effects of social determinants on health. It also taught new lessons, such as the critical importance of active epidemiological surveillance, the significance of mental health and well-being, and the utility of natural and traditional medicines. All these lessons, both old and new, are currently in play as the Cuban health system undergoes the arduous and not always smooth process of reorganization—again, in the thick of a major economic crisis and the ever-tightening U.S. embargo.

NEW CHALLENGES, NEW STRATEGIES

Today, the ability of Cuba's universal health system to provide comprehensive, integrative care to the country's 11 million inhabitants remains one of the unequivocal achievements of

Table 41.3. Cuban Public Health System: Infrastructure and Human Resources

Health Facilities

Type	Number
Family doctor and nurse offices	11,492
Dentist offices	1,215, with a total of 5,995 dental chairs
Community polyclinics	452
Maternity homes	142, with a total of 4,305 beds
Senior day care centers	228
Old-age homes	126, with a total of 9,475 beds
Hospitals	152, with a total of 38,642 beds
Research institutes	13

Human Resources for Health

Type	Number
Physicians*	76,506
Nurses (including auxiliary)*	103,014
Dentists*	12,144
Patient-to-doctor ratio	143 to 1
Patient-to-nurse ratio	117 to 1
Patient-to-dentist ratio	878 to 1
Medical school enrollment	48,951 (includes Cubans and foreigners)

Unless indicated, all data are through October 12, 2012, from Morales (2012).

* Data through December 31, 2011, from Anuario de Estadísticas de Salud (2011) and Ministerio de Salud Pública (2012).

the revolutionary government. By design rather than accident, one of the fundamental strengths shown by the health professionals and authorities planning and providing that care is the capacity to develop methodologies and systems to respond to emerging health problems, continued financial restraints, and paradigm shifts. Currently, a confluence of factors, both external and internal, is providing impetus for a reconfiguration of health service provision in Cuba. These factors are also presenting challenges to a woefully resource-scarce system that is showing strain fifty years after its inception.

The health picture in Cuba has changed substantially since the seminal efforts of the Rural Medical Service in 1960, the advent of the community polyclinic in 1974, and the establishment of the network of family doctor and nurse in 1986. Whereas malnourishment, communicable diseases, and diarrhea-related mortality used to be the most pressing health problems, Cuba's current health status is similar to more developed nations, characterized by crippling chronic disease—90 percent of all deaths in Cuba are caused by chronic disease and a rapidly aging population. Chronic diseases, the majority of which can be prevented and controlled by changes in lifestyle, argue for more effective intersectoral coordination and underscore the importance of patient responsibility for individual health. Meanwhile, across the country, people are living longer—life expectancy in Cuba today is 77.9 (up from age seventy forty years ago)—and by 2025 over a quarter of the population will be older than sixty, according to projections by the Center for Population and Development Studies (*Oficina Nacional de Estadísticas* 2008). This makes Cuba the "grayest" country in the region. Caring for elder Cubans places greater demands on the health system for geriatric, rehabilitative, and chronic disease care. Complicating matters are episodic outbreaks of emerging and reemerging diseases, including dengue and cholera.

Even the best-financed, best-administered, and best-equipped health systems struggle with preventing and treating chronic disease, ensuring healthy aging for a graying population, and detecting and controlling infectious disease. In Cuba's case, the global economic crisis, combined with the U.S. embargo, further limits the country's capacity to address health problems. Indeed, Amnesty International (2009) concluded that "the export of medicines and medical equipment [from the United States to Cuba] continues to be severely limited and has a detrimental impact on the progressive realization of the right to the highest attainable standard of health" (15). The UN High Commissioner for Human Rights went further still, calling the embargo "disastrous" for the economic, social, and cultural rights of the Cuban people (UN Human Rights Council 2007). According to Cuban authorities, the U.S. embargo has cost the health system over U.S.$21.6 billion since it was enacted in 1961 (Morales 2012).

The convergence of these economic and health factors over the past decade has led Cuban health authorities to mandate a renovation of the provision of health services to reinforce prevention (with an emphasis on curbing chronic and emerging diseases) and to identify efficient, effective practices to help control costs and provide sustainability for the health system—without sacrificing the strides made in population health. This amounts to the most dramatic change in the Cuban health approach since the advent of the program of family doctor and nurse; the changes detailing the reorganization of the health system were outlined in two documents released in 2010. *Necessary Transformations in the Public Health System* called for "reorganizing, downsizing, and regionalizing health services by maximizing the efficient, rational use of scarce resources, while guaranteeing quality access and providing sustainability to the health system." The complementary *Public Health Work Objectives and Indicators 2011* serves as the road map for how to achieve those goals in an equitable, systematic way. The changes are being implemented in a graduated process that focuses on cutting spending, increasing revenue, and taking steps to improve quality of care.

Spending cuts are being realized by closing or consolidating underutilized facilities; analyzing which specialty services are imperative to the specific health picture of an area and reorganizing delivery of those services to provide them more effectively; fortifying epidemiological surveillance and reporting; stepping up health promotion to lower the disease burden, thereby decreasing doctor and hospital visits; prioritizing clinical and diagnostic methodologies with a concomitant emphasis on the use of natural and traditional medicine; addressing patient satisfaction and complaints in a practical way; and strengthening intersectoral collaboration to promote health and well-being.

The reliance on health promotion to prevent illness and the clinical exam as a means to diagnose conditions once they manifest are key to Cuba's strategy for maintaining and improving health indicators. To achieve this, while addressing "the population's dissatisfaction" with the state of health services, the *Ministerio de Salud Pública* (Ministry of Public Health [MINSAP] 2011) has determined that the program of family doctor and nurse needs to be "revolutionized." To achieve this, MINSAP has detailed eight specific objectives and scores of actions related to the provision and organization of services at the primary care level, improved record keeping and consultations among medical professionals, goals for research and training, and techniques for involving other sectors in improving health. The time line for achieving these objectives nationally is five years.

The call for a revolution in primary care builds on the lessons that Cuba has developed over the past fifty years, specifically the need to continually evaluate and develop methodologies and systems to remain responsive and relevant in the face of changing epidemiologic, economic, environmental, and social circumstances. Many of the steps outlined by MINSAP for this revolution are not dissimilar from steps taken during the Special Period to help hold the line on population health gains. What is new, however, is the frank recognition of patient dissatisfaction as one of the triggers and the emphasis on the need for health professionals to have more flexibility and autonomy in decision making and implementing mechanisms to make this possible.

The other, perhaps more compelling factor triggering the need for transforming the health system is economic: the global financial crisis and the U.S. embargo, combined with devastating hurricanes in 2008 and 2012 that caused an estimated $12 billion in damages and the mismanagement of health system resources (Fariñas 2012; Grogg 2012; Martínez 2012), have impacted Cuba's capacity to sustain the quality of its national health system. For example, a program launched in 2004 to modernize fifty-two hospitals and over 400 polyclinics around the country stalled after a robust beginning, purchase of supplies and equipment is lagging, and salaries for health professionals remain untenably low. Such deprivation and shortages have a major impact on policy and performance (Keck and Reed 2012) and adversely affect health personnel and patients alike.

Economic realities have also come home to roost in relation to Cuba's decades-long commitment to international solidarity and cooperation in health and medicine. Since 1961, Cuba has collaborated with 103 countries in health and medicine, posting over 113,000 medical professionals to help bolster those countries' health systems; currently, 39,000 Cuban medical workers and support staff work in sixty-five countries (Morales 2012). On the training side, over 12,000 students—all of whom received six-year medical degrees on full scholarships provided by Cuba—have graduated from Havana's Latin American Medical School (ELAM) since its founding in 1999 (Gorry 2012). While some bilateral agreements for Cuban medical personnel are based on goods-for-services exchange (most notably Venezuela), the majority of the costs of medical internationalism, including ELAM scholarships, are assumed by Cuba. Moreover, posting so many health professionals overseas has had a negative impact on patient satisfaction since Cubans are accustomed to services on demand, and while there is no doctor shortage in Cuba, where the patient-to-doctor ratio is 143 to 1 as compared to 390 to 1 in the United States, waiting times have increased to see family doctors and specialists. ELAM students and graduates doing primary care rotations in family doctors' offices and polyclinics can also engender patient dissatisfaction because some Cubans prefer to be treated by Cuban personnel.

Tackling these challenges is complex and has compelled authorities to look for ways to raise revenue to promote sustainability. International medical cooperation, for instance, is still provided free of charge to the poorest countries, but fee-for-service agreements are increasingly being negotiated with wealthier nations experiencing shortages of human resources for health, especially in the Middle East. Likewise, tuition-paying international students are a growing segment of Cuba's medical education program, though maintaining six-year medical scholarships for global South students remains a priority. Medical tourism is another area the country is pursuing to promote sustainability. The greatest revenue gains, however, are coming from Cuba's biotech and pharmaceutical sector—the country's second-largest export earner after nickel. Indeed, between 1995 and 2010, Cuba's pharmaceutical and biotechnology revenues increased fivefold, and in 2011, the sector earned U.S.$711 million; it is estimated that by 2016, these revenues will surpass U.S.$1 billion (Scheye 2011), although this is probably a very conservative estimate.

Cuba began developing its biotechnology capacity in the 1980s in order to produce critical medicines that the U.S. embargo prevented the country from procuring on the international market and to address neglected tropical diseases and other conditions afflicting the global South. Today, there are twenty-four research institutions and fifty-eight manufacturing facilities in Havana's Scientific Pole, producing generic drugs, vaccines, diagnostic equipment, and innovative therapies unavailable elsewhere. Based on a "closed-loop" research, development, manufacturing, and distribution model whereby all entities involved work together to address pressing health needs, the Scientific Pole provides 66 percent of the 885 essential medications registered for use in the country's national health system. Importantly, of the thirteen vaccines that every Cuban child receives, eight are manufactured domestically (Morales 2012). Some of these, like the Cuban recombinant hepatitis B vaccine, are manufactured for domestic use as well as export: this particular vaccine has earned the country more than $200 million (*Mesa Redonda Informativa* 2012).

The Scientific Pole also produces vaccines unique in the world, most notably the only commercially available type-B bacterial meningococcal vaccine and a synthetic antigen vaccine against *Haemophilus influenza b*, a disease that kills half a million children each year globally. Nimotuzumab, an antitumor treatment, and Heberprot-P, a therapy for diabetic foot, also star in Cuba's pharmaceutical portfolio and are the only ones of their kind available anywhere. Heberprot-P is proving especially important since 10 to 15 percent of the 171 million diabetics worldwide will develop diabetic foot (10 to 15 percent of these eventually require amputation). Moreover, there is no other specific medication that can sustain the healing process of wounds and complex ulcers on the lower limbs at terminal stages in diabetic patients. Heberprot-P represents significant earning potential for the sector but also saves the Cuban health system precious financial and material resources since it means fewer surgical interventions and hospitalizations, obviates the need for rehabilitation for amputees, and decreases the years of potential life lost. Furthermore, it improves the quality of life for diabetic foot sufferers and helps them remain active members of society. Heberprot-P is registered in fifteen countries worldwide, is undergoing the registration and market approval process in several other countries, and has been applied to more than 80,000 diabetic foot sufferers in Cuba and elsewhere. It is worth noting that this cutting-edge treatment, along with all others developed in Cuba, is not available to patients in the United States due to the embargo.

As with medical education and international cooperation, Cuba's commitment to provide quality products and services at low cost to poor countries remains steadfast. The experience of TecnoSuma, the commercial arm of the Scientific Pole's Immunoassay Center, illustrates how Cuba has been able to maintain this commitment while saving money for its own health system and earning revenue at the same time. Launched in 1981, TecnoSuma develops diagnostic equipment and reagents for early detection of a variety of diseases, including congenital hyperthyroidism, HIV, and prostate cancer. It also designs and produces innovative medical technologies, such as a glucose meter designed specifically for tropical climates. The Tecno-Suma strategy, developed in close collaboration with MINSAP, is to provide effective, cost-efficient, and contextually appropriate diagnostic tools and technologies meeting the highest international quality standards. TecnoSuma is completely self-financed through its international sales—it has commercial offices in Mexico, Colombia, Venezuela, Brazil, Argentina, and China—and it estimates that import substitution for its reagents alone has saved the country U.S.$300 million.

These sales subsidize the price of TecnoSuma technologies to the Cuban health system (and other resource-scarce contexts), helping keep costs low. For instance, digital video colposcopes used to detect cervical anomalies cost over U.S.$10,000 on the international market, but the TecnoSuma product, SUMASCOPE, is provided to the Cuban health system for under

U.S.$300. All of TecnoSuma's two dozen products repeat this pattern. According to Aramís Sánchez, assistant general manager of TecnoSuma, "demand is high and growing: we're currently working at double capacity and expanding our facilities as a result. One of our best-selling products, the SUMASENSOR blood glucose meter, gets high marks for patient satisfaction, saves money, helps diabetics live more independently, and helps improve care since physicians can more accurately monitor blood sugar levels and adjust treatment accordingly" (quoted in Gorry 2012).

CONCLUSION

The underlying principle of health as a human right has driven Cuba's unwavering commitment to provide equitable, quality care to its entire population free of charge. Nevertheless, a principle is only as worthy and effective as the practices put in place to realize the goals it embodies. By focusing on health promotion and prevention, locating services closer to patients in a community-based model, establishing a scientifically rigorous and robust medical education system, and tailoring research and development to address local health problems and neglected diseases, Cuba has proven that better health is possible, even for poor countries. Through good times and bad, the health system and dedicated professionals staffing it have been able to improve and maintain health outcomes so that today Cuba, a poor and blockaded country, has indicators on par with developed nations. It is for these reasons that the Cuban rights-based approach has served as a model for other developing countries, including El Salvador, Venezuela, Angola, and Honduras.

A key component of this approach is to continuously evaluate policies and processes since the health picture and economic, social, and environmental factors change and practices and methodologies need to be adjusted in order to remain relevant and responsive. Cuba's experience during the Special Period showed that the health system—and the population's health more generally—can resist and rebound from economic crisis. However, today, the disease burden is more complex and weighty with a chronic disease epidemic that shows no signs of slowing and is complicated by the emergence of tropical and waterborne diseases as well as the rapid aging of the population. All of these factors make the task more difficult. The global economic recession combines with the embargo to strain the health system even further, evidenced by growing patient dissatisfaction, the interruption of sorely needed repairs to health facilities, and shortages in materials.

Cuba is currently undergoing the most dramatic economic reforms since the revolutionary government came to power. This process is introducing complexities to which the health system is not immune; for instance, the explosion of private restaurants necessitates sanitary measures and monitoring for which there are not always the human resources to implement. Moreover, some resellers of agricultural produce use illegal chemical ripeners to get fruits and vegetables to market quicker, a process that has raised questions about food safety and nutritional value (Fariñas and Delgado 2012). Such factors increase the need for comprehensive epidemiological surveillance and response and closer intersectoral collaboration, further challenging the successful transformation of the health system. Fortunately, health authorities and policymakers are constantly evaluating population health and the determinants affecting it to tailor an effective approach. Perhaps most important, the government, supported by popular support, continues to exercise the political will to provide quality health care for all.

REFERENCES

Amnesty International. 2009. *The US Embargo against Cuba: Its Impact on Social and Economic Rights*. London: Amnesty International.

Declaration of Alma-Ata. 1978. International Conference on Primary Health Care, Alma-Ata, Soviet Union. September.

Fariñas, Lisandra. 2012. "Economía de salud en la capital: Terapias contra el descontrol." *Granma*, June 21.

Fariñas, Lisandra, and Sheyla Delgado. 2012. "¿Comprar Verde por Maduro?" *Granma*, May 11.

Gorry, Conner. 2012. "Cuba's Latin American Medical School: Can Socially-Accountable Medical Education Make a Difference?" *MEDICC Review* 14, no. 3: 5–11.

Grogg, Patricia. 2012. "Community Drills Part of Cuba's Top-Notch Disaster Response System." Inter Press Service, May 22.

Keck, C. William, and Gail A. Reed. 2012. "The Curious Case of Cuba." *American Journal of Public Health* 102, no. 8: 13–22.

Martínez, Rosa. 2012. "Beautiful Santiago de Cuba after Sandy." *Havana Times*, November 3.

Mesa Redonda Informativa. 2012. "La ciencia cubana: Un factor de desarrollo económico." March 1. http://mesaredonda.cubadebate.cu/mesa-redonda/2012/03/01/ciencia-cubana-un-factor-desarrollo-economico-video/.

Ministerio de Salud Pública. 2011. *Programa del Médico y la Enfermera de la Familia*. Havana: Ministerio de Salud Pública.

———. 2012. *Anuario Estadístico de Salud, 2010*. Havana: Ministerio de Salud Pública.

Morales, Roberto. 2012. "Opening Plenary Address: The Cuban Health System." Cuba Salud 2012 Conference, Havana, December 3.

Oficina Nacional de Estadísticas. 2008. "El estado actual y perspectiva de la población cubana: Un reto para el desarrollo territorial sostenible." http://www.one.cu/estadoactual.htm.

Overseas Development Institute. 2010. *Millennium Development Goals (MDG) Report Card: Measuring Progress across Countries*. London: Overseas Development Institute.

Reed, Gail. 2008. "Cuba's Primary Health Care Revolution: 30 Years On." *Bulletin of the World Health Organization* 86, no. 5: 327–29.

———. In press. "Chronic Vascular Diseases in Cuba: Strategies for 2015." *MEDICC Review* 10, no. 2: 5–7.

Scheye, Elaine. 2011. "Cuban Healthcare and Biotechnology: Reform, a Bitter Pill to Swallow or Just What the Doctor Ordered?" In *Proceedings of the 21st Annual Meeting, Association for the Study of the Cuban Economy (ASCE)*. http://www.ascecuba.org/publications/proceedings/volume21.

UN Human Rights Council. 2007. *Situation of Human Rights in Cuba*. Report Submitted by the Personal Representative of the High Commissioner for Human Rights, Christine Chanet (A/HRC/4/12, January).

UNICEF. 2004. *State of the World's Children 2005*. New York: UNICEF.

World Bank. 2001. *World Development Report 2000/2001*. Oxford: Oxford University Press.

World Health Organization. 2011a. "Closing the Gap in a Generation: Health Equity through Action on the Social Determinants of Health." October. http://www.who.int/entity/social_determinants/thecommission/finalreport/en/index.html.

———. 2011b. *Rio Political Declaration on Social Determinants of Health: Rio de Janeiro, Brazil, 21 October 2011*. Geneva: World Health Organization.

Chapter Forty-Two

Fifty Years Later

Women and Social Change in Cuba

Clotilde Proveyer Cervantes, Reina Fleitas Ruiz,
Graciela González Olmedo, Blanca Múnster Infante,
and María Auxiliadora César

The Cuban government has prioritized fulfillment of the Millennium Development Goals, promoting the presence of women in leadership roles in order to guarantee and promote women's rights, power and political participation. The female presence in the Cuban Parliament grew after the election of 2008; women now occupy 260 of the 614 seats, or 42.34 percent of the National Assembly of People's Power. The rate of growth has been constant, though it is still proportionally small compared to the great number of women with the necessary skills and requirements to participate in this governing body. Table 42.1 displays the rate of women's involvement in the Cuban Parliament.

Comparing these numbers to the levels of participation of women in parliaments in other countries throughout Central America, there is little doubt that Cuba holds a prominent position in the region. Cuba now ranks third in the world for this indicator, the estimated average female representation in world parliaments being 17 percent.

Table 42.1. Women in the Cuban Parliament

Year	Percentage of Women
1976	21.8
1981	22.7
1986	33.9
1993	22.8
1998	27.6
2003	36.0
2007	42.34

Source: Federation of Cuban Women.

Despite a growing representation of women in the Cuban Parliament, women participate in the Council of State to a lesser extent. [In all] six women have served in the Council of Ministers from 2004 to 2008, and thirty-three have held responsibilities in the vice ministries.

WOMEN IN LEADERSHIP POSITIONS

Progress has been made in the distribution of management positions between men and women. In 2007, women made up 54.5 percent of management personnel in the medical field; among [dentists] the number rises to 65.3 percent. Despite these encouraging figures, this field follows the same pattern as other institutions: the pyramid narrows as it gets higher. Even though some women have been vice ministers of health, none has occupied the central position of the ministry. All this takes place in a health care system in which women constitute 70 percent of the workforce.

The participation of Cuban women in the different levels of the Cuban Communist Party (PCC) and in grassroots and labor organizations has been important to the process of women's empowerment. In 2000, 30.1 percent of the active members of the PCC were women. Nonetheless, women held only 22 percent of the leadership roles in the municipal committees and 23 percent in the provincial committees. For that same year, women made up 13.3 percent of the Central Committee and 8 percent of the members of the Political Bureau, the highest level of power in the party. [Authors' note: In April 2011, at the Sixth Congress of the Communist Party of Cuba, there were forty-eight women in the Central Committee (of a total of 115, or 41.7 percent—a dramatic increase of over 300 percent).]

In the National Association of Small Farmers (ANAP), women were barely represented in the leadership in 2000. Women held the presidency of 1.8 percent of the Agricultural Production Cooperatives (CPAs) and Credit and Service Cooperatives (CCSs). However, by 2008, there were sixty-one women leading CPAs and ninety-four presidents of the CCSs. Women now account for 23 percent of the members of the municipal committees of the ANAP and 24 percent of the members of the association's committees. Women represent 32 percent of the total membership of the ANAP.

[In terms of access to education for women] comparisons to data from the beginning of the 2000s show steady progress. In the past five years, women have made up the majority of the population with technical training in the country, representing more than 60 percent of higher-education graduates each year. In medical sciences, for several decades, more than 70 percent of enrolled students and graduates have been women.

WOMEN'S PARTICIPATION IN THE LABOR FORCE

[Regarding the nature of women's employment] the following ratios describe the employment of Cuban women by occupation:

- 46 percent of workers in the public sector and 65.6 percent of professionals and technicians are women.
- 72 percent of workers in the education sector are women.
- 70 percent of workers in the health sector are women.
- 51.6 percent of researchers and 48.9 percent of workers in science and technical units are women.
- 17.22 percent of workers in the cooperative sector are women.
- 25.4 percent of [self-employed workers] are women.

- Women's presence is smaller in other branches of the economic activity, including agriculture (17.4 percent), construction (15.7 percent), and mining (19.1 percent).
- Women have a larger presence (41.5 percent) in service jobs, such as businesses, restaurants, and hotels. In financial services, banking, and real estate, they represent 52.4 percent of workers and 51.3 percent in community, social, and personal services.

Women's employment in the education sector is much higher than in other sectors. Women make up 51.6 percent of researchers and 60.4 percent of the scientific reserve of the country. Of 199 Scientific Research Centers, 48 (24 percent) are managed by women.

In 2006, Cuban women made up 69.4 percent of the workers in the health care sector, [and] 56.2 percent of doctors in Cuba are women. Differences still exist between specialties, however. More women work in clinical roles and more men in surgery. Pediatrics is a clear illustration of this dichotomy of roles because in this specialty women are the majority. [They] make up 65.3 percent of pediatricians and only 30 percent of pediatric surgeons. Differences also exist in other specialties. Women are the majority in the branches of nutrition (71.4 percent), ophthalmology (73 percent), and general family medicine (64.5 percent). [They] are less represented in specialties that focus on higher-level public health issues and cutting-edge research, including oncology (36 percent), neurosurgery (16.5 percent), and cardiovascular surgery (7 percent).

INCOME GAPS

Gender discrimination is prohibited in the daily practice of the labor relations system and by Cuban law. [Nevertheless, this] study found that women received 2 percent lower salaries than men, with the exception of those workers in the Ministry of Education.

Salary losses due to absence from work were caused by illness (60 percent), child care and care of other family members (22 percent), and maternity leave (18 percent). Of the total absences recorded by gender, 77 percent were registered by female employees. This confirms that men rarely miss work for any reason other than illness. The disproportionately large amount of responsibility that women take on compared to men in raising a family translates into fewer days worked on average each month and, as a result, lower incomes for women.

This means that, although salary discrimination does not exist, there is still a salary gap between men and women. This affects women's contributions to social security, meaning that women's pensions are smaller than men's, reflecting women's greater difficulty in accessing retirement benefits to sustain them in their old age.

CUBAN FAMILIES AND GENDER RELATIONS

One of the most important transformations for Cuban families has to do with the educational advancement of women. This progress has helped a greater number of women obtain their economic independence and, as a result, set a much lower tolerance for violent practice generated by the patriarchal culture in couples' relationships. Educational advancement and greater legal flexibility for divorce help explain a higher divorce rate in the country. The crude divorce rate went from 0.5 per 1,000 inhabitants in 1960 to 3.1 per 1,000 in 2007. Case studies on the process for dissolving marriages in Cuba affirm that women are more likely to request a divorce. Other cases, however, still show situations in which women fear divorce because separation from their partners implies economic insecurity for them and their children.

There is now less prejudice facing Cuban women after a divorce and greater respect for their social function. This environment has led to an increase in the number of women who remarry. In 2007, 49 percent of divorced women eventually remarried compared to 51 percent of men.

Conflicts due to the growing role of women in society have led to the dissolution of many couples. Breakups and later remarriages create a new challenge for Cuban families: multiple parents. These arrangements often lead to the superimposition of education models that are conflictive from a gender standpoint.

In 1980, the abortion rate was 42.1 per 1,000 women, and in 2007, the number was 20.4, a reduction by just more than one-half. Use of birth control is an indicator of the freedom that Cuban women enjoy; easy access to contraception allows women to control their fertility. Access to birth control and the legalization and institutionalization of abortion offer real guarantees for women's rights to control their own bodies. On the other hand, the more frequent use of birth control among women and female control of fertility may also be an expression of men not assuming full responsibility.

VICTORIES ACHIEVED

- The formation of women as a new political actor, best represented by their organization the Federation of Cuban Women, which acts as an interlocutor with the government to draft national policy. The federation has shown significant results. These results have allowed Cuba to fulfill the benchmarks of Millennium Development Goal 3 related to gender equity.
- A radical change in the social, economic, cultural, and political situation of Cuban women, which is evident in all aspects of progress made toward gender equity.
- The reduction and/or elimination of many forms of violence against women in Cuba due in great part to the changes that have been made to women's overall situation, the increase in awareness of gender issues, and the social policies guaranteed by the Cuban state, which acts to guarantee both women's rights and the involvement of women as crucial actors in building integration and equality in society.
- Progress in legislation and legal proceedings, which create a measure of protection for women's rights in all areas of life.

CHALLENGES

- To implement a cross-cutting gender-based approach in designing and executing social policy, economic policy, and all institutional decisions.
- To strengthen a gender-based perspective in education and to perfect nonsexist socialization mechanisms in schools and other institutions with a socializing role (the family, workplaces, mass media, and so on).
- To perfect programs and actions that help resolve the contradiction between the high demands of female leadership and participation in society and the reproduction of patterns that subordinate women in gender relations, above all in the private sphere.
- To promote new measures to eliminate the "glass ceiling" that prevents women from reaching decision-making positions.

NOTE

Excerpted from Clotilde Proveyer Cervantes et al., "50 Years Later: Women and Social Change in Cuba," Oxfam, 2009. Reprinted by permission of the publisher.

Chapter Forty-Three

Cuban Educational Reform during the "Special Period"

Dust, Ashes, and Diamonds

Denise Blum

En educación estamos cambiando todo lo que debe ser cambiado (In education we are changing everything that must be changed).
—Fidel Castro Ruz

Cuba's economic recovery during the "Special Period" (1989 to the present) involved the introduction of increased tourism, private ventures, and U.S. dollars. These measures led not only to growing inequality and private enrichment but also to an exodus of teachers. In 1989, university professors and physicians were at the top of the salary scale, and teachers earned adequate salaries by comparison; thereafter, small private farmers, self-employed workers, and traders in the free agricultural and black markets became the highest earners. Many professionals shifted their state occupations to jobs in enterprises with foreign capital or in tourism, where they earned part of their wages or tips in hard currency; they also moved to the informal and black market jobs, where remuneration was higher. Labor needs dictated careers and education for those careers. This alignment, however, was part of major upheaval for the Cuban education system as it regressed into a state of emergency, if not crisis, as teachers were in short supply. The education budget for 1998 had decreased by 42 percent compared with 1989 (CEPAL 2000). While the government's education expenditures also declined in the decade that followed, "Castro prided himself in speeches for not closing a single school, daycare center, or hospital, and for not leaving a single person destitute" (Eckstein 2004, 610).

The role of education in a socialist system is significant, as education serves a necessary political responsibility in addition to skill learning and supplying branches of production with a qualified workforce. The education system is charged with forming a socialist mind-set in the children to perpetuate a socialist society as dictated by the government. (Capitalist societies and their education systems also socialize their own—capitalist—ideology. In a socialist society, however, this is overt and explicit in the curriculum and teacher training and quite visible in educational activities.) The purpose of this chapter is to document major educational reform measures during the latter part of the Special Period, marked by the "Battle of Ideas" campaign that emerged during the rescue of Elián González in 1999, Raúl Castro's presidency in 2008, and the evolution of those educational reform measures today. Because socialist education is explicitly political, examining the reform measures is key to understanding Cuban socialism.

The foundation of Cuban socialist education is the Revolution's educational ethos. It is characterized by four major tenets: (1) a commitment to revolutionary values, with a heavy emphasis on morality and nationalism, as reflected in the heavy emphasis of teaching patriotism, especially in the courses on civic education and Cuban history; (2) universality: keeping all ages participating in the schooling process even once employed; (3) inclusiveness, as seen in the collective operation of the classroom and schooling on a whole; and (4) efforts to improve educational attainment and social well-being through increased graduation rates (Pumar 2010).

The government maintains its ethos with a nostalgic reinscription of ideological codes from the past on the present through education. This may take the form of informal or formal education that retains and reinforces the government's efforts to generate popular support. Antonio Kapcia (2000) defines a "code" as a "set of related and cognate beliefs and principles that can be grouped together to make a coherent belief in a single, given, value" (13) as one of the building blocks of the wider ideology, linking past to present. In the context of education, these codes include patriotism, hard work, sacrifice, and collectivism. These codes are embedded in the legendary figures of José Martí and of Che Guevara, who feature prominently in Cuban textbooks and school activities to this day.

By metering the work-study principle (based on principles from Karl Marx and José Martí) in the Cuban education system, it is possible to understand the government's economic and moral challenges and successes in preparing young people for society. The work-study principle combines manual and mental labor, understanding labor as a part of a Marxist dialectical process that ideally is both creative and meaningful. Moreover, the work-study principle is one that is inextricably tied to the land and the collective spirit, recalling the Rebel Army in the Sierra Maestra in the late 1950s, and has been manifested in the historical boarding schools (in the countryside), "Schools in the Countryside" (a one-month mobilization program for agricultural work), and school and community gardens. As schools are aligned to the political and economic structures of society (Bowles and Gintis 1976), the ongoing major educational initiatives in Cuban schooling are worth discussing to understand the present and future of Cuba.

Furthermore, a cultural and political hegemony (Gramsci 1971) exists in Cuba between the ruling governmental officials and the people. My particular focus, however, is on the relationship between the state and youth and the ways in which the state tries to appeal and win the ideological support of the young people using the education system.

REVIVING REVOLUTIONARY FERVOR

Predictably, the introduction of capitalist measures in the 1990s led to a decreased loyalty to the Revolution in economic terms. The values of solidarity and collectivism functioned within social networks, but little support existed for a government that could not provide materially for its people. Additionally, the increased infusion of capitalist measures encouraged the accompanying values of individualism, competition, alienation, and consumerism: all quite oppositional to the Revolution. For the Cuban government, this alarming development had to be stopped (Breidlid 2007).

The Cuban government found an opportunity for renewed ideological support in the international drama that surrounded the custody battle of Elián González in 1999 during the Special Period. The upsurge in popular support to return the boy, who was being held in

Miami by relatives, to his father in Cuba was an ideological battle fought on all fronts: cultural, political, educational, and social.

The boy's rescue became an opportunity to revive nationalism and revolutionary fervor. Cubans commented that the Cuban people had not been so united in national purpose and moral conviction since the 1961 Literacy Campaign. In fact, once Elián was returned, some Cubans noted that this was one of the few contemporary battles with the United States in which protest, debate, and justice came to fruition. This victory was particularly important to galvanize political support with the Cuban young people, whom the government had growing concern regarding their disaffection. The international attention given both the ideological and the legal issues that emerged in the custody struggle became a primed moment to initiate and advance new educational initiatives.

In this passionate political climate, *Mesa Redonda* was founded in December 1999 with the motive of publicizing and giving more popular participation to the movement to rescue Elián and opening a space for critical dialogue on current issues. This radio program was among the first to use the term "Battle of Ideas." Invited panelists engaged in debate over national and international political, cultural, and sports issues. Today, *Mesa Redonda* continues as a news analysis television program that encourages critical dialogue over current issues.

During the Battle of Ideas campaign, innovations were implemented to address societal needs and secure youth participation and, consequently, sustainable ideological support for the Revolution. Two specific problems were targeted (1) the poor and overcrowded areas affected most severely by the rigors of the Special Period and (2) the discontent and rise in juvenile delinquency among Cuba's highly qualified university students. Initially, the *desvinculados* (disconnected, disaffected youth) were sent to approximately 60,000 homes to assess social problems, and, as a result, a whole raft of programs were set up, the most important being the school of social work (this field had not existed previously). The social work schools gave a potentially lost generation a reminder of those with fewer material resources and a stake in the Revolution that they could see materialize as a result of their work in socially useful tasks, while benefiting from a well-paid job.

After a year of intensive training at one of the social work schools, students could enroll in university courses provided that they carried out social work every Saturday until they graduated. Social workers worked not only with the elderly, those with disabilities, and the mentally ill but also with young prisoners, encouraging them to attend university or technical schools. By mid-2004, 21,000 social workers had been produced to work with the most disadvantaged and alienated sections of society, and through this process, the state hoped that the youth would experience a renewed commitment to the Revolution.

Cursos de superación integral para jóvenes (integrated development courses for youth), like the social work schools, were an incentive to engage young people who had become disaffected in society. Many young people saw more benefit in working the black market than in continuing with their education. These integrated development courses were offered at night to accommodate youth. Young people earned a nominal amount of money for attending these classes, which included community projects. Thus, young people acquired knowledge and culture to reincorporate themselves into society (Mayo Parra n.d.).

Other school reforms existed as well. In 2000, in Havana, where many veteran teachers had left to consider more lucrative ways of making a living, teaching labor was replenished with *maestros emergentes*: high school students who were recruited mainly from the eastern part of the island to teach elementary and junior high school while receiving pedagogical training on the weekends. In order to use young unprepared teachers in training effectively, *teleclases* (televised instruction) were used with two *maestros emergentes* to a classroom to accompany the standard televised course. The student-to-teacher ratios were lowered to improve the quality of instruction and personal attention to the student. Elementary schools had a twenty-to-one student-to-teacher ratio, while junior high and high schools had a fifteen-to-one ratio. This was a way to ensure that proper content was delivered, with the *maestros emergentes* merely reinforcing subject matter and maintaining a disciplined learning atmosphere. Unfortunately, the *maestros emergentes'* endeavor failed due to their inexperience, lack of pedagogical knowledge, and immaturity. Over 40 percent of the teachers in the classrooms were *maestros emergentes*, and the program was terminated in 2008 when Raúl Castro assumed the presidency.

Another initiative to remedy the teacher shortage was to provide training in multiple subjects for secondary teachers. In the junior high schools, the comprehensive *profesor general integral* was introduced in the 2003–2004 academic year, with one teacher teaching all subjects except for computer, art, foreign languages, and physical education. The focus was on interdisciplinary teaching and learning to cater more to the students as a group and also to emphasize the importance of holistic learning. However, this transformation at the junior high level increased a teacher's workload in preparing for multiple subjects. One consequence was teacher resistance and exodus, making it difficult to keep the classrooms adequately staffed.

Art instructor schools became a priority during the Battle of Ideas, and one school was built in every province. This idea was not new; the art instructor schools were also a priority in the 1960s. However, investment in this area had waned over the decades. With this initiative in 2000, cultural knowledge, skills, and appreciation were extended to every corner of the island, converting Cuba into the country "*más culto*" (most cultured) in the world. Fidel Castro reinforced his cultural mission using the José Martí maxim "*ser culto para ser libres*" (be cultured to be free), adding "in order to achieve an integrated knowledge of culture in our people" (Castro 2004) and noting the necessity of an interdisciplinary education.

Local university centers (*sedes municipales*) also served this interdisciplinary mission and provided greater access to those who had day jobs by offering college classes at night, with one *sede municipal* in every municipality. (There are 169 municipalities in the country.) This was part of the commitment to give educational access to all regardless of age. It is important to note that one can enroll in college for the equivalent of a BA or BSc only until age twenty-five. Therefore, the *sedes municipales* were established to give a second chance to those who were unable to enroll during the worst years of the Special Period and to encourage more students to enter higher education. They were not newly constructed schools; rather, already existing schools were used after hours.

In the area of pedagogical training, the *sede municipal* provided a mentor to each preservice teacher, as many were in the classroom teaching while taking classes. The idea behind the *sede municipal*, besides convenience and access, was to ensure that Cubans became more knowledgeable and skilled while considering the process of education as one of lifelong learning.

Seeking to involve older Cubans in the benefits of a new educational expansion, the *Universidad Para Todos* was established in 2000 to broadcast degree-level classes on television. Classes have been given in many subjects, such as French, English, Cuban history, geography, science, and the arts, by well-known Cuban scholars and scientists with the purpose of raising and integrating cultural and scientific knowledge on the island (Mayo Parra n.d.). In addition to using the television for teaching and learning, computer literacy was universalized starting in elementary school.

In 2003, over half of the sugar mills were closed in rural areas. Special schools were set up to retrain the thousands of unemployed sugar workers for alternate professions. In addition, technical training programs were created for those who had failed university entrance exams.

EDUCATIONAL ADJUSTMENTS UNDER RAÚL CASTRO

When Raúl Castro assumed the presidency in 2008, a new education minister was appointed, Ena Elsa Velázquez, and changes in the education system followed. Even though secondary school enrollment rose to 87 percent in 2006, after a 75 percent enrollment for the corresponding cohort in 1994–1995, this was still not comparable to 1989 enrollment levels of 88 percent (UN Development Program 2007). In response, the 2009 education budget was initially increased by 2 percent, but in mid-2009 several cuts were implemented. Boarding schools in the countryside (*escuelas en el campo*, grades 10 through 12), combining farmwork on the school grounds with academic courses, were closed due to the costs of resources, especially food, water, electricity, and transportation, to supply the country schools. Tenth through twelfth grades were studied in the city only. Moreover, with high school facility closures, the number of slots for high school students has declined by 50,000, or more than 20 percent, since 2008, with more students being channeled into the skilled trades, where slots jumped from 26,000 in 2008 to 74,000 in 2011 (*Oficina Nacional de Estadísticas* [ONE] 2012).

In 2011, the Cuban government announced important changes for the junior high schools. The students would have the same teachers for grades 7 through 9, the purpose being to place emphasis on the teacher-student relationship and to personalize the curriculum when necessary, attending to student needs. Teachers were no longer responsible for teaching most of the subjects, which was causing teacher burnout. Instead, their responsibilities were pared down to teaching only two different subject areas while still maintaining the title *profesor general integral*. In addition, *teleclases* were no longer relied on for content delivery. They were used for support and inserted for the first time to promote needed professions, especially teaching, agricultural work, and midlevel skilled workers.

Ideological reinforcement was needed in addition to guiding students into the needed career paths. Solidifying political responsibility meant that teachers were required to emphasize more patriotism in the classroom in order to prepare students for ongoing economic changes. Cuban history, which used to be taught only once in a child's schooling, was now required in every grade from fifth through twelfth, including schooling for midlevel technicians and skilled laborers (Barrios 2009). Civic education, normally taught in only ninth grade, was now taught in sixth grade too. Civic education provided an important means to inculcate the revolutionary codes for state allegiance, patriotism, sacrifice, and hard work. The revolutionary heroes of Che Guevara, José Martí, and Camilo Cienfuegos were well rehearsed.

UNIVERSITY EDUCATION AND CHANGING CAREER PATHS

The changes in the education system at the college level are of great importance and will have enormous repercussions in the long run. University enrollment in 2008–2009 increased by 167 percent compared with 1989–1990. However, in the 2012–2013 school year, enrollment dropped by 27 percent compared to 2008. Students are now encouraged to learn more practical careers in an effort to reduce costs. In addition, lower enrollment has been influenced by the recently required university entrance exams in history, language, and geography. Those who have more resources are able to hire tutors to prepare their children in school subjects as well as on exams. This undercuts the standard of equal opportunity enshrined in the Cuban Constitution. Opportunities are shrinking while competition is growing.

Nevertheless, Cuba does have more university graduates than those graduating from technical schools. In 2009–2010, 2.4 percent of students enrolled in agricultural studies, 7 percent in technical fields, and 24.8 percent in social sciences and humanities. These numbers are cause for concern, as this presents a surplus of academics and a shortage of workers. Access continues to be free and universal from prekindergarten through postsecondary education. However, enrollment rates do not reveal the whole story: between 17 and 30 percent of students who entered preuniversity or technical school do not complete their program (ONE 2009).

Increasingly more opportunities are being provided in technical fields and agriculture, with slots in the humanities being reduced. The goal is to strengthen and prioritize the training of technical personnel who are needed to revive the country's production sector, thereby reducing the dependency on imports. For that reason, education officials are designing strategies for vocational guidance and recruitment, from elementary through high school education, in an attempt to encourage young people to choose professions and trades related to production, especially agriculture—which have typically been understood as hard labor and professions for the less educated. Esteban Morales has summed this up well: "It stopped being attractive, even to farmers' children" (quoted in González 2012).

The enrollment figures, nevertheless, obscure other education challenges confronted in other countries of the Organization for Economic Cooperation and Development, such as the ongoing urban-rural divide. Although there are a greater number of students attending college, what is not seen are the declining high school and university graduation rates. Elementary education is a good indicator because it is mandatory and attendance policy is well enforced, one that contributes to high graduation and literacy rates. Significantly, the discrepancy between urban and rural graduation rates for elementary education students remains wide, with 1960–1961 and 2007–2008 graduation rates narrowing by only one percentage point (table 43.1). This difference clearly informs the extent to which the rural population will continue education at a higher level and how its representation and participation in society outside of agricultural work will progress or not.

CONCLUSION

With each period of educational change, the ideas of the liberating power of education, a socialist morality, and political responsibility are summoned, specifically using the words of

Table 43.1. Percentage of Graduates from Primary Schools in Urban and Rural Districts, 1961–2008

School Year	Urban	Rural
1960–1961	79	21
1970–1971	68	32
1980–1981	66	34
1990–1991	74	26
2000–2001	76	24
2007–2008	78	22

Source: ONE 2009.

the nineteenth-century writer and revolutionary José Martí to legitimate the message as well as Che Guevara, who advocated for moral rather than material incentives. The bonding of the moral and material is reflected in the schooled Marxist-Martiano work-study principle. The work-study principle, during the Battle of Ideas, was reflected in the mobilization of *maestros emergentes*, mainly from the eastern part of the island to Havana, and the mobilization of social workers to work with the disadvantaged in both rural and urban areas. Both of these initiatives were terminated in 2009 and 2010, respectively. Additionally, the long-standing, historical boarding schools and schools in the countryside that involved students in agricultural work were shut down in 2009 due to insufficient funds to provide transportation, utilities, food, and facility maintenance.

The boarding schools and schools in the countryside created new, enriching and lasting relationships for students and teachers, ones that broke down stereotypes and classroom hierarchies and addressed racism. Knowing the value of relationship building among student, teacher, family, and nation, the government is seeking new ways to create these bonds that promote collectivity and commitment to the Revolution and to being revolutionary. As Laurie Frederik (2012) clarifies, in Cuba "revolution" and "revolutionary" did not mean protest or rebellion. Rather, they had more to do with being patriotic and loyal to the socialist project at hand. The Revolution and being revolutionary called for strong moral fiber. Cuban psychologists and authors González Rey and Mitjans Martínez (2000) assert, "The creation of a sound moral personality, guided by deep convictions and values, is essential to the development of a socialist society" (28). As some ideas become ashes, others are dusted off and recycled from the past, and the diamonds of *inventos cubanos* and socialist values in education continue to be mined. Notably, the increased emphasis on morality is an indication of an economic system that may be in conflict with an education system that preaches solely socialist ideology.

Education plays not only a political role but also a societal role, a key tool for the state. Moreover, education plays a significant role in understanding Cuban socialism. The government offers more access to higher education while implementing entrance exams that filter out some students. Graduates from preuniversity schools are diverted to vocational schools rather than guided to universities. The vocational schools must prepare the young people to function in a more liberal economic market with private initiatives. As the vocational-technical schools take center stage, how will the system stabilize and improve the quality for a skilled labor force if the former structures and rules are removed and replaced by a market structure and rules?

The goal is to reclaim every Cuban for the Revolution—to maintain a functioning form of socialism even though capitalist measures (such as private property and entrepreneurship) have been established. The dual economy presents a dual value system of collectiveness and competition, making the old rigid schooling inadequate if not irrelevant. Young people are quite aware of this disconnect, as evidenced in the high enrollment but low graduation rates. Weaknesses in the educational system began with the crisis of the 1990s. Many were not corrected, and the government continues to make adjustments.

Orienting and recruiting students to meet societal needs has not been easy. Currently, with entrance exams, the quota of students permitted to enter the university has been lowered, except for medicine. Students are being redirected into vocational education to become mid-level technicians and skilled workers. For this purpose, the state has allocated more funding to higher education, specifically vocational training. The greatest needs, agricultural-related professions and teachers, are not as appealing to the youth. As a result, problems continue with scarcity of both teachers and agricultural workers/producers because of national issues and the global economic crisis.

At the beginning of the 2012–2013 school year, there was a 6.8 percent deficit in permanent classroom teachers, which has again forced administrators to fill positions with students who "lack experience" in teaching, as acknowledged by *Juventud Rebelde* itself (Barrios 2012). The article warns that the career of teaching is currently an "Achilles' heel." As evidence, it cites the fact that of the more than 31,000 university slots offered in education this current school year, only 19.7 percent of these have been filled, with the greatest shortages in Havana, Ciego de Ávila, Matanzas, and Artemisa, some of the hardest places to fill (Barrios 2012). Without a doubt, the teacher shortage is not only a problem in schooling but one of the family and society as well. Well-prepared, knowledgeable teachers are needed for the future of Cuban society.

The Cuban government, under Raúl Castro's leadership, continues to mine practical solutions to ongoing economic and ideological challenges: allowing property and car ownership and sales, permitting Cubans to travel more easily, lowering costs on cell phone usage, making available more public transportation, and providing access to a non-Cuban television network, Telesur, which provides a broader political perspective. In trying to solve the problem of economic stagnation, the policymakers inadvertently created new problems for the education system with their socialist commitment to a strong welfare state. Schools have a clear economic and political purpose: to absorb unemployment, fill a skills need, and prevent potential disaffection.

The cornerstone of socialist Cuban education is the work-study principle, which has all but disappeared. Vocational training has taken primacy, but the integration of the private sector into vocational activities remains an open question. Will the market structure displace state companies? What impact will a more open economic system have on vocational training, education, and moralism? Education is the principal weapon for resistance, creation, and socialism. Regardless of economic changes, educational reform will continue to involve the ideological and material struggle for the trust and support of the youth.

REFERENCES

Barrios, M. 2009. "Un nuevo punto de crecimiento en la educación cubana." August 29. http://tvcamaguey.blogspot. com/2009/08/un-nuevo-punto-de-crecimiento-en-la.html.

———. 2012. "Los maestros que nos faltan." *Juventud Rebelde*, October 13.

Bowles, S., and H. Gintis. 1976. *Schooling in Capitalist America*. London: Routledge and Kegan Paul.

Breidlid, A. 2007. "Education in Cuba—An Alternative Educational Discourse: Lessons to Be Learned?" *Compare* 37, no. 5: 617–34.

Castro, F. R. 2004. "La graduación del primer curso de las Escuelas de Instructores de Arte, en la Plaza Ernesto Che Guevara, Santa Clara." Speech given by Fidel Castro, October 20, 2004. http://www.cuba.cu/gobierno/discursos/ 2004/esp/f201004e.html.

CEPAL. 2000. *La Economía Cubana, Reformas Estructurales y Desempeño en los Noventa*. 2nd ed. Mexico City: CEPAL.

Eckstein, S. 2004. "From Communist Solidarity to Communist Solitary." In *The Cuba Reader: History, Culture and Politics*, edited by A. Chomsky, B. Carr, and P. M. Smorkaloff, 607–22. Durham, NC: Duke University Press.

Frederik, L. 2012. *Trumpets in the Mountains: Theater and the Politics of National Culture in Cuba*. Durham, NC: Duke University Press.

González, I. 2012. "Cuban Higher Education in Times of Reform." Inter Press Service, August 13. http://www. ipsnews.net/2012/08/cuban-higher-education-changing-in-times-of-reform/.

González Rey, F., and A. Mitjans Martínez. 2000. "Motivación moral en adolescentes y jóvenes." In *Selecciones de lecturas sobre introducción a la psicología* [Moral motivation among adolescents and youth], edited by L. Ibarra Mustelier and N. Vasallo Barrueta, 28–37. Havana: Servigraf.

Gramsci, A. 1971. *Selections from the Prison Notebooks*. New York: International Publishers Co.

Kapcia, A. 2000. *Cuba: Island of Dreams*. Oxford: Berg.

Mayo Parra, I. n.d. *Cambio educativo en Cuba: Antecedentes y contexto*. Mexico City: Memorias del VII Encuentro Nacional de Investigacíon Educacional, Universidad Pedagógica Nacional.

Oficina Nacional de Estadísticas. 2009. *Anuario*. http://www.one.cu.

———. 2012. *Anuario*. http://www.one.cu.
Pumar, E. S. 2010. "Cuban Education and Human Capital Formation." *Cuba in Transition* 20: 97–105.
UN Development Program. 2007. *Human Development Report, 2007/2008*. New York: UN Development Program.

Chapter Forty-Four

The Changing Dynamics of Sexuality

CENESEX and the Revolution

Emily J. Kirk

Since 2008, when power officially shifted to Raúl Castro and the first sexual reassignment surgery was carried out in twenty years, Cuba's National Center of Sexual Education (CE-NESEX) has increasingly become a topic of interest in international media coverage. Headed by Mariela Castro Espín, the daughter of current president Raúl Castro, and former Federation of Cuban Women (FMC) president, Vilma Espín, CENESEX has piqued the curiosity of many. Indeed, the center and the dramatic changes it has instituted have been used to exemplify what is often referred to as "Castro's Cuba"—the implication being that the island is led by a familial dictatorship. Similarly, significant amounts of both academic and journalistic literature on Cuba regularly present the Revolution as a monolithic and unalterable structure, employing a largely top-down approach. Yet the changes that have occurred in the evolution of the CENESEX and, in particular, its recent work seem to indicate the precise opposite.

The center was officially established in 1989 and its precursor (the National Group for Work on Sexual Education) (GNTES) in 1977 (Hamilton 2012, 49). It developed from a teaming of Cuba's unique brand of feminism and educative processes, instituting sexual health care, increasing related research, and developing dramatically more progressive attitudes from Cuba's historically homophobic values (Kirk 2011). The center refocused its primary aim in 2004 to concentrate on lesbian, gay, bisexual, and transgender (LGBT) issues and since 2008 has been responsible for considerable advances in Cuba, including celebrations for the International Day Against Homophobia, comprehensive care for transgender people, and a redefinition of the Communist Party's Fundamental Principles.

While originally a small national group with the aim of establishing needed sexual education across the island, CENESEX has evolved into an internationally recognized center, focusing primarily on achieving rights and respect for LGBT people through education. The center's contemporary role continues to push the boundaries of what is considered to be revolutionary, highlighting well the complexity of the Cuban Revolution.

CENESEX AND THE REVOLUTION

After decades of institutionalized homophobia, notable changes occurred following the 1989 establishment of CENESEX. The center (and, by extension, the GNTES) had previously made considerable efforts to dissuade institutionalized homophobia and *machista* attitudes regarding sexuality. These abuses included, among others, forced attendance at reeducation camps (the Military Units for the Aid of Production); restrictive legislation forbidding homosexuals from working in the fields of education, medicine, sports, and the foreign service; and a basic understanding of homosexuality as anathema to the Revolution (Lumsden 1996, 77; Turner 1989, 70).

Throughout the 1990s, CENESEX continued developing its work in sexual education, while Cuba as a whole continued to struggle with attitudes toward sexual diversity. The internal struggle became clear in 1992, as both president Fidel Castro and FMC president Vilma Espín made public statements regarding homosexuality. President Castro noted in an interview that he was "absolutely opposed to any form of repression, contempt, scorn or discrimination with regard to homosexuals" (quoted in Leiner 1994, 59). Similarly, in 1992, FMC president Vilma Espín publicly noted that oppression against gays and lesbians had to stop, adding that they should instead be respected and welcomed (Leiner 1994, 59).

It was evident that Cuba was facing a massive internal debate regarding sexual diversity, as the entrenched homophobia was being challenged through the revolutionary ideology of unity and equality, which had previously condemned it. CENESEX, following its complex development as a result of a Cuba's unique brand of feminism and processes of education, continued to push the boundaries of acceptability within the Revolution. Indeed, the FMC and student groups in particular worked within and alongside CENESEX, increasingly incorporating issues related to sexual diversity (Krause-Fuchs 2007, 70).

In 2004, both CENESEX and its sister organization, the Cuban Multidisciplinary Society for the Study of Sexuality (SOCUMES), joined the International Lesbian and Gay Association (ILGA), as the central goals of CENESEX shifted toward LGBT issues (Castro Espín 2012, 31). Indeed, the center placed significantly more emphasis on the employment of an integral approach to achieve juridical and societal respect for sexual diversity (Roque Guerra 2011). Sexual education was still the main focus of CENESEX, although achieving sexual diversity rights became central to the educative process. Thus, although it represented only one of the fourteen "Areas of Work" cited by CENESEX, the area of sexual orientation rights and gender identity has expanded since 2004.

Of particular note was the 2004 incorporation of a "Sexual Diversity" section on the CENESEX website. The principal goal of the new section was to provide educative material on sexual diversity and challenge prejudice (Roque Guerra 2012, 224). The CENESEX website has continued to be a vital medium of communication and is indicative of the center's development. To explain, while the mission statement refers to the importance of the management and application of appropriate sexual education, the information present on the website instead suggests two main interests: education and respect for sexual diversity. This is clear by the website's home page, which presents, among others, links to the Diversity Is Natural campaign, SOCUMES, their declaration of sexual diversity rights, and the *Cubans Against Homophobia* newsletter. Similarly, there is a clear trend in the increasing number of articles published in the center's research journal *Sexología y Sociedad* (Sexology and Society), which provides articles from both national and international experts on varying topics related to sexual health and sexuality. Although online copies are available only from 2008 on, there is a clear trend in the increasing numbers of articles focused on LGBT issues and respect for sexual diversity. In 2008, for example, only two of the sixteen articles published in the journal focused on LGBT issues, while they represented four of the twelve published in 2011 and one of the four that have since been added for 2012.

Following the center's 2004 shift, further liberalizations in the attitudes toward sexual diversity became evident. In particular, notable success has been achieved in the field of care for transsexual and transgender people. In 2005, CENESEX, expanding on a multidisciplinary initiative that the GNTES established in 1979, developed the National Commission for Comprehensive Care of Transsexual Persons, including various legal and social aspects (Acosta 2006; Castro Espín 2012, 31; Roque Guerra 2011; Roque Guerra 2012, 244). The primary aim of the commission was to provide comprehensive care, including diagnoses, therapy, and support. By 2008, the commission had received ninety-two applications—and twenty-seven applicants had received official diagnoses as transsexuals, nineteen of whom were undergoing the process to receive gender reassignment surgeries, and thirteen had already obtained permission to change their name and photo on their national identification cards (Acosta 2006, 2008).

The commission was later strengthened by the June 2008 establishment of Resolution 126 (Grogg 2009). The resolution, signed by Public Health Minister José Ramón Balaguer, authorized the development of a center to provide comprehensive health care for transsexuals, including free gender reassignment surgeries and therapy (Acosta 2006, 2008). The evolution of the commission also prompted the presentation of a Gender Identity Bill for the Council of State (Roque Guerra 2012, 224). For the first time since 1988, Cuban physicians began carrying out sexual reassignment surgeries (Castro Espín 2008). The resulting positive effects for the transsexual community were made clear, as in 2012 a forty-eight-year-old transgender woman and local Committee to Defend the Revolution president was elected as a delegate to the municipal government (Pedroso 2012; *The Guardian* 2012).

Indeed, CENESEX continuously increased the breadth of its work within the field of sexual diversity as a whole. In 2005, for example, CENESEX, collaborating with the National Center for the Prevention of STD/HIV-AIDS, held a gay film festival. That year also marked the first year Cuban specialists participated in the Henry Benjamin International Gender Dysphiria Association (Castro Espín 2012, 31). And the following year, CENESEX personnel (representing Cuba) attended the International Conference on Lesbian, Gay, Bisexual, and Transgender Human Rights as well as the ILGA World Congress. And by 2007, Cuba was commemorating the World Day Against Homophobia (Castro Espín 2012, 31–32; Roque Guerra 2012, 224).

The year 2008 would prove to be a milestone as the developments of the previous years came to the fore. Sexual diversity and related rights became a repeated theme of debate across the island among both officials and the general populace. The growth of these discussions was evident in the increase of publications that explored the topic of sexuality as a whole. Analysis of the popular magazine *Bohemia*, for example, is telling. While in the early 2000s articles that focused on sexuality and sexual health had become common, in 2008 these articles also increasingly introduced issues of sexual diversity. The May 2008 edition of the magazine was the first edition to have a full article (six pages) focusing on sexual diversity. The article, titled "Diversidad sexual: Desafiando molinos," incorporated an interview with Mariela Castro Espín and described in detail the challenges as well as prejudices faced by those of nonheterosexual orientation. It was also the first time CENESEX was featured in an article, with the center's efforts to dissuade prejudice through education being described in detail (*Bohemia* 2008, 24–29).

The second annual commemoration for the International Day Against Homophobia (May 17) also occurred in 2008, increasing dramatically from the smaller commemoration the previous year into a celebration. In total, Havana and six other provinces participated, and various activities were held. Notably, the second Conference for International Day Against

Homophobia occurred "with the support of cultural institutions, student organizations, the government, the UJC [Young Communist League], and the PCC [*Partido Comunista de Cuba* (Communist Party of Cuba)]" (Castro Espín 2012, 32).

It is important to note the significance of this day for Cuba, as previously these celebrations had never been held. In addition, seven of the island's fifteen provinces participated in the celebrations, another first. Significantly, May 17 is also the anniversary of the 1959 Agrarian Reform Law, proposed and drafted by, among many others, Ernesto "Che" Guevara, which redistributed large landholdings to the landless (Kapcia 2008, 29). It has since been celebrated annually and, understandably, is an important anniversary of revolutionary history. Thus, in Cuba, the significance of the celebration of May 17 in support of an International Day Against Homophobia goes beyond support for LGBT communities; it also indicates the importance of the celebration, as considerable numbers chose to share it along with another of great histori- cal importance.

Yet, while significant change was achieved particularly throughout 2008 and 2009, much of the success was eclipsed in November 2010 at the UN General Assembly's Social, Humani- tarian, and Cultural Affairs Committee. The participating Cuban diplomats voted in favor of an amendment, suggested by Mali and Morocco, that would result in the substitution of all specific references to abuses due to "sexual orientation" with a more general "discriminatory reasons on any basis." In effect, the wording that sought to denounce homophobia would be replaced with a diluted version, weakly arguing against discrimination in general. Significant- ly, Cuba was the only Latin American country that voted in favor of the amendment (Acosta 2010a). It was clear that while changes had occurred across the island, the official Cuban position on sexual diversity was still controversial as, in this important international forum, the Cuban officials took a step backward.

Following the vote, CENESEX and SOCUMES immediately—and publicly—criticized the decision. Dr. Alberto Roque, the leading physician at CENESEX who also works closely with SOCUMES, stated, "Failure to specifically mention discrimination on the rounds of sexual orientation gives the green light for many states and government to continue to treat homosexuality as a crime" (quoted in Acosta 2010b). The public and forceful opposition to the government's official position highlights well the growing influence of the center as well as its position as a body under the aegis of the state but one enjoying a considerable level of autonomy.

Indeed, while the new leadership was working on liberalizing state control, CENESEX was continually developing a notable national and international profile as the global media gradu- ally became more interested in its achievements. Sexual diversity became the cornerstone of the center's work and would continue as they increased the numbers of related talks, lectures, films, debates, plays, and campaigns across the island.

The center has also been working to develop and ratify an updated Family Code, building on the 1975 Code, which emphasized the importance of women and promoted equal distribu- tion of household responsibilities and child care. The code was essential for the development of women's rights; however, it focused on the nuclear heterosexual family. In effect, it sug- gested that to be a good family or revolutionary, one must be in a heterosexual partnership. While it presented a narrow view of the household, it did serve to advance more progressive attitudes regarding gender identities and roles. However, it was clear that a new code was needed—one that would illustrate and legitimize diverse family models.

As a result, CENESEX, in collaboration with the FMC, the UJC, and the National Union of Cuban Jurists, submitted an amended Family Code to the National Assembly of People's Power in 2012. It focused primarily on the legal recognition of same-sex couples. Originally, same-sex marriage was a suggested modification, but due to sensitivity to cultural values, reference to "marriage" was later changed to "civil unions." In addition, sections were also added in which the rights of nonheterosexual women would be able to utilize Cuba's reproductive technologies, which have previously been reserved only for married heterosexual women. The code has not yet been seriously considered in the National Assembly, a situation that many believe to be the result of fear of the legalization of same-sex marriage (Ramírez 2007; Roque Guerra 2010; Sierra 2008). Yet, since it has been officially submitted to the National Assembly, it must legally be discussed and put to a vote (interview with Manuel Vásquez Seijido, CENESEX coordinator for the Network of Jurists for Sexual Diversity Rights, February 13, 2013, Havana). The amendments remain a continuous topic of contention as the center continues its efforts to persuade the National Assembly to incorporate diverse family structures.

CENESEX has continued to press to change the island's historically homophobic legislation. As noted by center director Mariela Castro Espín, if the rights of LGBT Cubans were not ratified, then they were in essence left unprotected by the law (Sierra 2008). For this reason, constant efforts have been made to establish a juridical presence for LGBT issues. The Penal Code, for example, has consistently proved discriminatory. While homosexuality was officially decriminalized in 1979, the previously homophobic laws were replaced with vague and thus only superficially more liberal ones, leaving many in the hands of homophobic judiciaries. One such law was the highly subjective *Ley de la peligrosidad*, under which anyone could be arrested for engaging in "dangerous" or perceived "antisocial" behavior (Bejel 2001, 106). The center has continued to work toward updating these laws through advocacy and, in particular, education. Two of the center's departments—the Juridical Department and the Department of Services, Social Networks, and Sexual Rights—deal with issues regarding the advancement of LGBT rights. The process to change the Penal Code, as is the case with the Family Code, is extremely complex. It would require the various ministries at several levels to agree with the amendments, followed by a highly involved ratification process. Thus, it is likely that several other aspects of revolutionary Cuba will also have to change before significant and meaningful amendments are made.

Indeed, and despite significant changes in national attitudes, legislation regarding sexual diversity has not changed dramatically. Yet there have been some significant developments in the PCC's official stance. An important step occurred in 2010, when former president Fidel Castro (expanding on his 1992 statement in which he declared that he was opposed to discrimination against homosexuals) publicly assumed responsibility for much of the homophobia that had occurred in Cuba in the early decades of the Revolution. He explained that the leadership's decisions were based on the pervasive climate of machismo and on the growing U.S. threats (Reuters 2010). While policy changes were not suggested, the address did function as a vital step in the development of LGBT rights and respect. It engaged new ideas regarding sexual diversity and the role of the leadership and its policy and as a result forced many to rethink what it meant to be a true revolutionary.

Further reforms within the Communist Party occurred in 2011, when the National Congress of the Communist Party made significant changes to the Party's Fundamental Principles. In particular, two sections made telling amendments. Section 54 noted that discrimination on the basis of race, religion, or sexual orientation would not be tolerated, especially for anyone working in the public sphere, participating in political organizations, or in general working for the defense of the Revolution. Similarly, section 65 stated that all media outlets and sections of the press were required to present the "reality" of Cuban diversity, including gender, skin color, religious beliefs, and sexual orientation (*Cubadebate* 2011; *El Universal* 2011). These amendments were of paramount importance for legitimizing LGBT rights and respect as well as the condemnation of homophobia as a whole. Additionally, these changes illustrate the official direction being taken by the leadership, representing another step in developing a more progressive and accepting attitude toward sexual diversity—which had previously been considered anathema to the Revolution.

It is also important to note that, while generally considered internationally to be an activist organization, the breadth of academic research the center produces and publishes in the field of sexuality is considerable. A recent study published in the journal *Sexología y Sociedad*, for example, provides a detailed analysis of the sociopolitical impacts of society on transsexuals. The findings noted that transsexual people, particularly women, largely suffered due to a combination of, among other things, the social construction of gender identity, lack of social integration and therapy, and insufficient sexual education. The study also offered possible solutions and options for self-empowerment, suggesting improved education and therapy models as well as improved familial ties in order to prevent social exclusion.

In addition, CENESEX remains an educative center, offering extensive training for students as well as the populace. Courses currently offered include a master's in sexology, a diploma in clinical sexology, a diploma in integral care for family violence, distance education, postgraduate courses for professionals, and promotional training (which is designed specifically for activists). The teaching staff includes many of the approximately forty staff members, including sexologists, psychologists, physicians, and legal experts. The center is an integral element of the Ministry of Public Health and the National Public Health Care model while maintaining its active role in progressing attitudes toward sexual diversity through education.

CONCLUSION

CENESEX has developed from its initial position as a small national group to become an internationally recognized center focusing on rights and respect for sexual diversity through education. Major achievements in Cuba have characterized the center's recent history as sexual diversity has gradually been redefined as "normal" and as celebrations for the International Day Against Homophobia have taken place, LGBT film festivals have been a success, and the understanding of sexual diversity on the whole has been discussed, while the PCC has officially incorporated sexual diversity into its Fundamental Principles. Yet significant challenges remain, as the National Assembly seems disinterested in the amended Family Code, necessary protective legislation is lacking, and some discrimination is still present.

It is important to note that the changes made in recent years are not inherently revolutionary. Indeed, while heralded for the revolutionary success that CENESEX has promoted in recent years, these changes have not been that revolutionary—many countries have adopted similar policies. Instead, what is both remarkable and revolutionary is the speed by and manner in which CENESEX has developed and established sweeping changes—which have then been widely accepted by the Cuban public. A country that had previously institutionalized and imprisoned homosexuals just a few decades earlier and that still maintains in several ways a deep-rooted *machista* attitude now hosts internationally recognized antihomophobia celebrations and campaigns. Given this context, few have accomplished what the center has done.

Yet aside from the successes and challenges facing CENESEX, the center is also telling of the Revolution as a whole. Importantly, the center's evolution contradicts the traditional understanding of Cuba as a staunch monolithic structure, often referred to in the literature as

"Castro's Cuba." Indeed, as its evolutionary process highlights—working with the Ministry of Health, the Ministry of Education, the FMC, the PCC, the Union of Young Communists, the University Student Federation, and SOCUMES—the center has evolved through a complex model of negotiations. Instead of the presupposed top-down model of change within the Revolution, the development of CENESEX incorporates significant elements of a bottom-up approach to change, vastly differing from classic understandings of revolutionary Cuba.

A new way of understanding the Revolution is developing, one in which it is understood as a complex process of negotiations rather than as an unmovable, restrictive structure (Kapcia 2008, 179; Kapcia 2009; Ludlam 2012). The evolution of CENESEX supports this contention, as it illustrates well the nature of the Revolution as a negotiative model of processes. CENESEX was developed out of a teaming of Cuban feminism and education practices and continues to evolve through comparable means to achieve change—working within the Revolution and its constructions to push the boundaries of what is—or should be—considered revolutionary. CENESEX will continue to evolve throughout these processes, developing Cuba's national understanding of sexual diversity and providing a revolutionary model for others to follow.

REFERENCES

Acosta, Dalia. 2006. "Nueva propuesta sobre diversidad sexual." *Cultura y Sociedad*, no. 1, January.

———. 2008. "Health-Cuba: Free Sex Change Operations Approved." Inter Press Service, June 6. http://ipsnews.net/news.asp?idnews= 42693 (accessed February 2, 2012).

———. 2010a. "Cuba: Foreign Ministry Explains Controversial 'Sexual Orientation' Vote to Activists." Inter Press Service, December 2. http://www.lexisnexis.com:80/uk/nexis/results/docview/docview.do?start=29&sort=BOOLEAN&format=GNBFI&risb=21_T13960687041 (accessed February 2, 2012).

———. 2010b. "Cuba: 'Sexual Orientation' Vote in UN Panel Kicks Up Controversy." Inter Press Service, December 1. http://www.lexisnexis.com:80/uk/nexis/results/docview/docview.do?start=30&sort=BOOLEAN&format=GNBFI&risb=21_T13960687041 (accessed February 2, 2012).

Bejel, Emilio. 2001. *Gay Cuban Nation*. Chicago: University of Chicago Press.

Bohemia. 2008. "Diversidad sexual: Desafiando molinos." Vol. 100, no. 11: 24–29.

Castro Espín, Mariela. 2008. "La atención a transexuales en Cuba y su inclusión en las políticas sociales." *Revista Sexología y Sociedad* 14, no. 36 (April). http://www.cenesexualidad.sld.cu/la-atencion-integral-transexuales-en-cuba-y-su-inclusion-en-las-politicas-sociales (accessed January 3, 2012).

———. 2012. "A Cuban Policy Approach to Change." *Cuban Studies* 42: 23–34.

Cubadebate. 2011. "Proyecto de documento base de la primera conferencia nacional del Partido Communista de Cuba." October 14. http://www.cubadebate.cu/noticias/2011/10/14/descargue-proyecto-de-documento-que-discutirá-conferencia-nacional-del-particdo-pdf/ (accessed November 1, 2011).

El Universal. 2011. "Bloguero cubano aplaude apertura de orientación sexual." October 17. http://www.eluniversal.com/internacional/111017/bloguero-cubano-aplaude-apertura-de-orientacion-sexual (accessed October 17, 2011).

Grogg, Patricia. 2009. "Men and Women Defend Their Sexual Orientation against Prejudice." Inter Press Service, March 31. http://www.lexisnexis.com:80/uk/nexis/results/docview/docview.do?start=51&sort=BOOLEAN&format=GNBFI&risb=21_T13967991259 (accessed February 2, 2012).

Hamilton, Carrie. 2012. *Sexual Revolutions in Cuba*. Chapel Hill: University of North Carolina Press.

Kapcia, Antoni. 2008. *Cuba in Revolution: A History since the Fifties*. London: Reaktion Books.

———. 2009. "Lessons of the Special Period." *Latin American Perspectives* 39, no. 1: 30–41.

Kirk, Emily. 2011. "Setting the Agenda for Cuban Sexuality: The Role of Cuba's CENESEX." *Canadian Journal of Latin American and Caribbean Studies* 36, no. 72: 143–63.

Krause-Fuchs, Monika. 2007. *¿Machismo? No, gracias. Cuba: Sexualidad en la revolución*. Madrid: Ediciones Ideas.

Leiner, Marvin. 1994. *Sexual Politics in Cuba*. Boulder, CO: Westview Press.

Ludlam, Steve. 2012. "Interest Representation, Participation and Power: Political Dimensions of Cuba's Economic Reforms." Paper presented at the 2012 Cuba Research Forum Conference, Nottingham, United Kingdom.

Lumsden, Ian. 1996. *Machos, Maricones and Gays: Cuba and Homosexuality*. Philadelphia: Temple University Press.

Pedroso, Aurelio. 2012. "De travesti a concejal." *Rebelión*, November 19. http://www.rebelion.org/noticia.php?id= 159404 (accessed November 19, 2012).

Ramírez, Marta. 2007. "Lesbianas por la maternidad: Del teatro a la realidad." *Cultura y Sociedad*, no. 4, April.

Reuters. 2010. "Fidel Castro Takes Blame for 1960s Gay Persecution." August 31. http://www.reuters.com/article/
    2010/08/31/us-Cuba-castro-idUSTRE67U4JE20100831 (accessed November 1, 2011).
Roque Guerra, Alberto. 2010. "Homophobia: Challenges to the Cuban Family and Society." Remarks given at the
    opening of the panel on the family and society during the observation of World Anti-Homophobia Day, 2010,
    Havana. http://www.walterlippmann.com/docs2901.html (accessed November 1, 2011).
———. 2011. "Diversidad sexual en las políticas en Cuba: Avances y Desafíos." *Revista Sexología y Sociedad* 17,
    no. 45 (April). http://www.cenesexualidad.sld.cu/diversidad-sexual-en-las-politicas-publicas-en-cuba-avances-y-
    desafios-0 (accessed January 3, 2012).
———. 2012. "Sexual Diversity in Revolutionary Times." *Cuban Studies* 42: 218–26.
Sierra, Raquel. 2008. "Diversidad sexual: Abriendo paso a la comprensión." *Cultura y Sociedad*, no. 1, January.
The Guardian. 2012. "Cuban Transsexual Elected to Public Office." http://www.guardian.co.uk/world/2012/nov/18/
    cuban-transsexual-adela-hernandez-elected (accessed November 18, 2012).
Turner, Dwayne C. 1989. "The Homosexual Sons and Daughters of the Cuban Revolution: Steps to Liberation."
    Human Mosaic 23: 60–78.

Chapter Forty-Five

Transcript of Television Interview with Mariela Castro

Amy Goodman

Goodman: Talk about the work that you're doing in Cuba.

Castro [translated]: I am the director of the National Center of Sexual Education. This is an academic center that is part of the Ministry of Public Health. Its mission is to coordinate the national program of sexual education with a multidisciplinary focus which coordinates different sectors.

Goodman: Why have you chosen to make sexuality and the politics of sexuality your issue? You, yourself are heterosexual. You're married to a man. You have three children.

Castro: This is work that my mother began with the Federation of Cuban Women. She was the one who created CENESEX. Though professionally I worked with preschool children and adolescents, as I heard about the difficulties of LGBT people, I began to sympathize with their needs and problems. Many LGBT couples chose to come to counseling sessions with me, and as I listened to them, I started to study, to find tools to be able to help them.

Goodman: You've come to the United States at an interesting time. The president, President Obama, has just endorsed same-sex marriage, marriage equality. What are your thoughts about this?

Castro: I think it's very valuable that the president of the United States speaks out publicly in favor of the rights of same-sex couples. Being the most powerful country in the world, what the president says has great influence on the rest of the world.

Goodman: Yet we do not have across-the-board law that says that same-sex marriage is accepted. And in Cuba you don't either. What are you doing in Cuba to change the laws?

Castro: In Cuba, CENESEX is leading an educational strategy, with the support of the media, to promote respect for free and responsible sexual orientation and gender identity. We are also doing some advocacy with state institutions and civil society organizations, so that they support this educational strategy. Beyond the educational strategy and our media strategy, we are also promoting legislative initiatives that suppress the same rights for homosexuals and transgender people, so that, for example, the Family Code recognizes the rights of these people and also their possibilities as couples, the legalization of their union as a couple.

Goodman: Are you pushing for same-sex marriage in Cuba?

Castro: I am promoting marriage, but this was not accepted by many groups of people. And so, what we are negotiating is the legalization of consensual unions and that the legalization of these unions would guarantee, more than anything, their property rights, inheritance rights.

Goodman: So, do same-sex couples have the same economic rights as heterosexual couples?

Castro: All rights are guaranteed for all people. There is no exclusion for LGBT people. But where there is still not respect for their rights is around the guarantee that if one member of a same-sex couple dies, the survivor be recognized as the person who should receive the inheritance, or even just be allowed to enjoy the goods they had enjoyed as a couple.

Goodman: Presumably, you have your father's ear, the president of Cuba. How does he feel about making it fully equal between same-sex couples and heterosexual couples?

Castro: He is convinced that it is necessary, that it is part of the project of full justice the Cuban Revolution proposes.

Goodman: Is he as supportive as you are?

Castro: He has been supportive since before, from when my mother was working on these issues.

Goodman: And what about gay men and lesbians in the military?

Castro: In all of Cuban society, there are all kinds of people. In the army, as well, there are homosexuals and lesbians. They don't manifest it publicly, but they are there.

Goodman: If it is known, if they are open, would they be kicked out of the military?

Castro: I see that the rules have become more flexible. Of course, before, they were more rigid. I think that in all Cuban society, the policy and laws are becoming more flexible. And the same will happen in the army.

NOTE

Television interview with Mariela Castro conducted by *Democracy Now*, June 11, 2012. Reprinted by permission of *Democracy Now*.

Chapter Forty-Six

Surfing Revolico.com

Cuba's Answer to Craig's List

John M. Kirk

Perhaps nothing offers a more immediate (and interesting) panoramic view of the changes in Cuban society in recent years than a few hours trawling through the sections of this website. It was created in 2007 and is enormously popular on the island. The website boasts 5 million visits monthly and notes that 75 percent of its traffic comes from repeat customers. Most of the client basis consists of Cubans on the island, but as a result of the approximately 400,000 members of the Cuban diaspora who visit annually, the number of postings from Cubans abroad and even from foreigners is increasing.

A small core of employees run the site, as is mentioned at Revolico.com: "We are a small but functional team of computer programmers who one day felt the need to develop a simpler, more organized and efficient way of advertising and seeing what others were advertising. The idea arose, and we decided to give it a try." What began as a small advertising venture has now grown spectacularly and is regularly consulted by Cubans with access to a computer terminal. Many thousands of advertisements appear on the site. On November 19, 2012, for instance, a note from the site's webmasters stated that 8,095 ads were on the site that day and that a staggering 292,994 commercials had been placed on the Web during the previous sixty days.

I check the website from time to time to follow trends in terms of the interests of Cuban consumers. The information provided here is for several days, selected at random, in November 2012. There are six basic categories: Computers, Automobiles, General Buy/Sell, Employment, Services, and Housing. For the day in question, the largest number of ads was in the Computer section (119,605), followed by General Buy/Sell (84,468), Housing (35,045), Services (27,771), Automobiles (25,386), and Employment (for people offering services and seeking positions, 715).

Each of the categories is subdivided into various sections to make it easier for clients to find the appropriate merchandise. As is clear, most of the subscribers to Revolico are interested in electronics. The computer section alone has nineteen subsections, including PCs, laptops, printers, hard drives, DVD burners, and sound cards. Likewise, the General Buy/Sell category has a plethora of electronic goods, including MP3 players, iPods, video games, flat-screen televisions, and Xboxes.

Some prices help to give an idea of the cost of these items. Average computers, such as HP, Toshiba, and Acer, sell for 600 CUC (convertible pesos, roughly equal to the U.S. dollar).

A Toshiba satellite C650 laptop was offered for 400 CUC; a nineteen-inch Samsung LED monitor, 180 CUC; an eight-gigabyte flash drive, 12 CUC; and a Bluetooth USB, $6. Lexmark, HP, and Canon printer cartridges could be refilled for 4 CUC. One vendor noted, "I sell new PC parts brought from abroad. Please don't bother me by quoting other prices on the Revolico site. These are brand new." Advertisements were placed by technicians offering to install Windows 7 and 8 (5 CUC) as well as antivirus software (4 CUC).

Internet connectivity is a major problem in Cuba, and several enterprising Cubans offered access through their accounts. One person offered a month of e-mail service abroad for 15 CUC; another offered twenty-four hours of Internet for 5 CUC as long as the purchaser had "an email account and the possibility of connecting abroad." Many of these accounts are illegal, often the result of enterprising Cubans hacking into legal accounts of foreign businesses or bribing government officials with Internet privileges. Many of the services offered in this regard will probably be illegal. An exception was one advertisement offering sixty hours of Internet for 120 CUC, the owner adding that "this is a legal ETECSA [the national telephone company] account." One enterprising vendor offered services for 15 CUC, adding, "Our desire is to be an oasis in the midst of the desert."

Dozens of ads offered imported television programs, mainly from the United States. One person offered a weekly recompilation ("including materials in High Definition for clients with plasma TVs") in digital format of 300 gigabytes. Among the weekly package was a collection of twenty-five to thirty-five films as well as a selection of games, shows, soap operas, cartoons, music videos, twenty to forty documentaries, classic films, and sports (soccer, baseball, and boxing), comedy, and reality shows. Another offered for 1 CUC a wide selection of popular television shows, including *Miss Marple*, *American Idol*, *Boston Legal*, *Cold Case*, *Criminal Minds*, *CSI* (the Miami, Las Vegas, and New York series), *Downton Abbey*, *Grey's Anatomy*, *Dancing with the Stars US*, *Law and Order*, *The Good Wife*, *The Mentalist*, and *NCIS*.

Under the government of Raúl Castro, two of the major reforms now allow the buying and selling of homes and vehicles—for the first time in five decades. Popular media in North America have largely forgotten about these reforms now that the novelty has worn off. In Cuba, however, fierce negotiations take place over the prices for both these categories, and Cubans have learned quickly the need to be shrewd bargainers. The prices for cars seem high to the North American reader, but in Cuba—where for decades access to hard currency has not meant that one could go down to the local car showroom and buy a car—this is a major development.

Foreign journalists in Cuba often refer to the approximately $20 that represents the average monthly wage in Cuba. As this book illustrates, nothing is ever as it seems in Cuba since there are so many exceptions to every rule. And while many people do get by on minimum salaries, others have other, lucrative sources of income. As a result, a vigorous business exists of selling cars. It is generally a seller's market since demand far outstrips supply. Some examples are worth noting. A 1990 VW Jetta, for instance, is offered for 17,500 CUC, a 2006 Lada is offered for 16,500 CUC, and a 2009 Mazda 6 "American model," fully loaded (with air conditioning, heating, and independent climate controls among a long list of features), is offered for 80,000 CUC ("In the last analysis we're talking about a tremendous luxury car," notes the ad).

Part of the charm of Cuba is to see the older prerevolutionary American cars, a surprising number of which are still working. Their prices are high since they are used as working transportation vehicles. A 1952 Plymouth (complete with Toyota brakes and a reconditioned Renault engine) is on sale for 13,000 CUC. A 1957 Chevrolet (with a Mitsubishi engine and a

Hyundai gearbox) is on sale for 18,000. One keen vendor offers his 1953 Ford for 13,800 CUC, noting that it has a Russian (Volga) gearbox and radiator, German engine, and Toyota suspension. He notes that he easily makes 40 CUC as a *botero*, or private taxi driver ("and so in a year you can recoup your investment").

Numerous services are offered by Cubans to act as personal chauffeurs. One particularly adept salesman focused his advertisement on returning members of the Cuban diaspora (400,000 Cuban Americans return to the island annually): "Esteemed Visitor, You are returning after being abroad for some time to visit your family members and friends. . . . I recommend that you return to your barrio in classic American car, something which will provide a touch of distinction to your visit."

Another intriguing ad featured a company called SEATAXI, which is owned by a group of former pilots. They have several cars to drive clients around on a twenty-four-hour basis ("We are not bothered by getting up early in the morning," they note). They charge a daily rate of 50 CUC for one to ten days, 40 for eleven to twenty days, and 30 CUC for longer periods. One intriguing feature of their service is the "VIP treatment" they offer at airports, clearly because of their many years working there as pilots. For 25 CUC, clients can be met as they leave the plane and taken to the VIP lounge, where they can have a drink and wait for their luggage. They will be given preference in the Immigration and Customs lineups and can be spirited through the airport process. In a revolutionary socialist country like Cuba, this service would have been unthinkable a few years ago.

Two of the most popular categories of employment revolve around the professions of taxi driving and working in a *paladar*, or private restaurant. One ad is from the owner of a 1950 Chevrolet who was looking for someone to rent it as a taxi driver. He noted frankly, "The deal is simple: You will pay me 800 Cuban pesos—about $38—daily, and whatever else you make above this will be yours. You will have to buy the gas, and you can have the car between 7am and 6pm."

In terms of employment, two advertisements illustrate clearly the "new Cuba." One is from a twenty-two-year-old, a graduate in physical education who is well mannered and responsible. She is looking for a well-paid position and is prepared to pay 300 CUC to obtain one. Another advertisement is worth noting. A twenty-three-year-old woman placed an ad looking for a job in a *paladar*. She wrote that she was "attractive, with good work habits and was very responsible." She claimed to speak "almost six languages" and was respectful and organized. In addition, she noted that she had "a European capitalist mentality"—a claim that she would never have made even a few years earlier. The two young women who were looking for well-paid positions are typical of many young Cubans who grew up in the worst years of the "Special Period" and could not have helped being influenced by those very difficult years.

An advertisement that would also been inconceivable in recent years is from a person offering services to walk dogs and to look after them "while the client enjoys their vacation." The rise of prostitution during the early years of the Special Period has now largely decreased. Still, it is not rare to see foreign tourists accompanying Cubans (usually significantly younger) and paying them for services rendered. One ad was placed by a twenty-seven-year-old man who offered his "services to accompany women up to the age of 45." He noted that he was in excellent physical shape and offered his services for 20 CUC. He noted, however, that the ad was directed "only at people over 18," emphasizing the dubious nature of his interest. Sadly, the occasional advertisement also appears along the lines of a forty-five-year-old Frenchman who described himself as "well endowed and very hot." His sales pitch was brutally direct: he was looking for women from eighteen to fifty-five who possessed lots of body hair and would be prepared to participate in a number of sexual acts in return for a "financial arrangement."

One of the major reforms introduced by Raúl Castro made it legal for Cubans and foreign residents to buy and sell housing, a policy that had been impossible for some fifty years. It was a major development and has resulted in a flurry of advertisements on Revolico. Prices vary greatly, ranging from 6,000 CUC (for a two-bedroom house in Guantánamo) to 350,000 CUC for a four-bedroom house with three bathrooms, two kitchens, three terraces, and many fruit trees.

A final smattering of advertisements from the broader, more general category offers an almost surreal collection of goods and services. In no particular order, some of the great variety of goods offered include a case of twelve bottles of "excellent wine" for 12 CUC; pirated CDs of music, recorded to reflect the client's tastes, for 1 CUC; all kinds of medicines imported from the United States, ranging from Centrum multivitamin pills (17 CUC for 100 capsules) to Afrin nasal spray (30 milliliters for 8 CUC); pizza boxes (thirty by thirty centimeters) for 15 cents each; Rosetta Stone language program CDs for 10 CUC; silicone breasts ("made of cohesive gel, the latest models, both smooth and texturized") for 600 CUC; Great Dane puppies for 300 CUC; and piglets for 20 CUC. As can be expected, this "grab bag" of thousands of advertisements covers an enormous variety of goods and services.

So what lessons can be learned about Cuba today from consulting this website? Revolico.com, which has been in existence only since 2007, provides a popular service for many Cubans. It also illustrates clearly just how Cuba has changed in recent years since the public advertisements for many of these goods and services would have been illegal just a few years ago. Cuba has changed enormously since the Special Period was initiated but to an exceptional degree since Raúl Castro has come to power. Is this change for the better? That is, of course, for the reader to determine. Many of the features of contemporary Cuban society are welcome changes from the past. At the same time, the somewhat crass materialism is disappointing. In many ways, Cuba is emerging from the cocoon in which it was carefully isolated from the rest of the world and is in the process of being "Latin Americanized," along with the bootleg CDs, the street peddlers, and the plethora of private services being offered. What is also clear is that there is no going back for post-Fidel Cuba as Cubans take advantage of the reforms introduced by Raúl, for better or worse.

Cuba Chronology

2006–2013

2006

July 10: President Bush's Commission for Assistance to a Free Cuba issues its second report, recommending increased enforcement of the U.S. embargo and calling for an $80 million fund "to increase support for Cuban civil society."

July 31: As a result of major intestinal surgery, Cuban leader Fidel Castro "temporarily" turns over his responsibilities to six officials. Vice President Raúl Castro assumes the leadership of Cuba's Communist Party and becomes acting president of the Council of State.

September 11–16: Cuba hosts the fourteenth summit of the 118-nation Non-Aligned Movement (NAM) and becomes the chair of the NAM for the next three years. Castro is not well enough to attend the NAM summit or ceremonies in December to mark his eightieth birthday.

October 31: Cuba reports an economic growth rate in 2005 of 11.8 percent, based on measures that include estimates of the market value of free social services in Cuba and medical services exported to Venezuela and Bolivia. Cuba has deployed more than 30,000 medical personnel to South America.

2007

January: Former head of the National Cultural Council Luis Pavón Tamayo (1971–1976) appears on Cuban television, sparking fears within the Cuban cultural community about a return to the dark days of censorship on the island known as the *quinquenio gris* (gray period). Prominent members of the Cuban Union of Writers and Artists (UNEAC) respond publicly, denouncing the censorship and persecution of artists in the past and calling for debate about the role of culture within the Cuban Revolution. Minister of Culture Abel Prieto calls the television appearance a mistake and assures UNEAC that no change in cultural policy is being contemplated.

May: Cuba celebrates its first International Day Against Homophobia, with Mariela Castro, daughter of Raúl Castro, presiding. The celebration marks a major departure from the past and places Cuba at the forefront of initiatives regarding rights for lesbian, gay, bisexual, and transgender individuals in the Americas.

July: Fidel Castro does not appear at the annual July 26 celebration commemorating the start of the Revolution. Speaking in Fidel's place, Raúl Castro indicates Cuba's willingness to improve relations with the United States. He offers to engage in talks after the 2008 U.S. presidential election.

2008

February 24: Cuba's National Assembly formally elects Raúl Castro to serve as president of the Council of State, making him the official head of state. It also elects seventy-seven-year-old José Ramón Machado as first vice president of the Council of State.

March: Raúl Castro lifts restrictions on the purchase of mobile phones and computers and the ability of Cubans to stay in tourist hotels and rent cars.

July: In an effort to spur food production and reduce Cuba's importation of food, the government announces that it will lease fallow land to private farmers and reduce restrictions on the free market sales of produce.

August: A new labor law allows greater salary disparities by lifting the salary ceiling on highly skilled jobs, a departure from the emphasis on wage equality in place since the start of the Revolution.

August–September: Hurricanes Gustav and Ike cause the worst storm damage in the nation's history; 200,000 Cubans are left homeless. The storms destroyed 25,900 metric tons of agricultural crops, including 50 percent of the sugar crop, 90 percent of the tobacco crop, and 80 percent of the plantain and banana crop.

October: The European Union restores economic aid, including emergency hurricane recovery aid of more than $2.6 million in 2008 and $38.9 million in 2009. Aid programs had been cut five years earlier after Cuban authorities arrested more than sixty outspoken critics of the government and charged them with receiving material support from the U.S. government. Their sentences initially ranged to a high of twenty-seven years.

November: President Dmitry Medvedev of Russia and Hu Jintao of China visit to conclude trade and investment accords with Cuba. China agrees to purchase Cuban nickel and sugar. Their visits are signs of strengthened relations with both countries. Raúl Castro pays a reciprocal visit to Russia in January 2009.

December: A poll by the Institute for Public Opinion Research at Florida International University finds that 55 percent of Cuban Americans living in Miami want an end to the U.S. embargo. This is the first time that a majority of Cuban Americans have been in favor of ending the embargo since polling began in 1991.

2009

March: Cabinet Secretary Carlos Lage and Foreign Minister Felipe Pérez-Roque, former close aides to Fidel Castro, resign after admitting "errors." Their departure, along with six other officials, is the first major change in senior government officials since Raúl Castro's election as president.

April: In advance of the Summit of the Americas, U.S. President Barack Obama asserts that he wants a "fresh start" with Cuba, lifting all restrictions on family travel and remittances to Cuba for Cuban Americans.

June: Despite opposition by the United States, the Organization of American States votes to start a process to restore Cuba's membership, which the organization suspended in 1962. Cuba responds that it has no intention to resume active membership and plans instead to engage with regional organizations in which the United States does not participate.

Costa Rica and El Salvador establish diplomatic relations with Cuba, leaving the United States as the only country in the Western Hemisphere that does not formally recognize the Cuban government.

August: Raúl Castro announces the creation of an Office of Comptroller General to improve fiscal discipline and fight corruption. He also declares that Cuba can no longer afford all the free services and subsidies of consumer goods the government has provided in the past.

September: Colombian singer and Miami resident Juanes holds a concert in Havana's Plaza of the Revolution, drawing hundreds of thousands of fans. Approval of the concert by both the U.S. and the Cuban government signals greater receptivity to cultural exchanges.

December: Cuban authorities arrest Alan P. Gross, a USAID subcontractor, charging him with committing "acts against the integrity or territorial independence of the state" by installing sophisticated satellite communications transmitters, which may have included the capability of preventing detection of its signals for a radius of 250 miles. Gross and the State Department claimed that his goal was to provide Cuba's Jewish community with equipment that would enable its members to access the Internet without Cuban government interference.

2010

March: The new film by Fernando Pérez *El Ojo del Canario* (The Eye of the Canary) controversially depicts the childhood of Cuban revolutionary icon José Martí as that of a typical and, at times, troubled adolescent.

April: In a speech to the Congress of Young Communists, Raúl Castro asserts that the state payroll is inflated by as many as 1 million workers. He declares, "The Revolution will not leave anyone helpless . . . but this does not mean that the State will be responsible for providing a job to everyone."

May: After the intervention of Cardinal Jaime Lucas Ortega y Alamino, Raúl Castro agrees to allow the dissident group "Ladies in White," originally composed of the wives and mothers of political prisoners, to hold regular demonstrations.

July: Following discussions with Cardinal Ortega and Spain's foreign minister, President Castro agrees to free 166 political prisoners, including all of those still in jail as a result of the 2003 arrest of critics who were subsequently convicted of illegally accepting U.S. government funds.

September: The Cuban government announces plans to cut over 1 million state sector jobs, 500,000 of them in the next six months, and relaxes restrictions on self-employment and small businesses. Analysts see these measures as a shift toward an increasing acceptance of the private sector.

November: Raúl Castro's plans for economic reform on the island are unveiled with the distribution of the "Guidelines of the Economic and Social Policy of the Party and the Revolution," which outline 291 proposals for reform. After widespread public discussions, a revised version is approved at the 2011 Communist Party Congress.

The American Ballet Theatre performs in Cuba for the first time in fifty years.

2011

January: U.S. President Barack Obama relaxes restrictions on travel to Cuba for academic, religious, cultural, and educational purposes. In addition, U.S. citizens are permitted to send limited amounts of money to Cubans, though tourist travel remains prohibited.

February: An underwater fiber-optic cable, financed by the government of Venezuela and intended to increase Internet access in Cuba, finally reaches the island. Once operational, the cable would help Cuba overcome its status as the country in Latin America and the Caribbean with the lowest Internet access.

March: Former President Jimmy Carter travels to Cuba, meets with Raúl Castro, but is unsuccessful in obtaining a commutation of Alan Gross's sentence.

April: The Communist Party of Cuba holds its Sixth Congress, the first in fourteen years, and approves the "Guidelines of the Economic and Social Policy of the Party and the Revolution." The party also endorses term limits for all party and government leadership positions.

August: Hoping to further encourage private enterprise and improve productivity in the state sector, the National Assembly approves several economic reforms aimed at decreasing the state's role in the retail and service sectors and promoting private small businesses and cooperatives. Plans include the elimination of state subsidies and an increase in state wages.

October: René González, one of the "Cuban Five," is released on parole from a Florida jail but is required to remain in the United States. The Five are Cuban intelligence officers who were given long prison terms in 2001 after being convicted of conspiracy to commit espionage and murder. The Cuban government asserted that their mission was to monitor Cuban exile groups in South Florida that had engaged in acts of terrorism against Cuba.

September–November: The Cuban government allows individuals to buy and sell houses and automobiles directly to one another for the first time in fifty years.

December: Ahead of a papal visit by Pope Benedict XVI, authorities release 2,500 prisoners, including some convicted of political crimes.

Cuba's first zombie film, *Juan de los Muertos* (Juan of the Dead), wins the prize for the most popular film at Havana's international film festival. In February 2013, it receives the Goya Award for the best Latin American film.

2012

January: The Communist Party of Cuba holds its first National Conference, at which Raúl Castro calls for the promotion of youth, women, and Cubans of African origin into positions of leadership.

March 26: Pope Benedict XVI visits Cuba, where he calls for greater religious and political freedoms and meets with both Fidel and Raúl Castro. The pope condemns the U.S. embargo against Cuba, lamenting the "restrictive economic measures, imposed from outside the country, [which] unfairly burden its people."

April: The Sixth Summit of the Americas in Cartagena, Colombia, ends without a final communiqué. Several Latin American presidents declare that they will not attend another summit unless Cuba is included. The United States and Canada had blocked the proposal to invite Cuba to the next summit.

October: The government announces that land has been distributed to 170,000 private farmers. The land is leased to them for a ten-year period.

October 25: Hurricane Sandy makes landfall in eastern Cuba, killing eleven people, damaging 230,000 homes, and causing more than $2 billion in economic damages. It is the deadliest hurricane to hit Cuba since 2005, when Hurricane Dennis killed sixteen people.

November: The Scarabeo 9 deep-water oil-drilling rig is removed from Cuban waters. Intended to probe for oil deposits as far down as seven miles, the rig's departure places on hold Cuba's hopes of tapping an estimated 20 billion barrels of crude oil reserves.

As a result of Cuban efforts earlier in the year, the Colombian government and the Revolutionary Armed Force of Colombia (a guerrilla group engaged in armed struggle against the government since the 1960s) begin peace talks in Havana.

December: Venezuelan President Hugo Chávez flies to Cuba for major cancer surgery.

Cuba's National Symphony Orchestra ends a monthlong tour of the United States after giving some twenty concerts.

2013

January: Raúl Castro assumes the presidency of the Community of Latin American and Caribbean States, an organization of all the countries in the Western Hemisphere except the United States and Canada.

Telesur, the Latin American television channel based in Venezuela, starts daily broadcasts to Cuba, offering an alternative to Cuba's state-run television.

The Cuban government eliminates the "*tarjeta blanca*," an exit permit required any time a Cuban wishes to travel outside the island. In the future, Cubans with a legal passport will be able to travel freely.

February: Cuba's National Assembly reelects Raúl Castro as president of the Council of State. He declares that this five-year term as president will be his last, and he endorses the election of fifty-one-year-old Miguel Díaz-Canel Bermúdez as first vice president, placing a leader born after 1959 in the direct line of political succession for the first time.

At the Havana Book Fair, copies of Heberto Padilla's works are sold openly for the first time since 1971. The poet had left the island in 1980. He served thirty-seven days in prison in 1971, and the government subsequently banned his poetry and plays because of their "counter-revolutionary character."

Leonardo Padura receives the National Prize for Literature. A popular Cuban novelist, his works go to the edge of acceptable criticism in highlighting official corruption and hypocrisy.

March: President Hugo Chávez of Venezuela, Cuba's most ardent supporter in Latin America, dies after a long battle with cancer. His successor, Nicolás Maduro, pledges to maintain Venezuelan ties to Cuba.

June: Cuba opens 118 Internet cafés across the island, promising more in the future. Previously, Cubans could connect to the Internet only through work or school or at tourist hotels.

Cuba authorizes two baseball players to play in the professional Mexican league. The government also agrees to return to the Caribbean Series, a tournament of professional teams that Cuba left in 1960.

July: The United States agrees to resume immigration talks with Cuba, frozen for two years because of the imprisonment of Alan Gross.

Panama detains a North Korean freighter illegally carrying hidden Cuban military equipment (a Soviet-era missile radar system and fighter jets) through the Panama Canal. Cuba claims that the equipment was to be repaired in North Korea and then returned.

The government announces that there were 429,458 self-employed workers (up from 143,000 in late 2010).

October: The UN General Assembly condemns the U.S. embargo against Cuba by a vote of 188–2 with three abstentions. This was the twenty-second year in a row that the General Assembly has voted against the U.S. sanctions.

Index

About the Editors and Contributors

Philip Brenner is professor of international relations and affiliate professor of history at American University. He is the coauthor of *Cuba's Quest for Sovereignty: A Five Hundred Year History* (forthcoming) and *Sad and Luminous Days: Cuba's Struggle with the Superpowers after the Missile Crisis* (2002) and coeditor of *The Cuba Reader: The Making of a Revolutionary Society* (1988). A specialist on U.S. foreign policy toward Latin America, Dr. Brenner is a member of the board of directors of the Center for International Policy and the advisory boards of the National Security Archive and Center for Democracy in the Americas.

Marguerite Rose Jiménez teaches public policy in the Department of Public Administration and Policy at American University's School of Public Affairs. Her research focuses on public health history, vaccine diplomacy, and global health and development, particularly in Latin America and the Caribbean. She has published several articles on international medical cooperation, the Cuban economy, and U.S.-Cuban relations.

John M. Kirk is professor of Spanish and Latin American studies at Dalhousie University in Halifax, Nova Scotia, Canada. He has been traveling to Cuba since 1976 and has written and coedited several books about Cuba, José Martí, Cuban foreign relations, culture, and the Cuban development model. For the past seven years, he has been working on Cuban medical internationalism and is the coauthor of *Cuban Medical Internationalism: Origins, Evolution, and Goals* (2009). He is just finishing a second book on the topic. He is the editor of the Contemporary Cuba series with the University Press of Florida.

William M. LeoGrande is professor of government in the School of Public Affairs at American University in Washington, DC. He is the author of *Our Own Backyard: The United States in Central America, 1977–1992* (1998) and *Cuba's Policy in Africa* (1980), coauthor of *Back Channel to Cuba: The Hidden History of Negotiations between Washington and Havana* (2014) and *Confronting Revolution: Security through Diplomacy in Central America* (1986), and coeditor of *The Cuba Reader: The Making of a Revolutionary Society* (1988), and *Political Parties and Democracy in Central America* (1992). He has written widely in the field of Latin American politics and U.S. policy toward Latin America, with a particular emphasis on Central America and Cuba, with articles appearing in *Foreign Affairs*, *Foreign Policy*, *New*

Republic, the *New York Times*, the *Washington Post*, the *Los Angeles Times*, the *Miami Herald*, *Le Monde Diplomatique*, and other journals and newspapers.

CONTRIBUTORS

Carlos Alzugaray Treto is a former Cuban diplomat who currently serves as book review editor of the Cuban journal *Temas*. He has been vice rector of the Instituto Superior de Relaciones Internacionales; a senior scholar at the University of Havana's Center for the Study of the United States; a visiting professor at Beloit College, the University of Winnipeg, and the City University of New York; and a visiting scholar at American University, the European University Institute, and the University of the Basque Country. He is author of *Crónica de un fracaso imperial* (2000) and coauthor of *La integración política latinoamericana y caribeña: Un proyecto comunitario para el siglo XXI* (2001). His articles on U.S.-Cuban relations, Cuban foreign policy, and international affairs have appeared in journals and anthologies published in Cuba, North America, South America, Europe, and Asia.

Denise Blum is associate professor in social foundations at the School of Educational Studies at Oklahoma State University. She is an educational anthropologist and the author of *Cuban Youth and Revolutionary Values: Educating the New Socialist Citizen* (2011) and coeditor of *Globalization and Corporatization of Education: Limits and Liminality of the Market Mantra* (2014). Her research incorporates a political-economic approach while studying social and cultural issues related to schooling and identity.

Michael J. Bustamante is a PhD candidate in Latin American and Caribbean history at Yale University and a former research associate for Latin America Studies at the Council on Foreign Relations. He has published articles in *Foreign Affairs*, *Current History*, and the *Wilson Quarterly*, among others.

Marce Cameron is a journalist and the coordinator of the Australian Youth-Student Revolutionary Tour of Cuba and Venezuela as well as the membership secretary of the Australia-Cuba Friendship Society.

Mariela Castro Espín is director of the Cuban National Center for Sex Education (CENES-EX) and a global leader in the movement for LGBT rights. She is the president of the Cuban Multidisciplinary Centre for the Study of Sexuality, president of the National Commission for Treatment of Disturbances of Gender Identity, and director of the journal *Sexología y Sociedad*.

Soraya M. Castro Mariño is professor and senior researcher at the Center for the Study of International Politics, Institute of International Relations, Cuba. She previously was a professor at Havana University. She is the coeditor most recently of *Fifty Years of Revolution: Perspectives on Cuba, the United States, and the World* (2012). She also coedited issue 41 of *Cuban Studies* (2010), coedited and contributed to *Estados Unidos y América Latina. Los Nuevos Desafíos: ¿Unión o Desunión?* (2007), coauthored *Retreat from Reason: U.S.-Cuban Academic Relations and the Bush Administration* (2006), and coauthored *EEUU: Dinámica Interna y Política Exterior* (2003). She has published numerous articles in journals and chapters in books on U.S.-Cuban relations, U.S foreign policy, and the U.S. foreign policymaking process.

María Auxiliadora César is the coordinator of the Center of Cuban Studies at the University of Brasilia and a research associate in the Social Service Department. A trained sociologist and social assistant, her research has focused on social policies and their impact on well-being and gender.

Armando Chaguaceda is a Cuban historian and political scientist who specializes in Latin American politics. He is a member of the Institute of Historico-Social Research at the University of Havana and of the Social Observatory of Latin America and the coordinator of the working group Anticapitalisms and Emergent Sociabilities of the Latin American Council of Social Sciences (CLACSO) and an adjunct professor at the University of Veracruz. He is the author and editor of various texts, including *Democracy, Participation, and Citizenship: Latin American Perspectives* (2008).

Margaret E. Crahan is senior research scholar and Director of the Cuba Program at the Institute for Latin American Studies at Columbia University. She has held the Kozmetsky Distinguished Professorship at St. Edward's University, the Dorothy Epstein Chair at Hunter College, and the Henry R. Luce Chair at Occidental College. She is a member of the Board of Trustees of St. Edward's University, vice president of the Inter-American Institute of Human Rights, and a board member of the Latin American Program at the Woodrow Wilson Center. She is the author, editor, or coeditor of more than 100 books and articles, including *Religion, Culture and Society: The Case of Cuba* (2011), *The Wars on Terrorism and Iraq: Human Rights, Unilateralism, and U.S. Foreign Policy* (2004), and *Human Rights and Basic Human Needs in the Americas* (1982).

Simon C. Darnell is assistant professor in the Faculty of Kinesiology and Physical Education at the University of Toronto in Canada. He was a research fellow at the Department of International Development Studies at Dalhousie University and has worked with the Commonwealth Advisory Board on Sport.

Antonio Aja Díaz is a professor, researcher, and director at the University of Havana's Centro de Estudios Demográficos and the director of the Program on the Study of Latinos in the United States at Casa de las Américas. He has been a visiting scholar and professor at universities in Canada, France, Mexico, Puerto Rico, the United States, and Venezuela. He is the coauthor of *Cuba y Cayo Hueso: Una historia compartida* (2006) and author of *Al cruzar las fronteras* (2009).

Jorge I. Domínguez is the Antonio Madero Professor for the Study of Mexico and vice provost for international affairs at Harvard University. He currently serves on the editorial boards of *Political Science Quarterly, Foreign Affairs Latinoamérica, Cuban Studies, Foro internacional,* and *Journal of Cold War Studies* and has been director of Harvard's Weatherhead Center for International Affairs and president of the Latin American Studies Association. He is the author or editor of dozens of books and articles, including *Democratic Politics in Latin America and the Caribbean* (1998) and *Between Compliance and Conflict: East Asia, Latin America, the "New" Pax Americana* (2005), and is coeditor of *Cuban Economic and Social Development: Policy Reforms and Challenges in the 21st Century* (2012).

María Isabel Domínguez is associate professor and scientific director of the Psychological and Sociological Research Center in Havana, Cuba, where she specializes in themes related to youth and generations. She holds a PhD in sociology from the Cuban Academy of Sciences.

Tracey Eaton is assistant professor of journalism at Flagler College, heads the investigative Cuba Money Project, and writes the blog *Along the Malecón.* A former Fulbright scholar, he has been the Cuba bureau chief and Mexico bureau chief for the *Dallas Morning News*, metropolitan editor of the *Houston Chronicle*, and a staff writer for the *Miami Herald.*

H. Michael Erisman is emeritus professor of international politics and Latin America at Indiana State University in Terre Haute. He is the coauthor of *Cuban Medical Internationalism: Origins, Evolution, and Goals* (2009) and coeditor of *Cuban Foreign Policy Confronts a New International Order* (1991) and *Redefining Cuban Foreign Policy: The Impact of the "Special Period"* (2006). His extensive work on Cuba's foreign relations also includes *Cuba's International Relations: The Anatomy of a Nationalistic Foreign Policy* (1985) and *Cuba's Foreign Relations in a Post-Soviet World* (2000).

Richard E. Feinberg is professor of international political economy at the University of California, San Diego, and the book reviewer for the Western Hemisphere section of *Foreign Affairs* magazine. He served as a special assistant for national security affairs and the senior director of the Office of Inter-American Affairs under President Bill Clinton. He previously served as president of the Inter-American Dialogue and executive vice president of the Overseas Development Council. He has authored more than 200 articles, monographs, and books, including *Soft Landing in Cuba? Emerging Entrepreneurs and Middle Classes* (2013).

Reina Fleitas Ruiz is professor at the University of Havana. She received her doctorate from the University of Havana and is the coeditor of *Desarollo humano local: Una antología* (2004).

Edmundo García is a Cuban artist who lives in Miami and produces the radio program *La Noche se Mueve.* He is a frequent commentator about the work of Cuban exile writers and artists.

Kevin Gatter is completing a master's degree in comparative and regional studies at American University and is a staff member of American University's Center for Latin American and Latino Studies. He has done research on Easter Island's independence movement and is interested in issues about race and ethnicity in the Americas.

Graciela González Olmedo is a professor of sociology at the University of Havana. She has written widely on the impact that social change has had on women, including research on prostitution, and she is working on a major project about the role of women in Cuban society in the twenty-first century.

Conner Gorry has been writing guidebooks since 1998 and moved to Cuba a few years later. She is a coauthor of *Lonely Planet: South America on a Shoestring* (2002). She has written extensively on public health matters in Cuba and works for MEDICC in Havana.

Katrin Hansing is associate professor of sociology and anthropology at Baruch College in New York. Prior to her tenure at Baruch, she was the associate director of the Cuban Research Institute at Florida International University in Miami. She is the author of numerous publications, including the book *Rasta, Race, and Revolution: The Emergence and Development of the Rastafari Movement in Socialist Cuba* (2006), and recently completed her first documentary film, *Freddy Ilanga: Che's Swahili Translator* about Cuban-African relations.

Adrian H. Hearn is convenor of international relations at the University of Sydney China Studies Centre. His research examines the social challenges and opportunities arising from Asia-Pacific economic integration. He has explored these questions in collaboration with the German Institute of Global and Area Studies, AusAID, the Chinese Academy of Social Sciences, and others. He is a coeditor of *China Engages Latin America: Tracing the Trajectory* (2011) and author of *Cuba: Religion, Social Capital, and Development* (2008).

Ted A. Henken is professor of Latin American studies and sociology at Baruch College, City University of New York. He is the president of the Association for the Study of the Cuban Economy (2012–2014). He is the coauthor of *Small Enterprise and Public Policy in Revolutionary Cuba* (2014) and the coeditor of *Cuba in Focus* (2013). He has published articles on Cuba in *Cuban Studies, Latin American Research Review, Latino Studies, Encuentro de la Cultura Cubana*, and *Cuba in Transition* and articles about the Cuban blogosphere in *Nueva Sociedad* and *Espacio Laical*.

Rafael Hernández is senior research fellow at the Centro de Investigación y Desarrollo de la Cultura Cubana "Juan Marinello" and the editor of *Temas*, a Cuban quarterly in the field of social sciences and the humanities. He has taught at the University of Havana and as a visiting professor at Harvard University and Columbia University. He is the coauthor of *Looking at Cuba* (2003) and *The History of Havana* (2008) and coeditor of *Debating U.S.-Cuban Relations* (2012).

Monica Hirst is professor in the Department of Economics and Administration at Quilmes National University and professor of international relations at Torcuato Di Tella University, both in Buenos Aires. She served as chief researcher for the International Relations Program of FLACSO-Argentina for fifteen years and has been a consultant to the UN Development Program and the Ford Foundation. Her books include *Crisis del estado e intervención internacional* (2009), *The United States and Brazil* (1994), and *Democracia, seguridad, e integración: América Latina en un mundo en transición* (1996).

Robert Huish is assistant professor in the Department of International Development Studies at Dalhousie University in Canada. He is the author of *Where No Doctor Has Gone Before: Cuba's Place in the Global Health Landscape* (2013) and coeditor of *Globetrotting or Global Citizenship: Perils and Potential of International Experiential Learning* (2014). His research focuses on community-based health advocacy and the impacts of Cuban medical internationalism as a counterhegemonic force in the global South.

Antoni Kapcia is professor of Latin American history and director of the Centre for Research on Cuba at the University of Nottingham. He is the author of *Cuba in Revolution: A History since the Fifties* (2008), *Havana: The Making of Cuban Culture* (2005), and *Cuba: Island of*

Dreams (2001); coauthor of *Literary Culture in Cuba: Revolution, Nation-Building and the Book* (2012); and coeditor of *The Changing Dynamic of Cuban Civil Society* (2008).

C. William Keck is editor in chief of the journal *MEDICC Review*, professor emeritus in the Department of Family and Community Medicine at the Northeast Ohio Medical University, and adjunct professor of family medicine at Case Western Reserve University School of Medicine. A former director of health for the City of Akron, Ohio, he serves as chair of the Council on Linkages, a national organization that works to establish and strengthen linkages between academia and public health practice. He is the coeditor of *Principles of Public Health Practice* (2009).

Emily J. Kirk is a doctoral candidate at the University of Nottingham, where she is the curator of the Hennessy Collection at the Centre for Research on Cuba. Her current research focuses on CENESEX, and she has published articles on this and on Cuban medical internationalism in the *Canadian Journal of Latin American and Caribbean Studies*, *Cuban Studies*, and *Cubadebate*.

Hal Klepak is professor emeritus of history and strategy at the Royal Military College of Canada. He serves as consultant on inter-American security affairs to the Commander of the Canadian Army and in a series of posts as consultant to the Canadian foreign and defense ministries, international organizations, and academic boards. He is the author of *Raúl Castro and Cuba: A Military Story* (2012), *Cuba's Military 1990–2005, Revolutionary Soldiers in Counter-Revolutionary Times* (2005), and *Natural Allies? Canadian and Mexican Views on International Security* (1996).

Sinan Koont is emeritus professor of economics at Dickinson College, where he helped to develop and then taught a novel multidisciplinary course, "Cuba," which included a three-week student program in Cuba. He is the author of *Sustainable Urban Agriculture in Cuba* (2011).

Par Kumaraswami is lecturer in Latin American cultural studies and the codirector of the Centre for Latin American and Caribbean Studies at the University of Manchester, England. A specialist on Cuban cultural policy, especially with respect to literature, he is the coauthor of *Literary Culture in Cuba: Revolution, Nation-Building and the Book* (2012) and coeditor of *Rethinking the Cuban Revolution Nationally and Regionally* (2012) and *Making Waves* (2008).

Saul Landau was a columnist for *Progreso Weekly* and vice chair of the board of the Institute for Policy Studies when he died in 2013. He had been a professor of digital media at California State Polytechnic University and a visiting professor at American University. The author of more than twenty books and producer/director of more than forty films, he was the recipient of numerous awards, including the Letelier-Moffitt Human Rights Award, the George Polk Award for Investigative Reporting, an Emmy (for *Paul Jacobs and the Nuclear Gang*), and the Bernardo O'Higgins Award, the highest honor the Chilean government bestows on a noncitizen, for his work to help restore democracy to Chile. His film *Will the Real Terrorist Please Stand Up?* (2012) is a history of the U.S. terror campaign against Cuba that provides a context for his chapter on the Cuban Five.

Sandra Levinson is a scholar-activist who is a leading authority on Cuban culture. She helped to found the Center for Cuban Studies in New York in 1972 and serves as its executive director and curator of the Center's Cuban Art Space, which collects and displays Cuban art, photographs, and posters. A contributor to many newspapers and journals, she was an editor of *Ramparts Magazine* and has taught at universities in New York City.

Esteban Morales is a political economist who has focused on the challenges for small countries in the Western Hemisphere and on issues related to race. As a professor at the University of Havana, he served for eighteen years as the director of the Center for the Study of the United States. He is the author of *Race in Cuba: Essays on the Revolution and Racial Inequality* (2013), coauthor of *United States-Cuban Relations: A Critical History* (2008), and coeditor of *Subject to Solution: Problems in US-Cuban Relations* (1989). His coauthored 2011 study *De la confrontación a los intentos de "normalización": La política de los Estados Unidos hacia Cuba"* received the Premio Anual de la Crítica Científico-Técnica from the Cuban Book Institute.

Nancy Morejón is one of Cuba's most renowned poets who has published more than a dozen collections of poetry. Her work has centered on the themes of the Afro-Cuban experience and women and on Caribbean culture. In 1986, she won the Cuban Critics Prize for *Piedra Pulida*, in 2001 she won Cuba's National Prize for Literature, and in 2013 she was elected president of the writers' section of the Union of Writers and Artists of Cuba (UNEAC).

Blanca Múnster Infante is a professor of economics at the University of Havana and a scholar at the university's Center for Research on the World Economy.

Armando Nova González is a professor of economics and a researcher at the Center for the Study of the Cuban Economy at the University of Havana. A specialist in agricultural economics, he is the author of numerous articles, book chapters, and books on the political economy of Cuban agriculture, including *La agricultura en Cuba: Evolución y trayectoria (1959–2005)* (2006).

Manuel Orozco is a senior fellow at the Inter-American Dialogue. He is chair of Central America and the Caribbean at the U.S. Foreign Service Institute and senior researcher at the Institute for the Study of International Migration at Georgetown University. He is the author of *América Latina y el Caribe: Desarrollo, migración y remesas* (2012), *Remittances: Global Opportunities for International Person-to-Person Money Transfers* (2005), and *International Norms and Mobilization for Democracy* (2002).

Leonardo Padura Fuentes is the most popular novelist in Cuba as well as a screenwriter and essayist. His series of six detective novels featuring Inspector Mario Conde have been translated into twenty languages. In 2012, he was awarded Cuba's National Prize for Literature. His most recent novel is *Herejes* (Heretics), and the English language edition of *The Man Who Loved Dogs* was published in 2014.

Omar Everleny Pérez Villanueva is professor in the Department of Economics and a researcher at the Center for the Study of the Cuban Economy at the University of Havana. He is the author of *Miradas a la economía cubana*, volumes I (2009), II (2010), III (2012), and IV (2013), and *Reflexiones sobre la economía cubana* (2005, 2006) and coeditor of *Cuban Eco-*

nomic and Social Development: Policy Reforms and Challenges in the 21st Century (2012), *The Cuban Economy at the Start of the Twenty-First Century* (2005), and *Cuba: Hacia una estrategia de desarrollo para los inicios del siglo XXI*. He has been a visiting professor at Harvard University, Carleton University, Sorbonne University, and Columbia University.

Philip Peters is president of the Cuba Research Center (Alexandria, Virginia), a nonprofit organization founded in 2013. He produces the blog *The Cuban Triangle* and is the author of numerous monographs on politics and economics in Cuba. He previously served as vice president of the Lexington Institute and as a State Department appointee of presidents Ronald Reagan and George H. W. Bush. A frequent lecturer on Cuba to diverse groups, he has also testified before Congress and the U.S. International Trade Commission.

Camila Piñeiro Harnecker is a professor at the Center for the Study of the Cuban Economy at the University of Havana. Her research centers on alternative forms of economic organization such as self-management and democratic planning. She received her MA in sustainable development from the University of California, Berkeley, and is the editor of *Cooperatives and Socialism: A View from Cuba* (2012).

Clotilde Proveyer Cervantes is a sociologist and professor at the University of Havana. She has been a member of Cuba's National Group for the Prevention of and Attention to Domestic Violence. She is the coeditor of *Social Work in Cuba and Sweden: Achievements and Prospects* (2005).

Archibald R. M. Ritter is an economist and distinguished research professor at Carleton University in Ottawa. He produces the blog *The Cuba Economy* and has published numerous articles on Cuba's development policies. He is the author of *The Economic Development of Revolutionary Cuba: Strategy and Performance* (1974) and *Cuba in the International System: Integration and Normalization* (1995) and editor of *The Cuban Economy* (2004).

Ana M. Ruiz Aguirre is a PhD candidate in cultural studies at Queen's University (Ontario, Canada). Her research focuses on the way Cuban art and politics intersect and influence each other and Cuban society.

Daniel Salas González is a professor in the Department of Journalism at the University of Havana. He has written for the *Juventud Rebelde* newspaper and was a guest editor and contributor for *La Gaceta de Cuba*.

Jorge Mario Sánchez Egozcue is a professor of economics at the University of Havana and senior researcher at the Center for the Study of the Cuban Economy. He has been a visiting professor at the University of Texas, Columbia University, and Harvard University and has lectured at universities and research centers throughout Europe and the United States. He has been cochair of the Cuba section of the Latin American Studies Association, and his articles have been published in numerous scholarly journals.

Ann Marie Stock is a professor of Hispanic studies and the director of film and media studies at the College of William and Mary. She is the author of *On Location in Cuba: Street Filmmaking during Times of Transition* (2009) and editor of *Framing Latin American Cinema: Contemporary Critical Perspectives* (2009). She is the founder and director of Cuban

Cinema Classics, an initiative that makes available subtitled Cuban documentaries in the United States.

Julia E. Sweig is the Nelson and David Rockefeller Senior Fellow and director of Latin America studies at the Council on Foreign Relations. She writes a biweekly column for *Folha de São Paulo* and serves on the international advisory board of the Brazilian Center for International Relations. She is the author of *Cuba: What Everyone Needs to Know* (2009, 2013) and *Inside the Cuban Revolution: Fidel Castro and the Urban Underground* (2002), which won the American Historical Association's Herbert Feis Award for best book of the year by an independent scholar.

Carlos Varela is a singer-songwriter whose work is considered among the most representative of *la nueva canción cubana* (the new Cuban song movement). In 1980, his songs became part of the *Movimiento de la Nueva Trova* (Movement of New Folk Music), and he helped to develop *la novísima trova*, which is characterized by its politically charged lyrics and social commentary. He has performed in concerts worldwide, including in Spain, Mexico, Venezuela, Colombia, Chile, Sweden, Ireland, Canada, and the United States. He lives in Havana, Cuba. In April 2013, Carlos Varela and his band returned to Miami to celebrate his thirty-year career.

Sjamme van de Voort is a PhD student in the Department of Culture and Society at Aarhus University in Denmark. His doctoral project is "Building Cuban Culture: How Official Narratives Become Public Memory."

María del Carmen Zabala Argüelles is professor of economics at the University of Havana and academic coordinator of the university's program on social development and a member of FLACSO-Cuba. She is the author of *Jefatura femenina de hogar, pobreza urbana y exclusión social: Una perspectiva desde la subjetividad en el contexto cubano* (2010) and editor of *Pobreza, exclusión social y discriminación étnico-racial en América Latina y el Caribe* (2008).

CPSIA information can be obtained at www.ICGtesting.com
Printed in the USA
BVOW09s1042010714

357848BV00002B/2/P